Diminishing Returns

Diminishing Returns

The New Politics of Growth and Stagnation

Edited by

LUCIO BACCARO, MARK BLYTH,
AND JONAS PONTUSSON

OXFORD
UNIVERSITY PRESS

OXFORD
UNIVERSITY PRESS

Oxford University Press is a department of the University of Oxford. It furthers
the University's objective of excellence in research, scholarship, and education
by publishing worldwide. Oxford is a registered trade mark of Oxford University
Press in the UK and certain other countries.

Published in the United States of America by Oxford University Press
198 Madison Avenue, New York, NY 10016, United States of America.

Names: Baccaro, Lucio, editor. | Blyth, Mark, 1967- editor. | Pontusson,
Jonas, editor.
Title: Diminishing returns : the new politics of growth and stagnation /
edited by Lucio Baccaro, Mark Blyth, and Jonas Pontusson.
Description: New York, NY : Oxford University Press, [2022] |
Includes bibliographical references and index.
Identifiers: LCCN 2021060907 (print) | LCCN 2021060908 (ebook) |
ISBN 9780197607862 (paperback) | ISBN 9780197607855 (hardback) |
ISBN 9780197607886 (epub)
Subjects: LCSH: Macroeconomics. | Keynesian economics. |
Economic development. | Stagnation (Economics)
Classification: LCC HB172.5 .D56 2022 (print) | LCC HB172.5 (ebook) |
DDC 339—dc23/eng/20220304
LC record available at https://lccn.loc.gov/2021060907
LC ebook record available at https://lccn.loc.gov/2021060908

DOI: 10.1093/oso/9780197607855.001.0001

CONTENTS

ACKNOWLEDGEMENTS

This volume originates in a research project at the University of Geneva, directed by Lucio Baccaro and Jonas Pontusson and funded by the Swiss National Science Foundation (grant no. 100017_166186). An initial exploratory workshop took place at the Max Planck Institute for the Study of Societies in May 2018. Subsequently, two additional workshops were held: at Brown University in August 2019, where first versions of most chapters were presented and discussed, and at the Max Planck Institute for the Study of Societies in January 2020, where after another round of discussion the content of the volume was finalized.

The editors are indebted to Lucy Barnes, Jens Beckert, Robert Boyer, Daniela Gabor, Peter Hall, Anke Hassel, Silja Häusermann, Chris Howell, Sebastian Kohl, Costas Lapavitsas, Renate Mayntz, Bruno Palier, Fritz Scharpf, David Soskice, Alexander Spielau, Wolfgang Streeck, and Till van Treeck, for presenting or commenting on papers at the first workshop. They would also like to express their gratitude to Puneet Bhasin, Benjamin Braun, Björn Bremer, Sinisa Hadziabdic, Manolis Kalaitzake, Erik Neimanns, Erik Peinert, Sid Rothstein, Mischa Stratenwerth, Arianna Tassinari, Tobias Tober, Leon Wansleben, and Josh Weitz for frequent conversations and comments on the project embodied by this volume. Claudia Werner provided superb administrative support throughout. Finally, we, the editors, wish to thank chapter authors for their cooperation and their intellectual contributions to the project.

CONTRIBUTOR LIST

Dragos Adascalitei
Research Officer, European
Foundation for the Improvement
of Living and Working Conditions

Lucio Baccaro
Director, Max Planck Institute
for the Study of Societies
(Cologne)

Cornel Ban
Associate Professor of International
Political Economy, Copenhagen
Business School

Mark Blyth
Professor of international
Economics, Brown University
(Providence, RI)

Dorothee Bohle
Professor of Political Science,
University of Vienna

Fabio Bulfone
Assistant Professor, Leiden University

James Conran
Assistant Professor of Political
Science, University of Oregon
(Eugene, OR)

Lennart Erixon
Emeritus Professor, Department
of Economics, University of
Stockholm

Oddný Helgadóttir
Assistant Professor, Copenhagen
Business School

Jonathan Hopkin
Professor of Comparative Politics,
London School of Economics

Martin Höpner
Professor, Max Planck Institute for
the Study of Societies (Cologne)

Evelyne Hübscher
Associate Professor of Comparative
Politics and Public Policy, Central
European University (Vienna)

Alison Johnston
Associate Professor of Political
  Science, Oregon State University
  (Corvallis, OR)

Julia Lynch
Professor of Political Science,
  University of Pennsylvania
  (Philadelphia, PA)

Matthias Matthijs
Associate Professor of International
  Political Economy, Johns Hopkins
  SAIS (Washington, DC)

Jonas Nahm
Assistant Professor of Energy,
  Resources and Environment, Johns
  Hopkins SAIS
  (Washington, DC)

Özlem Onaran
Professor of Economics, University of
  Greenwich

Jonas Pontusson
Professor of Comparative Politics,
  University of Geneva

Aidan Regan
Associate Professor, University
  College Dublin

Alexander Reisenbichler
Assistant Professor of Political
  Science, University of Toronto

Thomas Sattler
Associate Professor of International
  Relations, University of Geneva

Herman Mark Schwartz
Professor of Politics, University of
  Virginia (Charlottesville, VA)

Jazmin Sierra
Assistant Professor of Political
  Science, University of Notre Dame
  (South Bend, IN)

Engelbert Stockhammer
Professor of International Political
  Economy, King's College London

Yeling Tan
Assistant Professor of Political
  Science, University of Oregon
  (Eugene, OR)

Dustin Voss
PhD candidate, London School of
  Economics

Sara Watson
Associate Professor of Political
  Science, Ohio State University
  (Columbus, OH)

Andreas Wiedemann
Assistant Professor of Politics,
  Princeton University
  (Princeton, NJ)

Introduction: Rethinking Comparative Capitalism

LUCIO BACCARO, MARK BLYTH, AND JONAS PONTUSSON

Drawing on previous work by the editors (Baccaro and Pontusson 2016; Blyth and Matthijs 2017), this essay and the volume that it introduces develop an approach to the comparative analysis of capitalism(s) centered on the notion of "growth models." We choose growth as a point of departure because we see capitalism as a social order whose stability depends on its capacity to satisfy expectations of material improvement.[1] However, as highlighted by the recent literature on "secular stagnation" (Storm 2017; Summers 2014a; Teulings and Baldwin 2014), growth has become increasingly difficult to generate across the advanced economies, giving rise to a host of new problems, from financial instability to the collapse of mainstream parties. Simply put, the questions that motivate our project are the following: If the main mechanism for securing the legitimacy of democratic capitalism is the ability to produce (and widely diffuse) economic growth, what happens when growth is harder to come by and less broadly shared? And how should we think about capitalist diversity—"varieties of capitalism"—in the context of global stagnation?

In this introductory essay, which frames the project, we make five interrelated arguments. First, we argue that existing theoretical frameworks in comparative political economy are ill equipped to tackle the politics of growth and stagnation because of their almost exclusive emphasis on institutions influencing firm competitiveness ("supply-side institutionalism") and their neglect of the level and composition of aggregate demand. Second, we argue that political economists need to take macroeconomics more seriously than they have done so far but also be more critical and take advantage of pluralism in macroeconomics.

Mainstream economics sees growth as primarily determined by supply-side variables, unlike post-Keynesian macroeconomics for which aggregate demand has both short-term and long-term effects on growth. We draw on the latter to set out the macroeconomic underpinnings of our analytical framework.

Third, we identify a broad stagnationist tendency in advanced capitalism, harking back to the crisis of "wage-led" growth, and we examine different national level responses ("growth models") to the common problem of boosting aggregate demand at a time of stagnation. We aim to overcome the dichotomy between "commonality" and "diversity" of capitalisms by developing a theoretical framework that accounts for both. Fourth, we discuss how international political economy factors, particularly the presence or absence of mechanisms for relaxing the current account constraint on growth, undergird the feasibility and durability of national growth models. We go beyond methodological nationalism and argue for the need to mobilize both CPE and IPE in analyzing contemporary capitalism. Fifth, we set out a broad, multifaceted approach to the domestic politics of growth models, charting a middle course between electoral and elite-centered approaches and distinguishing between the politics of policy choice and the politics of democratic legitimation. The remainder of the introduction develops each of the five points in turn. In a final section, we provide a summary of the various country chapters.

Part 1: Comparative Political Economy

We begin by articulating how our approach to comparative analysis of capitalism(s) relates to existing literature in comparative political economy, conceived as a subfield of political science and political sociology that emerged in the 1980s. In what follows, we briefly discuss three separate CPE research programs in the 1980s and 1990s—national models of capitalism, post-Fordist production regimes, and neo-corporatism—and then engage critically with the dominant CPE paradigm of the last two decades, the VoC approach.

From Strong States to Encompassing Bargains

Inspired by Shonfield's *Modern Capitalism* (1965), much of the early CPE literature sought to delineate national models of capitalism based on the different roles played by government, business, and organized labor in different economies. In the first instance, the point of this exercise was to explain the different responses of countries to the oil price shocks and industrial adjustment challenges of the 1970s. The distinction between "weak" and "strong" states featured prominently in initial articulations of this research agenda (Katzenstein 1978), but CPE scholars quickly incorporated the idea that the structure of interest groups and, in particular, institutionalized relations between union and employers must be considered as well. The result was a broad-based consensus on a threefold typology of advanced capitalist political economies: liberal, statist, and corporatist political economies (Hall 1986; Katzenstein 1985; Zysman 1983). Relying on institutional arrangements to explain shifts in the sectoral composition of economies, as well as adjustment processes within sectors, this CPE tradition in turn invoked historical legacies of state-building and the distribution of power among "producer groups" to explain institutional arrangements.

Less closely linked to political science, a second stream of CPE literature in the 1980s interpreted the economic dislocations of the 1970s as a crisis of Fordist mass production and explored the emergence of alternative methods of organizing industrial production. In the Anglophone literature, two contributions in this vein stand out: Piore and Sabel's *The Second Industrial Divide* (1984), and Streeck's work on the conditions of diversified quality production (DQP) (Streeck 1991).[2] Emphasizing industrial districts, characterized by local-level coordination among firms, Piore and Sabel challenged the relevance of national models. In contrast, Streeck (1991) linked the study of technological and organizational change on the level of the shopfloor to national diversity, arguing that core features of the German model—vocational training, employment protection, co-determination, and coordinated wage bargaining—prevented German firms from competing by cutting labor costs and, at the same time, enabled them to pursue DQP strategies (see also Sorge and Streeck 2018; Streeck 1997).

Commonly referred to as "neo-corporatism," the third strand of CPE theorizing in the 1980s sought to identify the conditions under which unions might deliver wage restraint in return for government policies to combat unemployment and/or expand social benefits. Scholars contributing to this research program emphasized the institutional power of organized labor, positing that encompassing unions have not only have an interest in exercising wage restraint, but also the capacity to do so, with the centralization of authority within unions and the absence of inter-union rivalries seen as preconditions of successful "political exchange" (e.g. Pizzorno 1978; Regini 1984).

In a different vein, Hibbs (1977) relied on the idea of a trade-off between unemployment and inflation to generate a partisan model of macroeconomic policy choices where Left parties, with workers as their core constituency, prioritize low unemployment while Right parties, with owners of financial assets as their core constituency, prioritize low inflation given the differing asset bases of their electoral constituencies. Combining Hibbs's partisan model with the insights of the neo-corporatist literature, Garrett (1998) argued that partisan differences with regard to macroeconomic management and social spending are most pronounced when unions are encompassing and economic openness renders wage restraint imperative.[3]

The assumptions that competitiveness is the key to economic growth and that wage restraint is the key to competitiveness represent a conspicuous feature of the neo-corporatist research program. It is fair to say, we think, that these assumptions were never systematically tested. Importantly for our purposes, the core assumptions of the neo-corporatist literature do not sit well with the fact that real wages grew faster than labor productivity in all OECD countries during the *trentes glorieuses* and that wage shares grew most rapidly in the countries that experienced the most rapid GDP growth (Bengtsson 2015a, 2015b). We shall return to this point in due course.

Synthesis: The Varieties of Capitalism approach

Presented in Soskice (1999) and the introductory chapter to the canonical volume edited by Hall and Soskice (2001), the VoC approach to comparative political economy integrated insights from the aforementioned research programs into a single, firm-centered analytical framework. In this well-known framework, solutions to a number of "coordination problems" confronting firms define two basic varieties of capitalism: Liberal and Coordinated Market Economies or, in shorthand, LMEs and CMEs. The key problems are as follows: to elicit the co-operation of employees while securing wage restraint, to secure the supply of workers with desirable skills, to finance investment and manage relations with owners (and other providers of finance) and, finally, to manage relations with subcontractors and competitors.

In LMEs, these problems are solved through markets. In CMEs, they are instead solved through institutionalized strategic coordination by firms. In both cases, the institutional context favors some firm strategies over others, and the solutions adopted by firms constitute an equilibrium outcome that is deemed to be a Pareto improvement over the initial position of the agents involved. This process, iterated, gives rise to self-reinforcing institutional complementarities that result in increasing returns and lock-in feedback effects. In short, decisions made by firms in, for example, an LME, *precisely because it is an LME*, reinforces the selection of specific LME strategies over time, resulting in distinct institutional clusters.

Hall and Soskice (2001) did not restrict themselves to describing the emergence and persistence of LME's and CME's, as previous CPE scholars had done, but also aspired to explain how these clusters emerge and reproduce themselves through self-selection. The concepts of "institutional complementarities"—whereby positive feedback mechanisms tightly bind institutions and their outputs in equilibrium—and "comparative institutional advantage"—whereby such institutional clusters allow variation across the two main possible types of CME and LME—drive their explanatory framework. Outcomes such as a state's innovation strategy, or the choice of social and public policies favored in particular cases, become explicable as a function of institutional solutions to these key coordination problems.

From the VoC perspective, the distinction between LMEs and CMEs does not have much, if any, bearing on overall efficiency and long-term growth rates (see Hall and Gingrich 2009). What distinguishes the two types of capitalism has to do with the economic activities that generate growth. While the institutional framework of LMEs favors the expansion of low-wage services and high-tech sectors engaged in radical (product) innovation, the institutional framework of CMEs favors incremental (process) in manufacturing and, more specifically, diversified quality production. Perhaps most importantly, the VoC framework strongly implies, contrary to conventional wisdom among market liberals, that international competition leads to a crystallization of LME–CME differences, as firms specialized in economic activities that are advantaged by existing institutions thrive, and governments seek to promote growth by engaging in reforms that render institutional frameworks more coherent (and thus enhance existing institutional complementarities).[4]

As with any analytical paradigm that aspires to reconfigure an existing field of inquiry, the VoC approach has been subjected to a wide variety of criticisms. For our purposes, three lines of criticism deserve to be briefly mentioned.[5] The first concerns the conceptual foundations and empirical adequacy of the binary typology of LME and CME, with critics commonly arguing that the coding of countries as LMEs and CMEs lumps together political economies operating according to quite different logics. A second set of critics have taken VoC scholars to task for failing to explain why some countries are LMEs while others are CMEs. Focusing on the implications of welfare-state provisions for skill formation, Korpi (2006) exemplifies this line of attack. A third line of criticism concerns institutional changes in advanced capitalist political economies since the 1980s. In this debate, the critics (notably Baccaro and Howell 2011, 2017; Streeck 2009) emphasize common trends across LMEs and CMEs, frequently construed as "liberalization," while VoC scholars insist on the persistence of fundamental differences between LMEs and CMEs (Hall and Gingerich 2009; Hall and Thelen 2009).

While we find all of these lines of criticism cogent and relevant, our attention lies elsewhere. Specifically, the core of the Hall and Soskice version of the VoC framework, as already noted, heavily emphasizes supply-side logics. As Baccaro and Pontusson (2016) and Blyth and Matthijs (2017) have both noted, the macroeconomy is curiously absent from their framework, if "the macroeconomy" is taken to mean something more than a set of factor price shifts to which firms respond more or less automatically given proximate institutional incentives.[6]

In our view, the CPE literature in general, and the VoC literature in particular, have been swayed not only by contemporary empirical developments, but also by prevailing ideas in economics. We submit that CPE scholarship has been profoundly influenced by the anti-Keynesian turn in macroeconomics, adapting to this development by focusing on supply-side issues and, for the most part, ignoring aggregate demand and distribution. While eager to assert that politics matter, CPE scholars have been reluctant to challenge mainstream economists on their home turf, preferring to show that their work nicely complemented mainstream economics. In contrast, we believe that the economics underpinning one's institutional analysis are crucially important and, to coin a neologism, that one should be as transparent as possible about one's "macroeconomic foundations."

Part 2: Macroeconomics

Turning to macroeconomics, our goal here is to elucidate the differences between New Keynesian (NK) and Post-Keynesian (PK) approaches and to suggest that the latter approach, broadly conceived, provides a better foundation for thinking about growth models or, at least, a useful foundation that resonates with the intuitions and insights of political economists working in political science and political sociology. More specifically, we argue that the PK approach provides a more convincing explanation of secular stagnation than the NK approach.[7]

The New Keynesian underpinnings of comparative political economy

The macroeconomic underpinnings of recent CPE scholarship are New Keynesian in that they deviate from neoclassical assumptions about instantaneous market clearing and rationality, but, to all intents and purposes, they keep the neoclassical assumption of supply-side dominance intact. Articulated by Carlin and Soskice (2009, 2015), the macroeconomics animating and supporting the VoC approach to comparative capitalism can be summarized as follows.

First, output in the short run is determined by aggregate demand, with demand being a negative function of the real interest rate. In the long run, however, monetary neutrality holds as expansion of the money supply changes neither preferences nor possibilities. Second, labor markets do not automatically clear and hence there is involuntary unemployment (Layard, Nickell, and Jackman 2005). Third, firms have the power to transfer costs onto prices while maintaining a fixed margin. The unique intersection of the "wage-setting" and "price-setting" curves identifies the equilibrium level of output and the equilibrium level of employment, around which an economy fluctuates in the short-to-medium run. Commonly known as the Non-Accelerating Inflation Rate of Unemployment (NAIRU), this equilibrium is entirely determined by labor productivity and the institutional framework of labor markets and product markets, and is unaffected by aggregate demand.[8]

Fourth, a competitive economy with fully flexible prices is the most efficient form of economic organization and remains a reference point for policymakers. However, wages and prices (except for the prices of financial assets) fail to adapt instantaneously to demand shifts, thus moving the economy away from the efficient competitive optimum. In these circumstances, monetary policy has real effects in the short run because it minimizes the welfare losses caused by price inflexibility. Fiscal policy could in theory play a similar role, but it is less efficient than monetary policy due to the long and variable lags through which it impacts the real economy, and because it inserts an element of discretion—politicians' own motives—into the functioning of the economy.

Fifth, given such a framework, the task of stabilizing the economy is best entrusted to independent central banks operating on the basis of clear response rules (e.g., raising the interest rate when inflation is above target). The monetary responses of an independent central bank allow an economy with inflexible prices to approximate the functioning of a fully flexible economy (see Goodfriend 2007; Woodford 2003). Hence demand management is only relevant in the short- to medium-run, minimizing losses caused by deviations from the fully flexible, competitive ideal type. In the long run, macroeconomic policy does not matter for economic growth, which depends entirely on supply-side forces such as demography, technology, investment in R&D, and human capital.[9]

The limits of a supply-side focus

Accepting the propositions articulated above as the parameters of what is politically and economic possible has profound consequences–most obviously for growth policies that seek to promote real wage growth as a way to stimulate aggregate demand—something we discuss later in the chapter under the rubric of "wage-led growth" (Lavoie and Stockhammer 2013). Trying to raise wages has clear limits in the world of mainstream macroeconomics and generates more drawbacks than benefits. At constant labor productivity, trying to increase the real wage is equivalent to trying to increase the wage share of GDP. However, this attempt is doomed to failure according to the NK model summarized above. In response, employers will immediately defend their profit margins by increasing prices. If workers insist on claiming a higher share of output, the NAIRU would have to shift to restore compatibility between workers' wage claims and employers' profit claims. The new NAIRU equilibrium would have the same real wage as before but a lower level of employment. So far, so neoclassical, despite the caveats.

CPE scholars inspired by NK macroeconomics typically posit that it is the monetary response of the central bank that brings the economy back to equilibrium after a demand shock (Franzese 2001; Iversen 1999). If the central bank forecasts higher inflation than its target, it responds by increasing the nominal interest rate for given levels of inflationary expectations. That is, it increases the real interest rate. In this world, the role of collective bargaining is at best to minimize the damage. The increase in unemployment needed to achieve disinflation is smaller if the bargaining system is coordinated and unions are encompassing (Tarantelli 1986). However, if unions are unable or unwilling to deliver wage restraint, collective bargaining forces the central bank to tighten its monetary policy. In Iversen and Soskice's formulation (2006, 432), "parties that care about employment" should be "more interested in designing policies that can reduce the equilibrium level of unemployment than in policies that generate brief bursts of employment."

Soskice (2007) argues that that a conservative macroeconomic policy stance is the optimal one under such constraints. In LMEs as well as CMEs, macroeconomic policy is pinned down in the long run by the equilibrium rate of unemployment. Thus, a demand stimulus can only lead to a higher equilibrium level of employment and output if accompanied by either supply-side reforms or voluntary wage restraint.[10] On these assumptions, it is quite possible that the equilibrium rate of unemployment is lower in LMEs than in CMEs, on account of weak unions and weaker labor market institutions, but it is difficult to see why (or how) a demand stimulus matters beyond the short run in either type of capitalism.

If the positive effects of expansionary macroeconomic policies are delivered only in conjunction with wage restraint exercised by encompassing unions, it is far from obvious that macroeconomic policy deserves to be brought back to the center stage of analysis in political economy. In fact, its role is remarkably limited. This is not just a peculiarity of an earlier generation of CPE research, but an enduring feature. For example, Beramendi, Häusermann, Kitschelt, and Kriesi (2015) have formulated a strong critique of "producer group politics" and a forceful plea for bringing electoral politics into comparative political economy, conceiving public policy as the interaction of political supply (party programs) and political demand (voter preferences). We discuss their view of politics later in the chapter. Here we focus on their political economy, which completely neglects macroeconomic policy, as if it could not be the object of democratic choice and should be taken as given, focusing solely on the distinction between "consumption-oriented" social programs (transfers), which are bad; and "investment-oriented" social programs (education, active labor market programs, etc.), which are good. Yet, the trade-off between the two types of social expenditures clearly depends on the rate of growth. If the economy stagnates, a rise in one implies a fall of the other. In an expanding economy, it is possible to increase both, and any rebalancing is likely to be less politically controversial.

Iversen and Soskice's latest analysis of contemporary capitalism (2019) has a similar neglect for the role of macroeconomic policy. In their view, growth comes from a particular organization of the supply side, and the supply side determines the patterns of political support and the location of the "decisive" voter as well. The distinction between LMEs and CMEs is no longer prominent. In its stead, the "knowledge economy" takes center stage. Growth depends on the ability to manage the prerequisites of a knowledge economy, which implies building clusters of innovation and investing in education and human capital development. Information technology has broken the old Fordist alliance between skilled and unskilled workers, and this reduces the political feasibility of redistribution. Importantly, Iversen and Soskice (2019) argue that in the knowledge economy, growth requires conservative monetary and fiscal policies, and structural policies ensuring competitive markets, international trade, and free capital mobility. Macroeconomic activism risks unsettling the supply-side conditions for growth.

In sum, as the literature reviewed in this chapter illustrates, a supply-side view of how the economy works has little ability to conceptualize the role of macroeconomic policy in the process of economic growth. As the next section argues, the contrasting tradition of Post-Keynesian (PK) macroeconomics has a greater potential to contribute to our understanding of the long-run trajectory of capitalism as well as its contemporary manifestations.

Post-Keynesian macroeconomics as a better lens

We see the PK tradition has providing much greater room for aggregate demand and macroeconomic policy than the NK tradition. In making this case, we draw on PK models inspired by Kalecki (see Hein 2012; Lavoie 2009; Lavoie and Stockhammer 2012; Lavoie 2014) and also on models elaborated by the French Regulation School (Boyer 1987; Boyer and Petit 1991). These macroeconomic models share some fundamental features: drawing on Keynes and

Kaldor, output is determined by effective demand in the long run as well as the short run (Lavoie 2018) and, drawing from Kalecki, distribution affects aggregate demand.

While the basic NK model provides a stylized representation of the economy in three equations (Carlin and Soskice 2006), the basic PK model (and its regulationist equivalent) posits two fundamental relationships: the *demand regime* and the *productivity regime*. These relationships determine the impact of a marginal change in the wage share (a marginal change in the real wage at constant labor productivity) on demand growth and productivity growth respectively. Their curves may be positively or negatively shaped. Importantly, they jointly determine the growth rates of variables, as opposed to their levels. That is, they jointly determine the *growth path of the economy*.

PK and NK economists alike start from the view that workers and firms have competing claims over the distribution of productivity, and that firms have market power, allowing them to set their prices as a mark-up on unit labor costs. The standard PK model of firm behavior also assumes, in contrast, that firms have some unused capacity and that their marginal costs are constant up to full capacity/employment. In addition, PK models typically incorporate Keynes and Kalecki's insight that workers have a higher propensity to spend their income than capitalists (Stockhammer 2015),[11] from which it follows that an increase in labor's share of income usually boosts aggregate demand in the short run. Depending on other parameters in the model, such as an expansionary effect of the wage share on capital accumulation or the expansionary effect of demand on productivity, it may also lead to an increase in the growth rate.

Whereas NK economists typically assume labor productivity to be given in the short term, and independent of aggregate demand, PK economists emphasize that labor productivity tends to increase as real wages rise and aggregate demand increases. They explain this regularity, commonly referred to as the "Kaldor-Verdoorn effect," with reference to several mechanisms (Storm and Naastepad 2012). First, expanding demand allows firms to realize productivity gains associated with economies of scale. Second, expanding demand also stimulates new investment, which renders capital more productive to the extent that it incorporates new technology. A related mechanism involves factor substitution: if the price of labor goes up while the price of capital stays put, capital intensity (capital per unit of labor) and labor productivity will both increase.[12] Finally, an increase in the wage share is generally the result of greater labor power and a strengthening of protective institutions. These "beneficial constraints" create incentives for managers to use of capital and labor more efficiently (Streeck 1997).

Returning to the implications of an attempt by workers to increase the wage rate, the NK conclusion that such an increase only increases inflation unless supply-side conditions change emerges from PK models only in the special case of an economy operating at full potential. This is a special case because PK economists contest the NK view that the long-run Phillips curve is (usually) vertical. Instead, they posit a horizontal or weakly upward-sloping Phillips curve, meaning that sustained wage militancy does not lead to infinitely accelerating inflation, but rather to a higher level of inflation combined with a higher level of output.[13]

As Stockhammer (2008a) points out, PK models do not have a built-in equilibrating mechanism and they are potentially unstable due to endogenous political and economic variables. For example, a shift in the balance of power in favor of labor increases the real wage, which leads to an increase in employment, which in turn strengthens the bargaining power of labor and so on. If productivity gains do not keep up with workers' escalating wage claims, this process is bound to generate inflation, which creates distributional tension between wage earners and the holders of capital and financial assets, a process has been used to explain macro shifts in the global economy as a whole (Blyth and Matthijs 2017).

In our view, the absence of an "equilibrium" to which the economy automatically tends to return, is an attractive feature of the PK, which brings it closer to the modus operandi of political economists. It makes it easier to conceive capitalism as inherently an unstable system, in which (temporary) stabilization is a political outcome. Drawing on regulation theory (e.g., Boyer 2004), "political exchange" between labor and capital, by which labor agrees to moderate its nominal wage demands in order to keep inflation at moderate levels, is the equilibrating mechanism at work in PK models.[14]

Summing up, although there are similarities between the PK and NK understanding of macroeconomic dynamics—for example, in both approaches wages and employment are determined by bargaining rather than market forces—the PK approach allows the analyst to discern a greater variety of growth models. Rather than seeing all economies as LME or CME variants of the same (fundamentally neoclassical) growth model, the PK approach allows us to distinguish different growth models by focusing on the role of demand, wages, and profits in an open economy, where real wage growth and aggregate demand have feedback effects on labor productivity.

Before proceeding further, a few words to clarify what we mean by "growth models" would seem to be in order. In the post-Keynesian literature, a "demand regime" refers to the short-term response of demand/output (expansion or shrinking) to a shift in the functional distribution of income (Bhaduri and Marglin 1990) while a "growth regime" encompasses the long-term implications of the distributional shift (typically through its impact on the investment function and/or on productivity). As understood by Post-Keynesian economists "demand regimes" and "growth regimes" are both counterfactual entities: they depend on some structural parameters of the economy (e.g. propensities to consume, sensitivity of investment to demand and profit share, real exchange rate and demand sensitivity of imports and exports). Actual growth, in turn, depends on whether public policy is consistent or inconsistent with the underlying demand or growth regime (Lavoie and Stockhammer 2012). In this volume, by contrast, we use the term "growth model" in a descriptive sense in order to distinguish among different growth models based on the decomposition of GDP growth. For example, we refer to Germany as an "export-led economy" because the lion's share of German GDP growth over the last three decades is attributable to export growth (Baccaro and Pontusson 2016; 2021).

"Growth models" are related to, but not the same as "growth strategies" as conceived by Hassel and Palier (2021a), among others. A growth "strategy" is a set of policies to generate growth and as such represents a deliberate intervention in the economy. In our conception, "growth models" reflect how economies are organized, not simply the macroeconomic policy priorities of governments. The transition from one growth model to another involves reforms as well as shifts in macroeconomic policy paradigms.

Post-Keynesian macroeconomics and secular stagnation

A crucial issue for this volume is to conceptualize the inherent tendency of contemporary capitalism toward stagnation. Growth is crucial for capitalist legitimacy and reproduction. A key question driving the volume is what happens when growth becomes harder to come by. Here, too, PK macro provides a distinct vantage point. To see why, it is helpful to compare the NK and PK analyses of "secular stagnation." Introduced by Summers (2014c), the NK account of secular stagnation invokes an unobservable entity, the "natural interest rate (r^*)," defined as the real interest rate that delivers potential output at a stable inflation rate. According to Summers and others (e.g., Teulings and Baldwin 2014), the natural rate of interest has been declining for years, becoming negative after the financial crisis of 2007 (Summers 2014, 35). Hindered by the "zero lower bound," monetary policy is currently unable to hit the natural interest rate (Eggertsson and Krugman 2012), creating household savings in excess of business demand for credit. This imbalance is eliminated through a quantity adjustment—shrinking GDP—to bring the supply of savings in line with planned investments at the feasible real interest rate (zero minus the inflation target of central banks). Although equilibrium is restored in this way, output remains below potential, hence stagnation.

Summers lists several reasons why the natural interest rate has become negative. New high-tech ventures such as Facebook or Whatsapp require much less capital than old manufacturing ventures. Growing life expectancy without a corresponding increase in working age implies that savings have to rise to finance retirement while the decline in the relative price of capital goods and consumer durables means that less capital is required for equal amounts of physical investment less capital. Finally, Summers suggests that growing personal and functional inequality has increased the average propensity to save (Summers 2014c, see also von Weizsaecker 2013).[15]

Summer's argument relies on a "loanable funds" theory of the interest rate. According to Summer's theory, which goes back to Wicksell, there is a supply curve of loanable funds (the saving schedule), which depends positively on the interest rate, and a demand curve (that investment schedule), which is negatively related to the interest rate. The interest rate equilibrates demand and supply. Where it not for the presence of a nominal rigidity, the zero-lower bound, the economy would operate at its full potential.

PK economists (notably Storm 2020) argue that this theory misunderstands the role of money and banks insofar as banks do not transfer savings from households to firms, but pre-finance investment by creating money ex nihilo. Furthermore, they see the demand and supply curves of loanable funds as not independent but linked to each other. For example, if the propensity to save increases due to greater inequality, shifting the supply curve, the demand curve also shifts because firms expect a lower marginal efficiency of capital.

From a PK perspective, the declining interest rate is not the cause of stagnation, but one of its manifestations. As demand shrinks central banks lower the interest rate in an attempt to stimulate demand—a phenomenon that has become commonplace since the late 1990s (Chappe and Blyth 2020). However, investments become increasingly investment-rate insensitive at increasingly low interest rates and aggregate demand may even decline with negative interest rates. In other words, the aggregate demand curve (which maps the relationship between aggregate demand and the interest rate when investments equal savings) bends backward at very low interest rates (Palley 2019). Furthermore, when the interest rate (the marginal efficiency of capital) hits zero and even becomes negative, firms modify their financing structure away from equity (which are bought back) toward debt. Simultaneously, investments in financial assets, which continue to have a yield higher than zero, are preferred to real investment, and so productive investment falls. This implies that the rigidity of the zero lower bound is the not the cause of secular stagnation. Even if a sufficiently negative real interest rate could be reached, the stagnationist tendencies would not vanish.

Inconceivable from an NK perspective, PK sees secular stagnation as resulting from policies that have lowered the labor share of income and increased the capital share by weakening unions and labor institutions and increasing the shareholder orientation of firms. These are the policies that have undermined the wage-led growth model, as we discuss in the next section. From a PK perspective, negative interest rates are counterproductive as they may induce households to save more in order to provide for retirement while leading financial institutions to try and boost yields by engaging in risky investments, thus increasing financial instability.[16]

Part 3: Growth Models

A focus on growth models allows us to see the secular decline of growth rates in advanced capitalist economies as issuing from a more basic set of forces, namely, the exhaustion of the wage-led growth model, the most stable and efficient growth model capitalism has been able to produce so far, and the limits to the post-Fordist growth models that have succeeded it.[17] In this section, we briefly discuss the reasons for the exhaustion of the wage-led growth model and identify alternative growth models in the post-Fordist era.

Wage-led growth and its exhaustion

The Fordist growth model emerged in the period after World War II as the evolution and replacement of the *mode of regulation* prevailing in the interwar period, when wages formed in competitive labor markets were highly sensitive to economic fluctuations. In the pre-Fordist era, consumption out of wages remained limited, and consumption out of profits was insufficient to generate economies of scale, causing accumulation to remain below its potential even though the technical conditions for mass production were already available at the time. To the extent that there were productivity gains, they were mostly realized as profits, which tended to be used to acquire financial assets rather than goods and services (Boyer 2004). The result was low aggregate demand (relative to potential), rentierism, and financial speculation. In Marxist language, there was a "contradiction" between the technical potential of the economy and the balance of social forces determining the distribution between wages and profits.

The key innovation that ushered in the Fordist era was the institutionalization of collective bargaining and the increase in trade union power that went with it. With collective bargaining, wages were no longer flexible and responsive to labor market conditions, but downwardly rigid and indexed to labor productivity. In this period advanced capitalist countries saw the emergence in some countries of a "historical compromise" between unions and employers, whereby unions recognized the capitalist order, setting aside any attempt to challenge managerial control of the labor process, let alone transform property relations, and employers accepted to share the fruit of technical progress with workers (Korpi 1983). By indexing real wages to labor productivity growth, Fordist industrial relations relaxed the demand-side constraint that had hindered growth in the interwar phase. In addition to collective bargaining, other institutional innovations contributed to generating an adequate level of effective demand, particularly the public welfare provisions (Esping-Andersen 1990) and the adoption of counter-cyclical (Keynesian) budget policies (Hall 1986). As a result, growth took off in the "glorious" 30 years after World War II (Armstrong, Glyn, and Harrison 1991).

The Fordist model was a well-functioning wage-led growth model (Lavoie and Stockhammer 2013). Real wage increases stimulated household consumption while expanding demand stimulated productive investment by firms (a mechanism known as the "accelerator" of investments) and permitted the realization of economies of scale and productivity increases, thus directly contributing to GDP growth. Higher wages and institutional rigidities also promoted the substitution of relatively expensive labor with relatively cheaper capital to increase capital intensity, further contributing to productivity growth (Storm and Naastepad 2012). In sum, the wage-led Fordist model rested on a virtuous circle in which real wage increases both expanded demand and simultaneously promoted the realization of productivity increases that would ultimately validate those real wage increases.

Over time, several problems emerged within the wage-led model. One of its main vulnerabilities was the pressure exercised by wage militancy on the rate of profit. Although real wages stimulated demand, lower profits per unit of output reduced the capitalists' incentives to invest (Marglin and Schor 1990). Limited capital mobility and financial repression, that is, real interest rates below the rates that would have prevailed in a global market, attenuated the pressure. But the progressive dismantling of capital account controls, largely completed in Europe in the late 1980s, provided capital with an exit option as it made it increasingly difficult for national policy-making authorities to undercut the global rate of return on capital, indexed to the global real interest rate.

The second vulnerability had to do with inflation. When trade unions pushed for wage increases above productivity gains and the economy was at, or close to, full employment, firms in oligopolistic markets reacted to the squeeze of their profit margins by raising prices. Attempts at reining in inflation generally involved the institutionalization of income policies (Bruno and Sachs 1985; Flanagan, Soskice, and Ulman 1983). These experiments worked better in relatively centralized or coordinated bargaining systems such as Germany and Sweden than in relatively decentralized systems such as France, Italy, and the United Kingdom (Cameron 1984; Soskice 1990). In Thatcherite Britain, inflation was eventually defeated through a shift to monetarism and an attack against the statutory prerogatives of trade unions, including the dismantling of tripartite policy-making fora (Goldthorpe 1984; Tarantelli 1986).

To summarize, the wage-led growth model was undergirded by a historical capital-labor compromise and facilitated by limited trade openness and capital controls. However, its growing dysfunctionality, and specifically its inability to contain inflation, spurred a shift in the class balance of power, leading to more aggressive policies by employers and the state to reduce worker power and shift risks onto workers (Glyn 2006). Building on these developments, a "shareholder revolution" in corporate governance increased the share of distributed profits in total profits and contributed to boost the profit share (Lazonick and O'Sullivan 2000). These regulatory changes threw sands into the gears of the key macroeconomic relations of the wage-led model. Far from being the rigid variable to which all other variables (prices, money, profits, government expenditures) had to adjust, wages once again became the adjusting variable.

Post-Fordist growth models

Econometric evidence suggests that most advanced economies were structurally wage-led until the mid-1990s and that all large economies remain "wage-led" in the technical PK sense (see Onaran and Obst 2016 and the literature cited therein, Onaran and Galanis 2014). According to these analyses, "profit-led growth" characterizes only a limited number of small open economies in which domestic demand is less important than foreign demand. At the same time, there is ample evidence that the wage share, after peaking between the 1970s and 1980s, has declined in most advanced countries as well as in many developing countries for which data are available (ILO 2008; OECD 2008). For a wage-led economy, a declining wage share means that growth must slow down.

The mainstream explanation for wage-share decline is that it is technologically determined, caused by the decline of the relative price of capital goods as a result of the ICT revolution (Karabarbounis and Neiman 2014). In contrast, and in line with secular stagnation and rentier capitalism arguments, PK economists (Stockhammer 2013) and economic sociologists (Kristal 2010) argue that the main cause of the generalized decline is the changing balance of power between labor and capital to the detriment of labor, as well as financialization (Hein 2012; Pariboni, Paternesi Meloni, and Tridico 2020).

The crisis of wage-led growth has led to the emergence of two alternatives: export-led growth and consumption-led growth financed by debt (Stockhammer 2015). Both model types seek to solve the problem of missing demand without relying primarily on real wage growth. Here we briefly articulate the distinctive characteristics of each of these growth models (see also Baccaro and Pontusson 2016).

Debt-financed consumption

The category of debt-led growth fits the trajectory of the US economy in the decade preceding the crisis of 2007–2008 (Rajan 2010; Schwartz 2009; Stiglitz 2009), but the underlying logic is applicable to the United Kingdom and other "Anglo" capitalisms as well. Households pledge their appreciating home assets as collateral for accessing loans with which they finance consumption even in the absence of real wage growth (Mian and Sufi 2011). With the diffusion of the "originate-and-sell" model of mortgage finance the actor that generates the mortgage is no longer the one that assumes the risk inherent in it. The mortgages are sold to financial intermediators—generally investment banks—who repackage and sell them to retail customers. These practices lower credit standards and facilitate the access to debt by households with riskier profiles. Financial innovation generates products such as "asset-backed securities," and the derivatives built on them, which give the impression that risk has been reduced through diversification but which in reality compound and spread risk.

The end result is an economy that "rides an asset bubble." That is, it grows at higher speed than its potential for some time but generates at the same time high levels of debt exposure and financial speculation. When such a bubble eventually bursts, banks stop lending to each other and to the real economy and a "balance-sheet recession" ensues as households hurriedly deleverage. That is, they increase their savings to lower their debt exposure (Koo 2011). To the extent that housing prices have a limited impact on nominal wages and consumer prices, an inflation-targeting central bank sees no reasons to intervene to deflate the bubble (Carlin and Soskice 2015; Woodford 2003) and so it grows, as does financial fragility.

An economy that grows through debt-financed consumption needs to attract international financial capital as a result of insufficient savings. Current account deficits are the norm and the ability to finance them defines whether the model is sustainable or not. For reasons to which we shall return, current account deficits are not a big problem for "core" countries such as the United States and the United Kingdom, but more peripheral countries do not have the same leeway. Sooner or later they are forced to rein in expenditures and increase savings in order to address their current account problem.

Spain and other Southern European countries are the most obvious examples of the latter scenario. Before the crisis, their growth process relied on debt-financed consumption, but the construction sector was clearly the key propelling force for accumulation (see Reisenbichler 2018). In such a growth model, a construction boom creates a favorable labor market situation for low-skilled construction workers, which reverberates to low-skilled workers in general. The construction boom is financed by domestic credit creation by banks, and housing demand is stimulated by laxer credit requirements.[18]

Until the outbreak of the sovereign debt crisis, Northern banks were happy to finance such a growth model by lending to Southern banks, thereby providing the capital needed to finance the current account deficit of these construction-led growth models (Baccaro 2020). After the sovereign debt crisis, however, Northern banks came to see lending to Southern banks as excessively risky and thus stopped the cross-banking flows. For some time, the "Target 2 payment system" of the Eurozone replaced the role Northern banks in funding Southern banks, leading to an increase in the liabilities of Southern countries vis-à-vis the ECB (Schelkle 2017). However, all Mediterranean countries were forced to reduce foreign debt by shrinking consumption and imports, either through direct conditionality or indirectly (Sacchi 2015). Simply put, the consumption-led growth model of Southern European countries before the crisis was more precarious than "core" consumption-led growth models like the United States and the United Kingdom due to the absence of reliable mechanisms for relaxing the current account constraint.

Export-led growth

Epitomized by the German case, export-led growth is an evolution of the Fordist model, but a peculiar and non-generalizable one. In the early phases of trade liberalization, export-oriented firms sought to compensate for rapidly saturating internal markets by expanding into foreign markets, which allowed them to prolong the Fordist logic of scale-induced productivity growth for some time. With the transition to export-led growth, however, the role played by wages in equilibrating the system is progressively reversed. In an export-led growth model, real wage increases are no longer the main driver of growth. Rather, foreign demand becomes central in determining growth dynamics.

Bhaduri and Marglin (1990) identified an export-led variant of the profit-led growth model. A fall of the wage share has an expansionary effect not so much through the impact of a higher profit share on investment and accumulation, but through the impact on the real exchange rate. If the wage share fall leads to lower domestic prices than in trade partners, while fixed exchange rates and a fortiori a monetary union prevent the nominal exchange rate from appreciating, a depreciation of the real exchange rate ensues, and this translates into greater exports and lower imports (Lavoie 2014, 532–536).[19]

As such, (nominal) wage moderation and an underappreciated real exchange rate become crucial for growth (Hoepner 2018). With sufficient price elasticity of exports, and with a sufficiently open economy, the growth model replaces domestic demand (which tends to stagnate) with foreign demand, and also generates a peculiar sectoral dynamic, with domestic demand-oriented sectors like construction shrinking in relative terms in comparison to similar countries while exposed sectors expanded (again, in relative terms).

The costs of competitive disinflation are generally borne by workers, but their distribution is asymmetric. While core workers in manufacturing, whose collaboration is crucial for production success (Sorge and Streeck 2018), receive real wage increases almost in line with national productivity increases, the real wage gains of low-end service sector workers are flat or even negative. The export-led growth model is sustainable in the long run only as an exception. All national economies cannot be export-led (a point to which we shall return shortly). Importing demand only works so long as some other economies generate that demand internally. If the global system flips to an export-led regime, global economic stagnation necessarily follows.

Balanced and failed growth models

As argued by Baccaro and Pontusson (2016), the Swedish case (and possibly other cases) combines a domestic and an export driver of growth. Like their German counterparts, export-oriented Swedish firms are under intense pressure to reduce costs just like their German counterparts (Baccaro and Howell 2017, ch. 6). At the same time, a German strategy of repressing internal demand in order to stimulate external demand is not feasible in Sweden due to the presence of a highly organized service sector, where unions still push hard for wage solidarity with the manufacturing sector. The Swedish growth model has therefore retained features of the old wage-led model but has also relied on debt-financed consumption.

Swedish growth appears to be a mix of different growth drivers: exports, wages, and debt have all played a role. Household debt has increased dramatically in the 15 years preceding the crisis in Sweden. The large public sector has pushed up the wages of service workers in comparable occupations, thus contributing to household consumption. Baccaro and Pontusson (2016) have argued that high levels of organization in the Swedish service sector have acted as a new form of "beneficial constraint" making it very difficult for Swedish firms to rely on a strategy of wage containment and forcing capital to shift from manufacturing to industries characterized by lower price sensitivity of exports, such as ITC and high value-added services.

It seems that by stimulating consumption, household debt also improves the job prospects of low-skill workers (likely to be employed in the service sector) and thus indirectly boosts their wages. It is not clear, however, how stable or durable the Swedish growth model is. The individualization of employment relations has been extensive in Sweden, not just in manufacturing but also, and possibly to a greater extent, in the public sector. Thus, the ability of service and public sector unions to push for wage increases in line with manufacturing and national productivity now depends almost exclusively on their remaining mobilization capacities, while the supporting institutions have been to a large extent dismantled, or at least profoundly modified (Baccaro and Howell 2017, ch. 7).

An alternative to wage-led growth is not always readily available. Here, Italy is a case in point. Once a very successful economy in terms of comparative growth rates (Locke 1995), it has stagnated since the mid-1990s. The Italian growth model is a case of exiting one growth model and failing to find another. Although household indebtedness has risen in the pre-crisis years, it has not risen sufficiently to rekindle domestic demand. At the same time, the export sector is too small to act as a locomotive for the economy as a whole and it is saddled with an overappreciated real exchange rate as a result of Euro membership. Attempts to turn the Italian economy into an export-led growth model in response to the Euro crisis have failed dramatically.

Peripheral growth models: Compradors, courtesans, and parts suppliers

For countries occupying more peripheral positions in the global economy, growth depends on attracting foreign capital through favorable regulatory provisions (including for taxes), independent of whether such capital then stimulates household consumption, investment, or exports.[20] Such states can act as compradors—business intermediaries—as in the case of the various UK-related tax havens in the Caribbean (Shaxson 2019a). They can also act as courtesans—for example, as conduits for tax avoidance and money laundering, as in the case of Latvia. And, finally, they can also act as specialized part suppliers in global supply chains (Blyth 2016), as in the case of the Eastern European firms supplying the German auto complex, or with Taiwan and the global semiconductor trade.

Building upon that latter distinction, the chapter by Ban and Adascalitei in this volume identifies core and periphery variants of growth models. The core export-led model has national firms at the top of global supply chains reaping the greatest share of profits. The periphery variant has national firms as suppliers of intermediate goods or as suppliers of low value-added, labor-intensive final services, and this limits the upgrading possibilities of domestic firms. The distinction between core and periphery consumption-led growth model depends on how constraining the current account is. Much the same dynamic is identified on a global level by Schwartz (2019a) where a core of IPR protected global firms reap very high profits, their essential suppliers retain reasonable profits, and the rest of the supply chain subsists on very low profits.

To sum, the post-Fordist growth models fall broadly into two camps. In the first, growth relies on domestic consumption, which is mostly stimulated through easier access to credit, or by a residual ability of workers to push for higher wages (as in the Swedish case). In the second, growth is stimulated by foreign demand. Additionally, growth may be stimulated by investment in housing, as in the Irish and Spanish cases before the crisis, or by finding niche or supply-chain strategies in the wider global economy, as in the periphery and micro-state cases. All of which brings us to a point where this delineation of growth models has to deal with the issue of scale. Clearly, growth is not a variable determined simply by the internal dynamics of national economies. Rather, it depends critically upon the (national) unit's place in the global system and how the unit's growth strategy is linked to the growth strategies of other units.

Part 4: International Political Economy

Scholars working in the subfield of political science known as international political economy (IPE) have long been interested in economic growth and stagnation, but at the level of the system (the global capitalist economy) rather than at the level of its country units. While some IPE scholars have also embraced insights from heterodox macroeconomics, CPE scholars have become increasingly cognizant of interdependencies among growth models identified and observed at the country level. As noted at the outset, another important ambition of this volume is to bring CPE and IPE perspectives on contemporary capitalisms into closer conversation with each other.

Thinking systemically about the politics of growth

Emerging more or less at the same time as CPE, the early IPE literature sought to explain why the end of the Bretton Woods systems did not lead to the decline of the United States as the dominant power in the global economy. The focus of this early literature was on the US current account and budget deficits and its declining share of world trade. Building on Kindleberger (1973), who saw international monetary stability as a public good, IPE scholars feared a return to 1930s protectionist blocs as a result of the decline of the US. Explanations as to why this in fact did not occur ranged from the institutional (Keohane 1984) to the structural (Gilpin and Gilpin 1987). For our purposes, what was interesting about this early IPE literature was that it did not view growth solely as property of national economies, but rather as a property of the system of national economies in which some kind of co-evolutionary effect was always present. As Japan rises, the United States falls, and so on.

Another branch of IPE with a close affinity with CPE is the literature on international monetary arrangements. Building off John Ruggie's idea of "embedded liberalism" as the normative order characterizing postwar monetary governance (Ruggie 1982), this literature sought to understand how unit-level growth strategies were enabled or disabled by international monetary dynamics: for example, how the end of Bretton Woods led to European monetary integration (McNamara 1998) or how national models of neoliberalism were activated by changes in capital mobility (Helleiner 1994). The point here is, again, that the system and the units need to be considered together for a complete account to emerge.

More recent work in IPE has made the links between IPE and CPE still more apparent. Taking a Kaleckian/regulationist perspective on shifts in what they term "global macroeconomic regimes," Blyth and Matthijs (2017) present an account in which the wage-led growth models that typified the Bretton Woods era were endogenously destabilized. As wage gains began to outstrip productivity gains, the wage share shifted such that capital began to fear both worker militancy as a political challenge, and inflation as an economic challenge, in the form of diminished expectations of future profitability. The result was the defection of capital from the institutional architecture of wage-led growth, both locally and globally, and a "system reset" in the form of globalization, integration, privatization, and liberalization (qua neoliberalism) designed to create the conditions for profit-led growth.

Yet another recent strand of IPE stresses the presence of dense networks in areas such as global finance (Oatley et al. 2017; Oatley 2019) and in hierarchies in international regulatory regimes (Farrell and Newman 2018). Framed in terms of "interdependence," this strand of theory and empirical research is less directly concerned with the macroeconomic underpinnings of growth, but enriches our understanding of growth in that it, too, shows us that growth is not solely a unit-level property and that global factors are involved in the reproduction of growth models at the national levels and in transitions from one growth model to another.

What IPE adds to CPE

Comparative political economists typically conceive growth as a property of the units. This is not an unreasonable point of view considering the high proportion of non-traded services in advanced economies and their reasonably large home markets. It therefore follows that a lot of demand is domestic, even under open-economy conditions, and that a political understanding of growth models and demand is essential. But if the growth models perspective is correct that the global economy has moved, over time, from a set of wage-led economies to a world where wage-led growth has become increasingly unfeasible and alternative drivers of demand, for example, exports or debt have replaced real wages as main driver, then the questions we need to answer are twofold: What is behind this global shift? And how does this alter our understanding of how growth comes is produced?

We are not interested in establishing relationships of causal primacy between the system and the country-level units, but in clarifying the interrelationships between the two levels. We see country-level developments as being conditioned but not entirely predetermined by systemic forces. One way to acknowledge the interrelationship is to consider that national growth models stand in a relationship of complementarity to each other. Most obviously, it should be recognized that for every meaningful net exporter there has to be an equivalently meaningful importer running a deficit somewhere else in the system. As Keynes noted, export-led growth tends to become rather beggar-thy-neighbor as all countries cannot be net exporters. Keynes' solution to this "fallacy of composition" problem—the Bancor (global outside money) to expand global demand and a clearing union to balance the accounts—never came to pass. Instead we got the US dollar, Bretton Woods, and then persistent, but seemingly stable, imbalances.

Insights from IPE allow us to take better account of how growth models are both embedded in, and enabled by, a global capitalist system and, conversely, how the stock of growth models determines the nature of that system. This proposition involves three distinct issues: the level of analysis used for examining growth, the role of international finance and the hegemonic rule of the US dollar, and secular stagnation.

Growth models at different levels of analysis

As the chapter by Schwartz and Blyth explains, there are four different ways that we might think about the relationship between national growth models and the global system. One approach, arguably the dominant approach in CPE, is to the treat the units (countries) in isolation, positing that independent unit-level

responses to common functional problems, such as managing inflation stemming from the wage-led growth model, lead to a shift in the system overall, for
example, toward open capital flows. A second approach also starts at the unit
level but focuses upon fallacies of composition at a higher level of aggregation,
such that common responses produce a global outcome that differs from the
individual strategies. For example, with relatively closed economies, any one
country could rely on the stable inputs that made Fordist production possible,
but once multiple economies do the same, such stable inputs could not be
produced, and the system is destabilized from simple aggregation.

The third approach introduces the question of asymmetric power at the
system level, positing that the differential capacity of units allows one or more
units to dictate the structure and payoffs to the system overall. Such a perspective invites us to consider how international institutions, for example, the US
patent regime and its instantiation in the TRIPS agreement (Wade 2003), benefit the growth models of some countries more than the growth models of other
countries, and helps to make sense of the distinction between "core" and "peripheral" growth models sketched earlier. This approach also draws our attention
to how some growth models are disabled by their insertion into wider systemic
relations, such as the pre-1990 Italian wage-led growth model into the EU, and
how some are enabled, such as the insertion of East European states into the
German export complex.

Analysis at this level uncovers how one can see the global economy as a single
but highly asymmetric field of power where differentially placed states and
global firms' investment activities massively impact unit-level growth models.
The fourth approach adds a path dependency to the third approach, positing that
the timing and insertion of unit-level growth models into the global economy
matter hugely. For example, Germany can arguably "do more exports" to get out
of crises precisely because export-led growth was written into its developmental
model from its inception in the 1870s in the form of repressed consumption and
excess production.

Growth Models and International Monetary Power

Within the PK macroeconomic framework sketched above, aggregate demand
is a crucial "growth driver," but there is still a balance-of-payments constraint
(Thirlwall 1979, 2011). If imports grow faster than exports, the country in question will have a tendency to produce systematic current account deficits. That is,
its stock of foreign debt will increase over time. But foreign borrowing cannot
continue indefinitely, and at some point the country will have to rebalance
through a price adjustment, an exchange rate devaluation, or through a quantity
adjustment. That is, a reduction of domestic demand in order to reduce imports.

Under the assumption of real exchange rate rigidity, Thirlwall (1979) shows that the growth rate that is compatible with the balance of payment balance is equal to the rate of growth of exports, which in turn depends on the growth of foreign demand and the foreign income elasticity of exports, divided by the propensity to import or, in other words, the income elasticity of imports (see also Thirlwall 2011). This point is important because it reintroduces supply-side considerations into the determination of the feasible growth rate.

If a country wants to increase its feasible growth rate, it cannot simply expand aggregate demand. It will have to increase the attractiveness of its exports, or reduce the desirability of imports, which requires appropriate supply-side policies that upgrade its production structure. In reality, as the previous discussion of Germany has highlighted, prices are not fixed, and the ability to export does not just depend on foreign demand, but also on the real exchange rate.[21]

As noted already, the current-account constraint does not bind all countries equally. Countries whose currencies are on top of the international hierarchy of money will be less affected, because the rest of the world will be willing to lend to them at favorable rates and for long periods of time. In other words, monetary power matters for growth models (Cohen 2015). Only the US Fed can create monetary liabilities—"outside money"—that have to be redeemed with the means of payment the central bank controls, as opposed to other assets. Massive US federal deficits, rather than being a source of weakness for the United States, may be a source of strength, as countries holding dollar assets have a stake in maintaining the global status of the dollar as store of value. While this argument is easiest to articulate with regard to the "exorbitant privilege" enjoyed by the US dollar (Cohen 2015; Gourinchas and Rey 2007; Maggiori, Neiman, and Schreger 2020), it also applies, to a more limited extent, to currencies like the British pound, which international financial markets are willing to consider as one notch below to the dollar in the international hierarchy of money.

Despite the decline of the relative weight of the US economy in the world economy, the dollar is by far the dominant currency in the international monetary system and has become even more dominant over time (Gourinchas, Rey, and Sauzet 2019).[22] Furthermore, global banks hold liabilities denominated in dollars, which they procure on the wholesale US money market, and match them with assets also denominated in dollars (Gabor and Ban 2016; Hardie et al. 2013; Sgambati 2019). Finally, the dollar is the most important currency for central banks' official reserves, with the euro a distant second (Gourinchas, Rey, and Sauzet 2019). Its role in trade invoicing, international banking, and official reserves makes the dollar the single most important issuer of "safe assets" around the world (Caballero, Farhi, and Gourinchas 2017).

Given that US Treasury bonds are the predominant form of safe assets for global investors, other countries have incentives to run current-account surpluses with the United States in order to accumulate safe assets denominated in dollars. This explains why the US balance sheet predominantly features bonds carrying low yields as external liabilities, while the external assets of the United States are mostly equity and portfolio investments carrying a higher yield (Schwartz 2009). In part, the United States finances international net borrowing through a yield differential between international assets and liability (estimated to be about 2% by Gourinchas, Rey, and Sauzet 2019).

The difference in yields and the composition of the US balance sheet (long in equities and other more remunerative assets, short in bonds) allows the United States to act as a global banker, borrowing short and lending long (Schwartz 2009, 2019a). However, the United States is also a global insurer. Since the dollar (as a liability of the US Fed) is the ultimate means of payment of the international monetary system, and since financial actors around the globe have liabilities denominated in dollars and ultimately need dollars to carry their payments through, if there is a crisis of confidence such as in 2007, the United States needs to step in and provide global liquidity through swap lines between the Fed and other central banks (McDowell 2012). Thus, although the United States has an "exorbitant privilege," there are also times in which it has an "exorbitant duty" to provide liquidity and keep its financial empire afloat (Gourinchas and Rey 2007).

In sum, the US ability to sustain its debt-financed consumption-led growth model is strictly dependent on the ability of the United States to relax the current account constraint on growth, which in turn depends on the role of the United States as international monetary hegemon. It also bears noting that the current account deficits of the United States not only provide international liquidity but are also a non-negligible source of demand for the rest of the world.[23]

International monetary power: Life outside the top

For comparison, similar considerations about the constraining role of international finance apply, in reverse, to export-led growth in Germany. Here there is less research to support the argument. However, it seems possible that the relative underdevelopment of finance in Germany, both its equity and its bond market, makes it easier for German economic actors to export capital than to import it, strengthening its structural current account surplus (Baccaro and Braun 2020).

First, the low depth and liquidity of the German equity and bond markets present German savers with few investment opportunities, and create incentives to export capital abroad, first and foremost to an increasingly integrated European financial market, but also to international capital markets more broadly (Braun and Deeg 2020). Second, foreign capital is unlikely to want to invest in German financial assets for the same reason, although recently the German housing market seems to have become a new investment opportunity for both domestic and international capital (Baldenius, Kohl, and Schularick 2019). Third, German banks currently have excess deposits, which they park at the central bank.

Partially confirming the earlier discussion, Mendoza et al (2009) present a macroeconomic model in which, in the presence of free capital mobility, different levels of financial development across countries generate global imbalances as well a specific composition of the countries' international investment positions. Countries with greater capacity for insuring risky assets, thanks to deeper and liquid financial markets, will tend to import capital and will display a higher proportion of risky assets on their balance sheet, while countries with lower financial development will export capital and will have lower investments in risky assets and greater investment in risk-free assets. The result is that countries with higher financial development will have negative net foreign assets, a negative position in foreign debt, and a positive position in foreign equities, and vice versa for the country with lower financial development. This model resonates with developments in the United States and Germany.[24]

The considerations mentioned highlight that the position of the national growth model in the international economic hierarchy, as a "core" or "periphery" country, is relevant for the sustainability of the growth model. As argued, a debt-financed consumption-led model is feasible only if the current account constraint can be relaxed in some way, either through the attractiveness of the country's supply of financial assets (Chang and Leblond 2015; Forbes 2010) or through other mechanisms.

Spain, for example, as argued in Chapter 11, ran a consumption-led growth model in the run-up to the financial crisis, and accumulated sizable current account deficits year after year, and yet the attractiveness of Spain as a financial center did not play a very important role. In the Spanish case, the mechanism that temporarily relaxed the current account constraint was the tendency of international financial markets to treat all sovereign bonds denominated in euros as if they had the same risk profile, thus leading to a convergence in bond spreads across the Eurozone (Chang and Leblond 2015). Hence, Spain was able to import capital in the form of cross-border banking loans, mostly from other Eurozone countries.

Whether a country is core or periphery is also important for export-led growth models. Both Germany and Central and Eastern European countries relied on export-led growth in the period preceding the crisis and after its worst stages were over (Ban and Adascalitei 2020 and Chapter 7). However, it makes a big difference whether key domestic firms are at the summit of global supply chains (Durand and Milberg 2020), and are thus able to reap a greater share of profits, as is the case for German supply chains, or whether they act primarily as suppliers to foreign lead firms, in which case the opportunities for upgrading and the share of profits are more limited, and the need to squeeze costs in order to remain competitive is greater, as is the case for Eastern European supply-chain firms.

More leverage on secular stagnation

An IPE perspective on growth models adds to our alternative account of secular stagnation in at least two ways. To begin with, the growing importance of late developers is arguably an important factor behind the slowdown of economic growth at the global level. All successful late developers, from to Germany to Japan and Japan, have repressed consumption in order to increase domestic savings and investment and then grow via exports. Seen in such a historical and systemic light, the decline of wage-led growth may be more historically determined than commonly recognized.

The second factor highlights more recent work in IPE and related fields on the generation of rents in the global economy (Philippon 2019; Schwartz 2019a; Christophers 2020). The key idea in this literature is that ownership of assets that generate income streams that have high barriers to entry or legal protections such as intellectual property rights have become a key source of profits across the global capitalist system. As Schwartz (2017) argues, how global firms, especially the most profitable among them, reap superior profits through their position in global value chains through their ability to leverage intellectual property rights to their advantage is again highly relevant for growth, and differentially so.

Over the past 20 years, a global industrial structure has emerged, in which a core of IPR-protected firms earns most of the profits and pay high wages to few workers and dictate the activities of their vertically integrated and capital-intensive key suppliers, which also pay relatively high wages to substantially more, but still relatively few, workers. Downstream lie the parts suppliers and service providers that are the subcontracted supply-chain firms with low margins and low wages that pay most workers. Whether firms and countries are a part of the high value-added US tech chain in Asia, or a part of the low value-added German auto chain in Eastern Europe, matters for how they grow. In addition, the new global industrial structure described by Schwarz and others affects the rate of growth at the system level. If rents are high and protected, levels of investment fall, as does labor productivity, while inequality rises in both profits and wages across the system.

Underpinning this differential growth is what scholars in a related literature drawn from sociology and legal studies have identified as "global wealth chains" (Seabrooke and Wigan 2017) or "global financial networks" (Haberly and

Wójcik 2021). In this body of work, the firm and the corporation are made analytically distinct, with the firm acting as a going concern in a fixed location while
the corporation is seen as a multi-jurisdictional network of legal entities that
operate across a variety of jurisdictions. Making this firm-corporation distinction allows these analysts to show that the agents who control the firm can use
the legal form of the corporation to assign what parts of the overall organization
produce value and count as profits centers. This enables top management to use
jurisdictions other than the firm's home for lower taxes and/or financial secrecy
(Robé 2011; Garcia-Bernando et al. 2017), all of which has consequences for
growth and distribution.

In short, insights from IPE and related fields teaches us that national growth
models are embedded in a global system and depend on a global currency that
keeps this system liquid, with an adequate level of demand. Moreover, the
sources of secular stagnation lie at the system as well as the unit level. The system
and its units must be seen as co-evolving.

Part 5: The Politics of Growth Models

As noted at the outset, the final objective of this volume is to advance our understanding of the domestic politics of growth models. The approach to comparative and international political economy set out earlier posits that (capitalist)
growth models are inherently unstable and that the reproduction of growth
models necessarily involves state intervention in the domestic economy (and,
by extension, conflict or coordination between states). Since the 1990s, the
dominant view among CPE scholars, including French regulationists, has been
one in which "politics" matters primarily for the creation and preservation of
institutional arrangements that incentivize economic actors to behave in particular ways.

In our perspective, by contrast, governments play a more actively directive
role, and they do so, first and foremost, through the macroeconomic policies
that they pursue. In addition, the analytical perspective set out here focuses attention on distributive conflicts involved in macroeconomic management. By
stimulating or depressing different components of aggregate demand, macroeconomic policy shapes the distributions of earnings and profits across sectors.
How then should we think about the politics of macroeconomic policy choices
and, more broadly, the politics of choosing (and sustaining) growth models?

In what follows, we begin to address this question by articulating a set of
ideas about politics that are broadly shared by contributors to this volume, and
by situating these ideas in relation to the existing literature. In so doing, we

engage with the "electoral turn" in comparative political economy advocated by Beramendi *et al* (2015) as well as the long-standing literature on "producer-group coalitions" or "cross-class alliances" (Gourevitch 1986; Swenson 1991, 2002; Thelen 2014, 2019). We also seek to incorporate insights from recent work in the tradition of "elite studies" (most notably Culpepper 2011) and the literature on the role of ideas in economic policymaking (Hall 1993, Blyth 2002, Schmidt 2008).

In our view, the debate between CPE scholars who emphasize the role of electoral coalitions and those who emphasize the role of producer-group coalitions is a stale debate that we should leave behind us. Whether mass (electoral) politics trumps elite (interest-group) politics or vice-versa depends on the issues at stake and specific conjunctures. Also, the forms that elite politics and mass politics assume obviously vary across countries and over time. It seems more useful, from a theoretical point of view, to conceive of mass and elite politics as separate dimensions of the politics of growth models.[25]

The core proposition that we advance here is that the stable reproduction of growth models hinges on two political conditions. First, the presence of a coalition of more or less organized interests, including corporate elites and unelected as well as elected government officials, with a common policy agenda. Second, the ability of parties that form part of the dominant growth coalition to mobilize electoral majorities that are compatible with the agenda of this coalition. The choices that voters make at the polls do not determine the macroeconomic policies that government pursue, but they constrain the policy choices available to dominant growth coalitions. The ability of governing parties to manage policy conflicts within the dominant growth coalition in turn affects their capacity to mobilize electoral support.

Crucially, the congruence of the politics of the dominant growth coalitions and the politics of electoral coalitions must not be taken for granted. Tensions between these two domains of politics, operating according to distinctive logics, give rise to moments of uncertainty or, in other words, periods in which it becomes more difficult, and sometimes impossible, for the dominant growth coalition to issue policies that effectively support the growth model and the growth model itself becomes politically contested.[26] In many liberal democracies, the financial crisis of 2007–08 represents the beginning of such a period of "messy politics." Our objective here is not to develop a unified theory of politics. Rather, we seek to combine elements of existing theoretical models in ways that open up space for new exploratory research as well as the elaboration of testable hypotheses. As will become evident in due course, different contributors to this volume emphasize different aspects of the broad approach to the politics of growth models sketched here.

Against the "electoral turn"

Advocating an "electoral turn" in comparative political economy, Beramendi *et al.* (2015) argue that "electoral partisan politics . . . should drive explanatory accounts of policy choice in political economy" (p. 62). While Kitschelt and Rehm (2015) insist that the policy positions of political parties are, broadly speaking, representative of their voters, Häusermann and Kriesi (2015) argue that voters in contemporary democracies are aligned on two basic dimensions, "universalism versus particularism" and "state versus market." For Kitschelt-Rehm and Häusermann-Kriesi alike, politics is essentially a contest between parties that seek to build and sustain coalitions of voters in this two-dimensional space.

Our critique of the "electoral turn" advocated by Beramendi *et al* (2015) is three-fold. As we have argued earlier, the lack of attention the politics of macroeconomic management is a conspicuous feature of the volume assembled by these scholars. In a telling passage, Häusermann and Kriesi (2015: 207–208) assert that macroeconomic and industrial policies have largely been taken out of the hands of national governments because of European integration and that parties of the Left and Right have tended to converge on these issues. These authors then point out that "important alternative economic issues such as labor market regulation and welfare policies remain within the discretion of national governments, and on these issues, both party policies and voter preferences continue to diverge."

This passage ignores the divergence of macroeconomic conditions generated by monetary integration and the close links between macroeconomic policy and social spending. More importantly, we question the idea that comparative political economists should restrict their attention to issues on which parties and voters diverge. While we do observe partisan convergence on macroeconomic issues in many countries (see the chapters by Hopkin and Voss and Huebscher and Sattler in this volume), the policy stance on which parties (and voters) converge is not the same across all countries. As comparativists, we are (ought to be) interested in explaining how and why policy consensus varies across countries and over time.

The neglect of corporate interests and the political influence of business is another conspicuous feature of the approach to the politics of advanced capitalism advanced by Beramendi *et al.* (2015). Their case for the "supremacy of electoral partisan politics" hinges entirely on the observation that organized labor and tripartite corporatism are in decline across the OECD countries (pp. 25–26, 388). Much of the 1980s literature on producer group politics focuses on more or less explicit bargaining between organizations representing business and labor, but the political influence of organized business and large corporations surely does not presuppose corporatist bargaining. To the contrary, the influence of corporate interests over government policy would appear to be inversely associated with union power and tripartite corporatism (as suggested by Hacker and Pierson 2010 as well as Culpepper 2011).

Finally, the way that Beramendi *et al.* (2015) conceive of electoral politics strikes us as problematic. Emphasizing electoral coalitions, these authors depart from some of the assumptions of median-voter theory, but they, too, posit that voters choose parties based on well-specified policy preferences and that every voter carries the same weight in the strategic calculi of vote-seeking parties. These assumptions, about parties as well as voters, run afoul of the well-documented observation that, across liberal democracies, government policy is consistently more responsive to the policy preference of affluent voters than to the policy preferences of middle-income and especially poor voters.[27] The mechanisms of unequal representation are open to debate, but any adequate theoretization of contemporary politics in liberal democracies must surely, somehow, take income and class biases in representation into account.

The politics of policy choice: Dominant growth coalitions

Starting with Gourevitch (1986), an important strand of comparative political economy conceives of politics in terms of coalitions among "producer groups," defined by class interests and sectoral interests, and of policy outputs as the outcome of struggles between competing coalitions.[28] Our approach to the politics of growth models builds on this literature, but also seeks to improve on it. While we disagree with some of the assumptions and propositions associated with "the electoral turn," we agree that many contributions to the producer-group literature have not paid sufficient attention to electoral politics. Setting the role of electoral politics aside for the time being, there are other blindspots in the producer-group literature that we want to identify and address as well.

To begin with, we contest the way in which the producer-group literature commonly conceives "cross-class alliances," to use Swenson's apt and oft-cited expression, in terms of two rather crude dichotomies: sheltered vs. exposed sectors and labor vs. capital. An obvious objection to this conceptualization of the core cleavages that underpin coalitional politics is that finance is entirely missing. Yet finance capital and the financial services industry have long been important powerful actors in some political economies—most notably, of course, the British political economy—and their influence has arguably increased in most political economies in the post-Fordist era (along with importance of financial assets as a source of income for upper-middle-class households). The growth models perspective that we have set out above also invites a more disaggregated view of the real economy and the macroeconomic policy preferences (or "requirements") of different sectors. For example, some exposed sectors are more exchange-rate-sensitive than other exposed sectors. And some sheltered sectors are more interest-rate-sensitive than other sheltered sectors. Moreover, it is important to recognize, we think, that sectoral interests, as distinct from class interests, are more salient for wage-earners with sector-specific skills than for wage-earners with more general skills (Iversen and Soskice 2001) and, in a similar vein, that sectoral interests are more salient for some capitalists than for others.

A second blind spot of the producer-groups literature concerns the way that it often conflates "producer group politics" with "policy-making through tripartite bargaining." In some countries, cross-class alliances have commonly taken corporatist forms, but the absence of corporatist institutions does not mean that cross-class alliances are unimportant, let alone absent.[29] Lobbying by sectoral business associations and informal networks linking corporate elites to elected and unelected governments officials constitute an alternative channel of producer-group politics that the CPE scholars have tended to ignore. Relatedly, we suggest that the sectoral interests of (some) skilled workers can be represented in politics not only by unions, but also by the firms for which they work and by the business associations to which these firms belong.

Pioneered by Culpepper (2011), recent work on the political influence of corporate elites represents a welcome addition to the CPE tradition emphasizing non-electoral politics or, Culpepper's terminology, "quiet politics." However, the elite literature fails to address our core questions to the extent that it focuses on ideas, values, interests and behaviors that all managers and owners of large corporations have in common. Again, we want to know why government policies favor certain sectoral interests (and certain corporations) over others, and why such biases vary across countries. In our view, these questions cannot be answered without reference to the growth models that different countries have adopted. Simply put, our working hypothesis is that representatives of sectors or firms that are key to the success of the growth model enjoy privileged access to policymakers.[30]

To convey a less voluntaristic and less pluralistic conception of "coalitions" than the prevailing conception in the producer-group literature, we propose to speak of "dominant growth coalitions." In our conceptualization, these coalitions are organized around "policy paradigms" in the sense that Hall (1993) uses the latter term. That is, a set of propositions about how the economy works and what the overarching goals of government policy should be. They are not coalitions among equals, but rather characterized by hierarchical power relations, with firms in leading sectors (and the owners of those firms) constituting the core of the coalition and other, more or less organized, groups occupying subordinate positions.

Representatives of the different groups that are part of the coalition negotiate what Hall (1983) refers to as first- and second-order policy changes, pertaining to policy instruments and specific policy settings, but the policy paradigm, or, in other words, the growth strategy upon which the coalition rests, is rarely subject for (re)negotiation. In ordinary times, when growth models operate smoothly, there is one growth coalition that is clearly dominant and subordinate groups within this coalition do not have readily available exit options. In the domain of macroeconomic management and long-term growth policies, much of what we think of as "coalitional politics" is about managing conflicts of interest and accommodating changes in the balance of power within the dominant growth coalition as distinct from struggles between competing coalitions.

In our view, the advocates of the electoral turn are mistaken to the extent that they treat political parties simply as vote-maximizing machines or inter-mediary organizations through which citizens' preferences are represented in the policy-making process. As suggested by Blyth and Katz (2005), governing parties of the Center-Left as well as the Center-Right can and should (also) be seen as part of the dominant growth coalition (see also Hopkin and Blyth 2018). Ministers and senior parliamentarians, along with their unelected policy advisors, participate regularly in policy deliberations that involve conflicts of interest within the dominant growth coalition and, in this context, promote the interests of one or another of the contending groups. Equally important, party leaders and the expert advisors on whom they rely play a key role in the elaboration of the paradigms that define the parameters of policy debate within the dominant growth coalition and in the projection of these paradigms to the public at large.[31]

Back to electoral politics

As noted above, we do not contest that elections matter. Rather, what we con-test is that elections are about choosing macroeconomic policies and, by ex-tension, choosing growth models. In our view, it makes more sense to think of electoral politics in terms of selling the growth model/the policies of the domi-nant growth coalition to the public at large and, in some circumstances, to pre-empt or deflect popular discontent. Needless to say the nature and scope of this challenge depends on how inclusive the growth model is, but also on global economic conditions. In a global context characterized by stagnation, post-Fordist growth models and the coalitions that support them have become less inclusive since the crisis of 2008–09 and, as result, it has becoming increasingly difficult for governing parties to mobilize electoral majorities. Furthermore, some growth models have more "degrees of freedom" than others and allow for a more encompassing support base without imperiling the functionality of the growth model. For example, Sweden's "balanced" growth model arguably accommodates service-sector workers better than Germany's export-led model (cf. Baccaro and Pontusson 2019).

In contrast to Beramendi *et al's* (2015) emphasis on issue voting, our approach to electoral politics emphasizes economic voting and the idea that claims to be competent managers of the economy are a key feature of the electoral appeals of mainstream parties. Featuring prominently in some the CPE literature of the 1990s, notably in Garrett (1998), economic voting deserves, we think, to be brought back to center stage. Most importantly for our purposes, economic voting provides a simple and quite convincing explanation of why elected policymakers are particularly inclined to attend to the needs and demands of leading firms and sectors. That is, the firms and sectors that drive economic growth in their country. In this sense, electoral politics mediated by governing parties might be seen as a constraint on the ability of subordinate coalition partners to challenge the policy preferences of leading sectors.

Building on the Gramscian notion of hegemony, it seems highly plausible to argue that mainstream political parties as well as government authorities play an important role in projecting the interests of leading firms and sectors as the "national interest." In Gramsci's (1992) core formulation, the success of such "framing effects" may require material concessions targeted on potentially disruptive subordinate groups, but the key to the political dominance of certain ideas about the way that society operates (or the way the economy operates) is "passive consent," the belief that, in the phrase typically attributed to Margaret Thatcher, "there is no alternative" or, "this is the way things function," which signals the ability of a hegemonic discourse to shape the perception of basic causal relationships. As the Trump experience illustrates, when all else fails, at least some governing parties are willing to turn to populist scapegoating to shore up the legitimacy of failing growth models. Without going further into this topic, suffice it to say that ideas that are backed by powerful actors and that resonate with material interests of those to whom the ideas are communicated play an important role in our understanding mass politics as well as well as our understanding of elite politics.

Our approach to the politics of growth models seeks to steer a middle course between the producer coalitions approach and the electoral approach by systematically distinguishing between the politics of policy choice and the politics of democratic legitimation. The former is shaped by a dominant growth coalition, which—we posit—is aware of the "requirements" of the growth model and has privileged access to government bureaucrats and the policy implementation sphere. Typically, the latter is *not* primarily about choosing the growth model, but about diffusing opposition to it such that the key policy foundations of the growth model remain in the background. We do not take a stance on whether the dominant growth coalition is composed of key sectors or key firms, leaving this to be determined on a case-by-case basis. Furthermore, we do not see the two political moments as tightly coupled. Especially in moments of crisis, a growth coalition may come apart because it is unable to secure a viable electoral majority, and political entrepreneurs may assemble new coalitions in the electoral sphere, which in turn forces a reconfiguration of the producer coalition and the growth model.

In sum, in this introduction we have developed a new approach to the politics of growth and stagnation, based around the concept of growth models, underpinned by Post Keynesian macroeconomic theory. We compared our approach to the "Varieties of Capitalism" (and "Electoral Turn") approaches along the axes of macroeconomic and core growth assumptions, the main theoretical models produced by each approach, key growth drivers, approach to economic policy, the effects of the international economy, views of secular stagnation, and underlying model of politics. Our objective is to provide an updated understanding of growth and stagnation that better tracks the polarized and contested world of today. A world where demand and distribution matter, and where growth, the universal salve of capitalism, is harder to come by. The following table I.1 summarizes key differences between the Growth Models and Varieties Approaches.

The Rest of the Book

The rest of this volume is organized modularly so that it can be read as a whole or in parts. The first part of the volume builds upon this introductory chapter to more fully specify the model of growth and stagnation that we operationalize in the empirical chapters. The second and third parts of the volume considers empirical cases at the regional and national level of aggregation, respectively, operationalizing the insights of the introduction and the chapters in the first part of the volume. The fourth and final part focuses on specific issues (financialization, politics, austerity, the welfare state), which either affect or are affected by growth models.

Further elaboration of the theory

Part 1 consists of three chapters. The first chapter, following this introduction, by Onaran and Stockhammer, gives us an "under the hood" explication of the Post-Keynesian (PK) macroeconomics that defines our approach. It first contrasts the methodological foundations of PKE and discusses differences and

Table I.1 **Varieties of Capitalism and Growth Models Compared**

Core Features of the Model	*Varieties of Capitalism*	*Growth Models*
Macroeconomic approach	New Keynesian	Post Keynesian
Core Growth Assumptions	Given by the Supply Side and R^*. Monetary dominance assumed and pursued	R^* is unstable and monetary policy insufficient. Demand can drive supply when there is capacity
Core Focus	Firm-level strategies to solve coordination problems	Shifts in demand, wages and profits in national economies with a focus on sectoral production of GVA
Main growth models	• Liberal Market Economies (LMEs) • Coordinated Market Economies (CMEs)	• Consumption/ Debt-financed • Export-led • Balanced • Commodity-Led • Peripheral
Growth drivers	Supply factors - changes in demography, technology, human capital	Demand factors - stimulated by fiscal and monetary policies
Macroeconomic policies	Ineffective in the long-run due to monetary neutrality. Short-run, macroeconomic policies create distortions from the assumed competitive equilibrium. Policy should focus on microeconomic reforms to labor and product markets	Policies that expand demand can stimulate investment and productivity growth. Aggregate demand and wage growth can positively effect productivity
International Dimension	Absent as the development of capitalism is determined by domestic firms' responses to price changes that may be local or global	Present insofar as some GMs such as export-led rely on shifts in foreign demand. More generally seen as a mediating condition for national GM growth drivers

(*continued*)

Table I.1 **Continued**

Core Features of the Model	Varieties of Capitalism	Growth Models
Secular Stagnation	Stagnation is driven by the secular decline of r*, which is in turn driven by supply side factors such as high-tech firms and aging populations. Growth is below potential to adjust the gap between household savings and business demand for credit.	Stagnation is policy driven. The decline of r* is a manifestation of stagnation, not its cause. The end of the wage-led growth model (weaker unions and labor institutions) is the main cause.
View of Politics	Implicitly producer group led, low salience of social conflict or distribution	Distinction between politics of policymaking, which is producer group-led, and politics of consensus building, in which electoral dynamics play a key role. Loose coupling between the two spheres.

similarities to mainstream economics and New Keynesian Economics. It then presents the main features of PKE: demand-led growth (the goods market), PK monetary theory (financial markets) and a theory of induced technological change that gives rise to path-dependent growth (the supply side). These moves allow an explication of the PK theory of demand regimes, which covers distributional growth drivers (wage/profit-led growth) as well as extensions that consider debt-driven and export-driven growth and how fiscal policy fits into the model. Finally, the chapter discusses financialization, the return of financial cycles and central role of real estate prices for recent macroeconomic performance. The chapter thus provides the macroeconomic framework that underpins the growth models approach that subsequent chapters draw upon.

The second chapter by Schwartz gives us a deep dive into the issue of secular stagnation, discussed above, by focusing on how corporate profit strategy and organizational structures changed from the Fordist era to what he calls the present "Franchise" era. Schwartz draws attention to how the spread of franchise structures tends to concentrate profits into firms with a low marginal propensity to invest and concentrate wages (critical for consumption) into those firms' small labor force, which also has a low marginal propensity to consume. Concentrated profits and wages provide a plausible causal explanation for secular stagnation.

For Schwartz, the critical issue in the shift from Fordism to Franchise is not simply the growing salience of "knowledge" or human capital in production, but rather the ongoing effort to wrap a legal property right around that knowledge and to separate the corporate ownership of those formal intellectual property rights (patent, copyright, brand and trademark—IPRs) from formal legal ownership of physical capital and from formal legal responsibility for employees. This gives rise globally to a three-tiered production system where IPR-rich firms capture a disproportionate volume of profit on account of their possession of legally defined monopolies. Physical capital-intensive firms capture more moderate volumes when they can use investment barriers to entry, tacit knowledge, and horizontal concentration (or some combination of these three) to deter competitive entry. Finally, labor-intensive firms capture only small volumes of profit despite high levels of labor exploitation. This chapter allows a deeper understanding of the findings in the later empirical chapters on FDI and global supply chains, as well as contextualizing the debate about financialization, by showing the ways in which the financial sector resembles the IPR dominated sectors.

The third and final chapter in this volume by Schwartz and Blyth focuses attention on which level of analysis we should focus on to understand growth and stagnation. Integrating insights from IPE into CPE (and vice versa) they discuss the degree to which the global system conditions unit level growth models, or conversely, the degree of independence those models exhibit in terms of their domestic growth dynamics. They lay out four approaches for understanding the relationship between national growth models and the global system.

The first approach, treats units (countries) in isolation, positing that independent unit-level responses to common functional problems lead to a shift in the system overall. Here the system is the sum of its parts. The second approach also starts at the unit level but focuses upon fallacies of composition at a higher, usually global level of aggregation, such that common responses produce a global outcome that differs from those at which individual strategies aimed. The third approach introduces the question of asymmetric power at the system level, positing that the differential capacity of units allows one or more units to dictate the structure and payoffs to the system overall. Analysis at this level views the global economy as a single but highly asymmetric field of power where differentially placed states and global firms' investment and supply chain activities impact unit-level growth models independence. Here the system conditions units and is more than the sum of its parts. The fourth approach adds path dependency to the third approach, positing that the timing and insertion of unit-level growth models into the global economy matters hugely. Here the system not only conditions units, but in the strongest form of the approach is causal for unit level growth models. Finally, the chapter considers the degree to which the global economy exhibits financial Minsky cycles akin to those at the national level. This helps us assess which of the four approaches captures the system and unit level dynamic most accurately. It also complements the chapter on financialization.

Growth Models at scale

The second part of the volume analyzes regional or national varieties of growth models. Chapter 4, by Johnson and Matthijs, examines the countries of the European Monetary Union (EMU), not as a single growth model but as a set of institutions that advantage some unit level strategies and disable others such that, as Schwartz and Blyth argue, the effect of the whole is greater than the sum of the parts. Johnson and Matthijs argue that that prior to 2009, EMU accommodated a diverse set of growth models, even strengthening the growth strategies of its export-led and domestic consumption-led members. However, come the crisis of 2009–2014, the EMU's export-led core countries re-wrote the Eurozone's new macroeconomic rules in a manner that championed export-led growth strategies as stagnant domestic demand within its peripheral countries led the Eurozone as a whole to build up growing current account surpluses with the rest of the world during the 2010s.

This strategy had a mixed record in the first half of the decade, working in some countries but not in others. However, in a world of trade wars and big power rivalries, it quickly runs into trouble. While the ECB continues to be the main source of offsetting declines in domestic demand, it is running up against serious political constraints and operational limits. In conclusion, Johnson and Matthijs argue that if the EU wants to put its future growth on a more sustainable footing it will need to re-write the euro's governing rules. Specifically it will need to rebalance the advantage given to export-led models by accommodating domestic demand driven models through more fiscal flexibility and an EU-wide industrial policy to compete with the US and China.

Chapter 5 turns to China itself. As the country tipped to surpass the US in size in a few years and, arguably, as the poster child for successful growth strategies over the past 30 years, how China grows matters for the world as a whole. Tan and Conran argue that China's economic expansion has been the product of a hybrid system containing two growth models, one based on exports concentrated along the coast, and the other on state-led investment in China's interior. The chapter then compares the political economic underpinnings of China's growth models with those of the countries in the West, in particular noting salient similarities (but also differences) with the German export-led model, the Irish FDI-led model, and the Spanish construction-led model. Their analysis suggests that China's heterogeneous growth regime may be compared with the Eurozone—another continent-sized economy with distinct regional growth models—rather than its member-states. They argue that the two component growth models are far from easy complements, with each one having distinct distributional implications, as well as specific pathologies that produce consequential spillovers for the global economy.

This chapter analyzes the political coalitions and state-capital relations underpinning the Chinese growth models to elucidate the unique dimensions that authoritarian capitalism brings to our understanding of growth models, while also highlighting commonalities that transcend regime types. In particular, it emphasizes the shared centrality of economic growth as a legitimation mechanism in both democratic and authoritarian capitalism. The analysis explores the degree to which authoritarian rule enables China to switch between growth models—emphasizing exports or investment as circumstances dictate—in ways that may be harder for democratic regimes. It also identifies limits to this "authoritarian flexibility" however, by examining the state-capital politics that have frustrated the PRC leadership's longstanding desire to shift towards a more consumption-driven growth model.

In chapter 6, Sierra examines Latin America, focusing on the distributive conflicts surrounding export-led growth models based on commodities that define the continent's economies. Sierra argues that the persistence of commodity-driven growth as the general growth model of Latin America is explained by an endogenous distributional dilemma. While governments have clear incentives to promote the interests of the rural sector due to its centrality in commodity-led growth, doing so affects their capacity to promote the urban sector, and thereby successfully switch growth models.

How did Latin America endogenize this switching dilemma? First, the formation of a strong export oligarchy in the post-colonial period led to a concentration of income and assets that allowed landed elites to retain the power to undermine policies that affected their interests, notably redistribution and broad-based industrialization. Second, unable to finance economic modernization through either rural elites or urban labor, Latin American governments ended up depending on foreign finance in the form of capital imports to attempt to bypass the switching dilemma, placing additional external limits on structural transformation.

Sierra then shows us through the cases of Argentina and Brazil how these Latin American Commodity dependent states have undergone three rounds of attempted GM switching, each of which has been undermined by this endogenous dilemma. She concludes that the politics of switching GMs is complicated insofar as governments must navigate the distributional tensions involved in compensating the losers of the switch, while at the same time providing incentives to the potential winners of the switch. Identifying these losers and winners, and how policies must often be designed to address their interests simultaneously, can shed light on the conditions under which GM switching may succeed.

Rounding out our examination of growth models at the regional level, chapter 7 by Ban and Ascalitei discusses the consolidation of an export-led growth model in Central and Eastern Europe. Focusing on three distinct time periods (2000–2008, 2008–2012 and 2012–2019), it shows that despite marginal shifts towards consumption-led growth through personal debt or wage increases, the core of the region's economic model continues to be heavily dependent on exports. The consolidation of the CEE export-led model has both systemic and national roots.

Specifically, growing international competition from Asia in the beginning of 2000s forced firms in Western economies to seek alternative sources of competitiveness that involved a mix of wage moderation at home and expansion towards the CEE countries. Capital hungry Eastern governments were all too happy to use FDI to restore the competitiveness of their outdated state-owned enterprises. Backed by a growth coalition that involved domestic and foreign capital as well as workers in the tradeable sectors, the export-led growth model took off and generated growth rates well above those seen in core countries. The 2000s also saw an increase in debt fueled consumption, which partially compensated for the lack of wage growth in the region.

The crisis provided an opportunity to put an end to hybridization and to reinforce the export-led component of growth through short-term austerity measures and deeper labor market reforms. These changes consolidated the export-led model that remained in place even amidst political reconfigurations that, at least rhetorically, aimed to fight the economic dependency of the region on FDI. After the crisis ended, however, the closing of the debt-finance consumption channel combined with the German export boom to the rest of the world and local demographic decline to put upwards pressure on wage-financed consumption increases without inflationary or external balance problems. Yet despite historically low spreads in the region's bond markets, this did not count as a full Kaleckian turn, however, with the region's contribution of consumption to GDP growth remaining far below both consumption-led growth models and balanced ones.

Country Case Studies

Following this discussion of growth models at scale, in part 3 of the volume we drop down to the unit level to discuss countries that exemplify what might be seen as the "ideal-typical" cases of growth models. Chapter 8 focuses upon the credit and consumption-led growth models of the US and the UK. In this chapter Reisenbichler and Wiedemann analyze the workings of credit-driven, consumption-led growth models and their underlying political support coalitions. They identify two distinct channels through which these growth models generate aggregate demand: the housing and income-maintenance channels, which suggests that housing markets can be transmission belts for the larger economy and influence aggregate demand and macroeconomic performance through credit, wealth, and capital flow effects. The income-maintenance channel, in turn, posits that credit markets help households maintain their income and economic status when earnings stagnate and expenditures rise to functionally substitute for wage growth and social policies, allowing households to go into debt to smooth income losses and meet rising expenditures.

They document these channels and their political support coalitions in the United States and the United Kingdom as exemplary cases of credit-driven consumption-led growth models. They also highlight how these credit- and consumption-led growth models are embedded in the international political economy. As capital controls were lifted across the OECD, the US dollar's role as a reserve currency gave the US an "exorbitant privilege," allowing it to sustain massive current account deficits that fuel household borrowing and foreign (largely Chinese) investment in U.S. Treasuries and mortgage-backed securities. This suggests that credit-driven, consumption-led growth models depend on surplus countries—which often run export-driven growth models—for capital inflows.

Chapter 9 focuses upon the locus classicus of expert-led growth, Germany. Baccaro and Hoepner build upon the Johnson and Matthijs chapter by arguing that exports are central to the German GM. They argue that the key ingredient of this growth model is undervaluation, which has two aspects. First, a set of institutions and policies that keep inflation lower than Germany's trade partners. That is, the construction of a bargaining regime oriented towards wage moderation, conservative monetary and fiscal policies, and strict credit regulation, especially with respect to housing credit, which prevents the rise of asset prices from spilling over into rising wages and prices. Second, a rigid exchange rate regime that minimizes the possibility of exchange rate adjustment, thus ensuring real exchange rate undervaluation. Together, these policies hold down prices in the domestic sector in order to enhance the competitiveness of the export sector. Since the emergence of the Euro and the consequent effects of the Euro crisis these effects have been turbocharged such that German growth continues to be highly reliant on externally generated demand, despite a partial rebalancing in the post-crisis period. This situation leaves Germany vulnerable to external economic and political pressures, as well as acting as the "price policeman" of the Eurozone, to the detriment of many of its members.

In chapter 10, Erixon and Pontusson examine Sweden's growth dynamics from the early 1990s through the 2010s. The chapter expands on, but also qualifies Baccaro and Pontusson's (2016) characterization of the Swedish growth model in the period 1994–2008 and argues that the distinction between wag-led and profit-led growth deserves more attention than the GM literature has given it so far. Erixon and Pontusson characterize the pre-crisis Swedish growth model as "export-led" *and* "balanced," with "balanced growth" understood in terms of complementarities between economic sectors characterized by wage-led growth and sectors characterized by profit-led growth. They argue that productivity growth is critical to the sustainability of balanced growth and that aggregate demand alone does not provide an adequate explanation for Sweden's high rate of productivity growth in the period 1994–2008. The chapter proceeds to show that exports played an important role in the recovery of the early 2010s and that domestic consumption, financed by credit as well as wage growth, has been the main demand driver of growth over the last decade. Yet exports remain very important to the Swedish economy. In Erixon and Pontusson's formulation, the crisis triggered a shift from a balanced export-led growth model to balanced consumption-led growth.

Building on the discussion in this first introductory chapter, Erixon and Pontusson suggest that three considerations explain the shift in the Swedish growth model. First, global economic stagnation rendered an export-led recovery a less viable/attractive option (for vote-seeking politicians) than it was in the 1980s and 1990s. Secondly, the interests of Swedish export firms have become more diffuse and financial interests have gained influence within the dominant growth coalition since the 1980s. Thirdly, electoral politics has increasingly focused on short-term competition for the support of middle-class voters as a result structural-economic changes, the rise of white-collar unions, and the persistence of the Left-Right divide.

Chapter 11, by Baccaro and Bulfone, examines the contrasting experience of Italy and Spain. Again drawing on the chapter by Johnson and Matthjis, Baccaro and Bulfone argue that in the pre-crisis period Spain was able to develop a credit-financed consumption-led growth model, which was made possible by the convergence of interests rates across the EU and the associated enhanced cross-border banking flows. In contrast, the Italian economy stagnated, as it was neither able to stimulate exports nor to stimulate domestic demand sufficiently. The different trajectory is linked to a combination of international and domestic factors, specifically, the conditions of entry into the European Monetary Union and the composition of dominant growth coalitions in the two countries.

In Spain, there was a clear coalition between developers, banks, and politicians, which was built around the needs of the mortgage finance/construction industry complex and associated services. In Italy, the growth strategy first sought to increase the competitiveness of the export sector through wage moderation, and then sought to favor the expansion of domestic demand, leading to some of the same policy trends as in Spain, such as rising housing prices and rising construction investment, but not nearly to the same extent. Exports were made more difficult by an overvalued real exchange rate and higher competition by newly developed economies, while a high level of public debt, which Italy inherited from the 1980s, led to the constant need for fiscal adjustment and made the stimulation of domestic demand more difficult. Consequently, there was no clear growth model and no clear dominant coalition in Italy. In the post-crisis period both countries were pushed into austerity and forced to increase the export-contribution to growth. However, the Spanish economy was able to rebound and continues to display greater dynamism than the Italian one.

Chapter 12 rounds out this discussion of unit level growth models with a discussion of some of the "courtesan" states of the OECD, whose growth model is largely determined by their position in the international economy and the skills of its economic and political elites to attract and keep capital. In this chapter Bohle and Regan argue that small states occupy different privileged positions in global wealth and value chains. In the globally interconnected world of big tech, banking, and financial services, they argue that small states increasing carve out particular niches in global wealth chains to service the needs of global investment capital—shareholders and high net worth individuals. These activities include everything from creating digital sales hubs to capture revenue, storing intellectual property, coding trade secrets, facilitating corporate tax avoidance, funneling tax evasion, enabling illicit banking practices, and opening the door to money laundering.

To illustrate how small states generate and are co-constitutive of global wealth chains, they examine two distinct cases. First, they examine the role of Ireland in facilitating the global corporate tax avoidance strategies of US multinationals, which increases the wealth of individual shareholders in big tech and pharma companies. Second, they examine the role of Latvia in facilitating illicit banking practices and money laundering, which increases the wealth of high-net-worth individuals in Russia. The paper concludes by arguing that the growth model literature needs to move beyond methodological and ontological assumptions of the *national* to understand the integrated and globalized nature of capital accumulation.

Policies and politics

The third and final part of this volume considers issues that importantly impact all growth models, albeit differentially. Chapter 13, by Helgadottir and Ban, brings a financialization lens to bear on the theory and practice of growth models. They argue that growth model theorists have not adequately theorized the constitutive role of finance in the production and maintenance of growth models. Their main argument is that each of the key growth models theorized in the previous section has distinct financialization dynamics that have shaped the contribution of exports and consumption to GDP growth in each of the growth models. Indeed, all of them have been deeply affected by financialization, particularly by shareholder value concerns and the increasing reliance of non-financial firms on financial activities, leading to growing corporate profits even as capital investment declines. This is not however homogenous process across cases.

They argue that the extent and mode of financialization explains why Sweden has maintained a higher level of capital investment than other cases, while still projecting robust consumption growth; why consumption has been such a resilient growth engine in Britain but not in Italy; and why the German growth model was constrained to stay competitive in export markets by repressing consumption. A clearer understanding of these component parts can also shed light on systemic dynamics. That is, financialization increasingly acts as the transnational "nervous system" connecting and enabling different growth models, as seen in how export-led economies that have generated surplus corporate profit have invested in debt-led models that rely on financial inflows.

Chapter 14 by Hopkin and Voss takes on the issue of politics as party politics. That is, the construction, maintenance, and sometimes the destruction of the political coalitions that underpin growth models and the role of political parties therein. This chapter suggests ways in which party politics can be brought into GM theory. Hopkin and Voss discuss how political parties have been differentially conceptualized by political economists and party specialists and illustrate the potential for bringing these literatures together. They offer empirical illustrations to show how growth models are shaped by party politics in the cases of Germany and the United Kingdom. They argue that electoral politics should not be seen as epiphenomenal or incidental to growth models, but neither is it realistic to claim that electoral politics shapes policy and institutional development in the direct way imagined by optimistic accounts of how parties "matter." Instead, they show how GM theory's emphasis on the politics of demand, the instability of contemporary financialized capitalism, and overbearing influence of the asset-holding classes, can be better understood by integrating new research on political parties into the picture. Finally, they show that the recent rise in populist or anti-system policies, and the ways in which this has reshaped the political economy, shows how growth models cannot insulate themselves from electoral pressures, particularly when they fail to deliver growth.

Chapter 15 turns to a policy that aims to restore growth but, in many cases, ends up reducing it: austerity. In this chapter Huebscher and Sattler examine how austerity not only impacts but benefits some growth models over others. Providing micro data to complement the arguments of Johnson and Matthijs, they argue that an export-led GM requires a reduction of fiscal deficits in order to promote cost competitiveness, while a demand-led GM requires fiscal flexibility to manage domestic demand. Huebscher and Sattler demonstrate that governments in fact subordinate their fiscal policy to the growth model of their country. Governments in export-led economies are two to three times more likely to pursue fiscal austerity than those in demand-led growth models. Relevant to the findings of Hopkin and Voss, they also find that the austere policies that many countries pursue are not in line with either voter attitudes or macroeconomic beliefs.

Contrary to the economic ideas that provide the intellectual foundation of fiscal austerity, voters believe that these policies are detrimental to economic growth, but there is great variation in the beliefs of left and right voters. These ideological differences translate into distinct fiscal policies under left and right governments in balanced growth models, but not in unbalanced models. These results point to a mismatch between government policy, especially in export-led economies, and voter views on fiscal policy, a mismatch that potentially contributes to the political disillusionment of voters and hence the rise of populist parties.

Chapter 16 turns to the welfare state and how it relates to growth models. In addressing this topic, Lynch and Watson reintroduce the distinction between the accumulation and the legitimation functions of the welfare state, articulated by Marxist state theorists in the 1970s. Positing specific social policy needs for each of the growth models identified by Baccaro and Pontusson (2016), these authors assess the extent to which growth-model logics shed light on recent welfare-state reforms in Germany, Italy, Sweden and the UK. Political legitimation of growth models, they argue, represents a more important consideration than accumulation needs in the politics of welfare-state reforms. Against this background, Lynch and Watson elaborate on different pathways whereby social policies serve to legitimate different growth models and illustrate such pathways with reference to the aforementioned country cases.

Finally, chapter 17 deals with the economic consequences of climate change. The climate crisis is perhaps the greatest constraint on all growth models and makes one wonder whether the planet will be able to afford having growth at all in the future. Successful emissions reductions require state-led transformations of virtually every sector of the economy. Nahm argues that across GM types a popular political strategy to overcome vested interest opposition to decarbonization has been to promise "green growth." That is, to build coalitions of decarbonization supporters that expect material benefits from green industrial change.

Yet states have varied dramatically in the types of green growth strategies that they have chosen and have only in some cases been able to deliver the promised economic co-benefits as a result of climate policy. Some states, including China and Germany, have emphasized export-driven green industrial strategies, yielding new jobs in manufacturing industries because of a clean energy transition. Others, such as the United States and the United Kingdom, have focused on the domestic consumption of clean energy technologies and imported a great share of such technologies from abroad.

Nahm argues that in terms of economics, divergent patterns of green growth reflect broader cross-national differences in growth models that emphasize different types of aggregate demand in the domestic economy. In terms of politics, differences in state-business relations, labor and wage politics, and distributional outcomes have shaped the types of coalitions that have emerged behind climate policy. Nahm concludes that while different growth models are in principle compatible with aggressive decarbonization, the configuration of economic and political coalitions supporting climate policy varies across growth models and the ability of states to actually pursue "green growth" has as much to do with their ability to find potential coalition partners as it has to do with technological or other limits.

Concluding Remarks

This volume aims to reshape the conceptual map in political economy. For too long political economy has accepted, implicitly or explicitly, the mainstream economic view about what deliberate policy intervention can and should try to achieve, and what issues can be meaningfully analyzed as "political" issues. In our opinion, this has led it into a *cul de sac* from which it is unable to see, let alone address, some of the most pressing problems of the age. We want to build, or rebuild, a political economy in which growth, distribution, and power are front and center. This leads us to take a critical stance vis-à-vis mainstream New Keynesian macroeconomics, which has provided the intellectual background (implicit or explicit) for a previous generation of research, and to strike an alliance with post-Keynesian economics, which we see as having elective affinities with political economy.

We think that the distinction between CPE and IPE is a matter of emphasis and not a fundamental divide. We acknowledge that a strongly unequal and hierarchical international economic "system" conditions heavily what is possible and feasible at the level of the "units," but it does not entirely determine it. There are meaningful differences in growth models and growth strategies at the national level, and these are shaped by politics.

Furthermore, we want to overcome the distinction between "producer group" politics and "electoral" politics and elaborate a theory that includes both moments. The politics of coalitions and sectoral elites is key for understanding the formulation of key policy decisions, but electoral politics plays an important role in the reproduction of the growth model, and as a constraint on what elites are able to achieve.

The growth model perspective has the ambition to change the way we do political economy. We see the economy as populated by competing groups vying for the control of key resources and attempting to shape the way the social world is perceived—in other words, an eminently political phenomenon.

Notes

1. We thank Wolfgang Streeck for suggesting this formulation.
2. The crisis of Fordism and post-Fordist production regimes also feature prominently in the analytical framework of the French regulation school (e.g. Boyer 2004) but note that French regulationists conceive "Fordism" as a macroeconomic regime (as we do in what follows).
3. Another strand of "macroeconomic CPE" in the 1980s and 1990s focused on strategic interaction between wage-bargaining agents and monetary authorities (see Hall and Franzese 1998). Scharpf (1991) stands out as the most comprehensive analysis of macroeconomic management in the CPE tradition.
4. In support of this general line of argument, Soskice (1999) suggests that multinational corporations are engaged in "institutional arbitrage," locating different activities in countries with different institutional configurations.
5. For more on debates surrounding the VofC approach, see the 2003 symposium in *Comparative European Politics* as well as Coates (2005) and Hancké et al. (2007).
6. More recently, Soskice and collaborators have pleaded with CPE scholars to engage with macroeconomics in a more sustained manner (e.g., Iversen and Soskice 2006, Carlin and Soskice 2009), but, as we argue in the next part of this essay, their efforts to "bring macroeconomics back in" amount to a reassertion of the dominance of supply-side factors.
7. The following discussion draws on and extends Pontusson and Baccaro (2020).
8. As discussed by Stockhammer (2008a), the NAIRU is a theoretical hybrid, which can be given New Keynesian, Post-Keynesian, and Marxian interpretations and also shares some features with the monetarist theory of the natural rate of unemployment (although the latter is a theory of voluntary, as opposed to involuntary, unemployment).
9. Such a view was implicit already in the Solow growth model (1957), articulated in the period of "high Keynesianism."
10. The logic of which has crippled Eurozone growth for over a decade.
11. A standard assumption in PK models is that workers consume all their income and the only source of savings is profit income.
12. It is noteworthy that recent work by Carlin and Soskice incorporates a feedback mechanism between aggregate demand and aggregate supply, thus moving their framework closer to the PK tradition. In Carlin and Soskice (2018), investment and productivity are modeled as being a function of demand and expectations about future demand (animal spirits). This implies that once output is below productivity, the supply-side potential of the economy is reduced by low investment. Consequently, productivity tends to fall below trend.
13. Working in the NK tradition, Blanchard (2016) finds that the Phillips curve is flatter than NK economists typically suppose.
14. Arguably, the current account constraint also stabilizes the system: to the extent that wage-led growth increases domestic demand and stimulates imports, while external demand remains constant, there is a tendency for the trade balance to go into deficit, which will have to be corrected, sooner or later, by reducing domestic demand (Thirlwall 1983). Taxes represent yet another potential mechanism of stabilization: as the economy approaches full

employment, discretionary taxes might offset demand pressures. In this case, re-equilibration is, again, a result of political intervention.

15. Another perspective on secular stagnation that has affinities with our approach is that of the new literature on "rentier capitalism" (Phillippon 2019, Piketty 2020, Schwartz 2019a, Christophers 2020). More on this below.

16. With time, Summers has moved towards the PK position, see for example his recent emphasis on the decline of worker power as cause of stagnation (Stansbury and Summers 2020)

17. We here use "wage-led growth" (the expression preferred by PK economists) and "Fordist growth" (the expression preferred by French regulationists) interchangeably.

18. One peculiarity of the construction-led model is that when investment is predominantly directed towards a low productivity sector like construction, the model comes with the additional problem of stagnant productivity.

19. Note that the effect of the wage-share increase on the real exchange rate implies that firms respond to a cost increase by changing prices and not just output, as Kaleckians traditionally assumed. However, the core idea of the PK framework remains relevant so long as firms do not transfer the full impact of cost increases into prices.

20. As consequence, standard growth decomposition based on national account data is often distorted and scarcely meaningful, as illustrated by the Irish case.

21. As such, it makes a big difference for the growth model whether export growth is primarily stimulated by real exchange rate depreciation or by an increase in their non-price competitiveness.

22. Most international trade is invoiced in dollars, especially in Latin America and Asia. This creates incentives for exporting firms, which receive payments in dollars, to match their dollar assets - bank deposits in dollars - with liabilities also denominated in dollars, thus contributing to the international demand for dollar assets. This in turn increases the price of these assets and reduces their yield and in the process also causes the dollar exchange rate to appreciate, or at least not depreciate, despite the further accumulation of foreign debt (Schwartz 2019a).

23. According to IMF World Economic Outlook data, the US current account deficit accounted for 2.2% of total demand in other countries in 2005–2006, but less than 1% in the 2010s.

24. As Hunnekes, Schularick and Trebesh (2019) point out, however, Germans who invest in so-called risky assets still face lower returns than their US counterparts due to their propensity to invest equities and FDI in other low-growth economies.

25. This formulation draws some of its inspiration from Culpepper's (2011) distinction between "quiet" and "noisy" politics (see also Busemeyer, Garritzmann and Neimanns 2020).

26. Inspired by French regulationists (notably Amable and Palombarini 2011; Amable 2017), a previous paper by Baccaro and Pontusson (2019) used the Gramscian term "dominant social blocs" to describe what we now refer to as "dominant growth coalitions." We have abandoned the notion of dominant social blocs because it seems to conflate elite politics and mass politics.

27. Gilens (2012) and Bartels (2016) provide extensive documentation of unequal representation in the US. Employing the same methodology as Gilens, recent analyses of German, Dutch and Swedish data uncover strikingly similar patterns of income and class biases in government responsiveness to citizens' demand for policy change (Elsässer, Hense and Schäfer 2020; Schakel 2021 and Persson 2020). For more fine-grained estimates using machine learning analyses that find a 70% probability of political attention to the 90th percentile and above, see McGuire and Delahunt (2020). See Elkjaer and Iversen (2020) for a contrarian view.

28. This approach has also been influential in international political economy: see, most notably, Frieden and Rogowski (1996).

29. Swenson's (2002) analysis of the New Deal illustrates this point nicely.

30. Elite-centered studies that take growth models into account include Brazys and Regan (2017), Bohle (2018), and Bohle and Regan (2021).

31. For our present purposes, it is not necessary to engage with the question of whether or not "cartelization" is a necessary condition for governing parties to assume these roles.

PART 1

THEORETICAL PERSPECTIVES

1

Growth Models and Post-Keynesian Macroeconomics

ENGELBERT STOCKHAMMER AND ÖZLEM ONARAN

Introduction

The global financial crisis and the following period of "secular stagnation" have raised questions about the state of modern economics and macroeconomics in particular. This has had repercussions for social sciences that deal with economic issues. In particular, in the fields of International Political Economy (IPE) and Comparative Political Economy (CPE), there is rising interest in non-mainstream macroeconomic theories (Blyth and Matthijs 2017; Baccaro and Pontussen 2016). In CPE there is a recognition that the field has in the past decades increasingly shifted to institutional and microeconomic questions and disregarded Keynesian considerations of macroeconomic instability and problems of fallacies of composition (Schwartz and Tranoy 2019). The purpose of this chapter is to give an overview of post-Keynesian economics (PKE) as a non-mainstream macroeconomic theory.

PKE is the radical wing of Keynesian theory; it builds on, but also goes beyond Keynes. PKE rejects methodological individualism and is based on the notion of fundamental uncertainty and conventional behavior. It highlights the role of institutions and class in determining economic outcomes. At the core of PKE is the assertion that growth is demand-led. The market mechanism in a recession is generally unable to establish full employment as wage cuts tend to dampen consumption and thus aggregate demand. Thus involuntary unemployment is the norm rather than exception. The financial sector is regarded as a source of flexibility as well as instability. Money is created endogenously as an outcome of banks' lending decisions. Credit can be used for different purposes; in particular it can be used to finance investment, but it can also be used to finance acquisition of financial assets. Thus, in deregulated financial systems asset price and credit booms will create forceful financial boom-bust cycles. PKE develops Keynes's short-run theory into a growth theory. An important element of this is that supply-side variables like technological progress and the inflation-neutral unemployment rate respond to demand pressures. As a consequence, the growth process is path-dependent and demand influences growth also in the long run.

This chapter then shows how these elements come together in the analysis of demand regimes and growth models (GM). The effect of key growth drivers such the wage share, private debt, or government spending is theoretically ambiguous, which gives rise to different regimes such a wage-led or profit-led demand regimes. Growth regimes also consider the supply-side effects in line with the notion of induced technological progress and path-dependent growth. Growth model describes the institutional configuration that give rise to a stable and sustained rise in key growth drivers. Debt-driven growth regimes are based on the assetization of housing and the financialization of households and give rise to financial instability. Overall, the chapter argues that PKE presents a more adequate macroeconomic foundation for CPE and IPE than mainstream economics.

The paper is structured as follows. Section 2 introduces PKE and its foundations. Section 3 discusses demand-led growth, section 4 is about the PKE theory of finance, and section 5 talks about the supply side of the economy. Section 6 analyzes the demand regimes and growth models and summarizes the empirical evidence. Section 7 discusses the post-Keynesian contribution to the debate on financialization. Section 8 presents a comparison of PKE with the old Keynesian, New Keynesian, and Marxist theories. Section 9 derives the economic policy recommendations and concludes.

PKE Foundations and Mainstream Economics

More so than other social sciences, economics has a sharp divide between mainstream and non-mainstream approaches, in particular since the 1970s. Mainstream (neoclassical) economic approaches are committed to methodological individualism based on the assumptions of utility and profit maximization of strictly rational individuals. Often (but not always) this is combined with the assumption of market clearing based on flexible adjustment of prices and wages. Various non-mainstream approaches reject methodological individualism, which include PKE, institutionalism, evolutionary economics, Marxist political economy, (parts of) feminist economics, and ecological economics. Among these PKE has the strongest focus on macroeconomic issues like the determinants of growth, employment, and financial instability.

PKE emerged from the Keynesian revolution by emphasizing the break between Keynes's approach and neoclassical theory. Keynes formulated his attack
on orthodox economics by arguing that self-healing mechanisms of the market
system are in general insufficient to generate full employment. While Hicks
(1937) and others (Samuelson, Solow) sought to develop a Keynesian-neoclassical synthesis based on a short run/long run and macro/micro distinction,
PKs emphasized the fundamental break of Keynes's approach with neoclassical
economics. The Keynesian-neoclassical synthesis became the basis for postwar
mainstream economics and can still be found in many undergraduate textbooks.
A major shift occurred in the 1970s and '80s with the Monetarist and New
Classical counterrevolution. These required strict rational behavior-based micro
foundations for macroeconomic models and led to a narrowing of the field of
economics and marginalization of non-mainstream economics.

Within the mainstream, New Keynesian Economics (NKE) accepted the neoclassical analytical framework and the need for rational-actor micro foundations,
but argued that in the face of transaction costs or information asymmetries
prices will not be perfectly flexible and markets will fail to clear (Mankiw and
Romer 1991). NKE developed a variety of models with market imperfections,
but during the 1990s the New Keynesian dynamic stochastic general equilibrium (DSGE) models and its textbook cousin, the "three equation" model became the NK benchmark models and Hope and Soskice (2016) suggest it as a
macroeconomic foundation for CPE. These models are essentially neoclassical
models with short-run price and wage rigidities, anchored in long-run supply-
side equilibrium. Importantly, markets are assumed to generate stable outcomes
and economic crises are analyzed as exogenous shocks.

The global financial crisis has led to mounting criticism of mainstream economics and to the rise of tensions within the mainstream, with a re-emergence
of the tension between "sweet water" (strictly neoclassical) and "salt water"
(New Keynesian) wings of the neoclassical-Keynesian synthesis. It also inspired
an empirically driven mainstream work, in particular on financial instability and
on the effectiveness of fiscal policy, that often comes close to post-Keynesian
arguments, but without a theoretical framework and due acknowledgment.

In contrast to mainstream economics PKE rejects methodological individualism. It argues that in a world of fundamental uncertainty, people cannot rationally optimize due to lack of information. Instead, Keynes argues people will
rely on simple behavioral rules (heuristics) and social conventions to guide their
behavior. This leads to a key role for institutions and social reference groups for
stabilizing behavior. Fundamental uncertainty has important macroeconomic
implications. First, it is about decisions with a long time horizon, like investment decisions, which are particularly affected: hence Keynes's emphasis on
(non-rational) animal spirits driving investment. Second, demand for money is

unstable, and in times of financial crisis there will be rush to liquidity as investors seek insurance from increased uncertainty by holding liquid assets. Third, as social conventions respond to others' behavior, they can give rise to herd behavior and expectational boom-bust cycles.

PKE extends Keynes's behavioral arguments with a concern for distributional issues and adopt a class-analytic approach. This complements Keynesian theory, which regards involuntary unemployment as a normal outcome in market economies. In the face of unemployment there will be asymmetric power relations between capital and labor. Unlike the full employment world of the neoclassical model, there is a meaningful firing threat in the post-Keynesian world. Moreover, a key macroeconomic variable, investment decisions, is in the hand of the capitalists (Dutt 1990). The post-Keynesian class analysis often features finance as a separate class. Shareholders, banks, or rentiers provide finance for firms and are remunerated in the form of interest or dividend payments. Thus, interest rates (and other financial variables) as well as wages are regarded as distributional variables. Simply put, by rejecting methodological individualism PKE adopts sociological foundations based on conventions, institutions, and classes. This makes PKE a natural complement to critical political economy approaches.

Much of the post-Keynesian research has focused on economic questions, but power relations are an integral, if often implicit, part of the post-Keynesian analysis. First, the distribution between labor, capital, and finance is regarded as a reflection of power relations rather than a technologically driven outcome of market processes (e.g., Stockhammer 2017a; Guschanski and Onaran 2021). Second, the state has a central role in the creation and maintenance of money and credit relations. The state and its central bank sit at the top of the hierarchy of monies and guarantees bank deposits. It also, effectively, guarantees the very existence of (some) banks in times of financial crisis, which are bailed out. Post-Keynesian monetary theory thus is closely related to state and debt theories of money and the legal theory of finance (Ingham 2004; Pistor 2013). Thus, PKE offers a rich framework for macroeconomic analysis that can fruitfully be combined with the political economy approach of the social sciences.

Demand-Led Growth

Macroeconomics explains aggregate variables such as economic growth, employment, inflation, or asset prices. At the core of the macroeconomic analysis in the short run is the goods market equilibrium, that is, aggregate income equals aggregate expenditures. The Keynesian assertion is that investment is the active and saving the passive (adjusting) variable. While in neoclassical economics the interest rate equilibrates the two and investment is merely the adjustment toward the optimal capital stock, PKE argues that investment is driven by animal spirits and business sentiment about demand and profitability as well as by financial factors. Private or public investment spending is associated with multiplier effects and will have a large impact on aggregate demand. Saving occurs out of current income. Thus, in the simple model, investment creates the corresponding saving via multiplier effects on income. In Keynesian theory, thus investment dynamics (rather than technology shocks) are key for understanding the business cycle.

These investment decisions will correspond to an equilibrium level of income (equilibrium in the goods market), which will not in general generate full employment (i.e., an underemployment equilibrium in the labor market). Importantly the adjustments caused by unemployment will often be dysfunctional and not bring the economy closer to full employment. In a period of heightened unemployment (i.e., a recession) there will be downward pressure on wages. Keynes (1936, ch. 19) argues that a (nominal) wage cut results in higher employment only if it stimulates aggregate demand. But in general, they will not do so. First, wage cuts tend to lower consumption expenditures and thus dampen aggregate expenditures. Second, a wage cut in a recession where firms have spare capacity is likely to lead to a downward pressure on prices. This can give rise to deflationary spirals that increase the real debt burden in an indebted economy and decrease demand. Only if investment were to react strongly (and positively) to the wage cut or in the face of strong export effects will there be expansionary effects of a wage cut. The demand regimes analysis of Bhaduri and Margin (1990, discussed in section 6) is one attempt to formalize these arguments.

In contrast to PKE, mainstream theories posit that economic activity will return to a supply-side determined equilibrium (different versions of the mainstream differ in how quickly that occurs). The most important supply-side anchor is the natural rate of unemployment (Friedman) or as it is referred to in NKE, the NAIRU (non-accelerating inflation rate of unemployment).[1] PKE thus rejects that the macroeconomic equilibrium is anchored in a supply-side determined equilibrium rate of unemployment that underpins mainstream macroeconomics. PKE argue that employment largely follows demand, that is, the labor market follows rather than leads the goods market. We return in section 5 to the treatment of the supply side and elaborate the notion of path-dependent growth.

Finance and Financial Instability

A key difference between mainstream and post-Keynesian analysis is in their treatment of finance. While finance tends to play a benign role in much of mainstream economics and banks tend to be regarded as passive intermediaries that channel savings from households to firms, PKE highlight endogenous money creation by commercial banks, the potential for financial instability, and endogenous (reoccuring) financial cycles. The desire to hold money in PKE is closely tied to the concept of fundamental uncertainty. In times of increased uncertainty, for example, during financial crises, the liquidity preference will increase as investors are wary of risky financial assets that may incur capital losses. Holding money (or more generally liquid and safe assets) is thus analyzed in the context of the portfolio decisions of investors, not as means of buying goods.

The creation of money is analyzed in a balance sheet context. In a modern economy money is overwhelmingly bank deposits, which are the short-term liabilities of the commercial banks. At the same time deposits are an asset for households or firms. Deposits are created when banks decide to lend, which extends their balance sheet both on the asset (loan) and liability (deposits) side (Kaldor 1982; Moore 1988; Lavoie 2014 ch. 4). Conversely, the repayment of loans shrinks bank balance sheets and destroys money. While this endogenous money view, originally formulated in opposition to the Monetarist view that the central bank controls the money supply, was initially highly controversial, in the last years central banks have increasingly accepted this view (McLeay et al 2014).

The fact that deposits are created by commercial banks does not mean that the state is not involved; most of the time it just stays in the background. In fact central banks and fiscal states ensure that bank deposits can serve as money by guaranteeing deposits (up to a certain maximum) and by effectively safeguarding the existence of (systemically important) banks (Ingham 2004). Bank bailouts are thus a necessary feature of stabilizing the monetary system and justify financial regulation. Moreover, government debt serves as the most important safe financial asset that underpins many private financial transactions and the balance sheets of private financial institutions. There is thus a link between state authority and the viability of the financial system.

Endogenous money creation gives the economic system a high degree of flexibility as credit can be created at will if the economic outlook of banks is sufficiently positive. However, credit can be used for different purposes. It can be used to finance socially useful investment, but it can also support speculative financial asset purchases. The pivotal role of credit also means that downturns will be exacerbated when banks' outlook darkens and when they restrict credit with the aim of repairing their own balance sheets. Hyman Minsky (1986, 2008, 2016) has been the pioneer to develop a theory of endogenous financial cycles, that is, financial boom-bust cycles that are systemic features of the capitalist market economies rather than a result of exogenous shocks.

Minsky's Financial Instability Hypothesis has been developed further and formalized in different ways. Nikolaidi and Stockhammer (2018) distinguish two main families. At the core of the first is a debt cycle that is driven by real expenditures (typically business investment) (e.g., Charles 2006, Fazzari et al. 2006). The Minskyan analysis highlights the balance sheet structure of firms and banks. Investment is typically at least in part externally financed and will thus increase their liabilities. During a boom with a high growth and healthy returns, firms and banks will gradually move toward riskier financial positions and their leverage will increase. Thus, during the boom financial fragility (proxied by debt-to-income ratios) increases. Eventually the growing debt burden will slow the expansion and at some point, rising interest rates or a change in business outlook will cause a financial downturn. Because of highly indebted units this may lead to bankruptcies and force firms to engage in fire sales of financial assets as they need liquidity to service their debt obligations. Short, it is the boom that creates the conditions for the subsequent bust.[2]

A second family of Minsky models emphasizes the role of expectation formation for asset prices such as stock prices or house prices (Ryoo 2016; Franke and Westerhoff 2017). If part of the investors form expectations of future prices based on extrapolating past trends, this will give rise to overshooting asset prices. If there are other investors that base their valuation of stock prices on the firm's fundamentals like sales, profits, etc., they may stabilize asset prices. Importantly, the interaction of those two investment strategies can give rise to endogenous speculative cycles. Both the debt and the asset price cycles feature prominently in recent empirical research, by heterodox economics as well as by empirically driven mainstream research (e.g., Borio 2014; Aikman et al 2015). This Minsky-inspired post-Keynesian research (and related research in Behavioral Economics, e.g., de Grauwe and Macchiarelli 2015; Bofinger et al. 2013) interpret financial crises as the outcome of systemic forces. Overall, this approach suggests that increased and reoccurring financial instability will be the outcome of deregulating financial markets.

A specific aspect of post-Keynesian theory of finance is the hierarchy of currencies, which is particularly relevant for developing economies (De Paula et al. 2016). These usually have less developed financial markets and therefore limited capacity to issue debt in their own currency. Foreign exchange denominated debt will thus play an important role and requires capital inflows. Financial liberalization will expose these countries to procyclical capital inflows and international financial cycles. During financial crises (whether they originate in the financial center or in the periphery), there will be a flight to safety and away from the financial periphery. The real debt burden will increase sharply as capital flight leads to devaluation (thus an increase in the value foreign denominated debt). Thus financial liberalization will both increase the volatility of growth and reduce the state's capacity to counter the crisis.

The Supply Side: Endogenous Technological Progress and Path-Dependent Growth

A distinguishing feature of PKE is that it regards growth to be demand driven not only in the short run, but also over longer periods. The rationale for this is that supply is not exogenously given, but technological progress is induced, and institutions adapt to changing circumstances. The resulting growth process is one that is path dependent, with demand shocks like financial crises having long-lasting effects, rather than one that is anchored in a (unique) supply-side equilibrium. Two channels have been highlighted. First, existing technology and productive equipment responds to demand pressures. Many modern production processes depend on a minimum scale to be economically viable and offer network effects, which means they exhibit increasing returns to scale. Moreover, new technologies are typically embodied in machinery, thus capital investment is a precondition for (realized) technological progress. In a recession with excess capacity, firms have little incentive to improve productivity further. The endogenous technological progress is often summarized as the Kaldor-Verdoorn law, which posits that productivity growth is a positive function of demand and wage growth (Palley 1996; Dutt 2010). From this perspective the collapse of productivity growth after severe crises like in Japan after 1991 and in much of the advanced economies after 2008 are not surprising, but an example of an induced technological slowdown.

The second channel relates to the labor market. The natural rate of unemployment or NAIRU is a specific supply-side constraint much discussed in macroeconomics. Modern mainstream economics treats the NAIRU as purely determined by labor market institutions such as the level of unemployment benefits or the strength of labor unions. The NAIRU thus serves as a supply-side anchor for economic activity. In contrast PKE argues that the NAIRU is endogenous, and it will react to economic performance and the actual unemployment rate. This is often referred to unemployment hysteresis, that is, that actual unemployment turns into structural unemployment. Possible mechanisms for this include deskilling or stigmatization of long-term unemployed and endogenous distributional norms. Skott (2005) and Stockhammer (2008a) present models where workers' wage claims are updated according to actual wages, that is, they get used to the current wage level.[3]

All of this is not to say that technology or, more broadly, supply-side constraints do not matter. Rather the point is that they are not the binding constraint that will determine growth in the long run. At any point in time there will, indeed, be supply constraints that can inhibit growth, but demand developments continuously shift these supply constraints (Fazzari et al. 2020). Unemployment hysteresis and induced technological change have far-reaching implications.

They mean that demand shocks, say the global financial crisis, will have long-lasting effects as they impact not only current output, but via depressed investment and rising unemployment also harm medium-term growth. On the flip side this means that government policy is potentially more powerful, if it is used in a countercyclical fashion, as fiscal policy has short-term as well as long-term effects (de Long and Summers 2012).

There are circumstances where PKE do emphasize supply-side constraints. This is best illustrated with respect to developing economies, though the underlying mechanisms are more general, and the following argument draws on structuralist models of development (Cimoli and Porcile 2014; Fischer 2015), which are close to PKE. Developing economies typically have large pools of hidden unemployment, their exports typically are in commodities or low-tech manufacturing and they need to import (up-to-date) capital goods. Most exports of developing countries are in primary goods or basic industrial goods, which face a low-income elasticity but high price elasticity. These structural features of the economy imply that dependent countries are less likely to be able to capture the gains of productivity growth and that a crucial element of the elastic supply conditions discussed earlier depends on the ability to import machinery. Their financial sectors are less developed and they lack the ability to borrow abroad in their own currency. This can create processes of divergence and core-periphery structures and balance-of-payment constrained growth.

Analyzing Demand Regimes

This section outlines a post-Keynesian framework to analyze demand regimes. They describe the effect of changes of key variables (growth drivers) in different macroeconomic constellations. In the debate on demand regimes and growth models the focus has been on the impact of changes in income distribution, but it is important to realize that the concept is broader than that. Think of aggregate demand depending on the wage share (*WS*), that is, the distribution of income between capital and labor, the volume of private debt (*PD*) and government expenditures (*G*):

$$Y = f\ (WS, PD, G)$$

Bhaduri and Marglin (1990) formulate a Keynes-Marx synthesis model to analyze the effects of the changes in the distribution of income between capital and labor on demand. A change in the wage share can have positive or negative demand effects; in particular it will have contrasting effects on the different components of demand. A rise in the wage share in aggregate income has a partial negative effect on investment (higher profits are expected to lead to higher investment), a positive effect on consumption (because capitalists save more than workers), and a negative effect on net exports (because higher wages imply a loss of international competitiveness). The net effect will depend on the relative size of the partial effects and may differ by country and time period. If the net effect of a rise in the wage share is positive ($\partial Y/\partial WS>0$), that is, if the consumption effect outweighs the investment and net export effect, the demand regime is called wage-led, if it is negative ($\partial Y/\partial WS>0$) it is called profit-led. In its analysis of demand regimes PKE has highlighted the effect of changes in income distribution on effective demand.

A similar set of distinctions can be made with respect to (private) debt. An increase in debt will have expansionary effects ($\partial Y/\partial PD>0$) as far as debtors have a higher propensity to spend than creditors. However, it will also have a negative effect on demand ($\partial Y/\partial PD<0$), as higher debt levels imply higher interest payments from debtors to creditors, which dampens aggregate demand (e.g., Dutt 2006). The effects of changes in private debt have an important temporal dimension: the short-run effect tends to be positive as income gets channeled to debtors with a high propensity to spend, whereas the long-term effects when debtors service their debt, will be negative. As the discussion to come will clarify, changes in household debt are closely linked to real estate prices, which under the conditions of financial liberalization are likely to exhibit cyclical fluctuations.

Finally, the effect of a change in government expenditures on demand is known as the fiscal multiplier effect. Supply-side economists argue that the multiplier is zero ($\partial Y/\partial G=0$) over long periods. More extreme, the argument of expansionary fiscal contraction, which briefly gained prominence during the Euro crisis, even suggests that reducing government spending (or more precisely, the budget deficit) will have a positive effect on growth ($\partial Y/\partial G<0$). Keynesians assert that the multiplier is positive but differ in their assessment how large it is and how long lasting. The synthesis-Keynesians and NKE would have positive multipliers in the short run, but a zero multiplier in the long run (when output returns to its natural level). PKE and, since the global financial crisis, some NKs argue that during recessions the multiplier is substantially larger than one ($\partial Y/\partial G>1$) and that in the face of hysteresis, these effects can be long-lived (DeLong and Summers 2013).

The demand regime of an economy is distinct from the growth regime and the growth model. The *demand regime* depicts the change of demand in response to key explanatory variables (e.g., the wage share or the private debt-to-income ratio). It is determined by the structure of the economy (e.g., responsiveness of corporate investment to profits and demand) and reflected in the parameters of the economic behavioral equations. The *growth regime* further considers supply-side effects in addition to demand effects via the growth of capital stock and productivity growth.

Finally, a *growth model* describes a period of sustained growth, where patterns of growth are sufficiently stable to identify key factors that have been driving growth. A demand regime is wage-led if a redistribution toward wages *would* induce higher growth, regardless of *whether* such a redistribution has taken place, or whether consumption has actually been the main contributor to GDP. In contrast, the growth model is defined by the actual patterns of distribution, asset valuation, and growth, that is, it presupposes a consistent change in the growth driver over a period of time. While the demand (or growth) regime and the growth model are logically linked, they are not the same.

To illustrate: the wage-led growth model of the postwar era has only been possible as there was a wage-led demand regime (and a wage-led growth regime) and there has been an upward pressure on the wage share. In contrast, in the interpretation of Lavoie and Stockhammer (2013) neoliberalism is marked by a pro-capital distributional change, even though the demand regime remained wage-led, along with a simultaneous financial deregulation, where debt-driven demand stimulation becomes the source of growth and defines the growth model. However, there are different interpretations of neoliberalism as in Baccaro and Pontusson (2016) who interpret it as a shift to a profit-led demand regime.[4]

Table 1.1 provides a simple framework to classify growth regimes along two axes. First, the demand regime can be profit-led or wage-led, that is, the effect of an increase in inequality, measured by the profit share, can be positive or negative. Second, actual distributional changes can be pro-capital (higher inequality) or pro-labor (lower inequality).

Table 1.1 **A typology of demand regimes and distributional changes**

		Actual distributional changes	
		Pro-capital	*Pro-labor*
Demand regime	Profit-led	Virtuous profit-led growth process ("neoliberalism in theory")	Stagnation or external demand stimulation ("Failed social reform")
	Wage-led	Stagnation or external demand stimulation, e.g., via debt-driven or export-driven growth ("actually existing neoliberalism")	Virtuous wage-led growth process ("social Keynesianism")

Source: adapted from Lavoie and Stockhammer 2013

This simple framework allows for a rich analysis that can be used to compare different economic theories as well as different country experiences in specific historic periods. Cell (1,1) depicts a constellation of rising inequality in a profit-led demand regime. This would give a virtuous, profit-led growth model. In fact this constellation depicts the trickle-down economy that many neoliberals of the early 1980s were propagating. Rising inequality here could be a healthy thing because it comes with growth, which will eventually benefit the poor. This is "neoliberalism in theory." Cell (1,2) has rising wages in a profit-led economy, which will not give rise to a viable growth model, but rather to stagnation. It is this scenario that Margret Thatcher was alluding to when she said "there is no alternative": social reform is doomed because it cannot generate growth. Cell (2,1) combine a wage-led demand regime with rising inequality.

This combination cannot deliver a stable growth model but creates a downward pressure on demand. However, growth can still occur if there are other stimulants of growth such as private debt and asset price bubbles. Indeed, from a post-Keynesian view, it is this cell where actually existing neoliberalism resides. Empirical studies summarized next mostly conclude that private domestic demand, that is, the sum of consumption and investment, is wage-led. Rather than generating a profit-led growth regime, neoliberalism has relied on financialization and globalization as means of demand stimulation. This has resulted in two distinct growth models, which are both unstable: debt-driven and export-driven growth. Both allow for growth, but are intrinsically unstable, because they require increasing debt-to-income ratios. In the case of the debt-driven model it requires debt in the country itself; in the case of the export-driven model it requires foreign debt of the trade partners who run a current account deficit. It is these rising mountains of debt that erupted in the 2008 crisis.

Neoliberalism has led to a polarization of income distribution expressed in rising profits and top incomes, but remarkably, this has nowhere translated into a business investment boom. Capitalists did *not* invest their profits.[5] PKE thus offers a simple framework that highlights the following features of neoliberalism: first, there is tension between what we called neoliberalism in theory and existing neoliberalism. Second, actual neoliberalism relies on external stimulation of demand, which typically comes with higher debt and is thus prone to instability. Third, there are at least two types of neoliberalism: a (domestic) debt-driven and an export-driven model. In other words, there is a finance-led as well as an industrial version of neoliberalism.

Empirical results and extensions

The debates on demand regimes have been dominated by the discussion of the effect of changes in the wage share, based on Bhaduri and Marglin (1990) which has become a benchmark model in post-Keynesian macroeconomics and given rise to an extensive empirical literature trying to identify whether actual economies exhibit wage-led or profit-led demand regimes (see Blecker 2016 and Stockhammer 2017 as surveys). The literature uses econometric analysis to identify the relevant effects and demand regimes. It may be difficult to follow for the nonexpert because it includes a variety of econometric estimation strategies, but it also reflects that different authors have extended the Bhaduri-Marglin model in different directions. Table 1.2 gives an overview summarizing this by means of the substantive extensions (i.e., which additional variables are included) and the estimation strategy.

The first generation of empirical tests of the Bhaduri-Marglin model, what we call "basic Kaleckian goods market" in Table 1.2, tries to disentangle the impact a change in income distribution has on investment, consumption, and net exports. Most of these studies find that domestic demand regimes are wage led, that is, the consumption effects overpower the investment effects, but that in open economies the net export effect can turn the total demand effects to profit led. This is an important issue as globalization means that economies are becoming more open and interconnected. Thus, a first extension of the model paid closer attention to the external trade side of the model, both in terms of allowing for changing impacts over time (due to globalization) (e.g., Stockhammer et al. 2009; Stockhammer et al. 2011) and to the interaction of different economies (Onaran and Galanis 2014).

This reveals an important fallacy of composition: while individual countries may become more profit led over time, because of globalization the world economy or regional blocks remain wage led. When countries trade among each other the positive net export effects of a wage cut cancel out in larger geographic units (because countries trade among each other) whereas the negative consumption effects add up. A seemingly rational pro-capital strategy at the level of an individual country is hence contractionary and counterproductive at global level (Onaran and Galanis 2014). This also holds for the Euro area: Stockhammer et al. (2011); Onaran and Obst (2016); and Obst, Onaran, and Nikolaidi (2020) provide evidence that the Euro area overall has a wage-led demand regime, even when individual European countries, in particular ones with small open economies may be profit led, because of the net export component of aggregate demand. But as European countries mostly trade among each other, these effects on net exports to a large extent cancel out at the European level.

A second extension of the model incorporates the impact of financialization by including variables like interest rates, household and business debt, financial wealth, and real estate prices (Onaran et al. 2011, 2019; Stockhammer et al. 2021).[6] Stockhammer and Wildauer (2016) find that for the pre-crisis boom the

Table 1.2 **Empirical studies and extensions of the Bhaduri-Marglin model**

		Estimation technique	Systems approach	Panel
		Single equation		
Extensions	*Basic Kaleckian goods market*	Bowles & Boyer 1995, Hein & Vogel 2008,	Stockhammer & Onaran 2004	Stockhammer & Wildauer 2016
	globalization	Stockhammer et al. 2009; Stockhammer et al. 2011; Onaran and Galanis 2014; Onaran and Obst 2016; Obst et al 2020		
	Financialization	Hein and Schoder 2011 (USA, D); Onaran et al. 2011 (USA)		Stockhammer and Wildauer 2015
	Goodwin models: aggregate goods market and distribution	Stockhammer and Stehrer 2011	Barbosa-Filho and Taylor 2006; Franke et al. 2006; Carvalho and Rezai 2014; Jump and Mendieta-Munoz 2015	Rada and Kiefer 2014
	Kaldorian: endogenous productivity growth	Naastepad and Storm 2006/2007; Onaran et al. 2019, 2021	Cauvel 2019	Hartwig 2014
	Feminist	Onaran et al. 2019, 2021		

financial effects, namely household debt and real estate prices) are substantially larger than the distributional effects and that growth in the Anglophone and southern European countries has mostly been driven by financial factors. This substantiates the notion of a debt-driven growth model. Perhaps surprisingly, there are currently few attempts to elaborate the role of fiscal policy in Bhaduri-Marglin models. Obst et al. (2020) and Onaran et al. (2019, 2021) are the few exceptions. They report that the impact of fiscal spending on demand is much stronger than that of changes in income distribution.

Other extensions elaborate the supply side of the model. The Kaldorian extension include the Kaldor-Verdoorn law and thus also estimate a productivity growth equation (Naastepad and Storm 2006; Storm and Naastepad 2012, 2013; Hartwig 2014; Onaran et al. 2021) and demonstrate the positive effect of demand growth and of wage growth on productivity growth. This has two important implications for the model. First, it includes the positive long-term effects of demand on the supply side and thus strengthens the concept of wage-led growth regimes. Wage growth can not only positively impact demand, but also supply. Second, by demonstrating the productivity effects, these findings weaken the link between demand growth and employment growth. While growth is more wage led, employment is less wage led.

The Marxist or Goodwinian extension is more theoretically motivated. The Bhaduri-Marglin model provides a theoretical bridge between post-Keynesian and Marxist theories. In the (Marxist) Goodwin model the business cycle emerges from the interaction between a profit-led growth process and an industrial reserve army that gets depleted during the boom and thus depresses the profit share, which leads to lower growth (the Marxist profit squeeze crisis). The Goodwinians thus extend the Bhaduri-Marglin model to include income distribution and then analyze the emergence of cycles. These studies typically do not offer a detailed analysis of the demand effects but focus on the interaction of demand and distribution. Several studies (Barbosa-Filho and Taylor 2006; Franke et al. 2006; Kiefer and Rada 2014) find profit-led demand regimes (typically with a focus on the USA). Thus in heterodox economics a controversy between Kaleckians and neo-Goodwinians developed (Blecker 2016; Stockhammer 2017) where Kaleckians have argued that neo-Goodwinians have misidentified demand regime as they do not adequately consider procyclical labor productivity (Cauvel 2019; Blecker et al. 2021).

Finally, feminist extensions integrate gender inequality, reproductive labor, and unpaid and paid care work (Braunstein et al. 2011; Seguino 2010). In a study on the United Kingdom, Onaran, Oyvat, and Fotopoulou (2019, 2022) consider multiple dimensions of inequality: functional income distribution between wages and profits, wealth concentration and gender inequality, and also allow for the feedback of the care economy on productivity growth. They find that gender equality has substantial medium-term productivity effects.

Most of the studies on demand regimes apply econometric techniques to identify the relevant effects. However, there is a shortcut that has been used in particular to identify growth models. Hein and Mundt (2013) use the growth contribution of the components of GDP (consumption, investment, government, and net exports) paired with some additional information (such as the net borrowing of households) to classify countries into (a weaker and stronger version of) export-led, domestic demand-led, and debt-led growth regimes. This approach has been updated for the post-2008 period (Hein et al 2020), which indicates that a majority of countries have moved to export-led growth. However, Kohler and Stockhammer (2021) argue that positive growth contributions of net exports can arise because of falling imports due to weak domestic demand. Thus growth contributions may understate the impact of financial downturns and fiscal austerity. In short the advantage of the analysis of growth contributions is its relative simplicity; its shortcoming is that it does not identify the drivers of growth and may thus misidentify actual growth regimes.

Financialization, Financial Cycles, and Finance-Led Growth

Financialization has become an important topic across a wide range of social sciences. It refers to the changing role of finance in contemporary economy and society and has been imbued with different meanings by different authors. PKE has made contributions to several of the debates around financialization, providing macroeconomic framing and empirical assessment of the arguments. We briefly sketch main features of post-Keynesian analysis of financialization as it is relevant for GM debates. Financialization has had different impacts on different sectors.

First, for non-financial businesses it has led to a strengthened role of shareholder and shift to "downsize and distribute" (Lazonick and O'Sullivan 2000). Stockhammer (2004), Orhangazi (2008), and Tori and Onaran (2020) have provided empirical evidence of the negative effect of shareholder value orientation on business investment. Second, household financialization led to an assetization of homes, which resulted in higher household debt. Household wealth and debt thus became (in some countries) major drivers of consumption spending (Stockhammer and Wildauer 2016; Hein 2013). This gave rise to debt-financed consumption (and residential investment) booms. Third, for the financial sector financialization meant a shift toward fee-generating income, securitization, and a rising importance of shadow banking. One important effect of this was that banks have shifted to providing loans to households rather than businesses (Jorda et al. 2016). Fourth, PKs have played a key role in demonstrating the distributional effects of financialization. Dunhaupt 2017; Stockhammer 2017; Kohler et al 2019; Guschanski and Onaran (2018) find a substantial negative effect of financialization on wage shares.

Two themes stand out in the post-Keynesian analysis of the macroeconomic effects of financialization. First, PKs analyze the distributional and demand impacts; second, informed by Minsky, a concern for financial instability. Regarding the first, various authors have developed some form of finance-led, debt-led growth models. In Boyer (2000) the key role is played by share prices; Stockhammer (2005) emphasizes the negative impact on investment while at the same time there is a positive effect on consumption (because of asset price inflation).

Similarly, Hein (2013) speaks of a regime of "profits without investment." Allowing for differentiation in the degree of household financialization, Lavoie and Stockhammer (2013) and Hein (2013) highlight different reactions to financialization and thus the emergence of different growth models within a finance-dominated accumulation regime: debt-driven vs. export-driven. All of these come with rising inequality but have different growth drivers. Regarding the second aspect, PKs analyze the potential instability of financialization: both rising household debt and the high leverage within the financial sector are regarded as unsustainable. This is not just based on the benefit of hindsight, but PKs build on a tradition of Minskyan theories of endogenous financial cycles and regard leverage ratios as indicators of financial instability (Minsky 1986; Wray 2016; Nikolaidi and Stockhammer 2017).

One theme that emerged in the macroeconomics of financialization is the centrality of the assetization of housing for the debt-driven growth models. While the emergence of debt-financed consumption is nowadays widely acknowledged, there is an irony here: most household debt is not consumer credit, but mortgage debt (Stockhammer and Wildauer 2018). It is not directly consumption related, but tied to real estate transactions, which in themselves don't have an impact on GDP. This means that additional steps are required to get from a house price boom to a consumption and residential investment boom. Mortgage equity withdrawal and re-mortgaging have provided important linkages. However, as only a small part of the mortgage credit gets spent on consumption, debt-driven growth requires substantial increases in household debt and it is sensitive to the house price cycles. An important feature of real estate is that it is widely used as collateral, thus it is (compared to, say, shares) relatively easy to get loans based on rising house prices, though the elasticity of national financial systems with respect to this clearly matters.

So far, the post-Keynesian argument has great similarities to what has been called "privatized Keynesianism" (Crouch 2009) or "house price Keynesianism" (Watson 2010) in CPE. However, the post-Keynesian analysis adds a distinct Minskyan flavor to this: real estate prices, like those of other financial assets are prone to boom-bust cycles. In the simplest models these emerge from the interaction of two valuation strategies: a fundamentalist and momentum trader (explorative) expectation formation (Dieci and Westerhoff 2012). Several post-Keynesian authors apply this to the housing market. Ryoo (2016) offers a full macroeconomic model with endogenous house price cycles. Stockhammer and Wolf (2019) highlight the cyclicality of house prices as a key feature of post-Keynesian analysis of housing. Arestis and Rosa Gonzalez (2014) highlight the reinforcing effects of household debt and house prices. This complements the recent housing CPE literature (Johnston and Kurzer 2020) that is stronger on institutional differences, but has so far had little to say on house price cycles.

Differences among PKE Old Keynesian, New Keynesian, and Marxist Theories

At this point it will be useful to contrast PKE to other economic theories. First, what are the main differences to old Keynesian and New Keynesian theories? The old Keynesians were the mainstream (neoclassical-Keynesian Synthesis) scholars that came to crystallize around the IS/LM model. The main difference here is that old Keynesians had a short-run/long-run dichotomy according to which the economy worked along Keynesian lines in the short run, but neoclassical in the long run (expressed in the Solow growth model). PKE differs in that it argues that aggregate demand matters also in the long run as supply constraint respond to demand due to hysteresis mechanisms. The NKs (since the 1980s) share the neoclassical long run feature but took another major step toward neoclassical theory: they endorsed the need for rational-behavior micro foundations of macroeconomics. NKE includes a wide range of arguments and models. The Stiglitz versions, while strictly micro-founded, also has long-run criticism of neoclassical general equilibrium. On the other side of the spectrum the New Keynesian DSGE model, which has become the cornerstone of modern macroeconomics, essentially presents a neoclassical general equilibrium model with wage and price rigidities. This is a far cry from PKE models.

A specific version of NKE is the three equation model that has been widely used as a macroeconomic benchmark model and that Hope and Soskice (2016) suggest as an alternative macro-foundation for CPE. This model consists of a demand equation, where aggregate demand depends on the interest rate; an inflation equation (Phillips curve) which explains inflation as function of output (and thus unemployment); and a monetary policy reaction function which depicts how the central bank sets interest rates in response to inflation. From a PKE perspective this model has several shortcomings (Stockhammer 2021).

First, it depicts the economy as anchored in a supply-side equilibrium; less technically it has a natural rate of unemployment. Second, it does not enable an analysis of financial instability and endogenous financial cycles. The main financial variable of the model is the interest rate which is set by the central bank. Private sector financial dynamics, reflected in asset prices or private debt, do not feature in the model. Indeed, it interprets financial crisis as caused by exogenous shocks. Third, it does not allow for the possibility of wage-led growth. A wage cut in a recession or a weakening of labor unions will always increase employment. Forth, it implicitly downplays the importance of fiscal policy as the main policy tool in the model of monetary policy.

Marxist theory is a wide field with different positions, and it is often difficult to pin down a distinct Marxist economics approach. There are similarities to PKE in that both use a class analytical approach. Whereas Marxists tend to root their analysis in the relations of production, which translates into a supply-side focus (e.g., Foley and Michl 1999), PKE focuses on demand-side issues and in particular finance. One area of overlap is the analysis of demand regimes where Marxists tend to emphasize profit-led regimes based on their assertion that profits get reinvested. Generally, PKE has a stronger focus on finance and regard finance (or shareholders) as a distinct class position. Both Marxist and PKE emphasize systemic source of instability, but for Marxists these are rooted in the capital-labor conflict, whereas post-Keynesian highlights financial cycles as source of instability. A major difference is in the ability of states and government spending to stabilize the economy in the face of crisis. While Marxists tend to flag the futility of government demand stimulations, PKE tends to emphasize its effectiveness.

Policy Implications

Before the global financial crisis, there seemed to be a consensus in mainstream economic policy (see Blanchard et al. 2010) along the following lines. Much of the stabilization (short-run demand management) function was assigned to monetary policy, which would be inflation targeting or follow a Taylor rule with a dual mandate on output and inflation. Financial stability was regarded as a microeconomic issue. Fiscal policy was to rely mostly on automatic stabilizers and would aim in the medium term at balancing the budget. Beyond the business cycle, unemployment was regarded as a supply-side issue. Financial deregulation was generally regarded as desirable and efficiency enhancing. This policy package was based on the New Keynesian approach, which assumed market clearing in the long run, but due to price and wage rigidities, a positive role for government in the short run. This consensus has been put into question since the global financial crisis, with some New Keynesians (e.g., Stiglitz, Krugman) moving closer to post-Keynesian positions.

PKE proposals, closer to Keynes's original proposals, differ in the short as well as long-run assignments (Arestis et al. 2001; Hein 2013; Palley 2015). Most importantly full employment is the overarching policy goal as PKE rejects the notion that market economies are anchored in a benign self-adjusting labor market equilibrium. In terms of stabilization fiscal policy has a more prominent role as monetary policy is regarded as less effective (for stimulating private expenditures) during a recession, in particular during financial crises. This is in line with a substantial recent New Keynesian literature that documents that multiplier effects are larger during recessions or when interest rates are at the zero lower bound (Blanchard and Leigh 2013, de Long and Summers 2012). Monetary policy has to support government policy and aim for high employment and growth as well as price stability. As financial markets are regarded as prone to instability and procyclical, the central bank has to actively lean against the wind over the financial cycle (similar in spirit to what central banks now discuss as macroprudential policies). PKE has a more positive assessment of labor market institutions, which serve as insurance mechanisms and help rebalance corporate power. Post-Keynesians encourage an institutional bargaining structure that involve unions and employers to achieve stable inflation.

Unlike mainstream economics, post-Keynesian policy recommendations do not entail a short run-long run distinction as growth is regarded as path dependent. Thus, high rates of demand and wage growth in line with productivity growth foster technological progress. Again there is a positive view of labor market institutions (e.g., Storm 2013). The long-term goal is to ensure high employment, which may involve sustained public deficits, in particular in the aftermath of financial crises when the private sectors want to deleverage or when the social return to public investment is sufficiently high. Industrial policy is encouraged as path-dependent growth and increasing returns (in some areas) may trap countries or sectors in low-road equilibria (Kaldor, Latin American structuralism).

Climate change does pose challenges to the growth orientation of Keynesian approaches as well as to mainstream economics, and it requires the incorporation of ecological externalities into post-Keynesian models and indeed there is a growing literature on post-Keynesian ecological macroeconomics (Dafermos et al. 2017; Rezai et al. 2018) and the transition to a low carbon economy will have to involve the post-Keynesian toolbox, but will require focus on labor rather than resource-intensive sectors (Onaran et al. 2021) and industrial policies to enhance energy efficiency (Pollin 2019).

Notes

1. Stockhammer (2008a) offers a comparative analysis of stable-inflation unemployment rates in NK, PK, and Marxist theories. An exogenous NAIRU is also part of the three equation model that Hope and Soskice (2016) recommend as a foundation for CPE.
2. Much of the Minsky literature is theoretical or empirically descriptive. Stockhammer et al. (2019) provide an empirical test for endogenous debt-investment cycles.
3. Some recent empirically driven NK work also asserts widespread unemployment hysteresis (Ball 2009; Blanchard et al. 2015; OECD 2017).
4. For Germany, Baccaro and Pontusson highlight exports as the reason for the shift to the profit-led growth model.
5. This is at odds with both neoclassical mainstream economics and large parts of Marxist theory, which assume that profits are reinvested.
6. One interesting detail in Stockhammer and Wildauer (2016) and Stockhammer et al. (2018) is that they find positive or nonnegative effects of the wage share on investment, which is at odds with the standard assumption of the Bhaduri-Marglin model. Stockhammer, Rabinovich, and Reddy (2018) document that corporate investment (for the United Kingdom and France) shows the expected negative effects of the wage share. It is important to keep in mind that investment consists of business investment and residential investment, which are likely to have different determinants. The standard argument of negative effects of the wage share on investment refers to business investment. In contrast, the wage share can have a positive effect on residential investment, if working class households own real estate property. A higher wage share can lead to higher mortgages and higher investment.

2

From Fordism to Franchise: Intellectual Property and Growth Models in the Knowledge Economy

HERMAN MARK SCHWARTZ

Introduction

What is the Knowledge Economy (KE)? How is slow growth since the 1990s—secular stagnation—related to the KE? In this chapter I argue that "Franchise economy" is a better label than KE, because it captures the essential elements of the current era: a shift in the key distributional conflict from fights between capital and labor to fights between different firms over profit volumes, and a related shift in corporate organizational structure enabling firms with robust intellectual property rights to capture greater volumes of profit. Those firms have a low marginal propensity to invest, slowing growth.

KE, as a positive description, is conceptually better than "Post-Fordism." Post-Fordism, and its class-conflict free cousins "post-industrial society" and "service economy," are Owl of Minerva labels. They belatedly recognized that growth models characterized by nationally homogeneous mass production by male semiskilled workers and consumption by female organized households backed by essentially centrist governments funding an ever-growing welfare state were largely gone by the early 1990s. KE correctly points to the growing salience of human rather than physical capital in production but simultaneously obscures how profit arises and which firms capture profit. KE analyses focus too much on Thorstein Veblen's (1904) *industry*, the Schumpeterian increases in productivity that make life better and easier, and not enough on *business*, firms' pursuit of profit maximization or "pecuniary gain," through sabotage of productivity increasing processes. KE analyses thus overlook how the concentration of profit into a handful of firms with a low marginal propensity to invest contributes to secular stagnation, and they obscure how knowledge-intensive financial services or social media might actually be value subtracting in the economy.

The Franchise economy label better captures the shifts in corporate strategy and structure generating stagnation and inequality by highlighting the sources and uses of profits. A franchise initially meant a royal grant of monopoly rights over trade, land, or some other activity and so encompasses Pagano's (2014) and Durand and Milberg's (2020) intellectual monopoly capitalism. Fordist corporate profit strategy sought oligopoly profit through control over physical capital, producing a dualized structure of large oligopolies and smaller firms with limited market power. Franchise firms seek monopoly profit through control of state-granted robust intellectual property rights (IPRs—patent, copyright, brand, trademark). In *ideal typical* terms, IPR-based strategies have shifted corporate organizational structures away from Fordism's vertically integrated firms toward a three-tier, de jure vertically disintegrated structure comprised of IPR-rich human capital-intensive firms, physical capital-intensive firms, and labor-intensive firms.

This de jure disintegration conceals dominant IPR-based firms' considerable de facto operational control over the bottom two layers. The franchise business model originating in the US hospitality sector is patient zero for the Franchise economy.[1] US franchisor firms are legally separate from their franchisees' firms but minutely specify franchisees' operations. De jure independent franchisee owners are de facto subordinate managers in de facto vertically integrated but de jure separate firms. *Franchise economy* thus captures both strategy and structure in both national and global commodity chains.

The combination of IPR-based profit strategies with legally disintegrated structures is both novel and a major source of secular stagnation. Knowledge has always been critical for production. But the tacit, uncodified knowledge characterizing pre-1870 competitive capitalism could not easily be sold and thus transformed into financial assets. Likewise, subcontracting arrangements characterized both agriculture (e.g., sharecropping) and industry (Herrigel 1996) in the 19th century. Chandler's (1977; Lazonick 1990) managerial revolution was built on the transformation of subcontractors' tacit knowledge into codified scientific and managerial knowledge, and on efforts to construct durable IPRs around that new intellectual property (IP) (Fisk 2009). Chandler's managerial revolution generated vertically integrated firms controlling both physical capital and IP. Disentangling the contribution of knowledge-related profits from physical capital-related profits was impossible. Moreover, firms that failed to generate or control the physical capital needed for continuous flow production fell into Fordist economies' bottom layer of disorganized, low-profit volume firms.

By contrast, the Franchise economy's three-tier, disintegrated corporate structure segregates IPR-generated profit streams from most physical capital- and labor-intensive processes. Middle-tier firms resemble shrunken versions of the old Chandlerian firms, possessing a significant physical capital footprint protected either by the scale of investment or considerable tacit knowledge, or both. The bottom tier provides labor-intensive, commoditized manufacturing and service products with limited or no barriers to entry. While the overall quantity of codified knowledge obviously has increased, the critical break with the past is the new combination of strategy and structure: stronger legal protections for information and its organizational segregation. Without legal protection, codified knowledge would yield no profits (Schwartz 2016; Pistor 2019). Without organizational segregation, those profits would be spread over a larger pool of labor and physical capital, as in Fordism. Without de facto control, IP based on brand and customer experience would depreciate more rapidly or yield smaller profit volumes.

This new structure contributes significantly to secular stagnation. The monopolies constructed by top-tier IPR firms allow them to capture a volume of global profits approximating that which financial firms capture in the US economy, though less at the global level. Profit volume matters as much or more than profit rates for the macro-economy, though top-tier firms often also have high profit rates. IPR-based monopolies have the typical monopolist's low marginal propensity to invest. IPR firms' relatively small employee headcounts also limit redistribution through wages as compared with integrated Fordist firms.

Meanwhile, an increasing share of the total labor force finds itself in precarious employment in the bottom layers, decreasing the consumption impulse to growth (Stansbury and Summers 2020). The concentration of profit and income into firms and households with, respectively, low marginal propensities to invest and consume generates secular stagnation and rising social unrest. Rising household and corporate debt in before 2008 temporarily bridged the gap between supply and demand (Streeck 2014a). Politically, the center of the struggle for profit shifted toward lobbying the state for firm-specific regulatory regimes, especially around IPRs. Various forms of bargained capitalism (Piore and Sabel 1984) gave way to Weber's (1978, 93, 108, 164–166, 638) political capitalism and Culpepper's (2011) quiet politics.

The chapter has five parts. Part one critiques three KE-type analyses. Part two revives Veblen to open a window into the Franchise economy. Part three examines the new organizational structure. Part four presents data on profitability and capital expenditure to back claims about secular stagnation in part five. The conclusion links the argument to the other chapters in this book.

From Fordist Manufacturing to the Knowledge-Based Service Economy?

Most KE analyses transpose the key Fordist distributional issues, namely efforts to control labor and inflation, into the present (Schwartz and Trานøy 2019), ignoring the sources of and struggles over profit. A handful of early studies of Fordism anticipated aspects of the Franchise economy because they attended to US state policy around "knowledge" dating back into the 1950s (Galbraith 1967; Bell 1973). Indeed, Fritz Machlup coined "knowledge economy" in congressional testimony in 1958 (Slobodian 2020, 73, 80–81). Sustained Federal R&D and procurement spending generated today's core information and communication technologies (ICT)—semiconductor chips, software, connectivity (Flamm 1988; Block and Keller 2015; Mazzucato 2015). ICT determined neither production relations nor corporate structure, however. ICT eased but did not determine emergence of the three-tier Franchise structure, which the US hospitality industry pioneered well before ICT emerged. Firms implemented new technologies in ways designed to control the increasingly militant workforces of the 1960s and 1970s (Noble 1984; Zuboff 1988; Brenner et al. 2010) and to reduce the increased cost of capital in the inflationary 1970s. Technology did not determine the income distribution in the Franchise economy (or Financialization plus Franchise economy).

By the 1990s the political economy literature approached the new economy through five different lenses: globalization, financialization, the service economy, reboots of varieties of capitalism, and a focus on intangibles. Each is partly correct, but all are "blind man and elephant" analyses. Schwartz and Blyth (here) and Ban and Helgadottir (here) respectively deal with globalization and financialization, so I only address the last three.

Service Economy Arguments

The authors in Wren (2013a, 2013b) built on Iversen and Wren (1998), Esping-Andersen's (1990) welfare state typology, and Varieties of Capitalism (Hall and Soskice 2001) to understand what they labeled the new service economy. Iversen and Wren (1998) argued that Baumol's (1967) cost disease created a policy trilemma across full employment, fiscal balance, and wage equalization, which heterogeneous national political economies translated into different outcomes. Wren's authors sketched policy strategies for dealing with Baumol effects and, critically, for generating higher wages and employment via high value exports. The core policy prescription—and conventional wisdom—was greater investment in education to boost human capital and thus promote the expansion of high productivity service sectors (Wren 2013b, 69).

These analyses focused too much on what was being made rather than how it was made. Services are a residual category, which forced an immediate but useful distinction between dynamic and non-dynamic services.

In Baumol's cost disease, dynamic sector (typically manufacturing) productivity increases cause wage increases that are transmitted to less dynamic sectors (typically labor-intensive services), driving wage costs above productivity there. Baumol's model assumes that even if the dynamic sector sheds labor, competition for workers will boost stagnant sector wages. But if high productivity growth sectors do not expand output in a sluggish demand environment, then the reverse is likely—labor shedding will crowd workers into the stagnant sector, driving down wages. Baumol's cost disease only operates in the context of the institutionalized, national-level collective bargaining of the Fordist class compromise, which linked wages across multiple sectors through pattern bargaining, concatenation, and wage legislation. Without institutionalized Fordist collective bargaining, dynamic sector productivity growth does not obviously boost employment in a wage-led economy (Baccaro, Blyth, and Pontusson here).

But a 20-year offensive by employers everywhere, roughly 1975 to 1995, broke the institutional links between dynamic and stagnant sector wages (Pontusson and Swenson 1996; Brenner et al. 2010; Murray and Schwartz 2019), producing dual labor markets (Häusermann and Schwander 2012). Organizational changes allowed employers to segment their labor force, breaking wage transmission mechanisms and weakening labor's bargaining power.

Dualization emerged even inside service economy analyses' paradigmatic dynamic service sector firms. Key software (or in Amazon's case, logistics) firms make widespread use of contract employees even for programming tasks. Microsoft pioneered the use of software engineer "permatemps"; nearly half of Google's 2018 workforce were temps and contract employees (Bergen and Eidelson 2018; Wong 2019). From the owner's point of view, the three-tier Franchise economy organizational structure with its legally segmented labor markets and contingent workers is the antibiotic curing Baumol's cost disease.

Finally, as financialization arguments assert, the high-profit, knowledge-intensive financial sector plausibly inhibits rather than enhances growth.

Everything Is Fine, Co-specifically Speaking

Iversen and Soskice (2019) rebooted *Varieties of Capitalism*'s emphasis on complementarities and coordination to explain the politics of the KE. They see the KE as a Schumpeterian growth wave centered on ICT and biotechnology

(Freeman and Louçã 2001; Perez 2009). They assume that production of these requires co-specific assets deployed in face-to-face interactions. This is undoubtedly true for parts of the biotechnology (but not pharmaceutical), software, and haute finance sectors. The information generating parts of these sectors mostly cluster in a handful of neo-marshallian urban industrial districts.

This argument has two major problems and one minor problem. First, the argument is almost purely deductive and functionalist with respect to state-firm relations. Iversen and Soskice (2019, 10, 24, 47, 190; Christophers 2016), argue that both the state and small, knowledge-based firms have an objective, functional interest in promoting competition in order to drive innovation. But the Fordist and KE eras both have highly concentrated sales and profits (Table 2.1) (Davis and Orhangazi 2021; Philippon 2019).

Second, like service economy arguments, they focus on industry, not business, reading the politics of the KE off the mechanics of production rather than firms' drive for profits. "Information" production (including cultural and emotional signifiers) can involve significant "co-specific" assets and small teams (Kitschelt 1991). But this fact does not explain why some firms expelled labor and physical capital, while others ended up with large labor or physical asset footprints. Physically separate R&D teams existed under the umbrella of integrated Fordist firms. Pressure for legal disintegration came from financial markets and labor control struggles rather than any technical imperative.

The third problem makes this clear. If co-specificity characterizes KE production, what explains why leading KE firms have so many essentially disposable contract workers, and rely so heavily on comprehensive non-compete agreements in which workers transfer rights to any ideas they generate on-site or off-site to the employer? Widespread use of contractors and non-competes shows that control over IPRs matters more than co-specificity. Non-competes would be irrelevant if employees' tacit and codified knowledge were truly firm- and co-specific.

Table 2.1 **Gini index for cumulative gross profit of US listed firms and global ultimate owners, select periods**

	Gini index for cumulative profits	*N of profitable firms*	*total N of firms*
US listed firms 1950–1980*	0.885	7599	8267
US listed firms 1992–2017*	0.922	11,038	19,678
Global Ultimate Owners 2010–2018**^	0.867	17,844	20,114

^ Global Ultimate Owners with cumulative sales over $0.5 billion and financial data

Source: Author calculations from *WRDS Compustat and **Bureau van Dijk Orbis databases

Moving to a new employer would gain an employee nothing. Put differently, everyone is co-specific until management decides that they are not.

The Unbearable Lightness of Intangibles?

Haskel and Westlake's (2017) in-aptly titled *Capitalism without Capital* likewise obscures intra-capitalist conflict, and, while noting some aspects of the reduced salience of capital-labor conflict, misses the social organization of production. They argue that intangible capital creates four novel S's: *spillovers* (intangibles or knowledge tend to spread to other firms), *scalability* (production can expand without a corresponding increase in physical capital), *sunken-ness* (the difficulties involved in selling "information" create difficulties extracting capital invested in an intangible), and *synergies* (the ability to combine knowledge to attain greater output).

Haskel and Westlake's technologically determinist argument ignores four important issues. First, they miss how IPRs transform intangibles like information into capital, that is, into a social relation yielding a stream of income. IPRs limit both scalability and synergy. Second, they largely ignore the state's role not just in establishing IPRs but in determining potential profitability via IPR duration and antitrust (Christophers 2016). Third, they exaggerate sunken-ness. IPR-rich firms routinely buy up IPRs to build barriers to entry. Google paid a nontrivial $12.5 billion to acquire bankrupt Motorola Mobility's 17,000 patents; a Microsoft-led consortium paid $4.5 billion to buy bankrupt Nortel Network's 6,000 patents. Less visibly, Microsoft has preempted competition by acquiring over 200 start-up firms. Fourth, if intangibles had significant spillovers and synergies, we would expect to see productivity rising across the entire economy, rather than visibly increasing dispersion between high productivity frontier firms and the rest (Andrews et al. 2016). Dispersion suggests—as Veblen would predict—that firms slow technological diffusion to defend their IPR-based monopoly profits. *Capitalism without Capital* actually lacks both capitalism—a system of accumulation driven by profits—and capital in its sense of a social relation, masking the sources of secular stagnation.

Understanding the Franchise Economy

These analyses all derive social relations of production directly from means of production, or, in Veblen's (1904) terms, they concentrate on *industry* to the exclusion of *business*. But *businesses* with robust IPR portfolios strategically repress competition through preemptive *offensive* acquisition of and litigation against potential rivals. Firms without robust IPR portfolios strategically repress competition through traditional *defensive* horizontal mergers and concentration (Philippon 2019; Davis and Orhangazi 2021). Firms with neither strategy resort to hyper-exploitation of labor.

Second, these analyses prioritize the conflict between capital and labor over the generation of surplus value (and thus the total pool of profits) while ignoring conflicts among capitals for shares of that profit pool. Interclass conflict undeniably matters in capitalism. But in the Franchise economy, capitalist intraclass conflict over the profit pool structures how interclass conflicts play out. Labor market dualization emerges from firm-level profit strategies oriented toward financial markets and rival firms rather than the other way around. The limiting factor on accumulation drives the shift toward intra-capitalist conflict in the Franchise economy. Capitalist growth requires the ability to access and exploit relatively abundant factors of production. Exploiting those factors requires social and political interventions that transform latently abundant factors into actually available factors, and then restricts access to generate profit.

A different limiting factor marked each of the French Regulation school's broad phases of competitive capitalism and Fordism (Harvey 1982; Perez 2009). Marketable and mortgage-able land was the limiting factor in the pre-1914 or pre-1945 agricultural era (Schwartz 2019b). Docile semiskilled labor and cheap oil were the limiting factors in the manufacturing or Fordist era (Piore and Sabel 1984). The limiting factor in the Franchise economy is the ability to monetize information, attention, and people's inner emotional states because *information doesn't really want to be free* (Doctorow 2014).

Digitized information theoretically is a public good, non-excludable and non-rivalrous in consumption (Ostrom 1990). Non-rivalry, an issue of *industry*, should create infinite supply. Digitized information is infinitely reproducible. From a *business* perspective, non-excludability prevents the profitable production and sale of information. For Veblen (1908a, 1908b), like Marx, the essence of capital as a social form was exclusion and preferably monopoly control. Machines simply embody the stock of social knowledge. Owners' control over that physical capital gave them the ability to simply hire proletarians who possessed the residual tacit knowledge needed to operate those machines (Veblen 1908a, 516–518).

The Franchise economy is built on information, per the unintentionally revealing KE mantra "data is the new oil." Yet the central problem in the Franchise economy is not data shortages, any more than land was in short supply relative to population in C19, or workers and oil in short supply in C20. Oil was central to Fordist growth, but hardly physically scarce. Rather, the central public and private problems around oil from 1920 to the early 1970s were using political violence to secure access to oil and then managing an overabundant supply to prevent price collapses. Cartelization—exclusion—secured steady, substantial profits for oil firms (Blair 1976).

Firms' central problem in the Franchise economy similarly is creating exclusion around information generated by consumers and workers. Political and legal processes generate exclusion, transforming otherwise free public goods into club (non-rival but excludable) goods, enabling monetization of information. That income stream then backs marketable assets.

The IPR-based firms now capturing the largest profit volumes all shield their data / knowledge from easy appropriation with some legal wrapper. Thus the entertainment complex lobbied for infinitely renewable copyright; pharmaceutical firms "evergreen"—extend—their patents with small formulary changes; software firms deploy patents, copyright, and end user license agreements (EULAs); haute finance increasingly uses patents; and a large variety of consumer goods and experiences are branded. Absent IPRs, profits from Disney's Mickey Mouse, Nike's Swoosh, Microsoft Office, Pfizer's Viagra, or Morgan Stanley's MSCI indices would drop. The key issues defining the Franchise economy are thus primarily legal ones about (re-)defining property rights around information.

This has four aspects. The first three relate to strategy and the last to structure. First, most important, the creation and expansion of legally constituted domestic and international monopolies through IPRs. Second, the decay of buyers' traditional property rights over both physical and intangible goods. Third, firms' struggles to wrap their otherwise standardized products in an IPR cloak while stripping IPRs off other producers' goods. Fourth, segregating the parts of production with a permanently falling cost curve—usually intellectual property "products"—into legal entities separate from the parts where marginal and average costs rise from exhaustion of economies of scale and rising costs of coordination.

Intellectual Property Rights and Antitrust

The US national security state and key IPR firms changed US domestic IP and antitrust law to create or enhance the profitability of IPRs after the 1960s. Legislation enabled the copyrighting or patenting of software in 1968, 1976, and 1980, strengthened trademark protection in 1988, and extended copyright on works for hire to 105 years in 1998 (Pistor 2019). The Supreme Court expanded the scope of IP protection in novel ways, as in *Diamond v. Chakrabarty* (1980), which permitted patenting of genetically modified organisms, and in *State Street Bank v. Signature Financial Services* (1998), which affirmed business process patents (important in finance). That said, the Supreme Court has also curtailed

IPRs, implicitly invalidating some business process patents in *Alice Corp. v. CLS Bank International* (2014).

Beginning with the 1973–1979 Tokyo GATT Round the US state undertook a concerted, 40-year campaign to extend US IPR law globally in order to secure revenue streams for US firms offshoring production and sales (Drahos and Braithwaite 2003; Sell 2003). This matured into the Trade-Related Aspects of Intellectual Property Rights (TRIPs) annex to the 1986–1994 World Trade Organization agreement. The now defunct Trans-Pacific Partnership (TPP) and Transatlantic Trade and Investment Partnership (TTIP) trade deals aimed at strengthening global IPRs. Weaker antitrust enforcement also enabled emergence of the three-tier Franchise structure. The threat or reality of antitrust litigation during the Fordist era motivated "hi-tech" firms like ATT or IBM to restrain their IP licensing fees. Chicago school "law and economics" arguments justifying monopoly if consumer surplus increased influenced the Justice Department, the Federal Trade Commission, and judges to bless mergers they would have banned in earlier decades (Christophers 2016; Peinert 2021). This enabled the emergence of platform giants providing "free" services to consumers.

Finally, Federal Trade Commission and National Labor Relations Board decisions enabled IP-rich franchisors to license brands and trademarks to their franchisees, to tightly control the nature of franchisees' operations, and to supply critical inputs while avoiding both legal responsibility for franchisees' workforces and antitrust litigation (Callaci 2018). Franchisors pioneered the three-tier Franchise economy organizational structure.

Non-intellectual Property Rights Erode

Politically created and enhanced IPRs have steadily eroded buyers' traditional property rights. IP "producers" employ variations on the software EULA to commoditize user data. Clicks, buying and lifestyle habits, searches, credit card-based purchases, and equipment usage become the data that platform firms sell to other firms seeking to target ads and that machine makers use to extract maintenance dollars. Users cannot easily retrieve the data they create.

But more subtly, buyers have lost the essentially unlimited property rights over purchased objects that they previously enjoyed. The courts have ruled that the mandatory EULAs accompanying not only software but also, for example, e-books, DVD video, smart TVs, and some capital goods convey only usage and not ownership rights. Producers retain ownership, including rights to discontinue, modify, or selectively withdraw software even when it is embodied in a physical object and even if this would disable the object (Perzanowski and Schultz 2016).

Firms use IPRs and EULAs to tie consumers to relatively continuous if not permanent streams of revenue via subscription. In the ideal typical case, users adopt some free version of the software (or purchase a closed device like Amazon's *Kindle* e-reader or a John Deere tractor) and then are locked into continuous purchases, providing a stable flow of revenue to the IPR owner. Music and video are now streamed via subscription rather than owned by consumers. Moreover, software enables firms to extend control into previously "fixed" physical objects. BMW, for example, plans to sell access to heated seats in some models on a subscription basis and proposed making Apple CarPlay a subscription service. Interestingly, Watt and Boulton's initial business plan involved leasing their patented steam engines in return for a percentage of the coal subsequently mined, while acting like a pure IP firm and licensing production. Watt produced few engines in its first 20 years of operation (Hodgson 2021).

The subscription model extends into conflict among capitals. Microsoft Office 365 is typically used at work. More generally the shift toward Software-as-a-service (SaaS) and storage as a service (the cloud) turns industrial software into a long-term stream of income, in contrast to the old "one and done" sales model. Similarly, users of GMO seeds or chickens essentially rent these, and are contractually banned from retaining or reselling them. "Owners" of jet engines, agricultural equipment, and medical scanners also surrender all data to the producing firm, and are banned by the 1998 Digital Millennium Copyright Act (DMCA) from hacking that equipment. In effect, they are on an annual subscription. Long-term streams of income are valued more highly in the equity market. This larger market capitalization is a potent form of Max Weber's *Kapitalmacht* that enables IPR-rich firms to preemptively buy up rivals and thus maintain their monopoly.

Standardization, Commodification, and Profit Strategies

Third, the nature of fights over standardization has changed. Continually falling real prices are more typical than late Fordist era inflation. As Veblen (1904, 234) observed, "Chronic depression, more or less pronounced, is normal to business under the fully developed regime of the machine industry." Competition drives productivity growth which in turn depresses prices, producing the classic product cycle and transforming bespoke luxuries into standardized commodities. Few firms escape deflationary pressure on profits. A mere 811 firms out of 62,000 listed firms globally from 1990 to 2018 account for all buy and hold net returns over the one-month US Treasury bill—a very permissive proxy for their cost of capital (Bessembinder et al. 2019). US stock market data from 1926 to 2015 show a similar pattern (Bessembinder 2018).

Put simply, the more standardized a product is, the more easily buyers can replace any given seller and the lower the barriers to entry for new suppliers.

Indeed, the big platform firms—Amazon, Google, Facebook, or Uber—are profoundly deflationary by making price discovery relatively frictionless. They split standardized goods into an IP part protected by IPRs, and a generic good or service with low barriers to entry. The former capture profits; the latter see their pricing power and profits evaporate, producing Veblen's deflation. Consider firms like Uber and Airbnb, which approximate economists' utopia of perfect markets by lowering the cost of price discovery and maximizing the use of existing assets. Their price discovery is profoundly deflationary for firms and workers in the bottom two layers. By 2018 Uber brought taxi fares down to levels that neither returned monopoly profits to Uber (Horan 2019) nor allowed vehicle owners to recoup capital costs and pay some socially minimum wage to drivers. The average US Uber driver earned a 10th percentile American wage in 2018 (Mishel 2018).

Firms seeking excess profits have only three strategies, all observable in the Franchise economy. First, broad sectoral swaths of the United States and many European economies use classic Veblenian horizontal concentration to buy up existing rivals and create a physical bottleneck in the flow of commodities (Philippon 2019). Concentration creates excess capacity, which top producers can use strategically to deter market entry by competitors (Steindl 1952, 9–13; Bulow et al. 1985). Horizontal concentration is a fundamentally *defensive* strategy to maintain or expand markups (De Loecker and Eekhout 2018; Davis and Orhangazi 2021).

IPR-rich firms' *offensive* acquisitions differ. They aim at preempting new entrants, with minimal market share, from disrupting their existing markets. Thus Google acquired Waze to protect the traffic analysis and mapping component of Google maps; Intel acquired Mobileye to prevent a challenge to its automotive chip business; Facebook acquired WhatsApp to preempt a challenge from messaging to its social platform. The pharmaceutical industry exhibits both types of mergers (Cunningham et al. 2019).

Second, a firm can acquire a bottleneck "platform" position aggregating buyers and sellers in a two-faced market. Amazon and Facebook most obviously and successfully use this strategy, followed by the less successful Airbnb, Uber, or Spotify, and in an even weaker way various restaurant franchises. Here profits arise from matching essentially standardized sellers and buyers and using the dual monopoly position to extract a toll on commerce, much as in finance. In the absence of IPR protection or control over other key elements, this strategy is vulnerable to competitive entry. Uber's centrality, for example, is vulnerable not only to Lyft but also to a whole range of local taxi app competitors backed by local regulators. Likewise Google (search) and the Canadian firm Shopify (ordering and payments) have combined to provide merchants (fulfillment) with an alternative to Amazon's platform. Shopify's order flow in 2020 was 40% of Amazon's third-party merchant flow.[2] Amazon's vulnerability to this kind of competition motivates its forward integration into warehousing and delivery and backward integration into the cloud.

The third, final strategy involves turning a standardized product into a universal standard protected by IPRs and IPR-funded offensive acquisitions. This captures the largest possible addressable market while excluding competition. Everyone is forced to license the standard, giving the producer enormous market power barely tempered by fear of antitrust authorities or buyer efforts to coordinate around a rival standard. Consider Qualcomm, whose 130,000 patents around the standard CDMA (3G) and LTE (4G) technologies linking cell phones to Wi-Fi and cell phone towers allow it to levy a 3% to 5% royalty on the selling price of nearly every cell phone sold globally. The salience of IPRs here is evident in the tripling of the number of patents filed for industrial designs and doubling of trademark applications between 2000 and 2015 (Durand and Milberg 2020; Haskel and Westlake 2017).

Generic Increasing Returns or Organizational Structure?

IPR-rich firms can reorganize commodity chains into the three-tier Franchise structure. In physical production, costs decline so long as economies of scale (or scope) exceed transaction, coordination, and variable costs. Eventually, though, coordination costs rise and variable costs swamp fixed costs, causing diminishing returns to scale. By contrast, production of IP goods has a continuously falling cost curve because digital (re-)production has falling marginal costs as compared to production of physical goods. Variable costs for the production of the Nth digitized program or unit of a dopamine-producing branded good are essentially zero.

Most analysts jump from this to claim that "network" effects, driven by increasing returns, are the predominant characteristic of the franchise/IPR economy. This is somewhat true, but misleading for two reasons. First, we still live in a material world (Madonna 1984)—almost all digitized information resides in or is used through physical goods. The iconic iPhone is quite tangible; Uber cannot function without cars and drivers.

Second, more important, the legal structure surrounding production determines who captures those increasing returns. The critical difference between Fordism and Franchise is the legal split between firms producing information and firms producing physical goods. Knowledge production under

Fordism also had increasing returns, as when stock animation cels and patterns were reused across multiple movies. But those returns were largely buried inside firms producing and owning physical goods. Movie production requires massive volumes of equipment and human creative and physical labor. Fordist era movies were produced in studios that owned equipment, sets, and film stock, and employed actors, writers, etc., on a non-contingent basis. Today, all of this is broken up across multiple legal entities (Hozic 2001). Each additional stream, rental, or ticket returns extra revenue to the owners of the IP in movies (including actors' images), but not to equipment or labor providers. In both eras producers retained property rights and consumers "rented" the experience. But Fordist era information goods were embodied in physical goods with rising average cost curves and produced by firms that internalized those rising average cost curves, while today firms possessing the relevant IPR can monetize the Nth consumer at no marginal cost. This is the organizational side of the standardization fight. Increasing returns thus are only visible because of the fissuring of corporate structures.

Strategy Drives the Three-Tier Industrial Structure

Put simply, the combination of IPRs as strategy and franchising as structure generates the defining characteristics of the Franchise economy: concentrated profits but weak investment, dualized labor markets across all three layers, and slow productivity and GDP growth. Firms' strategic responses to the Fordist labor control crisis produced the Franchise economy's *ideal-typical* three-tier production structure. On top are firms that successfully expelled standardized, often unionized, labor and big fixed, often asset-specific, physical capital while retaining only IP, critical employees, and the absolute minimum of fixed physical capital. The many new software firms were born that way. IPR-based monopoly allows these human capital-intensive firms to extract large volumes of profit from their value chain. These firms typically have a relatively high return on assets, and high revenue and profit per employee, given a large numerator (the IPR profit stream) and a shrunken denominator (labor and physical capital).

In the second level are firms with large physical capital footprints. As with the old Fordist firms, investment barriers to entry let them capture moderate profits. Firms deploying low-skill, low-wage labor to produce undifferentiated goods and services populate the bottom. These capture small volumes of profit despite high rates of exploitation. Where automobile firms and line workers emerged as the iconic firms and labor model in people's imaginary of the Fordist era, tech firms and "gig work"—the top and bottom layers—constitute the imaginary iconic firms and labor model today. Equally so, the Fordist imaginary

ignored poorly paid workers in marginal labor markets and the current imaginary ignores contingent labor across all three layers.

While hybrid firms exist, particularly if design and production are co-specific, and while the distribution of layers is geographically uneven, all advanced
economies and the global economy exhibit this three-tier structure.

Even in the Fordist economy's iconic automobile sector, core firms have shed
production of low and medium value components to concentrate on design and
assembly. GM and Ford de-merged their parts production, reducing the share of
value produced in-house to about 20% by the 2000s (Klier and Rubenstein 2008,
47). In turn, newly independent parts suppliers aggressively off-shored production of labor-intensive, low-skill parts production in an effort to remain profitable as core firms demanded 5% annual cost reductions (Klier and Rubenstein
2008, 51–52). This generated a global three-level structure. Similarly, VW shed
30% of its German workforce in 1974–1975, and 30 to 40% of VW's assembly
plant headcount today is "temporary" workers (Tolliday 1995, 122; Doellgast
and Greer 2007).[3] Difficulty transforming all tacit into codified knowledge
accounts for the residual hybridization of the automobile and similar sectors.
Nonetheless, the rising importance of software has produced alliances linking
Ford with Google, VW with Microsoft, and Hyundai/Kia with Apple, presaging
emergence of a purer franchise structure.

Literal franchise sectors, like fast food and hospitality, are closest to
the ideal type, and also show that this three-tier structure is not limited to
"tech." Most hotel brands currently neither own physical buildings nor employ most of the workers therein. Hilton Worldwide Holdings, for example,
has 16 brands and 5,900 registered trademarks franchised out to building
owners across carefully curated and gradated market segments.[4] By 2018,
Hilton directly owned or leased only 1% of the properties labeled with some
Hilton brand. Private equity firms, family trusts, and real estate investment
trusts typically own hotel buildings, which are a large physical asset. A different "Apple"—Apple Hospitality Real Estate Investment Trust—runs 242
hotels in the USA under various theoretically competing Hilton and Marriott
brands.[5] All of Apple Hospitality's buildings are managed under contract by
hotel management firms, who in turn contract in labor from firms like Adecco,
Hospitality Services Group, or GHJC Group. These jobs can be "gig"-like but
are more often standard, albeit precarious employment relations. As with fast
food and other franchises, the lead hotel "brand" firm controls the behavior
of firms and workers further down the chain in minute detail. Lead firms thus
enjoy all the benefits of vertical integration with few of the legal, administrative, or labor control problems.

The shift to the Franchise economy thus involved a partial resolution of the
capital-labor distributional conflict in capital's favor, as labor market dualization

and the secularly falling share of wages in OECD GDP shows. This reduced GDP growth by shifting income toward households with a low marginal propensity to consume. But equally important, it redistributed profits among competing capitals toward firms with a low marginal propensity to invest. Uber "invested" $14 billion as ride subsidies but only $1.6 billion on physical plant and software (Horan 2019).[6] Uber's bad math precisely illustrates the institutional shape of the dual axes of conflict in the Franchise economy. Capital-labor conflict is temporarily resolved by pushing workers as far outside the firm as is possible and transforming workers into miniature capitalists. They are then pitted against the better organized, better capitalized firms in a struggle over "profit," with predictable outcomes. As Max Weber observed long ago, *kraft ihrer Kapitalmacht* has a quality all of its own in the *preiskampf*.

Finally, consistent with the chapters by Schwartz and Blyth, Tan and Conran, Sierra, and Bohle and Regan (here), the three-layer structure is fractal, and can be found both inside national economies and across the global economy. Apple Computer, for example, has a de facto global three-layer structure involving itself, semiconductor firms like STM (Europe) or Toshiba (Japan), and assembly firms like Hon Hai (a Taiwanese firm operating in China). But it also has a parallel domestic structure involving itself, Qualcomm and Corning, and an army of contract service providers and programmers at its headquarters.

Who Gets What?

Not most workers. The knowledge economy or service economy is heterogeneous across firms within conventionally defined sectors, rather than being heterogeneous across conventionally defined, homogeneous sectors as the service economy, co-specificity, and intangibles arguments assert. Both high- and low-end (dynamic versus stagnant) service sectors have dual labor markets. This seems to run against the skill-biased technological change arguments for increasing wage dispersion in Wren (2013a) and Iversen and Soskice (2019). The key "tell" here is that inside each sector the real difference is between high and low profit firms.

Wages increasingly depend on who you work for in the three-tier economy, not what you do, as firms with bigger profits pay higher wages. Wage dispersion across firms rather than within firms accounts for much of rising income inequality in the United States (Barth et al. 2014; Song et al. 2019; Autor 2019). The higher profitability of IPR-rich firms flows into wages, with workers capturing between 30 and 42 cents of every dollar of patent generated surplus as higher earnings, and with longer serving and higher paid workers benefiting most (Kline et al. 2018, 1, 3; Berger et al. 2018, 3). In the past, unionization, sociological factors, and efficiency wages in continuous flow production dispersed oligopoly profits across a wider range of employees. The legal trifurcation of employment instead concentrates profit redistribution onto a much smaller employee footprint.

And not most firms. Table 2.2 compares the cumulative shares of sales, gross profit, and capital expenditure for the top 100 and 200 publicly listed US firms by cumulative gross profit in the broad Fordist (1950–1980) and Franchise (1992–2018) eras. Their disproportionate share of capital expenditure justifies looking at the top firms by sector to show why IPR-firms' low marginal propensity to invest generates the stagnation characterizing the Franchise economy.

Figure 2.1 shows the distribution of gross profit by sector for the top 100 US firms in each era. Figure 2.1 shows the obvious shift toward the hardware and software firms conventionally seen as the heart of the KE. But it also shows the shift toward pharmaceuticals, consumer branded goods (including food franchises), and of course, finance, which appears to be neither high tech nor IPR based but in fact is both. Space constraints prohibit full exposition of the voluminous financialization literature and why finance should be considered as an IPR sector (Schwartz 2017). A narrow slice of financial firms captures the bulk of profits by selling bespoke derivatives and managing IPOs and investment funds. The Gini for financial firms' cumulative profits is .95 for both gross and net income, 1992 to 2017. The production and (limited) reproduction of derivatives exhibits exactly the same characteristics as the canonical three-level IPR model. Much like software and biotech, small teams with high human capital produce derivatives in an ICT and software heavy production process (Bernstein 2008).

Subsequent to a 1998 federal court decision permitting patenting of mathematical and business algorithms, investment banks increasingly rely on Class

Table 2.2 **Top 100 or 200 US firms' share of cumulative sales, profit, and capital expenditure, 1950–1980 and 1992–2018, %**

Share of:		Firms	Sales	Profit	Capital expenditure
Top 100	1950–1980	1.2	41.7	45.8	47.8
	1992–2018	0.5	36.3	44.6	34.0
Top 200	1950–1980	2.4	54.6	58.2	59.4
	1992–2018	1.1	47.5	54.9	47.0

Source: Author calculation from WRDS *Compustat*

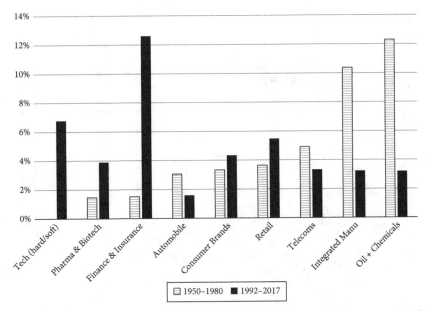

Figure 2.1 Top 100 US firms' share of all gross profits by sector, 1950–1980 versus 1992–2017, %. Source: Author calculation from WRDS Compustat

705 business process patents to protect new derivatives and processes. In 2014, for example, Bank of America filed roughly the same number of successful US patents as Novartis, Rolls Royce, or MIT, and JP Morgan as many as Genentech or Siemens.[7] Finally, the shift to a subscription model for payments enabled an entirely new asset class to emerge. Financial firms securitize subscription revenue streams, linking finance even more closely to IPR-based firms. Finance thus fits into the more general pattern whereby firms with robust IPRs are able to extract a disproportionate share of the value created in various commodity chains.

Just the US?

Is this a US-specific phenomena? Data limits prevent a diachronic OECD-wide comparison. But data for the past decade in the Orbis database and in the much more restricted set of firms in the Forbes Global 2000 list corroborate the US data, confirm that the global division of labor also exhibits a three-tier structure, and suggest that the global division of labor conditions national-level growth models. The top 200 firms in the Orbis dataset captured 45% of the cumulative profit of the 20114 consolidated entities with cumulative operating revenues over $500 million, 2010 to 2018. The decline of the old Fordist automobile

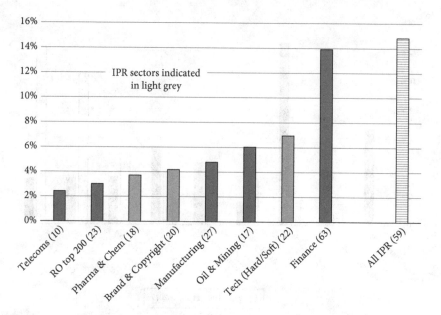

Figure 2.2 Top 200 global firms' share of cumulative profits, 2010–2018, by sector.
Memos: (#) = number of firms; All IPR includes all firms in light gray; manufacturing includes
automobiles; RO 200 = rest of the Top 200. Source: Author's construction from Bureau van Dijk
Orbis Database

plus oil complex (or autos, oil, and integrated manufacturing) in favor of the
new IPR plus financial firms is clearly visible in the distribution of those profits
(Figure 2.2). Within the top 200, the IPR sectors (tech hardware and software,
pharmaceuticals, consumer branded goods, and copyrighted goods) and finance
each captured one-seventh of all profits, while and the autos/oil/manufacturing
complex captured only a tenth.

Profits are distributed unequally not only across sectors, but also across countries, because the global distribution of the three different kinds of firms is uneven. Figure 2.3, for example, shows the distribution of profits by nationality of
ownership in NACE category 26 (computer, electronic, and optical equipment).
This category would include firms like Apple, Toshiba, Raytheon, Hon Hai, or
Fresenius. This sector accounts for 4.3% of cumulative profit for the Orbis-
20114, 2010 to 2018. US firms have disproportionately large profit volumes,
while profits relative to sales are disproportionately low for the numerous small
Chinese firms doing assembly or making low value components. The salience of
US firms' (non-Chinese) Asian collaborators is equally visible. The most profit-
able Asian firms are physical-capital intensive ones, like Taiwan Semiconductor
Manufacturing Company, which accounts for 31.3% of profits attributable to
Taiwanese NACE 26 firms, or Samsung, which accounts for 69.7% of Korean

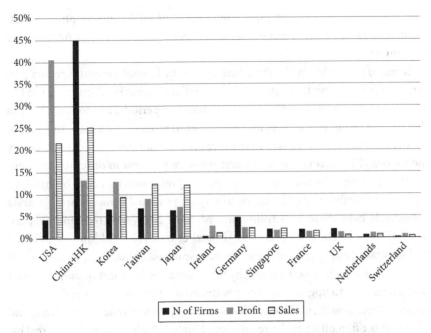

Figure 2.3 Share of firms, cumulative sales, and cumulative profits in NACE category 26 (computer, electronic, and optical equipment), 2010–2018, %. Memo: 6507 firms total.
Source: Author's construction from Bureau van Dijk Orbis Database

profits. Adding "inverted" US firms, like Seagate, which are technically credited to Ireland, would increase the US shares.

Macroeconomic Consequences

IPR-rich and financial firms in the Franchise economy have a lower marginal propensity to invest, slowing growth across all growth models. Fordist firms' strategy and structure promoted growth, albeit with a firm governmental hand on their back. Firms seeking oligopoly profits did so by expanding their control over physical capital. The natural depreciation of physical capital required reinvestment, sustaining investment levels. Integrated firms combined profit coming from control over IPRs with that coming from physical capital, enabling reinvestment. Efficient management of physical plant in the face of rising labor militancy required redistributing part of those oligopoly profits toward workers, sustaining growth in consumption. And the very physicality of production made it easier for governments to tax firms, enabling the expansion of government spending. Put differently, firms' strategy and structure generated the institutional base for the postwar wage-led growth models that post-Keynesian analyses posit, expanding all three components of GDP: consumption, investment. and government spending net of transfers. (Exports largely net out over the OECD.)

None of this holds in the Franchise economy. Capital expenditure as a percentage of gross profit for all listed US firms fell from peak Fordism, circa 1961 to 1965 versus the most recent comparable Franchise period, 2014 to 2018. Within that general trend, IPR sectors underinvest even more (Figure 2.4). The bulk of capital expenditures continues to come from the older Fordist sectors. Like any monopoly, IPR firms face only modest pressure to invest in order to stay competitive. Instead, IPR firms with large profits prefer to retain cash on hand, to pay out extraordinary dividends, or to acquire potential competitors. US firms collectively held about $1.9 trillion in cash as of 2016, with tech and pharmaceutical firms holding roughly 57% (Manzi et al. 2017). Additionally, Haskel and Westlake (2017) are correct about how scalability affects investment—IPR firms do not have to invest (as much) to produce the Nth unit of output. Much of the spending to upgrade or create software or chip designs takes the form of salaries. This has weak multiplier effects as compared to physical investment, and even that is often offset as the recipients of higher "tech" salaries bid up real estate prices and rents in prime urban areas.

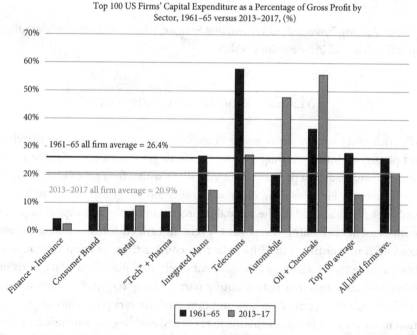

Figure 2.4 Capital expenditure as a percentage of gross profit for the top 100 US firms by indicated sectors, %, 1961–1965 versus 2014–2018 (ranked by share of gross profits, 1961–1965). Source: Author construction from WRDS Compustat data

Meanwhile, excess capacity deters investment by second-tier firms that need investment to scale. Automobile sector excess capacity ranges from about 10% in North America to 50% in China. This understandably makes firms cautious about new *net* investment although they do replace depreciated capacity. Apple's relations with its suppliers illustrate the tensions here. Apple invested US$200 million (from its $5 billion Advanced Manufacturing Fund) in Corning Glass to create a production facility for a new generation of Gorilla Glass™ (for mobile phone screens), because Corning was leery of expanding capacity.

Franchising and other forms of contracting out have broken up the old Fordist intra-firm wage leveling and profit redistribution mechanisms (Weil 2014). Workers at a given fast food franchise are not technically employees of the franchisor / brand owner. From a firm's point of view, this addresses the problem that at least part of labor-intensive production consists of non-tradable services—"last mile" jobs that must be done on-site in high cost urban areas (Autor 2019). Immigrants often populate this sector, bringing lower wage norms with them. Although this has gone furthest in the United States, temporary and minimum wage jobs have also proliferated in Europe (Häusermann and Schwander 2012).

Finally, the ease of tax avoidance for firms whose only real asset is IP limits government revenue (Zucman 2015). IP can be licensed or sold to shell firms in tax havens, which then collect profit by re-licensing that IP back to corporate units that actually make sales in higher tax localities. This has depressed government revenue to the point where it has produced a backlash from usually business friendly finance ministries. US legislation in 2020 will force the unmasking of anonymously held shell corporations, and the OECD's decade-long Base Erosion and Profit Shifting (BEPS) project of course has been pressuring governments to eliminate the more egregious tax avoidance schemes, like the infamous double Irish with a Dutch sandwich that relocated profits to shell companies with no legal tax domicile.

In sum, the three-tier industrial structure Franchise economy has a natural tendency toward secular stagnation. Firms with large profits invest little; firms that might invest lots have smaller profits. Inter-firm wage disparities concentrate income into higher income households with a low marginal propensity to consume, while the other 90% of households resort to varying degrees of debt to maintain a socially acceptable standard of living. That borrowing sustained growth and enabled physical-capital intensive firms to earn profit margins that induced moderate amounts of investment from 2001 to 2007 on the basis of an unsustainable housing boom (Schwartz 2009; Streeck 2014a).

That said, even without COVID-19 the Franchise economy was plausibly reaching its natural limits. In the core electronics sector, the semiconductor industry was hitting absolute physical limits to increased chip density. The two main end products for those chips, cars, and phones, both have hit the top of their logistic growth curves. By 2020, global cell phone penetration was roughly 70% with roughly 46% of the world's population owning a smartphone. And while electrification of the auto fleet will surely increase demand for chips, it equally surely will cause significant employment losses as the parts count for cars drops.

Conclusion

The knowledge economy has little to do with knowledge per se, but rather a lot to do with property rights around knowledge and the usual distributional conflicts in capitalist societies. The core dynamic of the Franchise economy is a shift from corporate strategies centering on a search for oligopoly power based on control over physical capital and instantiated in vertically integrated production structures, toward corporate strategies centering on a search for monopoly power based on control over IPRs and instantiated in legally disintegrated but functionally integrated production structures.

In this dynamic, Fordist era distributional struggles between capital and labor have taken a backseat to the distributional struggle among firms over profits. Not because the first distributional struggle is unimportant, but rather because capital largely won. In this context, the struggle over the enlarged pool of profit that greater exploitation enables has moved to the front. In that distributional struggle, the peculiar nature of the Franchise economy's "abundant resource"—digitized production, social and personal knowledge—has allowed a handful of firms to capture the lion's share of global profits by locking both data and social knowledge behind IPRs.

In short, it's not just concentration of profits—which characterizes both eras—but concentration into specific kinds of firms subsequent to a politically mediated legal fissuring of production activities and labor forces. Fragmentation reflects political choices made by dominant growth coalition (see introduction to this volume) that control the organizations regulating antitrust enforcement (Christophers 2016), define what qualifies for patent or copyright protection, and define who is legally the employer.

Whether the Franchise economy can persist in its current form is an open question. That said, government responses to COVID-19 might generate sustained expansionary fiscal and welfare policy. At the time of writing, the US Biden administration had secured a third, $1.9 trillion COVID-19 recovery package (*American Rescue Plan 2021*) and was proposing a similarly sized infrastructure and care economy package. This might generate a complementary investment response from second-tier firms as excess capacity is absorbed, while limiting labor exploitation by firms in the third tier. And antitrust authorities are taking increasing aim at the big platform monopolies, though not, at this time, the more general problem of horizontal and preemptive concentration. Much remains uncertain in this politically fragile moment, though.

Notes

1. I will use Franchise (capital F) to indicate the broader phenomenon and franchise (lower f) to indicate specific sectors using explicit franchise contracts.
2. Benedict Evans, "Shopify" @ https://www.ben-evans.com/benedictevans/2021/2/17/shopify.
3. Chris Brooks, "On eve of union vote, Chattanooga VW workers describe rampant workplace injuries," *Labor Notes*, June 11, 2019 @ https://labornotes.org/2019/06/eve-union-vote-chattanooga-vw-workers-describe-rampant-workplace-injuries.
4. Hilton Worldwide 2019 US Securities and Exchange Commission Form 10-K filing @ https://otp.tools.investis.com/clients/us/hilton_worldwide2/SEC/sec-show.aspx?FilingId=13217616&Cik=0001585689&Type=PDF&hasPdf=1.
5. Apple Hospitality REIT 2019 US Securities and Exchange Commission Form 10-K filing @ https://ir.applehospitalityreit.com/SEC_Filings.
6. Economist, "How real-estate barons have ridden the tech boom," May 9, 2019 @ https://www.economist.com/business/2019/05/09/how-real-estate-barons-have-ridden-the-tech-boom).
7. US Patent and Trademark Organization, "Patenting by organization, 2014," @ https://www.uspto.gov/web/offices/ac/ido/oeip/taf/topo_14.htm.

3

Four Galtons and a Minsky: Growth Models from an IPE Perspective

HERMAN MARK SCHWARTZ AND MARK BLYTH

Introduction

As the first chapter noted, the Growth Models (GM) research program attempts to provide scholars with three new tools. First is a conceptual vocabulary that breaks with equilibrium assumptions and typologies, aiming for a more dynamic and political account of different *national* growth trajectories and possibilities. Second is a set of techniques for more accurately measuring how different *national* models grow or not. Third is a focus on demand at the *national* level in terms of national productivity and profit regimes, and how such factors shape *national* growth dynamics.

The word "national" stands out both in such accounts and by design in the opening paragraph. In a world of nation-states that exhibit increasingly nationalist politics and policies, such a stance is far from unreasonable. However, an ontological nationalism, *the fact of nations*, should not by default determine a methodological nationalism, *the assumption that the national level is the sole locus of growth dynamics*. In contrast to the Comparative Political Economy (CPE) model outlined in the first chapter, this chapter argues for an International Political Economy (IPE) account of growth and growth outcomes in which the causes are not confined to the unit level. This chapter examines the consequences of taking this insight seriously for developing a more robust and usable body of GM theory. In doing so we invite scholars to incorporate both sets of insights into their analyses.

The difference between the IPE and Comparative Political Economy (CPE) lens lies in a concern with exogenous sources of growth and scale effects beyond the unit level. We view IPE as complementing and augmenting CPE approaches rather than competing with them. It complements, because extant CPE and IPE approaches have natural affinities already that simply need to be made stronger. But we also hope an IPE approach augments GM theory as a whole, making it more useful.

We develop two arguments to make this case. First, while CPE traditionally has developed with an OECD country-level bias, which makes the national level the appropriate—or at least traditional—focus of study, the gains from this methodological contrivance are attenuated when the scale of economic activity becomes continental and/or global. For example, a variety of national growth models exist within the European Union (EU), but can we, or should we, conceive of the EU itself as constituting a GM? If not, how do its institutions, and the requirements of membership constrain or enable, advantage or disadvantage, different national growth models?

As the chapter on the EU by Johnson and Matthijs in this volume demonstrates, FDI into Eastern Europe before the crisis of 2008 combined with post-crisis reforms to the EU's fiscal institutions post crisis to privilege export-led growth models over consumption-led models in the EU, in large degree. There is then, in the EU, a selection effect at the level above the national economy acting upon unit-level GMs.

Baccaro's chapter on Italy provides another example. Italy was (excluding Japan) the fastest growing OECD economy from 1960 to 1990, and then it basically stopped growing. Many (perhaps too many) plausible causes can be found at the unit level, ranging from dysfunctional politics to demographics. But equally so, it is rather obvious that an economy with the largest proportion of small firms of any rich OECD economy that embraces a supranational currency that limits devaluation as a rebalancing strategy might run into trouble in the face of increasing competition with German and then Chinese firms. Again, combining factors beyond the unit level with unit-level factors gives a more complete account.

China exhibits these dynamics further. With 1.4 billion people and the world's fastest growing large economy should we consider China as a single national growth model? The chapter on China by Tan in this volume rather sees China as a collection of quite different and regionally distinct GMs (private sector, state-owned enterprises, exports) pressed into service at different moments by a state that takes a long view on investment and growth. Likewise, should Latin American economies be understood wholly at the unit level when, as Sierra shows in her chapter, despite being quite different along many measures, they are all primarily commodity exporters with similar boom and bust cycles driven by external demand shocks? In short, something is missing from unit-level accounts of GMs that a focus on higher levels of analysis can augment in more than simply an additive way. This brings us to our second argument.

The choice facing GM scholars is how to weight and prioritize unit-level versus system-level factors in their own particular research. While it would be nice to simply compute the domestic level growth accounting from GDP decompositions and assume that scale drives such a choice—that is, the larger the unit the more "system" as opposed to "unit-level" factors should be weighted—reality often runs in a more complex direction. The United States, as Schwartz (2017, 2019a) has shown, indeed has a GM. And the sustainability of that GM is contingent upon the rest of the world tolerating US current account deficits while holding and using US dollars, which implies a global growth dynamic is relevant for even the largest economies. But at the other end of the scale, the GMs of microstates such as Luxembourg, or even individual US states such as Nevada, likewise depend upon global dynamics—in these cases the desire to avoid paying taxes—creating niches which they can occupy.

In what follows we provide five guideposts—"Four Galtons and a Minsky"—for scholars thinking about how to balance unit and systemic effects in their accounts. The four Galtons are analytic cuts at where growth lies and how it is produced based upon the notion of the fallacy of composition (that what is true at the unit level will be aggregately true at the system level as well). The "Minsky" in contrast complements the chapter by Ban and Helgadottir in this volume that sees financialization as a process cutting across, and common to, all growth models. Our Minsky however goes one step further than these authors by reminding us that credit cycles, which are integral to both growth and recession, are no longer purely or mostly unit-level phenomena but rather deeply related to the interaction of different growth models. As such, global finance increasingly matters for local growth despite claims by nationalist and anti-system parties that local GMs can be isolated or insulated from the global economic system.

Going Galton: Thinking about Systems and Units

What is the relationship between system and units? The methodological issue that we explore here parallels Francis Galton's critique of Edward Burnett Tylor's explanation for the presence of similar sets of cultural practices in Pacific Island societies (Hamel 1980). Tylor argued that similar practices represented functional responses to similar problems in all these societies, and so for statistical purposes they could be considered independent events. Galton, in contrast, argued that rather than springing up independently, these sets of practices had originated in a single spot and then diffused mimetically to all the other societies. Galton argued that Occam's razor favored external causality as the odds of independent similar emergence were low.[1] These cases were not independent.

Given Galton's insight, how should we think about GM units and growth in today's global system, given an increasingly complex global division of labor replete with transnational firms organizing flows of physical goods, data, financial instruments, people, and culture? For example, in the Baccaro and Pontusson (2016) version of GMs, most countries initially exhibited wage-led growth but diverged after the 1970s. This raises two Galtonian questions: Why the similarities before 1970–1980 and why the divergence afterward? Did unit-level or system-level factors drive similarity and then diversity?

This debate has any number of classic formulations, but a key touch point is the debate between Robert Brenner (1977) and Immanuel Wallerstein (1974) over the causes for the rise of a world economy differentiated into distinct production zones. Brenner argued a unit-level account where local class struggles produced specific production and class configurations that then aggregated to produce a world economy in which trade occurred. Wallerstein, by contrast, argued systemically—that an expanding global division of labor automatically called into existence the appropriate—and different—forms of production and state structure needed in any given locale.

Wallerstein drew heavily on the French *Annales* school's studies of European agricultural zones, which in turn, rested on the first serious work of economic geography, Johann Heinrich von Thünen's *Der isolierte Staat* (1826). Thünen's abstract model posited a market-based economy in which farmers located on a plain with uniform fertility and monotonically increasing transportation costs responded to the food demands of a central town. He showed that market forces would produce zones differentiated not only by their products but also—*and here is the really important part*—their production methods, including the degree of capital and labor intensity.[2] In Thünen's model (and other economic geography models, like Krugman and Venables, 1995), the market eliminates actors who choose the wrong product or production technique, producing relative local homogeneity—in a word growth models—but system-level diversity.

Returning to Galton, the point here is that what looks like a functional complementarity between, for example, export-led GMs and consumption-led (or, if you will, capital import-led) GMs does not arise from unit-level characteristics per se. Rather, given demand on scale A, the market will create spaces for products X, Y, and Z, and someone/someplace will emerge to serve that demand. Local characteristics may determine which of several potential producers becomes a dominant producer (Germany over France in the Eurozone, for example), but that determinant would be idiosyncratic.

The point, we stress again, is not that unit-level variables lack importance or causal significance, but rather that unit-level variables may well be brought into play and activated by system-level mechanisms. As such, they should not be understood in isolation from systemic mechanisms. To take one obvious example, export specialization requires a division of labor large enough to sustain that specialization. That is why export-led economies can only be export led to a significant degree if there are import-surplus economies out there. It's minimally a question of scale and maximally a question about the location of causality rather than one about matching balance sheets or accounting identities. Those import-surplus economies have to pay for imports somehow, which raises the issue of the degree to which the global structure of power generates the observed outcomes, what we will call Galton 3. Before doing that, though, we relate the specific arguments in CPE GMs to the more minimalist Galton 1 and 2 arguments about IPE or system-level causes.

Galton Types 1 and 2: IPE Meets CPE's Growth Models

CPE GM models bring three useful insights to the table that are compatible with existing work in IPE. First, per Keynes, Kaldor, and the post-Keynesian models elaborated by Stockhammer and Onaran in this volume, Say's law is backward. Rather supply creating its own demand, demand induces expansion of supply as firms opt to invest when excess capacity is absorbed (Baccaro and Pontusson 2016). Second, per Keynes, the income distribution matters since the marginal propensity to consume declines with rising income. Third, per both Hayek and the post-Keynesians, apparent institutional stability conceals the likelihood that economies can be in permanent disequilibrium because growth changes the availability of the different material and social resources powering those economies (Schwartz and Tranøy 2019), and also because capitalism is inherently conflictual across both classes and countries. In sum, demand drives supply due to differences in the ability and propensity to consume, and the more skewed the income distribution, particularly in moments of heightened investment uncertainty or class conflict, the weaker the domestic growth impulse.[3]

Given this understanding, the first and most obvious point of contact for the CPE version of GMs with IPE was the invention of "macroeconomic regimes" (Blyth and Matthijs 2017; Blyth 2016) as a concept that sought to explain the transition from the postwar Fordist growth models theorized by Boyer and Saillard (1981), to the more variegated Varieties of Capitalism (VoC) models of today (Hall and Soskice 2001; Hancke 2007). This literature argues that this transition emerged from a Kaleckian stand-off between investors and workers over the effects of inflation on profits and on future investment at the level of the system as a whole.

In particular, those Kaleckian stand-offs in the 1960s and 1970s exacerbated the pre-existing but mild global inflationary pressures that eventually motivated oil exporters to raise prices and thus trigger what looked like uncontrollable inflation. Blyth and Matthijs (2017) argued that this stand-off generated the shift from what CPE theorists would see as relatively homologous, Fordist wage-led regimes—where the policy target was full employment—to a set of more heterogeneous and specialized profit-led regimes—where price stability became the key policy target, and the restoration of profits became the key concern of elites.

The similarities between this particular IPE approach to understanding change over time and the CPE version of GM theory rests upon its purported causal mechanisms for the shift away from the postwar full-employment regime. Both the CPE version in Baccaro and Pontusson (2016) and the IPE version in Blyth and Matthijs (2017) settle on different Kaleckian mechanisms driving what the former call the shift from a wage-led to profit-led regime and the latter a shift to a neoliberal regime. Where the CPE version rests upon the insights of post-Keynesian/neo-Kaleckian macroeconomics regarding variation in wage shares and thus demand in unit-level economies, the IPE version rests upon a breakdown in the capital-labor productivity bargain underlying the regime at the level of critical components at the global level (but not the system as such). Both of these two versions of GM theory, the CPE and the IPE, are consistent with what we term a "Galton 1" scenario of independent responses to the functional problems of managing mass production, which in turn independently produced the inflation "bug" that crashed different national systems.

Building upon this, but moving up the system further to a "Galton 2" perspective, reveals that homogenous national growth models at the micro level generated endogenous decay because of two emergent fallacies of composition at the macro (global system) level.[4] This account stresses how Fordist domestic growth in most OECD economies rested on a tightly coupled material production system (Piore and Sabel 1984; Chandler 1977). Tight coupling could only work in the presence of stable prices, stable access to labor power, stable consumption, and stable inputs. Fordist *domestic* stability therefore relied on a stable class compromise or incomes policy in which wages grew with productivity (and sometimes inflation). But *globally* (and here is where the fallacy of composition crops up) Fordist growth relied on equivalent compromises securing a stable and predictable supply of raw materials, particularly oil.

The dual political compromises around this supply involved the United States and ex-imperial European states propping up governments in recently decolonized polities in exchange for a ceiling on prices on the one hand, and major oil or resource firms restraining output to set a floor on the other hand.[5] At the beginning of the 1960s the problem was largely one of preventing price declines. But as Fordist production practices and consumption norms spread to

Europe and Japan in this period, the demand for oil for transport and plastics began to exceed supply, shifting the problem to one of preventing price increases that might trigger global inflation.

Put differently, institutional mimesis around the Fordist growth model could occur at a national level in the 1950s to 1970 because economies were relatively closed for historical reasons, and because economies of scale in critical industries like transportation equipment were low enough to be satisfied in a national (or near national—consider Scandinavia) market. Any one economy could plausibly have succeeded at Fordist production of transport equipment without stressing oil supplies. But if all rich countries attempted a Fordist model, then cheap oil at predictable prices would disappear, producing a shock to those tightly coupled production systems. As such, what happens at the system level and the unit level differs in kind even if each is deeply causally imbricated with the other. The causal account differs depending on the Galton level invoked. In a level 2 Galton, no central power directs the adoption of Fordism. The degree to which Fordist GMs are adopted is a function of local conditions. Crisis emerges endogenously from simple aggregation.

Galton 3: GM Theory and the Issue of Asymmetric Power

The prior section dealt with Galton types 1 and 2, where the fallacy of composition generates an unexpected or unintended outcome from individually rational and independent national choices about GMs. But the world is not composed of the equal-sized units with equal power and resources. This brings us to "Galton 3," and the issue of whether some dominant actor(s) attempts to impose a preferred growth model, or to control and (re)-shape the market signals that drive actors' behavior in their local economy.

A version of this argument is found in Farrell and Newman's (2014, 2016, 2019) New Interdependence Approach and its related argument about "weaponized interdependence," which eschews unit-level explanations of international outcomes in favor of "a systemic account of world politics . . . where overlapping jurisdictions . . . emerge from [rule] overlap [to] create new opportunity structures for actors" (Farrell and Newman 2016, 716).

Farrell and Newman argue that globalization created a world of overlapping rules and novel jurisdictions where policy is no longer bound by the nation-state, in areas as diverse as financial affairs, digital privacy, and environmental regulation. In these contested areas, "rule overlap" empowers agents beyond the state to engage in bargaining, which leads to new political cleavages at a system level. Following this logic, Farrell and Newman (2016) suggest that control of key institutions at the level of the system is a key source of asymmetric power among states that is not reducible to the unit level.

Their most recent update to this approach, termed "weaponized interdependence," is deeply relevant for the concerns of GM theory (Farrell and Newman 2019). It takes this insight into the generation of asymmetric power further by developing a network analytic approach to understanding power at the level of the system. This version of the argument stresses that rather than globalization creating rule overlap, it creates critical nodes in the global network-architecture of regulation and access to flows (financial and informational) that comprise the system. Control of this architecture gives some states asymmetric power over others.

Seeing the system as a multilayered set of discrete network flows around finance, trade, information, etc., allows Farrell and Newman to explain how centrality in such networks, and increasing returns from centrality, create what they term "panopticon" and "chokepoint" effects that differentially empower the United States. For example, the ability to monitor almost all internet traffic due to so much of it being routed through northern Virginia (conveniently close to the US National Security Agency), or the ability to exclude third parties from the SWIFT payment settlement system (despite it being based in Brussels), strongly suggests power lies at the level of the system and is constituted by networks made possible by globalization.

A Galton 3 perspective thus draws our attention to the issue of asymmetric power between states, as well as growth coalition politics reaching across states. Both things are bracketed in the CPE literature. Systems are not level playing fields. Rather, as Farrell and Newman suggest, they are highly asymmetric, and they generate differential rates of return for those most central to the network. As such, the specific local growth model that a state happens to have is not just embedded in a wider "macroeconomic regime" as Blyth and Matthijs (2017) suggest. Rather, it is embedded in relationships of hierarchy and advantage that clearly structure the dynamics of growth at the unit level.[6]

Consider Eastern Europe in relation to Germany, or the pre-2008 British GM. The Eastern European FDI-led and (largely) export dependent growth model is only possible because of its embeddedness in the wider EU-level macroeconomic regime (pace Blyth and Matthijs 2017). The Eastern European GMs simply could not exist as viable growth models without a link via German supply chains to the Greater European Export Complex (Blyth 2016). Farrell and Newman's perspective thus encourages us to focus our attention on the asymmetric nature of this system and the outsized rents generated by Germany vis-à-vis the FDI dependent states. These differential returns stem from differential power, which is a systemic as well as a unit-level property.

Second, consider the United Kingdom's pre-2008 growth model, which Bacarro and Pontusson identify as an unbalanced consumption-led model driven by financialization and "the inflow of capital from abroad" (2016, 186). This is indeed a reasonable characterization of the United Kingdom seen as a single unit-level economy. But that view also omits another core component of Britain's GM. The United Kingdom is a central hub in the greater "Anglosphere," a globally interconnected network where the vast majority of global financial flows earn differential rents, part of which are spun off into the greater British (albeit mostly southeast) economy (Fichtner 2016; Oatley et al. 2013). Seen in this way, British growth is once again not simply a function of Britain's unit-level characteristics. Instead, Britain's position in the system, in terms of both centrality and hierarchy, matters for a fuller accounting of growth.

Indeed, we can imagine a stronger version of a Galton 3 explanation that would examine networks of firms and their embeddedness and differential profitability in global value chains in order to understand which firms capture value from those production chains and how. Similarly, we could imagine a version in which a dominant state consciously tries to reshape other countries' domestic political economies much as the United States, for example, has been doing since the 1920s (Costigliola 1984; Sørensen 2001; Maier 2015), and as Hirschman (1945) argued the German state did in Eastern Europe in the 1930s. This version of Galton 3 would argue that the world economy constitutes a single field of power in which firms as well as states operate, and in which firms and associations of firms provide the relevant growth coalition at a global scale, motivating much state behavior. Thinking about the relationship between the system and the units in this way resolves two major puzzles for the CPE GM literature, and one for the IPE literature that has to do with the mutual dependencies of exporters and consumption-led economies.

First, given that substantial net exports should generate extra growth, why do almost all export-led GMs have lower rates of growth than the consumption-led GMs? CPE GM approaches try to answer this by asserting that consumption-led economies have excessive, debt-financed growth, implying that the normal state of affairs is low rates of growth, and counterfactually, lower levels of consumption absent such financialization. But this only highlights the second problem. By definition, any GM with significant net exports will accrue external assets. The second question then arises. Why would export-led polities continue to accept this debt, knowing that consumption-led economies did not generate enough tradables to make good on those debts?

There is clearly more than just balance sheets going on here. This question is even more pressing once we realize that the major surplus economies receive subpar returns on the assets they accrue from export surpluses. This is obvious in the case of most Asian exporters, whose portfolios disproportionately hold US Treasury debt, which returns much less than corporate debt, equities, or FDI. But it is even more puzzling with respect to advanced economies like Germany, who seem to earn US dollars abroad only to use them to buy foreign assets that earn less than they would if they were simply invested at home (Hünnekes et al. 2019).[7]

Relatedly, IPE has its own version of this puzzle concerning growth and imbalances. The distribution of import and export surpluses is not random. From 1992 to 2017, the United States accounted for 50.6% of global current account deficits. On the other side, Germany, Japan, and China accounted for 43.3% of global surpluses, equivalent to 95% of the US deficit (Schwartz 2019a, 495). Chronic US current account deficits should call into question not only the viability of their associated global liabilities, but also the currency in which they are expressed. Yet the dollar seems more dominant than ever. And clearly that has something important to do with global growth since the holders of those dollars are export surplus economies who lose money doing so—and yet the system continues.

Galton 4: History Matters Because It Persists

Moving up to a fully system-level account may not be necessary, or even desirable for CPE GM theorists, since it makes the unit level all product and not at all productive. Yet such an approach, a "Galton 4," does contain some important insights that have to figure into unit-level explanations as Stinchcombe-ian historical causes that can usefully merge CPE's insights about the internal logic of local economies with IPE's insights about how those economies articulate with each other. The baseline consideration is this: the export-led economies are all successful late developers (Schwartz 2019a has an extended discussion) and that matters for explaining patterns of growth across *all* cases.

As Gerschenkron (1962), Streeck and Yamamura (2001), and the subsequent developmental state literature argued, successful late developers generally mobilize capital for development by suppressing domestic demand. That capital is channeled into successively "heavier" industries, which tends to starve agriculture, light industry, small- and medium-sized enterprises, and the service sector of investment capital. While policy-driven mobilization of domestic resources often creates viable, globally competitive firms at the technological frontier, it also leaves behind the scar of permanently deficient domestic demand, which causes output to flow overseas.[8] Germany may have become the export economy par excellence, but that move was embedded in its industrial founding, as it was in the foundings of all the other export-led states.

Relatively low household consumption in the late developers therefore forces firms to look outward for markets, which they find in the Anglo economies, and in high-growth developing economies. As an outcome of late development this is a structural and systemic factor more so than an expression of independent local choices. Germany can choose today to "do more exports" in response to a financial shock, but that is possible precisely because it has never done "more consumption."

This institutional lock-in around reduced consumption also tends to make financial systems in late developers relatively more bank oriented rather than capital-market oriented. Although financial systems everywhere have been shifting away from traditional lend and hold models (Hardie et al. 2013; Deeg and Hardie 2016), a huge disparity in the degree to which securities market as opposed to bank lending dominates still persists between the United States and other economies.[9]

Export-led GMs must recycle their surpluses in order to maintain their undervaluation regimes, *but they can only recycle their surpluses if there is an acceptable asset in which to deposit those surpluses.* And that asset is the US dollar. Current account surpluses put a large pool of dollars into exporters' hands. Exporters then channel their dollars through their local banking system. Local banks thus have growing US dollar-denominated liabilities (deposits), which in turn compel those banks to relend those dollars in global markets in order to have a corresponding asset. The dollar share of liabilities (deposits) and assets (loans) on the bank balance sheets of export-led economies thus grows, supporting US deficits.

Non-US banks' US dollar-denominated liabilities—that is, deposits—typically accounted for more than 49% of all cross-border liabilities, 1992–2017, and accounted for 57% in 2017. Indeed, non-US banks recycling trade surpluses as well as endogenously creating credit are the major source of dollar-denominated lending in global markets. Non-US banks generated 80 to 85% of offshore dollar lending, with virtually all of that funded from US dollars supplied by non-US entities (McCauley, McGuire, and Shushko 2015; Aldasoro et al. 2017; IMF 2018, figs. 1–23). This recycling of export surpluses also sustains the growth differential between the United States (and other Anglo- and consumption-led GMs) vis-à-vis the export-led models, even if this growth is based on consumption.[10]

Surplus economies' reliance on exports for growth and banks for intermediation thus pushes them into accepting and recycling US dollars, and thus maintaining the US dollar as the dominant global currency. In turn, the dollar's preeminence supports US preeminence in the global power hierarchy. This mechanism allows us to resolve the IPE and CPE puzzles noted earlier. It combines the different levels of analysis in those approaches by linking undervaluation regimes to the dominant global currency.

Thus, from a "Galton 4" perspective, the relationship between export-led and consumption-led economies is more than a simple mechanical one emerging from local choices independent of the system à la Brenner. Rather, export-led GMs have their origins in a Stinchcombe-ian historical cause, namely late development efforts triggered by the power imbalance between first Britain and the world, and subsequently the United States and the world. They have a Stinchcombe-ian continuing cause in the local structure of power, namely (excess) production and (suppressed) consumption built into firms and a local institutional environment shaped by late development and reinforced by the outcomes of two world wars.

These GMs make sense—that is, they can survive and prosper—economically only because a global hegemon generates new demand (via new, globally acceptable debt) that validates the excess investment in export-led economies. The global structure of power makes that demand acceptable to export-led GMs by validating the future utility of US dollar-denominated debts, even though, as noted before, some export-led GMs seem to be bad global investors.

This Galton 4 type explanation is no different from Polanyi's characterization of Britain's role in the global economy of the 19th century. Today, the US current account deficit performs the same role and it is a feature, not a bug. It provided a nontrivial 0.8% of global GDP (about $380 billion) *annual* stimulus to the global economy, 1992–2017. The counterfactual world in which the United States balances its external accounts by pushing its current account deficit under 0.5% of its GDP would see a parallel collapse of growth in the export-led GMs. That counterfactual world is one in which exporters stop accepting US dollars and allow their own currency to appreciate, or a world in which exporters translate surpluses into import substitution industry in the United States. In either scenario the export-led GM would disappear. So too would the financialized GMs, as the supply of new money dried up. In sum, from a Galton 4 point of view, GMs are deeply interdependent at the global systemic level, and growth is a property of both the unit and the system.

And a Minsky Atop It All

If much of CPE focuses on nation-level institutional dynamics, much of IPE focuses on money and financial dynamics. IPE particularly focuses on the US dollar's role as the "top" currency (Cohen 1996), and to a lesser extent as the vehicle tying growth at the global level to the unit level. CPE accounts increasingly recognize these dynamics by incorporating financialization as a component into their models, and by viewing it as a phenomenon that cuts across models (pace Helgadottir and Ban in this volume). IPE accounts agree with this stance, but once again IPE would push it in a different direction to highlight equally important, but less recognized, growth dynamics.

As noted, CPE accounts tend to view finance as a "fix" that ameliorates insufficient aggregate demand in national economies that have shifted from wage-led to profit-led regimes of growth (Baccaro and Pontusson 2016). Some CPE GMs are seen to rely excessively on finance for growth (although as noted before such models nonetheless seem to grow faster than the less financialized) while some are seen as more "balanced." IPE, by contrast, views finance as much more than an increment to aggregate demand at a domestic level in three ways, two of which we have covered already. But all three involve the fallacy of composition and endogenous decay.

First, exporters can only be exporters if there is a global currency to provide liquidity countering the deflationary dynamics that export-centered GMs produce. Specifically, if national-level competitiveness determines export share, and exporters are historically consumption constrained, then a rising share of export-led regimes in a system will endogenously depress global aggregate demand. The fallacy of composition means they cannot all remain successful net exporters. Keynes recognized this dynamic in 1944 and sought to supply a global currency—exogenous "outside" money—called the Bancor to offset these dynamics. The Bretton Woods arrangements failed to supply such a currency, and the US dollar instead provided a second-best, but vastly inferior solution.

Second, exporters in particular—and investors in general—need a global safe asset in which to park their earnings. Again, the US dollar and dollar-denominated assets play that role, mainly because there are no credible alternatives and because the United States still exhibits better growth dynamics than the alternatives, thus valorizing the debt it issues. But in a modern version of the Triffin Dilemma, a rising tide of export-led GMs would erode both US credibility and growth if the United States tried to accommodate all of their surpluses.

Third, these two factors have combined with the globalization and integration of financial markets we have seen over the past 30 years to produce global credit cycles—as clearly seen in the 2008 crisis—that can both augment domestic growth (Seabrooke 2006; Schwartz 2009) and severely damage it when it goes awry (Blyth 2013; Tooze 2018).

CPE accounts, to the extent that they paid attention to finance prior to 2008, tended to analyze it as a problem of how national-level firms acquired capital (Hall and Soskice 2001). Post crisis, finance had to be rethought in both CPE and IPE. Both disciplines rediscovered Hyman Minsky (1986), whose notion that endogenous credit cycles were both integral to and disruptive of growth provided a reasonable starting point. Minsky posited that after a financial crisis, regulators clamp down on what is permissible, producing an extended period of financial stability. As Minsky notes however, "stability breeds instability" over the long run. Actors mistake the lack of volatility as evidence of "financial repression" and their own ability to successfully manage risk. Consequently they lobby to remove constraints.

As actors succeed in liberalizing the supply of finance in a credit-constrained world, they initially reap high profits while boosting asset prices. This incentivizes the further expansion of banks' balance sheets to take advantage of these rising prices, moving the system from its "Hedge" phase to its "Speculative" phase. This second wave of credit expansion is however inherently unstable. It is itself predicated on realizing capital gains from rising asset prices that are in turn financed out of that credit expansion. Meanwhile, the ever-increasing demand for these assets leads to the entrance of new "less sophisticated" investors, which juices demand, and further masks risk. At this point, what Minsky calls "overtrading" occurs, and the "Ponzi" stage of the cycle becomes endogenously unstable as the returns on these hyper-inflated assets can no longer support their valuation. "Revulsion" then occurs as market actors all try to flee these same positions at the top of the market, causing the collapse in values each of them are individually trying to avoid. Minsky's argument thus rests on the fallacy of composition and endogenous decay.

As far as generic accounts of financial cycles, credit expansion, and deleveraging go, this is a pretty good basic model. IPE scholars would differ from the CPE renditions of Minsky by arguing Minsky cycles have become global, not local, events, plausibly since the 1982 Latin American debt crisis and certainly since the 1997 East Asian financial crisis. System-level crisis dynamics compromise the stability and survivability of national growth models.

As noted before, if exporters earn dollars and bank in dollars, then they must also be lending out those dollars to transform bank liabilities into assets. This creates a global network of lending and borrowing obligations that ties domestic credit cycles together as investors chase yield at a global level. In such a world, banks at a domestic level can create "inside" money in the form of loans that make deposits to chase this yield. But if those loans are made in US dollars—non-US banks originated 80 to 85 % of cross-border dollar-denominated lending in recent years—and the collateral values that are the counterparty to those loans fall in value, then these national-level banks doing the lending are suddenly short US dollars. By definition their own central banks cannot create dollars to bail banks out of their Minsky moment. This makes the entire global network dependent upon the US Fed as the global lender of last resort, which not only highlights the Galton 3 dynamics noted earlier, but also strongly suggests that credit cycles cannot be treated as local events. As such, when we talk about financialization at the unit level we would do well to remember that, particularly for dollar-long exporters, credit booms and busts lie just as much at the global as the local level (Schwartz 2019a).

Conclusions: IPE and GM Theory

An IPE perspective on GMs basically argues that unit-level GMs do not exist independent of the IPE, whether we regard that IPE as simply a set of market forces that create structural spaces for specific kinds of products and production processes (Galton 1 and 2), or as a hierarchical, power-driven system in which a dominant power with global Lender of Last Resort capacities passively or actively shapes everyone else's choices (Galton 3 and 4). IPE and systemic approaches in general highlight how the fallacy of composition at all levels creates endogenous dynamics that cause models at the unit level to change, whether by choice or market coercion or (something all growth model approaches elide) overt political intervention. As such, IPE and its CPE GMs should be seen as co-constitutive.

Saying that always sounds nice, but what does it actually mean? We think it means four things.[11] First, all GM scholars should recognize that systems not only differ in character from their component units, but also have dynamics that can significantly advantage or disadvantage unit-level GMs. For example, the crisis of Fordism opened a space for countries that had only incompletely adopted Fordist production techniques, like Italy, Denmark and, to a lesser extent, Germany. Future research could usefully build upon this insight, exploring why various countries did or did not capitalize fully on this opening.

Second, power, in the form of hierarchy, centrality, and the provision of global liquidity, matters. Systems are much more than the sum of the units that constitute them. One unit may have a privileged position in the system that allows it to generate exogenous demand or the use of actual and symbolic violence to rewrite the terms of trade or financial regulation. If capitalism tendentially trends toward deflation—something both Veblen and Schumpeter thought inevitable—then the power to issue money that everyone will accept is a major source of power that is exogenous to units and pertains to a specific unit's position in the system. Effects will vary across other units based on their own position in the system.

Third, history matters in the formation and maintenance of specific GMs. A polity's timing and manner of insertion into the global economy conditions local production and political structures to this day. While this conditioning is never as strict as path dependency arguments might have it, the global market does exert considerable pressure on actors to shape their behavior in ways that perpetuate their current growth model and thus the system structure. Today's export GMs didn't just decide to "go for exports" randomly. They were selected for it, and that historical selection has contemporary salience. For example, Chancellor Merkel's 2020 decision to allow Chinese telecoms firm Hauwei access to Germany's 5G network, despite US opposition, was heavily conditioned by Germany's continuing export dependence on China via its auto sector. As such, the ability of such states to wean themselves of exports toward less beggar-thy-neighbor forms of growth should be treated as an open question.

Finally and empirically, we hope that these "four Galtons and a Minsky" provide scholars with a set of parameters for judging not only "how much system and how much unit" they should stress in their accounts, but also how systems shape units. As suggested before, while it's not as simple as "the bigger the scale the more system matters," we should nonetheless be attentive to those scale effects and network effects that are increasingly important drivers of growth for all GMs.

Luxembourg is a unit-level GM (and a parasitic one at that). But it only exists as Luxembourg precisely because everyone else is "not Luxembourg." Niches matter because the system—minimally via a global division of labor—generates them. Likewise China may not be a single unit-level GM so much as a concatenation of different GMs, evolving together over time. But China is a unit-level actor in the global economy, and that matters for all the other GMs out there. In sum, the system matters, and the only questions are "how" and "how much" given the research question at hand? Both IPE and CPE need to embed their analyses in that simple but powerful fact. Choice of weight in analysis is perhaps then the weightiest choice GM scholars need to make.

Notes

1. To this we add a third possibility, namely imposition by an external power, rather than pure mimesis. In turn this suggests that looking at polities rather than specific global firms (or global networks of firms) as the units in a system may understate how power actually works in that system.
2. Schwartz (2007) has a full description of the Thünen model that also includes a consideration of manufacturing and unit-system dynamics. Note that openly resting his argument on Thünen would put Wallerstein into a zugzwang: to evoke Thünen was to confirm Brenner's criticism of world system theory as a form of neo-smithian Marxism in which the market did all the work and in which exploitation disappeared since prices plausibly reflected productivity at the margin. Arguing that exploitation was central and that the market did not arise spontaneously, by contrast, would raise the significance of Weberian arguments about the centrality of violence in state formation, suggesting that world economies were simply in transition toward world empire and that exploitation had no economic basis. Far better then, to bury Thünen under a blizzard of citations to work that had used his model.
3. Lavoie and Stockhammer's (2013) work underpins these insights, parsing the differences between profit-led and wage-led demand regimes.
4. See Schwartz and Tranøy (2019) for a discussion of endogenous decay as a causal factor (or not) in CPE analytic models.
5. As Maurice Bridgeman put it in a speech to the API in November 1963, "The problem facing each responsible company with shut-in production . . . is therefore this: How much oil can we sell annually without contributing to a fall in prices which would not only render many of

our own operations unprofitable, but—which is even more important—reduce the revenue of many of the principal exporting countries to a point which is politically unsupportable?" Quoted in Francisco Parra, *Oil Politics*, p. 39. Shut-in production is capped oil wells whose output could be increased. Note that from 1950 to 1980 US oil firms in the top 100 firms by cumulative gross profit for all publicly listed US firms captured 10.5% of all gross profits, more than the manufacturing firms (including automobile firms) in the top 100.

6. Given that about two-thirds of total global trade in 2014 involved production that crossed national borders at least twice before reaching end users, this kind of interdependence matters for all growth models (Constantinescu et al. 2018).

7. Hünnekes et al. (2019, 4–5) show that Germany's annual returns on its external investments have been between 2 to 5 percentage points lower than returns for comparable rich countries, and lowest among the G7 countries. Put differently, subpar investment performance left German firms and households €3 trillion poorer than they would have been had they achieved returns similar to Canadian offshore investors over the decade after 2008. Nearly a year's GDP! Furthermore, German domestic assets also outperformed overseas assets, suggesting a serious misallocation.

8. Thus Höpner (2018) argues that even Germany, the most advanced of the surplus economies and one with a relatively robust welfare state, has operated a pro-export undervaluation regime since 1950; barriers to mortgage credit likewise suppress German domestic demand.

9. In 2013 (the most recent data) the ratio between securitized debt plus bond debt versus unsecuritized bank loans was roughly 2.2::1 for the US market, while the ratio for Japan was 1::1, and the Eurozone and EU was only 0.62::1 (IMF 2015). Financial systems in most export-led economies continue to be bank dominated, with banks providing 80 to 90 percent of corporate funding in Europe versus 30 to 40 percent in the United States (Standard and Poor's 2015; Detzer et al. 2014).

10. Market actors react to the social fact of GDP growth, more so than worries about the sustainability of debt (until it is too late).

11. Also, both IPE and CPE GMs contain a useful shift away from the microeconomic- and supply-side concerns that marked CPE after the mid-1980s (Schwartz and Tranøy 2019).

PART 2

GROWTH MODELS AT SCALE

4

The Political Economy of the Eurozone's Post-Crisis Growth Model

ALISON JOHNSTON AND MATTHIAS MATTHIJS

Introduction: The Changing Growth Model Dynamics of the Eurozone

When Europe's single currency turned 20 years old on January 1, 2019, the euro's two-decade anniversary was met with solemn reflection rather than exuberant festivities. A few lessons were certainly learned since ECB President Jean-Claude Trichet's confident comparison of the euro with a "large, solid, and steady ship" 10 years earlier, just over a year before the Eurozone's sovereign debt crises would push the single currency to the brink of collapse (Trichet 2009). While real progress has been made in putting the euro on a more sustainable institutional footing, EU leaders have not resolved its original design flaws and continue to be consumed with national fiscal rectitude and member state competitiveness. They also have not been able to bring back the healthy growth performance of the Eurozone member states from the 2000s, with renewed divergence in living standards and employment between faster growing Northern "surplus" countries and stagnating Southern "deficit" countries becoming a structural reality during much of the 2010s. While the COVID-19 pandemic forced a dramatic rethink of EU economic governance, it remains to be seen whether this will end up being a temporary shift to deal with exceptional circumstances or will result in a more permanent and sustainable new settlement in which a variety of different growth models can flourish once again.

How can we make sense of the changing growth dynamics of the Eurozone's member states? Lucio Baccaro and Jonas Pontusson's (2016) work on national "growth models" and Mark Blyth and Matthias Matthijs's (2017) paper on different "macroeconomic regimes" have motivated scholars of comparative capitalism to rethink the way they analyze the organization of advanced industrial economies. While supply-side theories dominated earlier generations of comparative capitalism research, the growth model paradigm assigns aggregate demand primacy in the study of comparative political economy.

Nevertheless, like the prior Varieties of Capitalism (VoC) canon, growth model research often suffers from a "Galton problem" (see previous Chapter 3 by Blyth and Schwartz). Except for examining how globalization impacts capitalist systems more broadly (trends which the wider VoC literature has also been highly cognizant of, as seen for example in Streeck and Thelen 2009 or Thelen 2014 in addition to Hall and Soskice's seminal 2001 volume), the growth model literature has not fully considered how international actors and the arrangements they create shape the evolution of growth models within domestic political economies. As nation-states become more deeply embedded in regional and global international organizations and agreements, it is logical to presume that the rules that their governing elites voluntarily bind themselves to will also shape their championed domestic growth strategies going forward.

Nowhere are these dynamics more visibly at work than in the European Union's (EU) Economic and Monetary Union (EMU) or Eurozone. In this chapter, we provide an International Political Economy (IPE) account of how international institutions, and the power struggles within them, have the potential to change and consolidate member states' national growth models over time. The introduction of the euro in 1999 was truly an audacious experiment and was one—at least according to one of its key architects, Jacques Delors, president of the European Commission from 1985 to 1995—that was intended to respect national diversity through asymmetric integration (see the Committee for the Study of Economic and Monetary Union 1989).

In this chapter, we argue that prior to 2009, during the euro's first decade, EMU did indeed accommodate growth model diversity, even strengthening the prioritized growth strategies within its export-led and domestic consumption-led growth models through several institutional innovations and policy changes. However, these innovations also helped in delivering the debt crisis in the late 2000s and early 2010s. While EMU's export-led growth models weathered these crises relatively well, given their comparative lack of reliance on external borrowing, the domestic-consumption-based growth models fared very poorly (Johnston 2016, Matthijs 2016b). By "virtue" of being EMU's creditors, the export-led core countries rewrote the Eurozone's new macroeconomic governance framework in a manner that championed export-led growth strategies. These rules established a more restrictive fiscal policy, shifting the Savings-Investment (S-I) balance toward excess savings to better accommodate external surpluses, while the European Central Bank (ECB) from 2012 onward shifted to a much more accommodating monetary stance that weakened the euro vis-à-vis other currencies, boosting net exports with the rest of the world (Matthijs and Blyth 2018).

In other words, EMU's tolerance of growth model diversity radically changed during the second decade of the euro's existence. Domestic consumption, abetted by fiscal expansion, wage growth, or foreign borrowing, became an unviable growth strategy under EMU's austere "Memoranda of Understanding" (MoUs) and new guidelines for macroeconomic surveillance. Given the power asymmetry between EMU's export-led growth models and their domestic consumption growth model counterparts within the European Council, the former were able to shape EMU going forward in a way that explicitly prioritized export-led growth and effectively cut off growth strategies that revolved around buoyant domestic consumption. Countries whose growth models were reliant upon domestic consumption before the crisis were either forced into stasis (Greece, and to a lesser extent Italy, which was already on the road to stagnation after the euro's introduction) or toward export-led or FDI-led growth paths (Portugal, Spain, and Ireland).

EMU's promotion of export-led growth and demotion of domestic consumption-driven growth after 2010 had important political economy implications outside of the Eurozone as well. As a result of stagnant domestic demand within its peripheral countries, the Eurozone as a whole built up notable current account surpluses with the rest of the world. This worked relatively well in the first half of the 2010s, but in a world of increasing protectionism and geopolitical rivalries, this strategy quickly runs into trouble. And while the ECB's expansionary policies continue to be a key source for offsetting lackluster domestic demand—though its main effect has been to boost asset prices rather than average incomes—the Frankfurt-based central bank is running up against serious political constraints and operational limits.

If the Eurozone wants to put its future growth on a more sustainable footing, it will therefore need to rewrite the euro's governing rules, so they do not merely benefit export-led models but also accommodate domestic demand driven models through more fiscal flexibility and a globally competitive EU-wide industrial policy. While the EU started this process in response to the COVID-19 pandemic in the summer of 2020—by activating the general escape clause of the Stability and Growth Pact, setting up a 750-billion-euro Recovery and Resilience Facility ("Next Generation EU"), and committing to a strategy to increase its own "strategic autonomy"—we yet have to see whether these policy initiatives will gain a more permanent character or are a one-off response of fleeting solidarity.

This chapter proceeds as follows. Section 2 provides a brief review of the relevant literature and an analytical framework that helps us identify different growth models within EMU and advanced market economies more broadly. The third section explains how these models evolved during the first decade of the single currency and how institutional changes during that period accommodated EMU growth model diversity, but also increased the riskiness of certain growth strategies, particularly those that depended on external borrowing and debt accumulation. Section 4 documents how export-led growth models emerged as the "victors" of the sovereign debt crisis, allowing them to transform EMU's post-crisis macroeconomic regime away from allowing diversity toward Germany writ large, making EMU itself a driver of growth strategy change within its domestic consumption-led member states. The fifth section discusses the role of the European Central Bank as a second-best substitute source for supporting aggregate demand during the post-crisis period, while section 6 explains the other source of compensating demand, that is, net exports to the rest of the world, and why this new ECB liquidity-greased and export-led growth model is risky in a world rife with zero-sum big power rivalries. Section 7 addresses the EU's policy response to the COVID-19 pandemic and section 8 concludes.

The Politics of National Growth Models

The most important contribution of Baccaro and Pontusson (2016) to scholarship in comparative political economy (CPE) was their simple proposition that comparative capitalism needed to start taking aggregate demand seriously again. This was also a basic point Blyth and Matthijs (2017) made to ongoing debates in the IPE literature, in which they put forward the concept of "macroeconomic regimes" and argued in favor of shifting the focus from micro "supply" dynamics to macro "demand" effects, putting the choice of policy targets and the impact of fiscal and monetary policies on aggregate demand at the heart of their analysis.

Baccaro and Pontusson's sectoral framework rests on a simplified economic aggregation. National economies consist of an export sector (whose firms export manufactured goods, services, or "investment") and a domestic (consumption) sector (whose firms/employers cater to economic activity that revolves around domestic demand, including the public sector, consumer banking services, housing and construction, among others). As a theory of institutional comparative advantage, earlier VoC scholarship focused more heavily on firms and goods/services in the export sector, as the outcome they explained was variation in trade specialization. Countries either excelled in producing (high quality) manufacturing goods for which production rests on incremental innovation and industry specific skills *or* in goods (and services) that require radical innovation, substantial shifts in product design and product lines, and general skills that are easily transferable across industries (i.e., ICT and pharmaceuticals). In Hall and Soskice's original 2001 volume, however, little attention was paid to sectors that revolved around *domestic consumption*. When "sheltered" sectors were discussed, it was in reference to how they upheld skills accumulation which could be used to enhance countries' comparative advantages (see Estevez-Abe, Iversen, and Soskice 2001; and Mares 2001).

In contrast to the VoC literature, both export-based and domestic-consumption-based sectors feature prominently in the growth model literature. Though national economies are composed of the two sectors, their political influence differs across countries, and can also vary over time within them. One of the crucial distinctions between these two sectors is how wage growth contributes to their economic performance (Johnston 2021). Buoyant wage growth is beneficial for domestic demand but can stifle foreign demand through its impact on the real exchange rate. As wages and prices rise, a country's real exchange rate appreciates vis-à-vis its trading partners. Consequently, the growth in the wage share is a pivotal distributive struggle within national economies, and the political power of firms and workers in the export sector versus those in sectors dominated by domestic consumption determines which national growth (and wage) strategies countries will choose to pursue.

When conceptualizing worlds of growth models using an export/domestic sector lens, one can conceive of four possible growth strategies (as simplified in Table 4.1). In one world (bottom-left quadrant), the economic (and political) power of the export sector dominates, and wage suppression is pursued at the

Table 4.1 **The Universe of Growth Models in Advanced Market Economies**

		Export Sector Economic/Political Power	
		Strong	*Weak*
Domestic Sector Economic/Political Power	Strong	"Balanced" Growth Models (Scandinavia, France, Italy, pre-euro, Ireland pre-crisis)	Domestic Demand-Led Growth models (UK, US, Greece pre-crisis, Portugal pre-crisis)
	Weak	Export-Led Growth Models (Germany, Belgium, Austria, Ireland post-crisis)	Stasis (Italy post-euro, Greece post-crisis, Portugal post-crisis, Spain post crisis)

Source: Authors.

expense of the domestic sector. This is a strategy of *export-led* growth and is best typified by Germany, Austria, and Belgium. In another world (top-right quadrant), the economic and political power of the domestic sector (be it the public sector or domestic services/goods sectors) dominates. Robust domestic demand growth is spurred through either buoyant wage growth (e.g., Greece and Portugal before the crisis), strong credit growth (as seen in the debt accumulation regimes of the United States and the United Kingdom that revolve around financialization and home ownership—as shown in Bohle 2014 and Thompson 2012) or a combination of the two (pre-crisis Spain).

In the third growth model world (top-left quadrant), the power of the export and domestic sector is equally matched. This is the world of "balanced growth models," best typified by Sweden and its Nordic neighbors, but also by Italy prior to the euro and France (which has a strong public sector and notable industrial coordination between the state and the country's largest firms—see Amable and Hancké 2001). Persistent and significant wage moderation need not be a defining feature of this regime if the export sector consists of firms in knowledge-intensive, high-value added goods and services for which external demand is less elastic (see Baccaro and Pontusson 2016, 176–177; and chapter 10 by Lennart Erixon and Jonas Pontusson) and if the domestic (public) sector is receptive to modest wage growth and fiscal discipline.[1] Ireland, whose FDI-centric growth model also revolves around the technology sector (Brazys and Regan 2017), could be placed into this typology before the crisis given the significant contribution of the construction and real estate sectors to its growth performance and their influence over Irish policymaking during the 1990s and early/mid-2000s (Williams and Nedovic-Budic 2016). However, since the crisis, Ireland implemented austerity and strengthened credit limits on household borrowing, while doubling down on its Silicon Valley FDI-targeting enterprise strategies (Brazys and Regan 2017).

Finally, the "stasis" (or "no" growth but stagnation) world (bottom-right quadrant), an equilibrium outcome which no set of domestic elites wish to find themselves in, occurs when the export *and* domestic sector display weak output performance to the detriment of the entire economy. This world of stasis (best typified by Italy since the late 1990s) emerged as the new equilibrium in the 2010s for some of EMU's debtor countries (Spain, Portugal, and particularly Greece). All three were forced to impose draconian austerity measures and structural reforms on their domestic sectors (particularly the public sector) under their debt assistance programs. But, unlike Ireland, they did not have a sizable external-facing sector that could immediately be turned to for growth.

Of course, growth strategies are fluid and countries can fluctuate between different equilibria over time (Jones 2021). However, scholars in the wider growth model literature tend to grant greater agency to domestic elites, and do not fully consider how foreign elites and international institutions can force these (domestic) elites' hands in their pursuit of specific growth strategies. We argue that the introduction of the single currency had imperative effects on growth models within EMU's member states, and that the specific crisis response that was chosen during the 2010 to 2012 period was an important and asymmetric instigator of significant change.

EMU's Impact on Growth Models (1999–2009)

From the euro's inauguration in 1999 until the Global Financial Crisis of 2008–2009, EMU could accommodate multiple growth models in one seemingly harmonious system that was in broad balance with the rest of the world. The richer Northern core countries, characterized by export-led growth models, grew slower, while the poorer Southern periphery countries, characterized by strong domestic sectors, grew faster (see Figure 4.1). A combination of looser fiscal policy at the national level, and a more restrictive monetary policy at the Eurozone level, also served to benefit the domestic demand-driven economies through a stronger euro (externally) and a fiscal boost to demand (internally). Indeed, the gap in standards of living between both types of growth models

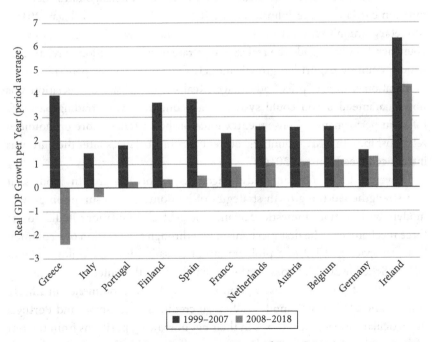

Figure 4.1 Real GDP Growth in the Eurozone, Pre- and Post-Crisis Average. Source: EU AMECO Database (2020) and authors' calculations

declined in that period, while income inequality widened substantially in export-driven growth models (because of wage moderation and higher interest rates; and r > g) but declined markedly in domestic demand driven models (because of faster wage growth and lower interest rates; and g > r) (Matthijs 2016b; Piketty 2014).

During this *belle époque* of the euro's first decade, EMU's institutional structure also exacerbated crucial differences between the Eurozone's export-led and domestic consumption-led growth models that would make their compatibility increasingly problematic. Numerous scholars have documented how the structure of EMU advantaged the Eurozone's export-led growth models at the expense of its domestic consumption counterparts over the course of the euro's first decade (Hall 2014; Iversen, Soskice, and Hope 2016; Johnston 2016; Johnston and Regan 2016; Matthijs 2016b; Höpner and Lutter 2018). These authors all highlighted that EMU's "export advantage" lies within how it changed the calculus of the real exchange rate between its member states.

The real exchange rate is merely a country's nominal exchange rate times the ratio of domestic to foreign prices. Under a system of multiple exchange rates, the nominal exchange rate acts as a competitiveness "buffer" between low-inflation (export-led) growth models and high-inflation (domestic consumption-based) growth models within the real exchange rate, because high inflation currencies also tend to have lower (less valuable) nominal real exchange rates than low inflation currencies (see Johnston et al. 2014 and Johnston and Regan 2016). Monetary union's removal of the nominal exchange rate between Eurozone countries, however, made the real exchange rate purely a function of relative inflation, granting export-led growth models that could deliver persistent wage moderation a direct "price" advantage. Real exchange rate depreciation was now guaranteed if you could systematically undercut your trading partner's inflation performance. Consequently, inflation had a much more pronounced relationship with EMU countries' current account balances after the euro was introduced (see Johnston 2016).

However, EMU not only advantaged its export-led growth models. It also strengthened the growth strategies of its domestic consumption growth models by boosting domestic demand via debt accumulation. It did so via three mechanisms. The first mechanism was through the creation of a common financial space that led to a proliferation of cross-border capital flows (Jones 2015a; Schelkle 2017). Cross-border capital flows further intensified an important source of domestic consumption that would gain prominence in EMU's consumption-led growth models—foreign credit. Greece, Spain, and Portugal in particular saw significant rises in their net borrowing positions from the rest of the world under the euro's early years, as well as notable deteriorations in their net international investment positions.

The second mechanism by which EMU enhanced domestic consumption growth strategies within its early years was through its impact on nominal interest rates. EMU introduced a common interest rate for its members, which allowed inflationary-prone domestic consumption growth models to enjoy the (low) interest rate benefits stemming from "peer effects" with low inflation countries (Brooks et al 2015). The third mechanism was through the reform of the Stability and Growth Pact between 2003 and 2005, which allowed EMU member states additional discretion over their fiscal policies, after France and Germany violated the 3% deficit rule, making it possible to further accommodate domestic demand growth strategies (Heipertz and Verdun 2010; Matthijs 2016a; Matthijs and Blyth 2018).

Until the Global Financial Crisis, markets largely discounted default risk for all Eurozone countries, causing yields on government bonds in the South to closely resemble those in their Northern neighbors (in 2007, on the eve of the Global Financial Crisis, the spread in nominal interest rates on long-term Greek and German government bonds was a mere 28 basis points—EU AMECO 2019). Consequently, EMU not only provided a greater availability of credit to its peripheral members whose growth models were dependent on robust domestic demand, but also this credit was considerably *cheaper* than the foreign capital they consumed under the European Monetary System (EMS). Cheap and plentiful credit supported significantly higher levels of domestic consumption within the periphery's public and/or private sectors. In Ireland and Spain especially, the influx of foreign capital combined with increasingly liberalized banking rules to enable households to go further into debt, which created unsustainable real estate bonanzas (Fuller 2018).

Everything changed with the 2008 Global Financial Crisis (GFC). Though the GFC emerged from the US' subprime mortgage crisis (see Helleiner 2011; Blyth 2013), liquidity concerns over "toxic" mortgage-backed securities created reverberations for countries with over-extended external borrowing positions in Europe. As Erik Jones highlights, "at some point, market participants question the sustainability of accumulated net foreign liabilities," and heavily (externally) indebted Eurozone members fell victim to sudden stops (Jones 2015b, 821). Inflows of foreign money abruptly dried up, and sovereigns were on the hook for both public and private debt.

By "virtue" of having suppressed domestic consumption and reduced their (net) external liabilities, EMU's export-led growth models entered the crisis on a sound footing. EMU countries with pre-crisis growth models that were partially (Ireland) or fully (Greece, Portugal, and Spain) sustained by extensive domestic consumption (which EMU's financial space exacerbated) were hardest hit by sudden capital flight, and their fiscal/financial positions became untenable without external debt assistance. The Council of the European Union was able to stave off contagion by creating a common bailout facility for Eurozone member states—first the European Financial Stability Facility (EFSF), which eventually became the European Stability Mechanism (ESM) (see Table 4.2).

As its creditors, the Eurozone's export-led growth models (led by Germany) were able to demand significant bailout conditions from debtor countries and were well placed to rewrite EMU's rules on macroeconomic surveillance to their own advantage. Naturally, they chose to write these rules in a manner that emphasized their own (export) growth strategies, while discouraging domestic demand expansion strategies, after framing the Eurozone debt crisis as a morality tale between "Northern Saints" and "Southern Sinners" (Matthijs and McNamara 2015). By May 2010, domestic consumption growth models were

Table 4.2 **Fiscal Responses to the Eurozone Crisis**

Date	Policy Implemented	Amount (€ bn)
May 2010	Bailout Package for Greece Agreed	110
	Eurogroup announces creation of EFSF	440
Nov 2010	Bailout Package for Ireland Agreed	85
Jan 2011	EFSM Created	60
Feb 2011	European Stability Mechanism (ESM)	500
Mar 2011	EC approves the Euro Plus Act	—
May 2011	Bailout package for Portugal Agreed	78
July 2011	First ESM Treaty Signed	—
Dec 2011	Six-Pack Agreement enters into force	—
Feb 2012	2nd Bailout Package for Greece Agreed	130
Mar 2012	Fiscal Compact Signed	—
	Eurogroup increases EFSF/ESM lending	200
Jun 2012	Fiscal Support Package for Spain Agreed	100
Sep 2012	ESM Launched	500
Dec 2012	Eurogroup: additional support for Greece	49
Feb 2013	Two-Pack Agreement enters into force	—
Nov 2014	Juncker Plan and EFSI Announced	315
Aug 2015	3rd Bailout Package for Greece Agreed	86
Dec 2017	EFSI Extended and Target Raised	185

Source: European Commission (2021), Council on Foreign Relations (2021), https://ec.eur opa.eu/info/sites/info/files/economy-finance/factsheet_timeline_of_eu_actions.pdf https://www.cfr.org/timeline/greeces-debt-crisis-timeline

facing what Blyth and Schwartz identified in Chapter 3 as a "Galton 3" problem. The unsustainability of the EMU harmony between its various growth models was laid bare by the crisis and would result in significant changes in the Eurozone periphery growth models.

EMU's New Regime: Export-Led Growth for All (2010–2020)

With Germany—and the rest of the Northern "creditor" countries—in the driving seat when it came to cobbling together conditional bailouts for the Southern countries in distress, EMU's new rules were bound to be driven by German ordoliberal thinking (Matthijs 2016a). As Merkel put it herself in a May 2010 speech to the Bundestag, "the rules had to be geared towards the strong rather than the weak" (Merkel 2010). In the Eurozone's case, the strong were those countries that did not rely upon domestic consumption growth and external or public debt accumulation. By virtue of being the "victors" of the crisis (and with their growth models vindicated), the Eurozone's export-led growth models were able to shift EMU from a comparatively agnostic institutional configuration of growth model diversity, toward a regime that much more explicitly prioritized and championed export-led growth. It is indeed telling that of the countries that remain in growth model "worlds" which include strong domestic consumption (Table 4.1) after the crisis, none—with the notable exception of France—are EMU members.

EMU's shift toward a supranational export-led growth model came through three programmatic developments.[2] The first was the establishment of austerity-based terms and conditions for the economic assistance programs within the EFSF (now ESM). The receipt of funds from the EFSF/ESM was conditional upon the implementation of draconian cuts to public sector pay and public employment, as well as to social programs that provided income supplements to poorer segments of society (see Hermann 2014) and social investment (see Perez and Matsaganis 2018). The first Greek bailout program in 2010 was so harsh in pushing Greece into recession that it was deemed a failure by 2012 and replaced with a second program which implemented a haircut (euphemistically called "PSI" or private sector involvement) on Greek public debt held by the private sector (Theodoropoulou and Watt 2015).[3] Spain's, Portugal's, and Ireland's Memoranda of Understanding (MoUs) also involved severe public sector wage and employment cuts, as well as substantial retrenchment in social programs (Glassner 2010).[4] Given its comprehensive approach to cutting all facets of public spending, EMU's MoUs perhaps had the most significant effect on pivoting the Eurozone's debtor countries away from domestic-led growth strategies, particularly those that stemmed from the public sector. Fiscal stimulus was no longer a viable growth strategy as long as these countries remained reliant upon EFSF/ESM funds.

Yet the EMU's debtor states were not the only countries who witnessed the evaporation of viable domestic consumption strategies. In 2011, the European Commission and the European Council (under heavy pressure from Germany and other Northern member states) introduced two key programmatic changes—colloquially known as the "Six Pack" and "Two Pack"—to EMU's macroeconomic governance and surveillance regime that would lead to EMU promoting an export-led growth model much more explicitly among all of its member states. Both of these reforms focused heavily on fiscal imbalances, in a Northern effort to reinvigorate the previously watered-down Stability and Growth Pact (European Commission 2019).

Four of the Six Pack's legislative initiatives targeted fiscal policy, strengthening the surveillance of fiscal balances (fiscal deficits could not exceed 3% of GDP per year, and total government debt had to be below, or "sufficiently declining towards" 60% of GDP),[5] enhancing and tightening the enforcement of fiscal rules (with sanctions in the form of a deposit of up to 0.2% of GDP[6] in an interest-bearing account for "significant deviations" from fiscal corrections). Where necessary, the European Commission was given direct oversight over national budgets, aided through the Two Pack's "European Semester" (European Commission 2011 and 2014). While the content of these fiscal rules was not entirely revolutionary, the terms of their enforcement (and voting rules behind them) entailed a considerable surrender of sovereignty by Eurozone governments (Matthijs 2017). Most prominent was the fact that sanctions under the Six Pack's "Excessive Deficit Procedure" would be made by "Reverse Qualified Majority Voting" (RQMV), by which penalties are approved by the European Council of Ministers unless a qualified majority of member states overturns them (European Commission 2014).

The constraints by the Two Pack and Six Pack on expansionary fiscal policy, and its detrimental effects for domestic-consumption growth models whose success depends on a buoyant public sector, is clear. However, the Six Pack also contained two pieces of legislation aimed at rectifying macroeconomic imbalances more broadly (including "external" imbalances), codified into the "Macroeconomic Imbalances Procedure" (MIP). The MIP marked the first time in its history that the European Union sought to regulate the external balances (i.e., current and capital accounts) of its member states—balances that governments only have indirect control over unlike their own fiscal accounts. Citing "serious gaps in competitiveness" as a major motivation for introducing the MIP (European Commission 2011), the Commission and the Council went beyond the Stability and Growth Pact's fiscal scope and used the crisis to draft policy that would impose limits on external imbalances produced by the *private sector*.

The MIP's Alert Mechanism Report identifies whether countries are at risk of "excessive imbalances" through a scorecard of 11 indicators. If a number of these indicators are breached, the European Commission executes an "In-Depth Review" of a member state's macroeconomic imbalances. Through these reports, the Commission can decide whether the "Excessive Imbalances Procedure" (EIP, the Excessive Deficit Procedure's macroeconomic imbalance counterpart), can be launched, and whether corrective action needs to be undertaken to rectify these imbalances. The Commission has not made it entirely clear what guides their decisions on whether corrective action should be taken, or how many scorecard indicators need to be violated for an In-Depth Review to be launched. However, the EIP does grant the Commission the power (although only for Eurozone countries) to levy fines of up to 0.1% of GDP per year if member states do not make a good faith effort to correct their macroeconomic imbalances (EU Commission 2019).

The MIP's scorecard demonstrates a clear preference for export-led growth. Two of its indicators place the onus of external adjustment partially or fully on deficit countries, exonerating surplus countries of any responsibility. The current account indicator—countries cannot have a (three-year moving average) current account deficit of more than 4% of GDP or a current account surplus of more than 6% of GDP—provides a clear adjustment advantage to (export-led) surplus countries by granting them an additional 2% cushion in avoiding sanctions. The Net International Investment Position (NIIT or the difference between a country's external assets and liabilities) indicator shields surplus countries from adjustment burdens *entirely*. Under the scorecard's rules, Eurozone countries must keep their NIIT above negative 35% of GDP—a feat the Eurozone's domestic consumption-based growth models, with the exception of Italy, have not managed to collectively accomplish since 2000 (see Figure 4.2).

There is however no limit on the net amount of (external) assets a country can acquire abroad. As a result of restricting domestic consumption, export-led growth models produce surplus savings. EMU and the Single Market created a common financial space in which these savings could be invested in endeavors abroad—given the localized nature of capital flows, mostly in other E(M)U countries (Gros 2012)—hence limiting inflationary pressures at home. Surplus countries' investment in assets in other EMU countries *automatically* worsened deficit countries' NIIT position. This component of the MIP scorecard is therefore a zero-sum game if external assets/liability accumulation is concentrated within the European Union. By ignoring where NIIT deficits come from in a comparatively closed financial space, the MIP scorecard effectively penalizes the

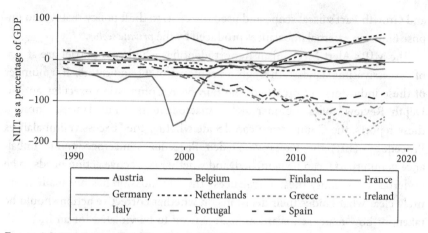

Figure 4.2 Net International Investment Positions in the Eurozone, 1990–2018.
Source: Eurostat (2019a). Horizontal black line is the NIIT deficit restriction of the MIP scorecard (-35% of GDP).

Eurozone's domestic consumption growth models for being a logical destination of investment for its export-led growth models' savings gluts.

Other components of the MIP scorecard champion export growth directly, or indirectly via the mechanisms (particularly wage moderation) that help generate it. Five-year trends in export growth must be above -6% of GDP (like the NIIT indicator, there is no positive limit). For Eurozone countries, nominal unit labor cost growth should not exceed 9% over three years, which limits the potential for wage-led growth. The scorecard also places limits on housing prices, recommending that annual real housing price growth should not exceed 6%. While the motivation behind the housing prices indicator was driven by Spain and Ireland's runaway real estate bubbles in the late 2000s, housing is the only nongovernmental sector whose growth potential has been singled out as needing restraint within the scorecard. The housing sector facilitated buoyant GDP growth in domestic consumption-led growth models (Spain most notably) and even "balanced" growth models (Sweden, Denmark, and Norway) during the Great Moderation (Schwartz 2009). Though the extent to which national governments can constrain their economies' housing market is not entirely clear, featuring housing prices in the MIP scorecard highlights the EU's desire to place constraints on sectors that fuel domestic consumption while actively championing strategies for export growth.

While the EIP has never been triggered by the time of writing, and hence the scope of the MIP's corrective arm is still unknown, the MIP scorecard clearly carries an expectation that Eurozone countries should demonstrate export competitiveness, while limiting expansion in the drivers of domestic demand. In perceiving domestic stimulus as a cause of problematic external imbalances, the Commission and Council have used the MIP as a weapon to recommend to their member states to limit their engagement in domestic consumption growth strategies.

More immediately, the contents of the MIP also conveyed *who* was expected to undertake external adjustment during the crisis. After the crisis, the Eurozone's (formerly) domestic-consumption based growth models have carried the bulk of EMU's adjustment burden, while export-led growth models continued to generate surpluses, within trade and foreign capital flows, particularly within the EU itself (Frieden and Walter 2017). As the Eurozone's new macroeconomic governance regime has attempted to nudge all of its member states toward export growth strategies, not all countries in a global economic system can be net exporters—net-exporting countries need net-importing trading partners in order to maintain their external balances. This means that if EMU forces an export-led growth model ideal onto *all* of its member states, it requires new neighbors to "beggar." But before that adjustment can happen, the Eurozone needed a new source to partially offset demand during and after its crisis, just like the global economy (as the previous chapter illustrates with respect to the case of the United States). Enter the European Central Bank.

More Than Just a Lender of Last Resort

When it comes to Eurozone monetary policy, there was a stark contrast in activity and policy innovation between Frenchman Jean-Claude Trichet (who served as ECB president between 2003 and 2011), and his Italian successor Mario Draghi, who took over the reins of the European Central Bank in November 2011 (until 2019). While Trichet had experimented with monetary easing during the fallout of the Global Financial Crisis, including 3-month, 6-month, and 12-month "long-term" refinancing operations and covered bond purchase programs in the fall of 2008 and spring of 2009, he proved much more reluctant to do so during the euro crisis in 2010 and 2011. Indeed, Trichet decided to *raise* interest rates (twice) in the spring of 2011, as the EU institutions were preparing for a Portuguese bailout, and the Eurozone was about to enter a new recession (Matthijs and Blyth 2018).

There were two main monetary policy innovations introduced under Trichet. First, the ECB adopted the "Securities Market Program" (SMP) in May 2010, through which it was able to purchase limited amounts of Greek government bonds on the secondary market. As the Eurozone debt crisis went on, it extended the SMP to Ireland, Italy, Portugal, and Spain, which committed the ECB to buying limited amounts of those countries' government bonds as a reward for their fiscal authorities' austerity and structural reform measures. The amounts of government bonds purchased remained limited, and therefore the SMP only succeeded in temporarily bringing down borrowing costs for those countries. Second, right before Trichet left Frankfurt on October 31 2011, the ECB introduced Covered Bond Purchase Program 2, with the aim of easing funding conditions for Eurozone credit institutions and enterprises, as well as to encourage credit institutions to maintain and expand their lending to customers. The initially targeted amount of purchases was 40 billion euro. But once Draghi took over, these relatively modest programs would quickly be superseded by much bolder measures (see Table 4.3 for an overview).

Right after taking office, Draghi reversed Trichet's controversial interest rate hikes of the spring of 2011, quickly lowering the ECB benchmark rate from 1.5% to 1.25% and then to 1%. In December 2011, Draghi reassured financial markets by announcing a whole new series of monetary policy easing initiatives, in the hope of restoring the "monetary transmission mechanism," repair Eurozone banks' balance sheets, stimulate investment, and boost overall economic activity. In an effort to support Europe's ailing banks, Draghi introduced very long-term refinancing operations (LTROs) in two tranches, one in December 2011 and one in February 2012, totaling over 1 trillion euros of very cheap loans to Eurozone banks for a maturity of three years. Furthermore, Draghi reduced the reserve requirements from 2 to 1%, increased the eligible collateral by allowing national central banks to accept additional credit claims, and widened the range of eligible asset-backed securities (ABSs).

During the summer of 2012, fear over the potential breakup of the Eurozone reached all-time highs as interest rates on Italian and Spanish bonds peaked at 7%. As financial markets were again in a tailspin, Draghi made an emphatic speech in London in July 2012, where he promised that "[w]ithin our mandate, the ECB is ready to do whatever it takes to preserve the euro" and reassured anyone who was still in doubt by adding the words "[a]nd believe me, it will be enough" (Draghi 2012). In September 2012 he followed up with a program of Eurozone-wide bond buying, called Outright Monetary Transactions (OMTs). The main difference with the SMP was that under OMT, the ECB could potentially buy unlimited amounts of sovereign bonds of struggling Eurozone economies, under the condition that those countries were willing to accept stringent economic and budgetary reforms. This program was hailed as the "big bazooka" the markets had been waiting for. Investors seemed to take Draghi at his word, as a modicum of stability in the bond markets quickly returned, and his OMT pledge was never actually tested.

As bond markets rallied, the Eurozone was still struggling through a recession and an economy on the brink of outright deflation. It was clear that monetary policy alone could not bring back growth. In July 2013, Draghi added "forward guidance" to his toolbox. He stated that "the Governing Council expects the key

Table 4.3 **Key ECB Monetary Policy Actions since 2010 Euro Crisis**

Date	Policy Implemented	EUR billions
May 2010	ECB starts buying public debt in secondary markets (SMP)	
Aug 2011	ECB reactivates secondary market purchases for Spanish and Italian debt	
Dec 2011	1st 36-month LTRO takes place	489.2
Feb 2012	2nd 36-month LTRO takes place	529.5
July 2012	ECB reduces all 3 policy rates by 25bps	
	Draghi gives "Whatever It Takes" speech	
May 2013	ECB drops MRO rate to 0.5%; MLF rate to 1%	
Nov 2013	ECB drops MRO rate to 0.25%	
Jun 2014	ECB announces 1st series of TLTROs	
	ECB drops MRO rate to 0.15%; MLF to 0.4%; Depo to −0.1%	
Sep 2014	ECB drops MRO to 0.05%; MLF to 0.3%; Depo to −0.2%	
Oct 2014	ABSPP and CBPP3 Plans Announced	
Jan 2015	ECB Announces Quantitative Easing (EUR 60 billion per month)	1100
Dec 2015	ECB drops Depo rate to −0.3%	
Mar 2016	ECB drops MRO to 0%, MLF to 0.25%, Depo to −0.4%	
Apr 2016	Expansion of Asset Purchases under QE by 20 billion per month	240
Jun 2016	CSPP Operations begin	
	2nd series of TLTRO begins	
Apr 2017	Asset purchases revert back to original EUR 60 billion/month level	
Jan 2018	Asset purchases lowered to EUR 30 billion/month	
Sep 2019	3rd series of TLTRO begins	

Source: European Central Bank, European Commission, Yardeni Research, https://www.ecb.europa.eu/pub/pdf/mobu/mb201412en.pdfhttps://www.yardeni.com/chronology-of-ecb-monetary-policy-actions-2014-present/

ECB interest rates to remain at present or lower levels for an extended period of time [...] we will monitor all incoming information on economic and monetary developments." The next summer, in June 2014, the ECB lowered its deposit rate to −0.1% and introduced so-called Targeted Long-Term Refinancing Operations (TLTROs) to fight deflation in the euro area. Negative deposit rates – further lowered to −0.2% in September 2014–encouraged banks to swap euros for dollars on their balance sheets, which weakened the euro's exchange rate. The TLTRO program consisted of two parts. First, banks would be able to borrow an amount equivalent of up to 7% of a specific part of their loans in two operations in September and December 2014. Second, additional amounts could be borrowed in further TLTROs, depending on the evolution of banks' eligible lending activities in excess of bank-specific benchmarks.

In the fall of 2014, Draghi introduced a third "Covered Bonds Purchase Program" (CBPP3), followed by an Asset-Backed Securities Purchase Program (ABSPP), before announcing the long-awaited "Public Sector Purchase Program" (PSPP) in January 2015. With PSPP or all-out "quantitative easing" (QE), Draghi committed the ECB to buy up a total of 60 billion euro of mainly public sector securities every month for a period of at least 18 months, starting in March 2015 and lasting until September 2016. This was another effort to boost inflation, which was hovering around zero at the time. QE was followed by further decreases in the negative deposit rate in December 2015 (to −0.3%) and March 2016 (to −0.4%) and an expansion of net monthly asset purchases to 80 billion euros per month in April 2016, before being scaled back in April 2017 to 60 billion euros/month and in January 2018 to 30 billion euros/month. By September 2019, Draghi announced that "we expect the net asset purchases to run for as long as necessary to reinforce the accommodative impact of our policy rates, and to end shortly before we start raising the key ECB interest rates" (Draghi 2019).

While the ECB has served as the "leader of last resort" (Blyth and Matthijs 2017) for the Eurozone since 2012, it is doubtful whether its accommodative stance can continue to be effective forever, apart from the one-off depreciation in the euro vis-à-vis its competitors that had a positive effect on net exports. Monetary easing alone is not enough. Not only will further easing face technical constraints in the future (i.e., the ECB may run out of high-quality assets to buy), it also faces growing political constraints with politicians in the North openly questioning whether the ECB can continue to overstep its narrow mandate for that much longer. Lacking any real fiscal stimulus at the Eurozone level, monetary easing is little more than "pushing on a string" (Van Doorslaer and Vermeiren 2021). It may create a wealth effect by driving up stock prices and other asset values, but it is not enhancing growth in median incomes or providing a permanent driver for domestic demand. During much of the 2010s, the Eurozone growth model therefore found itself stuck in a "liquidity trap" of its own making. In the presence of prolonged suppressed domestic consumption, the ECB could only do so much. EU businesses had to look for demand elsewhere. They found it in the more economically dynamic parts of the rest of the world.

The Profligacy of Strangers: External Balancing in a World of Renewed Geopolitical Rivalry

A key consequence of the Eurozone's anti-consumption, anti-debt, pro-export, and high savings bias is the emergence of a substantial EU and Eurozone current account surplus with the rest of the world after 2011 (Figure 4.3). The Eurozone's current account surplus of 396.4 billion euros in 2018 was actually larger than China's. This is an astonishing turnaround in a relatively short period of time and has acted "as a safety valve for a chronic shortage of domestic growth" as Eurozone domestic demand only grew by 0.4% on an annual basis since the euro crisis, compared to a very healthy increase in domestic demand between 2000 and 2007 (Torres 2019, 6). Former Bank of England governor Mark Carney used to refer to the United Kingdom's dependence on the "kindness of strangers" when asked whether there was a danger to the country's chronic current account deficits. The Eurozone's post-crisis growth model in effect relies

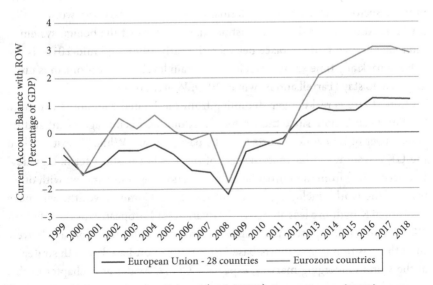

Figure 4.3 EU Current Account Balance (with ROW). Source: Eurostat (2019b)

on the "profligacy of strangers," but also on continuing future rapid growth in emerging markets, the durability of the US-led liberal international order, and permanent current account deficits in much of the Anglo-Saxon world.

While exports to the rest of the world can be an alternative source of demand for the Eurozone, it is doubtful whether this can last in the medium to long run for multiple reasons. First, there are domestic political limits to this new post-crisis growth model, as the fiscal rules are slowly but surely "killing public investment dead" in the words of Miguel Carrión (2021). While Eurozone electorates may be willing to accept temporary cuts to public spending and investment in order to get out of a crisis, they will revolt if their politicians are systematically unable to respond with tangible improvements to their lives. The rise of anti-system parties on both left and right in Southern Europe, and of the greens—who are running on ending the fiscal rules as we know them—in Northern Europe, are clear indications that this model only goes so far (Hopkin 2020).

Second, Donald Trump's election to the US presidency in 2016 underscored the fragility of the postwar American-led liberal international order. Trump's mercantilist campaign platform of "America First" and promise to "make America great again" gained significant traction among the American electorate. Zeroing in on America's bilateral trade deficits, Trump threatened to use both the structural power of the US dollar and the size and openness of the American market as strategic weapons of economic statecraft. During the Trump years, the US government put tariffs on solar panel and washing machine imports, and started treating imports in steel, aluminum, and the automotive industry as threats to national security (Bown and Kolb 2021). This directly hurt European exports in those sectors, especially from Germany. Even in a post-Trump world, under the "Buy American" Biden Administration, it is clear that the benign system of multilateral open trade in place between the early 1990s and mid-2010s is not coming back any time soon. Therefore, a certain level of protectionism is probably here to stay (Farrell and Newman 2019; Walter 2021).

Third, there is real danger stemming from the United Kingdom's exit from the European Union, since the United Kingdom has been a significant and reliable buyer of Eurozone exports over the past 50 years. While "Brexit" will hit the UK economy harder than the rest of the EU in the short term, a gradual UK decoupling from the Eurozone economy and deeper integration with other parts of the world, including the countries of the Commonwealth, will make the United Kingdom a less attractive destination for European exports (Matthijs 2020). Fourth, the post-crisis Eurozone growth model relies on a relatively smooth transition from exports-based to consumption-based growth strategies in the world's emerging markets, especially China. As the next chapter in this volume by Yeling Tan and James Conran shows, China's "transition" to consumption away from exports and investment will be very slow and gradual.

While the medium-term (in)sustainability of the move from domestic demand as a source of growth toward net exports with the rest of the world is clear, the main consequence of the EU's 2010 shift toward relying on the profligacy of strangers has been to effectively reduce the universe of Eurozone growth models from all four to the bottom two (see Table 4.1). But as we will discuss in the next section, the COVID-19 pandemic of 2020 to 2022 may prove to be the catalyst for a German shift vis-à-vis the Eurozone's post-crisis growth model. With Berlin's seeming embrace of financial solidarity and the French notion of "EU sovereignty"—in trade and financial affairs, in health, and in the green and digital economy—we should ask ourselves whether the fiscal and industrial policy U-turn is the beginning of a more sustainable Eurozone growth model or a temporary "one-off" response to extraordinary circumstances.

Rebalancing or Temporary Fix? EMU's Policy Response to COVID-19 in 2020

In an almost cruel twist of fate, the first EU member states to be badly hit by the COVID-19 pandemic in March 2020 were the domestic demand-led economies of Italy and Spain. As the rest of Europe watched a local quarantine in Lombardy turn into a nationwide lockdown, and the number of Italian infections and deadly casualties steadily rose, the initial response in most EU member states was to close their borders while issuing travel and export bans to places where the virus was spreading at alarming rates. The EU was struggling to come up with a collective response, as Commission President Ursula von der Leyen pleaded with EU members—to no avail—not to close their borders, while Christine Lagarde made her debut as ECB president with a disastrous press conference in which she asserted that the ECB was "not here to close the spreads" between Italian and German sovereign bond yields.

While EU member states kept complete control over their public health response—including serious curbs on individual freedoms through regional and national lockdowns—the ECB and EU finance ministers started acting resolutely from mid-March 2020 onward to shore up domestic demand. The initial missteps in communication with financial markets were quickly corrected by Lagarde when the ECB's governing council lifted all self-imposed constraints on bond purchases by rolling out a bold one trillion-euro Pandemic Emergency Purchasing Program (PEPP) that served to immediately calm down markets. That action alone eased borrowing constraints on Italy and other Southern European countries in one fell swoop. Given that the EU and national fiscal authorities were relatively slow to respond, the ECB acted once again as the "leader of last resort" and would continue to do so over the course of the pandemic (see Table 4.4).

Table 4.4 **Monetary Response to COVID-19**

Date	*Policy*	*(EUR billions)*
Mar. 2020	APP increases by 120 billion EUR through Dec. 2020	333.2
	ECB begins conducting additional LTROs	388.9
	Corporate Sector Purchase Program (CSPP)	
	TLTRO III Conditions eased to rates as low as −0.75%	
	Pandemic Emergency Purchase Program created	750
Apr. 2020	Further easing of TLTRO III conditions	
	7 PELTROs introduced at 25 bps below the MRO rate	26.57
	Temporary easing of collateral measures	
Jun 2020	Governing Council increases PEPP	600
Dec. 2020	PEPP envelope increased further	500
	4 additional PELTROs offered at one-year maturities	

Source: European Parliament (2021).

In April 2020, Eurozone finance ministers agreed to a financial package worth roughly 540 billion euros to fight the pandemic, on top of the 37-billion-euro Coronavirus Response Investment Initiative and Support Instrument set up by the European Commission a few weeks prior. That package had three additional elements. First, the Eurogroup agreed to 100 billion euro in loan guarantees for the European Commission to set up an instrument for temporary Support to mitigate Unemployment Risks in an Emergency (SURE). Second, they agreed an additional 200 billion euro in loan guarantees for the European Investment Bank to set up a European Guarantee Fund. Third, they approved an extra 240 billion euro in pandemic crisis support through the European Stability Mechanism (ESM) (Dendrinou, Chrysoloras, and Seputyte 2020).

The problem with the Eurogroup proposals was that all the financial support the EU was giving to individual member states was through loans and loan guarantees. Given that the ECB had just committed to buying unprecedented amounts of sovereign debt through its pandemic emergency purchasing program (PEPP), there was no shortage of liquidity. However, there was little desire on the part of heavily indebted Eurozone members that were badly hit by COVID-19 to go even deeper into sovereign debt. The calls to take the next step in completing the Economic and Monetary Union by introducing Eurobonds (or "coronabonds") were getting louder, especially from France and Mediterranean member states. A major EU fiscal package in the form of grants was clearly needed, buttressed by Northern creditworthiness and out of solidarity with their suffering Southern counterparts. It was also the only way for the Mediterranean countries to be able to escape the dreaded "stasis box" in Table 4.1, and move back toward a more "balanced" or "domestic demand-led" growth model.

In May 2020, German chancellor Angela Merkel would let go of her long-standing opposition ("No Eurobonds as long as I live!" she had stated back in 2012)[7] and make a U-turn on jointly issued EU bonds. By doing so, Merkel's Germany broke ranks with fellow Northern Eurozone travelers like the Netherlands, Finland, and Austria. On May 18, together with French president Emmanuel Macron, she put her shoulders under a "French-German Initiative for the European Recovery from the Coronavirus Crisis."[8] While most of the attention went to the second point of the proposal—the setting up of an ambitious "Recovery Fund" at the EU level worth 500 billion euros in grants to be distributed by the European Commission and financed through jointly issued bonds—the other three points were potentially more important for the strategic future direction of the European Union that could support domestic demand-based growth and once again accommodate a more diverse universe of growth models. The proposal included a joint Franco-German call for the EU to develop strategic health sovereignty with a joint "health strategy," speeding up both green and digital transitions, and enhancing EU economic and industrial resilience by giving a new impulse to the single market.

Just over a week later, the European Commission built on the Franco-German momentum by rolling out an EU stimulus plan of 750 billion euro, called "Next Generation EU," which would consist of 500 billion euro in grants and 250 billion euro in loans. The centerpiece of the Commission's plan was a 560 billion euro "Recovery and Resilience Facility" to address the economic fallout of the pandemic, consisting of 310 billion euro in grants and 250 billion euro in loans. Another 50 billion euro was proposed for the REACT-EU cohesion fund, in order to guarantee a green and digital recovery. The other 140 billion euro was earmarked to pad key existing programs in the EU budget, including for research, rural development, just transition, solvency support, strategic investment, health, and humanitarian aid. This hugely ambitious package was hailed by some observers as a potential "Hamiltonian Moment" for the European Union, in which the seeds of a future fiscal union were planted (see Table 4.5).

To many EU observers' surprise, the European Council meeting of heads of state or government in mid-July 2020 agreed to a compromise proposal that stuck to the substantial headline figure of 750 billion euro. After significant pressure from the so-called Frugal Five member states—Austria, Denmark, Finland, the Netherlands, and Sweden—the total amount in grants was lowered from 500 to 390 billion euro, while the total amount of loans was increased from 250

Table 4.5 **EU Fiscal Response to COVID**

Date	Policy	(EUR billions)
Apr. 2020	CRII+ Begins	37
May 2020	SURE program introduced	100
	Pan-European Guarantee Fund passed	200
	Pandemic Crisis Support provided by ESM	240
Dec. 2020	EU Leaders finalize Next Generation EU (NGEU)	750

Source: IMF Policy Tracker https://www.imf.org/en/Topics/imf-and-covid19/Policy-Responses-to-COVID-19

to 360 billion euro. The frugal five also negotiated substantial budget rebates for themselves as part of the final package. Clearly, "Next Generation EU" did not lay to rest the differences between North and South when it came to economic philosophy, with predictable consequences for future growth.

The EU's COVID-19 response marked a sharp deviation from the E(M)U's export-growth fetishism in the past decade. Instead of hindering economic activity in domestic sectors, "Next Generation EU" actively bolsters it (particularly for parts of the public sector). The pandemic made the consequences of widespread collapse in domestic consumption painfully clear—not even creditor countries could openly advocate further austerity, at least during the pandemic's worst stages. However, there are two main questions that continue to hang over the fiscal policy changes of 2020.

First, will the European Union be able to deliver on its ambitious recovery program and steer its growth model toward something more self-sustaining and less reliant on the largesse of the ECB and the profligacy of strangers? Second, will the innovations of 2020 prove to be the beginning of a Eurozone economic government with actual powers for macroeconomic stabilization and the accommodation of domestic consumption-based growth? Fortunately, at the time of writing, Germany's new Social Democratic Chancellor Olaf Scholz's "traffic light" coalition, with the Greens and Free Democratic Party (FDP), has indicated that it is willing to take a more dovish approach to further EU reforms. FDP Finance Minister Christian Lindner, deviating from his party's historical hawkish fiscal stance, claimed that the successful implementation of Next Generation EU and full recovery from the pandemic "is more important than the debate on fiscal rules" and that "we won't waste the crisis" (Nienaber 2022). Though a return to an austerity-based export-led growth model may be waiting in the wings, it is unlikely to come before Europe has fully recovered from the pandemic.

Conclusions

Using the Eurozone as a case study, this chapter provided an IPE account of how international institutions, and the power struggles within them, can change growth models within their member states. We argued that prior to 2009, EMU accommodated growth model diversity, even strengthening the prioritized growth strategies within its export-led and domestic consumption-led growth models through several institutional innovations and changes. However, these innovations also helped in delivering the debt crisis of the late 2000s, which EMU's export-led growth models weathered well, given their comparative lack of reliance on external borrowing, but its domestic-consumption based growth models weathered poorly.

By virtue of being EMU's creditors, EMU's export-led core countries rewrote the Eurozone's new macroeconomic rules (including the Macroeconomic Imbalances Procedure, the European Semester, and the Fiscal Compact) in a manner that championed export-led growth strategies. These rules established a more restrictive fiscal policy, shifting the S-I balance toward excess savings to better accommodate external surpluses, while the European Central Bank (ECB) from 2012 onward shifted to a much more accommodating monetary stance (weakening the euro vis-à-vis other currencies and thereby boosting net exports).

While the ECB continues to be an imperfect source of offsetting declines in domestic demand, it is running up against serious political constraints and operational limits. Furthermore, the adoption of a German-style export-led growth model for the Eurozone as a whole, by relying on external demand in the demand-driven Anglo-Saxon economies and fast-growing emerging markets, will also run into problems in a world where protectionism is on the rise. The COVID-19 pandemic looked like it could have been the straw that broke the camel's back on the E(M)U's export-led growth strategy. The pandemic required state-led responses from the EU and national governments to significantly boost domestic demand; and surprisingly, these responses have been largely delivered.

Whether this is a derogation or a trend break from the EU's promotion of export-led growth remains to be seen. The economic response to COVID-19 demonstrated that the EU has the potential to put its future growth on a more sustainable footing and rewrite its current fiscal and economic rules to accommodate different growth strategies. Moreover, the stance taken by Germany's new center-left government demonstrates that EMU's creditor countries' demands for draconian austerity from debtor countries with domestic consumption-led growth models may not last forever. Even the new Dutch government led by Mark Rutte and new finance minister Sigrid Kaag has signaled it is somewhat more open-minded when it comes to reforming the EU's fiscal rules. Time will tell if Northern elites will continue to show fiscal flexibility and greater solidarity with their struggling neighbors in the South after the pandemic subsides. If the Eurozone is once again to see different growth models flourish side by side, we must hope that tne policy shift brought about by the COVID-19 pandemic is permanent rather than temporary.

Notes

1. In contrast to other countries that introduced sweeping cost-saving New Public Management reforms into their public sectors, Sweden has managed to introduce these reforms while also keeping a generous welfare state and strong (public sector) collective bargaining intact (see Ibsen et al. 2011).
2. For an overview of the EU's fiscal responses to the euro crisis, see Table 4.2.
3. The ECB in particular, but also Germany and the European Commission, fervently opposed debt relief for Greece during the first MoU, despite support for it from the IMF (see Moschella 2016)
4. Despite its fiscal crisis resulting from a banking crisis, Ireland's minimum wage was cut by 12% (Lane 2011, 73).
5. In a 2011 memo, the European Commission clarified that the gap between a country's current debt level and the 60% rule should be reduced by at least 1/20th annually on average over three years (European Commission 2011).
6. In a clear and direct rebuke to Greece, these sanctions could be increased to 0.5% of GDP if "statistical fraud was detected" (EU Commission 2014).
7. See video footage here: https://www.youtube.com/watch?v=p2s0bGq-bTI ("Keine Eurobonds solange ich lebe").
8. German Federal Government (2020).

5

China's Growth Models in Comparative and International Perspectives

YELING TAN AND JAMES CONRAN

Introduction

The world's biggest growth story over the past half century has undoubtedly been that of China. That growth has propelled the country's population from one of the world's poorest into the ranks of the global middle class (GDP per capita grew from US$307 in 1978 to over US$8,000 in 2019).[1] Virtually closed in the Mao era, the Chinese economy has become deeply interwoven into global supply chains and products from the aptly named "workshop of the world" now comprise 15% of world trade.[2] The sheer scale of China's growth has not just lifted millions out of poverty in the country but has also had deep ramifications for the rest of the world—triggering awe and apprehension in equal measure. These effects range from global current account imbalances, which has fed into financial instability, to political polarization within the United States as documented in the "China shock" literature (Autor et al. 2020), and most recently a "trade war" with the United States that has yet to be resolved. Yet, while China's economic success is popularly understood through its role as a manufacturing exports powerhouse, this is only part of China's growth story.

This chapter argues that despite its position as the world's largest exporter, China's growth over the past four decades has been driven by more than a single model. Specifically, China's economic expansion has been the product of a hybrid system containing one growth model based on exports concentrated along the coast, and another growth model based on state-led investment in China's interior. We underscore how each growth model is intrinsically tied to China's increasingly central position in the global economy by examining several critical events: the 1998 Asian financial crisis, China's 2001 entry into the World Trade Organization (WTO), and China's response to the 2008 global financial crisis. The chapter argues that the two growth models are far from easy complements, with each one supported by different political coalitions, each producing distinct distributional outcomes, as well as exhibiting specific pathologies that have proven difficult for policymakers to resolve, and which produce consequential spillovers for the global economy.

While China's growth experience has perhaps been unique in world history, it is nevertheless useful to examine these dominant growth models in comparative perspective, in order to elucidate points of commonality beyond the Chinese case. Specifically, at the end of this chapter we compare the political economic underpinnings of China's growth models with those of the German export-led model, the Irish foreign direct investment (FDI)-led model, and the Spanish construction-led model. Through this analysis, we illustrate how China's internally heterogenous growth model may be compared with the Eurozone—another continent-sized economy with distinct regional growth models—rather than its member states.

In our comparison, we emphasize the unique dimensions that authoritarian capitalism brings to our understanding of growth models, while also highlighting commonalities that transcend regime types. In particular, we underscore the shared centrality of economic growth as a legitimation mechanism in both democratic and authoritarian capitalism, with the growth imperative arguably even more essential to legitimation in the Chinese context given the absence of democratic sources of legitimacy, and because of lower living standards in what is still a developing economy. The chapter also details the degree to which authoritarian rule enables China to shift between growth models—emphasizing exports or investment as circumstances dictate—in ways that may be harder for democratic regimes. There are, however, important limits to this "authoritarian flexibility," and the chapter illustrates them by examining the distributive and political conflicts of interest that have largely frustrated the PRC leadership's long-stated desire to shift toward a more consumption-driven growth model.

China as a "System of Systems"

A common view of China's growth presumes a reliance on exports, supported by wage and consumption repression (Felipe and Lanzafame 2018). However, it would be misleading to speak of a single "Chinese growth model," as the policies and political coalitions underpinning China's past four decades of growth have varied not just over time but also across different regions of the country. The export-led model, while important, has largely been a coastal phenomenon.

Equally vital to China's sustained economic expansion is growth based on state-led investment in infrastructure and urbanization, with targeted policies to stimulate housing and construction originating in the 1990s.

These growth models, one based on exports and the other on state-led investment, have been dominant at different points in time, made possible in part by China's sheer size and subnational diversity. China might therefore be more accurately described as a "system of systems," comprised of more than one growth model where growth drivers sometimes feed into each other in a complementary fashion but are equally likely to be acting at cross-purposes. If the Chinese growth model often appears to outsiders as an unstoppable juggernaut, on closer inspection its internal tensions, if not contradictions, are at least as important as they are for any other model of capitalism.

The Origins of the "System of Systems"

China's internal economic heterogeneity has its roots in the incremental and experimental approach to growth that China adopted in its reform period in the late 1970s and early 1980s after Mao Zedong's death. As Weber (2021) has demonstrated, there were influential advocates within the Chinese party-state of a "shock therapy" transition from central planning, but ultimately a more cautious and pragmatic reform vision emerged from these internal conflicts, setting China on the path to the "system of systems" described in this chapter.[3] Huang (2008) has argued persuasively that the ignition of economic activity in China's immediate reform period was rooted in rural and private entrepreneurship, rather than exports. Agricultural growth was revived by contracting collectively owned land down to the household while rural industry drove manufacturing expansion.[4] Against the backdrop of decades of economic isolation in the Mao period, efforts at trade liberalization took place through circumscribed experiments to create four Special Economic Zones (SEZs) along China's southern coast. Within these zones, tariffs on inputs would be reduced and manufacturing subject to lighter "administrative guidance." Outside these zones, however, command and control remained the dominant mode of governance.

This context of isolation and incremental reform, with limited foreign direct investment and trade liberalization meant two things. First, China's initial dynamic period of growth after the destruction and stagnation of the Mao era proceeded within an economy that remained largely insulated from external economic forces. Secondly, no single growth model dominated in this period. Instead, multiple growth drivers were at play, from rural private entrepreneurship to coastal SEZs. Economic activity took place on "dual tracks," with reform policies focused on introducing market incentives outside the core of the planned economy (Naughton 2007). Market expansion therefore took place around the plan, rather than seeking to replace it outright.[5]

A Dual Disequilibrium

China's experimental approach to development not only makes non-linearity and disequilibrium a key feature of its growth process but has also generated important political and economic consequences. The first is a distinct subnational diversity in China's domestic political economy across different geographical regions, which is the subject of rich scholarship ranging from SOE reform (Hurst 2009) to industrial policy (Segal and Thun 2001), private entrepreneurship (Tsai 2007), and land regimes (Rithmire 2015). Coastal SEZs became deeply integrated into global trade and investment networks, relying on foreign capital and exports as a source of growth and employment.

In contrast, China's interior regions remained insulated from the external economy. As China's national economy expanded, therefore, growth was undergirded not by a uniform adoption of market liberalization, but rather a patchwork of subnational political economies following quite distinct logics. While private capital might be more dominant in areas such as Wenzhou in Zhejiang province, state capital is more prevalent in the heavy industrial zones of the northeast. These regions, in turn, stand in contrast with the Pearl River Delta, where foreign capital is heavily invested. While such regional differences might be common to many countries, China's sheer geographic and demographic size magnifies the consequences of its subnational diversity. Guangdong province, dominant in foreign investment and export processing, is more populous than Germany, while Shanghai, dominant in state capital and finance, is roughly the demographic size of Australia.

Second, China's experimental process of reform expanded options for policymakers in terms of how the state should govern the market, resulting in competition within China's vast bureaucracy over different modes of economic governance (Tan 2021). While different types of capital (foreign, domestic private, and state) are dominant in different geographic regions, one can argue that from the 1990s onward, China's spectacular record of growth has by and large relied on two main drivers: exports and state-led investment. These two competing growth models have played a driving role in China's growth process at different points in time, with distinct distributional implications and pathologies.

To illustrate this dynamic, we focus on several critical events in China's development experience, beginning with the 1990s coastal development strategy, before examining the 1997 to 1998 Asian financial crisis, entry into the WTO in 2001, and the 2008 to 2009 global financial crisis. We discuss the rise (and fall) of dominant growth models in each period and how these shifts relate to changes in the international economic system, while also highlighting domestic consequences in terms of distributional and economic distortions. The section ends with a brief discussion of dynamics generated by the US-China trade tensions that emerged in 2018 and the 2020 COVID-19 pandemic.

Global Economic Shocks and China's Local Growth Models

We argue that China's domestic growth strategies and the international environment are mutually constitutive, with movements between different growth models intrinsically tied to China's deepening, and yet shifting, integration in the global economy. While transformations in manufacturing logistics and global supply chains facilitated the enormous expansion of processing trade that forms the basis of China's exporting prowess, such export-led growth requires healthy external demand. When this external demand has collapsed due to shocks ranging from financial crises to a global pandemic, the Chinese state has stepped in to keep growth going through state-led investment. However, these two growth models are uneasy substitutes. The deployment of each generates distinct distributional implications for what types of capital and sectors are privileged over time, and also produces pathologies that have consequential spillovers for the global economy.

The 1990s Coastal Development Strategy

In the 1990s China expanded its SEZs to most of the cities along the eastern coast, marking a geographical shift in the locus of growth away from the countryside and toward the urban coast. Following the model of the 1980s, these zones were designed to draw in foreign investment for low-end manufacturing and assembly of products eventually bound for global markets. The elimination of tariff and non-tariff barriers and entry of foreign firms greatly integrated China's coastal regions with the global economy, substantially shifting the country toward an export-led growth model. The dominance of foreign enterprises in these zones makes China's export-led growth model in the 1990s somewhat comparable to the Irish FDI model (except for scale) but distinct from the German export model (which is dominated by German rather than foreign firms). Indeed, China's export model in these regions during this period was arguably more comparable to the eastern European countries Germany uses as "assembly platforms" for its exporters (or what Nölke and Vliegenthart (2009) call "dependent market economies").

The impact of this coastal development strategy can be seen in Figure 5.1 showing the change over time in Chinese exports, consumption, and gross fixed capital income as a share of GDP. In the 1980s, the limited role of exports can be seen in the fairly stable consumption share (shown in the dotted line) and investment share (solid line) despite an increase in the export share of GDP (dashed line). This trend suggests that growth in the 1980s came more from supply-side gains in higher productivity of capital and labor in agriculture, while exports grew from a very low base. In contrast, the shift to a coastal exports strategy in the 1990s is associated with a declining trend in the consumption share with the investment and export shares rising simultaneously. These trends reflect major shifts in the composition of GDP that indicate a change in China's growth model, undergirded by the suppression of wages and a depreciated exchange rate regime that has been well-documented in other export-led models.[6]

As a result of this coastal development/FDI-driven strategy, China's export share of GDP rose from about 14% in 1990 to almost 21% in 2000. It should be noted that the success of this strategy, premised as it was upon processing trade, would not have been possible without the simultaneous reconfiguration

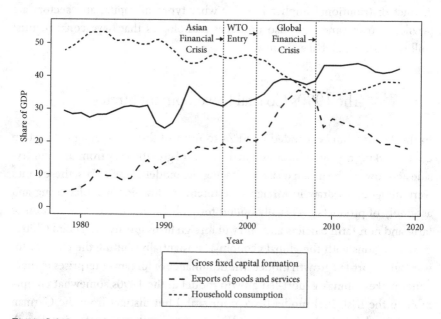

Figure 5.1 Investment, Export, and Consumption Shares of GDP in China (1978 to 2019). Source: World Development Indicators

of production into supply chains at the global level. The global fragmentation of production allowed China's coastal zones to position themselves not just as sites for low-cost manufacturing in labor intensive industries, but also efficient locations for product assembly. The national-level success of China's coastal growth model was then, as noted by Schwartz and Blyth in their chapter, conditional upon system-level transformations.

Despite its success, the coastal development strategy of the 1990s was very much geographically and administratively circumscribed, such that China's trading system during this period remained bifurcated into two regimes. While external integration through foreign capital and trading networks deepened along the coast, China's interior continued to be highly insulated from the global economy. These areas outside of the special zones operated under high tariffs and heavy administrative guidance, with trading rights restricted to state-owned enterprises (SOEs) (Naughton 1999). Trade in the interior was therefore dominated by state firms and coastal trade by foreign firms, leaving the domestic private sector—which mostly was prohibited from holding trading licenses—with a very minimal role in China's 1990s growth story (these trends are illustrated in greater detail in Figure 5.2 below). This dualistic system was only abolished in 2001 with China's entry into the World Trade Organization, discussed later.

The 1997–1998 Asian Financial Crisis and the First Shift in Models

The low level of economic development from which China embarked upon its post-Mao reforms, together with the sheer size of the country, meant that there was enough policy space for the government to enact more than one growth strategy. It is perhaps unsurprising, then, that export-driven growth was not the only locus of development that the government sought to promote in the 1990s. Instead, China looked simultaneously to external and internal sources of demand.

Even as China's coastal development zones expanded in the 1990s, policies were enacted to commodify state-owned land by separating ownership rights from use rights and commercializing the latter. The commercialization allowed the state to engage in land development, thereby making state-led investment via infrastructure, housing construction, and urbanization a viable growth driver. As Rithmire (2017) notes, "land development directly boosts GDP through investment and economic activity surrounding real estate investment. As many government reports and five-year plans note, increasing land for urban construction

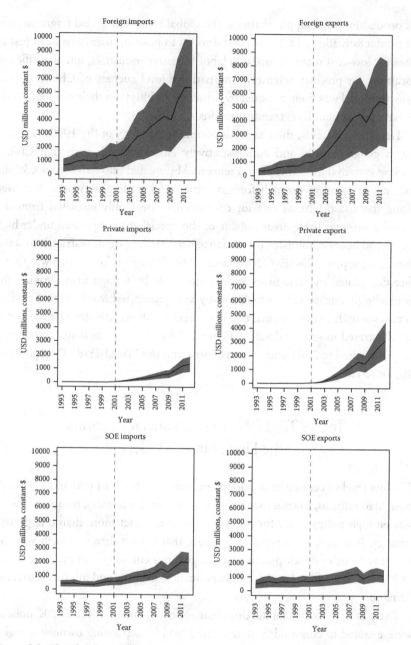

Figure 5.2 China's Bilateral Imports and Exports, Disaggregated by Firm Type (USD Millions, 1993 to 2013). Source: China Customs. Note: Shaded areas indicate 95% confidence intervals. The vertical lines indicate WTO entry in 2001. The figures do not include trade by other firm ownership types, such as joint-ventures.

means greater purchases of durable goods, greater employment in construction, and so forth, bringing along aggregate demand (p. 134)."

Land development as a growth driver became more salient for local governments after fiscal reforms in 1994 that reorganized tax-sharing arrangements in favor of Beijing. With local budgets falling by over 30% (Looney 2020, 183), fiscal reforms left many local governments burdened with unfunded mandates and a new imperative to locate alternative sources of revenue. Land development and urbanization soon emerged in the mid-1990s as an important source of revenue and growth for local governments. Land development benefited Beijing as well, as central control over how much land could be commercialized meant that the central government could use land as a macroeconomic tool, expanding the supply of land when it needed to stimulate aggregate demand (Rithmire 2017). State-led investment through urbanization and construction therefore became more salient policy instruments during periods of weak external conditions.

The first time this dynamic played out was in the Asian financial crisis that struck economies in east and southeast Asia in 1997 to 1998. While China was relatively shielded from the regional crisis due to capital controls and a lack of financial liberalization, the period nevertheless meant a deterioration of the external environment and drying up of FDI inflows. While annual net FDI inflows increased from USD 11 to 45 billion from 1992 to 1997, they plateaued and fell to around 41 billion from 1998 to 2000, reflective of poor external growth prospects in the region during this period.[7]

As Looney (2020) notes, the financial crisis "led many to conclude that the country was too dependent on exports" (p. 187). The Chinese government looked to alternative, internal sources of growth, and the context of repressed wages and low private consumption meant that government-led spending became a favored policy instrument. During this period, the Ministry of Land Resources increased its reliance on land transfers as a means of boosting domestic demand (Rithmire 2017). Sanderson and Forsythe (2013) note that "[b]etween 1996 and 1997, as the Asian crisis started, spending on infrastructure in China doubled, and by 2002, it had risen by nearly three times" (p. 7). At the same time, housing reforms in 1998 de-linked state employment from housing access, thereby opening up the sector to private purchases. This change was accompanied by a repeated lowering of the mortgage interest rate to boost private demand (Liu and Xiong 2020).

As such, state-led investment emerged as a growth strategy in the mid-1990s, at a time of weak external demand in the Asian region, and endured into the post-crisis years. However, the central government never abandoned its export-promotion strategy and indeed continued negotiating its entry into the WTO during this period. This dual track strategy can be seen in the 2001 Five-Year

Plan, issued the same year as China's entry. The national guiding plan listed urbanization as an important policy goal, further enhancing the role of housing (and thereby construction and infrastructure) as a growth driver even as China entered its most explosive period of export-led expansion.

2001—China, the WTO, and the Return of Exports

China's entry into the WTO in 2001 supercharged its export-led growth strategy and saw a sharp turn away from the dualistic trade regime described earlier. The ability to trade, previously restricted to state-owned and foreign firms, was extended to all enterprises, including private ones. A legislative overhaul brought trade and trade-related domestic policies into alignment with WTO rules and average import tariffs were lowered from over 30% to under 10%. From 2001 to 2007, China's export share of GDP rose from 20% to 35%—to date the steepest increase in China's export share as shown in Figure 5.1. At the same time, consumption share of GDP fell dramatically from 45% to 36%, by far the lowest among the world's major economies.

As a consequence, by 2009 China had become the world's largest exporter. This period of export expansion also sees China embedding itself in far more complex networks in the global economy. One major aspect of this interdependency is China's entanglement with consumption-led regimes such as the United States, which has led to global current account imbalances that many have linked to financial instability (Rajan 2011). Another form of interdependency lies between different export-led economies whose production networks are also tied to the Chinese processing trade regime that is heavily reliant on imported inputs. For example, China is Germany's third largest export market, and a major consumer of German capital equipment. Similarly, major commodity exporters have also come to depend on Chinese demand, with China displacing Japan and the United States as Indonesia's largest export market (based largely on energy and metals products) in the last five years, for example.[8]

China's expansion of its export growth model during its WTO-accession period further has a distributional impact on its domestic political economy. Figure 5.2 shows China's bilateral imports and exports from 1993 to 2012, disaggregated by firm type. Three trends from the figure are worth noting. First is the absence of trade by private enterprises in the 1990s, underscoring how China's export-led strategy in the pre-WTO period privileged SOEs and foreign firms, and discriminated against private ones. Second, the liberalization of trading rights as a result of WTO entry clearly triggered a big expansion of trade by private enterprises, but the magnitude of that increase is far outweighed by the surge in imports and exports by foreign enterprises located in China. Third, the value of SOE trade is barely affected by WTO entry, unlike imports and exports for private and foreign firms. In short, this figure illustrates how WTO entry shifted economic benefits away from SOEs (who lost their privileged access to trading rights) and toward domestic private firms and foreign firms invested in China.

2008–2009—The Global Financial Crisis and the Second Shift of Model

This turbocharged export growth model was severely disrupted in 2008 by the onset of the global financial crisis. In response to the collapse in external demand, China unleashed a massive 4 trillion RMB (over US$580 billion) stimulus channeled primarily toward infrastructure, echoing measures adopted during the Asian financial crisis a decade earlier. Figure 5.1 illustrates this dynamic, showing that as the export share of GDP fell dramatically from 2008 to 2009, the gross fixed capital formation share of GDP increased sharply over the same years. These trends reveal yet another major shift in the foundations of Chinese economic growth. Whereas the period from the 1990s to 2008 saw investment and export shares of GDP rising in tandem, the years following the global economic crisis see a major divergence in the investment and export shares. And while the fall in the consumption share of GDP during China's export-driven growth period comes to a halt during the crisis years, it sees only a minor increase in the 2010s. The unprecedented stimulus that explains this divergence was undergirded by shifts in elite thinking about China's growth model. As with the Asian financial crisis, the external shock led policymakers to reconsider China's reliance on exports as a growth driver. Although the government had begun to emphasize the importance of strengthening consumption from the 2000s onward, the need to rebalance China's economy became more urgent after the 2008 to 2009 crisis.

While China's export activity had been primarily located along its eastern coast, this new surge in infrastructure and construction projects was overwhelmingly concentrated in China's interior regions (Wallace 2014), reflecting not just an effort to defend overall growth rates, but also deeper macroeconomic and political calculations. While infrastructure investment in China's interior provinces had been underway since the late 1990s as part of the government's "Develop the West" initiative, the size of the 2009 stimulus far outweighed previous spending efforts. This geographical shift reflected not just the fact that rural regions were more undeveloped compared to the urban coast, but also coincided with broader policy deliberations over how to reduce the rural-urban wealth gap.

Looney (2020) recounts how the 2008 financial crisis tipped the balance in the policy debates away from exports once again. Poverty alleviation considerations were combined with efforts to rebalance the economy away from exports, leading consumption to become a key component of the government's efforts to build a "New Socialist Countryside." This meant channeling resources toward "consumption-related infrastructure," namely better power, water, roads, and telecommunications" (Looney 2020, 214). Political risk also factored into the overall calculus. As documented in Wallace (2014), the collapse in manufacturing along the coast led tens of millions of migrants to return to their rural hometowns. The rural focus of this state-led investment therefore additionally reflected political stability considerations as the regime directed more funds to areas receiving an influx of returned migrants.

The overall shift toward an investment-led strategy was reflected in the Third Plenum of China's 17th Party Congress in October 2008, which signaled a greater reliance on land development and urbanization as a growth driver (Looney 2020, 215). The long-term consequences of this policy shift can be seen in Figure 5.3 showing coastal-interior differences in the dominance of fixed asset investment (FAI) in the economy (black dots represent prefecture cities in interior provinces and gray dots represent prefecture cities in coastal provinces). The overall trend might be affected by data scarcity in the 1980s and early 1990s, but on the whole the figure shows that whereas coastal prefectures used to have

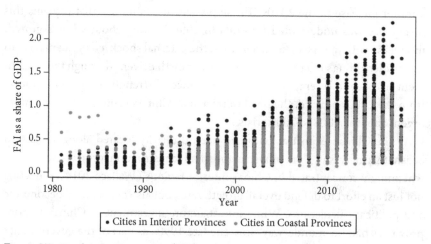

Figure 5.3 Fixed Asset Investment (FAI) as a Share of Prefecture GDP (1981–2018).
Source: CEIC Data

higher FAI shares compared to their inland peers, the trend reversed around the late 1990s. By the 2010s, many inland prefectures had FAI shares that far exceeded those of their coastal counterparts. Moreover, this trend has persisted well beyond the financial crisis, reflecting the importance of infrastructure investment as a growth driver in China's interior.

As with China's WTO entry, the switch toward an investment-led strategy brought about a reconfiguration of political beneficiaries. The stimulus was largely pushed out through China's state-owned banks and its SOEs, and thus this phase of investment-driven growth no doubt privileged state-owned firms, particularly those in the construction, steel, cement, railway and telecommunications sectors.

Investment and Exports as Demand Drivers—Neither Complements nor Substitutes

In short, China is too large and decentralized to be characterized as belonging to a single growth model. Instead, it could better be understood as a "system of systems" comprised of subsystems that are supported by distinct political coalitions. While the export-led model is concentrated along the coast and supported by external demand, benefiting domestic private and foreign-invested firms, the investment-led model is dominant in the interior of the country and reliant on domestic demand, privileging state-owned firms. These two subsystems are closely tied: the suppression of consumption and wages intrinsic to export-driven growth means that private investment is also constrained. A collapse of exports therefore implies that the only way to sustain demand is to turn to state-led investment.

That said, while the Chinese government has tended to boost its investment-led model at times of weak external demand, the two growth models do not stand in neatly as substitutes. This is in part due to China's size, making it capable of accommodating more than a single growth driver. But perhaps more importantly, domestic political economy logics push against such simple substitution dynamics wherein state-led investment would be rationally reduced once the external environment recovers. Instead, the overexpansion of any one demand driver is difficult for the central government rein in. Not only are the export and investment models supported by different economic actors with vested interests in the persistence of that particular mode of growth, both land development and exports are ultimately carried out by local governments whose leaders rely on positive economic figures for their political advancement and who therefore are locked in intense competition with each other for growth.

For example, the turn toward state-led investment triggered by the global financial crisis was implemented by China's local governments who transferred land rights to local government financing vehicles (LGFVs), allowing these firms to use land as collateral to issue bonds to finance infrastructure spending.[9] As Bai et al. (2016) have argued, while the use of these off-balance-sheet entities allowed China to blunt the impact of the financial crisis by increasing its public infrastructure investment, it also allowed local governments to use LGFVs to boost their growth rates and channel preferential deals to favored firms. Local governments, therefore, had no incentive to wean themselves off this growth strategy. Even as the central government ended its stimulus measures in 2010 and China's exports recovered, there was no observed retrenchment of state-led investment in the interior regions. Instead, as shown before, the infrastructure investment surge persisted for many years, generating a massive buildup of local government debt and problems of excess capacity that have proven immensely difficult for the central government to address.

Similarly, the export-led model is built on local governments whose economies are reliant on private and foreign manufacturing firms and a steady supply of migrant labor. The investment policies and regulatory structures in these jurisdictions are tailored to the goal of attracting export-oriented firm activities. Calls by the central government to rebalance away from exports toward consumption therefore directly threaten the revenues and growth prospects of these local governments located in coastal provinces.

The path dependencies associated with each of these growth models have generated pathologies which have also spilled over into the global economy. The most obvious global pathology of the export-oriented model, of course, would be the current account imbalances between the United States and China that helped lead to the 2008 global financial crisis. As Rajan (2011) puts it, "the global trade surpluses produced by the exporters search out countries with weak policies that are disposed to spend but also have the credibility to borrow to finance the spending" (p. 67). As for the investment-led model, as China's domestic demand for infrastructure and housing construction became more saturated, it started to export its excess infrastructure capacity to other countries under the aegis of the Belt and Road Initiative (BRI) (Cai 2017). Some of the provinces most active in advocating for and rolling out the BRI's infrastructure connections to Central and Southeast Asia, therefore, have been China's peripheral provinces in the western and southern interior (Jaros and Tan 2020).

In other words, both of China's domestic growth models are implicated in and fueled by dynamics in the global economy. The export growth model is reliant not just on domestic measures to suppress wage growth and other aspects of export costs, but also on the United States' consumption-based economy.

The investment-led model, in turn, is now being supported by capital and infrastructure-scarce economies in other parts of the world.

States and Markets: The Political Underpinnings of China's "System of Systems"

Building upon the above outline of the Chinese "system of systems," we now turn in more detail to its coalitional underpinnings and distributional implications to highlight how they differ from those of developed democracies. The first, most salient dimension to highlight is of course the direct involvement of the Communist party-state in many aspects of the economy. The strong role that the state plays in economic governance is arguably to be expected based on its low levels of development from the Mao period onward (Gerschenkron 1962). From a macroeconomic perspective, with a (largely) fixed exchange rate, plus capital controls and interest rates that were not liberalized until recently, the Chinese state's policy space for fiscal and monetary intervention is also outsized compared to advanced market economies. Most importantly, China's Communist regime and roots in the planned economy mean that the state remains directly implicated in Chinese capitalism through its monopoly on power and direct ownership of large sections of the economy. Therefore, the economic elite in China tend to overlap with the political elite much more directly than in capitalist economies with a clearer distinction between market and state.

This outsized role of the Chinese state has important implications for the balance of power within Chinese growth coalitions as compared to those in developed democracies. In developed democracies, dominant growth coalitions entail a symbiotic relationship between leading sectors or firms and the state. On the one hand, these leading sectors enjoy privileged access to policymaking processes (Introduction, p. 52) and they depend for their profitability on a range of state actions. On the other hand, the state—and thus the political parties who administer it—relies on these leading sectors to produce the economic growth that is so crucial to sustaining its electoral mandate. In the Chinese case, by contrast, the relationship between the party-state and capital depends on whether the leading sectors or firms are state-owned, private, or foreign. Rather than allowing privileged access to leading sectors, the Chinese party-state secures its political survival through direct *ownership and control* of strategic sectors and the preferential provision of resources to SOEs (Pearson 2015).

The privileged position of SOEs has been consistently reiterated through policy announcements over the years. For example, reforms in 1993 and 1999, while allowing for more space for market forces, have nevertheless reiterated the role of SOEs as the "principal component" and "pillar" of the economy (Tan

2021, 33). Policy announcements in 2005 to 2006 further emphasized the role of the state in "core" and "pillar" sectors, ranging from telecommunications and aviation to automotives and electronics. The shift back to an investment-led growth model prompted by the 2008 global financial crisis has only further boosted the importance of the state sector in the economy, reversing to some extent a steady expansion of the private sector in previous years (Lardy 2019).

In the case of domestic Chinese capital where a vibrant private sector has emerged, comprising 60% of GDP, the political relationship between private firms and the party-state is qualitatively distinct from what might be found in developed democracies. The amendment of the CCP's constitution in 2002 officially opened party membership to private entrepreneurs, allowing it to incorporate a growing private elite. Unlike developed democracies, which allow for more overt lobbying, private entrepreneurs in China seek to influence policymaking through more informal and covert means (Tsai 2007). Research shows that these private entrepreneurs seek advancement and protect their property by embedding themselves within the state, rather than standing apart from it (Hou 2019). Therefore, rather than the state relying on capital and providing privileged access to leading firms, China's private sector relies on the state for access to resources. In the Xi Jinping era, the CCP has taken more concerted actions to strengthen its control over the private sector, pushing for private firms to establish party branches within their organizations and further tilting the balance of power between state and private enterprise (Yan and Huang 2017).

Finally, foreign firms play a distinctive role in undergirding China's export growth model. Figure 5.2 clearly shows the degree to which foreign firms located in China benefited from the country's WTO entry, with their exports and imports expanding by a far greater degree in the WTO period compared to either SOEs or private firms. The dominance of these firms in China's export zones gives them a stake not just in China's export model but in the broader global system of interlocking growth models. Accordingly, policy analysts often refer to the foreign business community in China as a "ballast" that has stabilized US-China relations these past decades via their political support for the complementary (and yet unstable) linkages between the US consumption-led model and China's export-led model. It is no surprise, therefore, that as foreign firms based in China became increasingly concerned over issues such as the rise of state capitalism and policies favoring Chinese firms, economic relations between China and the United States and Europe have become more conflictual. Not only did the Trump administration raise a series of tariffs and export controls against China from 2018 onward, but the Biden administration has also upheld these tariffs and has further adopted new policies to ensure "supply-chain resilience" vis-à-vis China in critical sectors such as semiconductors.

While such concerns seem to have reached a crescendo amidst rising geopolitical tensions, the Chinese party-state has long been careful to circumscribe the role of foreign firms in different sectors of the economy. Foreign investment in various industries is controlled through a "Guiding Catalogue" that regulates the degree and form of capital investment. Industries with a high technology content are typically given an "encouraged" status to enable technology transfer. FDI in high-tech industries that also bear national strategic importance, or are dominated by SOEs (e.g., railways, aerospace, automotive), are typically restricted to joint ventures with a state-owned firm. This joint venture strategy reflects the party-state's conundrum in engaging with foreign firms in strategic sectors. On the one hand, the state is dependent on foreign firms for access to leading technology. On the other hand, it is careful to circumscribe the potential market influence of these firms so as to protect its own national champions. The resulting set of policy controls over FDI stands in stark contrast with how foreign capital is regulated in other FDI-intensive regimes and in developed democracies more generally, illustrating the degree to which party-state oversight affects the political underpinnings of China's hybrid growth models.

Importantly, China's reliance on the export- and investment-led growth models have distributive repercussions that go beyond the privileging of state capital over other forms of capital. Both regimes, it should be noted, suppress consumption. China's broader labor regime, which tightly restricts collective action, disadvantages workers (particularly low-wage earners) in different ways in each growth model. The export model is premised not only on a reservoir of migrant labor from China's poorer interior provinces, but on the structural precarity such labor is exposed to in the coastal regions as a result of the *hukou* system of household registration (wherein rural migrants are denied social services).

While the investment-led model is in part an attempt to address those regional inequalities, the dominance of the state sector in the investment regime has meant that the broad goals of poverty alleviation and rural development are operationalized in the narrow terms of infrastructure development and urbanization (Looney 2020). Finally, the shallow development of the Chinese welfare state following the dismantlement of the "iron rice bowl" (comprehensive benefits for SOE workers) in the 1990s has limited the degree to which wage increases result in greater consumption, forcing workers to accumulate "precautionary savings" in lieu of social insurance (He et al. 2018). All of this combines to produce income and wealth inequality that, according to the IMF, surpasses even Latin American levels (Jain-Chandra et al. 2018, 5).

The Party and the Legitimation of Growth Strategies

The dominance of the party-state in China's growth models is further amplified by the embedding of economic growth within a broader project of national rejuvenation. The CCP's projection of its status as a revolutionary party that has unified the country and restored its sovereignty and international prestige brings an added dimension to the coalitional politics of growth. That is, the party-state can deploy nationalism to legitimate its various growth models, strengthening the "passive consent" in Chinese society over what growth model is appropriate for the country. The suppression of wages and consumption that results from either an export- or investment-led growth model, therefore, is accepted not just as required for growth, but additionally necessary for rebuilding the Chinese nation.[10]

The CCP's monopoly on power also creates limits to the degree to which the Chinese party-state embraces growth as a means to legitimating its political authority. Here, the party-state faces a trade-off between fully committing to the maximization of growth and retaining control over certain aspects of the economy, either in order to secure ownership of national security and strategic industries, or to direct certain economic actors in pursuit of political goals. Lee (2018), for example, argues that the CCP does not seek to maximize profits, but rather aims for "profit optimization" to meet non-economic targets (p. 33). More recently, as China's economy has expanded and become more complex, the economy has come to pose greater risks of instability that might not be mitigated through existing levers of control. Thus, as Pearson, Rithmire, and Tsai (2020) argue, China's state capitalism is now more appropriately termed "party-state capitalism," with the party extending its political control over more arenas in the economy (such as the stock market) to address concerns over potential instability at the expense of growth.

The final political feature of the Chinese "system of systems" to highlight is the apparent "authoritarian flexibility" enjoyed by the party-state in being able to deploy an investment-led growth model at times of weak external demand, or otherwise shifting the pillars of growth in earlier periods. For example, Huang (2008) argues that growth in 1980s China was fueled by rural private industry, and that the 1990s saw a dramatic shift away from this strategy in favor of exports and state and foreign capital along the urban coast. Shih (2007) demonstrates this authoritarian flexibility in macroeconomic policy, arguing that China's central government is able to delegate power to the provinces in times of low inflation to spur growth and redelegate authority to central technocrats when the economy overheats in order to rein in the inflation threat. These shifts point to the dominant role of the party-state in the politics of growth in China and stand in contrast to developed democracies, where dominant growth coalitions have often proven resilient in times of crisis—indicating a reliance of these states on leading sectors and firms to a greater degree than seen in the Chinese case.[11]

There are nonetheless limits to China's authoritarian flexibility, well exemplified by the party-state's inability to rein in negative spillovers from each of the export- and investment-led growth models, despite policy announcements targeted at rationalizing the ill effects of an overreliance on either exports or investments. For example, in 2015 General Secretary Xi launched efforts to reduce the excess capacity created by the 2009 fiscal stimulus, yet implementation ended up being hobbled by subnational governments whose growth prospects were reliant on continued infrastructure investment (Naughton 2016; Jaros and Tan 2020). Additionally, the Chinese government's desire to shift away from a reliance on exports and investment has long been reflected in policy announcements urging broader structural transformation to move China toward a consumption-based economy. Yet, as Figure 5.1 shows, household consumption as a share of GDP remains under 40%, far below levels in the 1980s.

Chinese Growth Models in a Disrupted World

Just as the 1998 and 2008 financial crises highlighted the risks of an overreliance on an export growth strategy, so did events from 2018 to 2021. In 2018, the Trump administration launched a series of trade-related measures at China, including tariffs covering over $200 billion of China's exports to the United States and export restrictions targeted at its telecommunications companies Huawei and ZTE. In response, the Chinese government introduced policies aimed, once again, at reducing its exposure to the external economy. In 2018, Xi announced that "[u]nilateralism and trade protectionism are rising, forcing us to adopt a self-reliant approach . . . [China must] depend on itself for economic development" (Wang and Xin 2018).

In 2020, as the trade conflict with the United States persisted and amid a global pandemic that led many countries to reassess the benefits of relying on global supply chains nested in China for critical medical supplies, Xi announced a "dual circulation" strategy focused yet again at mitigating China's reliance on external trade. While China would still be plugged into the global economy through an "external circulation" of goods and services, the country would increase its emphasis on the domestic market (or "internal circulation"), with Xi noting that China would "gradually form a new development model in which domestic circulation plays a dominant role" (Tang 2020). Although policy emphasized that this domestic focus would involve expanding both consumption and investment

(Xinhua 2020a), in practice it has proven easier to increase the latter. Similarly, as the COVID-19 pandemic spread across the world in 2020 and most countries went into lockdown, external trade seized up. In response, China turned to its by-now familiar playbook of stimulating infrastructure construction, this time emphasizing "new infrastructure" related to the digital economy, from 5G tele-communications to new charging stations for electric vehicles (Xinhua 2020b).

Likewise, the government's limited progress in achieving its long-stated goal of shifting toward consumption-driven growth clearly suggests that despite one-party rule, and despite the leading role of the party-state in China's economic governance, there remain deep-seated vested interests that impose constraints on China's "authoritarian flexibility." Some of the sources of resistance come from within the party-state itself, from local governments reliant on either exports or investments to boost growth rates in support of their own political advancement, to SOEs in strategic industries such as steel, railways, telecommu-nications, and construction, whose viability depend on continued demand for infrastructure.

Importantly, it is easier for local governments to boost growth rates within their jurisdiction (and thereby enhance the promotion prospects of local leaders) through investment and exports, as such policies have more limited spillovers to other jurisdictions. Whereas infrastructure investment can be geographically targeted within a particular township or county, policies to boost consumption can end up increasing spending outside of one's jurisdiction through tourism or other imports, denying local leaders the opportunity to demonstrate growth performance to their superiors—and thus advance their positions within the party-state hierarchy. Thus, the geographical articulation of the party-state and the incentive structure of its cadres interact to produce a systematic bias against a more consumption-led growth model.

China in the Mirror of the EU's Dual Growth Model

China's size and internally heterogenous growth models, while unique in impor-tant respects, can nevertheless be fruitfully compared with another continent-sized economy containing a dual growth model: the Eurozone (EZ) (or the EU more generally). Thus, the Eurozone's export economy is centered in (western) Germany and the closely linked economies of northwestern Europe,[12] with the support of the supply-chain "platforms" of Eastern Europe, while more con-sumption and FDI-driven economies characterize the South and the periphery. This parallels, to a degree, the export-intensive economy in Zhejiang province, FDI-dominant provinces such as Guangdong and Jiangsu, and provinces in the western region such as Inner Mongolia reliant on infrastructure and construction.

What is to be gained from drawing such a parallel? First, comparing China with the EU helps us recognize that a hybrid growth model is no anomaly. Second, emphasizing the commonalities of China and the EU helps counter the widespread tendency to exaggerate the functional coherence of the Chinese model. Such hybridity emerged in different ways in the EU and China: in Europe, through the incomplete integration of a very heterogeneous set of capitalist economies, in China via the incremental layering of a market economy atop the planned economy. Yet in both cases we can say that the resulting growth models are not the efficient outcomes of any kind of evolutionary process but rather of the interplay of often conflicting political and economic imperatives. Indeed, when we consider the woes of the Eurozone growth model since the financial crisis of 2008, we can gain some insights into the vulnerabilities of the Chinese system, while also noting some revealing differences between the two blocs' responses to that crisis.

While the Eurozone crisis ultimately manifested itself as a sovereign debt crisis of the periphery (speedily labeled the PIIGS of Portugal, Ireland, Italy, Greece and Spain)—and was quickly framed as such by leading European policymakers—it has been widely noted that its causes were much more complex than this. The Eurocrisis as a whole arose from the fatal interaction of the Eurozone's heterogenous growth models (as the preceding chapter discusses in depth). In particular, the funneling of the current account surpluses inherent to the EZ's export-led regimes (above all Germany) into the European periphery helped finance debt-fueled construction booms in Spain and Ireland (even helping to shift the latter's growth model temporarily off the course of its traditional FDI- and export-led orientation).

The long-identified vulnerabilities of the Chinese growth model present obvious similarities to precisely the elements of the pre-2008 Eurozone economy that collapsed so spectacularly during the crisis. The debt-financed construction-intense growth models of China's interior regions bear a worrying resemblance to aspects of pre-crash Spain and Ireland, with the "shadow finance" system established by local governments fulfilling the role in China played by the domestic banking sector in the latter countries. And just as the housing booms in those countries were partly fueled by capital inflows from the Eurozone's surplus economies, the capital entering these investment heavy regions of China can ultimately be traced back to the export surpluses of the coast. The scaling back of China's pre-crisis policy of funneling those surpluses back into US treasuries and other assets has only further facilitated the shift toward the domestic debt- and investment-led growth model (Stetser 2018).

In this context it is striking that any parallel between these two continent-wide dualistic growth models does not extend to their responses to the 2008 crisis. Whereas the Eurozone spent a lost decade in the grip of fiscal austerity,

China's experience could hardly be more different. As noted before, 2008 was a critical inflection point for the Chinese model, with a massive stimulus program responding to the initial collapse of export demand and thereby doubling down on the local debt- and infrastructure-based growth sub-model and allowing the export-led growth model to subside in relative terms (see Figure 5.1).

Johnson and Matthijs (in the preceding chapter) see the Eurozone, under German leadership, as having moved toward a homogenization of its hybrid growth model along export-led lines, and it is possible to interpret the Chinese response to the 2008 crisis as a similar, though opposite, shift toward a less hybrid model, more singularly focused on investment, infrastructure, and above all "state capitalism." Indeed, these shifts are not entirely independent of each other—as the introduction to this volume notes, an export-led growth model is not universalizable. Thus, the Eurozone's accumulation of significant current account surpluses in the past 10 years could only have taken place if the rest of the world made correspondingly large moves in the opposite direction. China has certainly played its part in this regard, with its current account surplus declining from its 2007 peak of 10% of GDP to about 2% on average over the course of that same decade.[13]

At the same time, it is important to recognize that the Chinese economy remains highly internationally oriented—indeed, as noted before, we can observe in recent years some tendency to "internationalize" the domestic investment-led model via the BRI and the expanded international activities of both SOEs and other infrastructure-linked Chinese firms (such as, most controversially, Huawei). As such, the best way to understand these changes may be as a reversal of roles within a still fundamentally hybrid growth regime. Indeed, Xi Jinping's concept of "dual circulation"—emphasizing domestic demand as the primary driver of the economy while external demand plays a supporting role—can be seen as a doctrinal formalization of China's hybrid model.

Conclusion

This chapter has argued that the drivers of growth in large polities such as China need to be understood as existing in a "system of systems." Despite having a major impact on the domestic and international economy, exports form only one part of the Chinese growth story. Instead, China has relied on a hybrid growth model over the past four decades, comprising an export-led regime concentrated along the coast and an investment-led regime focused in the country's interior.

The relative prominence of these two growth models has depended not just on domestic policies but also the international environment. China's coastal development strategy of the 1990s and its entry into the WTO in

2001 both served to massively expand the export component of its growth, much of which was boosted by the expansion of global supply chains during this period. That said, events such as the 1998 and 2008 financial crises have prompted a greater focus on domestic investment and a reduced reliance on the external economy.

While China's growth experience is arguably unparalleled in world history, the hybridity of its internal growth models is not. Other large-scale economies, such as the Eurozone, share important characteristics of disequilibrium, internal incoherence, and contradiction. Just as China's export and investment growth models have created negative spillovers that have proven difficult to rein in, so the Eurozone's demand-driven and export-driven economies, bound as they were by a common currency, led to instability and ultimately crisis.

While the politics of growth in China and the EU are as different as their political regimes, they share a common thread in that growth in both regions feed into political legitimation. China's authoritarian regime, however, has allowed for a greater degree of policy flexibility compared to the developed democracies in Europe. While the troika's response in the Euro crisis was to impose austerity, the Chinese government used its policy levers and SOEs to stimulate state-led investment in its interior regions. Nevertheless, the coalitions underpinning China's hybrid growth models have imposed clear limits on this "authoritarian flexibility." The government's long-stated policy goal of shifting toward consumption-driven growth has met with stiff resistance, highlighting the power of vested interests in keeping China locked into some version of its current hybrid growth model, even as significant shifts take place in the primacy accorded to its different sub-models.

Notes

1. Data obtained from data.worldbank.org.
2. Data obtained from wits.worldbank.org.
3. The resulting process of economic policy experimentation is well documented in the literature and so this section only provides a short overview.
4. From 1978 to 1984, agriculture contributed more to GDP growth than industry in the majority of Chinese provinces (Looney 2020, 180.)
5. This incremental process has been alternately labeled "experimentation under hierarchy" (Heilmann 2008) or "directed improvisation" (Ang 2016) and expanded over time to include experimentation in governance approaches more broadly (Florini, Lai, and Tan 2012).
6. The dip in the investment share in the late 1980s is likely due to the 1989 Tiananmen crisis, which led to a fall in FDI and a stalling of the economic reform agenda that was only revived in 1992.
7. Data obtained from UNCTAD.
8. Data obtained from https://oec.world/en/profile/country/idn
9. The creation of LGFVs allowed local governments to circumvent rules restricting their ability to borrow or to run deficits.

10. The role of nationalism in forging a state-society consensus on the sacrifices required to achieve high-speed growth is by no means unique to China (see the discussion of Japan in Johnson 1982). What distinguishes the Chinese case is the revolutionary status of the party and the social transformations enacted under its rule.

11. Thus by 2017 the FIRE (finance, insurance, and real estate) sector had already recovered to its pre-crisis peak of about 20% of US GDP, while Germany's current account surplus is even higher as a share of GDP than before the Eurocrisis. In Ireland, the collapse of the housing bubble in 2009 did cause a subsequent shift from construction to exports and FDI—but this was itself a reversion to a growth model that had long been dominant until about 2005.

12. Germany and the Netherlands (as well as Denmark and Sweden outside the Eurozone) had current account surpluses ranging from 5% to 8% of GDP in 2020.

13. Data obtained from data.worldbank.org.

6

The Politics of Growth Model Switching: Why Latin America Tries, and Fails, to Abandon Commodity-Driven Growth

JAZMIN SIERRA

Introduction

Latin America's developmental trajectory is largely defined by its attempts to switch away from a Growth Model (GM) based upon the extraction and exportation of commodities. The region integrated into the world economy as an exporter of primary products (Cardoso and Faletto 1979) and these were the sole engines of economic growth until the Great Depression (Williamson 2011). Between the 1950s and 1980s, Latin America trended toward a more balanced growth model that combined wages and diversified exports as the main drivers of growth. In fact, by 1980, manufacturing's share of GDP reached a regional average of 26.7% (Bértola and Ocampo 2012, 188). In turn, the region's export basket diversified. Non-commodity goods grew from 8.1% of all exports in 1953 to nearly a quarter of all exports by 1980 (Bértola and Ocampo, 2012, 158). Yet, the transition toward a more balanced GM did not take root. The weight of natural resources in total regional exports remained close to 50%, well above the average of other developing countries (Figure 6.1). By the end of the recent commodity boom (2003–2015), Latin America accounted for 13% of world trade in agriculture as opposed to 3% of manufactured goods (FAO 2015). The UN Economic Commission for Latin America and the Caribbean described this process as a "re-primarization" of the region's economies.

Commodity-driven GMs have been detrimental to Latin America's development. Development requires structural transformation. Namely, a transition

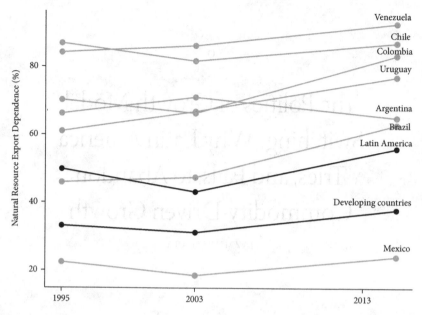

Figure 6.1 Natural Resource Dependence of Exports. Source: Ocampo 2017, 57

from a specialization in agriculture to diversification based on manufacturing
and services (Amsden 2001; Imbs and Wacziarg 2003; Rodrik 2004). No
country has improved its income status without such structural change
(Aiginger and Rodrik 2020). Only the manufacturing and (increasingly) service sectors can provide the employment and wage levels, and the productivity
gains needed for sustained economic growth and greater equality (Hausmann
and Rodrik 2003).

Being aware of this, Latin American governments have attempted to switch
from a commodity-driven to a more balanced GM that combines wages and a
diversified export basket as the drivers of growth. This required the pursuit of
industrialization, the redistribution of income, and the transfer of economic
and political resources from the rural to the urban sector. Attempts to switch
GMs were carried out by populist governments after the Great Depression,
by bureaucratic-authoritarian regimes during the Cold War, and by New Left
governments during the recent commodity boom. Despite significant variation
in ideologies, coalitions, and external conditions, these governments all failed.
As a result, no Latin American country has managed to transition from middle-
income to high-income status and the region remains the most unequal in the
world (Agénor et al. 2012).

In this chapter, I argue that the persistence of commodity-driven growth in
Latin America is explained by an endogenous distributional dilemma. While

governments have clear incentives to promote the interests of the rural sector due to its centrality in commodity-led growth, doing so affects their capacity to promote the urban sector, and thereby successfully switch growth models. The dilemma can be observed in three distinct, yet interrelated areas: macroeconomic policies, fiscal policies, and the domestic balance of power. First, commodity-led GMs generate appreciated exchange rates on the upside of the commodity cycle that leads to negative production and income effects in the urban sector. Second, they produce fixed assets and income concentration, making redistribution particularly difficult. Third, they empower rural elites that oppose the structural transformation of the economy.

How did Latin America endogenize this switching dilemma? First, the formation of a strong export oligarchy in the post-colonial period led to a concentration of income and assets that has persisted over time (Williamson 2015). This allowed landed elites to retain the power to undermine policies that affected their interests, notably redistribution and broad-based industrialization. This contrasts with the experience of East Asia, where the state enacted land reform and generated incentives for the oligarchy to invest in industry (Kaufman and Stallings 1991; Evans 1987).

Second, while successful late developers, such as Germany and Japan, generated the domestic savings and investment required for industrialization by repressing social and political demands of the working class (Gerschenkron 1962; Haggard 1990), this strategy was not available to Latin American countries where industrialization and labor activation went largely hand in hand (Collier and Collier 1991). Unable to finance economic modernization through either rural elites or urban labor, Latin American governments ended up depending on foreign finance in the form of capital imports to attempt to bypass the switching dilemma, placing additional external limits on structural transformation.

This chapter is organized as follows. I first develop a framework for understanding the distributive tensions built into commodity-led growth and why these generate a recurrent switching dilemma for governments that seek GM transformation. I next provide a historical overview of how distributive conflict between urban and rural interests emerged in Latin America, and how it conditioned the outcomes of state-led industrialization under populist and bureaucratic-authoritarian governments. I next discuss the contemporary experience of the New Left governments and show how the recent commodity boom that freed these governments from external financial constraints nonetheless kept these endogenous constraints largely in place. The comparison of historical and contemporary attempts of GM switching shows that once established, commodity-based GMs tend to persist despite their detrimental developmental outcomes.

Commodity-Driven Growth Models'
"Switching Dilemma"

When governments managing a commodity-driven GM seek structural transformation, they will attempt to replace commodity-driven growth with a balanced GM that combines internal and diversified external drivers of growth.
Achieving this balanced growth requires redistribution (stimulating household
consumption) and industrialization (changing the composition of the export
basket toward manufacturing and services). Switching has deep distributional
implications. It entails replacing the rural sector with the urban sector as the
main motor of economic growth while requiring a transfer of income from the
rural to the urban sector to achieve it. Governments must therefore navigate the
tension between distinct, and often clashing, rural and urban interests.[1] While
governments have strong incentives to promote the interests of the rural sector
due to their centrality to the existing growth model, doing so affects their capacity to promote the urban sector and successfully switch their growth model.
This "switching" dilemma can be observed in three distinct, yet interrelated
dimensions: macroeconomic and fiscal policies, and the balance of power (see
Table 6.1). I now turn to explaining each of these dimensions.

The first dimension of the switching dilemma centers on macroeconomic
policy. Governments seeking to switch GMs prefer an exchange rate that makes
local manufacturing and services competitive. Commodity-driven GMs, however, tend toward real exchange rate appreciation. During the upside of the

Table 6.1 **Commodity-Driven Growth Models' Switching Dilemma**

	Commodity-Driven Growth Model	*Switching Dilemma*
Macroeconomic Policy	Generates currency appreciation	Allow the currency to appreciate (or promote devaluation) and hurt (protect) urban and rural tradables
Fiscal and Regulatory Policies	Generates economic actors that hold fixed assets and concentrate income	Create an investment-friendly climate or redistribute resources to urban sector through fiscal (taxation) and regulatory policies (price controls, land reform)
Balance of Power	Generates structural and instrumental power of agricultural elites	Accept the veto power of rural sector or increase the power of the urban sector

commodity cycle export revenues increase foreign currency inflows leading to a rise in domestic prices. This inflationary effect is augmented if favorable external conditions lead to a relaxation of borrowing terms. While commodity producers can often compensate for currency appreciations through rising international prices, other tradables cannot. A stronger currency therefore affects both the international competitiveness of goods and services and their domestic demand because they must now compete with relatively cheaper foreign imports.[2] This results in a decline in production and employment in tradable sectors outside of agriculture (Bresser-Pereira 2018; Frenkel and Rapetti 2012; Frieden 2015) while the aforementioned inflationary pressures strain improvements in the real wage, affecting redistribution. Faced with these negative impacts, governments can intervene in currency markets to depreciate the currency, but in doing so risk diminishing their monetary reserves and generating further inflationary pressures.

The second dimension of the dilemma centers on the fiscal and regulatory policies required to transfer resources from the rural to the urban sector. This transfer can be achieved through taxes, price controls, and land reforms. As the main tradable, the rural sector is the leading supplier of the foreign exchange needed to finance imports, and crucially, can provide the "seed funding" for GM switching. For example, export duties of agricultural products are a particularly useful way of raising revenue. They require low levels of state capacity and can often be legislated by decree. When applied to wage goods—wheat, meat, milk—export taxes can also help curtail domestic inflation (O'Donnell 1988). And these economic sources are devoid of the conditionalities attached to foreign capital that may condition industrialization and redistribution.

Wealth taxation is particularly difficult under commodity-driven GMs. These models generate economic elites that hold fixed assets and concentrate income, making them more fearful of redistribution (Ansell and Samuels 2014). And while economic elites in unequal democracies may understand that some degree of poverty alleviation is necessary, heavily concentrated income in the very top percentiles means very concentrated losers for corporate and personal income tax (Fairfield and Garay 2017). Governments seeking to switch GMs therefore face the challenge of whether and how to transfer resources from the urban to the rural sector.

The third dimension of the switching dilemma centers on the balance of power (Korpi 1974; Schipani 2019) between rural and urban interests. Under the existing commodity-driven GM, rural interests hold significant economic and political power, and can effectively undermine attempts at switching. This is because economic sectors that are key to the success of the existing GM enjoy a privileged position within it. We can think of this privileged position as stemming from structural and instrumental power. Structural power stems from businesses' investment capacity (Lindblom 1977). If policies run counter to the interests of the GM's core actor, they will be avoided by policymakers without the need for coordinated political action. These conditions are largely met under commodity-driven growth, where reductions in the rural sector's production and investment can severely impact foreign reserves, fiscal revenue, and growth rates. This structural power may not be enough to achieve political influence, and economic elites may also invest in instrumental power (Fairfield 2011). Examples of the instrumental power of business include protesting, lobbying, campaign financing, and creating business associations. We can therefore expect that agricultural elites will leverage their instrumental power to defend the commodity-driven GM.

To balance against rural interests, governments can rely on urban labor. Labor favors switching toward alternative sources of demand because of the higher employment and wage levels that a balanced GM provides. Governments can redistribute power toward labor by granting collective bargaining, setting up corporatist institutions, and appointing union leaders to government positions (Schipani 2019). But increasing the bargaining power of labor may also compromise the switching of the GM. As noted earlier, nominal wage moderation is crucial for growth, particularly in contexts where productivity gains may be hard to find. Governments therefore face the further dilemma of whether or not to empower labor to counterbalance rural power.

The switching dilemma can shed light on the endogenous constrains given by commodity-driven growth for structural transformation. In short, when governments attempt to switch growth models, they must navigate the tension between policies that sustain the existing growth model and those that allow for its structural transformation. This includes compensating the losers while providing incentives to potential winners. Such a process will often lead to policy decisions that undermine the attempt to change the GM.

There are important variations among countries managing commodity growth that make the switching dilemma more or less salient. First, the dilemma is more likely to apply when the state must address rural and urban interests simultaneously. As the contrasting experiences of Latin America and East Asia show, this is more likely where the urban sector is activated and organized, and wage and consumption repression are not politically viable. Second, the dilemma is also more prevalent under Left parties or populist movements. These tend to hold a programmatic commitment to social and economic equality, and support state intervention in the economy to achieve it. Conversely, a Right party or populist movement is more likely to promote theories of comparative advantage, the protection of property rights, and the maintenance of social order.[3] Under a commodity GM, we can expect that the Right is more likely to protect it, while the Left is more likely to attempt structural transformation, and hence activate the switching dilemma.

Third, the ownership structure of commodity production matters (Cardoso and Faletto 1979; Haggard 1990). The dilemma is more likely to apply where commodity production is controlled by national capital, and the distributive conflict involves local actors. Where foreign capital controls commodity production, resource nationalism may help cement a broad coalition in favor of expropriating foreign interests and placing them under state control (Jones Luong and Sierra 2015). This, in turn, may mute distributive conflicts (Dunning 2008).

The Latin American Switching Dilemma

In this section I apply this framework to analyze why Latin American governments have tried and failed to achieve balanced growth in the 20th century. Latin America's insertion into the global economy as a commodity exporter, and its comparatively late industrialization, led to the presence of two powerful, yet often opposed, actors: a rural oligarchy and an urban popular sector (O'Donnell 1978; Evans 1987; Rueschemeyer et al. 1992).[4] Governments attempting to switch away from a commodity-driven GM had to address the distributive tension between the two, often leading to policy choices that undermined structural transformation.

Emergence of Commodity-Driven GMs

The commodity boom of the 1810s to 1890s consolidated the resource export sector (based on minerals and agricultural products) as the main driver of economic growth across Latin America. While this occurred across many former colonies, it was particularly pronounced in this region. By the end of this boom period, commodity exports represented approximately 20% of Latin American GDP while two major export commodities represented at least half of total exports in all countries (Williamson 2011, 47, 52).

Land and mineral assets were held by a small economic elite. Between 1880 to 1990, the GINI index of land ownership in Latin America was nearly 80, a stark contrast from the low 50s in the United States and Canada, and 44.3 in Asia (Bértola and Ocampo 2012, 101), and as a result inequality rose by 30% (Williamson 2015, 336). The economic relevance of the primary-product export sector was reflected in oligarchic political regimes (Halperín Donghi 1969). These were characterized by limited democracy where political parties were dominated by agricultural elites, often in coalition with a rising, yet still weak bourgeoise (Bértola and Ocampo 2012, 102). Policy reflected the interests of the agricultural elite with limited opposition.

But this was not the only game in town. Across Latin American countries, manufacturing was growing in economic relevance. Prior to the 1929 crash, manufacturing accounted from 16 to 20% of GDP in Argentina, Brazil, and Mexico (Bértola and Ocampo 2012, 129). This industrialization led to the emergence of new, urban economic actors: the bourgeoise, and the working and middle classes. This growing urban sector, however, did not yet represent a distributive threat to rural elites because it had not yet been politically activated. At this point, industrialists could be compensated without affecting agricultural interests via tariffs. In fact, by 1913 local industries were protected through manufacturing imports tariffs in Argentina, Mexico, and Brazil which ranged, respectively from 22, 45, to 60% (Williamson 2011, 219). Through these import tariffs, governments obtained the tax revenues that compensated for their inability to tax land (Bértola and Ocampo 2012, 132) making local industry protection a fortunate byproduct of a fiscal strategy (Williamson 2011).

GM Switching—Round One

The 1930s economic depression unleashed economic, political, and ideational changes that undermined the consensus surrounding commodity-driven GMs in Latin America. The collapse of markets for commodity exports and imports of foreign manufactures generated a spontaneous protection for local industry. Meanwhile, mass migration from rural to urban areas enlarged the urban workforce. These economic shifts were accompanied by a change in the intellectual climate. Scholars based at the United Nation's Economic Commission for Latin America began to question the comparative advantage assumptions of neoclassical economics (Prebisch 1962). They argued that price fluctuations and a secular decline in terms of trade of agricultural products vis-à-vis manufactures generated structural differences between center and periphery, to the detriment of the latter.

Political leaders that came to power in this period—as varied as Perón in Argentina, Vargas in Brazil, Aguirre Cerda in Chile, Cárdenas in Mexico, and Battle in Uruguay— replaced the traditional oligarchic political class and were supported through a cross-class coalition of urban industrial interests that included the bourgeoise and the popular sectors (Collier and Collier 1991). These urban actors had common, yet distinct, interests (Kaufman 1979, 199–200). Middle classes (professionals and service workers) sought increased access to the political system and social mobility opportunities. The working class sought formal protection of wages, job security, and working conditions. The industrial bourgeoise sought public policies that would protect their economic interests, mainly the provision of investment capital and protection from foreign competitors.

These new political coalitions coalesced around the goal of switching their particular country's GMs from export-led growth to "state-led industrialization," whereby the government would promote industrial production for domestic consumption and international exports (Bértola and Ocampo 2012). This entailed a sequential process that sought to substitute imports of manufactures (first consumer goods and then intermediate and capital goods) and then export domestic production (Hirschman 1968).

The first phase of the switching centered on import substituting industrialization (ISI) combined with fiscal and monetary expansion, and exchange rate appreciation The urban coalition benefited from this "macroeconomic populism" (Dornbusch and Edwards 1991). Working and middle class received job security and salary increases. Domestic industrialists were protected from foreign imports through tariffs and subsidies, and they tolerated income expansion because it created a domestic market for their goods. The combination of an expanding internal consumption market, industrial production with low capital requirements, and protection from foreign competition led this stage to be classified as the "easy phase" of state-led industrialization (O'Donnell 1988; Hirschman 1968).

The crux was how to finance all this? Such a profound switching of GMs not only implied replacing the rural sector with the urban sector as the main motor of economic growth, but required a transfer of income and power from the rural to the urban sector to achieve it (Cardoso and Helwege 1991, 49). The rural sector was indispensable for ISI through its inputs of raw material, hard currency, and cheap food for the urban population. For ISI to be financed domestically, governments would have to put in place a range of policies— price controls, export quotas, export taxes, and land reform— that directly affected rural interests.

GM Defense—Round One

It is here that the switching dilemma kicked in leading to decisions that undermined the attempt to change the GM. Take the example of taxes and exchange rates. Governments opted for overvalued exchange rates, which cheapened intermediary inputs, but depressed commodity exports and eventually acted as a barrier to industrial exports. An undervalued exchange rate that promoted commodity exports combined with taxes on these exports would have provided governments with the foreign exchange necessary to finance the acquisition of intermediary imports essential for manufacturing. However, as noted by Hirschman (1968, 27), "the power of the groups tied to the primary export sector would hardly have permitted so direct an assault . . . the great advantage of the inflation-cum-overvaluation arrangement was . . . that it resulted in an indirect rather than direct squeeze of politically and socially powerful groups."

A similar logic applies to land reform. Why did Latin American governments not follow the East Asian route of land expropriations to finance industrialization? The short answer is that most did not dare try to do so, and those that did, failed. Oligarchies in Brazil, Colombia, Chile, and Uruguay retained their political strength due to their stable clientelist relationships in the countryside. The lack of a large peasant population precluded Argentine elites from achieving this degree of social control (Halperín Donghi 1969), but Perón never considered altering rural property relations. The governments of Peru and Chile attempted to convert landed elites into an industrial bourgeoisie by providing compensation for expropriations that could be invested in new ventures. However, these funds were limited in size and lost value due to high inflation, and did not dissuade rural elites from reversing the expropriations (Kay 2002, 1089).

The Mexican and Venezuelan governments did carry out land reform and encouraged peasant mobilization, only to reverse these experiments later (Collier and Collier 1991). Take the example of Mexico where the conditions for a successful land reform prevailed. Not only did a nationalized oil sector serve as an alternative revenue source (Jones Luong and Sierra 2015), but the oligarchy had uprooted a large portion of the peasantry to consolidate land, precluding a cross-class rural alliance (Collier and Collier 1991, 114). Yet, the intensification of opposition from conservative sectors led to a dramatic decline of land redistribution (Hamilton 1982), a change in the constitution allowing large holdings once again (González Casanova 1982, 61), and repression of rural labor (Collier and Collier 1991, 408).

The distributive dilemma faced by governments in their attempts to switch GMs, and the suboptimal policy choices they made as a result, helps explain why by the early 1950s, primary ISI began to "exhaust itself" (Fishlow 1973). As domestic markets saturated, producers of basic consumer goods sought to advance toward heavy industry and exports, increasing their demand for foreign inputs. But the rural sector continued to be the only source of foreign exchange, and it now faced severed external constraints as commodity prices slumped after the Korean War just as protectionist barriers erected by advanced economies squeezed rural income (Kaufman 1979; Gereffi and Evans 1981).

In response, Latin American governments returned to more favorable stances toward agriculture (Kaufman 1979, 2010–2011). Unable to squeeze more resources out of it, they opted to improve its productivity (Zoomers 2002, 62). Support included subsidized credits for the purchase of agricultural machinery and equipment, research by government agencies for improving the quality of livestock and seeds, and currency devaluations (Kay 2002, 1078). The distributive effects of these measures were twofold. First, they implied a transfer of income away from the urban to the rural sector, thereby undermining the shift away from the commodity-led GM (Kaufman 1979, 2010–2011). Second, they (further) consolidated the power of a small group of producers (Zoomers 2002, 62) and increased their veto power. And while agriculture became more efficient, it could not meet the demands of the urban sector for affordable food and foreign exchange (Kay 2002, 1078). Unable to resolve the foreign exchange problem, "classical populism rapidly self-destructed" (Cardoso and Helwege 1991, 49).

GM Switching—Round Two

The "bureaucratic-authoritarian" era followed in countries with the most advanced industrialization processes: Brazil (1964–1985), Argentina (1966–1973, 1976–1983), Chile (1973–1989), Uruguay (1973–1985), and a milder version in Mexico (1976–1982) (O'Donnell 1973; Collier 1979). Several of these regimes—in Argentina (1966–1973), Brazil, and Mexico—continued to promote state-led industrialization, but addressed the shift dilemma by attracting foreign investments and assuming foreign debt (importing capital) and excluding the popular sector (diminishing expectations and consumption) (O'Donnell 1973; Evans 1987).

The exclusion of labor and the influx of foreign financing marked a strong departure from the populist era and allowed for heavy industry ISI and export promotion (Haggard 1990). Access to external finance initially eased the distributive conflict by releasing the agricultural sector from its role as the main provider of foreign exchange (Collier and Collier 1991, 394). However, dependence on foreign capital undermined the GM switch in two ways. First, FDI displaced domestic industry. In Brazil and Mexico, where governments provided the strongest incentives to FDI, half of the 300 largest manufacturing firms in each country were under foreign control by the early 1970s (Stallings 1990, 74–75). Second, dependence on foreign loans increased the likelihood of privileging budget discipline and price stability over the types of fiscal measures needed to transform the GM (Campello 2014; Kaplan and Thomsson 2016).

GM Defense—Round Two

These bureaucratic-authoritarian regimes, in turn, collapsed in the face of elite and popular discontent due to mounting external debt, foreign exchange shortages, and inflationary pressures. As a consequence, the "third wave of democratization" that followed went hand in hand with a deepening of market reforms. The transfer of resources from the rural to the urban sector was dismantled as government sought to support their country's comparative advantage rather than transform the economy (Ocampo and Ros 2011). This often-meant abandoning campaign promises to transform the GM. Stokes (2001) shows that half of the Latin American Left presidents inaugurated between 1982 and 1995 renegaded on their promises, and governed as conservatives through tax cuts and a reduction of industrial and social policies (Kaufman and Segura-Ubiergo 2001). Once the goal of switching GMs was surrendered, the distributive conflict that had emerged in the populist period was muted.

The China-Led Commodity Boom and the New Left: A Switch Too Far?

The recent commodity boom coincided with the election of Left governments across the region. By the end of the 2000s, two-thirds of the region was governed by the Left (Levitsky and Roberts 2011, 2). Despite important differences across these progressive forces, they shared a strong programmatic commitment to changing the GM by pursuing redistribution and industrialization (Sierra 2015; Schipani 2019). Existing scholarship suggests that the commodity boom offered the New Left a unique opportunity to shift the GM. The boom itself provided financial resources devoid of the conditionalities set by international financial institutions and private international investors (Murillo et al. 2011; Campello 2014). In addition, Latin America's landed elites had diversified by acquiring assets in industry and finance leading potentially to heterogeneous interests, and even indifference, toward several public policies (Frieden 2015; Paniagua 2018). Finally, the specificity of Chinese commodity demands generated incentives for rural producers to switch from exports of wage goods (beef and wheat) to exports of goods not consumed domestically (soy). This would relax the tension of the populist period between export promotion and domestic consumption (Richardson 2012).

The New Left, however, was unable to shift toward a balanced GM. Despite the return of industrial policy, the re-primarization of these economies prevailed (see Figure 6.1). Significant improvements in income distribution did take place (Huber and Stephens 2012; Sánchez -Ancochea 2021). But these were largely based on conditional cash transfers and non-contributory pensions financed through increases in consumption and payroll taxes (Holland and Schenider 2017). New Left governments did not claim agricultural wealth. The relationship between terms of trade and the revenue/GDP ratio for Latin America was weak during the commodity boom (Cornia et al. 2011). Income tax collection held steady at 1.4% of GDP compared to 8.4% in advanced economies (Holland and Schenider 2017, 992). Counterintuitively, during the commodity boom, Latin American countries subsidized, rather than taxed, their agricultural sector.

Despite favorable external conditions, these governments faced the same switching dilemma as prior governments in their attempts to leave behind commodity GMs. To illustrate these dynamics, I compare the strategies adopted by the Workers' Party in Brazil (2003–2016) and the *Frente Para la Victoria* (FVP), the left-wing of Peronism, in Argentina (2003–2015). Both Lefts set out to change the commodity-led GM by promoting domestic consumption through conditional cash-transfer programs, indexation of the minimum wage, and household credit (Schipani 2019); and supporting domestic manufacturing through subsidies and favorable exchange rates (Garay and Etchemendy 2011; Sierra 2015). They took, however, nearly mirror approaches toward the obstacles faced. While Argentina's FVP intervened in currency markets, taxed the agricultural sector, and excluded rural interests from policymaking, Brazil's PT allowed currency appreciation, subsidized the agricultural sector, and included rural interests in policymaking.

Argentina—GM Switching—Round Three

The FPV governments led by Kirchner (2003–2007) and Fernández de Kirchner (2008–2015) implemented macroeconomic and fiscal policies that deliberately undermined rural interests. Their macroeconomic choices were shaped by Argentina's prior market reform experience whereby price stability rested on a fixed and overvalued exchange rate of a one-to-one parity with the US dollar. This decade-long stabilization program was viewed as the cause of declining industrial competitiveness, wage stagnation, and unemployment. In his campaign, Kirchner promised a competitive and flexible exchange rate which would increase the competitiveness of all tradables (Frenkel and Rapetti 2012). In turn, the foreign exchange generated by a booming agriculture sector could be used to support industry. This expectation helped cement the FVPs alliance with the industrial bourgeoise who viewed a competitive exchange rate as crucial for its survival. The leadership of the peak business association, the *Unión Industrial Argentina* (UIA), expressed "unrestricted support" for Kirchner's economic policies even as the government intervened to secure wage gains.

But in the context of a commodity boom, where the dollar influx from commodity sales appreciated the currency, the government faced the same old difficulties (Frenkel and Rapetti 2012). The Central Bank used substantial reserves to sell pesos or peso-denominated bonds and buy dollars as a part of

exchange rate management. In turn, the undervaluation of the peso had inflationary effects. The growing inability to maintain the competitiveness of the *peso*
was reflected in the country's deteriorating balance of payments. Expectations
grew that a devaluation was imminent and prompted a massive sell-off of local
currency. The government responded in two ways, with contrasting effects on its
support from the urban popular and middle classes.

First, it engaged in price controls. Quantitative restrictions and bans of wage
goods (bovine meat, wheat, and milk) were introduced after 2006, and were subject to significant executive branch discretion in the absence of domestic laws
governing them (OECD 2019, 77). Price controls were also placed on products
sold domestically reducing the income of retailers. This policy was unsurprisingly opposed by rural producers and the retail industry, but was appreciated by
popular and middle-class consumers.[5]

Second, the government placed restrictions on the purchase of foreign exchange. Foreign reserves starting dwindling by mid-2011 and, in response, the
government implemented a *cepo cambiario* (dollar clamp), which required citizens to receive permission from the tax authorities to purchase foreign currency and placed a cap on the purchased amount. This effectively precluded the
middle class from protecting their savings against inflation by converting them
to dollars and contributed to their support for the conservative opposition in the
subsequent presidential election (Steinberg and Schiumerini 2020).

The FVP's fiscal policy centered on agricultural export duties. These are
legislated by decree and are the only federal tax revenue that is not shared with
subnational governments (OECD 2019, 76). After the 2001 economic crisis,
Kirchner's predecessor raised taxes on commodities to curve the devaluation's
inflationary effects and provide fiscal resources to contain social unrest. The
2002 Economic Emergency Law created an export tax on hydrocarbons, later
expanded to a 20% tax on all grains and soy derivatives. Toward the end of his
tenure, Kirchner increased these taxes to 32–35% for soy and its derivatives, and
25–28% for grains. In 2008, Fernández de Kirchner introduced a variable export tax where the rate would be proportional to the commodity's international
price. At the time of its introduction, the decree raised export taxes on soybeans
from 35 to 45%, and could reach up to 60%.

These export taxes had strong redistributive effects from rural to urban areas.
When introduced by Kirchner's predecessor, these fiscal resources were used
to finance a cash-transfer program for unemployed individuals. "Export duties
cannot be a permanent fiscal resource," argued the president of the Argentine
Rural Society, "This is part of our legitimate profits; it belongs to us. Let's remember that a cow, in addition to being milked, must be fed."[6] Yet commodity
taxes were necessary for the Left's redistribution toward the urban sector. Alberto

Fernández, Kirchner's first Chief of Staff and later elected president, noted: "We had to extinguish the fire, and the only way we could do it was by providing social assistance, and the only money we had to do it came from the taxes on [the exports of] soybeans" (quoted in Richardson 2012, 28).

Industrial business leaders with ties to the government publicly recognized that taxes on commodities were necessary for maintaining fiscal surpluses and macroeconomic stability. The fiscal resources obtained during the commodity boom had heavily favored them. The foreign exchange earnings of commodity exporters captured by the government had allowed the industrial sector to import capital goods (Rivera-Quiñones 2014, 75).

Argentina—GM Defense—Round Three

The 2008 tax hike however, faced strong opposition from agribusiness. The reaction of agricultural elites to the introduction of the tax in 2002 was muted: a combination of rising international commodity prices, a preexisting low tax rate, and the deep economic crisis that Argentina faced (Reca 2008). But their militancy against the tax hikes grew over time as they began to view the commodity taxes as an "illegal expropriation" of their "legitimate earnings." The main agricultural business organized protests and blockades from March until July 2008, which closed public transportation and generated food shortages. In response to mounting tensions, Fernández de Kirchner put the resolution to a vote in Congress. While the tax hike passed in the Chamber of Deputies with a small margin, the vote tied in the Senate, and the vice president (from a commodity-producing province) broke the tie by voting against the tax.

The political victory of agricultural producers was surprising. Since the return to democracy, rural elites had neglected to build political influence. The sector was divided into four different business associations according to property size, and were often in open conflict with each other. Each organization had declining memberships, small budgets, and limited personnel dedicated to lobbying for public policies (Richardson 2012, 44). However, the reaction of agricultural organizations to the 2008 tax hike also showed that when fundamental interests were at stake, they could organize to defeat a fundamental challenge to the commodity-led GM (Fairfield 2011).

The FVP was aware of the latent power of agricultural elites and sought to counter it in several ways. First, they were deliberately marginalized from policymaking. Prior to the 2008 fiscal conflict, rural associations were not consulted over policies that affected their interests and little accommodation was made to their preferences. The commodity tax hikes were not even discussed with agricultural business organizations prior to their enactment.[7] After the above-mentioned fiscal conflict, Fernández de Kirchner stripped away the powers of the Ministry of Agriculture, which was perceived as having ties to agricultural interests.[8]

Second, the FVP implemented policies that directly affected agricultural profits. Despite its inability to increase export taxes, the government held them at a sizable 35% for the rest of their term. Even after the mid-term election when the FPV lost its congressional majority, it used its sizable voting bloc to obstruct policies favorable to agricultural interests, including reducing export taxes.[9] Third, the government pursued a divide-and-conquer strategy towards rural business associations to reduce their instrumental power. It refused to meet with the main agricultural organizations jointly, insisting on individual meetings.[10] It also attempted to co-opt associations representing smaller producers by offering tax reimbursements to their members and punished the largest organizations by revoking their prerogative to regulate grain commerce (Richardson 2012, 71–72).

Lastly, the government relied on its urban coalition to counterbalance agricultural interests. The government made commodity taxation a political rallying cry for its allies. In a televised address defending her tax hike, Fernández de Kirchner declared that "It is impossible to attack the problem of the poor without distribution of revenue and without touching extraordinary profits" and lamented "the reaction of some who refuse to contribute in the redistribution" to "those who have least."[11] The president also made an effort to frame the actions of the agricultural sector as "protests of abundance" carried out by the "sector with the greatest profitability."[12] Meanwhile, the government further relied on the mobilization of labor outsiders and insiders to strengthen the urban-rural cleavage. Union and social movements leaders "decried the "rural oligarchy" for its aspirations to overthrow the democratically elected government" in rallies organized by the government (Richardson 2012).

These strategies were largely effective in keeping the power of agricultural elites in check. By the end of the FPV's tenure, and contrary to what the fiscal conflict suggested, the agriculture sector remained divided and sidelined from policymaking. But the Argentine Left paid a high political cost for implementing these policies. Divisions within Peronism emerged, as subnational leaders representing large rural interests distanced themselves from the FPV (Etchmendy and Garay 2011, 292). Municipalities reliant on soy production decreased their electoral support for the FPV and contributed to the election of a conservative challenger (Mangonnet et al. 2018). The subsequent Macri administration (2015–2019) did not share the goal of shifting the GM, leaving the structural transformation project once again truncated.

Brazil—GM Switching—Round Three

The PT governments led by Da Silva (2003–2011) and Rousseff (2011–2016) came to power firmly committed to transforming the Brazilian GM (Hunter 2010; Ban 2012; Sierra 2015). However, the PT largely avoided macroeconomic, fiscal, and political strategies that affected rural interests. The PT inherited an appreciated exchange rate from the prior period of market reforms. In the 1990s, the Cardoso administration (1995–2002) adopted a "macroeconomic tripod" that contained a floating exchange rate combined with inflation and primary surplus targets (Bresser-Pereira 2015). This tripod necessitated a high real interest rate and an overvalued currency that was supported by the country's financial sector while opposed by its tradable sectors (Bresser-Pereira 2015, 124). Cardoso's macroeconomic policies were successful at curtailing inflation, but investor confidence in the *Real* was affected by the series of financial crises in other emerging markets. This led Cardoso to devaluate the currency in 1999, and the tradables sector to enjoy a more competitive exchange rate.

Da Silva continued the macroeconomic policies of his predecessor, now in the context of an incipient commodity boom that strengthened the Brazilian real through the influx of foreign currency. In addition, the country became a target for short-term financial flows largely transmitted through the foreign exchange derivatives market that placed upward pressure on the real (Gallagher and Magalhães Prates 2014). The Da Silva administration refrained from intervening in currency markets, arguing that the maintenance of the macroeconomic tripod was justified by the need to avoid capital flight, stimulate capital inflows, and control domestic prices.

In this initial stage of switching the GM, tensions over macroeconomic policy were subdued. The PT benefited from a high growth rate anchored in improved terms of trade and the lingering effects of Cardoso's devaluation, which provided a competitive exchange rate for the first half of Da Silva's presidency (Bresser Pereira 2015, 126). In turn, social and labor policy combined large increases in the minimum wage (52% in real terms) that favored formal workers and a new conditional cash transfer, *Bolsa Família*, which favored informal workers. This expanded internal market, whose effects were felt in the second Lula administration, was beneficial to Brazilian manufacturing.

Rousseff assumed office in a more challenging context when distributive tensions emerged (Gallagher and Magalhães Prates 2014). Unlike Da Silva, Rousseff's presidency coincided entirely with an overvalued real. The average exchange rate went from R$3.08 per dollar when Da Silva came to power in 2003 to R$1.90 per dollar when Rousseff assumed office. While deindustrialization was present in the Lula administration, it accelerated under Rousseff, once again embedding debates about the exchange rates in larger discussions about the winners and losers of commodity GMs during a boom period. Specifically, the rise in commodity prices coupled with appreciated exchange rates generated an asymmetric trade shock. While agro-exporting municipalities increased their exports, employment levels, and wages, industrial municipalities experienced an opposite effect (Costa et al. 2016). Automakers, leather, and textiles were hit particularly hard (Jenkins 2015).

Overvaluation strained the PT coalition. The urban sector pressured the government to reign in currency appreciation. The major industrial business associations, the National Confederation of Industry (CNI) and the Federation of Industries of São Paulo (FIESP), argued that a weaker real would save exports and avoid layoffs.[13] Furthermore, Brazilian industry enjoyed access to real-denominated debt provided by the state-owned Brazilian National Economic and Social Development Bank under favorable terms (subsidized interest rates and long-term repayment horizons). Across issue areas, they had interest in a weaker real (Gallagher and Magalhães Prates 2014).

Workers in the export industrial sector supported these claims. These workers are not only among the most organized in Brazil, but they were also central to the PT coalition, and they were heavily affected by job losses due to the waning of industrial competitiveness once the macroeconomic dimension of the switch dilemma hit. For example, the labor markets in Brazil most affected by Chinese import competition experienced slower growth in wages between 2000 and 2010 due to these currency effects (Costa et al. 2016, 63). As such, the regulation of capital flows and foreign exchange derivatives to achieve exchange rate depreciation "became part of a broader job security package and had strong backing from workers" (Gallagher 2014).

Agricultural exporters remained largely on the sidelines of this debate. Able to compensate for a less competitive exchange rate with higher commodity prices, they were less affected by currency appreciation than industrial export and import-competing industries. In addition, Brazilian agribusiness held cross-cutting interests. They were also engaged in a capital-intensive agriculture, which imported substantial amounts of inputs from abroad that were more accessible with a strong real (Klein and Luna 2018).

The urban coalition was moderately successful in pressuring the PT to carry out currency interventions to weaken the real. But by 2013, the commodity boom began to wane and the exchange rate began to depreciate, rapidly. This raised import prices and led inflation past the Central Bank's annual target range. Rousseff, embarking on a re-election campaign, privileged inflation control over other public policy goals (Bresser Pereira 2015, 130), while the Central Bank intervened selling reserves (in the futures market) to avoid depreciation (Bresser-Pereira 2015, 130) thereby reversing most of the capital account regulations and foreign exchange derivatives regulation set a few years earlier (Gallagher and Magalhães Prates 2014).

With regard to fiscal policy the PT did not even try to increase taxes on agricultural exports during the commodity boom. The government continued to rely on a tax base that combined regressive consumption and production taxes (Ban 2012). To the degree that fiscal revenues were collected through international trade in Brazil, this occurred through import taxes, a strategy consistent with an overvalued exchange rate. Import taxes, furthermore, had an inflationary effect for domestic consumers of imported goods. Overall, reductions in inequality under the Workers' Party were obtained through higher growth rates and labor formalization, not fiscal redistribution (Serrano and Summa 2012). Counterintuitively, during the commodity boom the PT government provided net subsidies to the rural sector: transfers from consumers to agricultural producers represented 0.7% of Brazil's annual GDP (Fernández Milmanda 2019b).

Brazil—GM Defense—Round Three

The politics of GM defense were quieter in Brazil than in Argentina, a reflection of the PT's more moderate approach toward policies that could affect the agricultural sector. The PT was a more likely choice than Argentina's FPV for counterbalancing rural power. The reduction of land inequality had been part of the PTs programmatic core (Hunter 2010) and activists from the *Movimento dos Trabalhadores Rurais Sem Terra* (MST-Landless Movement)—a grassroots organization that calls for land reform and occupies public and private land—were part of the PT's historical coalition. But the PT also faced a politically stronger rural sector defending the existing GM.

Since the return to democracy, Brazilian rural elites organized their own *Bancada Ruralista* (Agrarian Caucus) in Congress with representatives from across the country and ideological spectrum (Fernández Milmanda 2019a). The Agrarian Caucus's legislative power peaked under the PT governments. Their caucus went from holding just below 25% of seats in 1995 to over 40% in 2007, doubling the largest political party in Congress (Freytes 2015, 114). In the context of a presidential regime with high party fragmentation, the PT faced the choice of alienating its political base by embracing agricultural interests, or forego constructing a legislative alliance that included the Agrarian Caucus (Sierra and Hochstetler 2017).

Despite its commitment to switching the underlying GM, the PT responded to agricultural interests. First, the PT largely cut ties with the Landless Movement in the lead-up to the 2002 presidential campaign (Hunter 2007). Second, Da Silva and Rousseff publicly acknowledged the contribution of agricultural producers to Brazil's trade balance and macroeconomic stability providing them with social legitimacy, going so far as to appoint Roberto Rodrigues, president of the *Associaçao Brasileira de Agrónegocio* (Brazilian Agribusiness Associations) to head the Ministry of Agriculture. Lastly, the PT used the state's control over domestic credit and investment to favor agricultural interests. The government granted debt rollovers to the sector and loans and equity investments through the BNDES (Sierra 2015; Sierra and Hochstetler 2017).

The PTs moderate stance toward agricultural interests was not reflected in other commodity sectors. Da Silva increased the role of the state in mining and petroleum, which largely affected international, but not domestic, commodity interests. After the discovery of significant oil reserves in the Bacia do Santos basin, Da Silva changed the hydrocarbon regulatory framework providing state-owned Petrobras a monopoly for extracting hydrocarbons from the new fields and demanding that foreign companies follow local content provisions. The legal change was unsuccessfully opposed by international oil corporations operating in Brazil (Freytes 2015, 72). This suggests that the PT's stance, rather than reflecting ideological moderation, was a response to the power held by agricultural elites under the existing GM.

Conclusions

This chapter sheds light on why the attempts by Latin American governments to switch from a commodity-driven GM to a balanced GM have largely failed. It argues that a key obstacle to structural transformation in Latin America is an endogenous dilemma whereby governments must navigate the tension between policies that sustain the existing GM and those that allow for its structural transformation.

This argument makes several contributions to our understanding of the conditions under which GMs can change. First, it provides a template for understanding the obstacles that governments face when attempting to switch GMs that are generalizable beyond Latin America and the specificities of commodity-driven GMs. When governments attempt to carry out GM switches, they must navigate the distributional tensions involved in compensating the losers of the switch while at the same time providing incentives to the potential winners of the switch. Identifying these losers and winners, and how policies must often be designed to address their interests simultaneously, can shed light on the conditions under which GM switching may succeed.

Second, it stresses that constraints on GM switching may be both external and internal. Existing scholarship has rightly pointed to external constraints on structural transformation, including declining terms of trade, conditionalities tied to foreign loans, and limited spillovers from FDI (Prebisch 1962; Amsden 2001; Rodrik 2004; Ocampo and Ros 2011). This conclusion is also likely influenced by the fact that, in the historical examples of successful GM switching (such as the East Asian Tigers), distributive conflict had not been activated prior to the attempt to switch. But most governments attempting to switch GMs are likely to face societal actors in a better position to block reforms, demand compensations, and secure new benefits. These internal dynamics place strong limits on structural change.

Focusing on endogenous constraints can also help address important empirical puzzles regarding the developmental trajectories of commodity producers. First, episodes of commodity booms, when external constraints are relaxed, tend to increase inequality (Prados de la Escosura 2007; Bértola and Ocampo 2012; Bhattacharyya and Williamson 2016). This chapter suggests that this occurs because such booms empower economic actors tied to the commodity-driven GM, making the redistribution of wealth more difficult. Second, while the Latin American New Left fared better than other governments in its ability to improve income distribution during a commodity boom, the wealth of the top deciles remained untouched (Sánchez-Ancochea 2019). Attention to the endogenous constraints built into GM switching can explain why the obstacles faced by the New Left had such historical echoes, and why the underlying commodity-driven GM was never deeply challenged.

Notes

For fruitful discussions and feedback, I am grateful to Mark Blyth and Luis Schiumerini, and to the participants of the New Politics of Growth and Stagnation Workshop (Cologne, January 2020).

This is defined as a growing share of natural resource goods in the export basket.

1. Although it is a simplification to state that all rural and urban actors have identical interests, I follow Lipton 1977; Wallace 2014; and Thomson 2019 in assuming that urban and rural actors have distinct interests that are politically consequential.
2. While urban labor could benefit from a strong currency that expands their consumption of foreign imports, research on attitudes towards exchange rates show that concerns over employment levels prevail (Broz et al. 2008).
3. Right populists who appeal to non-redistributive issues (i.e., nationalism, nativism, or security) pursue similar policies.
4. This overview speaks mainly to the experiences of countries that underwent strong "switching" attempts— Argentina, Brazil, Chile, Mexico, and Uruguay—and leaves relevant variations across these cases unaccounted for.
5. Jueguen, Francisco. 2016. "Precios Cuidados tiene un 75% de imagen positiva," *La Nación*. January 7.
6. *La Nación*. 2004. "Economías regionales. Reclamos por la eliminación de las retenciones al agro." August 23.
7. Longoni, Matías. 2012. "La Mesa de Enlace pide un espacio para discutir retenciones y sequía," *Clarín*. March 8.
8. Crettaz, José. 2008 "Un nuevo secretario para un organismo desmantelado." *La Nación*. July 21.

9. Bravo, Martín.2011. "Diputados: caerán los proyectos que más irritan al kirchnerismo," *Clarín*. November 9.
10. Sociedad Rural de Río Cuarto. 2013. "El campo ratificó que no irá por separado a reunirse con Yauhar." February 22.
11. *Clarín*. 2008. "El plan social con fondos de las retenciones contaría con casi US$ 1.300 millones anuales." June 9.
12. *La Nación*. 2008. "De Cristina Kirchner al campo: 'No me voy someter a ninguna extorsión'" March 25.
13. *O Estado de São Paolo*. 2009. "Indústria comemora decisão." October 20.

7

The FDI-Led Growth Models of the East-Central and South-Eastern European Periphery

CORNEL BAN AND DRAGOŞ ADĂSCĂLIŢEI

Introduction

In Europe's political economy the East-Central and South-Eastern European (ECSEE) occupy a distinct niche to their global (mostly Asian) rivals. In this global distribution of capital, these semi-peripheral countries developed a growth model anchored around export growth, with that export being dependent on the decisions and capabilities of the multinational corporations that own most of the industrial core of the region. We think that this is a distinctive growth path, and we call it a dependent export-led growth model. The purpose of this chapter is to unpack its workings and trace its historical roots and situate it in a comparative context. To our knowledge, this is the first attempt to read the political economy of this region through the lenses of the growth model literature.

For context, the short version of this region's developmental story is as follows: proximity to West European manufacturing sites at a time of nearshoring and increasingly short just-in-time production cycles (Csevalvay 2019; Éltető 2019) combined with China and Korea's entry into formerly privileged European industrial niches to enroll the region into their production networks. Local governments' pro-FDI industrial policies and state capacities (Bruszt and Vukov 2017; Medve-Balint and Scepanovic 2020), mostly deregulated labor markets, low corporate tax rates and poor corporate income tax collection (Adascalitei and Guga 2018; Ban 2016), further strengthened the region's lock on relocation plans of a considerable part of low and medium-skilled operations of West European orchestrating firms (Myant 2018b). The weak state capacity of some of these state compounded the difficulties (Vukov 2020). In the process, the ECSEE region converged on a growth model that for all its internal variation was of a solidly export-led kind. In many ways, today most of these economies are to German manufacturing what Mexico is to US-based manufacturing. The only exception is that there is freedom of movement for labor into the markets where the firms orchestrating the GVCs that operate in the region reside.

This chapter deploys both IPE (Blyth and Matthijs 2018; Blyth and Schwartz, forthcoming; Farrell and Newman 2014, 2016, 2019) and CPE perspectives (Bacarro and Pontusson 2016; forthcoming) on growth models in order to identify the specific mechanisms that power the FDI-led growth model. It also seeks to map out the possibilities for changes within the growth model following shifts in some of those mechanisms. Our argument is three-fold. First, the rise of Asian competition to the European export complex pressured the latter to remain price competitive in manufacturing via wage moderation at home and expansion in the near ECSEE abroad, with the former outcome extracted through and/or aided by the relocation of low- and medium-skill industrial capacity in this region.

Furthermore, with financialization, during the 1990s and 2000s American deregulatory and competitive pressure was applied on Europe's bank-based financial system (Goodheart and Schoenmaker 2016), leading the latter to extract higher yields from lending to Southern Europe (Blyth 2013), boost revenues from absorbing much of the CESEE financial systems and engage in risky financial activities there (Drakos et al. 2016; Allen et al. 2017).

Second, these international economic and political factors fit neatly with the CPE of the region and particularly its demand for investment and consumption. Thus, the decapitalization of many socialist era SOEs (in part via extremely hawkish monetary policy according to Gabor 2012, 2010a) and the scarcity of private local capital crashed investment amid runaway unemployment and put pressure on the budget deficit and the current account balance. In addition, the brand of neoliberal economics that structured the East European transition had eviscerated the possibilities of a socially embedded neo-developmentalist path (Ban 2016) that could have balanced the new imperative of global competitiveness with democratic demands for protection against the vagaries of the market mechanism (Bohle and Greskovits 2012).

Furthermore, since the domestic capital created by privatizations and regulatory rents was, on the whole, unable to compete internationally, starting with the late 1990s the East Europeans responded to these external dynamics by competing with each other for institutionalizing an economic growth model that relied heavily on FDI. But since this entailed, at least initially, keeping wages low amid growing disappointment with the results of the transition to capitalism, the FDI-led growth model replaced wage growth with credit-based consumption facilitated by the privatization of domestic banking systems to West European-owned ones, with bank ownership averaging 80% (Grittersova 2017). These banks relied heavily on external financing before the crisis and thanks to lower interest rates and the ease of forex lending, households in the region accumulated large debts to purchase homes or consumer durables (Bohle and Greskovits 2012; Becker and Jäger 2010). In this way, the growth model was welded together by a growth coalition bringing together foreign capital, the domestic capital that benefited from the former's relocation to the region and workers (especially workers with median incomes from the tradable sectors).

The combination of export and consumption growth oiled by FDI enabled the region to grow above Asia's already remarkable standards, arrest deindustrialization and gradually increase the value added of its exports. However, FDI in banking proved to be more of a source of systemic vulnerabilities, from the underfunding of domestic business to acting as a transmission belt for financial shocks in the "mother" countries and, in some cases, to balancing out payments crises and spiraling public debt (Gabor 2010a; Bohle and Greskovits 2012; Blyth 2013; Ban 2016).

As a result, the consumption convergence was arrested and (temporarily) reversed through austerity and structural reforms imposed by the East European version of the Troika in the bailout countries (Hungary, Romania, Latvia) and the competitive pressures that accompanied them in "non- program" countries (Piroska 2017; Lütz and Kranke 2014). As private sector wages began to fall, the East European economies became even more export reliant, thus cementing the growth model, except that this time around the credit crunch weakened the growth coalition underpinning it in political terms. To top it off, the very openness of the growth model became problematic, as it became clear that it cuts both ways: capital from core countries could move Eastward based on promises of wage moderation but workers from the East could also move Westward unsatisfied by the consequences of a shrinking wage share that had in turn been caused by the consolidation of the FDI-led growth model.

The result was growing pressure to increase wages as the bailouts and the recession began to wane (Ban 2019). Indeed, once the recovery cycle kicked in from 2015 to 2017, governments used the gaping space between slow wage growth and fast productivity growth to push up wages and consumption far above the Eurozone average. This welded back together the supporting growth coalition disrupted by the Great Recession, except that this time debt-financed consumption was less important. However, rather than count as paradigmatic change, these developments are best interpreted as a mere calibration within the FDI-led growth model. For all the "nationalist" rhetoric spreading in some Eastern countries, its fundamentals remain in place and are preset to prevent convergence with "core" Europe and lock in a middle-income trap instead. In short, our chapter supports the claim made by Blyth and Schwartz that "unit-level variables may well be brought into play and activated by system-level mechanisms."

Synthesizing IPE and CPE

Our analytical point of departure is located in IPE territory and is represented by an adaptation of the New Interdependence Approach (NIA) to growth model dynamics (Farrell and Newman 2014, 2016, 2019) and of Macroeconomic Regime Theory (Blyth and Matthijs 2017) at the international level. The aim of NIA is to emphasize "a systemic account of world politics . . . where overlapping jurisdictions . . . emerge from [rule] overlap [to] create new opportunity structures for actors" (Farrell and Newman 2016, 716). In this view, globalization created a world of overlapping rules and novel jurisdictions where policy is no longer bound by the nation-state, with control of key institutions at the level of the system being the key source of asymmetric power in political economy.

More recently, these authors embedded the NIA approach into a more network analytic perspective at the level of the international system, which enables them to focus on its hierarchical nature and specifically on critical nodes of private and public power in the global network-architecture of regulation and access to the financial and informational flows constituting the system. The more central one is in such networks, the higher the returns one receives from the system, something akin to "weaponized interdependence" (Farrell and Newman 2019). In other words, when we dig out the mechanisms of the prevailing growth model in the CEECs, this approach focuses our analytical attention onto the differential rates of return (rates versus dregs) that specific actors get from the deployment of the structural privileges attached to network centrality.

Ideas such as differential gains from globalization or that the fortunes of regions and countries are shaped by wider international relations of control and (inter)dependence should not be seen as the exclusive province of NIA. For almost 20 years, the rich political economy literature on Global Value Chains (GVCs) and Global Production Networks (GPNs) made the case that in open economies the dynamics of manufacturing and tradable service firms or wages depends on the integration of domestic firms (be it domestically owned or not) into GVCs and the extent to which the leading firms in the chains/networks extract concessions/rents (Hamilton and Gereffi 2009; Gibbon and Ponte 2008). The main implication of the focus on GVCs and GPNs and how they change over time is that local resource endowments, human capital, institutions, geography, and economic policy paradigms are no longer the main factors of development.

What distinguishes the NIA approach is that it nudges scholars to identify the state(s) that benefit the most as a result of the GVC/GPN organization and therefore trace not just the economics of its leading firms, but also the international political power of the state in question. Indeed, even the more Polanyian GPN perspective, which takes the political, institutional, and territorial determinants of the embeddedness of global production networks seriously (Coe et al. 2008) tends to recoil from focusing on who the ultimate beneficiary states are. Closer to home, the East European growth model is heavily dependent on GVCs organized around West European orchestrating firms, most of them belonging to the German manufacturing complex.

Thanks to the capacity of its firms to specialize in activities with ever higher barriers to entry, Germany extracted prime rents from this regime. Moreover, scholarship on the European crisis management disagrees on a lot but not on the fact that Germany is a key player in European economic governance (Matthijs and Blyth 2015; Schelkle 2017). Given this consensus and the fact that Germany is the main direct investor in the region, the crisis management regime cannot be divorced from the interests of German firms enjoying structural power in the European export complex.

Going "down" at the unit level, these external constraints can be modulated by domestic factors. Baccaro and Pontusson's (2016) supply side and macroeconomically centric analytical framework identifies the space for multiple growth models based on the relative importance of different components of aggregate demand (such as exports and household consumption) and relations among components of aggregate demand. Their emphasis on exports and external competitiveness builds on the CPE literature of the 1980s and 1990s but adds a critical Kaleckian layer to it by unearthing the forgotten importance of distributive struggles.

By looking at four EU 15 economies (Sweden, Germany, United Kingdom, and Italy) during the 1990s and 2000s, they found that the engine of their Fordist model of wage-led growth stalled, with productivity growth no longer feeding into household consumption and investment due to the erosion of strong collective bargaining institutions. As a result, they sought post-Fordist growth regimes to replace the faltering wage-led growth: wage and household debt increases in the United Kingdom, export-led growth in Germany based on price elastic goods, and a combination of exports of price-inelastic goods and consumption growth in Sweden. In contrast, Italy's stagnation is traced to the sluggish growth of both these domains. Each of these post-Fordist growth regimes have distinct drivers. Sweden's balanced growth model was powered by this country's capacity to compete through knowledge-intensive, high-value-added exports of goods and services. In contrast, Germany's adjustment was one based on the expansion of low-wage employment in private services. In contrast, consumption-led growth in the United Kingdom and Sweden was fueled by labor-market conditions favorable to unskilled (service-sector) workers.

Taken to Eastern Europe's internal economic diversity captured by the existing scholarship (Bohle and Greskovits 2012; Eihmanis 2018; Scepanovic and Bohle 2018; Ban 2019; Bruszt and Karas 2020; Ban et al 2021; Oellerich 2021; Naczyk 2021; Scheiring 2021), these insights would lead us to expect some variation in how the FDI-led growth model is domestically articulated based on the structural endowments of these economies. Specifically, we expect stronger attempts to balance consumption and exports in populous countries with large domestic markets (Poland, Romania), strict emphasis on manufacturing exports in small open economies with a manufacturing tradition/strategy (Czechia, Slovakia, Slovenia, Hungary), and strict emphasis on service exports in small open economies without a manufacturing tradition/strategy (the Baltics, Croatia). However, we do not hold a mechanistic view of how these structural constraints operate and/or path-dependently shape the life of the growth model. Instead, as the next section shows, we propose a theory of change and stability based on a dynamic view of the economics and politics that regulate it.

Explaining Change and Stability

The approaches synthesized in the previous section are both pessimistic about the likelihood of regime change while undertheorizing regime calibrations. To explain regime change, Macroeconomic Regime (MRT) Theory focuses on price shocks. For Blyth and Matthijs (2017), the key driver of the Gestalt flip from Fordist wage-led regimes—where the policy target was full employment—to specialized profit-led regimes—where price-stability became the key policy target, and the restoration of profits became the key concern of elites—was a Kaleckian stand-off between investors and workers over the effects of inflation on profits and on future investment at the level of the system as a whole. Specifically, the tight coupling of the wage-led regime demanded global compromises around securing a stable supply of raw materials, particularly oil at predictable prices. Or, this stability was disrupted by the spread of Fordism, which in turn applied a shock in the "home" of Fordism's tightly coupled production systems. In other words a growth model changes when its growth driver becomes so internally entrained and externally shocked that it can no longer fine-tune its endogenous socioeconomic contradictions.

We pursue this hypothesis in the case of the FDI-led growth model by focusing on the shock of the 2008 crisis and the entrained labor market of the transnationalized manufacturing export sector. Building on research done in economic geography, we expect that this entrainment was represented by the tendency of massive FDI inflows in labor-intensive manufacturing of the kind we see in CESEE to deplete the labor surplus, push up wages, decrease the rate of profit, and eventually compel firms to look for new spatial fixes to address their search for excess profit opportunities (Freyssenet and Lung 2000; Pavlinek 2020).

Indeed, while the conventional growth regime approach presumes demographic stability, the supply shock represented by the fact that the ECSEE periphery mass emigration reduced between a fifth and a tenth of the workforce (most likely on a permanent basis) is highly consequential from the point of view of the need to calibrate growth model theory (Atoyan et al. 2016). To more directly translate this into the ECSEE context, we suggest that the tight coupling of the region's FDI-led growth model entailed the need for stable prices, stable access to low- and medium-skilled labor, and a stable income policy in which wages grew below or at least in sync with productivity.

Forging the FDI-Led Growth Models of ECSEE: The Helicopter View

During the 1990s and 2000s the rising Asian competition incentivized German firms to organize production fragmentation and relocate low- and middle-skill production Eastward to defend its competitiveness. This process had a world historical importance for economic development in the ECSEE region. Theory tells that growth in low- and middle-income countries is driven either by finance (tax and regulatory havens like Singapore or Latvia) or manufacturing (like China, Mexico, and Korea, most of the NMS do the latter). In development economics, Dani Rodrik (2016) found that manufacturing decline in low- and middle-income countries is a structural change that has ended up being growth reducing in these countries. Avoiding premature deindustrialization is important also because as manufacturing shrinks, informality grows and, as a result of the labor force moving into services, the economy-wide productivity figures and, with them, the chances of claims to higher wages being met are set to suffer. Seen from a macro perspective, the ECSEE countries are a resounding success as exporters. When combined with geography and the growing importance of just-in-time production within European supply chains, this growth model placed the region on a path that avoided the common deindustrialization pathway of other emerging market economies that did not benefit from the unique geopolitical and institutional advantages of East Asia.

As Figure 7.1 shows, by the 2000s, manufacturing value added in GDP stabilized close or above German levels (with the notable exception of the Baltics, where manufacturing petered out in GDP in the same fashion it did in Ukraine or Brazil). The contrast with the traditional US "hinterland" (Latin America) and the fate of manufacturing in former communist countries outside the EU could not be more obvious and underscores the importance of

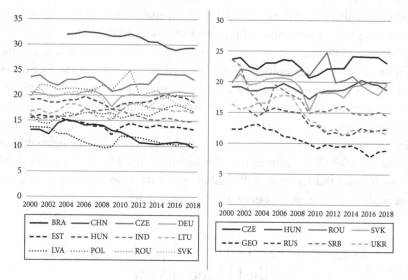

Figure 7.1 Manufacturing value added as a percentage of GDP. Source: AMECO database

the region's proximity to core European capitalism. Virtually every European Semester and IMF Article IV report indicates that exports of manufactures have been the main drivers of growth for the East-Central European region. This cross-regional comparison also begs for the insertion of the NMS in Rodrik's finding that "the sizable shift in global manufacturing activity in recent decades toward East Asia, and China in particular, with both Latin America and sub-Saharan Africa among the developing regions as the losers" (Rodrik 2016, 16).

Critically, this seems to be the case almost everywhere in the region. As Figure 7.2 shows, reliance on exports is particularly dramatic not only in the region's small open economies (whose export reliance is exceeded in the EU only by Ireland), but also in Poland and Romania, where exports are roughly as big as a share of GDP as Germany's. While in the early 1990s only former Czechoslovakia and Hungary could boast a share of exports in GDP close to Germany, 30 years later they were joined by Poland, Slovenia, and Bulgaria in increasing the share of exports in GDP above German levels, in some cases nearly doubling it. By comparison, Katzenstein's OECD small states in world markets seem either mediocre (Austria) or barely defending their laurels (Sweden). Indeed, the small open economies of Slovakia, Hungary, Estonia, Lithuania, Slovenia, and Czechia grew to have over 80% of GDP from exports (up from less than half in the early 1990s).

Also, while Romania and Poland had a similar share of exports in GDP with Southern Europe in the 1990s, around 2001 Poland broke off to become more

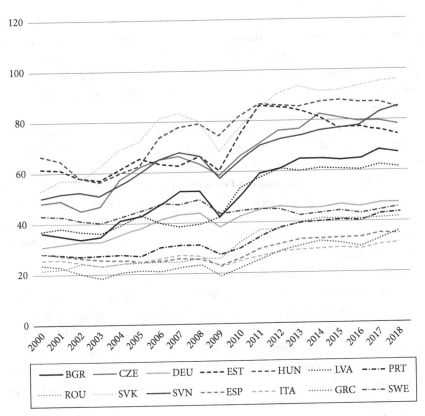

Figure 7.2 Exports of goods and services as a share of GDP. Source: authors' calculation based on World Bank WDI database

export reliant than Germany today. Around 2002 Romania followed the same path, growing to have a share of exports in GDP that was close to Sweden and, since the mid-2000s, by far outstripping those of Southern Europe and the United Kingdom. The finding challenges the intuitive conjecture that given their large domestic markets, Poland and Romania should be closer to the Southern European/UK consumption-led model rather than to Germany's export-led one. Furthermore, it may point at one of the reasons why manufacturing-based exports in Southern Europe contracted. Also, the shrinking of FDI inflows after 2008 and the plugging of the gaps with EU funds to the tune of 3 to 5% of GDP (Bohle 2018) was associated with robust export growth, with plateauing effects recorded only as of late.

   To make this more concrete, take the example of the geographic restructuring of the European automotive industry (the main export of most ECSEE economies) between 2005 and 2016, a period when average personnel costs per employee were five to eight times higher in Germany than in the ECSEE, while wage-adjusted labor productivity was between 40 and 60% higher in the region than in Germany. Combined with 50–70% higher tax rates in Germany, decentralized labor relations, EU-funded infrastructure improvements and a pro-FDI institutional environment, ECSEE played a critical role in addressing the declining profitability of Germany's or France's automotive sector (Pavlinek 2020).

The 2009 to 2012 crisis with the attending austerity period contracted European demand and increased surge of demand from extra-EU markets, where exports increased from 23% in 1999 to 37% in 2015, with finished cars as the main source of German (and generally European) exports. Germany accounts for 42% of regional sector production and this relocation made ECSEE have automotive-dominated export structures despite not being home to any headquarters. As a result of this shift, imports from outside the EU have been cut to a negligible weight.

In this regard Germany's dominant status is clear and keeping in line with the new economic interdependence hypothesis. In ECSEE and Europe as a whole, Germany is the only country with dominant trade relations in the regional automotive network in the sense that it engages in trade with a majority of the Member States. Even though France increased its relations of dominance, it does not come close to Germany's position. Since the crisis, both Spain and Italy, the only other countries with their own major auto groups, continued to shed relations with two dozen countries. Despite the emergence of East European countries as producers since the global financial crisis (their exports of such goods increased between 50% in the case of Slovakia and 80% in the case of the Czech Republic), Germany remains unchallenged as the top supplier of finished goods. Yet without ECSEE the German export performance since the crisis would be harder to imagine: the increase of high value-added finished cars was achieved by increasing imports of parts and components of ECSEE origin (Gracia and Paz 2017).

The spatial relocation of Western complex manufacturing toward the East is also evident when analyzing how the region has integrated into automotive GVCs. Figures 7.3–7.6 below show that the region has become gradually more integrated into automotive GVCs, with participation peaking in the aftermath of the crisis. Interestingly, integration was cemented through the development of backward linkages which measure the importance of foreign value added in the export of domestic goods. In other words, not only that the 2000s saw the emergence of ECSEE as the West's backyard workshop that gradually overtook Southern Europe in this regard, but also its establishment as a vital source of demand for Western intermediary goods.

All this did not come with the contraction of consumption. As Table 7.1 shows, on an annual basis the ECSEE countries had both exports and consumption

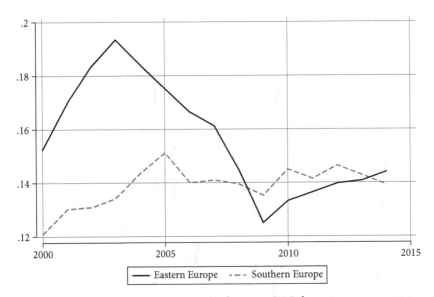

Figure 7.3 Participation in automotive manufacturing GVCs by region. Source: WIOD dataset CBDS Working Paper 2020/2 17

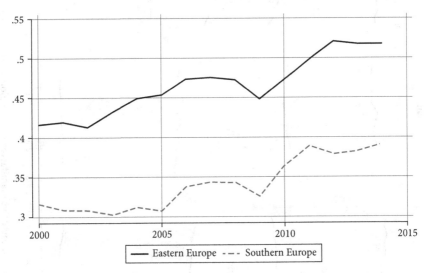

Figure 7.4 Forward linkages in automotive manufacturing by region. Source: WIOD dataset

figures above the EU average, with only two countries (Bulgaria and Estonia) having higher rates of consumption than of exports and Romania and Lithuania recording double the EU average for both exports and consumption growth.

As instructive as they can be, such macro views can be rather misleading for field maps. This is what the growth model approach in CPE is for and particularly

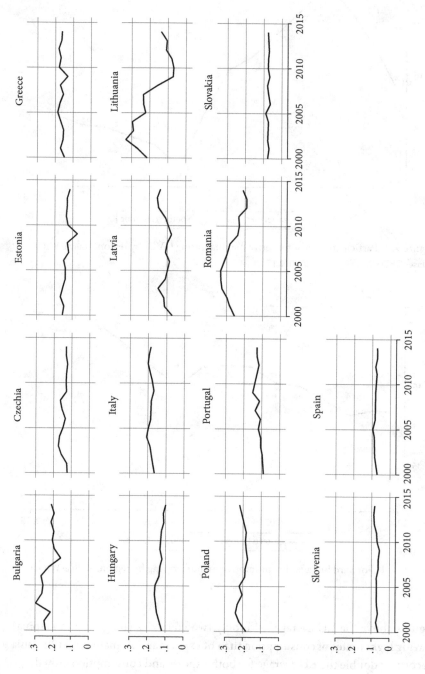

Figure 7.5 Backward linkages in automotive manufacturing by region. Source: WIOD dataset

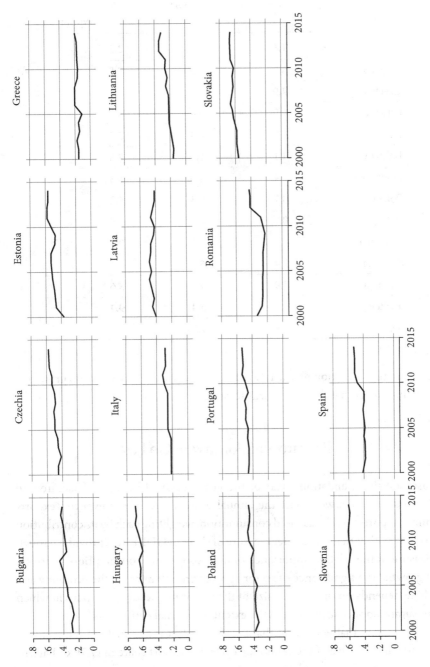

Figure 7.6 Forward linkages in automotive manufacturing by country. Source: WIOD dataset

Table 7.1 **GDP, Exports, and Consumption Growth Rates: 2000–2018 (Source: Eurostat)**

	GDP	Export	Household Consumption
European Union	1.6	4.6	2.5
Bulgaria	3.7	5.9	7.8
Czechia	2.9	8.4	6.4
Estonia	4.0	6.4	8.0
Latvia	3,9	7.3	7.7
Lithuania	4.1	10.0	8.3
Hungary	2.4	8.6	5.3
Poland	3.7	8.3	6.2
Portugal	0.7	4.6	2.9
Romania	4.0	9.5	**9.7**
Slovenia	2.4	6	3.5
Slovakia	3.9	9.1	8.6
Turkey	5.2	6.4	**9.1**
Serbia	3.3	12.7	5.2

the analytical attention on the ratio of export growth to consumption growth. It is to this aspect that the paper turns to next.

Baccaro and Pontusson Go East

Based on the foundational text of the growth model literature (Baccaro and Pontusson 2016), we report the annual growth rate of net exports (exports minus imports) and household consumption, weighting each by its contribution to GDP (rather than the cruder measure of share of GDP). This provides a rough measure of the relative importance of net exports and consumption as drivers of growth. The significance of sector-specific growth rates for the economy as a whole depends on the relative size of the sector in question, the ways in which consumption was financed, and the extent of external constraints.

The picture that emerges is that the driving factor of growth in the region is exports. Irrespective of the economic cycle, the export share in GDP of Eastern Europe ranges between Germany in Sweden but without ever coming close to Sweden's (let alone the UK's) consumption share. Indeed, none of these countries, not even the ones with large populations and internal markets (Romania and Poland) come close to being considered consumption-led models. Clearly, their insertion into the Great European Export Complex was unaccompanied by the possibility of extensive and permanent social compensation to labor.

Specifically, during debt-financed consumption (2000–2008) all the ECSEE states did much better than the EU average in terms of both export and consumption increases' contribution to output growth. However, as Figure 7.7 shows, while some of them were almost exclusively export reliant, others emphasized consumption a bit more. Thus, the Czech, Slovak, Slovenian, Baltic, and Hungarian economies were considerably more export oriented than the more populous countries (0.4% a year Romania, Poland), with Hungary and Slovakia's contribution of net exports to GDP close to average Swedish and German yearly levels for the 2004–2007 period recorded by Baccaro and Pontusson (around 1% a year). Slovakia and Hungary were the absolute outliers in terms of the export-led growth, while Romania was the outlier in terms of consumption. Although Romania slightly outdid Poland in terms of exports' contribution to growth, its consumption's contribution to growth was three times as large as Poland's. Indeed, the only countries with a solid balance between consumption and exports were Estonia (a medium- and high-end service economy) and Latvia (a financial entrepôt).

Yet if we do a back-to-back comparison with Baccaro and Pontusson's cases, even in the more consumption-oriented Eastern European countries, the yearly contribution of net exports to GDP growth was far above the "classical" cases of consumption-led growth (United Kingom and Italy). Poland and Romania's 0.4% yearly contribution of exports to GDP growth is higher than Italy's best cycles

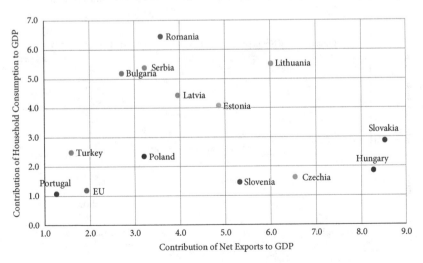

Figure 7.7 Export-led versus consumption-led growth: 2000–2008.

(0.05 and 0.19 respectively) and is far superior to the UK's negative figures, while Czechia, Slovakia and the Baltics average Swedish export performance. Similarly, yearly contribution of consumption to GDP growth met Italian consumption-oriented levels (0.65%) only in the countries pushing the hardest on the consumption pedal (Romania, Lithuania, and Bulgaria) while all the others, including Poland, was close to the German average threshold (0.26%). For all the private debt spike, in none of them did the contribution of consumption to annual GDP growth rise to Swedish (1.44 %) or UK (1.67%) levels. In short, during the 2000 to 2008 growth years, the ECSEE countries as a whole ranged between Sweden and Germany in terms of their export-consumption relations.

The dependent status of these economies (Nolke and Vliegenthart 2009) came to the fore during the Great Recession (2008–2012), when definancialization (Gabor 2010a) narrowed the possibilities of debt-financed household consumption (Ban and Bohle 2019) and deepened export orientation at the expense of consumption. Overall, the effect was growth of net exports in GDP growth at or above the German pre-2008 levels reported by Baccaro and Pontusson and a contraction of the consumption share below all historical precedents for all recession-hit ECSEE countries.

Indeed, as Figure 7.8 shows, all ECSEE countries but Poland (who had not gone through a recession) experienced a contraction in the share of consumption in GDP growth below average EU levels. As one would expect, the fall was particularly sharp in the countries under Troika conditionality (Romania, Hungary, Latvia) or close to this average for the rest, (with Estonia and Lithuania voluntarily shading the policies of Latvia, their Baltic neighbor). Even so, yearly growth in Polish consumption during this period was close to the pre-2008 German recession average (0.6%) and far from Sweden's balanced one (1.46).

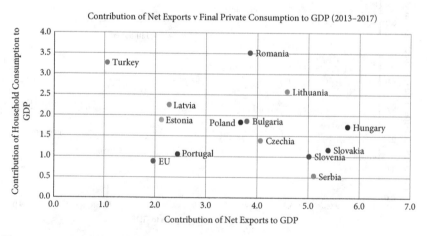

Figure 7.8 Export-led versus consumption-led growth: 2009–2012

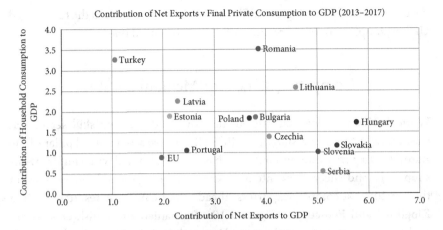

Contribution of Net Exports v Final Private Consumption to GDP (2013–2017)

Figure 7.9 Export-led versus consumption-led growth: 2009–2012

For all ECSEE countries the number was negative, an unprecedented occurrence in all of Baccaro and Pontusson's cases before 2008. As far as exports are concerned, while in consumption-oriented UK and Italy exports had negative growth as a share of GDP growth, in all ECSEE countries the growth rate of exports was positive, ranging from more than double German recession levels in Slovakia and the Czechia (around 1.6%) to recession-time Germany ones in Poland and Romania (around 0.6%).

As hypothesized, the FDI-led growth model felt a tweak after both the recession and policy conditionality came to an end because the entrainment of tight labor markets, the demands of the German export boom, and the low growth of credit eventually put upward pressure on wages. As Figure 7.10 shows, the overall export orientation endogenous to the model deepened: during the recovery cycle (2013–2017), the per annum contribution of exports to GDP growth shot up further still, with above 1% a year growth for almost all countries in the region. Hungary, Slovakia, and Slovenia exceeded the pre-2008 German recovery benchmark, with the "laggards" Estonia and Latvia hovering around the typical pre-2008 Swedish average. The tweak was that consumption recovered strongly in all ECSEE countries, with the strongest growth noted in Romania, Poland, the Baltics, and Bulgaria.

Again, when compared to the classical cases from Western Europe, consumption growth did not disrupt the overall balance of the export-led model, as its contribution to GDP growth ranged between pre-2008 Italian recovery levels (in Romania, Poland, Bulgaria, and the Baltics) to German ones (in Slovakia, Hungary, Czechia, Slovenia). To sum up, the export share in GDP growth ranged between Germany and Sweden while the consumption share ranged between the low German and Italian levels. Indeed, the figure shows that even at the best of times, not a single ECSEE country had come close to the full-fledged UK consumption-oriented regime or Sweden's balanced one.

Competing on Low-to-Medium quality?

While FDI was indeed channeled into low- and medium-skill sectors, at least initially, the conversion of the ECSEE countries as a critical pillar of the European Export Complex could not have been obtained with simple sweat-shop tasks and sheer work intensity. Czechia, Hungary and Slovenia are in the top 20 most complex exporters, ahead of the United States, Italy, United Kingdom, and France (see Figure 7.10). Romanian and Polish exports are in the same league of complexity as Denmark and the Netherlands. Indeed, China's exports are less complex than most East European exports except for Romania whose export complexity profile has grown since 2012 to al-most match that of China. This is a drastic change from the early 1990s, when only former Czechoslovakia and Hungary were in the top.[i] Of course, these complex exports are almost entirely produced within FDI-based corporate infrastructures, yet with the exception of Korea and China, the rest of Asia is extremely dependent on FDI as well. As always, the proof is in the pudding of the least complex exporters. Take the case of Romania, a country whose export profile was closer to the Maghreb in 1999 and who, 30 years later, is

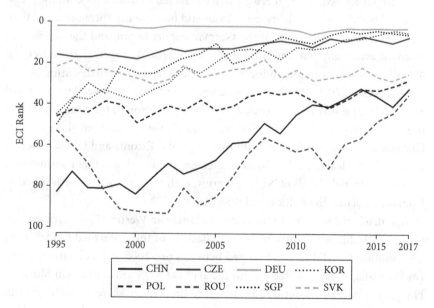

Figure 7.10 Country complexity rankings between 1995 and 2017. Source: MIT Economic Atlas

close to that of Visegrad and the Netherlands. This makes the ECSEE region a kind of unsung developmental success.

While "premature deindustrialization" definitely ravaged Latin America and some of the more industrialized parts of the former USSR (Rodrik 2016), it did not affect most of the ECSEE as much. On average, the dramatic deindustrialization of the 1990s was arrested (albeit not reversed to 1989 levels) only where one became a dependent market economy (Nokle and Vliegenthart 2009). Thirty years after 1989, the combination between (largely European) industrial investment and the region reclaimed its comparative advantages in medium-skilled segments of manufacturing industries and some high-end services such as ITC and medical. Moreover, when it comes to automotive, the main export of many ECSEE countries, their increasing share in the industry came at the expense of the Southern periphery and more traditional industrial centers such as Belgium and the United Kingdom (Gracia and Paz 2017).

Regarding the price elasticity in exports, our estimations in Figure 7.11 confirm the findings of Baccaro and Pontusson (2016) who show that the German exports have increasingly become price sensitive. Beyond this, they are quite surprising given the consensus in the literature that ECSEE countries specialize in lower value-added niches. Indeed, only two countries (Slovenia and Slovakia) confirm to the hypothesis of price sensitivity in exports, with the size of their coefficients comparable to the German level. The exports of the rest of the countries in the region are *not* price sensitive. This may suggest that other factors (e.g.,

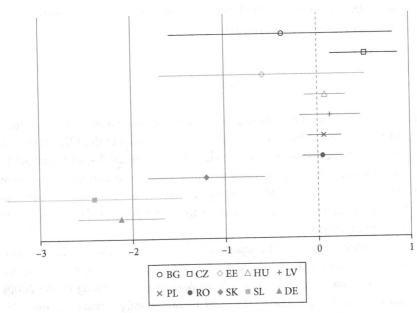

Figure 7.11 Price elasticity of exports (to changes in REER, quarterly data)

institutional environment, regulatory quality) account for the price competitiveness of East European exports (Bierut and Kuziemska-Pawlak 2017).

Our results should be interpreted with caution as they do not say anything
about how exports in different sectors react to exchange rate appreciation.
Therefore, the lack of sensitivity of exports to changes in real effective exchange
rate (REER) might stem from a disaggregation bias as some goods are more price
sensitive than others (Égert and Morales-Zumaquero 2008). Specifically, firms
exporting differentiated goods (for example, complex goods, pharmaceuticals,
etc.) are more capable to offset costs associated with exchange rate fluctuations
by setting prices in their own currency. Furthermore, and central to the ECSEE
export profile, imported intermediary goods can offset the effect of REER appreciation by decreasing production costs. As Figure 7.5 shows, this is certainly the
case in Eastern Europe where the import of intermediary goods from Western
markets is a core feature of the export-led growth model.

The main implication that this finding can have for future research in the
comparative growth model literature is that the price insensitivity of most
ECSEE exports enabled workers in their tradable sectors to extract concessions
on wages despite low levels of unionization and deregulated labor markets. As
the case of Romania's largest exporter (Dacia Renault) suggests (Adascalitei
and Guga 2016), given this export profile, firm-level unions in the most vulnerable parts of the periphery may project greater leverage than the more general
varieties of capitalism literature would lead one to expect. To paraphrase Blyth
and Schwartz, it may be that unit-level variables (firm-level labor union activism
in large GPN nodes) may well be brought into play and activated by system-level
mechanisms (the growth of price insensitive exports).

Conclusions

This chapter discussed the emergence, consolidation, and resilience of a distinct
growth model in Europe: the export-led growth model in the ECSEE region.
Focusing on three distinct business cycles (2000–2008, 2008–2012, and 2012–
2019), it shows that despite marginal shifts toward consumption-led growth
through personal debt (2000–2008) or wage increases (2012–2019), the core
of the region's economic model continues to be heavily and indeed increasingly
dependent on exports.

By combining IPE and CPE analytical frameworks, we showed that the consolidation of the ECSEE export-led model has both systemic and national roots.
Growing international competition from Asia in the beginning of the 2000s
forced firms in Western European (and predominantly German) economies
to seek alternative sources of competitiveness that involved a mix of wage

moderation at home and expansion toward the East. The internationalization of Western firms met capital hungry Eastern economies and states that were all too happy to use FDI to restore the competitiveness of their outdated SOE-dominated sector. Backed by a growth coalition that involved domestic and foreign capital as well as workers in the tradable sectors, the export-led growth model took off and generated growth rates well above those in core countries. The 2000s also saw an increase in debt-fueled consumption, which partially compensated for the lack of wage growth in the region.

The crisis proved to be an opportunity to put an end to this hybridization and reinforce the export-led component of growth through short-term austerity measures and deeper labor market reforms. These changes consolidated the export-led model that remained in place even amid political reconfigurations that, at least rhetorically, aimed to fight the economic dependency of the region on FDI. After the global financial crisis ended, however, the German export boom benefited the region and put upward pressure on wages without the risk of current account deficits. In many ways, the contrast with the austerity-burdened growth models of Southern Europe or the volatile commodity-led models of large parts of the Global South could not be starker. Yet, behind it all looms the question whether this growth formula could survive the imperatives of the green transition, the end of cheap money in the international financial system and the geopolitical turmoil ushered in by the Russian war on Ukraine and the specter of great power confrontation over the international issues as old as the Peloponnesian war.

PART 3

COUNTRY CASE STUDIES

8

Credit-Driven and Consumption-Led Growth Models in the United States and United Kingdom

ALEXANDER REISENBICHLER AND ANDREAS WIEDEMANN

Introduction

In recent decades, advanced industrialized countries have transitioned from Fordist production regimes to knowledge economies (Boix 2019; Hassel and Palier 2021a; Iversen and Soskice 2019). This post-Fordist transition entailed a decline in the wage share of GDP in most advanced economies, which led them to emphasize different aspects of aggregate demand, such as domestic demand and exports (Baccaro and Pontusson 2016; also see the introduction of this volume). This chapter examines advanced economies that have championed domestic demand in the form of debt-financed, consumption-led growth in response to these structural economic shifts. We focus on the United States and the United Kingdom as exemplary cases where household debt and private consumption are key engines of growth, but also sources of economic instability and inequality.

We argue that these economies generate debt-financed consumption through two major mechanisms that we term the *housing channel* and *income-maintenance channel*. The former suggests that rising property prices can unleash both household borrowing and spending. When house prices grow, homeowners' wealth increases along with their propensity to consume, while their growing housing wealth also improves their housing collateral against which they can borrow to finance spending on consumer goods or welfare services. The latter channel posits that credit markets allow households to maintain their socioeconomic status when earnings stagnate, incomes drop, and expenditures rise, particularly in the context of limited or eroding welfare states. Credit markets functionally substitute for wage growth and government transfers, enabling households to borrow money to smooth income losses and address rising expenditures.

Credit-driven, consumption-led growth models do not exist in a political vacuum. They are sustained by powerful political coalitions of producer groups in the financial services industry, asset-owning voters, and mainstream political parties. The key producer group is the so-called FIRE sector (i.e., finance, insurance, and real estate), which directly benefits from increasing financial transactions, the expansion of consumer credit, and growing property markets. In electoral terms, current and aspiring homeowners have an interest in accessible and expanding credit markets. While existing homeowners benefit from political measures that tend to increase home values, aspiring homeowners benefit from easier access to credit. Even poorer voters without much asset wealth increasingly rely on accessible credit markets to both smooth income losses and finance expenditures in light of limited government support. Finally, both center-left and center-right parties tend to favor policies that facilitate greater access to credit as growth strategies to generate consumption and domestic demand, particularly in moments of economic crisis (McCarty, Poole, and Rosenthal 2013; Reisenbichler 2021a).

Policymakers have reinforced credit-driven, consumption-led growth models—and the housing and income-maintenance channels—through fiscal and regulatory policies. One way to stimulate these channels is to adopt fiscal policies that provide tax relief on mortgage and other consumer loans. Another is to rely on regulatory policies that ease access to credit or support household borrowing through government guarantees on consumer debt. Together, these policy choices have created permissive credit regimes (Wiedemann 2021a, b) that improve credit access, reduce borrowing costs for households, and thus stimulate debt-financed consumption.

We examine the foundations and politics of credit-financed consumption by turning to the United States and the United Kingdom as exemplary cases. Both countries have permissive credit regimes that allow households to easily borrow money, build asset ownership, and maintain their living standards in the context of declining wages, rising living costs, and limited public welfare programs. In response to post-Fordist challenges of wage stagnation and fiscal austerity since the late 1970s, broad-based growth coalitions have fueled the housing and income-maintenance channels in order to boost debt-financed consumption. In the United States, policymakers championed fiscal subsidies for consumer debt, government guarantees for mortgages in the primary and secondary markets, and regulatory policies to ease credit access. In the United

Kingdom, politicians privatized the social housing stock, liberalized the financial and mortgage system, and relaxed credit constraints for borrowers.

While these measures have contributed to economic growth, both countries experienced a house price bubble that resulted in the financial crisis of 2008–2009. The crisis exposed the vulnerabilities of growth models that are based on credit and consumption. When the housing bubble burst in both countries, credit markets collapsed and household consumption dropped dramatically (Mian and Sufi 2014). To revive their growth models in the post-crisis years, British and American policymakers again fueled the housing and income-maintenance channels by adopting a battery of fiscal and regulatory measures, while central banks facilitated an ultra-low interest-rate environment and flooded capital markets with money. While the credit and housing markets of both economies recovered after the Great Recession, policies to support credit markets contributed to soaring asset prices in recent years. These developments have created distributional inequalities between the haves and the have-nots, potential financial instability, and housing affordability crises among younger, low-income, and minority households. Together, these factors risk undermining the US and UK growth models.

How Credit-Based Consumption Stimulates Economic Growth

We argue that credit-driven growth models stimulate economic growth through two distinct but related channels. The housing channel operates through real estate markets, in which rising house prices increase homeowners' wealth and loosen their credit constraints, thus boosting household borrowing and consumption. The income-maintenance channel, moreover, works through credit markets that allow households to maintain their living standards in light of stagnating wages, rising expenditures, and weak welfare support. Credit-driven growth models rely heavily on permissive regulatory and fiscal policy environments that make credit easily available to households. Such permissive credit regimes encompass deep financial markets, including capital markets for mortgages and pension assets, and allocate capital and credit disproportionately toward the household sector. Regulatory policies facilitate credit allocation to households by reducing credit risk for lenders, while fiscal policies incentivize household borrowing by subsidizing the costs of loans (Wiedemann 2021a, b).

The Housing Channel

Housing markets are key pillars of credit-driven growth models as they are able to stimulate domestic demand and economic growth (Fuller 2019; Hay 2009, 2011; Oren and Blyth 2019; Reisenbichler 2021a). The property market is an important sector of the economy (e.g., residential investment and construction) and contributes considerably to the business cycle. In the United States, for instance, declines in residential investment (and consumer durables) frequently preceded economic downturns, making it a "consumer cycle not a business cycle" (Leamer 2015, 45). More generally, housing affects the macroeconomy through household borrowing and spending. One core mechanism is that increasing house prices tend to stimulate domestic demand and consumption through wealth and credit effects.

The wealth effect suggests that increasing house prices—and, in turn, housing wealth—increases households' propensity to borrow and consume. As a result, higher housing wealth can directly influence consumption and domestic demand in the economy. As Fuller (2019) notes, gains in housing wealth can partially substitute for savings, as households "tend to save less and spend more, knowing that they have backup savings in the shape of accumulated housing wealth." On the flip side, Mian and Sufi (2014) demonstrate that, when U.S. house prices and wealth fell during the Great Recession, many households were left with unmanageable debt and forced to reduce consumer spending. In the United States, estimates suggest that a one dollar increase in housing wealth stimulates consumer spending by an average of eight cents (Calomiris, Longhofer, and Miles 2012). Similarly for the United States, Case, Quigley, and Shiller (2013) find that a house-price boom (equivalent to the one from 2001–2005 that increased housing wealth by $10tn) would increase consumer spending by 4.3%, while a 35% decline in housing wealth (such as the one from 2005–2009) would produce a 3.5% decrease in consumer spending. Studies on the United Kingdom, too, find positive associations between housing wealth and private consumption (e.g., Campbell and Cocco 2007; Disney et al. 2010).

The related credit effect implies that rising house prices increase borrowing and consumption by raising the value of housing collateral against which homeowners can borrow (Muellbauer and Murphy 2008; Aron et al. 2012). Growing demand for credit is often met by banks' increased willingness to lend due to higher levels of collateral; in turn, enhanced credit availability then translates into higher levels of aggregate demand. For the United Kingdom and the United States, Aron et al. (2012, 418) find that easing credit constraints stimulated consumption as "[f]inancial liberalization has enhanced the positive impact of housing wealth on consumption in the U.K. and U.S." When house prices fall, however, households' decreased net worth constrains their abilities to borrow, which in turn reduces overall lending and spending. Moreover, easier access to credit allows homeowners to use home equity loans to pay for welfare services, consumer goods, home improvements, business expenses, or other consumer debt. Greenspan and Kennedy (2008, 131) estimate that the extraction of US home equity loans amounted to $230bn per year between 2001–2006, which homeowners used for home improvements, personal consumption, paying off consumer debt, or investments in other assets. Similarly, Mian and Sufi (2011) show that US homeowners extracted 25 cents for every dollar in house-price gain from 2002 to 2006. For the United Kingdom, Cloyne et al. (2019, 2134) find that a 10 percent increase in house prices corresponds to an increase of 2–3% in household borrowing through extracting home equity.

The credit and wealth effects work particularly well in permissive credit regimes, such as the United States and the United Kingdom, as opposed to restrictive mortgage regimes in export-oriented Germany or Japan (Wiedemann 2021a). Johnston, Fuller, and Regan (2020) characterize the United States and the United Kingdom as some of the most credit-encouraging mortgage systems among advanced economies, measuring mortgage-interest subsidies, property transfer taxation, loan-to-value ratios, interest-rate restrictions, and the depth of the secondary mortgage market. In both countries, housing finance markets have fairly low transaction costs, low down payments, relatively high numbers of homeownership and turnover, and a variety of mortgage products available to households. While high down-payment constraints in Germany or Japan induce prospective homeowners to increase savings in times of rising house prices, lower down payments in the permissive credit regimes of the United States and the United Kingdom ease the credit restraints of prospective homeowners requiring comparatively lower savings (Muellbauer and Murphy 2008; Aron et al. 2012).

Ultra-low interest rates since the Great Recession and during the Covid-19 pandemic have contributed to surging house prices in the United States and the United Kingdom. Despite both countries' permissive credit regimes and down payments that are often as low as 5%, many young and low- to middle-income households in metropolitan regions cannot not keep up with growing house prices, which could limit the housing market's overall effect on private consumption in the years ahead.

The Income-Maintenance Channel

The second channel to sustain aggregate demand is through supporting households in maintaining their income and economic status when earnings stagnate, incomes drop, and expenditures rise unexpectedly. Debt-financed income maintenance has become a private alternative to public policies that traditionally bolstered households' income. For example, wage bargaining, social insurance against adverse economic events, and social investment in education and family policies have traditionally supported household income. Easier access to credit substitutes for real wage growth, automatic fiscal stabilizers, and other social policies by allowing households to borrow money to maintain their living standards—at least in the short to medium term.

There are several ways through which a credit- driven growth model helps individuals to smooth income losses and fund (rising) expenditures. Individuals' expenditures and consumption may suffer severely during periods of income losses. Such losses can stem from unemployment, parental leave, or sickness. These events not only negatively impact households' finances in the short run but can also permanently lower income during old age if pension benefits are tied to lifetime incomes. Traditional social policies support individuals through unemployment and sickness insurance during times of economic distress or through social investment policies such as paid parental leave. These policies help individuals and their families maintain prior living standards and consumption levels. From a macro-level perspective, social policies keep up aggregate demand and, during periods of economic declines, help mitigate recessionary effects as automatic stabilizers. In liberal welfare states, however, the financial impact of income shocks largely falls onto the shoulders of individuals (Hacker 2019) and may have more severe consequences for aggregate demand. Here, credit markets can operate functionally similar to social insurance policies and allow individuals to smooth income losses and maintain consumption (Wiedemann 2021a). In the absence of a comprehensive welfare state, homeownership also provides a private insurance and nest egg in old age. During temporary income losses, as described above, homeowners also often take out equity loans against the value of their homes.

Wage growth is another component to ensure that households have the necessary financial means to make a living. Credit often becomes the last resort to compensate for stagnating wages and growing inequality (Ahlquist and Ansell 2017; Rajan 2010). While in many countries the earnings of higher-income groups grew considerably, those of low- and middle-income groups increased little or even stagnated in real terms. These patterns of earnings inequality are most pronounced in the English-speaking countries, especially in the United States (Atkinson, Piketty, and Saez 2011). Over the period from 1979 to 2020, wages for the top 1% of Americans increased by 180%, whereas wages for the bottom 90% only grew by 28.2%. In 2020, average annual wages for the top

1% were $823,000, while average annual wages for the bottom 90% was only $40,000 (Economic Policy Institute, 2021). Earnings and income inequalities allow higher-income groups to recycle a share of their earnings through the financial system into loans to middle-or lower-income groups (Kumhof, Rancière, and Winant 2015), thus amplifying the effect of easier access to credit as a substitute for stagnating wages. In the absence of wage increases and redistributive efforts to curb excessive income inequality, easy borrowing allows households to maintain relative consumption levels and emulate consumption patterns of higher-income groups (Frank, Levine, and Dijk 2014). The expansion of debt is a politically feasible way to allow households, especially those in the middle class, to maintain their living standards in the context of increasing inequality. Distributing resources through credit markets is less costly, both fiscally and politically, as it avoids contentious questions of allocating tax revenues and fiscal redistribution. Credit markets offer policymakers a way to deal with growing societal demands and democratic overload in light of limited fiscal capacity (Krippner 2011; McCarty, Poole, and Rosenthal 2013).

Wage stagnation turns into a financial problem for households as living costs and expenditures for education, childcare, and healthcare have grown faster over the last decades than incomes (OECD 2019). A rising number of households live paycheck to paycheck and have little financial leeway to deal with unexpected income shocks, often struggling to meet daily expenditures (Kaplan, Violante, and Weidner 2014). Households' limited financial buffers are all the more precarious in the American and British credit-driven growth models, because they tend to provide marked-based welfare services such as education, childcare, or healthcare that are costly to individuals. Social investment policies that offer publicly funded education, subsidized or free childcare, and universal and comprehensive healthcare are either absent or very limited. Instead, households have to finance such goods and services on their own and often resort to credit markets.

In countries that rely on domestic demand as the key pillar of growth, income shocks, rising expenditures, and wage stagnation can therefore pose threats to aggregate demand and undermine domestic consumption. A weak welfare state aggravates not only labor market and economic risks but also the unequal distribution of economic growth, and it further contributes to wage stagnation of average incomes. All this is deeply problematic for a growth model that is heavily dependent on domestic consumption. Easier access to credit can, to some extent, fill this void by allowing households to maintain prior consumption levels and living standards and prop up aggregate demand. But at the same time, it also makes people, policymakers, and the economy much more vulnerable and exposed to credit markets.

The International Dimension

The US and UK credit-led growth models depend and thrive on their unique position in the international political economy. The chapter by Schwartz and Blyth in this volume emphasizes that the United States and, to a lesser degree, the United Kingdom are global financial power hubs, even though London's status as Europe's financial center remains uncertain after Brexit. Their central and prominent positioning in the global economic and financial order attracts significant capital inflows, as global investors consider their government bonds as safe assets and their currencies as global reserves. As a result, credit-led growth models in the global financial core have been able to sustain large current account deficits supported by global capital inflows. These capital inflows often come from export-driven growth models, such as Japan, Germany, and China, which run current account surpluses and channel excess savings abroad (Ansell, Broz, and Flaherty 2018). After lifting capital controls across the OECD, the US dollar's status as the major reserve currency gave the United States an "exorbitant privilege" (Eichengreen 2010), allowing it to sustain massive current account deficits that have fueled household borrowing due to foreign investments in US Treasuries and mortgage-backed securities (MBS).

When foreign funds flow into domestic capital markets, domestic credit markets expand and borrowing costs fall, bolstering the housing and income-maintenance channels of debt-financed consumption (Ansell, Broz, and Flaherty 2018). Housing bonds, such as mortgage-backed securities, are often considered to be the second-best option after government bonds in core credit-led economies (Schwartz 2009). In the United States, the federal government is backing most MBS through the government-sponsored mortgage giants, Fannie Mae and Freddie Mac, and their fully public cousin, Ginnie Mae, which make these bonds attractive to global investors. In 2018, China, Taiwan, and Japan were the largest foreign holders of US mortgage-backed securities, holding roughly $700bn or 10% of the entire US MBS market.[1] The UK's smaller residential MBS market (i.e., £133bn in outstanding residential MBS in 2019) also relies on foreign investors, especially from the United States.[2] Global capital inflows into the housing sector, in turn, increase housing demand as well as prices, while boosting housing wealth and easing credit constraints that are associated with higher consumer spending.

The Politics of Credit and Consumption: The Role of Growth Coalitions

Credit-driven, consumption-led growth models are underpinned by what Baccaro, Blyth, and Pontusson describe as "growth coalitions." These coalitions are constellations of political and economic actors who share a common interest in facilitating easy access to credit and debt-fueled consumption. They include producer groups in the financial services industries, voters that benefit from asset-price inflation and easy access to consumer credit, and political parties that claim to act in the "general economic interest" by stimulating credit and consumption.

The most important producer group is the FIRE service sector (i.e., finance, insurance, and real estate). These industries include banks, insurance companies, credit card companies, hedge funds, mortgage brokers, homebuilders, and realtors. While these industries do not always agree on policy details, they all profit from the expansion of consumer credit, property markets, and household consumption. These lobby groups are powerful constituents of the growth coalition, owing to their central structural position within credit-led growth models and their ability to frame political demands in ways that align with their growth models' macro-economic imperatives. While labor unions play a key role in moderating wages in (price-sensitive) export-oriented economies, they are not part of this coalition because they tend to promote fiscal and redistributive policies seen as incompatible with dynamic financial markets. In fact, the influence of labor unions and the labor share have declined in recent decades in most OECD countries, including in the United States and United Kingdom, while the role of capital has increased in globalized financial markets with mobile capital (Bergholt, Furlanetto, and Maffei-Faccioli, 2022; Iversen and Soskice 2019; Thelen 2019).

The key electoral constituency consists of current and aspiring homeowners—and asset owners more generally—who benefit from accessible and subsidized credit. Permissive consumer credit markets stimulate housing prices and other financial assets, allowing many households to move up or down the housing ladder and tap into home equity. As a result, housing is often viewed as an investment good embedded in a wider culture of finance. Renters, by contrast, often face the downside of dynamic real estate markets in the form of rising rents, while being effectively excluded from wealth gains and participation in an asset-based welfare state that heavily depends on real estate ownership. Middle- and upper-income households are the ones benefiting the most from such a "finance culture," because they are the predominant owners of property and stocks that tend to rise in value when financial markets and credit expand (Fligstein and Goldstein 2015).

Finally, political parties represent the interests of these "policy demanders" (Bawn et al. 2012) and are themselves shaped by the imperatives of the growth model. Mainstream political parties on the left and right tend to favor policies that aim to stimulate debt-financed consumption—the key element on which their growth model relies—which often produces surprising degrees of bipartisanship. In doing so, they also advance the interests of the FIRE industries and asset owners. Particularly in moments of crisis, center-left and center-right parties often agree to stimulate and double down on boosting the FIRE sector to generate growth (Reisenbichler 2021a).

What are the specific strategies available to policymakers to stimulate credit-led growth models? The toolkit of policy choices includes a wide array of fiscal and (de-)regulatory policies that make credit more easily and widely available, encourage the establishment of new consumer loan products, and/ or subsidize borrowing costs, all of which stimulate debt-fueled consumption through the housing and income-maintenance channels. Fiscal policies can encourage consumer debt through tax relief on interest payments (e.g., for student loans or mortgages); favorable tax treatment of debt-financed assets (e.g., for owner-occupied homes); or direct spending programs to finance the cost of homeownership. Second, (de-)regulatory policies include government guarantees on household debt that reduces the cost of borrowing for the consumer by absorbing financial risk from banks; liberalizing measures to encourage the proliferation of new consumer loan products; or initiatives to widen credit access to previously excluded groups. Such measures are the building blocks of permissive credit regimes that facilitate access to credit in the US and UK economies with limited welfare states, and they support income losses and social investment by relying on debt-financed consumption.

Credit and Consumption in the United States and United Kingdom

In the United States and United Kingdom the economic power of, financial and real estate sectors has grown at much higher rates than in other OECD countries (Kalinowski 2013) (see also the chapter by Ban and Helgadottir in this volume). Figure 8.1 compares the FIRE sector's value added as a share of GDP in the United States, United Kingdom, and export-oriented Germany. In the 2010s, the finance and insurance sector together added more than 7% of GDP, while the real estate sector contributed more than 13% in both the United States and United Kingdom. In Germany, by contrast, finance and insurance added only 4% of GDP and real estate only 10%. Relatedly, the status of New York and London as major financial centers in the global financial system attracts

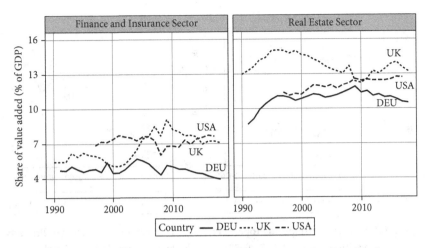

Figure 8.1 Value Added by Sector. Notes: Value added is measured as the value of output minus the value of intermediate consumption. Source: OECD National Accounts Statistics. 2020.

foreign capital that flows into consumer credit markets and is channeled into secured (e.g., mortgages) and unsecured debt (e.g., credit cards) (Eichengreen and Shah, 2020). The central sectoral position of the FIRE industries in credit-driven growth models makes them powerful players in these economies. Unlike in export-oriented Germany, easy access to credit and household borrowing is a key pillar to support aggregate demand in the United States and United Kingdom.

The importance of the FIRE sectors is also linked to relatively high levels of homeownership and household indebtedness. As Figure 8.2a shows, around two-thirds of the US population are homeowners, a number that has been fairly stable since the 1970s. In the United Kingdom, homeownership rates increased from around 50% in 1970 to an all-time high of 71% in the mid-2000s. This stands in stark contrast to Germany, where homeownership remains much lower compared to the United Kingdom and the United States. A related key feature of credit-led growth models—although certainly not limited to such economies—is rising house prices. Figure 8.2b shows that between the 1990s and the onset of the Great Recession, property prices have grown nearly three times in the United Kingdom and 2.5 times in the United States. Germany, by contrast, even experienced a decade of *falling* house prices from the mid-1990s until the mid-2000s, and only saw a steep increase during the 2010s.

Relatively high levels of homeownership, paired with growing property prices and turnover rates in housing markets, also have consequences for mortgage debt levels. Figure 8.3 shows the average mortgage debt and consumer credit as a share of households' disposable income. Since the mid-1990, households

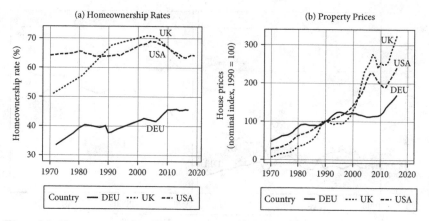

Figure 8.2 Homeownership and Property Prices (a) Homeownership Rates (b) Property Prices. Sources: Panel (a): Kohl (2017, 20–22). Panel (b): Jordà-Schularick-Taylor Macrohistory Database. 2019.

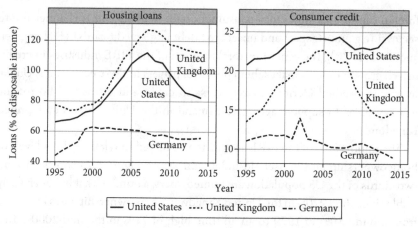

Figure 8.3 Household Debt as Share of Disposable Income. Notes: Consumer credit is measured as the outstanding amounts of loans of resident households and NPISHs for consumption purposes such as credit cards and overdrafts. Sources: European Credit Research Institute (ECRI). 2015.

in the United Kingdom and United States took on increasing levels of mortgage debt relative to their incomes. At the onset of the 2008–09 financial crisis, households in both countries held about 120% of their incomes in mortgages. After the Great Recession, mortgage debt declined as households began deleveraging debt. In contrast, Germany's mortgage debt levels only increased from the mid- until late 1990s and remained relatively flat since then. While mortgage debt is typically the single-largest type of household debt, American and British non-mortgage consumer credit—which includes credit card debt, car title loans, and student debt—also increased considerably in the years leading up to the financial crisis. After the Great Recession, US and UK households began deleveraging, while non-mortgage consumer credit plays a negligible role in Germany.

Finally, the US and UK economies are both characterized by high consumer spending and low savings in the economy. Figure 8.4a shows that, since the 1970s, US household consumption as a share of GDP climbed from roughly 60% in 1980 to over 68% in the 2000s. At the same time, gross savings as a share of GDP have declined since the late 1970s (see Figure 8.4b). After hitting its low point of 3% of disposable US household income in 2005—down from 14% in 1974—the personal savings rate rebounded to around 8% in the 2010s.[3] In the United Kingdom, household consumption has remained between roughly 64–69% for most years since the mid-1970s. While the UK's personal savings rate stood at 10% in 1995, it even entered negative territory between 2017 and 2019, but the pandemic lifted the savings rate to 8% again in 2020. In contrast, German household consumption as a share of GDP has dropped considerably from 58% in 1980 to about 52% today. In 2018, private consumption of US and UK households was thus nearly 15 percentage points higher than that of German households, while German gross savings as a share of GDP were 10 to 15 percentage points higher than in the American and British economies that year.

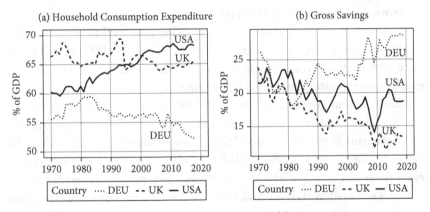

Figure 8.4 Household Consumption and Savings Rates (a) Household consumption Expenditure (b) Gross Savings. Notes: Panel (a): Households and NPISHs final consumption expenditure is the market value of all goods and services, including durable products, purchased by households. It excludes purchases of dwellings but includes imputed rent for owner-occupied dwellings. It also includes payments and fees to governments to obtain permits and licenses. Household consumption expenditure includes the expenditures of nonprofit institutions serving households, even when reported separately by the country. Panel (b): Gross savings are calculated as gross national income less total consumption, plus net transfers. Sources: World Bank national accounts data and OECD National Accounts data files. World Bank Data NE.CON.PRVT.ZS (panel a) and NY.GNS.ICTR.ZS (panel b).

The American Growth Model

The US growth model combines a permissive credit regime with deep and liquid financial markets that allow many households to easily borrow money, build asset ownership—in particular housing wealth—and maintain their living standards in the context of declining wages, rising living costs, and limited social policies. As we show below, the housing and income-maintenance channels are key to sustain debt-financed consumption in these growth models.

The Housing Channel

The US housing market is a central element of the US growth model (Prasad 2012; Reisenbichler 2021a; Schwartz 2009, 2020). To stimulate housing-based growth, in particular since the 1980s, policymakers from both parties have championed government guarantees in primary and secondary mortgage markets and tax subsidies for homeownership, while also liberalizing and financializing mortgage markets. As these measures widened access to mortgage credit and reduced mortgage costs for borrowers, they contributed to rising mortgage debt, house prices, and (debt-financed) household consumption from the 1980s until the early 2000s. When the 2000s housing boom turned into a full-blown financial crisis in 2008, policymakers adopted further programs to support housing as a way to restore the US growth model. While these measures stabilized housing and private consumption, they also fueled renewed house price surges in the 2010s, which in turn produced concerns about both financial instability and housing unaffordability in metropolitan regions.

The American growth coalition behind these policy choices encompasses housing-related interest groups, an influential homeowning constituency, and politicians from both parties. Well-organized interest groups, such as the National Association of Realtors (NAR)—and its 1.5 million members active in every single electoral district[4]—the Mortgage Bankers Association (MBA), the National Association of Home Builders (NAHB), and other financial institutions have been strong lobbyists in favor of expanding government support for housing. Indeed, the real estate lobby is one of the most powerful ones in the Beltway, with a lobby spending of $133m in 2020, which made it the fourth-largest lobby after the pharma, electronics, and insurance industries that year.[5] Relatedly, members of both the Democratic and Republican Parties have repeatedly supported measures to support housing and mortgage markets, a long-standing bipartisan consensus that is increasingly rare in American politics. Policymakers of both parties get behind these policies not only because they benefit the FIRE lobby and homeowning voters but also because politicians believe these programs to be strategies that can stimulate mortgage debt, housing activity and prices, and "ever-larger short-term consumption and spending" (Acharya et al. 2011, 171–172). That can stimulate mortgage debt, housing activity and prices, and "ever-larger short-term consumption and spending" (Acharya et al. 2011, 171–72).

Underlying the US housing channel is an architecture of fiscal and regulatory policies that subsidizes mortgage debt, lowers borrowing costs for homeowners, and widens access to mortgage credit, a set of policies that has evolved for almost a century. The US federal government stimulates housing markets and mortgage debt on at least three different levels. First, the US Treasury provides tax subsidies for homeownership and mortgage debt, such as the mortgage-interest deduction and capital gains exclusion on the sale of homes, which together amounted to $62bn in 2019.[6] Second, in the primary mortgage market, US government agencies offer private banks mortgage insurance against mortgage defaults (Thurston 2018). In 2018, the Federal Housing Administration and the US Department of Veteran Affairs guaranteed roughly $375bn in homeowner mortgage payments to banks.[7] Third, (quasi-)governmental agencies—such as Fannie Mae, Freddie Mac, and Ginnie Mae—guarantee the vast majority of MBS in the country, an astonishing number of more than $7 trillion dollars. These intertwining programs channel significant amounts of domestic and global capital in the housing market by purportedly reducing risk for financial actors and by reducing borrowing costs for consumers. Over time, policymakers have amended and expanded these government programs in repeated efforts to stimulate the country's housing market and domestic demand.

Especially since the 1980s, policymakers financialized the country's mortgage market by adopting several measures to stimulate mortgage lending, housing activity, and debt-financed consumption. Before then, the US housing finance market was relatively conservative and based on domestic deposits and savings (Fligstein and Goldstein 2012; Green and Wachter 2005). Yet, policymakers adopted sweeping (de-)regulatory reforms in response to increasingly illiquid mortgage markets and sluggish housing growth. First, they liberalized the primary mortgage market for lower-income households by allowing unconventional mortgage loans, such as Alt-A, adjustable-rate, and Jumbo mortgages (Schwartz 2009). Home equity loans were part of this liberalization effort and soon grew from only $1bn in the early 1980s to more than $300bn in outstanding debt in 2003, while the number of active loans increased from 23,000 in 1980 to 1.3 million in 2000.[8] Second, policymakers revolutionized the secondary mortgage market by creating a new housing finance system based on MBS attractive to domestic and global investors. The quasi-governmental agencies—Fannie Mae, Ginnie Mae, and Freddie Mac—soon became dominant actors trading MBS that came with a government guarantee (Morgan and Reisenbichler 2021). By the early 2000s, the government-backed trio underwrote $3.5tn in mortgage debt, constituting 35% of the residential mortgage market.[9] Finally, policymakers watched the growth of homeowner tax breaks without curbing these tax breaks when they had the chance, such as during Reagan's 1986 Tax Reform Act. As a result, the mortgage-interest deduction grew to $100bn annually just prior to the financial crisis (Hilber and Schöni 2016, 321).

The late 1990s and early 2000s saw booming housing markets and debt-financed consumption, but also a brewing housing bubble in the subprime market. The boom was in part produced by massive government support for the housing sector, low interest rates, global capital inflows, and aggressive profit-seeking behavior that mispriced risk in deregulated financial markets. Both the Clinton and George W. Bush administrations did little to stop the party—to the contrary, they developed their respective "national homeownership strategy" and "aggressive housing agenda" to stimulate housing markets especially in underserved parts of the population. In this period, many homeowners used their houses "as an ATM to finance consumption" (Acharya 2011, 171). In 2009, the amount of outstanding home equity loans was at an all-time high of $700bn, while the Financial Crisis Inquiry Commission estimates that US household extracted $2 *trillion* between 2000 and 2007.[10]

When the housing bubble burst in 2008, the result was a vicious cycle of falling house prices, growing mortgage defaults and foreclosures, household debt deleveraging, and faltering consumption (Mian and Sufi 2014). To revive the US growth model, the Bush administration quasi-nationalized the battered Fannie Mae and Freddie Mac to stabilize mortgage liquidity and reassure global investors—chiefly China—that the US government was backing agency-related MBS (Schwartz 2009). Fannie and Freddie have since remained in the hands of the US government, meaning that the American state currently guarantees $7.3tn in mortgage debt (Reisenbichler 2021a; Schwartz 2020). The Obama administration also adopted the Making Home Affordable initiative, part of the Troubled Asset Relief Program (TARP) of 2009, to reduce principal and interest payments of distressed homeowners, which restructured 1.8 million home loans and refinanced 3.5 million underwater mortgages at lower rates from 2009 until 2018 (Reisenbichler 2021b). While home equity withdrawal decreased after the financial crisis, outstanding home equity debt was still around $370bn in 2019 and remains a major component of debt-financed consumption in America.

In the fiscal realm, policymakers allowed distressed homeowners tax exemptions on debt forgiveness (through the Mortgage Debt Relief Act) at a cost of $1.4bn between 2008 and 2017 (Reisenbichler 2021b).[11] And it offered first-time buyer tax credits of up to $7,500 per household (first adopted under the Housing and Economic Recovery Act of 2008) to 2.3 million homeowners that cost taxpayers $16.2bn between 2008 and 2010 (Baker 2012). Finally, the Federal Reserve's ultra-expansionary monetary policy reinforced actions by elected officials, as it bought and retained over \$2tn in MBS as part of quantitative easing programs to reduce mortgage rates and stimulate the wider economy (Reisenbichler 2020).

However, as much as these policies helped produce an economic recovery, they also contributed to surging house prices in times of ultra-low interest rates that have excluded many young, minority, and low-income households from the property ladder. The pandemic has exacerbated these developments, due to prolonged expansionary monetary policy and increased demand for housing (outpacing supply). These developments have reinforced distributional disparities between asset owners and non-owners and created concerns about overheating housing markets even though mortgage lending is more conservative today than it was before the 2008–2009 crash.

The Income-Maintenance Channel

The income-maintenance channel constitutes the second building block of debt-financed consumption in the United States. The US growth model is highly dependent on household consumption to sustain aggregate demand, which, in turn, makes it vulnerable to income shocks, stagnating wages, and expenditure hikes that threaten to reduce household consumption.

Income shocks caused by unemployment, sickness, or temporary leave from work can negatively affect household consumption and therefore undermine aggregate demand. Through social consumption policies such as unemployment insurance, welfare states typically mitigate the effect of earnings losses on consumption patterns by offering income support during times of economic distress. The American welfare state, however, is much more limited than Social Democratic or Continental European welfare regimes and delegates responsibility to address social risks to individuals, employers, and private markets (Howard 1997; Morgan and Campbell 2011). Because of insufficient savings, many households have turned to credit markets and borrowed money to smooth income losses. Credit has become a private alternative to a public welfare state that allows households to maintain consumption in light of income losses (Wiedemann 2021a, 2022).

Over the past two decades, two trends have forced more households into debt. First, policy drift and welfare state retrenchment have shifted the burden of social risks even further away from the shoulders of society onto individuals themselves (Hacker 2019). The Personal Responsibility and Work Opportunity Reconciliation Act (PRWORA) of 1996 marked the most far-reaching form of welfare retrenchment under President Clinton, abolishing the Aid to

Families with Dependent Children (AFDC) program and replacing it with the Temporary Assistance for Needy Families (TANF), a program with stricter work requirements and time-limited benefits. In the early 2000s, President Bush began to implement welfare entitlement reforms under the guiding philosophy of "compassionate conservatism" that would shift responsibility for the provision of social welfare away from the government toward private-sector organizations such as markets and faith-based groups. His ideas of an "ownership society," in which economic prosperity is best rooted in personal ownership of assets, laid the foundations for an asset-based welfare state.

The second trend that contributed to rising household indebtedness is that, employment trajectories in the United States have become more flexible, interrupted, and unstable. The workplace has become "fissured" (Weil 2014) as firms outsource larger shares of their production and construct extensive networks of subcontracting and franchising to streamline operations and cut (labor) costs. The turn from stakeholder to shareholder models of corporate governance shifted the power from managers to shareholders and the focus from long-term interests such as stable firm-worker relationships to short-term considerations such as stock prices (Gospel and Pendleton 2005). These trends affect households' financial situation directly as they make household income more volatile (Dynan, Elmendorf, and Sichel 2012) and indirectly because interrupted employment patterns often disqualify individuals from social benefits if they no longer meet eligibility requirements. In this environment, credit markets have emerged as a private solution to address income losses during unemployment, sickness, and other periods of temporary leave from work. A 2004 study found that around one-third of US families drew on credit cards to cover basic living expenses during a four-month period (Draut 2005, 11). Easier access to credit is the fuel to keep aggregate demand up and running when incomes and earnings decline and the welfare state is not providing adequate support.

Credit markets further help sustain aggregate demand when living costs and prices for expenditures such as education, childcare, and healthcare have increased more than household incomes. Between 1996 and 2014, median household expenditures grew by about 25%. While expenditures recovered from the downturn during the Great Recession, incomes often did not. This pushed the median expenditure-to-income ratio for a two-earner couple with two children up to 75% (Pew Research Center 2016). Low-income American households today spend a higher share of their budgets (about 82% in 2014) on basic needs such as housing, food, transportation, healthcare, and clothing than they did three decades ago (Schanzenbach et al. 2016). But the financial burden of rising expenditures is not limited to low-income households. It also affects middle-income households who often live paycheck to paycheck and have little savings to weather income losses or expenditures hikes (Kaplan, Violante, and

Weidner 2014). In 2020, about 34% of American adults reported having difficulty covering everyday expenditures such as food, rent or car payments.[12] In
another survey, more than a third of American households stated they could not
cover unexpected expenditures of $400—or only by going into debt.[13]

Rising expenditures have become particularly burdensome because incomes
have not grown commensurately. Current real average wages have the same purchasing power as they did nearly 40 years ago. Gains have largely been concentrated among high-income earners. Since 1980, inflation-adjusted hourly wages
for workers in the bottom decile have increased by 8.9%, which corresponds to
an annualized inflation-adjusted growth rate of just 0.2%. Workers at the median
wage earned 16.8% more than four decades ago (0.4% annualized growth rate),
while those in the top decile gained 46.9% (about 1% compounded growth rate)
(Economic Policy Institute 2018). The reasons behind stagnating real wages are
hotly debated and include the decline of labor unions, a widening wage gap between workers with and without college degrees, restrictions on job-switching,
a growing pool of workers who are either in non-standard forms of employment
or outside the formal labor force, as well as the technological change and the rise
of low-wage service jobs (Atkinson, Piketty, and Saez 2011; Kristal and Cohen
2017; Mishel et al. 2012). Wage stagnation poses a key threat to a consumption-
driven growth model because it undermines households' ability to consume,
especially when the costs of living and other expenditures rise. Financial deregulation and easier access to credit provided policymakers across the political
aisles with a solution to prop up aggregate demand that had a limited fiscal im-
print on public budgets and, therefore, was politically feasible (Krippner 2011;
Rajan 2010).

The electoral dynamics between policymakers, voters, and interest groups
in the American growth model were in full display during and after the financial crisis. Mian, Sufi, and Trebbi (2010) show that politicians in areas with
high mortgage default rates were more likely to support the 2008 American
Housing Rescue and Foreclosure Prevention Act (AHRFPA), which provided
financial insurance for the Federal Housing Administration for renegotiated
mortgages as well as unlimited financial support for Freddie Mac and Fannie
Mae. Politicians who received campaign contributions from the financial
services industry were much more likely to vote in favor of the Emergency
Economic Stabilization Act (EESA), which allowed the government to recapi-
talize banks through direct purchase of assets and distressed MBS. People who
did not own a home but were similarly affected by the crisis through job losses
and have large outstanding credit card or student loan payments did not benefit
from similar protections and bailouts. Both programs reflect the political and
economic importance of homeowners as consumers and the FIRE sector as
both consumers and suppliers of credit.

The British Growth Model

Similar to the United States, the UK's credit- and consumption-driven growth model relies on a permissive credit regime and liquid credit and mortgage markets, which generate aggregate demand and, in turn, economic growth through the housing and income-maintenance channels.

The Housing Channel

Beginning in the 1980s, UK policymakers began to liberalize financial and mortgage markets, relax credit constraints, and subsidize homeownership by privatizing social housing in order to stimulate growth and promote asset-based welfare. The result was a debt-fueled growth model with "little incentive to save; instead, consumers were increasingly encouraged to think of their asset purchases as investments which they might cash in to fuel their consumption in retirement, as the state withdrew from pension provision, or in times of economic difficulty or unemployment" (Hay 2011, 7). After house prices and the economy collapsed during the 2008–2009 financial crisis, policymakers stimulated the housing channel to facilitate economic recovery. However, these demand-side policies contributed to soaring house prices in the context of low interest rates, leaving many households struggling to climb the property ladder amid growing concerns of overvalued housing markets.

The UK growth coalition consists of center-right and center-left political parties, housing-related interest groups, and homeowners. The financial sector and real estate industries, such as the City of London Corporation, UK Finance, the British Bankers' Association, or Home Builders Federation, are key forces in support of easy access to household credit and housing growth (Barnes 2016). The Conservative Thatcher government did much to stimulate housing as a vehicle for growth as well as to create powerful homeowning voting constituencies (Oren and Blyth 2019; Wood 2018). Subsequent Labour governments, including New Labour, followed the path of "house-price Keynesianism" as a growth and asset-based welfare strategy (Hopkin and Shaw 2016; Watson 2010). As Oren and Blyth (2019, 607) put it: "each policy selection, from Lawson to Brown, put the interests of the financial sector first, deepened the dependency of the economy on credit growth [. . .] and further shut down alternative paths for growth."

In a far-reaching attempt to privatize housing and boost private ownership, the Thatcher government introduced one of its signature policies: the 1980 "Right to Buy" program. More than 2 million council housing units have since been sold to tenants at a subsidized, below-market price. In the 1980s, however, many households faced significant hurdles in obtaining mortgages in what was then a fairly restrictive mortgage system dominated by building societies, while local authorities' efforts to offer public loans to tenants resulted in deficits that worked against the government's austerity principles (Oren and Blyth 2019; Wood 2018). In response, the Thatcher government adopted a series of reforms to allow for more competition between commercial banks and building societies in the mortgage market, such as the 1986 Building Society Act. Much like the US savings and loans banks that were the backbone of the pre-financialized mortgage market, UK building societies lost their predominant role in providing mortgage funding as capital markets took over that role through mortgage securitization, which became a core pillar of the British macroeconomic regime (Wood 2018).

These policy actions paved the way for a property boom in which house prices rose by about 10% on average between the mid-1990s and 2007 (Hay 2011, 19). Similar to the United States, a low interest-rate environment—paired with deregulated mortgage markets, global capital inflows, and investor appetite for mortgage bonds—contributed to the house price boom in the United Kingdom. Armed with increased net worth, UK households also tapped their home equity for credit-based consumption. According to Montgomerie and Büdenbender (2015, 394), home equity withdrawal constituted 4% of GDP between 2002 and 2007, with a peak of £63bn extracted in 2003 (a number that corresponds to 9% in consumer spending that year). When house prices declined by 20% and overleveraged households began to default on their mortgages, losses in household wealth constrained their abilities to borrow money and consume. As a result of mortgage defaults, toxic financial investments, and falling consumption, the UK's debt-fueled growth model was in crisis.

Once policymakers had stabilized the financial system, they turned to housing to promote economic recovery in the post-crisis years. The Cameron government adopted a series of measures absorbed under the 2013 "Help to Buy" program designed to stimulate housing markets and economic growth (Hilber and Schöni 2016). The program included an interest-free loan (for five years) of up to 20% (40% in London) of the home value for newly built homes, while households have to come up with a 5% down payment. This is an expansion of the 2011 "First Buy" program, which was designed to help low-income, first-time buyers to make a down payment. The "Help to Buy" program also included a guarantee scheme in the amount of £12bn, in place until 2017, which protected lenders from mortgage default and encouraged them to give out £130bn in mortgages to first-time buyers and low-income households. In response to the Covid-19 pandemic, the Johnson government initiated a new guarantee scheme capped at £4bn (up to £600,000 in home value) to encourage banks to extend mortgages with a down payment of only 5% in 2021. And it it temporarily offered tax relief on the stamp duty holiday (a tax on property purchases) from July 2020 until June 2021.

While these demand-side measures have stimulated housing markets and asset prices, they also exacerbated existing supply-side problems and the lack of affordable housing among young and low- and middle-income households. The UK's current affordability crisis is also the product of a rigid land-use planning system (i.e., greenbelt protections, height restrictions, etc.) with few fiscal incentives to develop and an outsized role for local politicians and NIMBYs in the property development process (Hilber and Schöni 2016).

The Income-Maintenance Channel

The UK's growth model also relies on the income-maintenance channel to support aggregate demand. Much like its American counterpart, the British growth model is heavily driven by domestic consumption, as Figure 8.4 shows. Yet, the strong reliance on consumption for aggregate demand makes the UK economy vulnerable to income shocks that affect the propensity and ability of households to consume. For the first time in nearly 30 years, UK households in 2017 collectively spent or invested on average around £900 *more* than they earned, turning households into net debtors (Office for National Statistics 2018).

A set of policy choices in the 1980s and 1990s paved the way for credit-based income maintenance to become part of the British growth model. The Conservative Thatcher and Major governments privatized and deregulated labor, finance, and product markets as well as several industrial sectors; they dismantled trade unions and Britain's already weak corporatist structures; and they retrenched many welfare state programs (Hemerijck 2013, 172–80). Guided by a new "workfare" rhetoric, the government tightened welfare eligibility criteria and coupled social benefits more closely to past employment. At the same time, middle-income households were encouraged to opt into private supplemental pension plans and health insurance and to become homeowners with property that can serve as a private nest egg during retirement (Rhodes 2000). The "Third Way" policy strategy under New Labour made social benefits further contingent upon paid employment and turned their focus of the welfare state to more active labor market policies with the goal to enable re-entry into the workforce. These policy changes were embedded in a more fundamental shift in aggregate demand: replacing Keynesian demand management with what Crouch (2009) called "privatized Keynesianism," meaning that the economy is no longer stimulated by wage growth or government spending and public debt but by individuals borrowing money to maintain income in times of stagnant wages and waning welfare. After the Great Recession, the Cameron government embarked on a series of austerity policies that severely cut government spending across a wide range of services, including welfare benefits. In 2010, it introduced "universal credit," a new type of benefit for working-age people, which replaced six existing benefit categories (i.e., income support, income-based jobseeker allowances, income-related employment and support allowances, housing benefits, child tax credits, and working tax credits) by merging them into a single payment with reduced benefit rates.

Welfare retrenchment aggravated the more unequal distribution of economic growth in liberal market economies. To alleviate the fiscal impact of income shocks and rising expenditures, governments sought to appease and acquiesce voters by providing easy access to credit, such as through subprime lending and cheap unsecured credit cards (Barnes 2016). Together, these policy bundles culminated in the rise of an asset-based welfare state in which households address income shocks or additional expenditures through equity release from their homes. Households without sufficient access to real estate assets, however, have to rely on unsecured forms of debt to address financial shortfalls. This asset- and debt-based welfare state has now become a cornerstone of a consumption-driven growth model, sustained by widely and easily available access to credit and critical to help households sustain aggregate demand.

Conclusion

This chapter examined credit-driven, consumption-led models and their underlying political coalitions in the United States and the United Kingdom. We identified two distinct channels through which these growth models generate domestic demand. First, the housing channel facilitates household borrowing and consumption through rising house prices and homeowners' wealth, which both increases households' propensity to spend money and improves their collateral against which they can borrow to finance consumption. Second, the income-maintenance channel strengthens aggregate demand by encouraging households to draw on credit markets to maintain their income and economic status when earnings stagnate, incomes drop, and personal expenditures rise in the context of limited welfare states. We showed that the (re-)production of these growth models hinges on a political coalition of policy demanders, which consists of producer groups in the FIRE service sector, asset owners, and center-left and center-right political parties, who all share a common policy agenda geared toward easy credit access and asset-price inflation to generate consumption.

We conclude, necessarily speculative, that the future of these growth models depends on how policymakers address internal vulnerabilities related to financial stability and distributional inequalities. First, credit markets are in-strumental in producing innovation and sustaining economic growth in these models; yet the very forces that bring about growth can also have destabilizing effects when financial actors engage in risk-taking behaviors, disrupt existing markets with new financial innovations, or exploit regulatory loopholes in pursuit of profits (Morgan and Reisenbichler 2021). For their part, politicians have strong incentives to prop up credit markets for growth but fewer incentives to restrain financial capitalism when markets overheat. The financial crisis of 2008–2009 was a case in point, revealing the internal contradictions of credit-driven consumption: expanding credit produces growth but may also lead to asset bubbles and financial crises. Concerns about financial stability have hardly disappeared in the post-crisis world of ultra-low interest rates and asset-price inflation. While permissive credit regimes have helped facilitate credit access when interest rates were higher in the past, the current combi-nation of permissive credit *and* ultra-low interest rates have contributed to soaring asset prices, a development that the Covid-19 pandemic reinforced. Policymakers have tightened financial regulations after the Great Recession but should be concerned about asset-price inflation that could result in future financial bubbles.

A second challenge pertains to the distributional implications of credit-driven growth models. Asset-price inflation during the past decades has benefited those with assets over those without and, therefore, has exacerbated distributional inequalities between the haves and the have-nots, as people without assets have not seen the same economic gains from stocks and property as those with assets (Fuller et al. 2020). In the case of housing markets, many younger, low-income, and minority households have been priced out of the property market, as their down-payment savings cannot keep up with house prices.

These inequalities pose important socioeconomic challenges, as concen-trated income and wealth are found to be detrimental to economic growth, in part because rich households have a higher propensity to save than lower-in-come households (Economic Policy Institute 2017). The United States and the United Kingdom are among the most unequal societies in the OECD, with the top 10% income groups capturing 45.5% of total income in the United States and 35.7% in the United Kingdom, respectively (World Inequality Database, 2021). Inequality-related drags on demand have thus far been compensated by permissive credit and low interest rates, but this begs the question as to how much further the housing and income-maintenance channels can be pushed. And as rising inequality enables high-income groups to use the financial system to recycle a share of their growing wealth as loans to low- and middle-income groups, this can contribute to rising indebtedness and financial crises (Kumhof, Rancière, and Winant 2015).

Notes

1. Karan Kaul &Laurie Goodman, *Foreign Ownership of Agency MBS*, Research Report, Ginnie Mae (2021), https://www.ginniemae.gov/newsroom/publications/Documents/foreign_ownership_mbs.pdf (last accessed Jan. 19, 2022).
2. Association for Financial Markets in Europe, *Securitisation Data Report* (2019), https://www.sifma.org/wp-content/uploads/2019/09/Europe-Securitisation-Quarterly-2019-09-23-AFME-SIFMA.pdf (last accessed Jan. 19, 2022).
3. OECD, *Household Savings* (2022), doi: 10.1787/cfc6f499-en (last accessed Jan. 19, 2022).
4. National Association of Realtors, *Monthly Membership Report* (2021), https://cdn.nar.realtor/sites/default/files/documents/monthly-membership-12-2021.pdf (last accessed Jan. 19, 2022).
5. Open Secrets, *Industries* (2020), https://www.opensecrets.org/federal-lobbying/industries?cycle=2020. (last accessed Jan. 19, 2022).
6. Joint Committee on Taxation, *Estimates of Federal Tax Expenditures for Fiscal Years 2019–2023* (Dec. 18, 2019), https://www.jct.gov/publications/2019/jcx-55-19/ (last accessed Jan. 19, 2022).
7. See Karan Kaul, Laurie Goodman, John Walsh, & Jun Zhu, *Mortgage Insurance Data at a Glance*, THE URBAN INSTITUTE (2019), https://www.urban.org/sites/default/files/publication/101403/u.s._mortgage_insurance_data_at_a_glance_-_2019_3.pdf. (last accessed Jan. 19, 2022).
8. Bureau of the Census, *Home Equity Lines of Credit—A Look at the People Who Obtain Them.* Statistical Brief, SB/95–15 (1995); Linda Cavanaugh. *Home Equity Lines of Credit—Who Uses This Source of Credit?*, US CENSUS BUREAU (2007) (last accessed Jan. 19, 2022).
9. See Housing Finance Policy Center, *Finance at a Glance*, THE URBAN INSTITUTE (2021) (last accessed Jan. 19, 2022).
10. Laurie Goodman & Michael Neal, *Good News for the Next Economic Downturn: Home Equity Use Is Low*, THE URBAN INSTITUTE (2019), https://www.urban.org/urban-wire/good-news-next-economic-downturn-home-equity-use-low (last accessed Jan. 19, 2022); Financial Crisis Inquiry Commission, *The Financial Crisis Inquiry Report*, Washington, D.C. (2011), https://www.govinfo.gov/content/pkg/GPO-FCIC/pdf/GPO-FCIC.pdf (last accessed Jan. 19, 2022).
11. Note that Trump's 2017 tax reform temporarily limited the mortgage interest deduction (until 2025) in an attack on blue states along both coasts where house prices are high.
12. See Center on Budget and Policy Priorities, *Covid Hardship Watch*, https://www.cbpp.org/research/poverty-and-inequality/tracking-the-covid-19-economys-effects-on-food-housing-and (last accessed Jan. 19, 2022).
13. See Federal Reserve, *Report on the Economic Well-Being of U.S. Households in 2019–May 2020* (2020), https://www.federalreserve.gov/publications/2020-economic-well-being-of-us-households-in-2019-dealing-with-unexpected-expenses.htm (last accessed Jan. 19, 2022).

9

The Political-Economic Foundations of Export-Led Growth: An Analysis of the German Case

LUCIO BACCARO AND MARTIN HÖPNER

Introduction

As argued by the introduction to this volume, large industrialized countries face a common threat of creeping stagnation due to the exhaustion of wage-led growth, which, in large advanced countries, was the key driver of growth until approximately the late 1980s to the early 1990s. To avoid stagnation, alternative stimulants of aggregate demand must be found. While other chapters in the volume focus on the way other countries have addressed the problem of faltering aggregate demand, for example, through easier access to debt (see Chapter 8), in this chapter we analyze the German solution to the problem, which is characterized by heavy reliance on foreign demand and by the emergence of an *export-led growth model*.

The key feature of the German growth model is *real undervaluation*, involving domestic prices growing systematically more slowly than foreign prices. Real undervaluation is the result of a bargaining regime oriented toward wage moderation; conservative monetary and fiscal policies; strict credit regulation (especially with respect to housing credit); and a relatively backward financial system, which provides few attractive domestic opportunities for financial investment and thus creates incentives for domestic capital to leave the country. In addition, an inflexible exchange rate regime translates domestic price containment into real exchange rate devaluation. The search for a sticky exchange rate regime is a constant of German postwar history (Germann 2021, Höpner 2018). In comparison with previous exchange rate regimes, however, such as the Bretton

Woods regime (1945–1973) and the European Monetary System (1979–1998), the introduction of the euro completely eliminated the possibility of nominal exchange rate adjustment by other members of the currency union, and thus provided the German export-led economy with a structurally undervalued exchange rate relative to competitors.

In this chapter, we provide a historical reconstruction of the emergence of export-led growth in Germany focusing on the period between 1991 and 2019. Our analysis begins with the reunification shock. Costs increased and domestic demand received a sudden boost, creating problems of inflation; deterioration of competitiveness; and, unusually, current account deficits. In retrospect, reunification was a fork in the road for the German political economy, which could have put it on a different, more domestic-oriented growth path, but ended up radicalizing its long-standing reliance on exports and competitiveness. The road not taken would have implied a greater role for domestic demand and some sectoral rebalancing, most likely to the detriment of the manufacturing sector but to the benefit of the service sector, construction, and Germany's underdeveloped public sector. The export industry would probably have continued to play an important role, but not as the main source of aggregate demand: rather, as the sector where the main innovation and upgrading capacities of the German economy reside. In retrospect, the life of the euro as a single European currency would have been much easier had Germany undergone this type of transformation.

However, the Bundesbank quashed both the inflationary spike and the domestic demand boom in the early 1990s, in the process causing the collapse of the European Monetary System (EMS) as well. In the following years, the German economy underwent a painful process of cost reduction, liberalization, and domestic demand compression. This was the period in which the export-led growth model took shape. The economy struggled with stagnation for some years, but progressively, as the export sector expanded in size, the demand stimulus provided by exports became sufficiently large to carry the whole economy along. In the transition period, the German economy experienced some peculiar sectoral dynamics: differently from other advanced countries, which experienced de-industrialization, the manufacturing sector maintained its size, while the construction sector shrank and the financial sector as well as the public sector remained underdeveloped in comparative perspective. In the period after the Great Financial Crisis (GFC), there was a partial rebalancing toward greater reliance on domestic demand.

The remainder of this chapter examines the undervaluation constellation in some detail. In the next section, we document the primarily export-led nature of German growth, the heavy weight of the manufacturing sector in comparative perspective, and the extent of price sensitivity of German exports. Following this we examine a set of policies and institutions which affect the trajectory of domestic prices: fiscal and monetary policies and wage policies. We then address the question of why there was no "private Keynesian" boost to domestic demand in Germany, by briefly analyzing the banking and housing sectors. The chapter concludes with a discussion of some challenges facing the German growth model.

The Demand Drivers of German Growth

This section is devoted to the analysis of Germany's growth drivers. We decompose total growth between the contribution of domestic demand and the contributions of exports. Different from standard decomposition exercises (e.g. Baccaro and Pontusson 2016), which focus on the contribution of *net* exports (i.e., subtract the value added of imports entirely from exports), and therefore underestimate the economic importance of exports and overestimate the contribution of domestic demand, we calculate import-adjusted demand contributions (e.g. Kranendonk and Verbruggen 2008).[1]

Table 9.1 reports the average growth contributions of (import-adjusted) domestic demand and exports between 1995 and 2018 in five-year averages by comparing Germany with two countries that are generally considered similar to it (Austria and Sweden) and two countries that are considered very different (United Kingdom and United States).

Over the 1995 to 2015 period, German growth was the lowest of the five countries under consideration and strongly dependent on exports (75%). The growth contribution of domestic demand was much smaller (25%). In the United Kingdom and the United States, growth was higher overall and largely pulled by domestic demand (89% in the United States and 82% in the United Kingdom). The growth profile of Austria was similar to Germany but less extreme (growth contribution of exports of 54%). In Sweden, growth was mostly pulled by domestic demand (66%) over the period, but the contribution of exports (33%) was non-negligible. In absolute terms, the growth contribution of exports was slightly lower in Sweden than in Germany (0.9% per year on average vs. 1%), and in Sweden it went together with a more positive contribution of domestic demand as well (1.7% vs. 0.3%).

Table 9.1 also suggests that exports were by far the most dynamic component of aggregate demand in every sub-period in Germany, including in 2006 to 2010, which was characterized by a large drop in international trade. Between 2001 and 2005, the contribution of domestic demand was negative by 0.3% per year, while the contribution of exports was positive (0.8%). Furthermore, there

Table 9.1 **Average contributions to yearly growth by five-year periods**

period		Import-adjusted Growth Contribution		total growth	Share of Total Growth	
		domestic demand	exports		domestic demand	exports
Germany	1996–2000	0.52%	1.36%	1.88%	27.68%	72.32%
Austria	1996–2000	1.15%	1.85%	3.00%	38.41%	61.59%
Sweden	1996–2000	1.80%	1.80%	3.60%	50.10%	49.90%
UK	1996–2000	2.95%	0.48%	3.43%	86.08%	13.92%
US	1996–2000	3.95%	0.37%	4.31%	91.50%	8.50%
Germany	2001–2005	-0.28%	0.82%	0.54%	-51.95%	151.95%
Austria	2001–2005	1.18%	0.61%	1.79%	65.76%	34.24%
Sweden	2001–2005	1.90%	0.72%	2.62%	72.66%	27.34%
UK	2001–2005	2.07%	0.36%	2.43%	85.14%	14.86%
US	2001–2005	2.52%	0.04%	2.56%	98.41%	1.59%
Germany	2006–2010	0.44%	0.81%	1.25%	35.53%	64.47%
Austria	2006–2010	0.61%	0.76%	1.37%	44.62%	55.38%
Sweden	2006–2010	1.70%	0.15%	1.86%	91.67%	8.33%
UK	2006–2010	0.08%	0.42%	0.50%	16.86%	83.14%
US	2006–2010	0.58%	0.42%	1.00%	58.21%	41.79%
Germany	2011–2015	0.65%	1.05%	1.70%	38.29%	61.71%
Austria	2011–2015	0.37%	0.71%	1.08%	34.08%	65.92%
Sweden	2011–2015	1.43%	0.77%	2.20%	64.92%	35.08%
UK	2011–2015	1.79%	0.29%	2.09%	85.88%	14.12%
US	2011–2015	1.85%	0.28%	2.13%	86.81%	13.19%
Germany	2016–2018	1.61%	0.38%	2.00%	80.81%	19.19%
Austria	2016–2018	1.20%	1.06%	2.27%	53.19%	46.81%
Sweden	2016–2018	1.55%	0.66%	2.21%	70.12%	29.88%
UK	2016–2018	1.15%	0.87%	2.02%	57.04%	42.96%
US	2016–2018	2.14%	0.14%	2.28%	93.80%	6.20%

The numbers in the table are average annual growth rates over five-year periods. For example, the values for 1996–2000 are the averages over 1995–1996, 1996–1997, 1997–1998, 1998–1999, 1999–2000.

Source: own elaborations on OECD Input-Output and Trade in Value Added data

was only a partial rebalancing of the growth drivers in the post-crisis period until 2015: The contribution of domestic demand continued to be smaller than exports (38% in 2011–2015).

However, domestic demand expanded considerably in 2016–2018, when German growth was larger than in other countries (except the US) and the extra growth came largely from an expanding domestic demand (which contributed 81% of total growth). These numbers suggest that the German growth model rebalanced somewhat in the latter part of the 2010 decade. It remains to be seen if the trend will continue after the COVID pandemic.

The Unusual Size of German Manufacturing and the Price Elasticity of Exports

The overarching importance of exports is accompanied by the heavy weight of the German manufacturing sector in terms of value added. Using data from the OECD STAN database, Table 9.2 reports the share of total value added of manufacturing, construction, and business services in Germany, Austria, Sweden, the United Kingdom, and the United States between 1991 and 2017. The manufacturing share of total value added remained constant at 23% in this period. As such, it was considerably larger than in Austria (19%) and Sweden (15%), let alone the United States (12%) and the United Kingdom (9%). Conversely, the construction sector was rather small in comparative perspective (4% of value added). The German business services sector as a whole was 10 percentage points smaller than its counterpart in the United Kingdom (47% vs. 58%).[2]

A crucial factor in the growth model framework is the price sensitivity of exports. If German exports were insensitive to domestic price changes, they would not be affected by a gain or loss of price competitiveness. In that case, policies that hold inflation down, in particular conservative fiscal policies and wage moderation (discussed later in the chapter), would reduce imports through the domestic demand channel, but not increase exports through the competitiveness channel. Moreover, an expansion of domestic consumption, which tends to raise domestic prices in relative terms, would not crowd out exports, and the trade-off between consumption and exports would not be stringent or would even be entirely absent.

The price elasticity of German exports is a controversial topic. It is often argued that German exports are not affected by price differences because German manufacturing competes on quality rather than cost. This position is buttressed by some econometric analyses, which suggest that the price elasticity of German exports is negligible or statistically insignificant, especially when the

Table 9.2 **Sectoral Shares of Value Added (at Constant Prices)**

Period	Country	Share of Total Value Added		
		Manufacturing	*Construction*	*Business Services*
1991–1995	Germany	23.12%	7.42%	42.33%
1996–2000	Germany	21.43%	6.34%	45.39%
2001–2005	Germany	21.86%	4.89%	47.23%
2006–2010	Germany	22.24%	4.17%	47.96%
2011–2015	Germany	23.03%	4.18%	47.52%
2016–2017	Germany	23.49%	4.09%	47.25%
1991–1995	Austria	16.65%	9.81%	45.14%
1996–2000	Austria	16.81%	9.61%	46.15%
2001–2005	Austria	17.07%	8.78%	47.82%
2006–2010	Austria	17.79%	7.82%	49.10%
2011–2015	Austria	18.48%	6.58%	49.86%
2016–2017	Austria	19.37%	6.20%	49.75%
1991–1995	Sweden	12.61%	7.30%	43.15%
1996–2000	Sweden	15.96%	6.38%	43.12%
2001–2005	Sweden	17.77%	6.25%	43.87%
2006–2010	Sweden	18.42%	6.29%	45.43%
2011–2015	Sweden	17.12%	5.19%	48.92%
2016–2017	Sweden	15.09%	5.14%	52.14%
1991–1995	UK	13.97%	7.21%	46.00%
1996–2000	UK	13.06%	6.31%	49.33%
2001–2005	UK	11.27%	6.22%	52.42%
2006–2010	UK	10.18%	5.78%	55.16%
2011–2015	UK	9.59%	5.48%	56.94%
2016–2017	UK	9.16%	5.77%	58.52%
1991–1995	USA	11.71%	6.32%	47.56%
1996–2000	USA	12.40%	6.15%	49.81%
2001–2005	USA	12.35%	5.60%	51.78%
2006–2010	USA	12.64%	4.44%	52.48%
2011–2015	USA	12.12%	3.75%	53.52%
2016–2017	USA	11.73%	3.88%	54.44%

Source: OECD STAN Database, own elaborations

estimating period ends in the early 2000s (Danninger and Joutz 2008, Horn et al. 2017, Neumann 2020, Stahn 2006). However, other econometric analyses find a non-negligible price elasticity of German exports (Baccaro and Benassi 2017, Breuer and Klose 2015, European Commission 2014, Thorbecke and Kato 2012).

To shed some light on this issue, we estimate the price elasticity of German exports between 1991 and 2019 by using data on exports at constant prices from the AMECO database[3] and data on the GDP of the Eurozone and main trade partners from the OECD Economic Outlook database.[4] Our main measure of the real effective exchange rate (REER) (capturing the price competitiveness of exports) comes from the Bruegel database.[5] This measure is based on the consumer price index (CPI) relative to 66 trade partners for Germany. We also check our results against an alternative measure of the measure of REER, from the Bank for International Settlements (BIS) database, based on CPI relative to 37 trade partners,[6] and a measure based on unit labor costs in total economy relative to the other EU15 countries excluding Germany, provided by AMECO.[7] After running a series of tests of stationarity and cointegration tests, we estimate the model below in first differences.[8]

$$\Delta \ln(x_t) = \alpha + \beta \Delta \ln(reer_t)$$
$$+ \gamma \Delta \ln(eurozone\_demand_t)$$
$$+ \vartheta \Delta \ln(US + UK + CAN\_demand_t) + \pi \Delta \ln(BRICS\_demand_t)$$
$$+ \varphi \Delta \ln(Row\_demand_t) + \epsilon_t)$$

The estimating equation states that German export growth depends on foreign demand (distinguishing between demand from the Eurozone, the US-Canada-UK bloc, the BRICS, and rest of the world demand), as well as the REER. Since our data are transformed in natural logarithms, the first difference approximates percentage change, and the regression coefficients can be interpreted as elasticities. The sensitivity of German exports to price changes is expected to be negative, although its magnitude and significance are subject to debate. The demand coefficients are expected to be positive. We distinguish between total export growth, export of goods, and export of services, and we report our results in Table 9.3.

Our estimates suggest that German exports are significantly price sensitive over the 1991 to 2019 period.[9] A devaluation of 1% of the real exchange rate is associated with an increase of export volumes of about 1% for total exports and exports of goods, and slightly less for exports of services. Exports are also highly sensitive to changes in Eurozone demand, with a positive elasticity of 2.5 for total exports, 2.75 for exports of goods (but only 1 for exports of services). Once controlling for Eurozone demand, all other sources of foreign demand are

Table 9.3 **Determinants of German Exports, First Difference Estimation, 1991–2019**

	(1) Total	*(2)* Goods	*(3)* Services
Eurozone demand	2.474***	2.755***	1.008*
	(0.422)	(0.469)	(0.528)
US UK Can demand	−0.00441	0.000617	−0.0416
	(0.279)	(0.310)	(0.349)
BRICS demand	−0.00915	−0.0187	0.0423
	(0.0354)	(0.0393)	(0.0443)
ROW demand	−0.200	−0.229	−0.0461
	(0.160)	(0.177)	(0.200)
REER (CPI-based, 66 partners)	−0.968**	−1.012**	−0.761*
	(0.352)	(0.391)	(0.441)
Constant	0.0171	0.0135	0.0356**
	(0.0111)	(0.0123)	(0.0139)
Observations	28	28	28
Adj-R2	0.705	0.698	0.281
Durbin test	ns	ns	ns

Data in natural logarithms
Standard errors in parentheses

*** $p<0.01$, ** $p<0.05$, * $p<0.1$ (two-tailed)

not significant determinants of exports. This does not mean that demand from other parts of the world does not matter, but only that it does not add explanatory power after controlling for demand from Eurozone partners.[10]

These results not only disconfirm a portion of the research literature, they also conflict with large parts of the German public discourse, according to which the German export success is exclusively due to the quality of German exports, rather than any price advantage. We think that popular discourse is affected by three misunderstandings. First, the concept of price elasticity is confused with lack of quality. The presence of significant price elasticity does not imply that German exports are of low quality, but only that price competition is on average a significant competitive factor in the international markets in which German exports operate. Second, the quality level of German exports is often exaggerated. Around half of German exports consist of automobiles, auto parts, machines, chemicals, and electronic products (see the details in Bundesministerium für Wirtschaft und Energie 2020), which is in line with the public self-image of high quality exports. But the other half is very diverse. Most Germans would probably be surprised to learn that their country is, for example, Europe's largest exporter of pig meat (Efken and Rieger 2015), and one of the three largest pig meat exporters worldwide. Third, there is also an element of blame-shifting to this emphasis on the price insensitivity of exports: if German export volumes are not significantly affected by prices, German price (and wage) moderation cannot be held responsible for the imbalances of the Eurozone. As our results indicate, this view cannot be supported.

Fiscal and Monetary Policy

We now provide a historical reconstruction of the mechanisms that underpin the undervaluation regime, beginning with budgetary and monetary policies. Policies that affect the inflation rate have an asymmetric impact on sectors. While domestic sectors such as private services and construction are both internal-demand driven and interest rate sensitive and therefore benefit from countercyclical (but potentially inflationary) fiscal and monetary policies, the export sector is instead exchange-rate sensitive (as argued before) and inflation averse. Within this conflict of aims between internal stabilization and export promotion, German monetary and fiscal policies have usually privileged the latter, due to two institutional features: central bank independence and fiscal federalism.

The *Bundesbank* and its precursor until 1957, the *Bank Deutscher Länder*, were independent and extraordinarily price stability oriented long before this became an international trend (Cukierman 1992). Their readiness to punish any seeming deviation from price stability shaped not only wage but also budgetary policies. Another institutional factor within which fiscal policies operated was fiscal federalism: The *Länder* and municipalities, which are responsible for most public investment and almost all public employment, had (and still have) a limited room for discretionary policies. They receive defined percentages of the *Verbundsteuern* (the income and turnover taxes) but cannot easily raise alternative sources of revenues. The municipalities have an additional tax at their discretion, a local business tax (the *Gewerbesteuer*), but the returns from this tax are particularly procyclical. Therefore, municipalities often have to cut, rather than raise, local public investments in times of crisis (Deutsche Bundesbank 2009, 22–23). These budgetary features create a conservative fiscal bias that contributes to keeping inflation down.

During our period of observation, the German political economy was heavily affected by the adoption of the euro. Due to the abolition of nominal exchange rate adjustments, every unit of competitive disinflation translated into a corresponding increase in price competitiveness against other Eurozone members. Moreover, interest rate policy was conducted by a multilateral central bank, which had to base its decisions on Eurozone averages, thereby necessarily confronting booming members with too low a real interest rate, and vice versa for busting economies. Furthermore, under conditions of stable nominal interest rates, rising inflation led to a falling real interest rate, and declining inflation to a rising one.[11] As a consequence, after the introduction of the euro, monetary policy was first too restrictive (in the 2000s) and then too lax (in the 2010s) when compared to the needs of the German economy. We therefore distinguish three phases: a first phase between the unification boom and the introduction of the euro, a second phase until the financial crisis, and a third one between the GFC and the pandemic crisis.

The 1990s: A period of hardship

Reunification affected the German political economy in multiple ways. The Eastern German hunger for Western products fueled a boom that soon overheated, with a real growth rate greater than 5% in 1991 and—very untypical for Germany—an inflation rate above 5% in 1992.[12] The *Bundesbank* reacted by raising the interest rate, the *Diskontsatz*, from 6% to an all-time high of 8.75% in four steps between February 1991 and July 1992. This measure effectively ended the boom and brought inflation down. But it also marked the beginning of a period of hardship that lasted until 1998, characterized by stagnating growth and revenues, huge transfer needs in order to build up state capacities in Eastern Germany, rising interest payments due to the positive gap between the interest rate on bonds and nominal growth,[13] rising unemployment, and rising costs of social security.[14] In addition, the real exchange rate of the DM appreciated both against other members of the EMS and against the dollar, resulting in a strong revaluation that reached its peak in 1995. In light of this vicious cycle, it became increasingly unclear whether Germany would be able to meet the Maastricht rule of a budget deficit of less than 3%, the decisive criterion for becoming a founding member of the euro, by the end of the decade.

The Christian Democratic-led government of Chancellor Kohl opted for a procyclical turn toward fiscal consolidation in 1996, with the so-called *Sparpaket* (cost-cutting package), which among other things included the reduction of workers' sick pay, a measure that provoked fierce protests among trade unions. This happened in the context of declining public gross fixed capital formation at all levels, but especially among *Länder* and municipalities. The budget deficit shrunk and actually went below 3% in 1997, but at a high cost: the negative output gap rose until 1998, the year in which a slight recovery set in. In all years between 1991 and 1998, the German employment rate was on the decline and reached its low of less than 64% of the workforce in the years 1997 and 1998.[15] In short, on the eve of the introduction of the euro in 1999, all economic indicators (except from the declining budget deficit) were negative.

Germany's first decade under the euro

Things became even worse for Germany until the mid-2000s. The introduction of the euro brought no initial relief. To the contrary, after a short upswing of the economy lasting until the year 2000, the euro made the recession that followed probably longer and deeper than it would have been without. In the five years between 2001 and 2005, the interest rates set by the ECB were too high for Germany. But this time, this was not because monetary policies intentionally cooled an inflationary boom down. Rather, the *Walters* effect ran against Germany: the ECB had to target the Eurozone as a whole and could therefore not offer the kind of zero-interest rate policy that Germany would have needed at the time. Throughout that period, Germany was perceived as the "sick man of Europe" (Scharpf 2018, 35–44).

There was a short period (136 days) in which the access to power of a red-green government coalition in the fall of 1998 could have brought about a turnaround in fiscal policy. This was one of the rare moments in which "parties mattered" for fiscal policy outcomes in Germany. Lafontaine, the first finance minister of the red-green government, adopted a clearly Keynesian approach. His budget plan contained an expenditure increase of 6%, including a particularly pronounced increase of the social budget of 12%, in order to stimulate internal demand (Zohlnhöfer 2003, 195–197). Also, Lafontaine repeatedly asked the ECB to adopt a more accommodating monetary policy. This phase ended on March 11, 1999, with Lafontaine's resignation.

The government nevertheless adhered to the reform of the private and corporate income taxes developed by Lafontaine.[16] This reform, passed in 2000 and adopted in three stages until 2005, decisively cut tax rates both at the bottom and at the top of the income distribution. The flipside of this reform was a revenue drop that was especially disastrous for the budgets of the *Länder* and municipalities.[17] However, the reform did not bring the boom the government had hoped for: growth slowed down in 2001 and even became negative in 2002. Rather than pushing fiscal expansion further, Lafontaine's successor Eichel opted for procyclical fiscal consolidation on the expenditure side.[18]

The period until the mid-2000s was economically disastrous in almost every respect. Economic growth remained lower than 2% in all years between 2001 and 2005, and even negative in two of the years, 2002 and 2003. Unemployment reached its peak of around 10% in 2003. In this economic environment, due to declining tax revenues, high cost of unemployment, and a positive gap between growth and borrowing costs, all fiscal consolidation attempts failed (Wagschal 2007). In this budgetary context, Germany exceeded the Maastricht deficit rule four years in a row, 2002–2005. This resulted in a reform of the stability and growth pact in 2005, which from then on referred to structural (cyclically adjusted) budget deficits and thereby allowed for more countercyclical measures.

The budgetary situation of the municipalities became particularly disastrous. Interestingly, as Hassel and Schiller (2010, 162–183) have shown in detail, this also paved the way for cross-party agreement on the far-reaching labor market and social policy reforms of that period, the *Hartz* reforms. Before that reform, the local governments had to pay the *Sozialhilfe* (social assistance) to long-term unemployed who were employable. In the context of declining revenues, this led to the virtual collapse of many local budgets, which in turn generated a consensus that a major reform of the system was unavoidable, the type of reform that political scientists usually would consider unlikely in a multi-veto point political system such as Germany. Since the *Hartz* reforms, the federal government rather than the municipalities have to pay the *Grundsicherung* for long-term unemployed persons.

In 2005, the recovery of the economy finally set in. The new Grand Coalition under Chancellor Merkel continued to focus on fiscal consolidation, now also on the revenue side: among its first measures was a sharp rise of the value-added tax from 16% to 19%. On the expenditure side, consolidation included the termination of the *Eigenheimzulage*, a subsidy for building owner-occupied property (Grasl and König 2010, 213–214). In 2004, the state had paid 11.5 billion euros for that subsidy; unsurprisingly, its abolition led to a further decline in the number of finished dwellings and made the situation of the construction sector, in crisis since the end of the unification boom, even worse. From 2006 on (until the GFC), Germany for the first time since 2001 met the 3% deficit rule, and unemployment went down to around 6%. In 2009, two years before the European fiscal compact, the government passed the constitutional debt brake, which went beyond the rules of the stability and growth pact and put further consolidation pressure on the *Länder*.[19]

In sum, the six distress years after the introduction of the euro were decisive for Germany, due to the cumulation of low growth, high unemployment, fiscal stress, consolidation, labor market and social policy reforms, and— discussed later in the chapter—extraordinary wage restraint. In these years, the relative size of the German export sector increased rapidly, from 27% of GDP in 1999 to 41% in 2006, and further to 44% in 2008, the year the financial crisis set in.

Fiscal conservatism after the financial crisis

After significant and economically successful fiscal expansion during the financial crisis, the government renewed the fiscal consolidation path chosen in the early 2000s. Since 2012 all budgets were balanced or in surplus, and the cumulated public debt was declining not only relative to the yearly GDP, but also in absolute numbers (Deutsche Bundesbank 2018, 77). This was not due to harsh fiscal reforms, but the result of declining costs of unemployment; rising revenues; and, above all, declining refinancing cost of public debt combined with a higher growth rate: the interest rate-growth relation had turned around, for Germany directly after the financial crisis and for the Eurozone on average in 2015.

But no expansion of expenditure occurred once consolidation was done,[20] although a broad consensus began to emerge about a serious lack of public investment (Boldrick 2021, 24). Since the early 2000s, net investments were mostly close to zero and even negative in many years, that is, gross investments were smaller than the writing-offs from capital consumption (Dullien et al. 2020). No major tax reductions occurred either, although taxes had been major topics in the 2009, 2013, and 2017 election campaigns of all major political parties. As Rixen (2015, 2019) shows, the Merkel governments elected in 2009 (coalition with the liberal party, FDP) and 2013 (Grand Coalition with the SPD) were the most tax-inactive governments in the history of the Federal Republic.

This over-conservative fiscal policy stance came and still comes as a mystery for many international observers. All numbers indicate that Germany could have done much more to renew its obsolete infrastructure, to promote digitalization, and to support ecological transition, among others (Klein and Pettis 2020, 168–169; Nölke 2021). Especially given the declining borrowing costs—in the summer of 2019, the finance ministry was even able to sell a 30-year bond with a zero-interest rate—Germany could easily tolerate a much larger public debt (Priewe 2020, 543).[21]

In light of the framework introduced in this volume, however, and of Germany's export-oriented growth model in particular, this fiscal conservatism makes perfect sense. Since the end of the financial crisis, the *Walters* effect had turned around for Germany: the interest rate set by the ECB was too low for Germany,[22] a matter much criticized in the public arena. Even more, Germany lacked any need for the ECB's bond acquisition programs. If fiscal expansion had occurred under such conditions and if it had fueled an inflationary domestic boom to the detriment of the price competitiveness of exports, interest rates could no longer have been used to cool the economy down. The tendency to protect price competitiveness at almost any cost also sheds light on the extraordinary

German resistance against the ECB's unconventional monetary policy, a resistance that also manifested itself in a constitutional conflict between the German Constitutional Court and the Court of Justice of the EU (Höpner 2021).

Wage Policy

Wage policy shapes domestic demand and cost-push (dis)inflation. The period under investigation can roughly be divided into two phases. The phase of extraordinary wage restraint (but with important variation across sectors) began after the unification boom and lasted until the financial crisis. Earlier in the chapter, we provided details about the unfavorable macroeconomic conditions under which this wage policy occurred. In all years between 1996 and 2007, the yearly economy-wide nominal unit labor cost increases were below 2%. The restraint reached its peak in the years 2004 to 2007, with four years of declining nominal unit labor cost in a row, indicating that wage policy not only contributed to below-target inflation, but even brought deflationary impulses.[23] Because wages in Southern Europe were overshooting at the same time and nominal exchange rate adjustments had been taken out of the macroeconomic toolbox in 1999, a large inner-European competitiveness gap emerged, accompanied by growing current account surpluses in Germany (5.7% of GDP in 2008).[24] Also, *real* wage growth was lower than productivity increases throughout that period, indicating a lack of demand-driven internal growth impulses.

In the second phase between the financial and the pandemic crises, a partial rebalancing took place in the Eurozone, to which not only wage restraint in the South, but also wage increases in Germany contributed. This happened in the context of Germany's swift recovery from the financial crisis, decent rates of growth,[25] and an almost linear decline in unemployment. The rebalancing gained momentum in the second half of the 2010s, but it was interrupted by the pandemic shock: since 2016, *real* wage increases exceeded productivity, indicating a rising wage share and an activation of wage-driven growth impulses; and after 2018, *nominal* wage increases finally exceeded the "golden wage rule" according to which nominal wages shall rise in line with productivity increases plus the inflation target.[26]

The rebalancing, however, did not go far enough to close the competitiveness gap that had emerged in the period before. During the first half of the 2010s, the current account surplus grew further and reached its peak of 8.6% in 2015, followed by a modest decline (7.1% in 2019, our last year of observation).[27] Evaluated purely on the basis of industrial job security, the long-lasting competitive wage disinflation paid out: Germany avoided the rapid deindustrialization taking place in countries such as France, Italy and Spain and kept its industrial employment almost stable, with 12.3 million industrial employees in 1999, 11.3 million in 2008 and 11.5 million in 2018.[28]

The export sector

The wage restraint in the industrial export sector can only be understood in the context of fundamental changes in the "German model" of industrial relations. Germany witnessed a dramatic decline in net union membership until the financial crisis, from more than 30% in the first half of the 1990s to 19% in 2008. In the same period, the bargaining coverage rate fell from around 80% to 60%.[29] This disorganization of wage bargaining affected the domestic service sectors much more than the industrial export sector. The same holds true for the welfare state reforms introduced by the Schröder government in 2003: although the promotion of atypical (subcontracted, temporary, and part-time) work put overall pressure on wages in the industrial sector as well, low-productivity services were much more affected. However, much functional change occurred within this relative structural stability (Streeck 2009, ch. I.2; Baccaro/Howell 2017, ch. 6).

The transformations started in the 1980s with flexible adjustment concessions in the field of working time. The critical juncture, however, occurred after the unification boom, when several shocks cumulated and fueled industrial employers' calls for more wage flexibility, especially among smaller firms in the metal sector. Among these shocks were the sharp interest rate increases brought about by the Bundesbank and the unusual overvaluation of the DM in the first half of the 1990s, both described in the last section. As a result, smaller supplier firms got increasingly squeezed by larger exporters. In Eastern Germany, the introduction of the DM fueled rapid de-industrialization. So-called hardship case clauses were introduced in Eastern Germany, which allowed for wage reductions in times of crisis. This phenomenon diffused rapidly, first uncontrolled and then formalized in the *Pforzheim* agreement for the metal sector in 2004, which ruled that the IG Metall had to agree to the use of opening clauses.

From the perspective of the trade unions in the metal sector, there was no alternative to controlled decentralization, not only because members weighted job security at least as high as wage increases, but also because employers' associations had introduced a new weapon: in order to keep and attract smaller firms, they had introduced "OT" (*ohne Tarif*) memberships for which the agreements did not apply. This phenomenon diffused across regions and sectors, perhaps beyond the initial intentions of the associations (Behrens and Helfen 2016, 454–455). The unfavorable economic context, the emergence of low-wage production locations in Eastern Europe, and industrial restructurings that weeded out service segments pressed actors to make use of the wage flexibilization opportunities which decentralization provided (Hassel 2014; Baccaro/Benassi 2017; Avlijaš et al. 2021).

The German labor regime was particularly suitable for such flexible adaptation (Dustmann et al. 2014, 182). Statutory wage extensions were almost entirely absent in the industrial sector, and the German form of supervisory board codetermination had strengthened the inclination of employee representatives to compromise for the sake of preserving jobs. The outcome of these adaptations was a flexible multilevel system of wage determination in which firm-level actors played a greater role than in the past. Not surprisingly, these actors put higher weight on job security than on overall macroeconomic, let alone transnational, benchmarks.

Domestic sectors

Export sectors have a pronounced interest in wage restraint not only in their own sectors, but in the sheltered sectors as well, since inflationary wage pressure can spill over intersectorally and because the industrial sector uses construction and various services. The international competition that promotes wage restraint in the exposed sectors is, however, absent in the sheltered sectors. This is why inflationary wage pressure often originates from non-exposed sectors, including public sectors, as happened in several Eurozone countries during the first 10 years of the euro (Johnston 2012; Hancké 2013; Höpner and Lutter 2018).

In the period under investigation here, German sheltered sector wage restraint was even *more* pronounced than in the exposed industrial sector: The bulk of wage disinflation happened in the low-end private services sector (but not in, in the terminology of Wren 2021, dynamic services such as finance and insurance), the public sector, and construction (Di Carlo and Höpner 2020). Here, nominal unit labor cost increases were not only smaller than those in industry but stagnated until 2003 and even became negative until 2007. This outcome is theoretically puzzling because it cannot be explained by the signals industrial wage bargainers sent to the rest of the economy—if such signals had been important, the wage increases in the sheltered sector would have been *higher* than they actually were (Di Carlo 2018, 12–14). The explanation can therefore only lie in sector-specific developments.

The erosion of unionization and collective bargaining coverage affected the private service sector much more than the industrial sector. In 2014, for example, 73% of employees in hospitality, 78% in information and communication, and 61% in health and social services were not covered by a collective agreement.[30] Furthermore, these sectors were not covered by a minimum wage, because the respective law was passed much later, in 2015. Since 2003, labor market and welfare state reforms put additional pressure on private service work (Avlijaš et al. 2021, 387f.). Due to this combination of factors, the gap between labor costs in manufacturing and in low-end private services became larger than in every other EU country (Albu et al. 2018, 7).

None of these variables, however, sheds light on wage restraint in the public sector, where trade unions remained strong and almost all employees were covered by collective agreements. As Di Carlo (2021, 16–19) has shown, this part of German exceptionalism can only be understood by considering that public wage policy is at the same time fiscal policy. In German fiscal federalism, *Länder* and municipalities, in which around 90% of public workers are employed, are chronically underfinanced. As the previous section made clear, the tax reform of the first red-green government forced the *Länder* into sharp fiscal consolidation. In response, they left the joint wage bargaining framework with the *Bund* and the municipalities and imposed fierce wage cuts. In these years, German public sector wage restraint was greater than in all other Eurozone countries.

In construction, the long crisis of the sector provided an unfavorable background for wage increases. In all years between 1994 and 2007, the size of the sector was shrinking. Beyond the widespread fear of losing jobs, wage policies were shaken up by the European free movement of workers, non-enforcement of the posted workers directive, and illegal work. In no other Eurozone member state, again, did wage restraint in construction go as far as in Germany until the financial crisis.

Thus far, we have explained German competitive wage disinflation by referring to the overall macroeconomic conditions and simultaneous, but causally unrelated, sector-specific developments which worked to the disfavor of labor. However, an *intersectoral* liberalization dynamic also played a role. Many European countries have prevented the decline of trade unions from translating into declining collective bargaining coverage rates by making use of statutory bargaining extensions (SBEs). This instrument was never widespread in Germany but existed in a number of internal sectors. Against the international trend, German SBEs eroded further since the early 1990s.

This is due to a German peculiarity, the veto power of *intersectoral* employers' associations in the *Tarifausschüsse*, the committees which have to approve SBEs in the national and subnational labor ministries, even if there is a *sectoral* consensus in favor of the SBE. Over decades, this veto had mainly been a "sleeping resource" without frequent activation. But the more the German export sector grew, the more decisive became export interests within the *Bundesvereinigung der Deutschen Arbeitgeberverbände* (BDA). In the course of the 1990s, it started to proactively exert its veto power.[31] This resulted in a sharp decline in SBEs which passed the approval process between 1991 and 2019 (see the details in Günther 2021). Here, the export sector directly contributes to the disorganization of wage bargaining in domestic sectors.[32]

The phase of incomplete realignment

As indicated before, the extraordinary wage restraint in the years until 2007 was relaxed somewhat between the financial and the pandemic crisis, and wages even exceeded the "golden wage rule" in the last two observation years, 2018 and 2019. This was not caused by a fundamental shift in the wage bargaining institutions. Both the losses in trade union membership and the erosion of collective bargaining coverage slowed down after the financial crises but did not stop or reverse. In the political sphere, the introduction of the minimum wage in 2015 and a slight re-regulation of temporary work in 2017 were surely supportive but did not fundamentally change the political-institutional conditions within which wage bargaining operated.

The main change took place, rather, in the macroeconomic environment: Germany almost reached full employment in the late 2010s, and skilled labor shortages emerged in some sectors. In addition, the conditions for wage increases in construction became more favorable since the sector began to profit from its role of "safe haven" under conditions of negative real interest rates and capital flight from the South. In light of this economic background, one could have suspected a more pronounced realignment to occur, one that would have fully closed the inner-European competitiveness gap.

Remarkably, the wage gap between the industrial sector on the one hand, and low-end private services, construction, and the public sector on the other hand, which had emerged until 2007, remained the same between the financial and the pandemic crises (Di Carlo and Höpner 2020). In the phase of incomplete realignment, wage increases in the sheltered sector never exceeded those in the industrial sector. This also includes construction, the most likely candidate for an over-average wage development that however did not occur, mainly due to the ongoing wage competition exerted from the transnational posting of work. Therefore, despite overall better wage increases, the export sector still profited from the increased wage dispersion across sectors.

Why No Privatized Keynesianism in Germany?

The previous sections have shown that developments in the labor market and collective bargaining system, monetary and exchange rate policy, and fiscal policy produced a tendency for German domestic demand to stagnate and for German prices to grow more slowly than in trade partners. This configuration of institutions and policies, combined with the adoption of the common currency, contributed to entrenching an export-led growth model in Germany. However, the explanation is not complete unless we address the following puzzle: Why didn't domestic demand expand through other channels, for example through the extension of bank credit to households (Wood 2019; Reisenbichler 2021a)? Why did the construction sector stagnate in Germany? In brief, why was there no "privatized Keynesianism" in Germany, unlike in other countries (Crouch 2009)?

In order to answer these questions, we need to consider developments in the German banking and housing sectors. The German financial system is traditionally considered a model of bank-based finance (Deeg 1999). According to the Varieties of Capitalism theory, this model is characterized by a close relationship between banks and enterprises. In a bank-based system, banks provide patient capital to enterprises, allowing them to focus on the long-term development of their businesses rather than on short-term profitability (Hall and Soskice 2001; Zysman 1983). In turn, banks are able to play this role of stabilization because they are able to avail themselves of deposits, a more stable source of funding than money markets.

Data from the World Bank Global Financial Development Database confirm the predominantly bank-based orientation of German finance. Figure 9.1 compares the size of the banking sector (total assets of deposit banks) in Germany, Italy, Sweden, the United Kingdom, and the United States against the stock market capitalization and the size of the private securities market (total amount of domestic private debt securities), all as a share of GDP. In Germany, banks are much larger than both the stock market and the private debt market (127% of GDP vs. 39% and 44%, respectively). In Sweden and the United States, instead, the stock market is larger than banks are, and in the United Kingdom only slightly smaller. The Italian financial system is similar to the German system and also sees a clear prevalence of the banking channel of finance.

However, the overwhelming importance of banks does not mean that nothing has changed in German finance. First, as argued by Hardie and coauthors (2013), banking everywhere has seen a generalized shift toward market-based practices. On the liability side, this implies that banks increasingly fund themselves not through deposits, but by borrowing short term on the money market. On the asset side, banks rarely keep the loans they extend on their books, but they sell them, either directly or as part of securitization packages, pocketing the associated fees. Even when loans are kept on the books of banks, their value is "marked to market," which means that banks have to heed rating agencies and

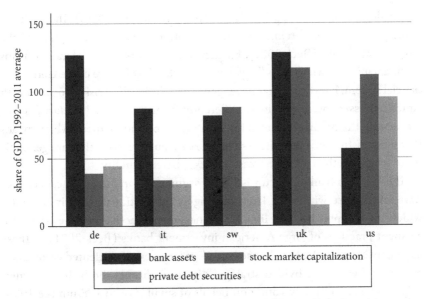

Figure 9.1 Bank Assets, Stock Market Capitalization, and Private Debt Securities.
Source: World Bank Global Financial Development Database.

market sentiment, and this undermines "relational banking" based on strong ties between banks and enterprises.

Furthermore, in the period before the financial crisis much banking intermediation took place through off-balance sheet vehicles, which are part of the "shadow" banking system (and are not subject to banking regulations). According to Hardie and coauthors (2013), the shift to market-based banking has affected all advanced countries, although to a different extent. While the Japanese banking system remains close to the traditional model of banking intermediation (funding through deposits and loans valued at cost and kept on the books), the United States is closest to the market-based end of the spectrum (funding through money markets, "originate and distribute" model of loan generation, fee-based business model). Surprisingly, Germany is closer to the US pole than to the Japanese pole according to these authors, indicating a significant evolution toward market-based banking.

Specifically, German banks responded to the decline in profitability of traditional banking activities by internationalizing their asset portfolio and investing in securitized financial products carrying a higher rate of return but also, as it turned out, higher risk. This explains the heavy involvement of the German banks, not only the large private banks but also some public regional banks (*Landesbanken*), in the Global Financial Crisis (Tooze 2017). However, differently from American banks, German banks did not massively engage in market-based liability management, because they were able to maintain a solid funding base in deposits even during the crisis (Hardie and Howarth 2013). Their liability management practices remained rather traditional, with the exception of the large private banks (Beck 2021). Furthermore, recourse to collateralized loans for financing (known as *Pfandbriefe*) is a long-standing feature of the German financial system. However, it has never generated the levels of risk associated with American asset-based securities. Differently from these, the *Pfandbriefe* loans are kept on the balance sheets of the institutions extending them, which means that these institutions bear the associated risks. Furthermore, they are generally more long term than other sources of market-based liquidity.

The German banking sector is highly segmented, and the greatest changes have taken place within the large and highly internationalized private banks, which have adopted both the liquidity management practices and the asset management practices of large American investment banks (Beck 2021).[33] These large banks used to be the "house banks" of large, export-oriented companies, to which they also provided strategic direction through both direct ownership of shares and proxy voting on behalf of small investors. From the 1990s on, however, the large private banks dramatically reduced their lending to the domestic private sector and this led to a decoupling of banks and enterprises. Braun and Deeg (2020) have argued that this decoupling is a secondary effect of the wage repression documented earlier in the chapter. By boosting firm profitability, wage repression increased the firms' ability to finance themselves through retained profits, and hence reduced their reliance on bank loans. To the extent that firms used external finance at all, they did so for the purposes of share buy-backs, that is, to reduce the stock of outstanding shares (Detzer et al. 2017, 164).

In the 1960s, 75% of the large private banks' assets was accounted for by lending to non-banks. However, this percentage declined to 25% in 2011 (Detzer et al. 2017, 60). Share ownership by banks also decreased from 12.5% in 1991 to 4.5% in 2011 (Detzer et al. 2017, 179). The regional government-owned *Landesbanken* also reduced their lending to the private sector starting from the late 1990s (Detzer et al. 2017, 630), while the small savings banks (*Sparkassen*), which had fewer profitability problems than the other banks, largely maintained their traditional model of banking, that is, they financed themselves through deposits and only marginally decreased their lending to the private sector as a share of total assets (Detzer et al. 2017, 62–63). Data from the BIS suggest a peculiar development of credit in Germany when compared with other countries, such as Sweden and the United Kingdom: credit to the non-financial sector actually declined from 2003 on (see Figure 9.2).

Figure 9.3, based on Bundesbank data, suggests that the decline in domestic credit is not so much due to lower loans to enterprises, which declined by only 2% of total banking assets (from 13% in 1999 to 11% in 2007); rather it is due to

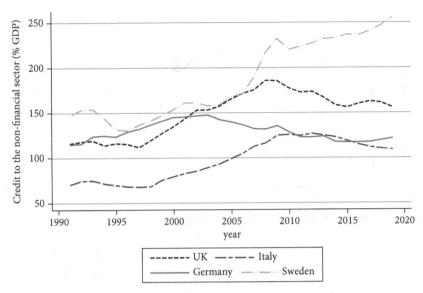

Figure 9.2 Credit to the Private Non-Financial Sector. Source: Bank for International Settlements

lower loans to households, which declined from 23% in 1999 to less than 17% in 2011. Importantly, interbank loans, that is, loans of German banks to other German banks, declined dramatically even after the crisis, from 27% in 1999 to 15% of total assets in 2019. Instead, loans to foreign banks increased from 7% in 1999 to 19% in 2007, to later decline to around 13% with the onset of the euro crisis. In the years in which international lending exploded, 80% of foreign loans were directed to European countries (Detzer et al. 2017, 79).

In brief, in Germany banks restructured their loan portfolios by replacing credit to the domestic economy with credit to foreign banks, especially European, and this explains the decline of credit to the domestic economy. Interestingly, the size of the German banking system (total assets as a share of GDP) shrank dramatically after the start of the euro crisis in 2011 (see Figure 9.4). Developments in the German banking system also contribute to explaining the peculiar trajectory of the German housing system. Figure 9.5 based on BIS data, shows that the trajectory of housing prices in Germany is anomalous in comparative perspective. Housing prices increased by 15% between 1991 and 1995 in Germany, as a consequence of the post-reunification mini-boom, but then declined until 2007, in a period in which housing prices more than doubled in the United Kingdom and Sweden (as well as other countries not reported in the graph), and increased rapidly even in Italy. After the crisis, German house prices grew rapidly, especially in large cities, but when considered over the entire 30-year period, they remain subdued in comparative perspective.

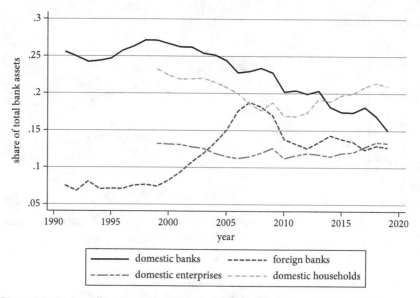

Figure 9.3 German Bank Loans as a Share of Total Assets. Source: Bundesbank

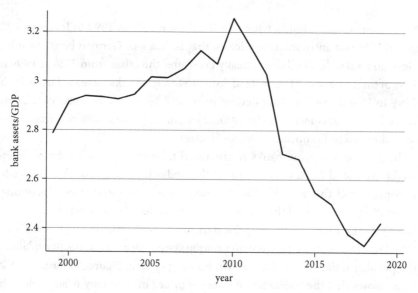

Figure 9.4 German Banking Assets as a Share of GDP. Source: Bundesbank

The stagnation of the German housing market has both demand-side and supply-side determinants, and their respective role is difficult to disentangle (Kohl 2017). The shrinking of domestic credit, especially to households, likely kept demand for housing low. In addition, the availability of cheap and legally protected rental alternatives to house ownership in Germany probably reduced

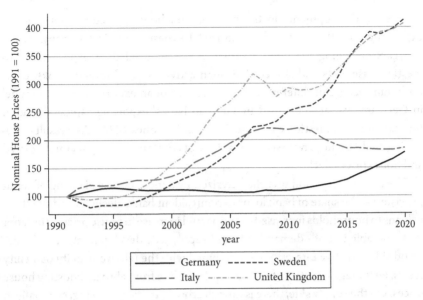

Figure 9.5 Housing Prices Bank for International Settlements

demand for housing loans. The German housing market is characterized by one of the lowest home ownership ratios in comparative perspective and more than 50% of the population live in rented apartments or houses. Until the recent spike in housing prices, the German housing market was one in which rents were affordable and there were few incentives for home ownership. The legal framework guaranteed protection from eviction and linked rents to the development of local prices. The stock of social housing was of relatively high quality as a result of massive public investment in the first decades after World War II. Additionally, there was no stigma associated to renting, even for middle-income households (Mertens 2015, 306).

Furthermore, the lending policies of banks are restrictive, as the key actors in the mortgage market are small and conservative financial institutions like the saving banks and local cooperatives. These controlled 29% and 20% of the market in 2012, while specialized mortgage banks (*Bausparkasse*) provided 7% of all housing loans in 2012 (Detzer et al. 2017, 246). Loan-to-value ratios are relatively low (70%), which implies that households are incentivized to save first before applying for a mortgage loan. Furthermore, the phenomenon of equity withdrawal in order to finance additional consumption is virtually absent, and early repayment of the mortgage in order to renegotiate it at more favorable rates is discouraged by penalties (Detzer et al. 2017, ch. 14). Last but not least, high real interest rates in the pre-crisis years, the result of a common monetary policy in the euro area combined with lower-than-average domestic inflation, discouraged investment in housing.

Overall, developments in the banking and housing sectors contribute to explaining why there was no "privatized Keynesianism" in Germany. In the 15 years preceding the GFC, German banks reduced their exposure to domestic households and shifted their loan activity toward foreign banks, especially European. Put differently, the emergence of an export-led growth model in Germany was accompanied by German banks' exporting capital abroad at the expense of domestic expansion (Fuller 2018; Jones 2021). As a result of declining credit to the private sector as a share of GDP, the housing sector stagnated and house prices declined.

The post-GFC period was characterized by a moderate rebalancing of credit provision—the share of bank loans to nonresident banks declined and the share of loans to households increased—and a rapid increase in house prices. The latter is attributable to both demand-side and supply-side developments. On the demand side, negative interest rates, combined with the relative scarcity of quality assets, encourage investment in housing, including from abroad, boosting house prices. On the supply side, there is now clearly a scarcity of housing, especially in large cities. The total number of housing completions (additions to the housing stock) declined from 600,000 in 1995 to 200,000 in 2012, and only slightly increased afterward, reaching 300,000 in 2019. Despite the scarcity, investment in housing has seen only a limited increase: from 5% of GDP in July 2008 to 6.6% in July 2019, while the stock of mortgage loans extended to households declined slightly from 37.7% of GDP to 36.6% in the same period (Bundesbank data). In other words, the scarcity of housing has not encouraged banks to extend more loans to households and has not greatly stimulated housing investment.

The housing boom is far from being distributionally neutral (Baldenius et al. 2019). It strongly benefits owners, that is, the rich, while the bottom 50% of the income distribution hardly benefits at all. In cities with lower per-capita income, rents have increased considerably, and poorer families spend up to 40% of their income on housing, up from 25% in the early 2000s.

Should the trend of growing house prices continue, it would not only create social tension, but also threaten the foundations of the German wage moderation regime. House prices reverberate across the economy and affect other prices in the economy. If the policy of affordable renting were to become a relic of the past, it is difficult to imagine that trade unions would not react by stepping up their demands for compensatory wage increases.

Conclusion

In this chapter, we have provided a historical account of the emergence of the export-led growth model in Germany. The reunification shock was a crucial moment, which could have shifted the German political economy onto a different track by increasing the importance of domestic demand for German growth. In all likelihood, had Germany shifted path, this would have greatly facilitated the life of the European Monetary Union, because its core economy would have contributed demand to other countries in the union (just like the United States does with the rest of the world), rather than subtracting it.

However, the Bundesbank strongly reacted, and arguably overreacted, to the appearance of some signs of growing inflation, modest in comparative terms but unusual in the German postwar context, and single-handedly quashed the domestic demand boom. Domestic actors responded by reinforcing familiar patterns of wage moderation and conservative fiscal policy, and this plunged the economy into semi-stagnation. The greatest restrictions came in 2000 to 2005, when the difficulties the German economy was experiencing—which are the classic problems a wage- and domestic demand-led growth model faces when deflation is forced onto it—were interpreted by policymakers as evidence that the internal adjustment was insufficient and more adjustment was needed. In these years, policymaking doubled down on internal devaluation and harsh austerity was accompanied by labor market and welfare reforms, producing exceptionally far-reaching wage restraint and a radicalization of the devaluation regime. The export-oriented sector greatly expanded at the expense of the private service sector and the construction sector, until, approximately around the mid-2000s, it became large enough to carry the whole economy along and rekindle growth and employment.

If developments until 2005 can be interpreted as export-led growth emerging as an unintended consequence of the adjustment to the reunification shock, what happened afterward, in 2005 to 2007, and especially after the financial crisis, is difficult to make sense of without attributing to policymakers a deliberate intent to consolidate and reinforce the devaluation regime. After a fiscal expansion in response to the financial crisis, Germany quickly returned to the path of fiscal conservatism, although (unlike in the early 2000s) clearly there was space for a more expansionary fiscal policy, which would have stimulated domestic demand, increased imports, and reduced current account surpluses, while simultaneously contributing to the supply of safe assets and thus facilitating the conduct of monetary policy at the EMU level. Institutions like fiscal federalism helped to enforce the commitment to "black zero" in fiscal policy.

Until the late 1980s, the German policy pattern could be described as a "policy of the middle way" (Schmidt 1987): as consensus oriented and avoiding abrupt policy changes and extreme outcomes. The pattern since Germany's transition to an export-driven growth model has been the opposite, however. In comparative perspective, the development of Germany has since been exceptional in many dimensions, and the outcomes have been extreme. This applies to the over-conservative fiscal policy stance as well as to the far-reaching welfare state reforms, the dualization of the labor markets, the large erosion of collective bargaining coverage, wage restraint, the sharp increase in the intersectoral wage spread, and the historically unique current account surpluses.

Remarkably from a political science perspective, this extreme development has nevertheless been based on a consensus shared by the decisive political parties. In our entire analysis period, there was no party-political contestation of the German path. In fact, the decisive decisions in the radicalization phase of 2001 to 2005 were made by a government led by social democrats: the harsh procyclical fiscal consolidation, the pressure on the social partners to decentralize wage setting, and the *Hartz* reforms. Certainly, the red-green government of these years was under particular pressure. But even in the most recent phase in which Olaf Scholz, a social democrat, was finance minister (since 2018), the government did not use the regained fiscal space until the onset of the pandemic crisis. If parties matter for growth models in the sense of this volume, this definitely does not apply to Germany.

In 2015 to 2019 there was a certain amount of rebalancing. In particular, wages increased, finally contributing to domestically driven growth. However, the rebalancing remains incomplete. In particular, large current account surpluses until 2019 signal that the domestic economy is still saving too much. At a time in which both households and enterprises are net savers, the public sector *must* go into deficit for net lending to the rest of the world (current account surplus) to go down. The political commitment to "black zero" was the main impediment to placing the German growth model on a more sustainable footing in the years leading up to the pandemic crisis.

The evolution of Germany's political economy has been shaped by the European Monetary Union in empirically complex and theoretically interesting ways. Germany's extreme export path and the euro are mutually enabling and undermining at the same time. The euro significantly changed the space of available options. Without the euro, Germany may not have been confronted with excessively high real interest rates during the long and severe recession of the first half of the 2000s. The Bundesbank could have responded with interest rate cuts and the state could have pursued fiscal expansion as long as these were non-inflationary. Had this happened, the *Hartz* reforms would presumably not have occurred either. At the same time, however, the euro also changed the payoffs of the undervaluation strategy. The tendency toward undervaluation was already typical for Germany before the euro, with a few exceptions, such as in the mid-1990s. But it was only in the euro that undervaluation could no longer be counteracted by realignments. Most likely, therefore, the extreme development of Germany's political economy would not have occurred without the euro.

At the same time, the German export-led growth model maintains a pathological, potentially undermining relationship to the euro. It threatens EMU by forcing other countries, especially the southern ones, to adjust through austerity and deflation, which are deeply unpopular (see Chapter 4 in this volume). That a breakdown of the euro would end German export successes is well understood by domestic elites and the general public. Economic elites are therefore willing to pay to maintain the euro, as Redeker and Walter (2020) have shown. The price, however, may become prohibitive, politically as well as economically. We believe that the long-term existence of the euro is by no means certain.

Although it now appears successful, the German growth model is in reality highly fragile because it depends on conditions which are not directly controllable by domestic policymakers. It requires a world economy that remains open to free trade and trade partners that are willing to tolerate large imbalances in bilateral relations, and the continued existence of the euro. After the experience of the Trump administration, the first assumption can no longer be taken for granted, and the second is not certain. Furthermore, the ongoing housing price boom in large German cities may undermine the unions' continued commitment to wage moderation. If rising house prices compromise the principle of affordable rents, wages and other prices may be pushed upward. The housing crisis also highlights the need for stepping up public investment, not just in housing but in infrastructure more generally. Finally, the urgency of ecological transformation, combined with the need for protection measures against the consequences of climate change, has been internalized by German voters. This requires the use of public debt for financing future investments. While this holds for many countries, such rethink stands in stark contrast to the fiscal pillar of the German growth model.

Notes

1. Space constraints prevent a detailed exposition of the methodology for the calculation of import-adjusted demand contributions to growth (for which we refer to Baccaro and Neimanns 2021, Appendix A.2. See https://www.mpifg.de/pu/mpifg_dp/2021/dp21-3_online_appendix.pdf.) The following remarks will suffice. Differently from Baccaro and Neimanns (2021), all data used here for the decomposition exercise are drawn from the OECD Trade in Value Added (TiVA) database. See https://stats.oecd.org/index.aspx?quer yid=106160 (last accessed on February 8, 2022). Import-adjusted demand contributions decompose imports between the part absorbed by domestic demand (for consumption, investment, government expenditures purposes) and the part absorbed by exports (imported intermediate products that are directly or indirectly incorporated into exports), and then subtract the relevant portions of imports from domestic demand and exports, respectively, when calculating contributions to total growth.
2. Extending the analysis to 2018 and 2019 using OECD National Accounts data suggests that the German manufacturing sector, while declining slightly in the latter part of the 2010s (to 21.2% of value added in 2019), remained larger than in the four other countries (18.6% in

Austria, 14.2% in Sweden, 9.7% in the United Kingdom, and 11.3% in the United States). The German construction sector increased a bit (to 5.37% in 2019), but remained smaller than in Austria (6.8%), Sweden (6.5%), and the United Kingdom (6.5%), although it was larger than in the United States (4.3%). The German public sector at large (including public administration and defense, education, and healthcare) accounted for 18.7% of value added in 2019, which is larger than in Austria (17.4%) and the United Kingdom (18.5%), but smaller than in Sweden (21%) and the United States (21.7%).

3. The variables are OXGN and OXSN, respectively (exports of goods and services at 2015 prices), which we then sum to produce a measure of total exports.

4. The variable is "Gross domestic product, volume, market prices" from the May 2019 edition of the Economic Outlook database. The figures for world GDP, originally in dollars, have been converted to euros using the OECD series on exchange rates between euros and dollars (PPPs and exchange rates dataset, variable: "Exchange rates, end of period"). The GDP of Germany (converted to 2015 euros using the OECD Economic Outlook variable: "Gross domestic product, market prices, deflator") was subtracted from both the eurozone and world GDP variables. By subtracting the eurozone GDP from world GDP we obtained the variable for the GDP of non-Eurozone countries.

5. See https://www.bruegel.org/publications/datasets/real-effective-exchange-rates-for-178-countries-a-new-database/ (accessed on April 23, 2021).

6. The BIS calls this a "narrow" index. The "broader" index, based on 60 partners, is only available from 1994 on.

7. The variable name is XUNRQ.

8. We examined the properties of the series using Augmented Dickey-Fuller tests. These tests suggest that all series are non-stationary in levels and stationary in first differences. We then tested for cointegration using both the Engle-Granger test and the Johansen test. These tests gave conflicting indications, with the former systematically rejecting cointegration and the latter not rejecting it. As a further check, we ran a single-equation error correction model and examined the properties of the error correction term, as suggested by DeBoef and Granato (1999) based on Kremers et al. (1992). This test did not reject the null of no-cointegration. Thus, we estimated our export equation in first differences. Note that given the absence of cointegration, the coefficients of the first difference specification can be interpreted as long-run coefficients. Results of the tests are available upon request.

9. Our estimates of the price elasticity of German exports are slightly bigger (in absolute value) than those reported by some analyses (e.g., Danninger and Joutz 2008; Neumann 2020), but in line with others (Thorbecke and Kato 2012; Breuer and Klose 2013). In unreported rolling-windows regressions, we noticed that the price elasticity coefficient increases (in absolute value) when more recent years are included in the sample. The greater magnitude of our estimates may be due to our more recent estimating sample.

10. The Durbin's test of serial correlation suggests that all models are free of serial correlation. Models with the BIS measures of REER produce very similar results. The models with the ULC-based measure of REER (based on comparisons with the EU14 only) perform worse statistically and deliver a slightly smaller price elasticity (around -0.7) and elasticity of foreign demand (around 2). Results are available upon request.

11. Economists discuss this as the *Walters critique*, named after Margret Thatcher's economic advisor Alan A. Walters, or as *rotating slumps*, a term coined by Olivier Blanchard.

12. If not indicated otherwise, all numbers referred to in this section are from Deutsche Bundesbank.

13. This "r > g" constellation emerged in 1992 and lasted for 12 years, longer than ever before in Germany after the Second World War (Data: Sachverständigenrat).

14. Between 1990 and 1998, social security contributions rose from 35.8% to 42.3% of the gross income. This only partly reflected the bad shape of the labor market. In fact, the Kohl government intentionally shifted significant parts of the financial unification burden to the social security system, in order to avoid tax increases.

15. Data: Statistisches Bundesamt.

16. In the period under investigation here, the government cut the nominal rate of the corporate tax, the *Körperschaftssteuer*, three times: in 1994, 1999–2001, and 2008. But different from

the cuts of the personal income tax, this did not translate into falling revenues, due to simultaneous broadenings of the tax base.

17. On the sharp drop of investments among municipalities, see Bremer et al. (2021).
18. This included further reductions of public gross investments in the years 2002–2004, with an especially harsh drop of -6.5% in 2004.
19. The German debt brake imposes a structural (cyclically adjusted) deficit of no more than 0.35% of the GDP upon the federal level, and a general ban on new debt on the *Länder*.
20. As Haffert (2019) shows, successful consolidation on the expenditure side is sometimes not followed by use of the regained fiscal space, but gives way to a permanent "surplus regime." This pattern occurred, among others, in Denmark, Finland, and Sweden in the late 1990s.
21. As Priewe (2020: 543) calculates, Germany could have refinanced a cumulated public debt of 147% of the GDP in 2019, without having to pay more interest on debt than it did in 2007. The actual cumulated public debt in 2019 was 59.8% of the GDP.
22. The ECB's interest rate on the main refinancing operations was 1% or lower since 2011, and 0% since 2016; the interest rate on the deposit facility was negative since 2014.
23. Data source: OECD.
24. Data source: IMF.
25. Note, however, that the German growth rate already went down to 0.6% in 2019, while it had been above 1.5% in all five years before, and that productivity increases were very close to zero in our two last years of observation, 2018 and 2019 (data source: OECD).
26. Data source: OECD.
27. Data source: IMF.
28. Data source: Comparative Political Dataset (AMECO data).
29. Data source: Comparative Political Dataset (ICTWSS data).
30. Data: Statistisches Bundesamt.
31. Between 2000 and 2018, more than 180 SBE applications were vetoed by the respective committees (data source: Deutscher Bundestag 2019, 4–11).
32. Such intersectoral conflicts also occur between the export and the construction sector. A particularly prominent example within our period of observation was *Gesamtmetall*'s resistance against the extension of domestic working conditions toward posted employees from other countries when the German *Entsendegesetz* (Posted Workers Act) was passed in 1996.
33. "By 2012, private banks accounted for 38% of banking assets, the publically owned savings banks for 29.4% and the cooperative banks for 11.8%" (Detzer et al. 2017, 4).

10

Rebalancing Balanced Growth: The Evolution of the Swedish Growth Model since the Mid-1990s

LENNART ERIXON AND JONAS PONTUSSON

Introduction

This chapter explores the evolution of the Swedish growth model over the last three decades. Relative to Baccaro and Pontusson (2016), we seek to go beyond an analysis based on growth accounting, and to qualify the characterization of Sweden as exemplifying a "balanced growth model." What distinguishes the Swedish experience from the German experience prior to the Great Recession of 2008–2009, we will argue, is not that exports and domestic consumption were coequal demand drivers of growth in Sweden while exports alone drove growth in Germany. Both economies were export-led but export growth generated more consumption growth in Sweden than in Germany, and thus boosted growth of import-competing goods and sheltered services. It is in this specific sense that the Swedish growth model of 1994 to 2007 can be characterized as "balanced" and as a continuation of the Swedish growth model of the early postwar period.

With this reformulation as our point of departure, we will proceed to explore how Swedish growth dynamics since the Great Recession differ from the growth dynamics of the pre-crisis period. Extending the analysis of Baccaro and Pontusson (2021), we demonstrate that a shift from foreign demand to domestic consumption as the primary demand driver of economic growth occurred in the wake of the Great Recession. The 2010s are also distinguished from the pre-crisis period by the increased importance of credit-financed consumption. At the same time, however, we emphasize that the Swedish economy remains highly trade dependent and that export-oriented manufacturing firms remain economically important and politically influential. In short, the Swedish growth model is still a balanced growth model, but the balance is different from what it used to be. To capture this shift, we refer to Sweden in 1994–2007 as an "export-led balanced growth model" and Sweden in the 2010s as a "consumption-led balanced growth model."

Our Swedish case study makes several analytical contributions to the growth-models perspective set out in the introductory chapter of this volume. As articulated in the introductory chapter (and in previous work by the editors), the growth-models perspective draws inspiration from the distinction between wage-led and profit-led growth commonly made by heterodox economists (e.g., Palley 2017; Lavoie 2017), but effectively replaces this distinction with the distinction between consumption-led and export-led growth. In this chapter, we bring the distinction between wage-led and profit-led growth back to center stage and treat it as conceptually distinct from the growth contributions of different components of aggregate demand. Our case study illustrates how the relationship between profits and components of aggregate demand can be explored empirically and some of the potential insights generated by doing so.

Relatedly, we want to suggest that insights might be gained by applying the distinction between profit-led and wage-led growth in a more disaggregated way than what is common among heterodox economists. Ignoring public services, our analysis distinguishes three aggregate sectors of the Swedish business: manufacturing, exposed services, and sheltered services. As we shall see, growth in (export-oriented) manufacturing has clearly been profit-led while growth in sheltered services has been wage-led and growth in exposed services cannot be so easily categorized as either profit-led or wage-led. The distinction between manufacturing and sheltered services holds for each of the time periods covered by our analysis. What distinguishes the post-crisis period (the 2010s) from the pre-crisis period (1994–2007) is the relative importance of the three sectors and the dynamic links between them.

Yet another analytical contribution that we seek to make is to bring productivity growth back into the picture. Baccaro and Pontusson's (2016) emphasis on the demand side of growth model was meant as corrective to the supply-side emphasis of the varieties of capitalism and the authors stated clearly that striking a better balance between demand- and supply-side considerations should be the long-term objective (pp. 27–18). Moving in this direction, our Swedish case study, however, seeks to illustrate how productivity growth affects macroeconomic dynamics.

In terms of methodology as well as substantive argumentation, our analysis of the Swedish growth model and its evolution over the period from 1994 to 2020 combines Baccaro and Pontusson's (2016, 2021) emphasis on balance between domestic and foreign demand drivers with Erixon's (2011) emphasis on the leading role of export-oriented manufacturing firms and the importance of productivity growth. In due course, we will also engage with the contention by Belfrage and Kallifatides (2018) that Sweden transitioned to a "finance-dominated growth model" in the time period covered by our analysis.[1] Akin to the perspective advanced by Ban and Helgadottír in this volume, we argue that the concept of "financialization" captures important long-term developments that predate the shift from export-led to consumption-led growth and that financial logic has not, at least not yet, displaced profit-making through the production (and export) of goods and services as the core logic of the Swedish growth model.

The rest of the chapter is organized as follows. We begin with the briefest possible introduction to the Swedish growth model until the mid-1990s. Against this background, we will devote separate sections to economic growth dynamics in 1994–2007 and 2010–2019. These are conceived in terms of demand drivers and the role of corporate profits in growth, with the over-time comparison featuring prominently in the second section. In subsequent sections, we address productivity growth and financialization across both time periods. Finally, we sketch an account of the politics of managing and adjusting the Swedish growth model.

The Swedish Case

Taking off in the last quarter of the 19th century, Swedish industrialization was fundamentally export-led. In the first instance, industrialization involved processing of wood and iron and exporting paper, pulp, and steel, but a number of innovative engineering firms exporting capital goods also emerged in this period (notably Atlas-Copco, Alfa-Laval, ASEA and Ericsson). The Swedish Social Democrats consolidated political power in the 1930s by striking a deal with the Agrarian Party, with the latter supporting proto-Keynesian recovery measures in return for agricultural tariffs (Gourevitch 1986).

This deal catered to the interests of domestic industries and was initially resisted by the export-oriented industries. However, the class compromise in the 1930s encompassed a second deal as well, the Saltsjöbaden industrial peace agreement of 1938, of which export-oriented employers were very much a part. As emphasized by Swenson (2002), the Saltsjöbaden agreement institutionalized cooperation between the LO (the confederation of blue-collar unions) and export-oriented employer associations to keep wage growth in construction and other sheltered sectors under control. The breakthrough of Swedish Social

Democracy in the 1930s hinged on the coexistence of these two, quite distinct, cross-class alliances.

The 1940s and the 1950s saw the rise of a new "fraction of capital"—engineering firms, like Volvo and Electrolux, producing consumer durables by Fordist methods (Erixon 1997). Accounting for a rapidly growing share of value added, this group of firms came to occupy a pivotal position bridging the traditional divide between export-oriented and home-market industries. Benefiting from the sustained boost of both domestic and foreign household consumption in the postwar era, Fordist mass producers were uniquely able to generate rapid productivity growth by scale advantages and the vitalizing role of international competition. Strong labor contributed to the productivity-enhancing reduction of profit margins in the open sector, especially by the blue-collar unions' pursuit of solidaristic wage policy from the early 1960s onward. Consistent with the logic the Regulation School's interpretation of the *trentes glorieuses* (e.g., Boyer and Saillard 2004), Fordist mass producers were the natural business ally of postwar social democracy in Sweden.

As documented by Erixon (1985, 1997) and Pontusson (1992a), the growing importance of export markets and foreign investment by the large Swedish engineering firms rendered the politics of class compromise increasingly fraught from the late 1960s onward. The Fordist growth engine ground to a halt while several traditional export industries linked to raw materials, steel and shipbuilding in particular, turned into "declining industries" in the context of the OECD-wide downturns of the 1970s. Volvo and other Fordist mass producers experimented with new, more flexible, production strategies in 1980s (Swenson and Pontusson 1996), but the recovery strategy adopted by the new Social Democratic government of 1982 was based on regaining cost competitiveness through a massive devaluation supported by voluntary wage restraint and tight fiscal policies (Erixon 1989; Pontusson 1992b). The Social Democrats also implemented an extensive program of financial deregulation in the second half of the 1980s (Blyth 2002, ch.7).

While the new macroeconomic policy paradigm of the 1980s contributed to sluggish productivity growth by reducing the pressure on firms to innovate, financial deregulation generated speculative bubbles in real estate and financial assets, setting the stage for a financial crisis in the context of the OECD-wide recession of the early 1990s. Largely due to policy choices in the 1980s, the early 1990s recession was deeper and longer in Sweden than in any other OECD country but Finland. With real GDP contracting for three consecutive years (1991–1993), the crisis of the early 1990s was worse for Sweden than crisis of the early 1930s (Edvinsson 2005, 253, 262).

Export-Led Growth 1994–2007

Except for a brief and shallow recession in 2001–2002, the Swedish economy grew at a steady and healthy pace from 1994 until the Great Recession of 2008–2009. Over the period from 1995 to 2007, Swedish GDP growth averaged 3.3% per year, roughly twice the rate of German GDP growth. Only a handful of long-standing OECD member states—Australia, Finland, Iceland, Ireland, South Korea, and Spain—performed better than Sweden by this measure. The Swedish recovery from the crisis of the early 1990s was export led in much the same way as the previous recoveries (Erixon 2015a). Having dropped in the second half of the 1980s, the export share of GDP increased from 26.0% in 1992 to an all-time high of 49.8% in 2008. Among West European countries, only Finland and Ireland exceeded the growth of exports registered by Sweden in the second half of the 1990s. Though falling behind Germany, the growth rate of Swedish exports remained impressive in the 2000s. From 1997 onward, Sweden also stands out as one of the OECD countries with the highest rates of household consumption growth. As reported by Baccaro and Pontusson (2016), domestic demand contributed significantly more to economic growth in Sweden than in Germany, although significantly less than in the United Kingdom, over the period 1994 to 2007.[2]

Figures 10.1 and 10.2 present our own estimates of gross profit shares over the period 1993–2018, with the gross profit share defined as gross profits (depreciation plus net profits) in percent of gross value added at current factor prices. While Figure 10.1 shows the evolution of the gross profit share for the business sector as a whole and for manufacturing and mining, Figure 10.2 decomposes the business sector into manufacturing (plus mining), exposed services and sheltered services.[3] Table 10.1 in turn tracks the allocation of total value added across these aggregate sectors from 1993 to 2018. As indicated at the outset, our objectives here are two-old. First, we want to insist on the conceptual distinction between export-led and profit-led growth. Second, we want to underscore the importance of sectors not only for the distinction between export-led and consumption-led growth, but also for the distinction between profit-led and wage-led growth.

Setting the post-crisis period aside for the time being, the gross profit share in the Swedish business sector declined from about 54% in 1995 to less 46% in 2002 and then recovered somewhat in 2003–2006 (reaching 51% in 2006). Based on data for all business, economic growth in the period from 1994 to 2007 can hardly be characterized as profit-led, but it is immediately clear from these figures that sectoral differences matter. The decline in the overall profit share over this period turns out to be entirely attributable to two factors: first, a steady

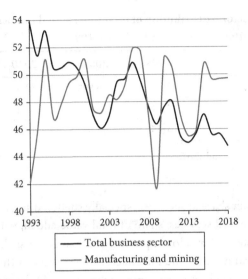

Figure 10.1 Gross profit share in percent of gross value added, total business sector (less agriculture, forestry and fishing) and manufacturing and mining, 1993–2018. Source: Own estimates based on the National Accounts Database of Statistics Sweden (Statistikdatabasen), Table *Förädlingsvärdets delkomponenter (ENS 2010) mnkr efter näringsgren SNI 2007* (Swedish industry classification based on NACE, rev. 2). Note that our calculations for the total business sector exclude agriculture, forestry and fishing.

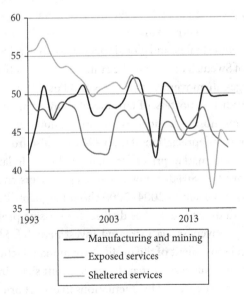

Figure 10.2 Gross profit share in percent of gross value added, manufacturing and mining, exposed services and sheltered services, 1993–2018. Source: Owned calculations based on National Accounts (see Figure 1). See also footnote 3.

Table 10.1 **The sectoral distribution of total value added by business (excluding agriculture, forestry, and fishing), 1995 -2018.**

	1995	2005	2010	2018
Manufacturing and mining	29.8 %	25.9 %	22.5 %	20.3 %
Exposed services	23.1	28.5	27.3	29.0
Sheltered services	46.5	44.9	46.6	49.5

Source: See Figure 10.1 and also footnote 3.

decline of the profit share in services, especially sheltered services; and, second, an increase in exposed services' share of total value added, with tradable services being characterized by a lower profit share than either sheltered services or manufacturing and mining. The manufacturing recovery in the second half of the 1990s was preceded by a sharp increase in the profit share and, in this part of the Swedish economy, the profit share was by historic standards high over the entire period from 1995 to 2006.[4]

As in the early 1980s, currency depreciation played a key role in the mid-1990s to increase the profit share in the manufacturing sector. In this instance, the falling value of the *krona* was the response by the financial market to the government's decision to switch to a flexible exchange-rate regime in late 1992. The *krona* then appreciated in 1995–1996 but deteriorated again in 1996–2001 as the prime rate by the Central Bank, governed by an inflation target from 1995 onward, reduced interest rates, and global speculative dynamics unrelated to the competitiveness of Swedish companies became an increasingly important determinant of exchange-rate movements (Alexius and Post 2008).

Traditional Swedish exporters of automobiles, investment goods, and raw materials—products mostly classified as low- or medium-tech—benefited from the sustained currency depreciation of the 1990s, but also from high foreign demand and rising world-market prices for their products.[5] In large measure, the profits boom enjoyed by Swedish raw-materials producers and manufacturing firms in the 1990s and again in 2004–2006 should arguably be seen as endogenous to the growth of exports and as distinct from rising profitability leading to increased competitiveness via increased investment (cf. Skott 2015). The strongly procyclical movement of the profit share in manufacturing and mining underscores this point, suggesting that the gross profit share in this part of the economy can largely be explained by fluctuations in export prices.

The key role of the ICT sector in the export-led recovery of the second half of the 1990s deserves to be noted in this context. Linking manufacturing (computer equipment) and services (information technology and telecommunications), the ICT sector as a whole, and especially the tele-products segment in which *Ericsson* acted as a spider in a strategic industrial network, was characterized by large technological opportunities and by fierce struggles for market shares. As a result, these firms experienced only a modest increase in their profit share in the second half of the 1990s (Erixon 2011, 309–311). More broadly, it is noteworthy that the service sector's share of Swedish exports increased from about 18% in the mid-1990s to 22% on the eve of the Great Recession even though the profit share in exposed services did not rise over this period.[6] On these grounds, "export-led" is arguably a better label for the Swedish growth model of 1994–2007 than "profit-led."

The diversification of exports through the expansion of high-tech manufacturing and a range of IT and business services distinguishes the Swedish experience of 1994 to 2007 from that of the 1980s. To some extent, the expansion of new, more knowledge-intensive, exports also distinguishes the Swedish experience from that of Germany in the period 1994–2007. As suggested earlier, however, the key contrast between Sweden and Germany has to do with the fact that export-led growth generated much more household consumption in Sweden than in Germany and thus more rapid growth of services catering primarily to domestic demand. As shown in Table 10.1, in Sweden, sheltered services' share of total value added declined slightly from 1995 to 2005, but this was entirely a result of growth in sheltered services lagging behind growth in exposed services. Firms in sheltered services actually grew their value added more rapidly than manufacturing firms. Critically for our purposes, this occurred despite a big decline in the profit share in sheltered services from 1994 to the early 2000s (see Figure 10.2).

In the sheltered private sector, which accounts for about 45% of total business value added, the growth process must be characterized as wage led. Crudely put, in this sector, profits' share of value added fell, but profits (and employment) rose by virtue of more output being produced in response to the demand created by wage growth. Profit-led growth in manufacturing and wage-led growth in sheltered services arguably complemented each other in the sense that the former generated initial recoveries, in 1994–1996 and 2003–2004, while the latter boosted growth in the later phase of each cycle (1999–2000 and 2007–2008).

As suggested by Baccaro and Pontusson (2016), the coupling of export-led growth with consumption growth in the Swedish case, and the contrast with Germany in this respect, can at least partly be explained in terms of wage formation dynamics. It is generally accepted that the Swedish system of peak-level wage bargaining collapsed in the 1980s and that a new system of "pattern bargaining," coordinated via centralized mediation, was institutionalized in the 1990s (see, e.g., Baccaro and Howell 2017, ch.8).

Formally speaking, this system resembles the German system of pattern bargaining in that it allows for collective bargaining at the firm level and, indeed, for bargaining between firms and individual employees. Also, both systems are premised on the idea of "wage moderation" by the manufacturing sector, considered to be the core of the exposed sector of the economy. In the Swedish case, this principle has taken been taken to mean that wage growth in the Swedish economy should not exceed wage growth in the Eurozone as a whole, the so-called Europe norm (*Europanormen*) (Erixon 2022).

For all the formal similarities between the two bargaining systems, wage developments in Sweden and Germany diverged sharply in 1994–2007. We suggest that the pattern-bargaining system made the export multiplier stronger in Sweden than in Germany. In the Swedish case, coordinated wage bargaining not only involved the exercise of wage restraint by workers in exposed sectors of the economy, but also the diffusion of wage increases in exposed sectors to sheltered sectors (Westermark 2019). In Germany, by contrast, more rigorous wage restraint in exposed sectors—in the first instance, manufacturing—was facilitated by the decoupling between exposed- and sheltered-sector wages, with the latter falling dramatically (see Baccaro and Pontusson 2016, 24–25). As workers in sheltered services tend to be less skilled and less well paid, low-end earnings inequality increased significantly less in Sweden than in Germany over this period. Not only was the average rate of wage growth faster in Sweden, but low-end Swedish wages grew particularly fast by comparison to low-end German wages.[7] To the extent that low-income households consume more of their income than high-income households, the more egalitarian profile of Swedish wage growth arguably contributed to the divergence between Swedish and German consumption growth.

Again following Baccaro and Pontusson (2016), divergent wage developments between Sweden and Germany can at least partly be attributed to differences in union strength and the size of the public sector.[8] Sweden's powerful public-sector unions were more able to ensure that the wages of their members would keep up with wages in manufacturing and exposed services than their German counterparts and public-sector wages for low-skill workers in turn set a floor for wages of low-skill workers in private services.

The Swedish experience of 1994–2007 highlights a feature that the literature on coordinated wage bargaining has tended to ignore, namely that coordinated bargaining with exposed-sector leadership sometimes serves not only as a mechanism of wage restraint, promoting export/profit-led growth, but also as a mechanism of wage-growth diffusion, promoting consumption/wage-led growth. As suggested by the Swedish case, whether or not coordinated wage bargaining takes on this dual role arguably depends on power relations more than formal institutional arrangements. In addition, we want to emphasize that wage growth-diffusion occurs not only through collective bargaining but also through market mechanisms, including consumer demand generated by earnings in export sectors as well as competition for labor across different sectors of the economy.

Consumption-Led Growth in the 2010s

By comparison to the crisis of the early 1990s, and the crises of the 1970s, the economic downturn triggered by the global financial crisis of 2007–2008 was very sharp but also short lived in Sweden, much like Germany and other Northern European countries. Swedish GDP contracted by 0.5% in 2008 and by a whopping 4.3% in 2009. GDP grew by 6.0% in 2010, but this spectacular recovery also proved short lived. Over the period 2008–2019, Sweden's annual GDP growth averaged 1.7%, roughly one and a half percentage point lower than the growth rate between 1995 and 2007. Also, Sweden's growth performance in 2008–2019 no longer deviated significantly from that of other OECD countries. Relative Germany, Sweden's GDP growth was slightly higher and GDP per-capita growth slightly lower.

The financial crisis and subsequent recession hit Sweden first and foremost by reducing global demand for the Swedish export products. The volume of exports fell by nearly 15% while employment in manufacturing and mining fell by 10% in 2009. Exports recovered sharply in 2010, but this recovery also proved short lived as the United Kingdom as well as the Eurozone member states embraced austerity policies in 2010. Swedish export growth in the 2010s was slower than in previous recoveries, but only slightly slower than German export growth at 4.2% compared to 4.8% per year (OECD 2020: Statistical Annex, Table 18).

As in the 1990s, the economy recovery of Sweden from 2010 onward followed in the wake of a sharp depreciation of the value of the *krona* and a restoration of the profit share in manufacturing. The depreciation of 2008–2009 was neutralized by appreciation in 2010–2013, but a further depreciation in relation to the US dollar—comparable to that of 1996–2001 in duration and magnitude (33% as compared to 40%)—followed in 2014–19. As a result, the profit share in manufacturing remained high, by historic standards, for most of the decade (see Figures 10.1–10.2 above).

In contrast to 1994–2007 however, these favorable conditions for export-oriented business did not translate into export-led growth. Arguably, the exchange rate has become a less important determinant of export competitiveness as the share of knowledge-intensive services in total exports has increased and the reliance on global value chains has increased the share of imported inputs in manufacturing, but we do not observe the decoupling between the exchange rate and the profit share in exposed sectors that this argument would seem to imply. As suggested before, sluggish foreign demand appears to have been the main constraint on export-led growth in the 2010s.

There was an important shift in the relative balance between foreign and domestic drivers of Swedish GDP growth in the aftermath of the Great Recession. Falling from all-time high of 49.8% in 2008 to 44.5% in 2009 (current prices), the share of exports of goods and services in GDP fluctuated between 42 and 47% from 2009 through 2019 (OECD National Accounts Issue 2, 2016 and 2020). Similarly, the data on the sectoral composition of total value added in the business sector presented in Table 10.1 bring out a clear contrast between the pre-crisis and post-crisis periods. While the share of value added by exposed services increased at the expense of sheltered services as well as manufacturing from 1995 to 2005, the share of value added by sheltered services increased at the expense of exposed services as well as manufacturing from 2005 to 2018.[9] It also deserves to be noted here that sectors conventionally characterized as "exposed" cater to domestic demand as well as foreign demand. This holds for manufacturing, but especially for "exposed services."

Relatedly, Figure 10.3 shows that investment in Swedish manufacturing fell behind investment in German manufacturing from 2008 onward. By contrast, even when excluding dwellings and finance, overall fixed capital investment by business increased much more in Sweden than in Germany over the course of the 2010s. With sheltered as well as exposed services being characterized by lower profit shares than manufacturing in the 2010s, classifying the Swedish growth model in this decade as "profit-led" would seem to be something of a stretch. At the same time, it is clearly the case that post-crisis period is distinguished from pre-crisis not only by lower GDP growth, but also by a declining profit share for the business sector as a whole.

The shift in Sweden, as in many other OECD countries, toward services in the 2010s was to a large extent policy led. The center-right coalition government avoided fiscal stimulus in 2008–2009, but the large Swedish public sector mitigated the recession by strong automatic (built-in) stabilizers. Albeit committed to the public-surplus norm established in the 1997, the subsequent fiscal policy by the center-right coalition became expansionary. The government was primarily guided by the efforts of the leading party, the Conservative *Moderata Samlingspartiet*, to increase labor supply by earned income tax deductions.[10] The return of the Social Democrats to power in 2014 (in coalition with the Swedish Green Party) meant a stricter application of the budgetary surplus norm (a public-debt-to-GDP anchor of 35% was added in 2019), but monetary policy compensated for the deflationary turn in fiscal policy (Leeper 2018).

Figure 10.3 Gross fixed capital formation (at constant prices) in the total business sector (excluding dwellings, finance, and insurance) and in manufacturing and mining, Sweden and Germany 1995–2019 (1995=100). Source: OECD database, 8A Capital Formation by Activity, ISIC rev 4. Note: The business sector has been derived here by subtracting Public administration and defense, compulsory social security (VO), Education (VP), and Human health and social work activities (VQ) from the economy (see the ISIC rev 4 classification). The exclusion of services provided by private companies in these sectors has only a marginal impact on total investments in the business sector in the two countries.

After a tightening of monetary policy in the early 2010s, motivated by the fear of a financial bubble, the *Riksbank* prioritized the fight against deflation from 2012 onward. To reach its inflation target, the *Riksbank* launched quantitative-easing programs and reduced the repo rate. For the entire second half of the 2010s, the Swedish repo rate was effectively negative, boosting demand not only for government bonds and real estate but also consumer demand by reducing borrowing costs (Andersson et al. 2020).

Private consumption was sustained by pattern bargaining in the 2010s. Despite the depreciation of the *krona*, real-wage growth in Sweden again exceeded that of most other OECD countries in the 2010s. As in the pre-crisis period, Swedish wage-bargaining dynamics served to diffuse wage growth from the manufacturing to other sectors of the economy and squeezed corporate profits in sectors characterized by limited mark-up opportunities and relatively low productivity growth.[11] In Western Europe, Sweden, Austria, and Norway stand out as the three countries with the highest rates of nominal wage growth in the private sector in 2008–2019. Sweden and Norway also stand out having

significantly higher rates of household consumption growth than most OECD
countries in this period.

On an economy-wide basis, Swedish wage growth closely tracked productivity growth prior to the Great Recession. In the post-crisis period, by contrast,
wage growth exceeded productivity growth by a wide margin, suggesting a more
important role for wage bargaining as a growth engine when exports and profits
in the exposed sector (the ICT sector in particular) fall short. As already noted,
however, monetary policy probably played a crucial role in sustaining private
consumption in the 2010s (primarily by the household cash-flow channel and
the stimuli of household disposable incomes). Let us briefly explore the dynamics of productivity growth before and after the crisis of 2008–2009 and then
address the question of financialization.

Productivity Growth

To motivate the discussion in this section, Table 10.2 provides an overview
of Sweden's labor productivity performance over the period 1995–2019, with
Germany, the United Kingdom, and the United States serving as comparative
benchmarks. Measured across the entire corporate sector, Swedish labor productivity grew twice as fast as German labor productivity between 1995 and
2007. Though the contrast is less stark, Sweden also outperformed the United
Kingdom and the United States (and indeed most other OECD countries) in
terms of labor productivity growth over this period. Importantly, this holds for
productivity growth in private services as well as manufacturing. Indeed, the
biggest difference between Swedish and German productivity performance in
the first half of the 2000s pertains to private services. What is most striking from
a comparative perspective is the broad scope of productivity gains in Sweden in
the decade before the crisis of 2008–2009. Productivity growth in storage and
transportation as well as wholesale and retail trade and hotels and restaurants
was significantly higher in Sweden than in the United States and the United
Kingdom, let alone Germany, and productivity growth in the financial sector,
including insurance companies, was also significantly higher than in Germany.

The sharp deceleration of productivity growth across the OECD area in the
wake of the Great Recession is consistent with the Kaldor-Verdoorn proposition
that aggregate demand determines the rate of productivity growth via the use of
scale advantages and the technological upgrading that new capital investment
entails. In 1995–2007, Sweden outperformed most OECD countries with respect to both GDP and productivity growth and this, too, would seem to support the Kaldor-Verdoorn theorem. However, it is far from obvious that GDP
growth and productivity growth are consistently associated with each other

Table 10.2 **Average annual percentage changes in labor productivity (value added per hour worked) in the non-agriculture business sector (excluding real estate), manufacturing, and the private service sector (excluding real estate). Sweden, Germany, United Kingdom and the United States, 1995–2007 and 2008–2019.**

		1995–2007	*2008–2019*
Total business			
	Sweden	3.9	1.2
	Germany	1.9	0.8
	UK	2.7	0.4
	USA	2.5	1.4
Manufacturing			
	Sweden	6.1	1.5
	Germany	3.2	0.9
	UK	2.5	0.5
	USA	4.4	0.2
Private services			
	Sweden	3.4	1.7
	Germany	1.4	0.8
	UK	3.3	0.6
	USA	2.7	n.a.

Source: OECD database, National Accounts, Productivity and labour costs, ISIC rev. 4. Data on productivity growth in the private-service sector for the United States 1995–2007 are imported from a discontinued time series not fully comparable with data for the other countries (OECD database, National Accounts, Productivity by Industry, ISIC rev. 3). Data for the United States on labor productivity in manufacturing and in the total business sector (less agriculture) are imported from the US Bureau of Labor Statistics.

across countries and time. It is noteworthy that British productivity growth was significantly slower than Swedish productivity growth despite very similar rates of GDP growth in 1995–2007. Also, Sweden combined sluggish productivity growth with robust GDP growth in the 1980s (Erixon 1989, 2008) and productivity growth in the country did not pick up appreciably as GDP growth recovered in the 2010s.

ICT specialization is a common characteristic of many countries with high productivity growth in the pre-crisis period. According to Edquist (2009), the

ICT sector alone accounted for nearly half of productivity growth in the Swedish corporate sector between 1995 and 2000 and the use of ICT in other sectors of the Swedish economy became an increasingly important source of productivity growth from the late 1990s onward. It is a commonplace to attribute Sweden's emergence as a leader in ICT adoption as well as in ICT innovation to its "national innovation system," as extended, and partly modified, by new government initiatives in the late 1980s and the 1990s (see, e.g., Ornston 2013; Thelen 2019). The Swedish innovation system has long been characterized by high rates of R&D investment by corporations and public authorities and by extensive R&D collaboration between firms and between the corporate and public sectors. Dominated by large engineering firms and pharmaceutical firms, the innovation system used to be geared toward incremental innovation within well-established industries (Edquist and Lundvall 1993; Erixon 1997; Bitard et al. 2008). Already in the 1980s, Social Democratic governments introduced measures to promote radical innovation and venture capital and the center-right coalition government of 1991 extended such measures (Ornston 2013).

Arguably, the deregulation of telecommunications and other public monopolies by the bourgeois parties also stimulated ICT innovation in a context characterized by public investment in infrastructure and public subsidization of corporate R&D expenditures (Bergh and Erlingsson 2009). Perhaps most importantly, governments in 1990s dramatically increased spending on education, broadened access to tertiary education, and undertook a range of measures to promote basic ICT competences as well as computer ownership and internet access for the population at large.[12] By stimulating domestic demand for ICT products and services, these measures boosted the earnings of Swedish ICT firms, but their main contribution to economic growth was to facilitate the introduction of productivity-enhancing ICT equipment and practices in other sectors of the economy.

As suggested by the literature on Nordic innovation systems, the larger institutional framework of public welfare provisions, active labor market programs, employment protection, and cooperative industrial relations contributed to pre-crisis productivity growth by facilitating employees' acceptance of changes in work organization and technology as well as more flexible employment contracts (Pontusson 2011). That said, the national-innovation-systems literature alone does not provide an adequate explanation of Swedish productivity growth, for there are no obvious institutional or policy changes that can invoked to explain the deceleration of corporate R&D expenditures and productivity growth in the wake of the economic crisis of 2008–2009. The use of data-processing software continued to expand in the Swedish business sector in the 2010s, but the productivity-enhancing potential of ICT usage in many service sectors appears to have been exhausted (cf. Gordon 2014).

Following the logic of the Rehn-Meidner model, wage pressure can also be invoked to explain Sweden's strong productive performance prior to the crisis of 2008–2009. While recognizing the need for wage restraint, Rehn and Meidner famously argued that wage solidarity, that is, higher percentage increases for workers in low-wage industries and firms, would promote overall labor productivity growth by incentivizing less productive industries and firms to invest in new (labor-saving) technologies while incentivizing more productive firms to expand employment.[13] As noted, the new system of coordinated wage bargaining that was institutionalized in the late 1990s aimed at adjusting nominal wage growth in the exposed sector to the pace of nominal wage growth in the Eurozone.

At the same time, coordinated bargaining with strong public-sector unions served to ensure that wages in sheltered sectors (private as well as public) would keep up with wages in the exposed sector. Especially in view of the extensive room for firm-level bargaining with the framework established by the Industrial Agreement of 1998, central wage-bargaining arrangements to achieve wage moderation can hardly account for the fact that manufacturing productivity growth in Sweden outpaced that of other European countries in 1995–2007. A plausible case can be made that wage pressure from pattern bargaining contributed to the high rate of productivity in services (cf. Westermark 2019), but a plausible case can also be made that strong productivity growth enabled employers in sheltered sectors to cope with the wage pressure generated by exposed-sector-leadership in the wage-bargaining process. Our purpose here is not identify causality, but rather to emphasize that wage growth and productivity growth are mutually supportive.

The deceleration of Swedish productivity growth in 2010s runs counter to the argument about wage equalization as a source of transformative pressure, for equalization remained a prominent feature of wage bargaining in 2010s (see footnote 11). At the same, however, the crisis clearly dampened average wage growth and this, along with currency depreciations in the second half of the 2010s, may well have contributed to the deceleration of productivity growth, especially in the exposed sector.

The main takeaway of the preceding discussion is that none of the causal variables that we have identified provides a satisfactory stand-alone account of Swedish productivity growth over the last three or four decades. Temporal change, as well as cross-national variation in productivity should be seen, we think, as the product of complex interactions between aggregate demand, technological opportunities, and institutional frameworks. Put differently, the Swedish productivity miracle of 1994–2007 rested on a fortuitous combination of factors that was unlikely to persist indefinitely.

A Financialized Growth Model?

Let us now turn to the topic of financialization and, more specifically, to Belfrage and Kallifatides's (2018) contention that financial deregulation in the late 1980s and further neoliberal reforms in the early 1990s ushered in a new, finance-dominated, Swedish growth model. As articulated by Belfrage and Kallifatides, the rise of finance to a dominant role involves three specific claims. First is that credit has become the primary source whereby households finance consumption. Second is that the financial sector has become the leading sector of the Swedish economy. Third is that investment decisions by non-financial corporations have increasingly been driven by financial considerations. Let us briefly consider each of these claims.

As shown in Figure 10.4, household indebtedness increased dramatically in Sweden in the 1990s and 2000s, much like the United Kingdom and the United States and in marked contrast to Germany. Still more strikingly, the financial crisis of 2007–2008 did not reverse the growth of household indebtedness in Sweden, as it did in both the United Kingdom and the United States. As noted by Andersson and Jonung (2015), among others, the rise in household indebtedness in Sweden primarily involved mortgage lending by banks and closely tracked rising house prices through the early 2010s (see also Anderson and

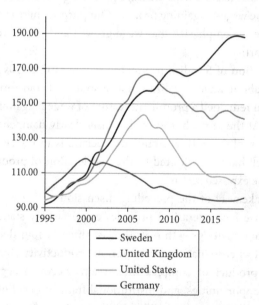

Figure 10.4 Debt of households and nonprofit institutions serving households (NPISHs) as a percent of net disposable income (NDI) in Sweden, Germany, United Kingdom, and the United States, 1995–2019. Source: OECD database, Financial Indicators.

Kurzer 2020). Credit contributed to household consumption already in the period leading up to the Great Recession, but the role of credit as a source of domestic demand increased significantly as wage growth slowed in the 2010s.

Consistent with the financialization story, the total value of bank loans in Sweden tripled from 2001 to 2018, but bank loans were overwhelmingly offered to house buyers and financial corporations. Only 13% of new bank loans over this period went to non-financial Swedish corporations (Kazen Orrefur 2019, 22–23) despite the fact that their debt rose substantially in relation to both GDP and profits in the 2010s by international standard.[14] By financing investment in financial assets as well as dwellings, private banks—essentially four banks (Nordea, SEB, Handelsbanken, and Sweden)—created a huge amount of new money in the 2010s. It is important to keep in mind, however, that the creation of bank money was very much encouraged by the interest-rate policy of the *Riksbank*.[15] Moreover, the financial sector's share of total business value added has fluctuated between 4% and 5% since the mid-1990s. By this measure, the Swedish economy remains less financialized than many other OECD economies.[16]

Turning to the behavior of non-financial corporations, Figure 10.5 shows the evolution of their operating surplus (i.e., profits from the production of goods and services) and returns on financial assets (financial profits) from 1997 to 2019. Notwithstanding the steady rise of stock-market prices, industrial profits exceeded financial profits throughout this period. It is also

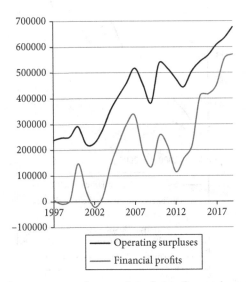

Figure 10.5 Annual operating surpluses and profits on financial assets in Swedish non-financial companies in 1997–2019 (million SEK). Source: Company data from Statistics Sweden (*Företagsräkningsposter enligt Företagens ekonomi*).

noteworthy that the two types of profits have moved in tandem. In other words, aggregate financial profits do not seem to operate by a different logic from aggregate industrial profits. The gap between them appears to have diminished in the mid-2010s, but this partly reflects their divergence in the wake of the financial crisis. Comparing 2015–2019 to 2000–2007, it is not obviously the case that financial profits have become more important to non-financial corporations over time.

A crucial question in this context is whether or not investments in real estate and financial assets have crowded out productivity-enhancing investments in equipment, R&D, and "intangibles" such as software. Figure 10.6 addresses this question by comparing the evolution of gross fixed capital formation by business in "financialized Sweden" and "non-financialized Germany." For each country, we present a curve for the entire business sector and another curve for businesses other than finance and housing construction. As these figures concern fixed capital formation, the financial sector is of minor importance and the comparison here is really between investment in housing and investment in other business sectors. As expected, we find that real-estate investment has lagged behind other forms of real investment in Germany since the early 2000s while real-estate investment has increased faster than other forms of investment

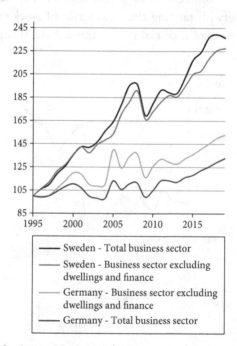

Figure 10.6 Gross fixed capital formation (constant prices) in the total business sector and the business sector excluding real estate and finance (including insurance). Sweden and Germany, 1995–2019 (1995=100). Source: See Figure 3.

in Sweden over the same time period. However, the more striking cross-country contrast that emerges from Figure 10.6 is that gross capital formation increased at a much faster rate in Sweden than in Germany even if we exclude dwellings. In short, the comparison with Germany calls into question the proposition that the Swedish construction boom of the 2010s crowded out investment in other forms of fixed capital.[17]

In our view, the concept of "financialization" captures several long-term economic developments with important implications for macroeconomic dynamics, but it is misleading to speak of the emergence of a new Swedish growth model distinguished by the leading role of the financial sector or by the dominance of financial speculation over real economic activities. To posit the development of such a growth model in the 1990s calls into question the common—and, we think, reasonable—supposition that finance dominance is anathema to productivity growth. As for the consumption-led recovery of the 2010s, it is important to recognize that Swedish real wages did grow at a relatively healthy pace and that wages at the bottom of the earnings distribution kept pace with average wages. Developments in the last few years could plausibly be invoked in support of the idea that a finance-dominated growth model has finally emerged, but the durability of these developments remains an open question.

Business Diversification and the Politics of Macroeconomic Management

Following Thelen (2019), we want to highlight the diversification of Swedish business over the time period covered by the preceding analysis and to suggest that this diversification facilitated the pursuit of consumption-led growth in 2010s. Again, the comparison with Germany is instructive from this point of view. In Sweden, much like Germany, export-oriented manufacturing was the leading sector of the postwar era and remained dominant through the 1980s, but the two countries subsequently diverged. To use Thelen's felicitous characterization of this divergence, Germany "doubled down" on its reliance on traditional manufacturing exports while Sweden "branched out."

The key role that the ICT sector came to assume in the economic recovery of the 1990s represents the most obvious indicator of structural changes within the framework of (balanced) export-led growth (Erixon 2011, 308–312). A traditional telecom company that embraced the "ICT revolution" in the 1990s, Ericsson alone accounted for nearly one-fifth of Swedish exports in 1999–2000. The share of ICT products in total export diminished in Sweden in the early 2000s, but it still remains higher than in Germany and most other European countries (World Bank database, ICT goods exports 2000–2019). As we have stressed throughout this preceding discussion, the role that the ICT has assumed since the mid-1990s extends far beyond exports of "ICT products." Software services became an important source of export earnings in the decade prior the crisis of 2008–2009. Since 2015, Ericsson is actually classified by Statistics Sweden as a producer of services. Also, new products generated by the ICT sector contributed to rapid productivity growth across the Swedish economy and thus boosted the competitiveness of a wide range of exports.

Linked to the rise of the ICT sector, the steady growth in the importance of service exports constitutes another important dimension of the diversification of the Swedish growth model since the mid-1990s (cf. Baccaro and Pontusson 2016). While service exports accounted for 6% of GDP and 18% of all exports in 1993–1995, they accounted for 10% of GDP and 22% of all exports in 2006–2007. The retreat from export-led growth that occurred in the wake of the global crisis of 2000–2009 was all about raw materials and manufactured goods. From the mid-2000s to the mid-2010s, goods exports declined from 36% to 30% of GDP while services exports increased from 10% to 14%. By 2014–2016, exports of services accounted for a whopping 47% of Swedish exports, as compared to 17.4% of German exports.[18] On the premise that competitiveness in world markets for services, at least the kinds of services that Sweden primarily exports, is less a function of labor costs than competitiveness in world markets for manufactured goods, the shift to services exports might be invoked from to explain the combination of export-led and consumption-led growth that characterizes the Swedish case over the period 1994–2007 and, to a lesser extent, the 2010s as well (Baccaro and Pontusson 2016).

Initiated by the center-right government of 1991, tolerated by Social Democratic governments between 1994 and 2006, and further promoted by the center-right parties after 2006, the privatization of education and welfare services represents another important form of business diversification. The consumption of education, healthcare and elderly care remains almost entirely funded by government(s), but private for-profit providers have become increasingly prominent in this domain. From 2002 to 2014, public disbursements to for-profit providers in education increased by 247% from 2003 to 2014 (Svallfors and Tyllström 2019, 748–749). Over the same time period, disbursements to for-profit providers in healthcare increased by 106% and disbursements to for-profit providers in elderly care increased by 130%. While overall employment in these three sectors increased by 20% from 2000 to 2015, employment by for-profit providers increased by 65% (accounting for roughly 20% of total employment in 2015). Importantly, large companies controlled by the Wallenbergs's investment company (Investor) and other financial groups have come to dominate this new sector of business activities, sometimes referred to as the "welfare-industrial complex" by Swedish commentators.[19] As Svallfors and Tyllström (2019) emphasize, organized business has become less vocal in its opposition to the welfare state at the same time as corporate actors have become directly involved in reshaping the welfare state (see also Busemeyer and Thelen 2020).

As late as the 1980s, large export-oriented engineering firms constituted a cohesive group at the core of the coalition of organized interests that supported the Swedish growth model. Twenty or 30 years later, it is more difficult to identify Sweden's dominant "fraction of capital." The point here is not so much that new actors have emerged, challenging the interests of export-oriented manufacturing, but rather that the manufacturing firms and their owners have diversified and that the interests of export-oriented manufacturing firms have become more ambiguous. As exports have shifted to more knowledge-intensive products and services, export-oriented firms have become less concerned with domestic labor costs. At the same time, the growing reliance on global supply chains in more traditional manufacturing has made devaluation less attractive as means to address labor costs. Arguably, this diversification of businesses and their interests leaves more freedom for government officials and parliaments to determine macroeconomic policies.

The fact that Swedish governments pursued more expansionary fiscal and monetary policies than German governments in the 2010s can partly be explained by the fact that Swedish business did not rally behind domestic austerity, but party politics deserve to be considered as well. With the entry of the populist Sweden Democrats into parliament in 2010, neither of the two partisan coalitions that have competed for government power since the 1970s commanded a parliamentary majority in the 2010s. In this new situation, the center-right coalition government of 2010 and the Social Democratic-Green coalition government of 2014 both eschewed austerity measures that seemed likely to weaken their re-election prospects. Austerity would have required a German-style grand coalition government. It tempting to argue that the deep Left-Right divide in Swedish politics precluded such a coalition, but there is a further twist that deserves to be noted. In contrast to Germany, there has never been a truly dominant center-right party in Sweden (cf. Castles 1978). Competition among the bourgeois parties makes it difficult for anyone (or any two) of these parties to enter into a formal coalition with the Social Democrats. Since the transformation of the Agrarian Party into a centrist bourgeois party in the 1960s, fragmentation on the Right of the political spectrum has effectively reinforced the Left-Right divide. Against this background, the lack of clear parliamentary majorities helps explain the consensus on macroeconomic management being delegated to the *Riksbank* in the 1990s.

Conclusion

As we have seen, financialization and diversification of non-financial business activities constitute long-term developments that have changed—and continue to change—the structure of the Swedish economy. These developments have important implications for macroeconomic dynamics, first and foremost through the implications for the politics of macroeconomic management. Yet neither development taken by itself nor the two taken together provides an adequate basis for identifying a new "growth model" in the sense that this term is used by Baccaro and Pontusson (2016) and other contributors to the emerging growth-models literature.

Sweden exhibited high GDP growth and especially high productivity growth from the mid-1990s until the Great Recession. We have established that Swedish economic recoveries in the late 1990s and early 2000s were primarily export-led and partially profit-led. These recoveries might have generated high consumption and productivity growth by the extensive diffusion of wages and technologies from export-oriented manufacturing firms into other sectors of the economy. It is likely that the export multiplier was reinforced by the wage bargaining system, generating wage-led growth in sheltered sectors. At the same time, the importance of the ICT sector for productivity, export (of both products and services) and investment across sectors added a technology-led (supply-side) component to the Swedish growth model anchored in the national innovation system.

By comparison, exports and productivity played a much less important role in the recovery of the early 2010s. As in the pre-crisis period, relatively egalitarian wage growth stimulated consumption growth, but cheap money also appears to have emerged as an important support for sustained household consumption in this period. Crucially, the shift in macroeconomic dynamics triggered by the Great Recession cannot be labeled as "profit-led," for sectors characterized by lower profit shares than the manufacturing sector grew their shares of investment as well as value added in the course of the 2010s (and the profit share in the business sector as a whole continued to decline).

The post-crisis shift can largely be explained by sluggish foreign demand for Swedish exports (especially manufacturing exports) and by expansionary macroeconomic policies—most importantly, over the long haul, monetary policy—pursued by the government and the *Riksbank*, boosting housing construction and household consumption. This shift was arguably facilitated by institutional reforms that were made in the 1990s, including the new bargaining system and monetary policy as well as financial deregulation and tax treatment of mortgages. Importantly, we argue that the shift itself did not involve much political contestation or any noteworthy new institutional reforms. The ease with which Sweden moved from export-led to consumption-led balanced growth may be reason enough to characterize this shift as an adjustment of the (balanced) growth model rather than a transition from one growth model to another, but we leave this as an open conceptual question for the time being.

Contrary to proponents of the idea that a finance-dominated growth model has emerged, we do not see any structural obstacles that would prevent the Swedish economy from becoming export-led again if foreign demand for Swedish exports were to pick up in the 2020s. That said, we hasten to reiterate that high productivity growth provided a crucial underpinning of the fortuitous combination of growth through exports and domestic consumption that Sweden achieved in 1994 -2007. In the absence of a new spurt of productivity growth, the restoration of export-led growth would require policies to suppress domestic consumption along the lines of the export-led strategy pursued by German governments and, as suggested before, this would in turn require a rather major reconfiguration of party politics.

Notes

1. A similar line of argument is advanced by Buendia and Rey-Araújo (2021). In contrast to our analysis, these authors emphasize the transformative role of neoliberal reforms in the early 1990s and downplay the impact of the Great Recession on the Swedish growth model.
2. This also holds for the import-adjusted estimates presented in Baccaro and Höpner's chapter in this volume.
3. Our coding of services as "exposed" or "sheltered" is based on the regional concentration of different service industries as reported by Eliasson and Hansson (2016). By our specification of the cut-off between exposed and sheltered service sectors, "exposed services" include transport and storage (H49–H53), edition, film, video and TV (J58–J60), telecommunications (J61), information technology (J62–J63), financial and insurance activities (K64–K66), business administration (M69–M70), scientific and technical activities (M71–M72), advertising and marketing (M73), and other business activities (M74–M75). "Sheltered services" in turn include electricity, gas, and water supply (D35–E39); construction (F41–F43); wholesale and retail trade (G45–G47); accommodation and food service activities (I55–I56); dwellings (L68A); other real estate activities (L68B); administrative and support service activities (N77–N82); education (P85); art, entertainment, and recreation (R90–R93); human health (Q86); and social work activities (Q87–Q88). Note that the analysis presented here fails to take account of overtime changes in these (sub-) sectors' exposure to international competition.
4. See Erixon (1987, 47) and Bengtsson (2014, 298) on the evolution of the profit share over a more extended period of time.
5. The Swedish *krona* strengthened in relation to the US dollar in 2001–2008, prompting a small rise in relative unit wage costs, but this did not prevent a second exports and profits boom starting with the 2001–2002 recession.
6. While finance and insurance only accounted for 7.1 percent of Swedish service exports in 2013–16, IT services accounted for 20.8 percent of Swedish service exports and "business services" for another 25.9 percent. The remaining categories worthy of notes are transport (26.8 percent), travel (15.8 percent), and intellectual property (11.1 percent). Source: OECD Database on Trade in Services.
7. From 1998 to 2007, average hourly earnings in the private sector grew at an annual rate of 3.1% in Sweden and 2.1% in Germany (OECD Main Economic Indicators). From 1994 to 2007, the Swedish 50-10 earnings ratio rose by 4.8% (from 1.25 to 1.31) while the German 50-10

ratio rose from by 12.2% (from 1.63 to 1.83). Sources: OECD Main Economic Indicators and Relative Earnings Database.

8. In 2011, public-sector union density in Sweden was 83% compared to 27% in Germany. In Sweden, private-sector density was 65% and public-sector employees accounted for 42% of all union members. In Germany, private-sector density was 16% and public-sector employees accounting for 37% of all union members. Source: Visser (2019).

9. By adjusting for imports, the decomposition of GDP growth by components of aggregate demand presented in Baccaro and Höpner's chapter in this volume obscures the post-crisis Swedish shift to consumption-led growth. Note also that Baccaro and Höpner's estimates fail to capture developments in the second half of the 2010s.

10. A commonly used measure of discretionary fiscal stimulus, the underlying primary government balance was reduced from 3.1% of potential GDP in 2009 to -0.1% in 2014. The underlying primary balance in Germany was the same in 2009 and 2014 (1.7%). Source: OECD Economic Outlook 106 database.

11. Relative to 1994–2007, the pace of overall earnings inequality growth decelerated in the 2010s, with the 90-10 ratios rising by .49 per year between 2010 and 2019, as compared to 1.01 between 1994 and 2007 (OECD Relative Earnings Database). See Erixon (2022) for a more extensive discussion of the macroeconomic role of wage formation in the 2010s.

12. According to Thelen (2019, 306–307), public spending on education increased from 5.3% of GDP in 1990 to 7.4% in 2000, with spending on tertiary education accounting for nearly half of the increase (rising from 1% in 1990 to 2% in 2000). Thelen also documents sharp rises in the percentage of the population with tertiary education and the percentage of households with computers and internet access.

13. See Erixon (2008, 2015b) on the Rehn-Meidner model and its continued relevance.

14. See OECD Financial Indicators Database.

15. Note also that the debt-to-equity ratio of non-financial corporations did not increase Sweden in the 2010s (OECD Financial Indicators Database).

16. While recognizing this point, Belfrage and Kallifatides (2018, 884–886) claim that profits of financial corporations exceeded the profits of non-financial corporations in 2005–2014. If profits are measured as a percentage of value added, as they ought to be, the differential between financial and non-financial profits would have to be huge in order for this claim to be true!

17. Note also that R&D investment by Swedish business declined in the 2000s but recovered slightly in the 2010s (Statistics Sweden, *Fasta bruttoinvesteringar, ENS2010 efter näringsgren SNI 2007 och investeringstyp, 1980–2019*).

18. Source: OECD Balance-of-Payments Database.

19. According to a report by Public Education Authority cited by Svallfors and Tyllström (2019, 749), the 10 largest for-profit providers account for one-fifth of primary education and one-third of secondary education in 2014. See also Busemeyer and Thelen (2020).

11

Growth and Stagnation in Southern Europe: The Italian and Spanish Growth Models Compared

LUCIO BACCARO AND FABIO BULFONE

Introduction

Comparative political economy usually treats Italy and Spain as similar, even "most similar," cases. For Varieties of Capitalism, they are both "mixed" models of capitalism, neither sufficiently liberal nor sufficiently coordinated, and thus less efficient than "pure" types such as Germany or the United States (Hall and Gingerich 2009; Molina and Rhodes 2007). For the welfare state literature, they are both "Mediterranean" countries, in which transfers (pensions in particular) receive the lion's share of social expenditures, while investments in human capital development are neglected (Beramendi et al. 2015; Ferrera 1996).

Despite these similarities, Italy and Spain have had very dissimilar growth performances in the past 30 years. While Spain was one of the fastest growing economies in the Eurozone, Italy went through a phase of prolonged stagnation. As a result, while per-capita GDP was more than 30% higher in Italy than in Spain in the early 1990s; by 2019 the gap had declined to 1.5%.[1] Furthermore, while Spanish growth beat the Eurozone average between 1999 and 2007 (19% vs. 15%), Italian growth was well below it (9%). After the euro crisis, which severely affected both countries, Spain rebounded while Italy continued to stagnate (see Figure 11.1). How do we account for these starkly different growth trajectories despite the alleged similarity between the two countries?

To answer this question, in this chapter we emphasize the interaction between international economic constraints and domestic conditions. Italy and Spain were both heavily influenced by their common membership in the euro,

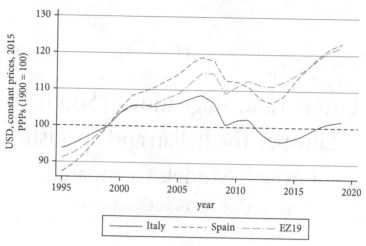

Figure 11.1 GDP per capita. Source: OECD

and before that by their effort to qualify for it, but in very different ways. Briefly stated, we argue that while Spain was able to implement a growth strategy that, although highly unstable and inherently inegalitarian, was consistent with the growth possibilities afforded by EMU membership, Italy stands out for its inability to do so.

The process of monetary unification had two opposite effects on members of the currency union that we call "Walters 1" and "Walters 2" (Walters 1990). Walters 1 applies to countries with higher-than-average growth of domestic prices. In these countries the convergence of nominal interest rates brought by the euro (both short-term and long-term rates) led to lower real interest rates, which in turn stimulated construction, boosted the demand for credit (to which banks responded by increasing the supply of credit), and expanded other service sectors relying primarily on domestic demand. However, these countries also saw an appreciation of the real exchange rate vis-à-vis other members of the currency union, which worsened the price competitiveness of exposed sectors such as manufacturing, forcing them to choose between upgrading, in order to reduce their sensitivity to price increases and their attractiveness for foreign buyers, or shrinking.

Walters 2 is the opposite. In countries characterized by lower-than-average inflation rates, the real interest rate deriving from the combination of a common monetary policy and the national inflation rate became higher than would have been required for full employment, but the real exchange rate devalued. This configuration penalized interest rate-sensitive construction and other domestic service sectors while favoring exchange rate-sensitive manufacturing. For the latter a currency union was a boon because it ruled out nominal exchange rate adjustment by other members of the currency union and guaranteed a structurally undervalued exchange rate regime (Höpner 2018). Both Walters 1 and Walters 2 give rise to unbalanced growth, yet growth nonetheless. The way Walters 2 unfolded and shaped the growth strategy of Germany since the mid-1990s has been analyzed in Chapter 9. This chapter is (mostly) about Walters 1. We argue that while Spain was able to ride Walters 1 in full, at least until the crisis, Italy was unable to exploit either Walters 1 or Walters 2 but wavered between the two, seeking first to boost the external competitiveness of its manufacturing sector, before partially shifting to a Spanish domestic demand-led strategy.

As a result, Spain embraced a financialized, credit-fueled, domestic market-led growth strategy, presiding over a huge increase in the volume of banking credit, a large expansion of construction investment, and a stellar increase in house prices (Cárdenas et al. 2021). In so doing, it accumulated massive current account deficits, but thanks to the general optimism prevailing in the early decade of the euro, it could easily finance them through net capital imports. Put differently, the euro allowed Spain to relax its current account constraint on growth for some time, therefore allowing it to consume, and grow, at a rate faster than that normally compatible with external stability (a mechanism discussed in the Introduction to this volume).

Italy, instead, entered the euro with a "German" strategy of competitive devaluation, based on the commitment of trade unions, negotiated in social pacts, to deliver both nominal and real wage moderation (Baccaro and Howell 2017, ch. 5; Regalia and Regini 1998). Between 1995 and 2000, Italy's nominal wage growth was as low as Germany's and lower than in other Eurozone countries.[2] Furthermore, fiscal policy was marked by sizable primary surpluses in an effort to lower the large public debt stock. These deflationary impulses muffled the expansionary impact of Walters 1. The strategy changed in the early 2000s, concurrently with a shift in government from the center-left to the center-right. Wage moderation was relaxed if not abandoned, particularly for public sector workers, and fiscal policy became less restrictive with a steady reduction in primary surpluses. In this period, Italy displayed some features of Spain's growth trajectory, for example, the increase in house prices, but there was no credit boom and no large rise in construction investment. Overall, the stimulus to domestic demand was insufficient to rekindle growth in Italy, due to a combination of budgetary constraints and misguided spending.

It must be emphasized that both growth strategies were difficult to implement in Italy due to the particular conditions in which Italy accessed the EMU. By eliminating the possibility of exchange rate devaluation, the euro contributed to a structurally overvalued real exchange rate for Italy, making export-led growth more difficult to achieve. At the same time, the high level of outstanding debt (twice as high as the Maastricht parameter) severely reduced the fiscal space, making domestic demand-led growth equally difficult to achieve.

In the early 2010s, both countries were heavily affected by the euro crisis (even though there had been no domestic boom in Italy in the preceding years) and responded similarly by destroying domestic demand and engaging in "internal devaluation" (Armingeon and Baccaro 2012). However, the crisis did not lead to a reversal of fortunes. In fact, while Spain was able to somehow rebalance its domestic demand-led growth model, stimulating a domestic demand-led recovery without severe repercussions for the current account balance, Italy was again stuck between a renewed export-led push and excessively timid attempts to stimulate domestic demand.

The remainder of the chapter fleshes out the argument in three steps. First, we analyze the demand drivers of Italian and Spanish growth. Second, we examine a number of policy drivers, looking at monetary policy, fiscal policy, wages and productivity growth, and trends in credit and household debt. Third, we reconstruct the growth strategies and growth coalitions of the two countries in three periods: in the run-up to the euro, in the pre-crisis period, and in the post-crisis period. In the conclusion, we discuss these findings.

The Demand Drivers of Growth

As we did for Germany in Chapter 9, we decompose total growth between the contribution of domestic demand and the contribution of exports using import-adjusted demand components (for more details on the methodology, see Baccaro and Neimanns 2021, Appendix A.2).[3] Import-adjusted demand contributions distinguish between imports absorbed by domestic demand (for consumption, investment, and government expenditure purposes) and imports absorbed by exports (as intermediate products that are incorporated into exports), and then subtract the relevant portions of imports from domestic demand and exports, respectively, when calculating contributions to total growth. The data used for this decomposition are Input-Output tables from which the import share of exports is derived and OECD Trade in Value Added data for exports and imports.[4] Compared with traditional growth decomposition exercises, which subtract all imports from exports, the decomposition based on import-adjusted demand focuses on domestic value added incorporated in final domestic demand and exports. We compare Italy and Spain with the two largest Eurozone economies: France and Germany.

Considering the 1995–2015 period as a whole, Spanish growth was the highest of the four countries with an average annual growth rate of 2.1%. Furthermore, the contribution of (import-adjusted) domestic demand was more important than the contribution of exports for Spanish growth: 64% vs. 36%. Italian growth was the lowest of the four countries at 0.5% per year, and was also primarily pulled by domestic demand, which contributed for 61% of total growth vs. 39% for exports. The French growth composition was similar with domestic demand contributing 69% and exports the remaining 31%, but total growth was lower than that of Spain at 1.6% per year. German growth was lower than both Spanish and French growth at 1.3% per year and was mostly due to (import-adjusted) exports with 75%.

As suggested by Table 11.1, which reports growth contributions distinguishing between different five-year sub-periods, both Italian and Spanish growth were largely pulled by domestic demand until the financial crisis. After the euro crisis, in 2011–2015, growth became negative in Italy at -0.7% per year on average, and essentially zero in Spain. In this period, the growth contribution of (import-adjusted) domestic demand became negative in both countries, by -1.2% in Italy and -1% in Spain, while exports gave a modest positive contribution to growth with 0.55% in Italy and 1% in Spain. The relative growth contribution of exports increased in France as well, to 70% of total French growth, and remained high in Germany with 62% of total growth. Although there was a shift toward export-led growth in Spain and Italy, this was a consequence of the euro crisis destroying domestic demand and imports in these two countries, and of exports maintaining a small positive contribution in a context of stagnation.[5]

After 2015, while Spain returned to relatively fast growth at 2.8% per year on average between 2015 and 2018, Italian growth remained subdued at 1.3%. In this period, the average yearly import-adjusted growth contribution of domestic demand was 1.8% and 0.6% per year for Spain and Italy, respectively, and the contribution of exports was 1% and 0.7%. Thus, Spanish growth seems again to be primarily pulled by domestic demand, accounting for 65% of total growth in 2016–2018. Meanwhile, Italy's paltry growth seems to have been primarily export led at 55% of total growth. Interestingly, in absolute terms, the growth contribution of both domestic demand and exports was greater in Spain than in Italy in every sub-period. To explain the greater dynamism of the Spanish economy than the Italian economy since the 1990s, we look at factors that may affect domestic and foreign demand: monetary policy, fiscal policy, wage and productivity trends, and the attractiveness of exports.

Monetary Policy

Spain benefited from the "Walters 1 effect" to a greater extent than Italy. Inflation was on average 3.1% per year in Spain and 2.6% in Italy between 1995 and 2007 compared to 1.6% in France and 1.5% in Germany. With a common monetary policy at the European level and with international financial markets attributing essentially the same level of risk to both Northern and Southern countries

Table 11.1 **Average contributions to yearly growth by five-year periods**

Average Contributions to Yearly Growth by Five-Year Periods	Period	Import-Adjusted Growth Contributions		Yearly Growth	Shares of Growth	
		Domestic Demand	Exports		Domestic Demand	Exports
Italy	1996–2000	1.56%	0.48%	2.05%	76.36%	23.64%
Spain	1996–2000	2.52%	1.58%	4.10%	61.54%	38.46%
France	1996–2000	1.67%	1.26%	2.93%	56.84%	43.16%
Germany	1996–2000	0.52%	1.36%	1.88%	27.68%	72.32%
Italy	2001–2005	1.01%	−0.10%	0.92%	110.64%	−10.64%
Spain	2001–2005	3.22%	0.07%	3.28%	97.90%	2.10%
France	2001–2005	1.61%	0.08%	1.69%	95.49%	4.51%
Germany	2001–2005	−0.28%	0.82%	0.54%	−51.95%	151.95%
Italy	2006–2010	−0.11%	−0.14%	−0.25%	44.74%	55.26%
Spain	2006–2010	0.61%	0.39%	1.00%	61.45%	38.55%
France	2006–2010	0.87%	−0.03%	0.84%	103.22%	−3.22%
Germany	2006–2010	0.44%	0.81%	1.25%	35.53%	64.47%
Italy	2011–2015	−1.22%	0.55%	−0.67%	n.r.	n.r.
Spain	2011–2015	−1.03%	1.03%	0.00%	n.r.	n.r.
France	2011–2015	0.31%	0.72%	1.03%	30.11%	69.89%
Germany	2011–2015	0.65%	1.05%	1.70%	38.29%	61.71%
Italy	2016–2018	0.59%	0.71%	1.30%	45.24%	54.76%
Spain	2016–2018	1.79%	0.97%	2.76%	64.91%	35.09%
France	2016–2018	1.31%	0.44%	1.75%	74.66%	25.34%
Germany	2016–2018	1.61%	0.38%	2.00%	80.81%	19.19%

The numbers in the table are average annual growth rates over five-year periods. For example, the values for 1996–2000 are the averages over 1995–1996, 1996–1997, 1997–1998, 1998–1999, 1999–2000.

n.r. = not reported

Source: own elaborations on OECD Input-Output and Trade in Value Added data

(Dellepiane-Avellaneda, Hardiman, and Heras 2021), but with different inflation rates at the country level, monetary policy was more expansionary in Spain
than in Italy.

In both countries, the Walters effect manifested itself even before the start
of the euro when long-term nominal interest rates began declining in anticipa-
tion of joining the common currency. As a result, the Spanish (long-term) real
interest rate saw a marked decline. It was 6.1% in 1995, but by 1999, when the
euro was launched, it had already declined to 2.6%. It continued to decline further, reaching a low of 0.1% in 2005. The difference in long-term real interest
rates with Germany passed from 0.7% in 1995 to -2.3% in 2004. Interest rates
suddenly shot up with the financial crisis, from 0.8% in 2008 to 5% in 2009, and
remained 3% on average in 2010–2014, but then declined again, reaching zero
in 2017 and -0.3% in 2019, when the ECB adopted hyper-expansionary and unconventional monetary policy in an effort to fight deflation.[6]

In Italy, real interest rates also declined massively, from 7.5% in 1992 to a low
of 1.3% in 2006, but remained considerably higher than in Spain at an average of
2% between 1999 and 2007. After the crisis, Italian interest rates also shot up at
on average 3% in 2009–2014 vs. 3.3% in Spain, but later did not decline as fast as
in Spain at 1.4% in 2015–2019 vs. 0.5%. In both Italy and Spain then, monetary
policy in the post-crisis years was considerably tighter than in Germany with a
difference in real interest rates with Germany at 2.3% in Italy and 1.4% in Spain
in 2015–2019. To summarize, both countries experienced monetary easing in
the pre-crisis period, followed by a monetary crunch during the euro crisis, and
then again monetary easing. However, real interest rates were lower in Spain in
both periods of monetary easing and only slightly higher during the crisis-in-
duced monetary crunch.

Fiscal Policy

Furthermore, fiscal policy was more expansionary in Spain than in Italy. The
two countries started the 1990s with very different levels of public debt to GDP
ratios, with 42% of GDP in Spain and 98% in Italy in 1991, rising to 61% and
109% respectively at the start of the euro in 1999. In order to reduce debt, Italy
ran a large primary budget surplus in the 1990s at 2.9%, on average, between
1991 and 2000. In contrast, Spain ran a small primary deficit in the same period
of -0.9%.[7] Between 2003 and 2006, Spain tightened up its fiscal policy progressively as the economy boomed, registering a primary surplus of 2.3% on average
in this period, while in Italy the primary surplus declined under the Berlusconi
government from 2.6% in 2001 to 0.2% in 2006 (Barta 2018, ch. 3).

After the crisis, the fiscal response of the two countries differed sharply again. While Spain had a strongly countercyclical response to the crisis, resulting in a primary deficit of –6.3% of GDP between 2008 and 2014, Italy maintained a positive primary balance in this period of 1% on average. In 2015–2019, the primary balance was again in deficit for Spain (–1%) and in surplus for Italy (1.4%). In brief, with the exception of a few years in the early 2000s, Italy's fiscal policy was considerably more restrictive, and less countercyclical, than the Spanish one.

Low growth also made it more difficult to manage Italy's large public debt. With interest rates above growth rates (r>g) almost every year, the Italian public debt had an inertial tendency to increase as a share of GDP (Baccaro and D'Antoni 2020). Persistent primary surpluses did nothing to reduce it. In fact, they may have set in motion a vicious circle of surpluses lowering the growth rate, thus requiring further surpluses in order not to exceed the Maastricht parameters (Storm 2019). After a small decline to 104% in 2007, Italian public debt shot up to 136% of GDP in 2019. Starting from a smaller initial level, Spanish debt also increased from 61% in 1999 to 97% in 2019.[8]

Real Wages and Productivity

Interestingly, Spain's domestic demand boom has nothing to do with growing real wages (Cárdenas et al. 2021). In fact, the average annual growth of real hourly wages, deflated with the consumer price index, was slightly negative in the period between 1995 and 2007 at -0.01% per year. This was not only in the economy as a whole but, surprisingly, even in the booming construction sector at -0.75% per year (see Table 11.2).[9] In this period, Spain had even greater real wage moderation than Germany. The only Spanish sector with a positive real wage dynamic was the public sector, where real wages grew by 1.45% per year on average.[10] Real wage growth was slightly greater in Italy than in Germany in 1995–2007 at 0.67% vs. 0.16%, but lower than in France over the same period (1.39%). Overall, real wage growth did not stimulate aggregate demand at all in Spain and only moderately in Italy (Perez and Matsaganis 2018). An important constraint on real wage growth was the dismal trend of labor productivity, which only grew by 0.22% in 1995–2007 in Spain, and by 0.47% in Italy, compared with 1.72% in Germany and 1.57% in France.

Despite real wage stagnation (as well as a commitment to negotiated wage moderation in both countries, see Molina 2014; Baccaro and Howell 2017, ch. 5), nominal wages grew faster in Spain and Italy than in Germany between 1995 and 2007, with 2.9% per year on average in Spain, 3.3% in Italy, and 1.7% in Germany. This trend, combined with stagnant labor productivity in the two

Table 11.2 **Real Hourly Wage and Labor Productivity Growth**

		Spain			Italy			Germany			France		
		1995–2018	1995–2007	2008–2018	1995–2018	1995–2007	2008–2018	1995–2018	1995–2007	2008–2018	1995–2018	1995–2007	2008–2018
Labor productivity		0.66%	0.22%	1.14%	0.44%	0.66%	0.18%	1.25%	1.73%	0.68%	1.25%	1.65%	0.78%
Real Hourly Wage	Total Economy	−0.01%	−0.05%	0.03%	0.33%	0.67%	−0.06%	0.75%	0.16%	1.45%	1.12%	1.39%	0.80%
	Manufacturing	0.21%	0.12%	0.31%	0.97%	0.96%	0.98%	1.05%	0.91%	1.20%	1.49%	1.58%	1.36%
	Construction	−0.34%	−0.75%	0.10%	0.52%	0.42%	0.63%	0.44%	−0.29%	1.30%	1.24%	1.31%	1.15%
	Public Sector	0.46%	1.45%	−0.63%	0.50%	1.38%	−0.54%	0.57%	−0.14%	1.42%	1.14%	1.43%	0.79%
	Business Services	−0.34%	−0.54%	−0.12%	0.04%	0.32%	−0.29%	0.83%	0.13%	1.67%	1.02%	1.30%	0.68%

Source: OECD STAN Database, own elaborations

Southern countries, produced a loss of competitiveness for Italy and Spain vis-à-vis Germany and other northern members of the Eurozone.

In the post-crisis period between 2008 and 2018, Spanish labor productivity picked up again, with an average annual growth of 1.14%, which was higher than in both Germany and France, and was mostly concentrated in the period until 2014. The increase in labor productivity was a likely consequence of the reduction of employment and the shrinking of the low productivity construction sector after the crisis. However, real wage growth was virtually nil in Spain in this period (0.03%), including in the public sector (-0.63% per year). In contrast to Spain, Italy's productivity performance deteriorated further in the post-crisis period, declining to an average annual growth rate of 0.18%, while the real wage growth was slightly negative overall. Compared to the pre-crisis years, the Italian public sector also saw negative real wage growth (-0.54%).

With nominal wages increasing faster than Germany, combined with the stagnation of labor productivity in both Spain and Italy, a significant loss of price competitiveness (an increase in relative unit labor costs) occurred in both countries, which translated into real exchange rate appreciation vis-à-vis other members of the euro, especially Germany (Scharpf 2011) (see Figure 11.2).

As a result of these trends, there was a deterioration of the current account in both countries that was more accentuated in Spain than in Italy, due to the greater dynamism of Spanish domestic demand, which stimulated import growth. Between 1999 and 2007, Spain's average current account deficit was 5.6% of GDP, while Italy's current account deficit was only 0.5% in the same

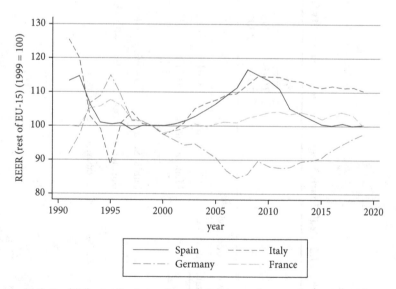

Figure 11.2 Real Effective Exchange Rates (relative to other members of EU15).
Source: AMECO

period. In 2007, the Spanish current account deficit was a whopping 9.4% of GDP, while the Italian deficit was 1.4%. During the euro crisis, both countries were forced to bring their external balance in surplus, by 2% on average between 2012 and 2019 in Spain and 1.9% in Italy. This was attained by destroying domestic demand and cutting imports.[11]

Bank Credit and Household Debt

If real wages were stagnant in Spain, domestic credit skyrocketed, giving a powerful boost to domestic demand. Data from the Bank for International Settlements (BIS) indicate that total credit to the Spanish private non-financial sector went from less than 80% of GDP in 1995 to a peak of 223% in 2009. Credit increased in Italy as well, but much less than in Spain: from less than 70% of GDP in 1995 to a peak of 126% in 2010, with the increase concentrated in the 2000s. In contrast, Germany's export-led economy was characterized by shrinking volumes of credit to the private sector (see Figure 11.2).

Spanish (non-financial) firms received the lion's share of expanding credit: their share went up from 62% of GDP in 1995 to 168% in 2009, but households also expanded their share considerably from 31% in 1995 to 85% in 2009. By comparison, Italy's numbers were much smaller: household credit went from 31% in 1995 to 62% in 2009, and firm credit from 52% to 83% in the same period.

A popular argument emphasizes the role of gross capital imports in "financing" the Spanish boom (e.g. Dellepiane-Avellaneda, Hardiman, and Heras 2021, 11). Yet, the key actors in bringing about Spain's credit boom were domestic banks (see Figure 11.3, panels A and B). While the stock of foreign loans was non-negligible, it peaked at only 53% of GDP in 2007.[12] By contrast, the stock of loans extended by domestic banks was three times larger, exceeding 150% of GDP in 2007–2010. Small credit banks played a key role in the credit boom and most of their loans went to the construction sector (Ruiz, Stupariu, and Vilariño 2015).

The credit boom had important consequences for the structure of the Spanish economy and for households' balance sheets. Investments as a whole grew from 22% of GDP in 1995 to 30% in 2006. Specifically, construction investments increased from 14% to 21% of GDP in this period.[13] The construction sector, already large in comparative perspective (9% of value added in 1995), peaked at 12% in 2006. By comparison, the German construction sector shrank from 7% of value added in 1995 to 4% in 2007. Spanish house prices more than tripled between the early 1990s and the mid-2000s (see Figure 11.4), while household debt rose from 64% of disposable income in 1995 to 149% in 2007.[14] In brief,

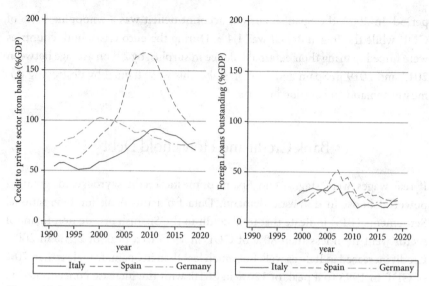

Figure 11.3 Stock of Domestic and Foreign Loans. Left graph only includes credit from
domestic bank. Source: BIS long series on credit to the non-financial sector(left graph);BIS
consolidated banking graph statistics and OECD(right graph)

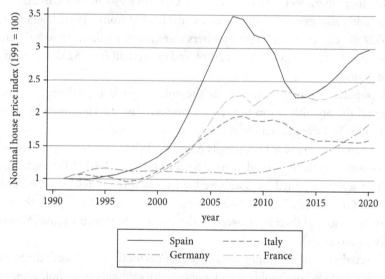

Figure 11.4 House prices. Source: OECD Analytical House prices Indicators.

all the available indicators point to a credit-driven construction boom, which
fueled domestic demand in Spain.

Many of the same trends also characterize Italy, but to a much lesser extent
than in Spain. For example, housing investment increased only from 10% of
GDP in 1995 to 12% in 2006. House prices rose by 190% between 1991 and

2007, as opposed to 349% in Spain. Household debt increased from 38% of disposable income in 1995 to 79% in 2007. In Italy, too, there were expansion of credit, an increase in construction investment, and a rise of household debt, but they did not stimulate domestic demand sufficiently.

The Export Sector

Although Spanish growth was largely credit driven in the pre-crisis period, the performance of Spanish exports has also been remarkable: Exports grew by 112.35% between 1995 and 2007, which is less than in Germany (150%), but more than in Italy (72%) and France (89%). However, in this period Spanish imports grew even faster than exports as a consequence of the domestic boom (170%), which explains the trade deficit. In the post-crisis period (2008–2019), Spain and Italy drastically cut import growth, which was only 4% in Spain and 9% in Italy, and this brought their trade account to surplus.[15] Despite export growth, however, the Spanish export sector remains considerably smaller than the German. In 1995, the export share of GDP was 22% in Spain, 25% in Italy, 22% in Germany, and 23% in France. In 2019, the corresponding shares were 35%, 32%, 47%, and 31%, respectively.

A Spanish peculiarity is that services weigh more heavily than in Italy, accounting for 32% of total exports vs. 19% in 2019. Travel is the largest export-producing service sector in both countries with 48% of total service exports in Spain and 40% in Italy. By comparison, the share of travel exports is 13% in Germany and 22% in France.[16] Travel largely coincides with the labor-intensive sale of touristic services to nonresidents. Estimates of the price elasticity of Italian and Spanish exports provide an indication of their technological sophistication. If exports are highly price sensitive, an increase in domestic prices relative to foreign prices (variation in the real exchange rate) will lead to an important reduction of export growth.

Regression analysis suggests that Italian and Spanish exports respond to variation in relative prices in a similar way. Exports of goods are highly price sensitive in both countries. The long-run elasticity is -1.3 for Spain and between -1.1 and -1.5 for Italy, depending on the real exchange rate indicator used. Services exports seem less affected by price competitiveness than goods, with an elasticity of -0.4 in Spain and insignificantly different from zero in Italy. By comparison, the corresponding elasticities for Germany as reported in Chapter 9 are -1 for goods and -0.8 for services. Furthermore, exports of goods are highly sensitive to demand in the Eurozone for Spain, with an elasticity of 2.5 in the Spanish case, and a short-run elasticity of 3 and a long-run elasticity between 1.5 and 2 in the Italian case. In contrast, especially for Italy, the foreign demand elasticity of services exports is lower than for goods exports. The details of the regression analysis and associated tables are in the appendix at the end of this chapter.

Overall, the analysis conducted in this section reveals both similarities and differences between the Italian and Spanish growth models. Both are primarily domestic-oriented economies, with growth being pulled mainly by domestic demand. However, Spanish domestic demand has been much more dynamic than Italian demand, both before and after the crisis. Differences in monetary policy partially explain the difference. Spain benefited more than Italy from the "Walters 1" effect, which implies lower real interest rates. Furthermore, with the exception of the 2003–2006 years, fiscal policy was more relaxed in Spain, thanks to the lower level of debt than in Italy. Most importantly, credit expansion was much greater in Spain than in Italy, and the credit boom stimulated construction investment, raised house prices, and boosted household consumption even in the absence of real wage growth.

The booming domestic economy led to a severe deterioration of the external balance in Spain in the years before the crisis. Yet, the accumulation of external debt did not increase Spain's interest rate premium and was easily financed through net capital imports year after year (Sinn 2014). However, the euro crisis led to a sudden increase in interest rate spreads, turning monetary policy to contractionary mode. Fiscal policy also became heavily restrictive as a result of austerity policies and internal adjustment in response to the euro crisis. Credit creation shrank, causing a contraction of both investment (-4% per year on average in 2010–2014) and household consumption (-1.3% on average in the same period) in Spain.

While the euro crisis also affected Italian domestic demand heavily despite the absence of any pre-crisis boom (investments declined by 4% per year in 2010–2014 and household consumption by 1%), Italy's post-crisis recovery was much weaker than Spain's recovery. Between 2015 and 2019 household consumption grew at an annual rate of 2.3% in Spain and 1.2% in Italy. Investment grew by 4.6% per year in Spain and 2.6% in Italy. Starting in 2015, Spanish house prices moved upward again, while they remained flat and then declined slightly in Italy. This period of renewed growth of the Spanish economy was accompanied by the correction of some of the previous excesses. Total credit to the private non-financial sector declined from 168% of GDP in 2009 to 91% in 2019, practically the same level as in the mid-1990s, and the real exchange rate depreciated relative to other EU15 countries to similar levels as in 1999, indicating improved competitiveness. By comparison, in 2019 Italy's real effective exchange rate was still 10% higher than in 1999.

Spanish exports also experienced healthy growth, both before and after the euro crisis, in contrast to Italy where export growth was more modest. As a result, at the end of the 2010s Spanish growth was higher than in other large

European countries, and appeared more balanced than in the pre-crisis period, with approximately 60% growth pulled by (import-adjusted) domestic demand and 40% by exports, and a modest current account surplus. Instead, Italy continued to stagnate.

Growth Strategies and Growth Coalitions in Italy and Spain

Having analyzed the basic features of the two economies, in this next section we reconstruct the evolution of Italy and Spain's "growth strategies" (Hassel and Palier 2021), distinguishing between the phase of qualification for the European Monetary Union (EMU), the pre-crisis period in the euro, and the post-crisis period.

The run-up to the euro

One important difference between the two countries is that Spain started to prepare for monetary integration well before Italy, implementing an orthodox macroeconomic agenda centering on inflation control, tight fiscal policy, and labor market reforms in the early 1980s. In Italy, instead, macroeconomic adjustment had to wait until a decade later. Therefore, Italy had to implement a radical budgetary adjustment in a short period of time to qualify for EMU membership, with a negative impact on domestic demand. As a result, once it became part of the currency union, it was less well placed than Spain to take advantage of the decline in interest rates.

In preparing to join the European Economic Community in 1986, the Spanish Socialist Party (PSOE), which took office in 1982, took the decision to essentially put the most dynamic segments of its manufacturing sector in foreign hands while seeking to build national champions in banking, construction, and utilities. The PSOE deemed the continued support for manufacturing companies in sectors like carmaking, mining, shipbuilding, and steelmaking as excessively onerous for the public purse. For this reason, in the 1980s the executive implemented a two-step program of industrial restructuring. First, state-owned companies were brought back to profit through the implementation of layoffs and other cost-containment measures (Etchemendy 2004). Second, the restructured companies were sold to large multinationals at a favorable price for the buyer.

This strategy was most notably implemented in the carmaking sector, with the government selling the restructured carmaker Seat and truck-maker Enasa to the German VW and the Italian Iveco, respectively (Chari 1998, 165–171). As a result, Spain positioned itself as an assembly platform for US, French, German, and Japanese companies (Charnock, Purcell, and Ribera-Fumaz 2014), and eventually emerged as the second largest car producer in Europe. By 1991 foreign companies controlled 95% of the carmaking industries and foreign penetration was above 90% across other key manufacturing sectors (Charnock, Purcell, and Ribera-Fumaz 2014, 64). The restructuring of the manufacturing sector had positive repercussions for Spain's public finances, as it removed loss-making companies from the government's balance sheet (Etchemendy 2004).

The PSOE followed a radically different strategy when restructuring sectors populated by powerful insiders such as banking and utilities. Rather than selling domestic companies to foreign multinationals, the government implemented a series of measures aimed at favoring the emergence of globally competitive Spanish multinationals, as in the cases of the utilities Endesa (electricity), Telefonica (telecommunications), and Repsol (oil and gas). The government partially privatized them by combining public offerings targeted at small investors with private auctions in which large share blocks were sold to selected domestic investors such as banks and construction companies (Etchemendy 2004). The pace of the partial sell-offs of profitable companies accelerated after 1992 when the PSOE implemented the first of two convergence plans of deficit reduction and cost containment aimed at preparing Spain for accession to the EMU (Murphy 1999).

Although broadly successful in their industrial outcomes, the sectoral policies of the PSOE came at a heavy cost in terms of employment (Charnock, Purcell, and Ribera-Fumaz 2014). Like the Franco dictatorship before, the PSOE government tried to tackle the employment crisis by stimulating the construction sector. With the Land Act of 1990 the government gave more leeway to local governments to develop their urbanization plans. Furthermore, the executive used a large part of the EC structural funds to upgrade the infrastructural network (López and Rodríguez 2011) leading to the mushrooming of airport terminals, highways, and high-speed railways (Murphy 1999).

In contrast, Italy's preparations for EMU began a decade later in the 1990s. This delay in implementing the macroeconomic adjustment was due to the fact that the required reforms were incompatible with the preferences of the "social bloc" supporting the ruling Christian Democratic Party (DC) (Amable, Guillaud, and Palombarini 2011). The hegemonic force in Italian politics between the 1950s and the early 1990s, the DC relied on the support of a heterogeneous coalition of socioeconomic interests including the large manufacturing companies of the North-West, SMEs owners mainly located in the North-East, shopkeepers, and Southern public sector workers (Amable, Guillaud, and

Palombarini 2011; Barta 2011). The heterogeneity in the preferences of these groups made the implementation of substantial budgetary cuts virtually impossible. For instance, tackling rampant tax evasion would alienate the support from SME owners and shopkeepers, while large firms opposed the phasing out of the generous subsidy schemes that favored them. For its part, the Southern electorate opposed a reduction of public employment, and party officials were hostile to a radical privatization campaign as state-owned firms were a vital channel to feed political clienteles. Furthermore, the growing constituency of aging workers opposed pension reform (Ferrera and Gualmini 2004).

Macroeconomic adjustment therefore had to wait until the collapse of the DC and other parties in the early 1990s, and it was politically steered by the center-left, an alliance between left-liberal parties and technocrats united in their support for the process of European integration (Deeg 2005; Rangone and Solari 2012). The center-left embarked on a wave of reforms including marginal labor market deregulation, wage compression, the privatization of manufacturing companies, banks and utilities, the reform of the welfare state, and corporate governance liberalization (Rangone and Solari 2012; Simoni 2020). The pace of reform accelerated after 1996, when the center-left won the elections on the promise of bringing Italy into the EMU as a founding member. Given the precarious state of public finances, meeting the Maastricht criteria required a Herculean effort of fiscal consolidation achieved mainly through an increase in taxation coupled with the swift sell-off of many profitable state-owned companies including the telecommunications incumbent Telecom Italia (TI) and the highway operator (Bulfone 2019).

The long-term political survival of the center-left coalition depended upon the formation of a producer pact between large companies and unionized workers. This producer coalition would underpin an export-led growth strategy based on wage moderation, similar to the strategy implemented by Germany. Buoyant growth would in turn allow the center-left to expand its reach to excluded groups, such as SME owners and Southern voters (Amable, Guillaud, and Palombarini 2011).

In contrast to Spain where the manufacturing sector was smaller and shrinking, Italy's manufacturing sector was the second largest in the Eurozone after Germany (De Cecco 2007). Often celebrated internationally for its flexibility and ability to occupy high market niches in mature sectors (Locke 1995; Piore and Sabel 1984), it had two main problems. First, it had an overrepresentation of small companies with a lower capacity to invest in innovation than large companies. Second, it needed periodic devaluations of the currency in order to remain competitive (De Cecco 2007). While accession to the common currency promised to act as a "beneficial constraint" for companies by encouraging them to upgrade and reduce their price sensitivity, permanence in the common currency required heavy doses of wage moderation in order to replace the lost ability to devalue (Baccaro and D'Antoni 2020).

Although the center-left managed to steer Italy into EMU, the expected growth boost did not materialize, which led to its electoral defeat in 2001. Two reasons concur to explain the failure of the center-left growth strategy. First, the enormous size of the fiscal adjustment required to initially qualify for EMU membership, and then to reduce public debt, depressed domestic demand thereby limiting the impact of the reduction in interest rates. Second, an export-led strategy in Italy was unlikely to succeed due to the lack of a sufficiently large export base. As noted earlier, even though Italy hosted the second largest manufacturing sector in the Eurozone, it was still considerably smaller than that of Germany. Since the 1990s the most dynamic segment of the manufacturing base has been composed of small companies that emerged from the old industrial districts to become highly internationalized mid-sized companies (Colli 2010). Despite their strong performance, these companies lacked the critical mass necessary to drive the growth of the whole Italian economy through exports. Furthermore, the size of the Italian export base was decisively reduced by the lack of large multinationals. In fact, since the early 2000s the strong performance of mid-size companies was mirrored by the crisis of large family-owned manufacturing multinationals like Pirelli or Benetton (De Cecco 2007). Paradoxically, this crisis was further accelerated by another reform implemented by the center-left: the privatization of state-owned utilities. In fact, the sell-offs gave manufacturing families the opportunity to diversify their activity into sheltered public service sectors like telecommunications and transports, thereby diverting resources from their core manufacturing business (Bulfone 2020; Colli, Rinaldi, and Vasta 2016).

From accession to EMU to the crisis

During the first EMU decade, whereas Spain doubled down on its strategy to expand the construction and banking sectors, Italy shifted from a strategy focused on fiscal adjustment and wage moderation in order to boost exports to one catering to domestic interests. For Spain, public policy showed a remarkable degree of continuity across governments of different political orientation. The recession of the early 1990s paved the way in 1996 for the rise of the right-wing Partido Popular (PP) under the leadership of José Maria Aznar. Despite the undeniable differences between the PSOE and the PP on issues like civil rights or security, the two parties had largely overlapping macroeconomic agendas. When in office, the PP embraced an orthodox economic policy agenda centering on fiscal rectitude, inflation control, and labor market deregulation. As with the PSOE before, the goal of this effort was to have Spain join the EMU as a founding member (Murphy 1999). In doing so, the PP was able to reap the fruits of the plan of deficit reduction implemented by the PSOE since the early 1990s.

By 1997 Spain had a declining level of public debt (64% of GDP) while (thanks to the previous devaluation of the peseta) the growth rate was above 3% of GDP (Murphy 1999, 65). Continuity between the two parties is also evident in their strategy to favor the emergence of national champions in sectors like banking, utilities, and construction. The PP presided over a last round of consolidation in the banking sector, which led to the emergence of Banco Santander and BBVA. When dealing with the restructuring of the state-owned utilities Endesa, Repsol, and Telefonica, the executive first promoted politically close managers at the head of the companies, then completed the privatization process by further strengthening the shareholder-cores of domestic banks and construction companies created by the PSOE (Etchemendy 2004).

Furthermore, the PP implemented a series of measures aimed at favoring the construction sector (Tortella et al. 2013). These included the deregulation of the mortgage market, which led to the development of the second largest securitization market in Europe (Dellepiane-Avellaneda; Hardiman and Heras 2021; López and Rodríguez 2011), and most notably, the 1998 reform of the Land Act, which loosened the procedures for obtaining building permits and considerably increased the stock of land available for construction (López and Rodríguez 2011).

It is noteworthy that this was the third instance since the Civil War in which Spain relied on the construction sector to recover from an economic crisis. The first housing bubble dated back from the 1960s when the Franco dictatorship heavily subsidized homeownership to limit social unrest, while the second followed Spain's accession to the EC in 1986 (Charnock, Purcell and Ribera-Fumaz 2014, 92–93). Hence, the *occurrence* of the housing bubble is not surprising per se, as the proximity between the executive, domestic banks, and construction companies had already unleashed similar dynamics in the past. What made the bubble of the early 2000s unprecedented was its *size*. Infrastructural investment grew in parallel with the building of new dwellings, the mushrooming of airports, and the development of the third largest network of toll roads in the world after the USA and China (Cardenas 2013). The construction boom was favored by two developments that increased demand for housing: record immigration from Latin America and Eastern Europe (Charnock, Purcell, and Ribera-Fumaz 2014) and the purchase of second homes by foreign nationals.[17]

Large banks and construction companies reaped profits from the bubble, monopolizing the premium segments of housing and infrastructural markets (Buendía 2020). The availability of capital, and the seemingly unlimited demand for new dwellings, allowed replicating a similar alliance at the local level with the involvement of regional and provincial governments, local constructors, and savings banks (*cajas de ahorro*). The benefits of the bubble reached large segments of the population. With housing prices rising strongly, middle-class and upper-class families owning multiple dwellings considerably increased their private wealth (Lopez and Rodriguez 2011, 3–4). Furthermore, the expansion of construction created important employment opportunities for low-skilled workers, resulting in a dramatic decrease of the level of unemployment, which went below 8% in 2007, but, as shown before, produced no increase in real wages. Finally, lower-income groups were encouraged to use their primary residence as collateral to finance additional consumption (Buendía 2020, 430).

Hence, buoyant growth allowed for the consolidation of a growth coalition in Spain with banks, construction companies, utilities, and wealthy owners of multiple properties at the core, savings banks and local governments further away from the core, and owners of a single property or construction workers in a more marginal position. The continuity between the economic policies of the PSOE and the PP is perhaps the clearest indicator of the strength of this coalition. Despite having criticized the uncontrolled growth of construction when in opposition, once in power the PSOE waited until 2007 before intervening to cool down the bubble (Buendía 2020).

In Italy, instead, there was a change in growth strategy in the early 2000s. After obtaining admission to EMU with the first group of countries at the end of 1996, the center-left government continued to implement a deflationary strategy of large fiscal surpluses and negotiated wage moderation until the end of the decade. In these years the wage share declined, bottoming in 2001. However, the center-left was voted out of office in 2001 as the strategy of internal devaluation failed to boost growth while alienating large segments of the electorate. Led by Silvio Berlusconi, the center-right relied on the groups most severely affected by the budgetary adjustment of the center-left: SME owners, shopkeepers, professionals, and public sector employees (Afonso and Bulfone 2019). To please them, the center-right portrayed its reformist agenda in clear opposition to the export-led strategy of the center-left, promising to prioritize domestic demand by implementing tax cuts, an increase of minimum pensions, salary increases in the public sector, and a plan of infrastructural investments targeted specifically to Southern Italy (Pasquino 2007).

The growth-enhancing impact of these measures was minimal. In fact, while the center-right did indeed implement some demand-expanding measures, including wage increases in the public sector, increase of the minimum pensions, and some marginal reductions of income taxes, these came along with measures that had the opposite effect. In particular, to tackle unemployment the center-right facilitated the creation of low-pay fixed-term jobs (Rangone and Solari 2012), hindering both productivity and real wage growth and depressing demand (Baccaro and D'Antoni 2020).

Furthermore, the center-right's reformist agenda was hampered by misguided investment priorities. For instance, rather than stimulating the construction sector, which in those years was showing a rather healthy development, the government used the bulk of the available financial resources to reduce taxes on owner-occupied dwellings (Baldini and Poggio 2014). This suggests that the center-right was more interested in protecting household wealth and rents, including those deriving from tax evasion (Dewey and Di Carlo 2021), than in stimulating a domestic demand-led rebound of the economy. Moreover, the policies of the center-right eroded the primary fiscal surplus accumulated by the center-left weakening Italy's fiscal position in the run-up to the crisis (Barta 2011).

The post-crisis period

As already argued, the crisis hit both countries hard and caused a similar policy response centered on austerity and structural reforms (Perez and Matsaganis 2018), despite differences in the size of the boom and current account deficits between the two countries. While Spain was spared from the early phase of the Global Financial Crisis (GFC), by 2009 the sudden stop of capital inflows from core member states and the bursting of the housing bubble brought to the surface the fragile foundation of the construction-led growth model (Tortella et al. 2013). The meltdown of construction hit the banking sector, in particular the savings bank segment, hard. The PSOE government initially responded to the crisis by implementing a stimulus package that led to the worsening of deficit and debt figures. With interest rates on sovereign bonds spiraling out of control, Spain had no choice but to turn to the European Stability Mechanism (ESM) to finance the restructuring of its banking sector, obtaining a loan of up to €100 billion in 2012. The newly elected PP government took advantage of the crisis to inaugurate a phase of harsh austerity, labor market deregulation, and collective bargaining disarticulation (Bulfone and Tassinari 2021).

The crisis of the construction-led model caused a shrinkage of the supporting dominant growth coalition. While the actors at the core were spared from the most negative repercussions of the crisis, those occupying more peripheral positions bore the brunt of austerity in full. Owing to their geographical diversification and retail focus, large commercial banks like BBVA and Banco Santander survived the crisis quite well (Quaglia and Royo 2015). In the post-crisis period, they even took advantage of the difficulties faced by their competitors at home and abroad to further expand the geographical scope of their activity. The savings bank segment was in contrast completely wiped out through a series of mergers engineered by the Bank of Spain. Of the original 45 savings banks, only two retained their status, while the other entities resulting from the mergers were forcefully turned into commercial banks (Ruiz, Stupariu, and Vilariño 2015).

Similarly, while local construction companies went bankrupt, large groups like Acciona and the ACS Group leveraged the expertise gained at home to design and realize large infrastructural projects abroad. Less directly involved in the housing bubble and bolstered by the enduring regulatory protection they received on the domestic market (Jordana 2014), large utilities like Repsol, Telefonica, and Iberdrola could further pursue their campaign of foreign expansion. Construction workers and lower-income homeowners were instead severely hit by the crisis, losing their jobs and having their properties repossessed. The shrinking of construction and of many construction-related service activities brought the total level of unemployment to the record level of 26% in 2013.

After the double-dip recession of 2009–2013, in 2014–2019 the Spanish economy bounced back, growing on average more than 2% per year. Like in the past, domestic consumption was the main driver of growth (Álvarez, Uxó, and Febrero 2018). Consumption was in turn stimulated by the combination of a post-crisis rebound in public investment, and a recovery of the construction sector with the particularly strong performance of the real estate, architectural, and civil engineering sectors. However, housing investments as a share of GDP and fixed capital formation in general remained about 10 percentage points below the peak of the pre-crisis years, and this reduced the gap between investment and saving (Cárdenas et al. 2021). Although more limited, the growth contribution of exports was also positive, as shown earlier. The combination of lower investment, lower imports, and exports growing at the same rate as before the crisis allowed Spain to combine the resumption of growth with moderate current account surpluses.

While Spain was caught in the Eurozone crisis due to the bursting of the housing bubble and the repercussions this had for its banking system, Italy was targeted by financial markets due to the combination of slow growth and high public debt. The ECB agreed to support the sovereign bonds of Italy and other Southern European economies on the condition that they implemented austerity measures and deregulatory labor market reforms (Armingeon and Baccaro 2012). Paralyzed by internal infighting, the Berlusconi government stepped down to be replaced by a technocratic cabinet led by the former EU Commissioner Mario Monti. The Monti government inaugurated a new phase of executives supported by the Partito Democratico (PD), the key party of the center-left coalition, lasting between 2011 and 2018. As in the 1990s, the reform agenda of these executives focused on fiscal adjustment through tax increases, expenditure cuts, and labor market liberalization. This time, the main target of the liberalizing zeal of the government were workers on open-ended contracts, while both the Monti government and the PD-led government of Matteo Renzi implemented some timid measures to re-regulate temporary employment (Picot and Tassinari 2017).

Acknowledging the failure of the producer pact of the 1990s, Renzi tried to increase the electoral appeal of the PD by introducing some measures to stimulate domestic demand (Bulfone and Tassinari 2021). Most notably the Renzi government introduced a monthly allowance of 80 euros, targeted at middle-income salaried workers and (in order to attract support from shopkeepers and SME owners) a controversial reform to increase the limit for cash payments (Afonso and Bulfone 2019).

Renzi's strategy failed in electoral terms, paving the way for the electoral success of the populist Five Star Movement and the radical right Lega in 2018. The two parties formed a "euroskeptic" coalition, which sought to increase the public deficit slightly beyond the threshold established by the European Commission, but with limited success. The Lega-Five Star alliance implemented some measures aimed at boosting domestic demand, above all the introduction of a universal guaranteed minimum income for the poorest segments of the population, and some measures of labor market re-regulation (Bulfone and Tassinari 2021). However, it did not achieve much and was replaced one year later by a government coalition between the Five Star Movement and the PD, which relinquished any attempt to challenge the European fiscal rules.

Conclusion

In comparative analyses Italy and Spain are often paired because of their alleged similarity. Yet, their growth trajectories in the past 30 years are highly dissimilar. While Spain has grown faster than the European average both before and after the euro crisis, Italy's growth performance has been the worst among the large advanced countries. In this chapter, we have explained this divergence by examining the way the two countries have adapted (or failed to adapt) to the constraints and opportunities offered by European Monetary Union. The euro has enabled two growth strategies, both unstable and complementary, which we have called "Walters 1" and "Walters 2." Walters 1 is a credit-fueled domestic demand-led strategy. The strategy became feasible because, at least before the financial crisis, the euro relaxed the current account constraint, making external imbalances sustainable for some time. Walters 2 is an export-led growth strategy and is contingent on a tight control of domestic wages and prices (see Chapter 9).

We have argued that Spain was able to push a Walters 1 strategy to its fullest extent. Spain's growth was heavily reliant on the expansion of construction and real estate activities, financed through a large increase in the provision of credit.[18] This growth strategy rested on a heterogeneous but coherent coalition of domestic interests including banks, construction companies, utilities, large hotel and hospitality chains, and wealthy owners of multiple residential properties. The strategy remained essentially unchanged as different parties (the PP and PSOE) alternated in government. The roots of this growth coalition go back in time. Spanish capitalism is historically characterized by the prominent position occupied by a restricted group of banks, utilities, and construction companies (Etchemendy 2004; Pérez 1997). In comparison to large service companies, domestic manufacturing groups have historically been confined to a more marginal position within Spanish capitalism (Cabrera and Rey 2007).

Italy instead entered into EMU with a Walters 2 strategy aimed at increasing external competitiveness through negotiated wage moderation and accumulating primary budget surpluses. However, this strategy failed to produce growth and did not pay off electorally. From the early 2000s on, the internal devaluation strategy was replaced by a new strategy, implemented by a center-right coalition, which sought to mimic some of the features of the Spanish growth strategy, but was more interested in protecting small wealth and rent holders than in stimulating domestic demand through a Spanish-style credit and construction boom.

It should be mentioned that Italy faced greater hurdles than Spain, therefore making both growth strategies unlikely to succeed in the Italian context. This is due to the fact that Italy entered into the euro with a level of public debt that was almost twice as large as Spain's (and the Maastricht parameter). As a result, it faced a vicious circle, as in the absence of growth, debt had an inertial tendency to increase as a share of GDP, requiring constant adjustment (Storm 2019; Baccaro and D'Antoni 2020). In any case, Italy's struggle to keep public deficit and debt under control made domestic demand reflation more difficult. In retrospect, the choice to enter into EMU should have been accompanied by a prior restructuring and reduction of the level of debt. However, this option was considered politically unfeasible and was never seriously entertained (see De Cecco 2007, 770).

Furthermore, it is doubtful that the Walters 2 strategy could ever have been successful within the euro. First, the Italian export sector is smaller, less sophisticated, and more price sensitive than the German one. Second, the strategy worked in the 1990s because nominal wage moderation was accompanied by a large devaluation of the nominal exchange rate between 1993 and 1995, but with the introduction of the euro the possibility of devaluation was ruled out and all competitiveness gains needed to come solely from domestic wage and price deflation.

Although this chapter has emphasized the contrast between the dynamism of the Spanish economy and the stasis of the Italian economy, it has also shown that the Spanish growth strategy rests on shaky economic and social foundations

(Perez and Matsaganis 2018). It is based on the accumulation of debt rather than real wage growth. It should therefore not be regarded as a blueprint for Italy or other countries.

Notes

1. Source: OECD Level of GDP per Capita and Productivity database, data in USD at constant prices, 2015 PPPs.
2. The average annual growth rate of hourly nominal wage was 2.6% per year in both countries in this period (based on OECD STAN data).
3. See https://www.mpifg.de/pu/mpifg_dp/2021/dp21-3_online_appendix.pdf. All data used here for the decomposition exercise are at constant prices.
4. For this decomposition exercise, we use data from the OECD Trade in Value Added (TiVA) database. See https://stats.oecd.org/index.aspx?queryid=106160 (last accessed on February 8, 2022).
5. Table 11.1 omits to report the shares of total growth for Italy and Spain in 2011–2015. This is because divisions by a negative number or by a number very close to 0 are difficult to interpret.
6. Data on interest rates are from AMECO: "Long term real interest rates, deflator private consumption (ILRC)."
7. Data on primary balance: OECD Economic Outlook, General government primary balance as a percentage of GDP.
8. Data on public debt: AMECO, General government consolidated gross debt.
9. However, as highlighted by Cárdenas et al. (2021, 206), the wage bill increased faster than unit wages because of higher employment intensity of growth, in turn a consequence of lower growth of labor productivity.
10. The public sector is defined as public administration and defense; compulsory social security; education; human health, and social work activities.
11. Source: AMECO.
12. However, net capital imports were necessary to finance the current account deficit.
13. Source: OECD National Accounts.
14. Source: OECD National Accounts.
15. Source: AMECO.
16. Source: OECD International Trade in Services Statistics.
17. According to an estimate net foreign investment in housing ranged between 0.5 and 1% of Spanish GDP between 1999 and 2007 (Garcia-Herrero and Fernandez de Lis 2008).
18. See Wood (2019) for a similar strategy in Denmark.
19. The variables are OXGN and OXSN, respectively (exports of goods and services at 2015 prices), which we then sum to produce a measure of total exports.
20. The variable is "Gross domestic product, volume, market prices" from the December 2020 edition of the Economic Outlook database. The figures for world GDP, originally in dollars, have been converted to euros using OECD exchange rates between euros and dollars (variable: "Exchange rate, national currency per USD"). The GDP of Italy and Spain, respectively, was subtracted from the EZ variable. By subtracting the EZ GDP from world GDP we obtained the variable for the rest of the world (ROW) demand.
21. The variable name is XUNRQ.
22. For Spain, all ECM models provide no evidence of error correction, which would be expected if there was cointegration. Results are available upon request.
23. A time trend is inserted in the model when this is necessary to eliminate serial correlation.
24. Again, a time trend has been added when needed to eliminate serial correlation.
25. The t-values of the error correction term are always larger than the Mackinnon critical values and allow for rejecting the null of no-cointegration at 5% for models 1, 3, 4, and 5; and at 10% for models 2 and 6.

Appendix

Estimation of the price sensitivity of Italian and Spanish exports

This appendix provides estimates of the price sensitivity of Italian and Spanish exports distinguishing between exports of goods and services. The purpose is to assess the extent to which they respond to movements in European and world demands, and their sensitivity to changes in the real exchange rate. Furthermore, we investigate whether there are notable differences between Italy and Spain.

Data and methods

Our data cover the period between 1991 and 2019. We use data on exports at constant prices from the Ameco database,[19] and data on Eurozone and world GDP from the OECD Economic Outlook database.[20] We use two measures of price sensitivity from the Ameco database and the Bank for International Settlements (BIS), respectively. The first is the real effective exchange rate (REER) based on unit labor costs in total economy relative to the other EU 15 countries.[21] The second is based on the consumer price index relative to 27 trade partners.

Augmented Dickey-Fuller tests suggest that all series are non-stationary in levels and stationary in first differences. We tested for cointegration using both the Engle-Granger test and the Johansen test. These tests produce conflicting results: while the Engle-Granger tests suggest no cointegration in all cases, the Johansen tests suggest the opposite. Thus, we ran single-equation error correction models (ECMs) for both countries and examined the properties of the error correction term, as suggested by DeBoef and Granato (1999) based on Kremers et al. (1992). These additional tests provided evidence of cointegration in the Italian case, but no evidence of cointegration in the Spanish case.[22] Thus, we estimated the Spanish export equations in first differences and the Italian export equation with an ECM.

The Spanish estimating equation is the following:

$$\Delta ln\left(y_t\right) = \alpha + \beta \Delta ln\left(reer_t\right) + \gamma \Delta ln\left(eurozone\_demand_t\right) + \vartheta \Delta ln\left(row\_demand_t\right) + \epsilon_t$$

In words, we hypothesize that Spanish export growth depends on demand from EZ countries and from ROW countries, as well as on the REER. Since data are in natural logarithms, the first difference approximates percentage change, and the regression coefficients can be interpreted as elasticities. Among the regression coefficients, β is the sensitivity of Spanish exports to price changes and is expected to be negative: if Spanish domestic prices increase relative to other countries, exports should decline. The coefficients γ and ϑ capture the sensitivity of exports to variation in demand from the Eurozone and the rest of the world, respectively, and are expected to be positive. The error term ε is assumed to be white noise. We report regression coefficients in Tables A.1 and A.2, distinguishing between CPI-based and ULC-based measures of the REER.

Overall, results from models with the with the CPI-based of REER measure (Table A.1) and with the ULC-based measure of REER (Table A.2) are very similar. Spanish exports are highly sensitive to the growth of demand in the Eurozone countries with an elasticity of about 2.5, slightly higher for exports of goods than for exports of services, which indicates that if European aggregate demand increases by 1%, Spanish exports increase by approximately 2.5%. The impact of ROW demand is instead very different. This has no impact on total exports and a slightly negative impact on exports of goods. One way to explain this unexpected finding is to hypothesize that as developing countries grow, they make it slightly more difficult for Spain to export because they encroach on Spain's trade specialization. Spanish exports are also significantly sensitive to prices, especially the exports of goods, for which the elasticity is -1.3%, indicating that if Spanish domestic prices increase by 1%, Spanish exports decline by 1.3%. The price elasticity of Spanish exports of services is lower, around -0.4%. Furthermore, the Spanish exports of goods also display a significantly negative time trend, which may indicate declining non-price competitiveness over time.[23]

Coming now to the Italian export equation, we hypothesize based on the results of the cointegration tests that there is a long-run relationship between exports, REER, and demand from Eurozone countries and the rest of the world. The existence of the long-term relationship implies that Italian exports respond to deviations from their long-run equilibrium: if they are below equilibrium, they increase, vice versa if they are above equilibrium. Thus, the first difference specification needs to be augmented with a term (the error correction coefficient (λ)) capturing the speed with which actual exports respond to deviations from their equilibrium value. The ECM model neatly distinguishes between short-term and long-term effects of the independent variables. Table A,3 reports the results of the estimation.[24]

First, the error correction term is always well behaved, that is smaller than 0 and greater than -1, as well as highly statistically significant, providing further evidence about the existence of cointegration.[25] The λ coefficient suggests that about 60% of the disequilibrium is reabsorbed within 1 year. An increase in Eurozone demand has a very strong short-term (1 year) impact on Italian

Table A.1 **Determinants of Spanish Exports 1991–2019, First Difference Estimation, CPI-based REER**

	(1) Total	(2) Total	(3) Goods	(4) Services
Euro17 Demand	2.378***	2.293***	2.459***	2.355***
	(0.265)	(0.360)	(0.284)	
ROW Demand	−0.119		−0.237**	
	(0.0767)		(0.105)	
REER (CPI-based)	−0.890***	−0.531***	−1.351***	−0.439***
	(0.272)	(0.148)	(0.372)	(0.155)
Time trend	−0.00166***	−0.00175***	−0.00211***	
	(0.000523)	(0.000535)	(0.000716)	
Constant	3.357***	3.531***	4.252***	0.0103
	(1.050)	(1.074)	(1.436)	(0.00613)
Observations	28	28	28	28
Adj-R2	0.810	0.799	0.733	0.724
Serial correlation test	ns	ns	ns	ns

Standard errors in parentheses
*** $p<0.01$, ** $p<0.05$, * $p<0.1$ (two-tailed)

Table A.2 **Determinants of Spanish Exports 1991–2019, First Difference Estimation, ULC-Based REER**

	(1) Total	(2) Total	(3) Goods	(4) Services
Euro17 Demand	2.558***	2.512***	2.705***	2.460***
	(0.233)	(0.227)	(0.322)	(0.306)
ROW Demand	−0.0410		−0.109*	
	(0.0444)		(0.0615)	
REER (ULC-based)	−0.898***	−0.790***	−1.301***	−0.450**
	(0.186)	(0.144)	(0.258)	(0.196)
Time trend	−0.00197***	−0.00193***	−0.00258***	
	(0.000435)	(0.000432)	(0.000603)	
Constant	3.971***	3.887***	5.196***	0.00785
	(0.874)	(0.866)	(1.210)	(0.00667)
Observations	28	28	28	28
Adj-R2	0.862	0.863	0.801	0.698
Serial correlation test	ns	ns	ns	ns

Standard errors in parentheses
*** $p<0.01$, ** $p<0.05$, * $p<0.1$ (two-tailed)

Table A.3 **Determinants of Italian Exports 1991–2019, Error Correction Model**

	(1) Total	*(2)* Goods	*(3)* Services	*(4)* Total	*(5)* Goods	*(6)* Services
Error-correction term	−0.650***	−0.568***	−0.595***	−0.622***	−0.616***	−0.590***
	(0.118)	(0.128)	(0.132)	(0.126)	(0.129)	(0.157)
Short-run coefficients						
Euro17 Demand	3.128***	3.237***	2.643***	2.990***	3.105***	2.641***
	(0.308)	(0.329)	(0.428)	(0.312)	(0.342)	(0.424)
ROW Demand	0.0241	−0.0517		0.000509	−0.0342	
	(0.0653)	(0.0774)		(0.0561)	(0.0615)	
REER (CPI-based)	−0.404**	−0.529**	−0.431**			
	(0.185)	(0.208)	(0.190)			
REER (ULC-based)				−0.416***	−0.474***	−0.393*
				(0.145)	(0.160)	(0.195)
Long-run coefficients						
Euro17 Demand	1.997***	2.036***	.887***	1.461***	1.620***	.912***
	(.214)	(.329)	(.093)	(.268)	(.292)	(.128)
ROW Demand	−.172*	−.331**		−.183*	−.265**	
	(.080)	(.124)		(.090)	(.105)	
REER (CPI-based)	−1.013***	−1.470***	−.251			
	(.241)	(.339)	(.306)			
REER (ULC-based)				−.868***	−1.136***	−.166
				(.218)	(.251)	(.321)
Time trend	No	Yes	No	Yes	Yes	No
Constant	−14.65***	−20.09***	−0.0541	−18.74***	−24.76***	−0.721
	(3.207)	(3.965)	(1.433)	(4.264)	(5.034)	(1.766)
Observations	28	28	28	28	28	28
Adj-R2	0.870	0.865	0.733	0.865	0.852	0.732
Serial correlation test	ns	ns	ns	ns	ns	ns

Standard errors in parentheses
*** $p<0.01$, ** $p<0.05$, * $p<0.1$ (two-tailed)

exports, with an elasticity of about 3, slightly higher for goods and slightly lower for services. A loss of competitiveness, measured as an increase in the REER, has a short-term negative impact on exports of about .4, approximately equal for goods and services. In the short run, changes in demand from the rest of the world have no impact on Italian exports.

The long-run estimates depend somewhat on the indicator used for the REER term, and they are greater for the CPI-based measure than for the ULC-based one. If Eurozone demand is on a steady growth path of 1%, Italian exports of goods increase by 1.5 to 2% per year (less than 1% for export of services). As for Spain, growth in the rest of the world has a small, but statistically significant negative effect on the export of goods (but not services), suggesting a certain degree of substitution. The long-term impact of a loss of competitiveness is also rather high for goods (elasticity between -1.1 and -1.5), while it is insignificantly different from zero in the case of services.

Overall, Italian and Spanish exports respond to movements in foreign demand and relative prices in a similar ways. Export of goods are highly sensitive to demands in the Eurozone, with an elasticity of 2.5 in the Spanish case, and a short-run elasticity of 3 and a long-run elasticity between 1.5 and 2 in the Italian cases. For both countries, the exports of goods show signs of being negatively affected by the growth of developing countries, controlling for Eurozone demand. Further research is required to disentangle this impact. Finally, exports of goods are highly price sensitive: the elasticity is -1.3 for Spain, and between -1.1 and -1.5 for Italy (long-run elasticity). In both countries, service sectors seem less affected by price competitiveness than goods.

12

Global Capital and National Growth Models: The Cases of Ireland and Latvia

DOROTHEE BOHLE AND AIDAN REGAN

Introduction

As stated in the introduction to this volume, the Growth Model (GM) research program seeks to address three issues. First, it aims to develop a new framework that allows for an understanding of the configurations, dynamics, and different forms of capitalism in the 21st century with a special focus on 'post-Keynesian' macroeconomics and the sources of demand. Second, it seeks to understand the political coalitions underpinning these specific configurations, and third, it seeks to do so by combining the insights of comparative (CPE) and international political economy (IPE). Although the GM perspective is in principle open to identifying a variety of GMs, its focus has so far has been on mid-size OECD countries, and a central distinction remains the extent to which these rich democracies secure income growth through domestic consumption and/or net exports.

Our chapter contributes to the GM research agenda by focusing on the role of small countries in servicing the interests of global capital. Analytically, our paper adopts the perspective developed by Herman Schwartz and Mark Blyth (Chapter 4 of this volume) in that it situates the specific national growth models of two small European states in the economic networks and power structures of the global system of finance and investment—what they call "Galton 3." Our specific focus is on one area that has so far received little attention in the growth model research program—global wealth chains (Seabrooke and Wigan 2014) and multinational corporations that operate transnationally. As such, our chapter complements the chapters by Ban and Ascalitei on Foreign Direct

Investment (FDI); Schwartz on the knowledge economy; and by Johnson and Matthijs on the EU's post-crisis growth model. Whereas Schwartz analyzes the monopoly strategies and business models of the knowledge economy's lead global firms, we show how small states make a living from servicing the economic interests of these firms. Whereas Ban and Ascaliti focus on "real investments" of transnational companies, and Johnson and Matthijs on the adverse consequences of the EU's new economic governance on national growth models, we show how the ability of mobile capital to move and arbitrage between different European jurisdictions enables the richest corporations and individuals to accumulate wealth.

A central contention of the chapter is that in 21st-century capitalism, a major determinant of growth (and stagnation) dynamics is the concentrated accumulation of wealth and capital—be it individual or corporate, legal or illicit—its uneven geographical distribution, and its variegated links with production and value creation, financial systems, and state institutions. This increased concentration of wealth, particularly in the hands of large corporations, is a function of the increasingly intangible nature of capital assets, which increasingly enables the movement of profits into tax havens and low-tax jurisdictions. But while these global wealth chains and capital assets are organized globally and transnationally, they do offer nation-states or sub-state units the opportunity to capture parts of the international chain, with due consequences for domestic economic growth, employment, and macroeconomic policies. Small countries often specialize in servicing the needs of global wealth by offering tailored and nontransparent banking services (e.g., Switzerland), illicit financial activities to launder money (e.g., Latvia), platforms for licensing intellectual property (e.g., Ireland), or zero-tax jurisdictions (e.g., Bermuda). But while growth models in small states might be entirely shaped by the economic niche they occupy in global markets, servicing the needs of global wealth is by no means restricted to these small countries. Subunits in larger states offer similar services, such as Nevada and Delaware in the United States, the City of London in the United Kingdom, or Beijing and Shanghai in China. As research in economic geography increasingly shows, what is measured as national growth in our national accounts is increasingly a function of *city-level* growth, creating intra-regional inequalities within countries (Iversen and Soskice 2019).

Furthermore, as a rich literature in IPE shows, an increasing share of the accumulation of global wealth and capital takes place in offshore jurisdictions, which coexist and interact with the onshore economy of nation-states in complex ways (e.g., Palan 2006; Palan et al. 2013; Sharman 2017a). These offshore jurisdictions, particularly those common law jurisdictions that were connected to the British empire, have been central to the historical evolution of global capitalism. Or to use the metaphor of Lonergan and Blyth (2020), offshore financial centers within city-states are not a bug within the global capital market system, they are part of the software that make it work. Yet, CPE has so far paid scant attention to the offshore economy and how it interacts with national political economies.

Our chapter seeks to probe this relationship between global capital and national growth models within two cases: Ireland and Latvia. The aim of these cases is explorative, not comparative. We chose these two cases as representing *very different cases* of the off and onshore network of global wealth chains, and which exhibit interesting variation for domestic growth. Both assume very different roles in the patchwork quilt of global capital. Ireland is a case where global value chains and productive investment increasingly interacts with global wealth chains. It thus allows us to explore the developmental consequences of the foreign investment and wealth "creation" for the Irish growth model, particularly in the tech and pharma sectors. Latvia, on the other hand, has crafted itself into the "Switzerland of the Baltics," with its banking sector being directed at attracting (illicit) wealth from high-net-worth individuals from Russia. This, as we will show, has an anti-developmental impact. The remainder of the chapter is structured as follows. The next section will briefly introduce our main concepts, especially global wealth chains and offshore finance, and justify why we think these recent phenomena need to be studied within the GM perspective. In sections 3 and 4, we will present the Irish and Latvian cases. The final section concludes.

Global Wealth Chains and the Offshore Economy

IPE has a long tradition of studying the rise and increasing power of transnational corporations, their role in organizing global value chains, and the concomitant transformation of national economies and the state (e.g., Stopford and Strange 1991; Gereffi et al. 2005; Dickens 2015). More recently, Leonard Seabrooke and Duncan Wigan (2014, 2017), have suggested an important addition to this research agenda by introducing the concept of global wealth chains (GWC). In contrast to research in global value chains, which focuses on the governance of global production and distribution, wealth chains examine the shifting of assets into and among offshore and onshore jurisdictions. Seabrooke and Wigan define GWC as "linked forms of capital seeking to avoid accountability during processes of pecuniary wealth creation," that is, they are capital investments and movements that "seek to escape fiscal claims, legal obligations, or regulatory oversight" (2014, 257). Wealth chains operate through offshore jurisdictions, that is, jurisdictions that specialize in designing regulatory and legal systems with the specific purpose of attracting disproportionate volumes of mobile capital (2014, 258). Central to this is the ability to legally define and code capital assets for offshore purposes. As these authors argue, the coexistence of wealth and value chains has important repercussions for our understanding of state development.

Why focus on global wealth chains? because of their sheer size. Zucman (2017) estimates that 8.7 trillion USD, equivalent to 11.5% of the entire world's GDP is held offshore by ultra-rich individuals. Other authors put this number much higher, up to 36 trillion USD, which would almost equal 50% of the world's GDP (Henry 2016, quoted in Shaxon 2019). An important share of that wealth stems from the illicit activities of corrupt elites from all over the world, especially in resource-rich countries and "kleptocracies." In addition to these super wealthy individuals, multinational corporations "use legal financial engineering to shift large sums of money across the globe, easily relocate highly profitable intangible business, or sell digital services from tax havens without having a physical presence" (Damgaard et al. 2019, 13). This manifests itself (among others) in "phantom investments"—foreign direct investments that take place within large corporations and have no real business activities, but are done mostly for tax avoiding purposes. This intra-group phantom activity now makes up more than 40% of the stock of global FDI and is growing faster than genuine FDI flows (Damgaard et al. 2019, 13.). Zucman (2017) estimates the resulting loss of corporate tax revenues for the United States in the order of 20% of the annual corporate tax take.

Second, wealth chains and the world of offshore finance are inextricably linked to the major transformations of capitalism since the end of Fordism. Palan (2006) notes a "veritable explosion of offshore" in parallel with the liberaliza-tion of capital markets, especially financial markets, and the transnationalization of production. While the offshore economy (rise of Euromarkets, tax havens, and export processing zones) initially played an important role in easing the transnationalization of productive capital, since then a more fundamental transformation of global capitalism has taken place, which puts the mobile in-vestor, and the reinforcement of her property rights at the center of politics. To put it differently, as Gill (1998, 25, quoted in Palan 2006, 13) writes, "[t]he mobile investor becomes the sovereign political subject." This is what Gill calls global constitutionalism, in which offshore "is often treated in terms of basic human rights: the right of small states to determine their own laws, the right of individuals to place their savings where they wish; the right of corporations to avoid punitive taxation and regulation" (Palan 2006, 15).

Underpinning this brave new world of the sovereign investor is a structural change from manufacturing to the "knowledge economy." In the post-Fordist "knowledge economy," where information has become coded as intellectual property rights, lead firms in global value chains generate huge profits from intangible assets—intellectual property, data, trade secrets, patents—rather than tangible investments, such as a factory (see the chapter by Schwartz in this volume). Just five technology firms—Apple, Amazon, Alphabet, Microsoft, and Facebook—make up 20% of the total market capitalization of the S&P 500, an unprecedented level of dominance by such a small sectoral grouping. These corporate groups enjoy enormous freedom in determining where their intangible assets are "created" and "located." They have developed great creativity in moving them into their own subsidiaries and holding companies within jurisdictions that specialize in raising little or no taxes. Consequently, the lion's share of global MNCs' income has shifted offshore (e.g., Palan 2006; Schwartz in this volume; Zucman 2017; Damgaard et al. 2019).

Third, the rise of offshore is also intrinsically linked to another hallmark of contemporary capitalism, namely the rise of inequality, both within and between countries (and between firms, see Schwartz 2016). Offshore tax havens are helping to drive the soaring wealth inequality among individuals and firms that has plagued (not only) advanced capitalist democracies (e.g., Piketty 2014; Saez and Zucman 2019; Schwartz 2016). It has also boosted large-scale corruption in "kleptocracies," where elites are mostly concerned with channeling state resources away for their private luxury consumption (Helgadóttir 2021). As Bullough (2018) argues, while kleptocracy and elite corruption is nothing new, it is only the rise of offshore economy that has allowed high-level corruption on a very large scale. All of this implies that global wealth chains and offshore are a crucial feature of contemporary capitalism. While IPE (and investigative journalism) have produced insightful evidence of global wealth and the offshore world, and international organizations have started to seriously engage with the latter, CPE mostly ignores networked offshore economies. They are depicted as something marginal, taking place in faraway exotic islands, but being of no concern for their field of interest. CPE's focus is on the value added of "productive" firms at the national level and measuring national units of activity through the national accounts. However, even the most cursory glance at some of the issues raised by this new world of sovereign investor capitalism shows how central it is to comparative political economy. If a huge chunk of Irish, Dutch, Swiss, and Luxemburg investment is phantom activity within globally connected MNC's, national accounts cease to become a source of useful information, and instead grossly distort existing economic relations (Mügge and Linsi 2020).

Crucially, major offshore centers are found in the OECD world. Of particular importance are small European states such as Switzerland, Luxemburg, the Benelux countries, and Ireland, and smaller Asian states such as Singapore and Hong-Kong. Switzerland and Luxemburg are known champions of financial secrecy. On the 2018 financial secrecy ranking issued by the Tax Justice Network however, the United States ranks second, Germany ranks just behind Luxemburg, and the Netherlands are not far behind either.[1] Luxemburg and the Netherlands host nearly half of the world's phantom FDI (Damgaard et al. 2019, 12), while the city of London is among the greatest financial offshore centers in the world. Ireland made headlines recently with almost two-thirds of the stock of what's classified as foreign investments being phantom (500 billion)—namely US MNC's storing capital within Irish based subsidiaries (Bohle and Regan 2021). Latvia, which according to the GM literature would qualify as a debt-financed consumption-led model (Baccaro et al., Chapter 1 in this volume; Bohle 2018), has recently seen its Central Bank president accused of taking bribes from local lenders linked to money laundering. Meanwhile the Scandinavian reputation for honesty and trust has been taking a severe hit in recent years because of their banks' exposure to massive financial crime (e.g., *The Economist* 2019).

In sum, national capitalist democracies are deeply entangled in the transnational web of global finance. It is not by chance that small states and city-states entirely or dominantly make their living from servicing the needs of global capital. As the literature on small states has shown, these often are endowed with fewer resources than large states, whether in terms of population, domestic markets, natural endowments, competitive industries, or advantageous geographical location. As a result, they are constrained in the growth strategies they can employ. At the same time, however, this vulnerability can turn into advantages for small states, as it forces them to develop innovative growth strategies. As Cooper and Shaw (2009, 2) formulate, "What small states lack in structural clout they can make up through creative agency." Thus, many small states structure their national economy around one commercial activity in which they create comparative advantage. It is our argument that they now increasingly carve out special niches in administering global wealth (for a summary of the literature on small states, see Bishop 2012; Bohle and Jacoby 2017; and Halperin 2015).

There is little work that links global wealth chains to national growth models, or CPE. Yet, we submit that wealth chains and small states are highly relevant for understanding the dynamics of the global political economy. On the one hand, the offshore economy is part and parcel of the secular stagnation since the global financial crisis. Instead of investing capital productively, lead corporations in global value chains move their profits offshore, "sitting on a huge heap of cash holdings" (Schwartz 2016), with negative consequences for global demand. Given that offshore wealth is not or relatively lightly taxed, it also reduces government spending and public investment. On the other hand, global wealth chains allow smaller countries to attract investment and generate income they might not otherwise have. Global wealth chains also create jobs: from legal advisors, tax accountants, to "directors" of shell companies. Depending on the niche in the global wealth chain a country occupies, wealth chains might significantly undermine the legitimacy of national institutions. The process of shifting capital assets and profit is hardwired into the DNA and legal structure of the global financial system and transnational corporations—and it's made possible by small nation-states. Furthermore, many nation-states have constructed their growth models by specializing in servicing the needs of global capital.

It is to this latter question that we now turn. We will take a closer look at two small European states whose growth, employment, domestic institutions, and developmental outlook is deeply shaped by their partaking in the global wealth chains of large financial and foreign-owned multinational corporations. Ireland's traditional focus on attracting high value-added segments of pharmaceutical and technology companies has recently been complemented by its role as a "treasure island"—a place to store intellectual property and the capital assets of global US firms who seek to "optimize" their tax strategies. This coexistence of value production and wealth positively affects Ireland's growth model. Latvia, on the other hand, has fashioned itself as the "Switzerland of the Baltics" and, as such, has become a major transit destination in the complex money laundering operations of Russian oligarchs and kleptocrats. While this business is in an economic enclave with little direct connections to the domestic economy, the interests of private banks have captured major state institutions with detrimental consequences for Latvia's growth model. What occurs in Ireland is legal, transparent, and central to the innovative corporate structures of the new global digital economy. What occurs in Latvia is illicit, murky, and central to the offshore capital holdings of rich individuals. But they are connected in that they both service the economic demands of wealth accumulation in the global political economy.

Treasure Ireland: Phantom Investment and Leprechaun Economics

Ireland is a highly globalized economy, measured in terms of export/import intensity, and inward and outward Foreign Direct Investment (FDI). According to the globalization index developed at the KOF economic institute at the ETH in Zurich, Ireland is the second-most globalized economy in the world. Ireland achieves this status by acting as a *platform* for US multinationals to sell directly into the international and European market (Brazys and Regan 2017, 2021; Barry 2019; Kinsella 2012). In this section, we will show how Ireland occupies a privileged position in the global hierarchy of foreign investment; how this growth model is connected to corporate tax avoidance—a crucial link within the global wealth chains of US multinationals; and the extent to which this shapes the domestic Irish growth model.

Tech Investment: The Rise of Computer
Service Exports

Measured as a percentage of modified Gross National Income (which we use instead of GDP to reduce the impact of corporate tax avoidance in the national accounts), Irish exports have grown from 80% of national income in 1995 to almost 150% in 2018 (Brazys and Regan 2021). This is nearly three times the European Union average (Byrne and O'Brien 2015). In the same time period, household consumption, as a component of aggregate demand, declined from around 58% to 40%. Net exports as a percentage of GNI now constitute 30% of total final aggregate demand. The EU is Ireland's largest export market, but on a country-by-country basis, it is the United States that is the main export goods market for US firms in Ireland. From a purely GM national accounting perspective, it is reasonable to conclude that Ireland is an export-led growth model, but this doesn't really tell us much about the politics of foreign investment that drives this export growth.

Over 90% of Irish exports come from the foreign-owned multinational sectors in technology, business services, and life sciences (pharmaceuticals and chemicals). In 2004, export of *goods* accounted for over 65% of Irish exports. By 2018, this had declined to around 40%. Computer and financial *service* exports now dominate the export basket—and these are notoriously difficult to measure in the national accounts. If we just look at manufacturing goods exports (this is what the national accounts were designed to measure), there has been a sectoral shift from electronics to pharmaceutical goods. The share of electronics in total goods exports has declined from around 30% in 2000 to around 6% in 2018 (Purdue and Huang 2016). Manufacturing exports in Ireland are now dominated by chemical and pharmaceutical goods (US pharma companies producing and selling back to the US market).

Between 2004 and 2018, *service* exports increased from around 30% to over 55% of total exports (see Brazys and Regan 2021). It was this growth in computer service exports that led to a sectoral shift in the Irish growth model in the aftermath of the financial crash (Brazys and Regan 2017). ICT services accounted for over 35% of Irish exports in 2020, three times more than in 2000. These exports are dominated by US multinational firms in the big tech sector (think Google, Apple, Amazon, Facebook, and Microsoft). These multinationals trade in international markets that are *not* price sensitive, and trying to accurately identify what constitutes their gross value added, and what underpins their digital sales revenue, is notoriously difficult. But it is fair to assume that they are far less concerned with controlling wage and labor costs than automobile manufacturers. Their investment decisions are much more motivated by concerns about ease of doing business and corporate tax policies, than the cost of paying for high-quality graduates. The important point to note from the perspective of a GM framework is that Ireland's export-growth model is shaped by the foreign investment strategies of US multinational corporations. Ireland has become (and Dublin more precisely) the global digital sales and advertising hub for the big tech sector. The value added of these global corporate groups may not be produced in Ireland, but it is where they declare their revenue, and where they house a large part of their intellectual property. And this is what matters for profitability and wealth creation. But how much of this is real, and how much of it is phantom investment for tax avoidance purposes?

Big Tech Investment and Tax Avoidance

The total capital stock of foreign investment in Ireland is enormous—approximately 800 billion USD. According to estimates by Damgaard 2019 et al., around two-thirds of this (around 500 billion) is phantom. It is capital that large multinationals—with a real presence in Ireland—move *within* subsidiary companies that are registered in Ireland. For example, the global corporate group of Alphabet, the trillion-dollar parent holding company of Google, is made up of over 400 subsidiaries. Around 30 of these subsidiaries are registered in Ireland (see Figure 12.1 for a snapshot of this structure). Just one of these subsidiaries—Raiden Unlimited, with no registered employees—is the holding company of an additional 40 sub-subsidiaries in 15 different countries. A large part of the economic activity that accrues from MNC's that are rich in intellectual property, such as Google, is a function of moving profits within their own subsidiaries to reduce the taxable income from their global earnings.

Ireland's headline 12.5% corporate tax rate on all tradable income is often assumed to be the incentive behind the profit-shifting strategies of US multinationals. But most global multinationals, in almost all EU jurisdictions, can find ways to bring down their *effective* corporate *tax rate*. Even in France, multinationals are estimated to pay an average effective corporate tax rate of between 15 to 20%. The rationale behind companies doing this is to maximize their profitability. Higher profitability means higher stock market valuations. Higher stock market valuations mean shareholders get wealthier. It is also a source of power for firms—they can more easily buy up potential and real rival firms because their shares are collateral for any borrowed funds. As Saez and Zucman (2019) have argued, the fundamental objective and outcome of corporate tax avoidance is increasing the wealth and capital income of individual shareholders. These shareholders—wealth holders—are highly concentrated among the top 0.1% of the wealth distribution.

In Ireland, it is not so much the headline corporate tax rate that matters but the various tax incentives that allow multinationals to shift their intellectual

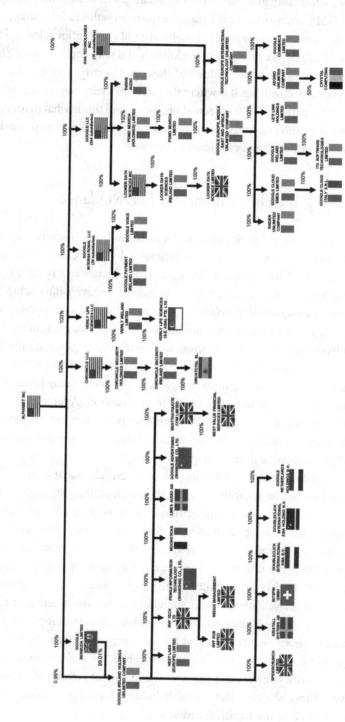

Figure 12.1 Key Irish subsidaries of Google's global corporate structure.
Source: Bureau van Dijk (2020). Available at: "http://fame.bvdep.com/"http://fame.bvdep.com

property through and/or incorporate their headquarters in Ireland. This is what makes Ireland so attractive to the business owners of US multinationals. The most well-known tax avoidance scheme that multinationals have used in Ireland is the Double-Irish, which was phased out from 2015–2020. It basically worked as follows: US MNC's would set up two Irish registered companies. Under US law, they were one Irish company. But under Irish law, they were two companies. One of these companies could be registered in Ireland but domiciled and tax resident in the Bermuda's IIRC. Google, for example, would shift the profits from the Irish-based to the Bermuda-based company—which legally licensed Google's intellectual property. This allowed them to store their profits—tax free—in the Bermuda's IIRC, until they decided if and when to repatriate the profits back to the United States, which they did when Donald Trump incentivized them to do so. This scheme was shut down in 2015 in response to pressure from the EU and the OECD's Base Erosion and Profit Shifting (BEPS) project. But the Irish government phased the closure over five years to allow companies using the Double-Irish scheme to restructure their global tax operations. This gave plenty of time for tax accountants and corporate lawyers to develop new profit-shifting structures.

Similar variants of this profit-shifting scheme existed within Ireland, and in those jurisdictions with whom Ireland has signed bilateral tax treaties. For example, Apple, another trillion-dollar company, created a different variant of the scheme via the licensing of intellectual property through multiple Irish-registered companies. They shifted the profits of their sales from international markets into and between these different subsidiaries to such an extent that the taxable income effectively became stateless. In 2016, the EU found that this tax structure broke EU competition law, and that knowledge of the scheme in two tax notes by the Irish state constituted illegal state aid. Ireland was then forced to apply its 12.5% corporate tax rate on these profits, which amounted to around 13.5 billion USD. This was the first time the EU used competition law to tackle the base erosion and the profit shifting strategies of multinationals. Apple and Ireland challenged the case in the European Courts and won. Their argument was that this was not something that was unique to Apple, and therefore Apple did not get preferential tax treatment. They rightly argued that the profits that were shifted into Ireland were liable for US taxes, not Irish taxes.

Ironically, since 2015, the international attempt to clamp down on aggressive BEPS strategies has been a boon for Ireland. For example, in 2016, soon after the Apple tax case, Ireland's economy recorded a staggering 26.5% growth rate, leading to the infamous trope "Leprechaun Economics" (see Krugman 2017). It has since emerged—although not officially recognized—that this spectacular growth was partially related to Apple *onshoring* 300 billion USD worth of their intellectual property and intangible capital assets to Ireland via Jersey. No one knows what exactly this IP is—whether it is the Apple brand, know-how, trade secrets, or just the contractual license to use the Apple product in European sales. All we know is that it is highly valuable and must be counted in the Irish national accounts. Apple can legitimately claim that moving these assets to Ireland is not a BEPS strategy because they have a physical presence in Ireland—employing over 4,000 people, albeit only in a select few of their legal entities, as the whole point of registering so many subsidiaries in Ireland is to use complex financial-accounting engineering to reduce the taxable income of their global earnings.

Other tech companies have adopted a similar strategy. For example, post-2015 Microsoft has onshored its IP via Singapore to Ireland, leading to a similar massive growth in the capital stock. Big Pharma companies, such as Abbvie; and the consultancy firm, Accenture, would appear to have done likewise. Generally, the strategy of big pharma companies to is pursue corporate inversions. These corporate inversions effectively move the US parent company to Ireland, such that they declare their global financial accounts in their Irish-domiciled head-quarters, and direct their global investments from Ireland—on paper at least. These tax-incentivized activities not only distort Ireland's GDP figures, but the entire trade balance of the Eurozone (Lane 2020).

The Role of the State in Ireland's Growth Model

The post-2015 onshoring of intangible capital assets to Ireland was not a co-incidence. It was a direct response to the closure of the Double-Irish tax structure. In 2009, during the financial crisis, the Irish state introduced a finance bill that contained measures specifically designed to attract intangible capital—the "capital allowances for intangible assets" (CAIA). In 2015, they expanded the definition of "intangible." The CAIA basically allows MNCs to purchase their own capital assets and then write the cost off as a capital allowance for tax purposes. Initially, they could write off the entire cost, which is what Apple did in 2016, but in response to public pressure, it was later reduced to 80% of the cost. The new scheme was ultimately designed to provide a strong incentive for US MNC's who used the Double-Irish structure to shift their intellectual property out of the Caribbean into Ireland. And it worked—Apple, Microsoft, Dell, Twitter, Oracle, Cadence, among many other firms—all pursued a variant of this "Green Jersey" tax strategy. The outcome was a boon in corporate tax receipts accruing to the Irish state. In 2020, corporate tax accounted for 20% of the total tax take in Ireland, and almost 80% of this came from between 10 to 20 multinationals.

Similar tax activities can be observed in the murkier world of financial and banking services. The Irish corporate tax regime allows for the creation of special purpose vehicles (SPVs). SPVs legally structure themselves to act as a conduit to move capital and avoid tax. Unlike the big tech and pharma sectors, these really are "post-box" shell companies that typically have no employees, and pay no tax to the Irish government. One type of SPV—"section 110"—are investment funds that funnel cash out of Ireland to more secretive banking jurisdictions, such as Luxemburg or Switzerland. These SPV's have created a massive shadow banking sector in Ireland, which, remarkably, the Central Bank has limited power to regulate, mainly because they know very little about them. The International Financial Stability Board (IFSB) estimates that the shadow banking sector in Ireland is the third largest in the world, with an estimated 2.5 trillion USD worth of capital assets being administered in the Irish Financial Services Center (IFSC). This means that Ireland is a central hub in the global network of off and onshore finance. Typically, Ireland is not the final destination for these investment funds, rather it acts as a conduit for these shell companies to store capital and wealth before shifting it to other locations. The main direct benefit to the Irish growth model is the creation of high-paying jobs in the financial service sector, and in the law firms that registered these shell companies.

Does all of this mean that Ireland is nothing more than a tax haven, and that these activities have no bearing at all on the Irish growth model? No, These schemes and incentives are baked into the systemic structure of global capital of which the Irish growth model is but one part. To use the analogy of Blyth and Schwartz in this project—the system shapes the unit. If the license to use the intangible capital assets of big tech and pharma corporations were not housed in Ireland, they would have to be housed somewhere else—and mostly likely, the USA. Ireland services the global capital interests of US big tech and pharma groups, particularly their sales, revenue, and advertising needs. This leads to real growth and real jobs. For example, according to Brazys and Regan (2020), between 2002 to 2018, and when we strip out all the phantom-like economic activities, Ireland recorded over $85 billion in real green field site investments (either new projects or the expansion of existing activities). This amounts to around 2,000 projects. Over 70% of these are in the big tech and pharma sectors. In terms of employment, there have been around 350,000 net jobs created in Ireland since 2012, and over one-third of these are associated directly with the FDI sectors. In ICT, over 50,000 jobs have been created, of which over 75% are located in Dublin. These are all real activities that are directly associated with a state-led developmental policy aimed at attracting foreign investment as a means to construct an export-led economy in Europe. Furthermore, the Irish state benefits massively in terms of revenue. As mentioned earlier, in 2020, the corporate sector accounted for almost 20% of total Irish taxation. That's one in every five euros collected in taxes. To our knowledge, there is no other country in the OECD where this is the case.

The Irish growth model is part of a global wealth chain that spans from Silicon Valley via Ireland to the EU, Asia, and further afield. The global corporations that shape the Irish growth model have economies that are larger than many states, and more consumers than there are citizens in China. These are truly *multinational and multi-jurisdictional* corporations that significantly impact the global distribution of wealth. Small nation-states—such as Ireland—are a crucial link in how they protect their global profits. This has provided the conditions for the Irish state to carve out a rather unique growth model, which, from a narrow self-interested perspective, has clearly benefitted the domestic Irish political economy.

The Switzerland of the Baltics: Illicit Wealth Chains and Latvia's Growth Model

While Ireland's growth model is shaped by the legal tax and profit-shifting strategies of US multinationals, Latvia's growth model is tied into destructive illicit wealth chains. Since independence, the country has assumed an important role in laundering illegal funds stemming from the post-Soviet space. Money laundering, as recent investigations such as the Panama papers have revealed, is by no means a marginal phenomenon in the contemporary political economy, and Europe has assumed a central place in this. Since the Great Financial Crisis, 18 of Europe's 20 largest banks have been fined for money laundering, exposing the continent's bloated banking sector, lax approach to financial crime, and the close state-bank ties (Raggett 2019). Some of Europe's smaller political economies have become veritable post-Soviet "laundromats," with their financial sectors striving on illicit wealth. This section introduces one of them, Latvia. It first looks at the conditions that made ample illegal funds available, then takes a closer look at Latvia's position in channeling illicit wealth to its final destination, and the state strategies that put Latvia in this position. It concludes with the implications for the Latvian growth model.

The Rise of Kleptocracy on the Ruins of Communism

One of the most important sources of illicit wealth is large-scale corruption of state elites across the globe, and particularly from resource-rich countries. Scholars have argued that the rise of offshore finance has fundamentally altered the scale and *Gestalt* of large-scale corruption. Whereas before, corruption would be largely confined within the national borders, and be synonymous with "steal and spend," the fact that jurisdictions across the globe accept any sums of money with no questions asked, has enabled corrupt elites to "steal, obscure and spend" ever larger amounts of money (Bullough 2018). Arguably, nowhere has kleptocracy[2] reached such dimensions as in post-communist Russia and other Soviet successor states. The large-scale transformation of a closed and state-controlled economy enabled state looting by political and economic elites on an unprecedented scale. Already in the 1980s, the Soviet secret service KGB started moving money out of the state. Once communism collapsed, there was not only ample opportunity to systematically loot the state, but there was also "an unusual coalition of former members of the party elite, the military complex, and veterans of the security and law enforcement apparatus, supported by the strong arm of organized crime" ready to do so (Shelley 1997, 482). Large-scale privatization was almost entirely hijacked by old and new criminal elites, and the resource boom of the 1990s and 2000s enabled additional appropriation and accumulation of individual wealth.

With Putin's coming to power in the 2000s, the kleptocratic system consolidated (Dawisha 2014). Drawing on a close circle of friends from his childhood and KGB times, the power of Putin and his friends grew in proportion with their wealth. It is the moneys drawn from bribetaking, kickbacks, rigged privatization deals, illicit exports, real estate deals, etc., that was looking for ways to become legit. As such, kleptocracy is a system not confined to a national political economy. As Bullogh (2018, 34) notes, "The essence of kleptocracy is that it is globalized, not confined behind national borders. It is pointless to ask whether Russia is a kleptocracy. It is more appropriate to examine how Russia's elites are part of a kleptocratic system by which their thefts from the national budget are connected, via Scottish limited partnerships and Moldovan or Latvian banks, to the London property market." While Russia is the one of largest generators of illicit money, similar large-scale looting of the state has taken place in the broader post-Soviet space. The next section takes a closer look at the role of Latvia in this globalized kleptocratic system.

The Latvian Pipeline of Post-Soviet Money

For its tiny size, Latvia plays an important role in moving money flows around the globe. According to Daniel Glaser, a former top official in the US Treasury, in 2015, about 1% of all US dollars moving around were going through the country. Glasner estimates that this is 30 times more than would be expected for a country of Latvia's size (Meyers et al. 2018). Latvian banks have been involved in almost all major post-Soviet money laundering scandals that have been revealed in recent years. They laundered a large share of money channeled away by the daughter of the former Uzbek President Islam Karimov, and were involved in the infamous Magnitsky affair, which ended with the death of a lawyer hired by an American holding company that got into conflict with Russian giant Gazprom over the embezzlement of their funds. Latvian banks also made their appearance in "some of the biggest and most complex money laundering schemes operating in Eurasia, running over extended periods of time—sometimes years—and involving thousands of shell companies and tens of thousands of transactions," such as the "Russian laundromat," and the "big Moldavian bank robbery." Table 12.1 lists major money-laundering scandals in which Latvian banks were involved during the past decade. It also shows the limited efforts made by public authorities to persecute the offenders.

Thanks to the work of investigative journalist we have a good understanding of the services Latvian banks provide to their clients. They work in tandem with their depositors, which are "platforms of anonymous shell companies registered in multiple offshore locations" to launder and move massive funds into the international system. Stack calls this form of money laundering "trade-based," as it is either based on "complex schemes of fraudulent trade transactions . . . by means of misrepresentation of price, quantity, and quality of imports or exports," or, as in the case of the Russian laundromat, based on the setup of fictitious loan relations (Stack 2015, quoted in Greco 2018, 18).

Latvian banks have adopted a specific business model, exporting what Greco (2018, 3) calls financial logistics services. Specifically, Latvian banks mostly provide short-term on-demand deposits, which facilitate the transit of funds into the international financial system. The transit function which is at the core of the Latvian business model distinguishes it from banks in countries like Switzerland and Cyprus, which "are focused on attracting non-resident customers' money for long periods and maintaining the value of deposited funds." (Greco 2013, 3). Latvia achieves its aim of a transit location through a strong network of Western correspondent banks, that is, banks that act as intermediaries for the Latvian banks. It was through the correspondent accounts of Western banks that Latvian institutions could transfer their clients' money to the final destination without having to open branches all over the world. Many major Western banks, including JP Morgan, Deutsche Bank, or Commerzbank offered their correspondent services to Latvian banks, often with the explicit encouragement of the respective financial regulators.[3] Thus, in the apt words of Bershidsky (2018), "through a strong network of correspondent relationships with Western banks, [Latvian banks] serve as a pipeline for post-Soviet money to safer havens, a pipeline as capacious as the ones that have pumped Russian gas to Europe. . . . Switzerland, in other words, was not so much a model as a destination" (Bershidsky 2018).

Table 12.1 Major Money Laundering and Criminal Cases Involving Latvian Banks, 2008–2018

	Banks involved	Description	Consequence
2001–2012	ABLV Parex	**Gulnara Karimova**, daughter of former Uzbek President Islam Karimov operated a massive bribery scheme in the order of USD 866 million using shell companies and offshoring schemes. Allegedly, Karimova deposited some 446 million USD in the two Latvian banks.[a]	Not until 2017–18, when ABLV's license was withdrawn, and the bank liquidated under pressure of the US Treasury
2007–	Trasta Komercbanka Aizkraukles Baltic International Bank Baltic Trust Bank Paritate Bank Rietumu Banka Privatbank	**Magnitsky Affair:** Sergei Magnitsky was a lawyer for Hermitage Capital who tried to investigate the theft of money from the fund after Hermitage got into conflict with Gazprom. In 2012, Hermitage Capital informed the General Prosecutor of Latvia, that 7 Latvian banks had been involved in money laundering (Latvian banks laundered at least 63 million USD out of the 230 million USD) for a group of Russian criminals close to Putin.[b]	No strong response, it took until 2016 that Trasta's bank license was revoked.
2008–2012	Rietumu Banka (5th largest Latvian bank by assets in 2017)	Rietumu banka was involved in a massive **tax evasion scheme** with a French offshore company by helping to launder EUR 850 million[c]	Rietumu Banka was fined in July 2017 in France 80 Million euro
2011	Krajbanka	Allegedly, the board approved the issuing of large loans to offshore companies. These companies were controlled by the bank owner, and used to channel assets out of the bank.	FKTK ordered bank to suspend financial services, and withdrew its license in 2012[d]

(continued)

Table 12.1 Continued

	Banks involved	Description	Consequence
2011–2014	Trasta Komercbanka (One of the oldest private banks in Latvia) & 11 additional Latvian banks, including ABLV	**Russian Laundromat**: a massive 20 billion USD money laundering scheme. 13 billion USD were transferred to Trasta, from where they went into 96 countries, whose location in the EU was seen as advantageous.[e]	The Laundromat was exposed in 2014 Trasta's license was only revoked in 2016, after its involvement in other scandals
2014	Privatbank Pasta Banca ABLV	**The big Moldovan Bank Robbery**: In November three Moldovan banks were robbed of USD 1 billion on one single day. Up to 20% of the money was allegedly channeled through three Latvian banks	In 2015, Privatbank was fined with 2 million euro, the highest fine ever.; the bank was also to change its board, and individual fines were imposed[f]
2011–2013	ABLV Banka Regionalna Investiciju Banka	**Kurchenko affair**: Kurchenko, a Ukrainian business man, billionaire and associate of Yanukovych has been channeling money through two Latvian banks. Kurchenko's schemes gave his companies an illegal turnover of about 1.6 million USD.[g]	ABLV's license withdrawn in 2017, and went into liquidation in 2018
2016	Trasta Komercbanka	Implicated in the laundering of at least 300.000 Euro as part of a larger fraud that sucked money out of the Franco-Belgian Bank Dexia[h]	FKTK consistently failed to notice the frauds Trasta was involved in prior to 2016, when the licence was finally revoked

2009–2015	ABLV	**Violations of North Korean sanctions.** In 2017, the FCMC	Withdrawal of license of ABLV in July
	Norvik Bank	in cooperation with the US Federal Bureau of Investigation	2017, liquidation in 2018
		detected breaches of statutory requirements in five Latvian	
		banks that had enabled the circumvention of the sanctions	
		imposed against the North Korea. The five banks were	
		involved in the violations indirectly; they all confessed to the	
		wrongdoing and later cooperated with the investigators[i]	

Source: Aslund 2017, various press and other reports (see footnotes)

[a] https://eng.lsm.lv/article/society/crime/100-million-dollar-bribe-to-uzbek-presidents-daughter-went-via-latvian-bank.a312056/; https://www.rferl.org/a/children-of-uzbekistan-elite-playground-latvia-golden-visa-program/27734370.html

[b] Transparency International 2018, Dawisha 2014.

[c] http://www.baltic-course.com/eng/finances/?doc=139030

[d] https://eng.lsm.lv/article/economy/banks/latvijas-krajbanka-appeal-case-gets-underway.a276201/

[e] https://www.occrp.org/en/laundromat/the-russian-laundromat-exposed/

[f] https://en.rebaltica.lv/2016/02/how-a-latvian-laundered-billion-usd-changed-moldova/

[g] https://www.occrp.org/en/daily/4545-ukraine-kyiv-court-seizes-billionaire-kurchenko-s-14-offshore-accounts

[h] https://eng.lsm.lv/article/economy/economy/latvian-bank-linked-to-another-russian-money-laundering-operation.a164643/; https://eng.lsm.lv/article/economy/economy/another-bank-linked-to-money-laundering-and-hacking.a159750/

[i] http://www.fktk.lv/attachments/article/7194/FCMC_annual_report_2017.pdf

Fusing Private and Public Power to the Detriment of Growth

Why have Latvian banks assumed such an important role in laundering illicit wealth in the post-Soviet space, and how has it impacted Latvia's growth model? Briefly put, it was a conjunction of private actors grabbing the opportunities offered by historical legacies in the context of global capital market liberalization and influential state actors' vision of the future Latvian economy after independence. Latvia's post-independence growth model was predicated on fusing the interests of Latvia's private commercial banks with its powerful Central Bank, with the explicit goal of developing Latvia into an international financial center. This led to the marginalization of Latvia's manufacturing sector, and repeated boom-bust cycles. During Soviet times, the Latvian port of Ventspils served as an export terminal for oil, providing access to foreign currencies. When KGB officials started moving money out of the Soviet Union, they could rely on the help of Latvian intermediaries (Sommers 2014, 33). The first private banks, for instance, the notorious Parex Bank, typically started as offshore currency exchange offices, and turned this into a business model after Latvian independence. This was facilitated by the global context: the offshore economy was alive and kicking when Latvian banks joined liberalized financial markets, and massive state looting and rising commodity prices gave ample opportunities for Latvian banks to exploit the dark side of globalization. Latvia's location between east and west, and its entry to the European Union gave its banks a comparative advantage over other locations in the post-Soviet space. This comparative advantage was at the core of the economic vision of Latvia's state elites, and most notably the country's first Central Bank president—Einars Repše. After independence, Latvia's new state elites adopted radical neoliberal reforms (Bohle and Greskovits 2012), and the newly created Central Bank assumed a pivotal role. It was tasked with defending the parity of the Lats, one of the most important symbols of the country's regained independence. After the GFC, it was tasked with securing EMU accession.

Einars Repše, was a central figure in Latvian politics for around 15 years and had a clear vision for his country. As noted by Aslund (2017, 10; italics added): "Prime ministers and finance ministers were replaced almost every year, while Repše stayed put. His economic ideas were clear and firm. He was a monetarist, who believed in a conservative monetary policy leading to stable prices, and he believed in an open economy. His ideal was Switzerland, *and he desired that Latvia would develop into an international banking paradise characterized by the rule of law and monetary stability.*" While he held a tight grip on monetary policy and the exchange rate, the opposite was true for the banking sector. Latvia's supercharged neoliberal reforms were instrumental in destroying much of the productive capacity of the country, while monetarism combined with lax regulation, lax supervision, outright corruption, and a staunch belief in "free markets" opened the door for a mushrooming of banks (Aslund 2007, 10). Despite repeated banking crises, illicit financial flows remained the hallmark of Latvia's state elites' dealings with the banks. Revealingly, Repše's successor at the helm of the Central Bank, Ilmārs Rimšēvičs, became one of the architects of the resurgence of the Latvian nonresidential banking sector after the Global Financial Crisis (Eglitis et al. 2014; Meyers et al. 2018). He was also responsible for appointing the supervisors of Latvia's banking system. Although he received repeated warnings about money laundering claims, he decided not to follow these leads. Instead, he shielded the banks from increasing pressure, and, in 2018 he was charged with taking a 250.000 euro bribe from Trasta Komerzbanka, the number one culprit in the "Russian laundromat" (see Table 12.1; for the corruption case see Meyers et al. 2018). Latvia's state elites' responsibility in nurturing a banking sector whose core activities consist of money laundering can perhaps be best described as purposeful non-enforcement and forbearance of illegal economic behavior.[4] In line with recent research on the purposeful non-action of states (e.g., Dewey and Di Carlo 2021), Latvia's state elites believed that enforcing stricter anti-money laundering regulations on their banking sector would hurt the economic interest of the most powerful sector of the economy, and thus the country as a hole. Interestingly, Latvia's elites were not alone in believing this. They found a powerful ally in the EU, where regulators explicitly claimed that supervising money laundering was none of their business.[5]

There is thus a strange asymmetry here: while in the wake of the GFC and the euro crisis, austerity was forced onto public sectors and entire populations, European banks remained largely untouched, free to engage in widespread money laundering, as witnessed in the cases of Danske, Swedbank, and most other major European banks. A giant hole in European supervision is the flip side of Latvia's (and other countries') thriving banks (Merler 2018). It is only recently, and only under significant pressure of the United States, that Latvia and the EU have started to crack down more systematically on money laundering.

What are the implications of Latvia's domestic banks predominantly serving as money laundering platforms for the country's growth model? At a superficial glance, not many. In contrast to other champions of money laundering and tax evasion, Latvia's banking sector is not oversized. In 2012, bank assets amounted to 130% of GDP, which was only slightly more than a third of the EU average, and far below the ratio in countries like the United Kingdom, Ireland, or Luxemburg where bank assets amounted to roughly 500, 700, and 2,200 percent of GDP respectively (Eglitis et al. 2014, 3). Latvia's banking sector also does not offer ample employment opportunities. The share of employment in the financial sector is consistently below EU average (Eurostat). In contrast to other offshore locations, Latvia does not have a higher share of lawyers, accountants, or employees in the real estate sector. It also cannot boost its budget from tax income related to its offshore activities. Given that the services Latvia's banking sector offers are mostly transit services, the offshore economy seems more like an enclave than strongly linked to the rest of the economy. Yet, there are powerful mechanisms that link the country's offshore economy to the way the country has been growing since independence.

In terms of Latvia's growth patterns, what is characteristic is its boom-and-bust character, which is shaped by repeated banking crises. All major banking crises with the exception of the first in 1995 had their origin in international developments, but were transmitted by domestic banks, which were also champions of money laundering (e.g., Fleming and Talley 1996; Aslund and Dombrovski 2011). For instance, while the literature mostly depicts Latvia's deep crisis of 2008 and fast recovery as a case of overheating before the crisis, and successful internal devaluation after (e.g., Aslund and Dombrovskis 2011), this overlooks the fact that Latvia had to ask the IMF for a bailout because it bailed out one of its largest domestic banks, Parex, whose core business was money laundering (Meyer et al. 2018). While the government's decision to bail out Parex pushed it into the arms of IMF and EU conditionality, the decision not to pursue external devaluation can be traced to both the structural power of the foreign-owned banking segment and the Central Bank's cozy relations with the banking community (e.g., Hilmarsson 2018). As a result, ensuing export-led growth occurred by default rather than design, with austerity and massive emigration pushing down demand, and external demand for agricultural and forestry products and transit services rising.

A second powerful mechanism of how the black hole in the center of Latvia's economy sucks the lifeblood out of its economy is the fusion of the private interests of Latvia's bankers and those of state elites. A Central Bank governor with close interest in income from illicit wealth is unlikely to administer monetary policy that supports growth of the real economy, or support regulations and policies for a banking sector serving broader developmental goals. And indeed, Latvia never developed a banking system that would support the real economy. As domestic banks were never very interested in issuing loans to the domestic sector, it is foreign banks that took up this role. Given the lax supervision, these banks engaged in highly profitable but irresponsible lending practices. Taking advantage of the ECB's expansionary monetary policy in 2004–2007, the foreign banks engaged in large-scale carry trade of cheap international credit, unleashing a credit boom to households which turned bust in 2008 (Aslund and Dombrovskis 2011, 29).

These observations have broader implications for discussing growth models. In the Latvian case, the shift from debt-financed consumption to export-led growth around the GFC tell us very little about what enabled consumption-led growth to begin with, how the change after the crisis came about, and whether the rise of export-led growth is in any ways linked to developments in the real economy, such as rise of wages or productivity gains. And more to the point of our chapter, Latvian growth cannot be understood without exposing the dark hole that links the country's powerful economic actors and institutions to the globalized illicit wealth chains. Once again, as in the Irish case, the system shapes the unit.

Conclusion

How does this relate to the growth models research program in this volume? We think there are three takeaways that are worthy of consideration. First, the national macroeconomic measurements that are used in comparative research are becoming increasingly unreliable. They were designed for a 1960s economy, and increasingly obscure the reality of global financial capital, and the relationship between global wealth and value chains. They also obscure the reality that global multinational firms are composed of hundreds of subsidiary firms in multiple locations. Being a tax haven in today's world of global financial capitalism no longer just means bank secrecy and turning a blind eye to tax avoidance. It increasingly means being actively part of an international chain that enables multinational corporations and high-net-worth individuals (often through complex investment funds) to create, move, protect and store capital, while facilitating profit-shifting within their transnational corporate structures. The national accounts, therefore, are premised on two outdated assumptions. The first is that profits are linked to a physical presence, and second, that we can value things objectively that are traded. Most profitable companies today rely on intangible capital assets that do not require a physical presence to sell their goods. This means that intra-company trading dominates FDI, allowing multinational groups to shift profits into their subsidiary firms across multiple jurisdictions, while hoarding cash and assets. Similarly, as argued by Katarina Pistor (2019), in today's global financial system, the ability to legally code complex debt contracts into financial assets is one of the most important instruments for turning capital into wealth. Analyzing how the transnational nature of capital and wealth accumulation interacts with national growth models provides an opportunity to seriously link IPE with CPE research.

Second, it is reasonable to ask whether this only applies to very small set of countries, particularly those that might be classified as "late developers." Small states have always maximized and leveraged their position within global markets—from the Netherlands to Singapore. In the past, this meant pushing for liberalized trading relations in goods and services, epitomized in the negotiation and constitution of the European single market, and adopting a proactive industrial policy. Today, in a world increasingly shaped by a hierarchical network of global corporations and finance, it seems a logical political evolution for small states to integrate themselves, and maximize their position, within these global wealth chains—through servicing the capital and profit-oriented needs of transnational firms and wealthy investors. In Ireland, this has had a real effect on national income and jobs, and positively affected the country's national economic development. This connection to real income growth seems much less obvious in the Latvian case. These two countries occupy very different positions in global wealth and value chains, and we analyzed them for explorative and illustrative purposes only. But one could reasonably argue that what we are observing today is less a networked chain of small nation-states servicing the needs of global wealth accumulation, but a series of *city-states* that link up the major metropolitan areas of the global economy—from Frankfurt to London, to New York and Shanghai—within the globally integrated financial system. For example, when we talk about the "Irish" growth model, it is really a story of Dublin, and the heart of Latvia's wealth-pumping machine beats in Riga. Similarly, when we talk about the UK growth model, it is really a story of London. Examining the changing economic geography of city-states within the global financial system—and all the intra-regional inequalities that this generates—is a promising avenue of future research in comparative and international political economy.

Finally, the growth models research program is predominately focused on unpacking the national accounts and identifying the drivers of aggregate demand (and in turn, the functional distribution of income). This is a very worthy exercise, as it allows us to identify the enablers and disablers of growth at the macro-level. But the real prize is unpacking this macro-level data, and identifying the underlying sectoral drivers of growth, and how these have changed over time—both in response to technological changes, and global markets. This system-level analysis necessitates taking capitalism seriously, and as Streeck (2011, 2012) has consistently argued, taking capitalism seriously means taking how it is *governed*—politically and socially—seriously. Central to this is analyzing how capital escapes the fiscal constraints of democracy. This is a crucial challenge of contemporary global capitalism.

Notes

1. https://www.financialsecrecyindex.com/en/explore/database
2. We use the term kleptocracy relatively loosely, to denote a system where government mostly exists with the aim of enriching personal wealth and political power of the elites. For a discussion of the concept and its recent transformation in the academic debates and policy circles, see the contributions in *Journal of Democracy*, Vol. 29, 1, January 2018.

3. https://www.occrp.org/en/the-fincen-files/european-regulators-failed-to-spot-suspicious-money-flooding-through-latvias-banks
4. We thank Donato di Carlo for this formulation.
5. Ironically, Valdis Dombrovksis, the Latvian prime minister who oversaw the resurgence of money laundering in Latvian banks after the GFC was appointed executive vice president of the European Commission in 2014. Since then, he however has turned into an advocate of tough reforms to close the supervisory gaps in the EU. (https://www.icij.org/investigations/fincen-files/europes-anti-money-laundering-chief-defends-his-record-in-wake-of-fincen-files/)

PART 4

POLICIES AND POLITICS

13

Financialization and Growth Models

CORNEL BAN AND ODDNÝ HELGADÓTTIR

Introduction

Financialization is a noted blind spot of the Varieties of Capitalism (VoC) literature. Even in the aftermath of the financial crisis of 2008, VoC failed to systematically engage with the broader literature on financialization—a fact that a number of critical scholars have seized on (e.g., Becker and Jager 2012; Stockhammer and Kohler 2020). Highlighting the practical limitations that result from this gap, scholars working on topics such as housing financialization (Aalbers 2008; Bohle and Seabrooke 2020) and corporate financialization (Lazonick 2010) from a comparative capitalism perspective have gone "off-grid" to create their own typologies to supplement the conventional ones advanced by Hall, Soskice, and others.

Crucially, this blind spot is not incidental. Rather, the ability of VoC to engage with financialization is limited by its analytical prioritization of the supply side of the economy with firms as its driving force (introduction to this volume; Baccaro and Pontusson 2016). This does not mean that finance is completely absent from VoC. Rather, it means that the analytical role that finance can play within VoC is reduced to a rather narrow definition of finance, primarily as it applies to corporate governance. While not inaccurate, this partial definition stands to bracket crucial aspects of financialization, such as the growing structural power of the financial sector, the financialization of the state, and the ways in which financialization has become part of everyday life—not to mention the cumulative impact of all these shifts on aggregate demand.[1]

What is more, in deprioritizing the demand side, VoC also obscures the extent to which financialization can be examined as a reaction to lagging demand and growth in a stagnant international political economy. In other words, when compared to VoC, the growth models approach has the competitive advantage not only of being capable of systematically engaging with financialization broadly defined, it can also help us understand what drives the process to begin with it. The study of financialization should therefore be at the heart of growth models scholars' efforts to "bring back" the demand side.

Nevertheless, the growth models literature has yet to fully capitalize on this potential comparative advantage by systematically incorporating finance into its analysis. The foundational article of the growth models approach mentions financialization only in passing (Baccaro and Pontusson 2016, 180, 186). Meanwhile, post-Keynesian work on financialization has only gone so as far as linking it to demand regimes, leaving CPE work on growth models largely underexplored (Stockhammer and Kohler 2020; see also special issue in *JPKE* edited by Gennaro Zazza in 2018).

This chapter addresses this productive gap at the intersection of the two literatures by focusing on the relationship between financialization, growth, and growth models. It does so first by developing a theoretical framework that brings together the regulation school's framing of financialization as a "social fix" and economic geographers' insistence that it is also a "spatial fix," albeit one that is not equally available to all states. Secondly, we synthesize existing literature to offer up a broad definition of financialization that emphasizes the fact that it extends across several sites; we emphasize corporations, households, the financial sector, and the state. Finally, we analyze four cases—Britain, Italy, Germany, and Sweden—that illustrate both the added value of applying a financial lens to growth models and emphasize the variable ways in which financialization appears in different models.

Financialization and Growth Models

A rich literature suggests that a macroeconomy can be profoundly shaped by finance even when it is not finance-led but merely "finance-dominated" (Stockhammer 2008b and in this volume). Therefore, the effects of financialization should be understood primarily through their impact on aggregate demand, which is the prime causal mover of the growth models approach, but one that continues to be examined primarily as a function of exports, wages, and debt in the growth models literature. Or, as Stockhammer puts it:

> The term finance-dominated rather than finance-led is used to highlight
> that financialization is shaping the composition of the components of
> aggregate demand and their volatility. An accumulation regime is de-
> fined as finance-led if an increase in the hurdle rate set by financial

markets for investment projects, leads to an increase in growth. No presumption of this sort is made here. Rather, it is argued that a finance-dominated accumulation regime should be defined in such a way that financialization can positively or negatively affect growth. (Stockhammer 2008b, 185)

This is a crucial distinction for a number of reasons. One is that purely finance-led growth models are not at all common in the global political economy. Specifically, they are limited to a few city states listed in the Global Financial Centers Index (GFCI), a ranking of the competitiveness of financial centers based on over 29,000 financial center assessments from an online questionnaire together with over 100 indices from organizations such as the World Bank, the OECD, and the Economist Intelligence Unit. Everywhere else, financialization is a component of growth alongside consumption and exports. In fact, our review of the secondary literature suggests that although there are few finance-led regimes, no growth model is untouched by financialization (perhaps barring Cuba, Bhutan, or North Korea). When it comes to this topic, some scholars (Grahl and Teague 2000, 171) focus primarily on the international level, speaking of a globalized regime of accumulation with financial predominance (*à dominante financière*) that can be seen everywhere in structural transformations within nation-states and through the increased prominence of private financial institutions at the international level.

Ultimately this pushes capitalism toward what some call "profits without investment" or "consumption-based capitalism" (*capitalisme consommatoire*) (Cordonnier 2006; Van Treck 2009). Over time, however, this "fix" can start threatening aggregate demand and the maintenance of high growth rates (Aglietta and Bretton 2001; Smart and Lee 2003, 156). A raft of studies in the post-Keynesian tradition has showed that in theory, finance-dominated growth models require weakly negative effects of increasing shareholder power on the productivity regime to be sustainable over time. They also require expansionary effects of shareholder power on capital accumulation. Empirically, however, neither of these conditions holds. In reality, then, the most common outcome of "financialization" seems to be a "contractive" regime (Hein 2012). This happens through several channels.

One is that higher dividend demands and share buybacks reduce overall investment in the capital stock (Hein 2012) while increasing the share of gross domestic products going to those with a lower propensity to spend (Dünhaupt 2017). Financialization also leads to union decline through as a variety of new interconnections between financial capital and firms generate downward pressure on labor organization (Kollmeyer and Peters 2019). The cumulative upshot of all these dynamics is lower aggregate demand. This, however, does not preclude diversity in the financial mode of regulation across growth models, leading to a variety of hybrids.

Crucially, the "spatial fix" that financialization can provide also varies considerably. Like capitalism itself, financialization is a territorially variegated phenomenon. In this regard we build on economic geography's translations into political economy (Schelkle and Bohle 2020) to emphasize the causal and profoundly political implications of the multi-scalar nature of growth models and financialization. In this conceptualization, "financialization should not be seen as a homogeneous one-size-fits-all model based on ideal-types, but rather be seen as a process that modifies existing trends and trajectories within particular locations of economic activity" (Doucette and Seo 2011, 151).

Indeed, geographers have long stressed that financialization is an inherently spatial phenomenon, with local, national, and macroregional institutional frameworks act as filters of how financialization functions (see Aalbers 2019 for an overview), leading them to talk about varieties of financialized capitalism. Thus, human geographers have contributed to the idea that there are not only varieties of capitalism whose parameters cannot be wired from the expectations of the VoC framework, with coordinated market economies such as those of Belgium or the Netherlands being critical nodes in the global geography of financialization (van Treeck 2009; Aalbers 2008, 2017). More recently, political economists took these insights seriously with careful comparative work looking at the nexus of politics and financialization, with a particular focus on the "multifaceted process of conflicted public choices and tradeoffs in social practices of finance, to which political responses vary" (Schelkle and Bohle 2020, 762).

In this regard we follow research in geography (Brenner, Peck and Theodore 2010), heterodox economics (Karwowski et al. 2020), and comparative political economy (Schelkle and Bohle 2020) by looking at the clusters of national economies meeting the description of a particular growth models as sites of variegated economic practices and relations cutting across regime borders while remaining varied within them. This means doing a multi-scalar analysis of financialization in growth models: (1) at the international level where its global features are forged and reproduced; (2) at the level of national institutional contexts of development, patterns of corporate ownership or transnational connections within value chains and, finally; (3) at the level of the global financial centers within them to the extent that they exist (Table 13.2).

The last levels of analysis are particularly important and new for this debate. Thus, growth models that have global financial centers are better positioned to reap the benefits of financialization than those that do not via the less volatile lending cycles associated with such centers (Tschoegl 2000). Critically, having a global financial center means a smoother flow of foreign capital financing external deficits (Stockhammer and Kohler 2020), thus reducing the likelihood of a balance of payments crisis, with all the attendant demand-destroying pro-cyclical fiscal policies that come with these events in the neoliberal era. The view that values financial centers as a distinct level of analysis chimes with the network-based approach in international political economy that sees the con-temporary global financial system as a network, with a particular focus on its hierarchical structure in which financial centers and globally systemic financial institutions sit at the top (Oatley et al. 2013). Moreover, if growth is driven by productivity gains that are concentrated in sectors reliant on high tech and so-phisticated labor skills, and if, in turn, these are concentrated in cities serving as nodes of global/regional finance and value chains, that further contributes to national growth models' special privileges in global financial markets (Sassen 2016; Curtis 2016).

Typologies of Financialized Growth: Consumption-Led Models with Strong Financialization—The United Kingdom

In their foundational framework, Baccaro and Pontusson show that in consumption-led growth models, household consumption increases faster than the export rate (Baccaro and Pontusson 2016, 187). Britain is the pro-totypical case here: while household consumption accounted for 2 to 3% of GDP growth per year, the contribution of net exports to GDP was consist-ently negative (Baccaro and Pontusson 2016, 187).

But what fuels this consumption? A key feature of financialization at the in-ternational level (understood as the liberalization and deregulation of national financial systems) was that it allowed some countries to spur domestic demand through households' debt-financed consumption and, to a lesser extent, firms' debt-financed investment. Indeed, Stockhammer (2008b, 2019) has explicitly argued that a major characteristic of such finance-dominated "debt-led" models is that consumption expenditure, powered by debt rather than wages, tends to be a driving force for economic growth. Homing in on the British case spe-cifically, Oren and Blyth (2019) argue that the differential between consump-tion and the export rate was actually a precondition for the financialization of the Thatcher revolution, which worked by bonding together mortgage markets and household debt. Since the Thatcher juncture, the UK growth model has depended directly on debt- financialization, a trend seemingly reinforced by the 2008 crisis (Wiß, 2019).

Alongside the diminished role of wages vis-à-vis debt, a further feature fueled of this growth model is the augmented role of financial returns. This is in line

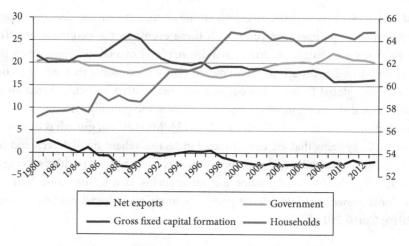

Figure 13.1 Contributors to British GDP. Source: Leeds et al. (2013), with authors' emphasis

with Robert Boyer's argument that once there are sufficient stocks of property in a national economy, expenditures on capital gains, dividends, interest, and pensions can compensate for weakened wage-based demand. In such a world, the population as a whole (and, we might add, the nonresident investors active in it) tends to hold a significant amount of financial assets and a general decline in wages as a share of output can even act as a stimulus, via the wealth effects generated in equity markets. Or, in Boyer's terms, "[w]hen equity effects are well developed, and the financial markets lead to a generalization of investment behavior determined largely by profitability, then a virtuous system of financial growth can be said to exist. In this system, raising the profitability norm does have a favorable effect on demand" (Boyer 2000, 127).[2]

Updates of Boyer's thesis have factored in real estate, showing how finance-led regimes of accumulation and property-based modes of regulation appeared in some Asian city states (most notably Hong Kong) relatively early (Smart and Lee 2003). Given that in such cases the rise in wealth-to-income ratios is driven by rising housing prices, as well as price changes in other financial assets (rather than home ownership per se or national savings rates) (Johnston and Regan 2019; Bohle and Seabrooke), the assetization of dwellings is of the essence here (Aalbers et al. 2020; Mader et al. 2020).

Crucially, however, this is a model that tends toward financial instability. Overall, the inflow of credit into the housing market, and hence indirectly via "equity withdrawal" into consumption, coupled with direct lending for consumption, increased instability in the economy, which has been a key characteristic of the United Kingdom (Montgomerie and Budenbender 2015). Similarly, Kamath et al. argue that "[t]he cumulative effects of this financing for consumption was a major factor in the long boom of the 2000s where consumption, which composed the dominant share of GDP, grew at a rapid rate. However, by 2011, this cycle of inflated consumption was collapsing and was a major cause of the prolonged recession that occurred in the UK post 2007 (2011)."

In terms of distribution, financialization also damaged the bargaining power of labor and increased inequality via its effect on corporate norms and strategies (Guschanski and Onaran 2018). Furthermore, since high-velocity financialization benefits from a low-tax environment, the British growth model produced demands for tax competition, which public infrastructure fell over time, shrunk the wage share, undermined investment in productivity-boosting public infrastructure, and changed the composition of public spending (Onaran and Boesch 2014).

As a result, financialization forced wage stagnation and given the profit surge, this reduced the share of wages in UK GDP (from 76.2% in 1975 to 67.7% in 2007 and to 65.8% in 2015). Adding another layer to our understanding of finance-led growth models, recent research on global wealth chains looks at the linkages between asset management and tax dodging through highly financialized city states like Hong Kong or Singapore or metropolitan areas like London that replace and/or add to real estate wealth as a form of boosting demand (Seabrooke and Wigan 2014, 2017). All of these dynamics have contributed to increasing income and asset inequality. To top it off, unlike continental systems, the United Kingdom has

> a social investment market in which pressures to reduce public spending are reinforced by a financial ecosystem able to provide easy capital to public authorities seeking new funding for social services otherwise unavailable because of the limits imposed by austerity measures (. . .) this neoliberal trajectory continues a financialisation trend routed in a macroeconomic regime the main source of revenues of which is intermediated by the financial sector, as an autonomous industry detached from the real economy. (Ciarini 2019, 465)

At the state level, UK-style consumption-led models shaped by high-velocity financialization may have some niche manufacturing and service sectors boosted by access to sophisticated credit products and institutions (such as risk-accepting angel investors). Yet, overall, exports of goods and (non-financial) services play a secondary role in generating demand. Therefore consumption-led models with strong financialization tend toward deindustrialization. The political "fix" for this situation was even more household credit, with Bank of England research showing that as consumption grew faster than real earnings, households resorted to secured borrowing both against their appreciating properties and unsecured credit-card debt (Barwell and Burrows 2014). Overall, the levels of UK household debt grew from approximately 55% in 1987 to 100% of GNP in 2007, with mortgage debt as the main contributor. This boosted net worth for house owners through revaluation effects (Burrows et al. 2015), which in turn legitimized the politics of the consumption-led and financialized model (Hopkin 2020).

Finally, the United Kingdom could not have had Sweden's balanced growth model because its brand of financialization was so thoroughly transformative of corporate strategies that it left little room for investments that increase non-financial firms' competitiveness. Indeed, despite increasing corporate profits, since the 1980s, UK firms have been dogged by weak private investment, with their revenue originating increasingly in financial activities. Thus, the Greenwich Political Economy Research Center on the investment behavior of non-financial corporations (NFCs) in Britain, found growing dividend payments and increasing financial revenues of firms due to their surging financial activities. Furthermore, Hein et al. (2017) found a sharp change in the sectoral composition of the economy toward the financial corporate sector with higher profit shares. There was also a particularly strong "shift of managers' preferences in favor of financial investments over real investment in the capital stock" (p. 248) without this leading to a fall in the wage share, however.

In turn, these transformations crowded out private investment in physical machinery and equipment (Tori and Onaran 2018). The transformation was structural: operating income devoted to the enlargement of NFCs' core activities and reinvested income declined from 80 to 90% in the 1980s to 40 to 50% in the past 10 years, while the stock of financial assets increased to 90% as a ratio to fixed capital in the late 1980s, with 2008 putting a minor dent into this trend. Overall, the rate of accumulation (investment/capital stock) crawled at an average of 25% for the past 40 years for the whole period, while the interests on debt and

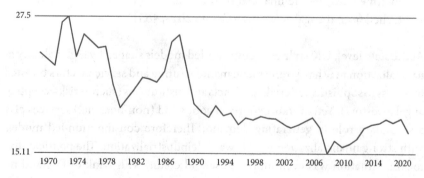

Figure 13.2 United Kingdom: Share of capital investment in GDP. Source: https://www. theglobaleconomy.com/United-Kingdom/capital_investment/

dividends paid to the shareholders increased substantially since the mid-1990s. Indeed, the investment rate would have been 16% higher without the rise in interest and dividend payments, and 41% higher without the increasing financial incomes (Tori and Onaran 2017).

Taken together, then, the UK style of financialization consists of several interlocking and mutually reinforcing developments that pertain not just to corporate governance but which also bond state-level policies to household behavior via structural shifts in the financial sector. Of course, this version of the relationship between financialization and consumption-based growth models is not available to any state. Rather, it requires a sophisticated financial center insured by a globally important central bank that provides low-cost finance and high-yield investment opportunities to firms and households while intermediating the plethora of yield searches that global banking and market-based non-bank financial institutions seek (Helgadóttir 2016). Or, as Walter and Wansleben showed, the Bank of England was a pioneer not just in regard to these functions, but also in "organizing the alignment of monetary policy with the changing structures of finance," thus drawing it "into a kind of 'ontological complicity' with the dynamics of financialized capitalism" (2020, 629).

Consumption-Led Models with Moderate Financialization: Italy

Italy is a case of an economy in long-run decline, held back both by shrinking consumption and investment over the last several decades. Average real GDP growth was 5.4% in the cycle lasting from the late 1960s until the mid-1970s, 2.6% from the mid-1970s until the early 1990s, 1.3% in the financialized cycle of the 1990s to the early 2000s and negative more often than not between 2008 and 2013. Indeed, as the Table 13.1 below shows, the GDP contributions of domestic demand, private consumption, investment and public consumption have all fallen drastically between the 1980s and the 2000s. Alongside this, Italy witnessed a decline in corporate investment and a rise in profits. Looking at the statistics, then, it is clear that the 1980s marked a critical juncture for Italian financial balances.

Although the Italian policy regime turned to financialization around the same time as other European countries, its uptake was moderate. Between the mid-1990s and the mid-2000s, the liberalization of capital movements and the birth of the euro opened global markets up to Italian private investors and the Italian market to international institutional investors. To boost opportunities for investment, the Italian government sold 119 billion euros worth of public assets between 1993 and 2009 and used financial innovation to comply with the

Table 13.1 **Main Demand Aggregates in Italy**

	1961–1974	1975–1992	1993–2002	2003–2007	2008	2009	2010–2011	2012	2013
Real GDP growth, cyclical averages (in percent)	5.38	2.6	1.61	1.3	-1.16	-5.49	1.09	-2.37	-1.85
Contribution to the increase of GDP of: domestic demand including stocks	5.28	2.62	1.34	1.32	-1.2	-4.43	0.55	-5.11	-2.7
private consumption	3.44	1.74	0.8	0.63	-0.47	-0.92	0.38	-2.45	-1.6
public consumption	0.63	0.51	0.09	0.31	0.11	0.16	-0.18	-0.53	-0.16
gross fixed capital formation	1.08	0.41	0.38	0.3	-0.8	-2.46	-0.16	-1.52	-0.85
changes in inventories and acquisitions less disposals of valuables	0.14	-0.09	0.07	0.08	-0.04	-1.2	0.51	-0.62	-0.08
the balance of goods and services	0.1	0.04	0.27	-0.02	0.04	-1.07	0.54	2.75	0.84

Source: Gabbi et al (2014), with authors' emphasis.

Economic and Monetary Union admission criteria that in turn enhanced the power position of "reformists" relative to the country's traditional political and business establishment (Lagna 2015, 2016). Nevertheless, measured in terms of financial assets' share in GDP, the results were rather modest outside of a few financialization islands such as Milan (Anselmi and Vicari 2020): financial assets' contribution to GDP rose from 3.5% in 1987 to barely 8% in 2006 (Gabbi et al. 2014).

The financialization of housing in finance was real, but, similar to Germany, it remained weak, limiting the scope for financing consumption as in the United Kingdom (Fernandez 2016). Shareholder value maximization entered the Italian corporate boardroom, yet rather than multiplying the investor base (thus expanding consumption in the middle of the income distribution), it allowed and facilitated local actors (mostly wealthy families) to retain their dominance (Salento 2016). The financialization of pensions is real but is one of the most hamstrung by prohibitions of direct investments in loans and real estate; many restrictions are in place for investments in corporate bonds and investment funds (no such restrictions are in force in the United Kingdom). The assets of pension funds are low (considerably lower than in the United Kingdom), and investments are concentrated in state bonds (Natali 2018).

What, then, is the added value of using a financialization lens to examine the Italian macroeconomic landscape? Here, the answer lies in a closer look at corporate governance and the growing entanglements between Italian non-financial corporations (NFCs) and the financial sector as well as the knock-on effects of this on household purchase power and access to credit. As in all the other cases under analysis, Italian NFCs saw a steady increase in operating surpluses over the period we examine. However, unlike other cases such as the United Kingdom and Germany, Italy did not see a substantial increase in dividend payments. The dividend income share hypothesis therefore does not seem to apply to Italy; in fact, its levels fell from 12% in the early 2000s to 9% in 2013. Other metrics that measure similar effects suggest a moderate and temporary increase in financial payouts. For example, the share of distributed property income in the gross operating surplus saw a modest increase from 50 to 60% between 1990 and 2005. However, unlike the situation in the United Kingdom, this trend reversed in the aftermath of the crisis of 2008. Similarly, unlike in the United Kingdom, the market for non-public resources for welfare provision and social innovation remains in its infancy even after 2008 and despite the permanent austerity budgets (Ciarini 2019, 473).

Does the observed increase in financial payouts mean that the surpluses of Italian NFCs were channeled into capital investment? To the contrary, there was a deceleration of private investments in capital stock, even as firms saw mounting payouts. Gabbi et al. report that firms with surpluses, levered up and

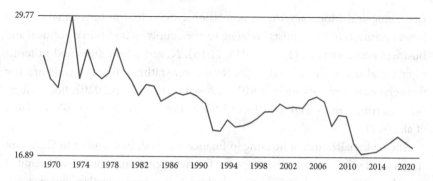

Figure 13.3 Italy: Capital investment as percentage of GDP. Source: https://www.
theglobaleconomy.com/Italy/capital_investment/

took on more debt, thereby experiencing a clear improvement in liquidity and
the ability to finance new capital investment should they have chosen to do so.
In reality, however, after an initial recovery in the 1990s and early 2000s, capital investment contracted sharply, leading to a marked slowdown of productivity growth and a progressive deterioration in competitiveness. This, in turn,
contributed to a steady loss of export market share and a significant contraction
in manufacturing activity, and an increased focus on labor cost reduction and relocation (Salento et al. 2013). Predictably, all this resulted in negative changes to
real wages, diminishing households' ability both to save and consume.

If they were not reinvested, where did the corporate surpluses go? The answer is that much of them seem to have gone to the financial sector, whose operating profits took off in the 2000s, easily exceeding those of NFCs—a trend
that has remained on course since the crisis. Indeed, the ratio of NFCs financial
assets to GDP grew by 20 percentage points from 1995 to 2006—from 39 to
59%—and remained stable at around 60% until 2012. This is testament to the
fact that financial investment has become a more profitable alternative to real investment, especially in the pre-crisis period of credit expansion and low interest
rates, facilitated by the euro (Gabbi et al. 2014).

In turn, households at the top of the income distribution benefited disproportionately from increases in stock market prices. At the end of 2012, households
in the top income quintile held 60% of financial assets, of which almost 80% were
risky assets, such as equity. Outside of this shareholding class, growth in household worth to income ratio was mainly driven by a sharp increase of real estate
assets (85% of total assets, with a growth of 100% between 1990 and 2007). By
contrast, the average household's ownership of financial assets reached its peak
in 2000 and never recovered from the dotcom bust.

This was part and parcel of a larger trend toward greater economic inequality
as between the mid-1980s and 2009 the top 0.01 and 0.1 saw their income shares

practically double. Over a similar period, those in the top 1% saw their income share grow from 6.9% to 9.4% while those in the top 10% saw their share go up from 27.2% to 33.9% (Gabbi et al. 2014). As for average household debt levels, Italy's remain the second lowest in the EU, a situation that owes largely to an inefficient legal framework applicable to housing finance (e.g., very long foreclosure period) and to the legal ban on equity withdrawal (Schwartz and Seabrooke 2009; van Gunten and Navot 2018).

All of this played a role in diminishing aggregate demand. This was compounded by the terms of Italy's integration into the euro: the historical "accordo sul costo del lavoro" (Cost of Labor Agreement) was signed in 1993, becoming the cornerstone of Italian labor market reforms. The agreement linked salaries to a target inflation rate both in the private and the public sectors. Otherwise put, despite high collective bargaining coverage, labor saw its incomes squeezed in the long run, based on an agreement it entered into of its own accord (Salento 2016).

Further, the 2008 crisis increased the share of non-performing loans on banks' balance sheets, which damaged their capitalization and therefore incentivized their deleveraging drive, with negative consequences for credit access for the average household. In these conditions, the slowdown in real domestic demand growth from 5.28% in the 1960s, to 1.32% in the 2000s before the crisis is hardly surprising. Without this multilevel financialization story, our understanding of the depressed Italian consumption would be impoverished (Gabbi et al 2014).

Finally, the financialization lens also helps illustrate the point that from an international finance perspective, not all consumption-led models have the same ability to generate new "fixes." Here, financial geography plays a crucial role: our analysis of the UK case suggested that the impact of financialization on consumption-oriented growth models is filtered by a state's position in the global financial hierarchy: association with a global financial center can channel global liquidity into cheap local credit. This has a decisive impact on the ability to prop up aggregate demand, especially in the face of crisis. Thus, having a global financial center means less vulnerability to cross-border sudden stops in capital flows. This, however, is not without inherent risks of its own and, as Oren and Blyth showed (2019) the architects of the United Kingdom as a financial center were well aware of the fragilities built into this model. Similarly, the Kumhof study cited earlier showed that the debt-enhancing effects of inequality are stronger with more liberalized financial markets (say United States, United Kingdom).

Nevertheless, UK financial institutions, firms, and households did not face massive capital outflows due to the systemic importance of the city of London in the global geography of finance capital and the intervention of the Bank of England to stabilize the country's sovereign debt (and thereby halt the doom loop between corporate and state debt). By contrast, Italy did face such outflows, and this led to additional pressures to adopt procyclical contractionary measures that undermined aggregate demand after the crisis (Jones 2015b).

To sum up, Italy's consumption-led growth model has been characterized by a strong profit increase without a commensurate investment increase. This can be attributed to strong entanglements between NFCs and the financial sector, and the upshot has been a deterioration of real wages and aggregate demand. Before 2008 this model was less well equipped than the British one to prop up consumption through credit, particularly through the wealth effects of real estate credit (Fernandez and Aalbers 2017). After 2008, it proved to be even more fragile as it did not have the privileged access to a global financial center that was at the heart of the British post-crisis credit "fix." Nor did it have Britain's advantage of external devaluation and the Bank of England's lender of last resort function. The long-run fall in investments and the negative movement of real wages account for the inability of households to post large positive financial balances, which in turn led to the fall of domestic consumption-based demand. The finding that consumption-led growth is more likely to boost real wages (including wages at the bottom of the pay scale) than export-led growth (Baccaro and Pontusson 2016) should therefore be interpreted with this in mind, giving appropriate causal weight to the unique privilege (and risks) that states with global financial centers have.

Export-Led Models and Weak Financialization: Germany

In Baccaro and Pontusson's original framework, Germany is the representative case for export-led growth models, characterized by a high level of industrialization, a complex state-led enterprise policy bolstering its export sector, and a deep reliance on foreign markets for demand.[3] In models of this kind, exports grow faster than consumption and there is an assumed trade-off between the two with wage restraint as a precondition for export competitiveness. As Baccaro and Pontusson note, this growth of exports at the expense of household consumption in export-led models stands in marked contrast to the balanced growth model of countries like Sweden, where net exports and household consumption contribute more or less equally to GDP growth (2016, 189).

But does the financialization angle add traction to the analysis of export-led growth models? We think that it does, primarily as it directs our attention to the self-reinforcing feedback loops between exportism, inequality, and current account surpluses. But let's start with the basics: financialization has been on the rise nearly everywhere over the last 30 years. However, export-led growth models are less financialized than consumption-led ones. What does that mean, concretely? For one thing, it means that even as Germany has witnessed extensive financial liberalization and financial activity has been increasing as a proportion of GDP, German financial markets have remained comparatively underdeveloped (Krahnen and Schmidt 2004; Dünhaupt 2017; van Treeck 2009).

Household financialization in Germany has also been limited. While other European countries and even some other export-led models—Korea is one example—have witnessed real estate bubbles fueled by easy credit and foreign investors' forays into national real estate markets, these trends have been much less prevalent in Germany, where real estate prices and mortgage debt have been remarkably stable and Germany remains a rather un-financialized outlier on this front. Thanks to conservative and opaque real estate financing vehicles that did not attract, a real estate bubble did not develop in the 2000s, with net wealth staying relatively stable in Germany during this period. Moreover, decades-long government intervention in the real estate sector led to a diversified supply of housing (including adequate volumes of rentals), which reduced pressure to buy (Wijburg and Aalbers 2017).

The German financial sector has also retained some of its national idiosyncrasies, even in the face of pervasive global financial homogenization over the last few decades. Thus, in Germany, traditional banks continue to account for most credit intermediation. Moreover, Germany retains its tripartite banking system in which private banks are one branch, cooperative banks another and public banks (Sparkassen and Landesbanken)—long associated with the German Mittelstand—are the third. While Germany has been taking some steps away from a purely bank-based model, it has not moved decisively toward a fully market-based one (Hardie and Howarth 2009; Deeg 1999). Indeed, some of financialization's key markers (corporate leverage, large financial sector) are not prevalent in Germany or Austria (Karwowski et al. 2020). And with the exception of Deutsche Bank, Germany's private banks have not emerged as prominent global investment banks. This is not only because they were rather late to join the global fray, but they also faced domestic competition from public banks, cooperative banks and, more recently, American investment firms and funds (Berghoff 2016).

Nor has the trajectory of German corporate governance fully aligned with dominant international practices. For instance, Fiss and Zajac (2004) argued that large German firms' adherence to shareholder value was best described as "symbolic management" to appease foreign investors (see also Vitols 2002). Moreover, while dividend payments in high-velocity financialization contexts such as the United Kingdom average 40% of retained corporate earnings, the German share is only about half that, leaving German firms with more to invest than their British counterparts. Some large German manufacturing firms have even delisted from the New York Stock Exchange in recent years. Further, as German NFCs tend to have large surpluses, they do not rely on markets for additional external finance, nor do debt securities play a particularly important role. Taken together, this translates into less pressure to shed labor than in more financialized systems.

Indeed, as Jackson, Höpner, and Kurdelbusch (2006) have argued, the introduction of a shareholder model in Germany has had different results than in the United Kingdom or Italy. Like elsewhere, large German firms such as Siemens engaged in selling and spinning off major parts of the company. Yet, in a testament to the resilience of consensus culture and the coordinating mechanisms specific to German corporate life, this did not come with intense boardroom conflict and mass layoffs in manufacturing. Not only did labor unions, employer associations, and works councils survive,[4] profit sharing between shareholders and unionized labor made unionization more attractive for some workers even as income inequality rose and the wage share fell (Detzer and Hein 2017). However, while inequality raised the share of savings in investment funds from 15% in the 1980s to 23% in the 2000s, and of securitized assets in total wealth holding by a similar magnitude, that level of growth is still far below the United Kingdom and United States, where both ratios are around 40%. Similarly, the level of wealth held in investment funds per capita is three times lower than in the United Kingdom and Sweden and six times lower than in the United States.

Since the mid-1990s, however, the continuity and resistance to change that has characterized German institutions has come under greater pressure. The German housing market, long seen as operating outside of financialized capitalism, was transformed in the aftermath of the crisis of 2008, with real estate prices booming as they had done earlier in many other European countries as a result of both national and international investors investing in real estate as an alternative to low-yielding equities. This also pushed more households to buy homes in a marked turn away from the traditional German reliance on rental housing (Wijburg and Aalbers 2017).

The combination of the growing politicization of the German public banking system and EU competition rulings that cut them off from public guarantees incentivized greater internationalization of this pillar of the financial system. In venturing into foreign markets, they followed the lead of the private German banks, which had sought this option to deal with the segmented and constrained domestic market (Hardie and Howarth 2009; van Treeck 2009). Thus, Germany's international financial integration increased strongly between the late 1990s and 2008, so that German investment abroad (mostly in Europe) dwarfed international financial investment in Germany, though this development was scaled back in the aftermath of 2008, as German financial institutions moved to decrease their exposure to riskier European bonds.

The norm of shareholder value maximization also took root more robustly in Germany over this period, boosted by the growing tendency of international institutional investors to invest in German firms. This coincided with increased investment in financial activities at the expense of investment capital stock in NFCs, leading to a sharp contraction in capital investment. More specifically, a steady increase in profits from the early 1990s until the Great Recession coincided with decreased investment in capital stock between the mid-1990s and the early 2000s. Bank credit, as well as corporate bond issues as the major external source of finance in Germany, were not necessary for real investment finance but were widely used for the acquisition of financial assets since the mid-1990s. Thus gross debt capital stock ratios have increased significantly, whereas gross debt-balance sheet ratios have not. Simultaneously, dividend payments increased as financialization ended the era of abstemious shareholders. (Detzer et al. 2017).

While Germany is one of the countries where wage and income distribution has been unusually stable for a long time, a recent report from the German Institute of Economic Research (DIW), the first to include super rich Germans, shows that wealth inequality in Germany is much greater than official statistics had previously suggested. Moreover, that it is the most skewed of the large European countries. In Germany as elsewhere, then, functional and personal income seem to be increasingly redistributed income to groups with higher savings propensities (Zalewski and Whalen 2010; Lin and Tomaskovic-Dewey 2013). This upward redistribution weakens the already moderate national consumption, further increasing reliance on external demand.

Decreased investment in capital stock, the growth of economic inequality, and low domestic demand—all part and parcel of German financialization—stand to put pressure on what Bacarro and Pontusson identify as the key to the

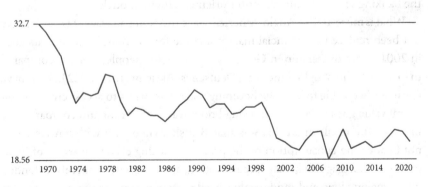

Figure 13.4 Germany: Share of capital investment in GDP. Source: https://www.theglobaleconomy.com/germany/capital_investment/

export-led model: wage moderation. The question here is whether export-led growth in Germany has started overlapping considerably with profit-led growth. If it does, as the above discussion of more recent developments in the German model suggests, then the question of whether wage restraint may come to be seen not as part of a solidaristic growth model, but a system in which wage earners are held captive by the mode of production comes to the fore. Here, then, there may be an important latent Kaleckian story of distributional conflict as the economy as a whole relies on large financialized companies that bank on wage restraint to ensure export competitiveness, even as they generate enormous wealth for owners, contributing to growing inequality at both ends of the spectrum.

The political risks associated with this stand to be exacerbated by the fact that unlike many other states, Germany has constrained many of the elements of financialization that contribute to its usefulness as a "social fix." For example, the fix of growing private indebtedness has attenuated the political impact of rapid growth in income inequality in many places. However, Germany did not compensate for stagnant wages over the several last decades with household credit, the nostrum that has permitted a number of political economies to kick the can of societal conflict down the road.

Here, again, Germany's export-led growth model is likely causal: unlike more consumption-led models, it has not been forced to use credit to generate domestic demand, since it does not rely on it to begin with. Indeed, following an initial increase in household debt after unification, after 1999 this kind of debt went on a continuously downward trend, with personal consumption loans via credit cards staying below the modest threshold of 10% of GDP. One important reason for low credit-card debt seems to be a very conservative banking system: a negative balance on a credit-card account typically has to be paid at the end of each month and overdraft facilities on checking accounts are limited and depend on monthly income, hardly the type of practices accommodated in the banking sectors of consumption-oriented growth models.

What is more, unlike Anglo-America, wage restraint and wage stagnation have not been replaced by financial market income for the middle class: at its apex in 2001, share ownership in Germany was 20% for people over 14, compared to over 50% in Anglo-America (Deutsches Aktieninstitut 2022). Nor have Germans been able to leverage booming real estate prices to access credit as collateral value goes up as their housing boom was both recent and comparatively modest. The result of all this was that British-style equity withdrawals could not finance the consumption of the property-owning classes. Instead, of high-powered mortgage debt and securitization, financialization merely extended into remaking low- and moderately priced rental housing into an asset class for investors within the paradigm of the "derisking state" (Gabor 2021).

Balanced Growth Models and "Dirigiste Financialization": Sweden

The Swedish case—a topic of perennial fascination for comparativist political economists—is crucial to this analysis precisely because of the variety of contradictory political diagnoses that have been attached to it. Sweden relies much less on household consumption than, for example, Italy and the United Kingdom, with the contribution of household consumption to annual GDP growth hovering around the zero mark in recent years. Imports of goods and services in Sweden were reported at 43.29 % in 2018 while exports account for a significant and growing proportion of GDP, reaching just under 46% of GDP in 2018. Baccaro and Pontusson (2016) characterize Sweden as a balanced growth model. However, when we take financialization into account, the Swedish balancing act is revealed to be a more precarious tightrope walk than it seems at first glance. Since the 1980s, Sweden has indisputably undergone a fundamental transformation of its economy, including a swift and profound turn to financialization (Blyth 2002). The question of how sustainable this shift is and how compatible with the Swedish social democratic tradition nevertheless remains an open one.

As ever, the devil is in the detail. We argue that some key elements of Swedish financialization have been managed so as to contribute to aggregate demand, maintain investment levels, and furnish some of the public goods that were previously provided by or brokered primarily by the state (i.e., housing, pension savings). Yet, many of these benefits rely on Sweden's ability both to manage the delicate balancing act of being a "dirigiste financialized state" and to act as a "safe haven" for international investors, leveraging uncertainty, global imbalances and underconsumption elsewhere to its national benefit.

The unusual nature of Swedish corporate governance is one key to understanding Swedish financialization and its capacity to preserve aggregate demand, investment, and high wage levels in what has been termed an "export-led mercantilist" economy (Hein et al. 2017). Crucially, publicly listed Swedish firms are far more likely than their counterparts elsewhere to put a firewall between share ownership on the one hand and corporate control and voting rights on the other. This is achieved by issuing different classes of shares with different voting rights attached to them. Established Swedish industry groups tend to disproportionally hold A-shares, which grant significant voting rights, while giving other investors, including the large share of foreign investors, access to B-shares, that carry much fewer votes (Stenfors 2014).[5]

In this way, industrial leaders have been able to retain effective control of large Swedish firms and ward off the most disruptive consequences of internationalized financialization. Sweden, like other countries, has witnessed increasing share-holder value orientation by management, and increasing dividend payments are testimony to this (Hein et al. 2017). Nevertheless, the insulated nature of Swedish corporate governance can serve to attenuate pressures to pay out dividends and keep costs down, giving Swedish corporations both greater leeway and a greater sense of purpose to invest in capital goods.

Financialization was weak in two further critical ways: the profit share of the financial corporations converged with the profit share of the non-financial corporations and there was no shift of the sectoral shares in gross value added toward the financial sector. As a result, Sweden did not record strong downward pressures on the aggregate Swedish wage share and, therefore, on consumption. Indeed, from 2006 onward, propped by very high labor-bargaining coverage, the share of wages exceeded that of retained earnings and rentier income (Hein et al. 2017).

If, for example, we compare Sweden to Germany, another economy that is very reliant on exports, we see that although there was a drop in capital in-vestment in Sweden in the 1990s, it has been steadily climbing (from 19% in 1993 to 24% in 2020), especially in the era of low and/or negative interest rates. Similarly, business investment in Sweden is one of the highest in the EU (nearly 16% of the GDP between 2013 and 2020).[6] Meanwhile, in the relatively more financialized Germany the drop was much greater (from 25% in 1993 to 21% in 2020) and since the early 2000s the trend has mostly been one of stagnation. In another contrast to Germany, the share of business investment in GDP averaged 11.5% during the same period, a figure higher than in the United Kingdom (9%) and Italy (10%) yet much lower than in Sweden.[7] This could threaten Germany's ability to continue to act as a producer of cutting-edge goods and technologies, making it ever more reliant on wage restraint for competition. By contrast, Sweden, with a more dynamic capital investment outlook, may be more likely to stay at the competitive edge, permitting higher wages to continue to contribute to aggregate demand and maintain the social contract that is at the basis of its political model. Compounding these factors is Sweden's share of government investment in GDP (4.5%), twice higher than in Germany, Italy, and the United Kingdom.

Another key to understanding the Swedish case is the way in which the state has leveraged orthodox macroeconomic policy choices to accrue the maximal benefits of financialization (rapid credit expansion, low/negative interest rates), thereby easing its shift toward more market-oriented policies. The best illustration of this is the housing sector, where Sweden has pivoted away from reliance on rental markets and public housing, both of which were common in the 1970s. Today, more than 70% of Swedish households own property, with the vast majority financing purchases through mortgages. The

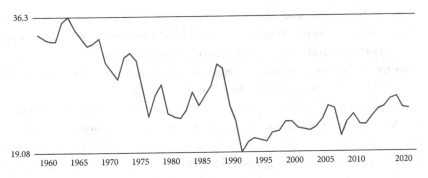

Figure 13.5 Sweden: Share of capital investment in GDP. Source: https://www.
theglobaleconomy.com/germany/capital_investment/

expansion in mortgage credit that this required has been staggering. As Alexis
Stenfors notes:

> The Swedish covered bond market has more than doubled in size and
> is currently the fourth largest in the world. By the end of 2013, the
> outstanding volume amounted to SEK 1,930 billion (around 50% of
> GDP), more than twice that of the Swedish government bond market,
> which stood at around SEK 800 billion. The largest bondholders in
> this segment tend to be domestic banks (21%), insurance companies
> (28%) and pension/mutual funds. In addition, it has increasingly be-
> come an investment outlet for international investors, which now stand
> for more than a third of the market. (2014, 125)[8]

Crucially, however, investment in Swedish mortgage bonds has increased rapidly in spite of the fact that they offer very low yields. Over the course of the last
20 years, mortgage bond yields have dropped from being around 10% to being
1 to 2% (Hedin et al. 2012). The very low interest rates that Swedish borrowers
have access to have been crucial to the expansion of homeownership in Sweden.
In turn, these low interest rates have been underpinned by Sweden's orthodox
macroeconomic policy choices. In the 1980s Sweden was a modest debtor state
but has since become an important creditor, registering high current account
surpluses from the 1990s onward. Concomitantly, government spending as a
share of GDP has gone down from nearly 65% in 1995 to just over 52% in 2011.
This has garnered Sweden a reputation as a "safe haven" for investors—a status
for which many are willing to sacrifice some yields, at least in the current global
economic climate, the continuation of which cannot be taken for granted.

On the flip side, as the state has withdrawn from direct participation in
housing provision, seeing its responsibility instead as that of a facilitator of

favorable borrowing and regulatory frameworks, private indebtedness has skyrocketed. Where the Swedish household indebtedness/disposable income ratio was around 100% from 1970 to 2000, it now stands at 170%. There is, in other words, "a very clear link between low real interest rates, house prices and household debt" in Sweden (Stenfors et al. 2014, 117).

In addition to the high levels of private indebtedness, this system has a number of other built-in fragilities. One is that after operating in an environment of low interest rates for many years, a number of Swedish households have shifted away from fixed interest rate mortgages and to variable interest rate mortgages. Thus, in the mid-1990s around 10% of mortgages had variable rates, compared to around 70% in 2013 (Stenfors et al. 2014). Similarly, a number of households have borrowed in foreign currencies. These borrowers may prove very vulnerable to any future fluctuations in interest or exchange rates.

What is more, in terms of distribution, Swedish financialization has departed from the egalitarian and solidaristic norms of classic Swedish social democracy, benefiting some social groups and age groups much more than others. As a result, economic inequality has increased very rapidly in Sweden, albeit from a lower baseline than almost anywhere else. This stands in contrast to the consensus-based and egalitarian Swedish tradition. The potential for political risk and the extreme reliance on low interest rates could therefore upend the Swedish balancing act. To date, however, Sweden has been a nimble dirigiste player in the world of financialization and that dexterity will be required in the future as well.

Conclusions

This chapter attempted to locate the analytical value added of a financialization lens for the established growth models approach. The main argument is that each of the growth models theorized by Bacarro and Pontusson have distinct financialization dynamics that, we argue, inform the observed variation in terms of the contribution of exports and consumption to GDP growth in each of the growth models. Indeed, all of them have been transformed by financialization and particularly by shareholder value orientation and increasing reliance of nonfinancial firms on financial activities, leading to growing corporate profits even as capital investment declined in all cases. From this perspective financialization was indeed a fix to the decline in profits.

However, in terms of the observed variation, the extent and mode of financialization explains why Sweden has higher capital investment than all the other cases while still projecting robust consumption growth, why consumption has been so robust in Britain but not in Italy, and why the German growth model was constrained to stay competitive in export markets by repressing consumption. The chapter also synthesizes the compatible definitions of financialization to propose a systematic multipoint measure of the intensity of financialization in the various growth models posited in the literature (albeit, for now, not operationalizing all of them).

As they stand, the interdependences between the variously financialized growth models are riddled with contradictions and conflict. As Blyth and Matthijs (2018) suggested, the politics of the declining neoliberal era produces "anti-creditor pro-debtor political coalitions that have been systematically eating away at mainstream center-left and center-right party vote shares since the crisis" (2018). To top it off, the challenges of apocalyptic climate change challenges the very idea of growth, making us wonder whether degrowth models is what the IPE/CPE nexus should be about in the not-so-remote future.

Future research on the financialization and growth nexus could benefit from engaging with these issues as well as from moving at the subnational level explore the conjecture that if growth is driven by productivity gains that are concentrated in sectors reliant on high tech and sophisticated labor skills and if, in turn, these are concentrated in cities serving as nodes of global/regional finance and value chains (Sassen 2016; Curtis 2016), then the concentration of some key elements of growth models in metropolitan areas over other national subunits can give an indication of how politically stable their future is.

As a vast literature on territorial inequality has showed (Santana and Rama 2018; Jennings and Stokker 2019), metropolitan concentration of gains in the growth model is a strong predictor of electoral volatility of the center-cannot-hold kind and, with it, of the risks of volatility in the growth coalitions underpinning various financialization and growth model combinations. This is also true in growth models with financial centers where these "metropolitan effects" on the growth coalitions that underpin growth models can overwhelm the buffering economic effects that financial centers have for financing the economy and the current account in particular (for example, Brexit and Trumpism).

Notes

1. Concrete examples of the ways in VoC *does* engage with finance can help illustrate and clarify this point. In one example, Hall and Gingerich (2004: 23) argue that firms in LMEs are embedded in different kinds of equity markets than firms in CMEs and that this has important consequences for their capacity to make credible commitments to their employees about wages and job security. They conclude that in LMEs, "firms are more dependent on dispersed equity markets, face the prospect of hostile takeovers, and confront regulations that give shareholders more power relative to stakeholders, the autonomy of the firm and its managers will be more dependent on current profitability. Here, labor markets allowing for high levels of labor turnover and competitive wage-setting will be more efficient, because they enable managers to reduce wages or staffing levels more quickly in response to fluctuations in current profitability

and allow the kind of labor relations that permit firms to exploit the high levels of capital mobility available in such economies."

2. More specifically, Post-Keynesians looking at financialization from a macroeconomic point of view (Boyer 2000; van Treeck 2009) have suggested that in finance-dominated consumption-led growth models, financialization has expansionary effects on consumption under two conditions: the recipients of financial incomes have a comparatively higher propensity to consume than debtors and (2) asset price inflation (financial securities, real estate) has positive wealth effects on the consumption demand, with both conditions being met by the UK (Stockhammer and Wildauer 2016; Tori and Onaran 2018). In contrast, contractionary effects on consumption kick in if the recipients of financial incomes have a lower propensity to consume than debtors, and if financialization redistributes income from workers to firms with a higher propensity to save (as measured via the difference between the labor share and the share of firms with cash savings) (Stockhammer 2019).

3. Here, however, it bears mentioning that for a large country, Germany is an extreme case of the export-led model. For example, the total trade flows in and out of Germany are two-thirds the size of German GDP, making its trade-dependency more like that of small economies such as Ireland and Hungary than other large economies, even ones that are very reliant on trade. For example, international trade is twice as important to Germany as it is to China. Germany also runs the second largest trade surplus in the world, after China, with more than 200 billion euros in surplus (this is equal to 7 percent of GDP, twice the level of Japan). And with annual exports that hover around a trillion euros annually, Germany dwarfs the export performance of any other country of comparable size (https://www.conradbastable.com/essays/the-germany-shock-the-largest-economy-nobody-understands?fbclid=IwAR2ygkCJDRoViI-CC7tZ JzTOuW6zjvxGChK-w9UutjzNjORT2m3X9Th8KPk).

4. albeit weakened by factors unrelated to financialization, most importantly offshoring to ECE (Berghofff 2016)

5. Other Scandinavian cories have also pursued this strategy but nowhere nearly as aggressively as Sweden.

6. https://ec.europa.eu/eurostat/databrowser/view/sdg_08_11/default/table

7. https://ec.europa.eu/eurostat/databrowser/view/sdg_08_11/default/table

8. Authors' emphasis

14

Political Parties and Growth Models

JONATHAN HOPKIN AND DUSTIN VOSS

Introduction

The growth model (GM) perspective has offered a much-needed jolt to comparative political economy, but it has suffered from a pathology that has long afflicted research in the field of political economy: a neglect of how electoral politics constrains and shapes policy through the mediation of organized political parties. This chapter makes a start to remedying this, suggesting ways in which party politics can be brought into GM theory. We discuss how political parties have been differentially conceptualized by political economists and party specialists and illustrate the potential for bringing these literatures together. We offer empirical illustrations to show how growth models are shaped by party politics.

We argue that electoral politics should not be seen as epiphenomenal or incidental to growth models, but neither is it realistic to claim that electoral politics shapes policy and institutional development in the direct way imagined by optimistic accounts of how parties "matter." Instead, we show how GM theory's emphasis on the politics of demand, the instability of contemporary financialized capitalism, and overbearing influence of the asset-holding classes can be better understood by integrating new research on political parties into the picture. Finally, we show that the recent rise in populist or anti-system policies, and the ways in which this has reshaped the political economy, show how growth models cannot insulate themselves from electoral pressures, particularly when they fail to deliver growth.

Growth Model Theory and Party Politics

Growth model theory seems to relegate political parties and elections to a marginal role in the political economy. The concepts of "hegemonic social blocs," or "dominant growth coalitions," which cement a particular pattern of power rela-tions upholding a growth model, seem fundamentally at odds with stylized ac-counts of democratic governance emphasizing the role of competitive elections, redistributive politics, and accountability. Taken to its logical limits, the role of parties in this perspective would be simply to provide a theatrical simulation of democracy, generating the illusion that citizens get to choose who governs from a restricted menu of relatively powerless representatives. From a Gramscian per-spective, the dominance of the social bloc would be ideational as much as ma-terial, with alternative interpretations of the economy being off limits or even inconceivable (Lukes 1973). But even mainstream party politics scholars have offered accounts of elections as essentially changing little (Katz and Mair 1995).

In this relative discounting of the cycles of electoral politics, growth model theory is far from alone. The dominant paradigm of the early 21st century, Varieties of Capitalism (VoC) (Hall and Soskice 2001), with some caveats, also tended to see institutional forms as driven by the preferences of non-parliamen-tary social interests, and liable to persist independently of the vagaries of election results. Neither did VoC's main rival, which we could loosely call "convergence theory," see much relevance in electoral dynamics, with its account of progres-sive liberalization relying as much on the impersonal forces of globalization and technological change as on the mobilization of political and electoral clout by neoliberal politicians (Baccaro and Howell 2012).

There are however, a number of reasons why growth model theory can ben-efit from more attention to party politics. First, if we take seriously the concept of hegemony, the focus on ideas and ideology is far from irrelevant to parties. If anything, parties can be seen as the key agents of developing and propagating the justificatory apparatus of a particular growth model, generating support for it, and adapting understanding of it to changing political and economic circumstances (Blyth 2003; Hopkin and Blyth 2019). Nor should parties' role be limited to merely "selling" the growth model—by helping to articulate new understandings of the economy parties' "ideational infrastructure" (Bick 2021) can redefine the boundaries of growth models. There is a role for parties as propagators, interpreters, or even initiators of new ideological justifications for ways of managing capitalism (Piketty 2020).

Second, the focus on the demand side of the economy brings voters back in, albeit perhaps indirectly. There is a big difference, in terms of electoral politics, between an export-led and a consumption-led growth model, in that export-led models imply an accumulation of savings at the expense of consumption, with significant potential to provoke electoral backlash unless a social consensus around the model has been carefully built, while consumption-led models tend to imply high levels of electoral instability as credit conditions fluctuate and the balance of power between creditors and debtors evolves.[1]

Third, by focusing on how capitalist interests can influence policy without needing to form institutionalized relationships of cooperation across class lines, we can move beyond the optimistic pluralist accounts of interest formation and policymaking that guide much of the electoral politics and public policy literature. Not only is it important to look at how social blocs vary in terms of the size and heterogeneity of the electoral coalitions they appeal to (Baccaro and Pontusson 2019), but we also need to understand how powerful groups can shape growth models to their needs in ways which bypass formal and visible policy processes altogether.

Bringing Parties Back In

Growth model theory shares with most mainstream comparative political economy a relative neglect of the complexities and nuances of parties and elections (Hall 2020). This is mirrored by the relatively oversimplified models of the political economy that most parties and elections scholars tend to work with. In this section we chart the development of party politics scholarship to identify the research contributions that can inform our understanding of the political economy.

Parties and Political Economy: From Cleavages to Strategic Choices

To risk caricaturing a vast and varied literature, the classic political parties' scholarship tended to work with a very under-theorized understanding of the political economy. As a result, some of the standard concepts and categories often still used in the parties' literature presupposed a particular configuration of socioeconomic forces that was in fact quite specific to the period in which they were developed. Parties' scholars in the postwar period did often reflect on theories of macrosocial change in their analysis of party development, such as long-run processes of economic modernization, but social categories such as workers, petit bourgeois, and the nebulous "middle class" underpinned discussion of parties' social roots. As a result, a certain understanding of the class structure and social-cultural divides in early and mid-20th-century Europe, and its mutation into a something more fluid and egalitarian during the postwar boom years, continued to influence researchers far beyond those periods.

In the electoral sphere, the scholarly debate developed very roughly as follows. The early, more conflictual phase of party democracy saw the establishment of party systems that starkly reflected economic class structures and long-standing social-cultural and territorial divides, both in the types of political representatives that were elected, and in the ideological and programmatic positions they adopted (Lipset and Rokkan 1967; Sartori 1976). But the lack of data and limited statistical power meant much less was known about voter behavior. When electoral surveys began to be widely available, they soon revealed a much weaker correspondence between social structure and voter choices than initially thought, leading to long debates on class dealignment, which coincided with an increasing preference for individual-level explanations of electoral outcomes. Alongside the growing political influence of neoliberal thinking, this resulted in a rapid detachment of the study of political parties as organizations that structured political ideas and projects from the study of voter behavior, increasingly seen as a set of reasonably coherent individual choices (e.g., Rose and McAllister 1986). The main resistance to this trend came from scholars reluctant to give up on a view of class politics that had transformed almost beyond recognition (Heath, Jowell, and Curtice 1988).

This growing emphasis on electoral choice had several limitations. Although most electoral surveys do ask basic questions about occupational, housing, and economic resources, they generally stick to a relatively simplified conceptualization of economic interests, which hinders more sophisticated analysis of the economic foundations of voting patterns, relative to the usually extensive battery of questions on attitudes and explicit policy preferences. This has encouraged a view of parties' relationships to voters in which parties provide a "supply" or "offer" of policies and personalities which comes up against voter "demands," which seems relatively optimistic about the extent to which what citizens want shapes politics and policy.

The "high point" of this type of analysis is the "valence" model of voting in which voters cast judgment of politicians' performance in meeting a set of voter needs that are broadly uncontroversial: law and order, a growing economy, and a reasonable level of governing competence (Clarke et al. 2010). The growing influence of the "valence" model tended to downplay the role of political parties and other actors "shaping" electoral preferences (Dunleavy and Ward 1981) and left electoral studies unprepared for the return of conflictual electoral politics in the 2010s.

Alongside the trend in electoral research toward voter choice models, political parties scholars also ditched earlier models of more structured party competition (Duverger 1954; Sartori 1976) in favor of conceptualizations of political parties as power- and vote-seeking strategic actors operating with a substantial degree of autonomy from social forces (Kirchheimer 1966; Panebianco 1988; Muller and Strom 1999). This reflected the very real organizational decline of parties, at least in terms of the idealized concept of the "mass party" that had shaped earlier generations of research (Duverger 1954).

By the 1980s it was becoming clear that parties had fewer grassroots members, weaker ideological moorings, and fewer reliable supporters than in the early phases of democratic politics. This sparked a "party decline" literature, which, while reflecting a very real phenomenon of increasing organizational and cultural fragility of political parties, had the unfortunate byproduct of reducing interest in their internal workings and the ways in which they developed ideas on how to govern the economy.

For our purposes, it is worth illustrating how these different conceptions of parties map onto analyses of the political economy. Mass parties that articulated and represented stable social cleavages underpinned the "managed capitalism" of the postwar boom, by giving structure to the distributional politics of an expanding welfare state (Esping Andersen 1990) and overseeing the corporatist bargains over wages and investment that held inequality at bay while delivering returns to capital (Hibbs 1977; Scharpf 1991). The difficulties of the 1970s, where growth slowed and corporatist bargaining broke down in many places as voter expectations accelerated beyond what governments were able to deliver, weakened the party types that had brokered social peace (usually social democrats and Christian democrats). The end of the postwar compromise and the shift to neoliberalism required a different kind of party. The "party decline" identified in the parties literature thus coincides with the crisis of the wage-led growth model identified by growth model theorists (Baccaro and Pontusson 2019; Hopkin and Blyth 2019). The shift to neoliberal modes of economic management had its counterpart in party politics with the shift to "cartel parties," first conceptualized by Katz and Mair (1995), who offered an account of party politics after the mass party era that was both realistic and historically grounded.

Parties and Political Economy: "Cartels" and the Neoliberal Growth Regime

For Katz and Mair the contemporary "cartel party" was the end point of a process whereby governing parties had effectively detached themselves from civil society to become embedded into the state, as indicated by their increasing material reliance (at least in Europe) on public funding and the implicit or explicit collusion between them to exclude outside forces from the political system. The oligopolistic pattern of behavior they described insulated political institutions from voter pressures, and alongside a gradual and almost universal decline in party membership and voter participation across the Western democracies short-circuited the standard channels for political accountability and citizen input into policymaking (Mair 2013). Far from the representative party government theorized in various ways by the pioneers of party studies (Schattscheider

1960; Downs 1957; Lipset and Rokkan 1967), democracy appeared to no longer involve much in the way of consultation with the *demos*.

The cartel party thesis had major implications for the political economy that were spelled out in subsequent contributions by Katz, Mair, and coauthors. Blyth and Katz (2005) elaborated a set of implications for economic governance of the cartel model, extending the implicit collusion of the core party system beyond party funding and barriers to entry, to consider also the ideological and programmatic boundaries of partisan competition. Shutting out outsider parties also facilitated shutting out different ideas, which became especially important once the establishment parties tired of responding to voter demands for ever-higher living standards and found it convenient to step back from active management of the economy and redistribution (Melzer and Richard 1978). The cartel party model was therefore an ideal electoral and legislative arrangement for entrenching the neoliberal growth model, shutting out alternative, more interventionist political economy models, delegating key policy levers to non-elected officials, and downsizing voter expectations (see also Blyth and Matthijs 2017).

From the Cartel to the Electoral Turn

The cartel model fitted neatly with the valence model of voting and with the political style of the post-Cold War 1990s and 2000s. The demise of the only real rival to liberal democracy and market economies, the loss of confidence of social democratic parties and labor movements, and the dramatic expansion of global capital markets, left progressive politicians in the West reluctant to challenge the kind of neoliberal thinking that had come out of the Cold War triumphant (Hopkin and Blyth 2019). Voters were therefore left with a choice between barely distinguishable partisan alternatives, sold to them based on superficial personality appeals and claims to governing competence (Crouch 2004; Hay 2007).

With adequate economic growth, this system appeared sustainable, albeit with obviously declining public enthusiasm and trust in politicians and institutions (Pharr and Putnam 2000). But the Global Financial Crisis overwhelmed this model of governance, drawing out the full extent of voter disaffection and disenfranchisement. Short of voter trust and forced to take unpopular decisions such as bank bailouts and austerity measures, parties, as Peter Mair put it at the time, "now appear to exacerbate rather than alleviate the problem" of securing democratic consent (Mair 2011, 13).

This pessimistic view has been countered by the so-called electoral turn literature, which recognizes constraints on responsible party government but still gives center stage to the "changing *supply and demand sides of politics*, that is, politicians" political-economic policy proposals and commitments, but also citizens' policy preferences (Beramendi et al. 2015, 2). Their model of "constrained partisanship" is primarily pitched against the classic political economy literature that gave primacy to the corporatist dealings of social partners and interest groups. But it also challenged the cartel politics thesis, with its implication that parties matter but party differences matter less (Mair 2011, 4), and therefore that elections ultimately fail to constrain policymakers very much (see Kitschelt 2000).

Instead, the claim the "electoralists" seek to make is that producer groups may matter, but that elections matter too, and indeed their importance has been growing. Rather than issue or valence voting, contemporary party politics still revolves around the competition between different occupational groups battling over material resources, but along updated and refined policy dimensions, such as trade-offs between consumption and investment as well as between different degrees of government interventionism (Kitschelt 1994; Kitschelt and Rehm 2014). In the next section we show how the debate between the cartel politics thesis and the constrained partisanship model can help inform our understanding of growth models, how they vary and how they change over time, and their implications for the distribution of economic resources and the stability of the democratic system.

The Party Politics of Growth Models: Securing Consent

One of the strengths of the growth models' approach is the potential to develop a more fluid understanding of how electoral and party-political dynamics shape economic policies and institutions. The heavy focus on path dependency in much of the political economy literature of the last few decades leaves parties as either important mainly in key formative moments of welfare regimes, but relatively less decisive afterward (Esping-Andersen 1990), or simply as expressions of social interests filtered through electoral institutions that are more decisive than the parties themselves (Iversen and Soskice 2006). Yet we know that political parties and their leaders disrupt and reshape capitalist systems, pushing societies onto alternative paths (Gamble 1994). To better understand how political parties do this, and under what conditions they can be tools for fundamental changes in the political economy, we need to understand parties as organizations.

One of the main limitations of coalitional approaches to the political economy is that they very often leave out the crucial detail of how, exactly, political organizations like parties mobilize support, and how they use their political and electoral capital to pursue particular political and policy ends. Even when the constraints on politicians are taken seriously, this omission can still result in an oversimplified, indeed naive accounts, of how votes inform policy and the organizational structures within which they operate are black-boxed. The cartel politics perspective is a good antidote to this kind of thinking. By questioning simplistic implied "principal-agent" relationships between voters and interest groups on the one hand, and party leaders on the other, we can theorize more realistically how different interests shape political decisions.

Blyth and Katz (2005) show that in a post-mass party world, voters should not be seen as principals delegating authority to the political party as agent, but rather as agents serving the purposes of principals who need votes to legitimize their rule. This is the consequence of parties no longer needing to extract human and financial resources from citizens (in the form of grassroots activism and membership subscription) because they have learned to secure those resources from elsewhere (state funding or wealthy private donors or a mix of both) (Hopkin 2004). If party systems take the form of an oligopolistic market for political representation, then voters are "price-takers" who have marginal influence on what political leaders are supplying to the market.

Parties may no longer need activists and identifiers to the same degree, but they do need some organizational resources to be able to function and hold their own within the party system. Technological changes in mass communications provide new opportunities to attract voters using the sophisticated tools of marketing, targeting, and persuading also used by private companies. These tools are very capital intensive, compared to the labor intensive patterns of mobilization adopted by mass parties, and require significant investment (Hopkin and Paolucci 1999). Happily, parties can offer a return on this kind of investment by adopting policy positions and securing policy and implementation decisions that can make the investment in political mobilization pay off (Ferguson 1995; Hacker and Pierson 2010; Skocpol and Hertel-Fernandez 2016).

In short, the contemporary cartel party is, by virtue of its relatively capital-intensive mode of political organization, ideally suited to an era in which the interests of capital are likely to triumph in any battle against the interests of labor. Increasingly free of the need to satisfy ever-escalating demands of voters and activists than alternative models assume, it can act as a mediator between the policy requirements of investor groups and the often-inchoate preferences of voters, and in some cases, as we shall see next, act straightforwardly as an agent for the former.

The Party Politics of Growth Models: Building and Reforming Dominant Growth Coalitions

By conceptualizing parties as agents of the configuration of capitalist interests invested in a particular growth model, rather than as political entrepreneurs seeking to act on behalf of an electoral coalition that is organized around a particular model, we can get closer to the conceptualization of a dominant growth coalition laid out in the introduction to this volume. In this account, the dominant growth coalition reflects sectoral interests, driven largely by capitalist producer interests, but also including a cross-class alliance of capital and "labor aristocracy."

The primacy of capital in this account is reflected in the claim that dominant growth coalitions are not coalitions of equals, and that instead the reshuffling of the bloc is usually at the expense of a section of its labor component. This is consistent with capital enjoying structural power and with the clout that capital enjoys as crucial funders of political campaigns, especially in the more liberal market economies. But beyond these more materialist dimensions of capitalist power, hegemonic forces can embed advantages in fundamental institutions of economic governance which establish the boundaries of legitimate economic policy. Understanding political parties' role in entrenching or challenging these institutions is key to understand how they shape and maintain growth models. Parties, beyond being organizations with leaders and voters, are also carriers of ideas or "generalizable principles" (White and Ypi 2016) that bind party supporters together and form the basis of a broader social appeal.

The classic scholarship on parties in the early and mid-20th century saw ideological differences between parties, and the correspondence of these ideological differences to specific social interests that parties sought to articulate, as central to democratic politics. The post-mass party model of democracy is instead seen as ideologically vacuous, with competition between strategically flexible actors pursuing votes following the demands of the median voter. But the lack of ideological distinctiveness does not mean the absence of ideology. Instead, a very clear preference for orthodox macroeconomic positions, pro-business regulation of markets, and limits on redistribution has been a shared, if rarely explicit starting point for political debate among established political parties since the 1990s (Blyth and Katz 2005; Hopkin and Blyth 2019).

This dominant ideology is even more powerful for being largely unrecognized in many cases, with political arguments occurring along entirely different, often superficial lines creating the impression of a vibrant pluralistic democracy while fundamental social conflicts remain buried. Party collusion in the cartel model is a good example of Schattschneider's insight that "the definition of the alternatives is the supreme instrument of power" (1960, 66). Once a growth model is entrenched, party competition revolves around distributional battles within the dominant growth coalition and payoffs to others adjacent to it, but with some claims to a share of the proceeds of growth. Because of the difficulty of organizing marginalized groups with no business interests willing to invest in a party alternative, large sectors of the electorate may be poorly served and entirely dissatisfied with the model, but unable to do anything about it, lapsing into abstention or a reluctant vote for the mainstream forces least hostile to them. The "party decline" trend described earlier captures such a scenario.

However, this "consent as acquiescence" may be harder to sustain if growth stagnates or some major economic shock disrupts the political equilibrium, as we have been able to observe in the decade following the Global Financial Crisis. If such consent is a widely observed pattern in the Western democracies over the past few decades, we need to go deeper to understand how this pattern of cartel politics reproduces distinctive growth models, and how in certain circumstances these models can be challenged.

Growth Models without Growth: Democracy and the Anti-System Challenge

In the rich democracies, from the 1990s until the late 2000s—a period of relative macroeconomic stability—political parties acquired a role as a kind of broker between the representatives of key economic sectors and the wider electorate. Their key function rested in defending the interests of dominant growth coalitions while shaping distributional policy so that the benefits of economic gains were sufficiently spread out to obtain support for, or at least acquiescence in, the economic model. In this phase, the parties' role was mostly one of "selling" the growth model to the public, or indeed in some cases suppressing contestation to it by switching the political conversation to less threatening issues such as sociocultural policies ("identity" politics). The convergence of established parties around the key policies and institutions underpinning each national growth model, and the delegation of key policy decisions, ensured that elections served to legitimate the model rather than entertain alternatives. The space for contestation was limited to variations in the distributional bargains necessary to secure consent.

We distinguish between two kinds of dominant growth coalitions: a narrow "dominant" coalition *that* is the main source and beneficiary of growth, and a much wider, "secondary" coalition, consenting to, and benefiting from, the growth model on the former's terms. The core of the "dominant" coalition consists of the organized economic sectors whose interests are unambiguously and tightly bound up with the institutions that underpin the growth model. In the export-led model, for example, this is the cross-class coalition within the export-oriented manufacturing sector, comprising owners and managers of firms and their core employees, their families, as well as the residents of areas heavily dependent on these firms for local economic prosperity.

Yet as Baccaro and Pontusson (2016) point out, however well organized and influential such groups, they are highly unlikely to constitute a majority of the electorate. As such, the main task for parties lies in building and maintaining a dominant growth coalition by mobilizing the support of voters whose interests are less obviously protected by the existing growth model, but who nonetheless enable growth through the provision of services, or public goods, or, more generally, through the provision of the *infrastructure* required for the successful operation of a distinct growth model.

In general terms, parties can draw on three strategies when building a dominant coalition: they can *integrate* groups of voters and/or particular interests into the dominant growth coalition; they can *buy them off* using redistributive policies such as welfare spending priorities, regulatory policies, and patterns of public employment and investment that effectively redirect some of the productivity gains of the growth model to groups beyond the immediate beneficiaries; or they can choose to *marginalize* them by exclusion. Party political strategies to achieve this vary across growth models along the lines of well-understood differences between welfare regimes (Hassel and Palier 2021a). In times when this cross-coalitional bargain is tenable, the political underpinnings of a particular growth model can be considered stable.

But this condition makes the politics of growth models particularly susceptible to the dilemma of democratic capitalism (Streeck 2014a). Absent physical domination, democratic political economies are only stable when there are sufficient resources available to redistribute in a somewhat equitable fashion. Tensions between the electoral (democratic) and the elitist (capitalist) domains arise particularly in times of crisis and pose serious challenges to the ability of parties to maintain a dominant growth coalition. When parties fail to uphold the boundaries of their dominant growth coalitions, for instance, because former beneficiaries become part of the excluded, growth models become politically contested. The 2008 crisis and subsequent periods of austerity and stagnation have exhausted the political legitimacy of the post-Fordist growth models in the hardest-hit countries, opening avenues for institutional change.

The latter phase gave rise of populist—or anti-system politics (Hopkin 2020) and placed in office new political forces, many of which have openly advocated major institutional changes. Anti-system politics is, by definition, directed at existing political and economic arrangements. Some aspects of these arrangements may be tangential to growth models but for the most part anti-system political movements take aim at these models, both in terms of their distribution of economic risks and rewards and in terms of the distribution of political power implicit in them. We can restate anti-system politics in terms of the fundamental features of growth model analysis as follows.

First, growth models relate to sources of demand. The 2008 crisis was at its heart a crisis of demand, as the financial meltdown squeezed credit. Different growth models were differently exposed to this crisis of demand, but all the industrialized democracies initially opted for fiscal and monetary stimulus before the post-Keynesian consensus reasserted itself in the form of fiscal austerity (Blyth 2013). The consumption-led models were particularly hurt by the turn to austerity, especially those in the Eurozone, and the shortfall of demand had direct electoral consequences, draining support from established political parties and providing opportunities for anti-system parties to challenge the "usual suspect" insiders (Hübscher, Sattler, and Wagner 2020). The cross-national evidence clearly points to anti-system voting rising most strongly in austerity-stricken countries that had adopted consumer-led growth models (Hopkin 2020).

Second, the distributional consequences of growth models are central to their stability. Inequality has been rising consistently since the 1980s across the advanced industrialized states, but the consequences of different growth models for the income distribution are important. There is a striking correlation also between current accounts and inequality since the export-led models tend to have welfare and labor market institutions that redistribute income more efficiently than the consumption-led models. This has implications for the electoral sustainability of the model, since more widely dispersed income gains naturally reinforce the position of the established parties and secure greater political stability, which is particularly challenging in the context of declining labor shares of income (Piketty 2013; Baccaro and Pontusson 2016).

The welfare state and collective bargaining provides workable solutions to the problem of the narrow electoral base of dominant growth coalitions in export-led economies. More egalitarian income distributions bring more voters into the pool of beneficiaries of export-led growth, while a low inflation and low consumption equilibrium provides some degree of financial security to households outside the dominant coalition but electorally incorporated into it. In consumption-led models household inequality is higher, and consumption levels more unpredictable, meaning that continued consumption growth, even at the expenses of high levels of indebtedness and financial instability, are necessary to preserve the political order.

The connections between different growth models and patterns of electoral behavior therefore became clear in the last two decades. The share of the vote going to anti-system parties grew as the size of the groups perceiving little benefit from existing growth models expanded. These patterns of anti-system voting are not limited to the consumption-led economies that suffered harsh austerity after the Global Financial Crisis. Indeed, the export-led countries were also affected, and well before 2008, as constraints on consumption (through wage restraint, labor market liberalization, and welfare retrenchment) fed through into voter discontent.

Figure 14.1 shows that anti-system voting grew first in the "creditor" countries (export-led and hybrid models, in Northern and continental Europe) from the mid-1990s, and then grew very rapidly in the "debtor" countries (consumption-led models) as the credit crunch hit in the late 2000s. These patterns reflect not only trends in overall growth but also the changes to the distribution of income (Matthijs 2016). Before the crash of the late 2000s, consumption-led models had superior growth rates and saw favorable trends in income inequality, as wages and government spending rose. The rapid reversal of these trends is very visible in the uptick in anti-system voting in the debtor countries as austerity hit in the 2010s.

The greater inequality and instability implicit in the consumption-led model implies a more precarious life for political parties as they attempt to stretch as far as they can the benefits of the model beyond the narrow dominant growth co-alition, while foregoing the kinds of fiscal instruments that would be necessary to do so. The resulting political upheavals when domestic demand is squeezed open new space for political challengers, since the established parties are by def-inition associated with the failings of the model.

In the next section, we employ more detailed case studies that trace the experiences of different countries throughout the cartel party era and into the period of global financial crisis. They show that parties have often succeeded

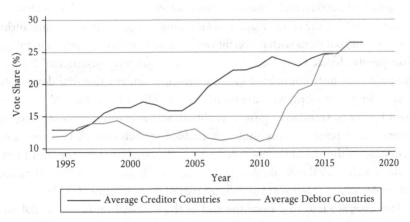

Figure 14.1 Anti-System Vote Shares, by Growth Model 1994–2018 (Creditor vs. Debtor Countries)

in building dominant growth coalitions to ignite encompassing change to a country's growth model, and they explore the means and strategies they have used to do so. But they also demonstrate that these coalitions are almost always very fragile constructs that operate under the premise of inclusion and exclusion, and as such, are prone to widening representation gaps and political contestation.

Party Politics and the German Growth Model

As other contributions to this volume argue, German growth is pulled primarily by real exchange rate-sensitive manufacturing exports. The key interests of the dominant export-manufacturing sector are structured around a mix of aggressive deflation and restrained domestic consumption to boost export competitiveness (Baccaro and Pontusson 2016; Höpner 2019). Among other things, this requires the expansion of low-wage employment and rationalization along supply chains while at the same time protecting the interests of the most productive and highly coordinated manufacturing sector under a least-encompassing class compromise. As a result, Germany's export-led growth model is characterized by an intense *Verteilungskampf*, that is, a *within* class "distribution struggle" between better and worse protected workers (Klein and Pettis 2020, 154ff.). This conflict is structured around a fundamental tradeoff between job preservation and wage growth, the outcome of which determines the country's real exchange rate and thus, its external competitiveness.

Between the early 1990s and the financial crisis of 2008, this tradeoff had been decided in favor of export-manufacturing capital and protected workers who remained a part of the dominant growth coalition, and at the expense of marginalized outsiders who were not. This outcome was the result of a *corporate* bargain in which the top managers of Germany's largest export-manufacturing firms forged coalitions with powerful work councils and core workers to rationalize supply chains. Only later did "employment for wage stagnation" become the politically institutionalized guiding principle under the social democratic Schröeder government, who thanks to long-established personal links to dominant figures of Germany's growth coalition, was able to implement sweeping labor market reforms. This shift was enabled by Schröeder's transformative leadership of the Social Democratic Party (SPD), latching onto the "third way" trend launched by the Anglo-American center-left in the early 1990s (Blair and Schroeder 1998) to jettison a significant part of its commitments to labor.

However, we find that since the end of the financial crisis substantial momentum change has taken place that re-strengthened the position of labor, as the mainstream parties—the SPD and Christian Democratic Union (CDU) failed to effectively shield the dominant growth coalition from the fallout from its liberalizing labor market reforms. Over time, parts of the manufacturing-based growth coalition became themselves subject to socioeconomic insecurity, destabilizing the dominant coalition and reversing the capital and labor shares. In what follows, we trace the joint efforts of business leaders, core workers, and social democrats in the emergence of Germany's "Janus-faced" export-led growth model (Germann 2021, 196; Cioffi and Höpner 2006), but also highlight the endogenous instability of this dominant coalition.

Breaking the Old Coalition

During the 1990s, formidable reunification efforts put severe pressure on the German model. In the 1980s the center-right coalition under Kohl had pledged a neoliberal, Thatcherite policy turn, but failed in the face of opposition from both trade unions and employers, and party-internal conflict within the Christian Democratic Union party (CDU) about the best way forward (Wood 2001). The CDU's neoliberal shift resonated with considerable portions of the electorate but clashed with the growth model that the social partners remained committed to, and the CDU's traditional commitment to collective bargaining and social integration acted as a brake on more radical reforms (Zohlnhöfer 1999).

Coalitional dynamics began to shift in the early 1990s as employers, increasingly focused on international competitiveness, established opening clauses for sectoral agreements, shifted capital investment and low-paid jobs to the East European periphery, and allowed capital and core workers to enforce strict "wage moderation and the reduction in non-core payments." As a result, real wages in high-end manufacturing and low-end services, which had progressed in lockstep with labor productivity until the mid-1990s, suddenly began to diverge dramatically (Baccaro and Benassi 2017, 102–103).[2] Figure 14.2 shows that the labour of income dropped sharply in the first half of the 2000s. This threatened to drive a wedge between beneficiaries and victims of economic change within the Social Democratic base, a tension resolved by SPD leader Gerhard Schröeder in favor of the interests of export-oriented firms; and, secondarily, their core workers. Internally, this move involved increasing the influence of corporate supporters of the SPD such as the *Managerkreis* (Manager's Circle), affiliated to the party foundation, the Friedrich Ebert Stiftung, who pushed hard for the abandonment of traditional welfare and labor market structures in favor of a more Third Way approach (Pautz 2010).

Notably, it was Peter Hartz, head of human resources at Volkswagen since 1993, who personified the "export-oriented elite" that decided the corporate distributional conflict over productivity gains in favor of capital. Hartz was longtime

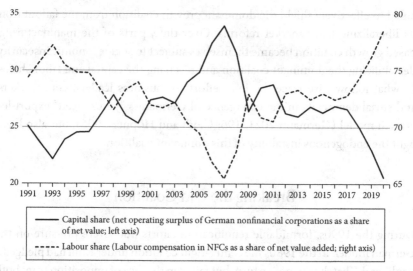

Figure 14.2 Capital versus labor share in German nonfinancial corporations (in %), 1991–2020. Source: Destatis; authors' calculations, cf. Klein and Pettis (2020: 155)

friend of Schröeder's, and Schröeder's SPD-led government commissioned and implemented Hartz's proposed reform packages that reinforced the German export-manufacturing growth models. These reforms were aimed at reducing seemingly structural and high unemployment numbers by flexibilizing the labor market. They deregulated temporary work, encouraged part-time employment, cut unemployment benefits, and introduced a marginal low-pay mini-job scheme that was exempt from social contributions. Jobseekers also faced sanctions for rejecting "reasonable" job offers, which added to increased wage dumping (Martin and Swank 2012, 211ff.; Lunz 2013, 18).

The SPD leadership retained significant agency in entrenching the German export-led growth model. These conditions enabled Gerhard Schröeder to build a new dominant growth coalition. First, while most trade unions stood in forceful opposition to the *Agenda* plans, Schröeder was successful in forging a coalition with strategically important unions, most notably the IG BCE, a powerful industrial affiliation of the German Confederation of Trade Unions (DGB) covering mining, chemicals and energy. Traditionally, this union could draw on excellent government connections as the mining industry had always been dependent on state subsidies. Moreover, the IG BCE had implemented its own social policy program which remained unaffected by federal reforms. An important requirement for the financial sustainability of such union-internal social policy program was that its large companies remained productive and profitable and that its members continued to be paid among the highest wages of the entire economy (Schiller and Hassel 2010). So, if wage cuts for these segments were off the table, the IG BCE was very open to reforms that improved the overall competitiveness of the German export sector in general and of the IG BCE's supply chains.

Second, frictions among different trade unions and rifts between large exporting businesses and small sheltered enterprises disorganized opponents. Organizational interdependencies between major unions and the SPD's party structure were essential in managing critical unions and convincing peripheral voters. In total, one-third of SPD members were organized in trade unions, with a majority of them in public and service sector unions, such as ver.di and GEW. These unions did not represent the now-dominant growth-producing sectors and were opposed to the reforms as they would have to shoulder the brunt of liberalization efforts. In addition, Schröeder gave important government positions to former IG Metall and IG BCE officials and reform-advocates like Walter Riester and Gerd Andres, while the left wing of the SPD came away empty-handedly. This combination helped the SPD leadership to secure crucial support from leading unions while deepening the rift within the labor movement itself.

After securing this division of the labor movement the reform coalition was able to organize encompassing popular consent in the elections of 2002 that went well beyond the narrow interest sets of members from the growth-producing sector. This electoral support was achieved due to the third crucial condition, a hegemonic discourse of crisis politics that allowed the reformists to present the interests of the narrow dominant sector as those of the nation as a whole and left little room for alternative political projects (Jacoby 2020). Structural pressures from globalizing markets, emerging economies in the Eastern periphery, and the ongoing deterioration of the fiscal position because of tremendous reunification efforts added to a general loss of economic confidence. In an influential policy paper of 2003, the *Seeheimer Kreis*, the SPD's market-liberal wing, tapped this general sentiment by arguing that the reform package met but the "minimum requirements for addressing the dramatic economic and financial situation in Germany" (Seeheimer Kreis 2003, 2; our translation). In addition, the SPD stressed dramatic fiscal pressures on municipalities and promised financial relief of €3bn at the federal level plus €2.5bn at the communal level in the first year after the introduction of reforms (Hassel and Schiller 2010, 286). Schröeder's TINA politics reached its peak when he combined the final vote on the reforms in parliament with a vote of confidence.

This strategy of "governing by panic" (Woodruff 2016) was a decisive move that helped the SPD tie their hands before the voters, anchor external competitiveness as a guiding principle and objective in public discourse, gain crucial electoral consent, and effectively close the market for political ideas. But this was only possible because Schröeder had, in typical cartel politics style, marginalized opposition within the party base by leveraging institutional power from the government and leaning on liberalizing forces outside the SPD (especially the corporate world), at the expense of its internal representative structures (Busch and Manow 2001). The success of this strategy, at least in the short term, is a clear example of how parties can shut down debate on the growth and distributional consequences of major economic policy shifts by insulating the leadership from grassroots pressure and presenting voters with a fait accompli.

This strategy was successful in creating a new dominant growth coalition of sufficient size to be survive two rounds of elections. However, the longer-term consequences for the SPD were less positive as it hemorrhaged support after losing power, having cut off part of its traditional support base in favor of the interests of leading companies in the manufacturing export sector. These adjustment efforts promoted by the SPD government were not shouldered evenly by labor (Hassel 2014). Employment protection legislation (EPL) for regular workers in Germany increased since 1985 (Thelen 2014, 131). Yet at the same time, the Hartz reforms cut EPL for temporary employees by half (OECD 2021a). Similarly, marginal employment (so-called mini jobs) more than doubled and involuntary part-time work almost tripled between 2002 and 2006 (Destatis 2021; OECD 2021b). As a result, poverty rates doubled between 2005 and 2015 from 5 to 10% (Klein and Pettis 2020, 152).

Reforming a Dominant Growth Coalition Under Stress

After a long period of retrenchment, the Global Financial Crisis set off a series of changes which ended up favoring labor whose share of income rebounded as the growth coalition between top managers, core workers (Diessner et al. 2021) and the SPD began to fracture after the implementation of the Hartz reforms. To sustain Germany's dualized labor markets (Hassel 2014), the boundaries between protected workers in core manufacturing industries and marginalized service workers in atypical employment had to remain distinct. But the forces of liberalization could not so easily be contained, and the logic of supply-chain rationalization soon spilled over into formerly more protected core segments of the labor force including sociocultural professionals and skilled workers in manufacturing industries (Marx 2011; Eichhorst et al. 2015). The erosion of the clear distinction between protected insiders and marginalized outsiders combined with structural underinvestment and suppressed domestic consumption to destabilize the export-oriented growth coalition while creating dissatisfied economic losers on both sides of the political spectrum (Nachtwey 2018).

The coalitional shift, which has unfolded since the late 2010s, manifests itself economically in collective agreements. Since 2011, agreed pay increases have scored substantially above the sum of inflation and total labor productivity rate (the Meinhold-formula) suggesting consistent real wage growth (Schulten and WSI-Tarifarchiv 2020, 8). As Di Carlo and Höpner (2020) explain, this period of "silent rebalancing" has been carried by a set of different sectors. Tighter labor markets increased bargaining power. Low-end service sectors, which suffered severe retrenchment from the Hartz reforms saw an income boost thanks to the introduction of the minimum wage in 2015 and a partial re-regulation of temporary agency work. Public sector employees, who are highly unionized but nonetheless contributed the largest share to overall wage restraint after Schröeder's *Agenda* had deteriorated states' public finances, saw their incomes rise when public investment increased, as did the construction sector. Together, these sectoral adjustments weakened Germany's unit labor cost competitiveness and to some extent rebalanced the export-led model relative to the period of stark entrenchment during the Schröeder era.

With a strong proportional electoral system and high degree of federalism making coalition formation more likely to reflect the interests of large parts of the electorate, Germany's institutional setup poses a greater challenge to growth model sustainability than in more majoritarian types of democratic regime. Even in 2005, the weakness of the main governing parties was emerging, with the SPD and CDU polling their lowest joint vote share since 1949, and the Global Financial Crisis accentuated the shrinking size of the electoral support base of the dominant growth coalition. The shift toward a distribution of economic gains more favorable to labor coincided with the rise of anti-system politics in the form of the rise of the AfD and the Linke in particular, and the collapse in the vote share of the center-left (Hopkin 2020). As in many other democracies with proportional representation electoral systems, the political repercussions of the crisis played out through an increasing polarization and fragmentation of the party system, weakening the cartel politics arrangements of the 1990s and early 2000s.

Despite these pressures the dominant growth coalition was able to survive through an increasing recourse to electoral "grand coalitions" between the two main governing parties, who had in the past generally alternated in power in coalition with pivotal forces such as the liberal FDP and latterly the Greens. But the shrinking vote share of the traditional parties demonstrated the limits of a growth model that squeezes large parts of the electorate, and the instability of such a politics when growth fails to deliver widespread gains.

In sum, the case of Germany demonstrates that even the most entrenched growth models are a consequence of political compromise, which by definition suggests the possibility of an alternative to the status quo. Not only does it require a delicate combination of political agency and coalitional mediation to redesign the social underpinnings of economic growth, but it turns out that sustaining fragile coalitions comes as an even graver challenge to political parties.

The Party Politics of Building a Consumption-Led Growth Coalition

Britain is a consumption-led growth model, with demand fueled by credit injections from a loosely regulated financial system that draws in capital from around the world. But its origins are to be found in an unambiguously partisan reform project in the 1980s, with the dramatic collapse of manufacturing resulting from the adoption of harsh deflationary policies under the first Thatcher government, and the reforms to the financial sector under her second administration. By the end of the 1980s, Britain had shifted from being a country struggling to maintain its balance of payments, to an economy consistently running substantial current account deficits that only closed in times of recession. But this new growth model had required a sharp reconfiguration of social forces and the party system that articulated their political representation.

The shift in the growth model reflected a significant shift in the influence wielded by different producer groups in the main political parties. Manufacturing industry, traditionally well represented by the Conservative Party, was initially supportive of the Thatcher project, which it saw as a solution to industrial unrest, inflation, and a squeeze in real profits (Glyn 2006). But as the disinflation and sterling appreciation of the early 1980s decimated much of British manufacturing, the business groups represented by the CBI (Confederation of British Industry) became increasingly critical of the Thatcher government, and as a result lost influence in party leadership circles to the more finance-oriented and ideologically neoliberal Institute of Directors (IoD) (Grant 2001, 339).

Trade unions, however, traditionally aligned with the Labour Party, were not just sidelined but threatened with near extinction from large swathes of the economy by a series of hostile pieces of legislation. As a result, the Labour Party progressively distanced itself from the unions over the late 1980s and 1990s. The kind of intra-industry cross-class coalition that underpins exemplars of the export-led growth model was fragile at best in postwar Britain, partly because the majoritarian two-party system made cross-party policy cooperation impossible (Iversen and Soskice 2009). By the late 1990s, with both major parties reluctant to side with manufacturing industry representatives, and labor in massive retreat, it had disappeared without trace.

Changing Demand Drivers and Changing the Growth Coalition

The decline of manufacturing coincided with the launching of a rapidly expanding and internationally open financial services sector, which become the key source of growth in Britain from the mid-1980s on. Reforms to financial markets not only attracted large amounts of foreign capital to London's stock exchange, as in the United States, but much of this capital also fed through to the housing market thanks to a loosening of restraints on mortgage lending and a decline in real interest rates. As a consequence, the economic cycle became more and more tied to housing market cycles, as the "wealth effect" of rising home equity drove consumption and often further borrowing based on equity withdrawal. UK Housing booms would typically begin in London and the South-East, where the direct beneficiaries of financial sector compensation growth and rising financial asset prices mostly lived, before spilling out into the rest of the country, with distance from London and the social composition of areas predicting the extent of house price inflation.

The emergence of this consumption-led growth model had significant consequences for voting patterns (Ansell 2014). Already existing patterns of class-based and region-based voting were accentuated, as the regions that had traditionally relied on manufacturing employment became even more heavily Labour, while the Conservatives further entrenched their domination of the South-East by picking up votes among working-class homeowners (Dunleavy and Husbands 1985).

A particularly electorally successful policy was the Thatcher government's "right to buy" initiative, which obliged local councils to sell public housing to tenants at heavily discounted prices, effectively creating a new constituency of lower income homeowners and landlords who were disproportionately likely to switch their political allegiance to the Conservatives. The scale of the shift was substantive enough to affect elections, with around two million sales to tenants since the early 1980s (Murie 2016). In this way the Conservatives expanded support for the credit-led model beyond the direct city beneficiaries to a wider coalition of homeowners and mortgage holders.

After briefly doubling down on its support for manufacturing and public sector workers and suffering a series of defeats, Labour rectified its "Southern discomfort" (Radice 1992). That is, its unpopularity with upwardly-mobile homeowners, particularly in Southern England, by aligning with Conservative positions on housing and its related economics of easy credit combined with tight public finances (Hopkin and Alexander Shaw 2016). As a result, policies focused on maintaining this housing-based credit expansion survived changes of government.

For example, Labour returned to power after the recession and housing crash of the early 1990s collapsed the housing market, pushing highly leveraged mortgage holders into negative equity, many of whom were forced into foreclosure. This recession hit the South-East particularly hard and provided the Labour Party with an opportunity to win over sections of the indebted Southern middle classes in the 1997 election. Support for the Conservatives among non-unionized working-class homeowners dropped from over 40% throughout the 1980s to only 23% in 1997 (Heath, Jowell, and Curtice 2001). Unsurprisingly, Tony Blair's post-1997 Labour government presided over another even more sustained housing boom that was only halted by the 2008 financial crisis.

Labour cemented the electoral hegemony of the new dominant growth coalition in two key ways. First, it refused to reverse the "right to buy" policy, nor did it make any attempt to build significant numbers of social housing units to make up for the millions sold off. By restricting the availability of non-market alternatives, growing demand for housing fed through into a growing private rented sector, backstopped by colossal public subsidies of rents for low-income households, which doubled after 2000 to reach a peak of almost £25 billion in the mid-2010s (more than 1% of GDP).[3]

This expenditure benefited around four million households, but indirectly contributed substantially to rental income for housing associations, local councils, and private landlords. This latter sector also received a boost under Labour with legislation establishing a new form of rental contract—assured shorthold tenancies—which facilitated tenant turnover, thus turbo-charging the emerging "buy to let" industry of small landlords buying up properties with mortgages to be paid off with rental income. Favorable tax treatments—such as generous tax deductions for landlord expenses—and the fall in interest rates after Labour opted for Bank of England independence, all made a buy to let a popular investment vehicle for middle-income, middle-aged Britons sitting on substantial home equity, many of whom were the beneficiaries of the earlier 1980s boom.

Toward an Asset-Based Growth Coalition

By 2020, almost three-quarters of people aged 65 years and over in England owned their home outright,[4] and around 5.5 million adults lived in households that owned at least one rental property, making small landlords a quantitatively significant electoral sub-constituency within the broader group of homeowners (around half of landlords owned only one rental property). A disproportionate share of this wealth was held in London and other Southern regions of England,[5] not surprisingly, given the high housing prices there. This constituency has enjoyed particularly careful attention from political representatives, with, around 20% of MPs being landlords themselves,[6] while most also own second properties purchased with the help of generous allowances for work-related accommodation expenses. Companies working in the real estate management and construction sectors were also generous contributors to UK political parties, particularly the Conservatives.

By the 2000s the British growth model's foundations in ever-rising house prices had become entrenched, with all the main political parties complicit in favoring the interests of the property-owning majority over other constituencies. Despite supply shortages becoming recognized in government as a reason for house price inflation, no serious effort was made by successive Labour and Conservative administrations to boost homebuilding, which had never recovered from the loss of the public sector contribution to building after 1980.[7]

The Resilience of a Seemingly Unstable Model

The period after 2010 is worth particular attention, because the aftershock of the 2008 crash seemed to undermine the foundations of both the British growth model and the cartelized party system. The deleveraging—both public and private—sparked by the financial crisis had predictably negative effects on demand, leading to a decade of real wage stagnation. What is more, homeowners began to decline as a percentage of the population after 2000, and the availability of credit to private individuals collapsed. The political costs of this stagnation contributed to the Brexit vote of 2016, which overturned a prime minister and drove fundamental shifts in the British political debate in the second half of the decade (Fetzer 2019; Adler and Ansell 2020). On the face of it this seems to challenge our understanding of the model and its relation to government policy and party politics. However, there are considerable continuities which lead us to conclude that the 2010s have seen a consolidation rather than any fundamental change in the British growth model, involving a shift from consumption growth to asset growth as the basis for political consent.

Real wages barely grew in the United Kingdom after 2008, returning to their pre-crisis level only in February 2020,[8] just before the deep recession provoked by the Covid pandemic. Yet asset values enjoyed substantial growth in the same period. Average real household wealth increased by around 40%, and median real household wealth by around 28% between 2006 and 2018.[9] This shift of growth away from consumption to wealth brought with it a shift in the composition of the supporting coalition for the growth model. From 2015 on, age and property ownership emerged as the key predictors of support for the governing Conservatives, while younger voters, and especially those in private rented accommodation, leaned heavily toward the opposition Labour Party. Policy under the Conservative governments after 2010 tended to reinforce this age divide.

The ultra-loose monetary policies followed by the Bank of England boosted asset values, while restrictive fiscal policies were skewed in distributive terms toward older age groups. Welfare cuts were particularly targeted at low-income working-age households, who suffered substantial real income losses because of several rounds of retrenchment measures, while pensions and health expenditures were protected from austerity. Indeed, pensions were indexed to price rises or average wage rises, whichever was highest, a policy known as the "triple lock." Meanwhile a 2011 reform to university tuition fees dramatically increased indebtedness among younger Britons.

Unsurprisingly households benefiting from home ownership and pensions raises were disproportionately likely to offer support to the Conservatives. Policies threatening the home ownership dividend were off the table for both parties. The long-awaited revaluation of local taxation bands (not a property tax but based on property values in the 1990s) continued to be postponed, and a botched attempt by the May government to address the shortfall in funding for social care through part-appropriation of homes was seen as responsible for her failure to win a majority in the 2017 election. In 2017 and 2019 support for the Conservatives was around 60% in the 65+ age group while it was lower than 30% among the under 35s. Support for Labour presented a mirror image, with its vote declining in roughly linear fashion by age group.[10] Helped by turnout being much higher among older voters, the Conservatives have been the largest party in each of the last four elections.

Our focus on balance sheets and age-skewed asset distributions suggests an answer to the conundrum of how to maintain the coalition for a consumption-led growth model when demand is hit by a credit crunch. The coalition underpinning the British growth model has certainly undergone a period of high instability since 2010, with "hung" parliaments for 7 out of 10 years, two prime ministers being unseated between elections, and of course the anti-system revolts represented by the rise of Scottish and English nationalism and Corbyn's left-wing takeover of the Labour Party. But the re-composition of the growth coalition around a Conservative electorate of largely small, retired property holders suggests an alternative form of consent to the credit-fueled consumption of the 1990s and 2000.

Favoring asset growth over income growth should in principle be incompatible with the demands of electoral politics, given that wealth is far more unequally distributed than income. However, an asset-based growth model does deliver a combination of very unequal distribution, in which most of the gains flow to the very top, with a broad base of small-scale beneficiaries, which in a context of low mobilization and fragmentation of the non-wealth-holding electorate, can deliver the dominant growth coalition.

This asset-based growth model has tended to support whichever party is able to preside over rising house prices: party alternation has only occurred twice since the 1970s, in 1997 and in 2010, immediately following the only periods of falling house prices during that period. Parties are therefore active suitors of financial and homeowner interests, and government policies reflect their need to bolster political consent through asset price inflation and, where possible, credit-led consumption growth.

Conclusions: Growth, Parties, and Dominant Growth Coalitions

This chapter has provided a theoretical and conceptual map for analyzing how party politics shapes, maintains, and sometimes reforms growth models. We have tried to move beyond static understandings of social blocs overreliant on the role of producer interests to incorporate the electoral dimension and political parties' role as brokers of a variety of interests in the political economy, illustrated through two cases of representative growth models. The implications for growth model theory can be briefly summarized as follows.

First, looking at party politics offers us a more nuanced picture of how growth models can evolve over time, moving beyond rigid institutionalist assumptions around the relationship between electoral systems and types of capitalism. Party competition and government alternation take place within the context of a growth model but cannot be dismissed as epiphenomena. Instead, parties can shape not only how consent is secured for a growth model but can also reconfigure the dominant growth coalition itself. Party systems can be arenas where producer groups shape policy to suit their needs, but they can also determine changes in interest group relations, and even the exclusion of previously powerful groups, such as trade unions and manufacturing firms in the United Kingdom. Examining how parties and leaders manage processes of growth model reform and replacement provides insights into the political foundations of different models. It allows us to move beyond the dichotomy of producer group dominance or electoral dominance that has conditioned the debate on growth models.

Most analysis of the party politics of economic policy takes parties as unitary actors representing relatively compact social interests and as a result misses the internal dynamics that shape how parties evolve and choose to represent different groups and manage the conflicts between them. By looking at how parties finance their activities and represent different socioeconomic sectors in their internal structures, we can see much more clearly how growth models are underpinned by policy. Again, this kind of analysis can reveal producer group dominance, for example through parties' financial dependence or the recruitment of personnel, but it can also reveal how different leadership groups can mobilize or demobilize voter groups in support of a particular set of policies. In short, elected politicians have strategies and these strategies can be growth model "makers" as well as just "takers."

Notes

1. Comparative analysis seems to suggest that export-led models are more politically stable than consumption-led ones (Hopkin 2020), but that in turn poses interesting questions about how political parties mediate between the needs of the growth model and demands for consumption of voters. This mediating role is even more challenging in an age of central bank independence where parties of government lack control over the main policy lever affecting macroeconomic policy.
2. Meanwhile, between the early 1990s and the early 2000s, the share of net value added by non-financial corporations that went to owners, shareholders, and creditors increased from 22.7 to just under 30%.
3. IFS, "Doubling of the housing benefit bill is sign of something deeply wrong," Mar., 4, 2019 https://www.ifs.org.uk/publications/13940
4. ONS, "Living longer: Changes in housing tenure over time," https://www.ons.gov.uk/peoplepopulationandcommunity/birthsdeathsandmarriages/ageing/articles/livinglonger/changesinhousingtenureovertime
5. ONS, "Total wealth in Great Britain: April 2016 to March 2018," https://www.ons.gov.uk/peoplepopulationandcommunity/personalandhouseholdfinances/incomeandwealth/bulletins/totalwealthingreatbritain/april2016tomarch2018#regional-distribution-of-total-wealth-in-great-britain
6. Solomon Hughes "Government by Landlord," *Tribune*, May 20, 2020, https://tribunemag.co.uk/2020/05/government-by-landlord
7. A key indicator of how the housing-led growth model had been entrenched was the response after the 2008 financial crisis, which focused first on saving financial institutions, and then on boosting consumption through a combination of interest rate cuts and central bank interventions to support asset markets (offset, after 2010 by cuts to welfare and social spending on working-age households introductive by Conservative-led governments).
8. ONS, "Labour market economic commentary: February 2020," https://www.ons.gov.uk/employmentandlabourmarket/peopleinwork/employmentandemployeetypes/articles/labourmarketeconomiccommentary/february2020
9. Figure 14.2 "Mean and median total household wealth, Great Britain, July 2006 to March 2018," in ONS, "Total wealth in Great Britain: April 2016 to March 2018," Dec. 2019, https://www.ons.gov.uk/peoplepopulationandcommunity/personalandhouseholdfinances/incomeandwealth/bulletins/totalwealthingreatbritain/april2016tomarch2018#trends-in-average-wealth-in-great-britain
10. British Election Study, "Age and voting behaviour at the 2019 General Election," Feb. 2021, https://www.britishelectionstudy.com/bes-findings/age-and-voting-behaviour-at-the-2019-general-election/#.YHMHRi1Q3_Q

15

Growth Models Under Austerity

EVELYNE HÜBSCHER AND THOMAS SATTLER

Introduction

Fiscal policy is an integral part of a country's growth model (Baccaro and Pontusson 2016; Blyth and Matthijs 2017). An export-led strategy, for instance, requires that governments limit fiscal deficits—that is, by implementing fiscal austerity—in order to promote cost competitiveness and, hence, to enhance export opportunities for domestic firms. In contrast, governments in demand-led models should be less concerned about fiscal deficits because they need fiscal flexibility to manage domestic demand. This chapter shows that, consistent with the implications of the growth-models perspective, governments subordinate their fiscal policy to the macroeconomic strategy of their country. We find that the decision to pursue fiscal austerity varies significantly across countries. This variation is in line with a country's growth model. The amount of fiscal austerity implemented in export-oriented economies before the Great Recession is about two to three times greater than the amount of austerity in demand-led economies. Differences in austerity are more strongly related to growth models than to other economic or political variables, including fiscal deficits, government partisanship, or political constraints.

Our analysis also contrasts this systemic, models-based view with the popular approach in political economy to explain economic policies from a voter-driven, bottom-up perspective. Contrary to this view, we find that growth models dominate voter preferences: governments tend to favor the fiscal policies that reinforce their country's growth model even if these policies stand in conflict with the preferences of voters. Specifically, voters are quite critical of austerity, but this skepticism does not prevent governments in export-led countries from systematically implementing spending cuts. In addition, government responsiveness is lowest in growth models that are closest to a specific "ideal type": while on average left voters are much less supportive of austerity than right voters, these diverging preferences only translate into distinct policies under left and right governments in balanced growth models, but not in unbalanced models, that is, heavily export- or demand-led, models.

Together, these results suggest that a country's overarching macroeconomic strategy is critical to understanding fiscal and macroeconomic policymaking. It better explains variations in fiscal austerity than voter preferences, and it limits the ability or willingness of party governments to respond to the fiscal preferences of their supporters in countries that mirror ideal growth models. This points to a mismatch between government policy, especially in export-led economies, and voter attitudes. This mismatch is likely to contribute to political disillusionment of voters and possibly contributes to political perturbations, such as the rise of populist parties (Hopkin 2020; Hopkin and Blyth 2019)—especially in those countries where austerity is implemented without the postulated positive effects on growth.

Fiscal Policy and Growth Models: Popular Perspectives on Austerity

A common perspective in comparative and international political economy puts popular preferences at the center of the analysis of economic policymaking (e.g., Beramendi et al. 2015; Lake 2009). In this bottom-up view, voters demand or oppose economic policies, which incentivizes governments to pursue or avoid these policies. Change in economic policy then can occur either through a swing in voter preferences or through a change in government partisanship when new government parties represent societal groups with interests and beliefs that are different from the supporter of previous government parties. Voters can prevent economic policies by threating to punish government parties in the next election or by vetoing policy change at various stages of the policymaking process (Hallerberg and Basinger 1998; Henisz 2004; Immergut 1992).

Applied to fiscal policy, this implies that variation in the pursuit of austerity primarily arises from variation in voter attitudes toward fiscal cuts; change in government partisanship; or differences in political constraints, such as veto players. But evidence that this is the case is limited, for two reasons. First, voter preferences cannot explain variation in fiscal policies across countries with different growth models. For a long time, and potentially in line with the voter-driven perspective, the political economy literature suggested that voters dislike fiscal deficits and, hence, support deficit-reducing policies (Alesina et al. 2011; Alesina et al. 1998; Brender and Drazen 2008). More recent findings, however, raise doubts about the enthusiasm of voters toward austerity. Although voters may be critical of deficits and debt (Brender and Drazen 2008), they are even more critical of austerity when they are confronted with concrete propositions to cut spending in specific areas, such as pensions, unemployment insurance, or education (Bojar et al. 2022; Bremer and Bürgisser 2018; Hübscher et al. 2020). This opposition is remarkably stable across countries (Hübscher et al. 2020) and over time (Hübscher et al. 2015).[1]

Second, fiscal policies should diverge more strongly across party governments than they actually do if voter preferences were a key driver of these policies. We know from previous research that voters hold different attitudes toward austerity depending on their ideological orientation: left voters are significantly more likely to reject austerity than right voters (Hübscher et al. 2020). But despite this large ideological variation, government partisanship only has a limited effect on austerity policies: left and right governments are about equally likely to implement austerity packages (Hübscher 2016, 2018; Hübscher and Sattler 2017).[2] Others find that left governments are more likely to cut welfare spending, which is in contradiction to the voter-driven perspective (Armingeon et al. 2016).

Fiscal Austerity through a Growth-Models Lens

Given these limitations of the voter-driven approach, growth models offer a fresh political perspective on the determinants of fiscal policy and overall macroeconomic policy. Fiscal policy, that is, fiscal expansion or restraint plays a crucial role restraint, for a country's macroeconomic model. Public investment and consumption directly contribute a significant share toward a country's *domestic demand*. Public expenditures also indirectly affect demand via their effect on citizens' consumption behavior, for example, by increasing or decreasing wages in the public sector or by providing more or less generous social assistance programs. In countries that pursue a consumption- and demand-led model, fiscal flexibility, therefore, is an important instrument to stimulate domestic demand and hence growth.

Public spending policies also have fundamental consequences for *international competitiveness* of domestic firms and their export opportunities. Public deficits induce inward capital flows when international investors buy government bonds. These inflows push countries toward a current account deficit (Chinn and Prasad 2003; Jones 2015b, 2016) and, hence, are detrimental to exports. Public sector employment and wages also feature prominently in real-economy models of trade imbalances. Trade surpluses are easier to achieve in systems with wage coordination, in which the sheltered sector, such as the public sector, accepts to limit wage growth in line with the interests of the exposed, trading sector (Johnston 2016; Johnston et al. 2014; Manger and Sattler 2020).

In countries that pursue an export-led model, fiscal restraint, therefore, is the preferred fiscal strategy.

These diverging fiscal strategies have their ideational origins in different economic literatures that postulate distinct mechanisms linking fiscal policy to economic growth. A large macroeconomics literature highlights the positive impact of fiscal policy on growth via so-called fiscal multipliers. Vice versa, research in this tradition points to the adverse effect of fiscal austerity on growth (Chowdhury and Islam 2012; Guajardo et al. 2014), especially during recessions (Jordà and Taylor 2016). In line with these insights, recent research shows that fiscal multipliers and hence the detrimental impact of austerity on European economies were much larger during the past crisis than the ECB assumed (Górnicka et al. 2018). Researchers in this tradition, therefore, have called for a more active fiscal policy in order to stimulate growth (Blanchard 2019; Blanchard and Summers 2017).

The intellectual counter position to the fiscal flexibility view does not explicitly consider the link between fiscal policy and international competitiveness and exports. But it also points to a supply-side argument that connects low deficits and fiscal restraint to economic growth via "expansionary fiscal contractions." As Blyth (2013) describes in detail (see also Dellepiane-Avellaneda 2014), an influential view advocates that fiscal austerity in fact does not inhibit growth, but can even induce economic expansion (Alesina et al. 2019; Giavazzi and Pagano 1990).[3] To the extent that fiscal consolidations have negative effects, these are traced to an inadequate strategy to consolidate: in particular, tax-based consolidations are seen as detrimental to growth, while growth is unaffected by spending-based consolidations.

From a growth-models perspective, fiscal and macroeconomic policies should be much less variant over time than the voter-driven perspective suggests. Specifically, fiscal austerity can be expected to change less with government ideology and voter attitudes and should primarily vary across countries that pursue distinct macroeconomic strategies. Largely, the main macroeconomic policies should be "locked in," either institutionally, ideationally, or politically. Institutionally, debt brakes, for instance, can ensure that governments of export-led countries do not deviate from the prescribed low-deficit policies. Ideationally, the public discourse can help to secure wider political support for the preferred policy by disseminating the economic arguments that motivate the country's growth model (Barnes and Hicks 2018; Ferrara et al. 2021). Politically, the influence of the growth coalition pushes political parties and governments toward the policy that is in line with the growth model (see esp. Chapters 1 and 15 in this volume, and Haffert and Mertens 2021). To the extent that policies vary over time, policy adjustments mostly follow the need of the particular growth models and vary less according to political ideology.[4]

This does not necessarily mean that ideology and government partisanship do not play any role at all. Instead, partisanship may matter most in countries with more balanced growth models, that is, in which both domestic and external demand equally contribute to economic growth, but it should matter less in countries with more unbalanced growth models. In export-led models, the dominant social interests are aligned in favor of fiscal austerity, which pushes both left and right governments in that direction. In demand-led models, social interests demand fiscal flexibility and oppose austerity, which again should be considered by both left and right governments. In mixed models, however, governments have greater political room to pursue distinct fiscal policies that vary according to their ideological viewpoints and the attitudes of their supporters.

What Do Voters Want? Beliefs about Austerity and Growth

Following the discussion in the previous section, we begin our empirical analysis with an analysis of voters (cf. Häusermann and Kriesi 2015). Specifically, we study the beliefs that they hold about the link between fiscal policy and economic growth. This allows us to explore to what extent these beliefs are consistent with the ideational narratives that accompanied fiscal consolidation measures taken by governments over the past decades. It also allows us to see how voter attitudes vary, both across countries and across subgroups of voters. We will then compare these attitudes with the actual behavior of governments, which we will analyze in the next section.

We conducted surveys in two countries—Germany and the United Kingdom—because they represent polar extremes in terms of their growth model (see Chapters 9 and 10 in this volume and section 4 of this chapter). The survey took the form of a vignette-based online experiment (Mutz 2011), which allows us to examine how respondents evaluate the government's fiscal strategy and its impact on economic growth. All respondents read about a situation in which their country experiences a situation of low growth and high fiscal deficit.

We then present two different scenarios how the government intends to address this situation. In both scenarios, the government aims at reducing the deficit and increasing growth albeit through fundamentally different mechanisms. Each mechanism corresponds to one of the different economic theories discussed in the previous section. In the first scenario, the government follows a Keynesian approach that highlights "fiscal multipliers": it proposes to increase public spending in order to stimulate growth, which should then lead to a lower fiscal deficit. In the second scenario, the government follows a non-Keynesian

Table 15.1 **Design of Experiment**

Introduction (shown to all respondents)		
The UK [German] economy has experienced slow economic growth for several years. At the same time, the UK [Germany] has experienced a sizable deficit in the public budget for several years. The UK's prime minister [German Chancellor] then announces in a televised speech how to deal with the situation.		
Group 1 (Control)	**Group 2 (Austerity)**	**Group 3 (Expansion)**
The prime minister says that despite this situation, the government will keep the current level of public spending on government programs, such as public infrastructure, healthcare, schools, and public pensions, unchanged.	The prime minister says that the government will cut public spending on government programs, such as public infrastructure, healthcare, schools, and public pensions, in order to reduce the public deficit. The prime minister says that the resulting reduction of the public deficit will also stimulate economic growth.	The prime minister says that that the government will increase public spending on government programs, such as public infrastructure, healthcare, schools, and public pensions, in order to stimulate economic growth. The prime minister says that the resulting increase in economic growth will also reduce the public deficit.

approach that highlights the possibility of "expansionary fiscal contractions": it proposes to cut public spending in order to reduce the deficit, which should then stimulate economic growth. The control group members read about a scenario, in which the government does not change fiscal policy. Respondents are randomly exposed to one out of these three scenarios and the difference in their responses toward the scenarios represent the political effect of one policy solution compared to another.[5] Table 15.1 shows the exact wording of each scenario.

After having been exposed to one of the scenarios just mentioned, the respondents answered a set of questions that are used as outcome variables in our analysis. More specifically, respondents were asked (1) to what extent they approve of the government's policy strategy, and (2) how, according to them, the decision will affect economic growth.[6] This allows us to examine to what extent respondent's assessment of fiscal policy is consistent with the economic ideas discussed before.

Figure 15.1 shows the mean values of all three treatment groups for the approval of each policy option with 95% confidence intervals. It becomes immediately clear that a decrease in spending is the least preferred option in both countries.[7] A decrease in spending is also significantly less popular than the status

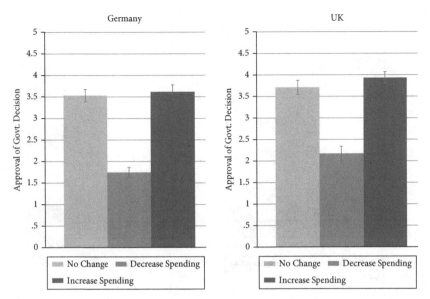

Figure 15.1 Approval of policy (approval varies between 1 and 5, with higher values indicating higher levels of approval)

quo with popular disagreement being stronger in Germany than in the United Kingdom. In both countries, an increase in spending is the most popular policy option. In the United Kingdom this policy option enjoys significantly more approval than the status quo, which is not the case in Germany. This finding could be interpreted as evidence that—on average—voters in Germany may be more critical of spending increases than voters in the United Kingdom, which is in line with our expectations for an export-led economy. However, these differences are small compared to the general disagreement with fiscal cuts in both countries.

We also examine voters' beliefs about the relationship between the different types of fiscal policies and economic growth. Figure 15.2 shows how respondents expect the economic performance of their country to change as a result of different fiscal policies. We find that an overwhelming majority of respondents believe that an increase in public spending will have a positive effect on economic growth. Specifically, the ratio of respondents who expect an increase in spending to have a positive effect ranges from 50% (in Germany) to 60% (in the United Kingdom). In contrast, only a relatively small faction of respondents (10% to 20%) think that austerity measures will have a positive effect on the economy. If voter preferences were in line with the country's growth model, we should find that German voters, on average, expect austerity to have a positive effect on economic growth and an increase in spending to be negatively associated with economic growth.

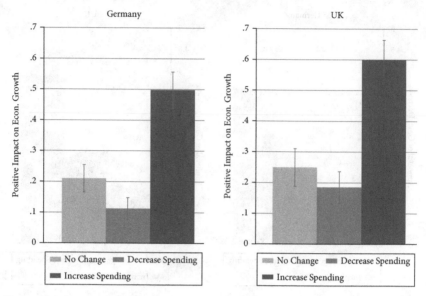

Figure 15.2 Expected impact of policy on economic growth

Finally, we examine how these evaluations differ with respondents' political ideology, notably their self-placement on the left-right axis. Figure 15.3 shows that in both countries the predicted level of approval for spending increases is high across the whole ideological spectrum, with the United Kingdom showing a slightly higher level of support for spending increases (across the ideological spectrum). Furthermore, support for increases in spending at the very left of the ideological spectrum is only slightly different from the level of support at the very right.

In contrast, approval of austerity varies greatly in the United Kingdom with the left being highly critical of austerity and the right showing a significantly higher level of approval. While the overall pattern in Germany is similar (in particular for approval of increases in spending), the level of support for austerity is approximately the same as in the United Kingdom at the left of the political spectrum but does not increase as much as it does in the United Kingdom when moving toward the right of the political spectrum. In fact, the level of approval of austerity at the left is only slightly different from the level of approval at the conservative end as indicated by the 95% confidence intervals.

We again perform the same analysis for the expected impact on economic growth in Figure A.1. More left voters expect that spending has a positive effect on economic growth than right voters. In the United Kingdom, there is a shared belief across the ideological spectrum that an increase in spending will have a positive effect on economic growth, while there is a clear divide across the

Approval of Government Policy (Treatment) (by Respondent' Ideology)

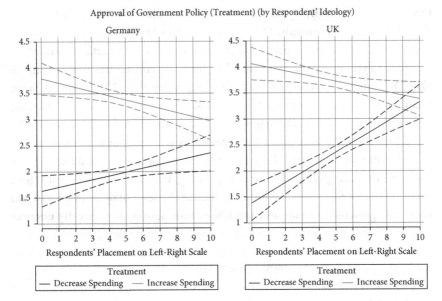

Figure 15.3 Predicted effect of spending increases (gray) and spending cuts (black) on policy approval as left-right position of voters' changes (with 95% confidence interval).

ideological spectrum when it comes to respondents' evaluation of the impact austerity. While the left expects that cuts have a negative impact on growth, voters on the right expect a more positive effect of austerity on growth.

The evidence on voter attitudes in this section suggests that voters are rather skeptical about the ideational narrative that has shaped the latest series of fiscal consolidation episodes. The beliefs of a majority of voters are not consistent with the economic arguments coined by economists and exponents from international organizations, which were overwhelmingly in favor of austerity policies (until the most recent past). While there is variation in the level of opposition toward austerity across the political spectrum, a majority of respondents find the Keynesian arguments about the connection between fiscal policy and economic growth more convincing. Furthermore, opposition to austerity is similar in countries following a demand-led as well as an export-led growth model.

What Do Governments Do? Patterns of Growth Models and Austerity

The previous section found that voters, on average, are quite critical of the idea that austerity will be good for economic performance. At the same time, there is a strong difference between left and right voters. In this section, we examine to what extent these diverging views translate into different fiscal policies under different party governments. Or whether fiscal austerity is in fact much more tied to systemic factors, in particular, the growth model of a particular country.

Our analysis uses data from the IMF on fiscal consolidation events in 16 OECD countries between 1978 and 2007 (Devries et al. 2011). This data set includes all political announcements of fiscal measures that aim at reducing the public deficit as reported in government documents and policy reports. The indicator reflects by how much these measures were supposed to improve the fiscal balance (as % of the GDP). As opposed to commonly used fiscal policy measures that are grounded in actual spending, this indicator does not reflect variation of macroeconomic indicators, such as the level of unemployment and economic growth. The indicator used, therefore, allows us to directly uncover political dynamics in fiscal consolidation and has become the standard indicator of fiscal consolidations in recent research (Alesina et al. 2015; Armingeon et al. 2016; Guajardo et al. 2014; Hübscher 2016).

To identify differences in growth models, we use an indicator by Baccaro and Neimanns (2021) that captures the contributions of exports and internal demand to aggregate growth of a country. Although we also look at export and demand contributions separately, we generally use the difference between export and demand contributions to growth because both dimensions are theoretically relevant for our purpose. A value around zero means that export and internal demand contributes about equally to growth, that is, the growth model is balanced. Negative (positive) values mean that internal demand (exports) contribute disproportionately to growth, that is, the growth model is more unbalanced. This indicator is available from 2000 onward. Since we want to examine cross-country differences, we use the mean of the indicator for each country between 2000 and 2007.

Figure 15.4 shows how austerity (left graph) and growth contributions (right graph) are distributed across countries. The figure reveals a number of insightful patterns that are consistent with the growth model perspective. First, the overall size of consolidation implemented in these countries varies significantly. It ranges from a total of 23% of GDP in Italy to just about 3% in France. If we only look at spending-based (as opposed to tax-based) consolidations, the Netherlands with fiscal cutbacks of more than 13% of its GDP is the biggest consolidator. France implemented the smallest spending cuts with a total of about 1% of its GDP. In other words, the cross-country variation in fiscal austerity is considerable. As we will show below, this variation can only partially be explained with core macroeconomic fundamentals, such as the state of public finances.

Second, and crucial for our purpose, the pattern of fiscal consolidations seems to be largely consistent with the growth models view. Among the countries with particularly low levels of austerity are the United States, the United

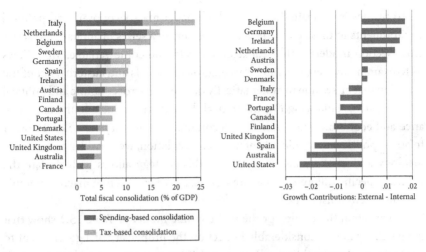

Figure 15.4 Austerity and growth contributions per country (until 2007)

Kingdom, and Australia, in which, according to the graph on the right in Figure 15.4, internal demand contributes much more to growth than exports. In contrast, countries, where export contribute most to economic growth, like Germany, Belgium, and the Netherlands, dominate the top of the austerity ranking. The differences in fiscal policy between these two groups are sizable. The total amount of consolidation by the export-led group is about two to three times the size of the amount by the demand-led group. A more systematic analysis of the bivariate relationship between growth contributions and austerity confirms this preliminary conclusion (see Appendix A.2 Available at www. thomassattler.org.). There is a clear correlation between growth contributions and total austerity. Most of this correlation is due to the relationship between export contributions and austerity, but the pattern between demand contributions and austerity also goes in the expected direction.

The question now arises to what extent these differences are related to varying macroeconomic fundamentals, especially fiscal deficits, and political circumstances, in particular government ideology, across countries. When zooming in on how austerity events are spread over time while also plotting information on a country's deficit, we find that austerity is only partially related to fiscal deficits. For instance, the United States and the United Kingdom refrained from implementing austerity even during periods of prolonged—and at times substantive—deficits. This pattern becomes more pronounced from the mid-1990s leading up to the "Great Recession."[8] Germany, and other more export-oriented countries, such as the Netherlands and Belgium, battled fiscal deficits much more proactively by implementing austerity measures or managed to run surpluses for a number of consecutive years, which rendered austerity unnecessary.

To further investigate the role of the broader macroeconomic and political environments in these countries, we also estimate a series of annual time-series cross-section models with fiscal austerity as the outcome variable. This allows us to examine the relationship between growth models and austerity, net of the variation that arises due to systematically different macroeconomic and political circumstances. Following our theoretical discussion, we include the fiscal balance and economic growth as macroeconomic explanatory variables. In order to assess political determinants of fiscal consolidation, we consider government ideology and institutional constraints.[9] This strategy allows us to isolate the country-specific differences that are not related to variation in macroeconomic or political circumstances.

As expected, the results for the first baseline model in Table 15.2 show that fiscal deficits have a considerable impact on the propensity of a government to implement austerity. Specifically, a one-unit increase in the fiscal balance (1% of GDP) leads to a decrease in consolidation activities of ca. 0.07% of GDP. Political and institutional factors do not have a significant impact on fiscal consolidation. While the sign on the coefficient on government partisanship goes into the expected direction (more conservative governments implement bigger consolidation packages), the coefficients are not robustly statistically significant.

Although the economic variables, especially the fiscal balance, have an important influence on fiscal consolidations, the baseline model with country-fixed effects show that a large part of the variation is country specific and unrelated to fundamental macroeconomic indicators. The explained variance in the specifications that include country dummies is more than twice as big than the explained variance in the specifications without. This confirms our expectation that countries vary in their fiscal strategy in a way that the standard economic and political variables do not capture.

We, therefore, re-examine to what extent the growth model of a country can explain the cross-country variation after having factored out the impact of macroeconomic fundamentals. In the model in column (3), we simply add the growth model variable, which has a statistically significant impact on austerity. The model in column (5) accounts for the multilevel nature of our data (Gelman and Hill 2007). It accounts for the fact that growth models are (almost) time invariant, whereas the control variables, like macroeconomic fundamentals, vary over time. We use a "partial pooling" approach, which fixes the coefficients on the time-varying variables but allows the intercept to vary with the growth strategy. The intercepts then represent the typical austerity level in a country per year when the control variables are at their means.[10]

Figure 15.5 shows how these country-specific austerity levels that we estimated from model (5) are related to the countries' growth strategies. The

Table 15.2 **Determinants of Fiscal Austerity**

	Baseline / OLS		Full / OLS		Full / Multilevel	
	(1)	*(2)*	*(3)*	*(4)*	*(5)*	*(6)*
GrowthContr(i)			5.105***		5.682*	
			(1.955)		(2.962)	
Abs(GrowthContr)(i)				–5.676		–5.539
				(5.141)		(6.270)
Ideology(i,t)	0.021	0.049***	0.029*	0.124***	0.037**	0.126***
	(0.015)	(0.018)	(0.016)	(0.037)	(0.018)	(0.043)
Abs(GrowthContr) (i)*Ideology(i,t)				–7.155***		–7.132**
				(2.039)		(2.948)
Constraints(i,t)	0.203	–0.915*	0.102	0.379	–0.126	0.189
	(0.224)	(0.477)	(0.230)	(0.244)	(0.291)	(0.284)
Deficit(i,t-1)	–0.069***	–0.083***	–0.068***	–0.067***	–0.075***	–0.073***
	(0.010)	(0.011)	(0.010)	(0.010)	(0.008)	(0.008)
Growth(i,t-1)	–0.037***	–0.028*	–0.037***	–0.035**	–0.033**	–0.032**
	(0.014)	(0.015)	(0.014)	(0.014)	(0.014)	(0.014)
Constant	0.311***		0.326***	0.397***	0.325***	0.391***
	(0.026)		(0.028)	(0.077)	(0.040)	(0.084)
Fixed/Random effects	—	FE	—	—	RE	RE
Sd(Cons)	—	—	—	—	0.11	0.09
Sd(Ideo)	—	—	—	—	—	0.04
Corr(Cons, Ideo)	—	—	—	—	—	-0.09
p	0.000	0.000	0.000	0.000	0.000	0.000
R2	0.20	0.41	0.21	0.22	—	—
N	477	477	477	477	477	477

Robust standard errors in parentheses. *** $p < 0.01$, ** $p < 0.05$, * $p < 0.1$.

empirical relationship is clear: the more important external demand is for growth, the more austerity a country implements (up to a maximum of 0.5% of GDP per year). Vice versa, the more important internal demand is for growth, the less austerity a country implements (with a minimum of slightly more than 0.1% of GDP per year).[11]

Finally, we re-examine the role of partisanship through the growth models perspective. As discussed in section 2, partisanship should only matter in countries with more balanced growth models and not in those with unbalanced

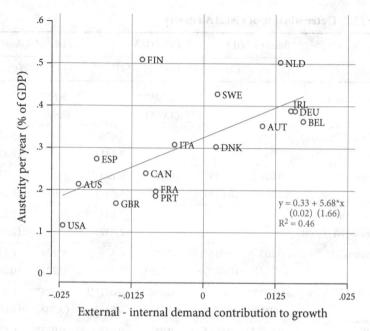

Figure 15.5 Estimated relationship between growth contributions and austerity (based on model (5) in Table 1)

ones. This requires a revised empirical specification, which we present in columns (4) and (6) of Table 15.2. In these specifications, we interact the partisanship variable with the absolute value of the difference between external and internal demand contributions. The latter variable reflects to what extent exports or internal demand contribute disproportionately to growth: if the variable is zero, then the growth contributions of exports and internal demand are equal, that is, the model is balanced; if it is positive, then the growth contribution of either exports or internal demand dominate, that is, the model is unbalanced.

To simplify the interpretation of the interaction, we compute the marginal effects of government ideology based on model (4) in Table 15.2 and plot them in Figure 15.6.[12] The blue line represents how the impact of ideology on austerity changes when the growth model becomes more unbalanced. The gray bars represent how countries are distributed along the scale of the moderating variable. As we can infer from the figure, ideology has a very strong and statistically significant impact in balanced growth models. In the most balanced model, a change from a typical center-left government to a typical center-right government increases the expected austerity level per year by 0.32% of GDP.[13] This effect decreases and becomes statistically insignificant when the growth model becomes more unbalanced.[14]

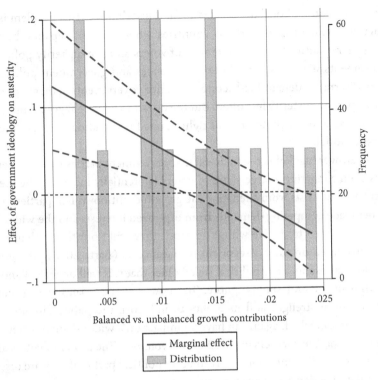

Figure 15.6 Effect of ideology across different growth models (with 95% confidence intervals)

When we tie these findings back to our analysis of voter preferences in the previous section, we can conclude that the voter-driven perspective seems to work better in balanced models, but not at the unbalanced "extremes" on the continuum of available growth strategies. In the balanced models, party governments implement distinct fiscal policies in line with the diverging demands from their leftist or rightist voter base. In the unbalanced models, dominated by a demand-led or an export-led economy, this link between voter preferences and government ideology is broken.

Reconciling Micro and Macro—Or Why Do Governments Ignore Voters?

The results from the previous two sections raise the question why governments in important cases seemingly ignore voters and implement policies that are at odds with the attitudes of a majority of voters and the government party's own constituencies. Ultimately, nonobservance of voters can be politically risky and create political dissatisfaction and instabilities. This problem is particularly prevalent in export-led countries where the discrepancy between anti-austerity attitudes of the majority of voters and pro-austerity policies by governments is most severe. Voter preferences and government policies are less in disarray in demand-led economies since governments in these countries tend to pursue austerity less often. But the question why right governments are unresponsive to the preference of right voters for spending cuts also prevails in these models.

Our answer highlights the trade-off that government parties face between the costs from alienating a large share of voters (potentially including the median voter) and the costs from alienating the growth coalition. When parties in government face competing demands from organized interests and the wider electorate, they need to decide whose demands they will prioritize in their policy decisions based on their assessment of these costs (Barta 2018). The growth coalition represents a key political stakeholder that it is well organized and that governments cannot simply ignore. The power of this coalition is grounded in its financial strength and its ability to influence the public discourse and public opinion, which again can have an impact on a wider share of voters (see Chapter 1 and the chapters in part 2 of this volume). The power of voters arises from the threat that they will resort to other political parties if they are dissatisfied with the policy of the government party.

For a long time, parties seemed to perceive the costs of alienating voters as the lesser of two evils. In fact, the convergence of the main political parties on a similar economic agenda in many political systems itself helped to contain these costs because it limited the options that were available for alienated voters. Most mainstream parties eventually began to prioritize the interests of the growth coalition and to converge on pro-market policies throughout the postwar period, which led to an overall decline in political competition (Baccaro and Howell 2017; Lynch 2019; Przeworski 2019). A prominent example of this process is the development of "Third Way" politics, an attempt of the left to overcome their traditional alliances in order to reform the economy while embracing neoliberal ideas (Bremer and McDaniel 2020). This development prepared the ground for the austerity narrative that emphasized the importance of balanced budgets, the importance of a lean state, and the abandonment of countercyclical public spending.

This mainstream party convergence initiated a process of dealignment between voters and established parties, but this development was slow moving and not seen as a problem that parties need to address urgently. In particular the growing distance between political parties and their constituents, or the cartelization of political parties (Katz and Mair 1995, 2009), resulted in an alienation of voters from their parties and a further push of parties toward organized interests and the state. As a consequence, a slow but steady decline in votes and an increase in swing voters rendered the supporter base of mainstream parties less stable over the years.[15] Both trends can be interpreted as a latent withdrawal of voter support from the political-economic model by parts of the electorate. Nonetheless, political parties actively pursued this mutual process of dealignment in order to uphold the macroeconomic policies prescribed by the growth model. For a long time, this development was not perceived as problematic because in most countries the established parties shared government responsibility and were the only ones who had a realistic chance to participate in government, which limited political competition from other parties.

Only the financial crisis and the following Great Recession generated new political dynamics that put this political-economic equilibrium to a test. The Great Recession disrupted the complacent policy community and also served as a trigger for disenchanted citizens to mobilize against their government and for new parties to be established. The majority of these newly established parties and movements took a decidedly anti-austerity and/or antiestablishment stance and managed to stir up the party landscape in a number of countries.[16] Other parties, which already existed for a longer time, gained more prominence again in the wake of the financial crisis and were able to present themselves as viable alternatives to mainstream parties.[17]

Conclusion

We draw three main conclusions from this analysis. First, austerity policies vary greatly across countries and in line with a country's growth model. Countries that pursue export-led models are much more likely to implement austerity than those that are more demand-led, even if we account for macroeconomic and political circumstances. Second, fiscal policies vary along ideological preferences of government parties only in balanced, but not in unbalanced growth models. Together, these results suggest that governments subordinate fiscal policy to the greater macroeconomic strategy, which is specific to their country and which is unrelated to objective macroeconomic factors. Moreover, this fiscal strategy seems to be part of a broader political consensus among political elites that cuts across political parties on the left and the right in many countries.

The mismatch between government policy and voters' fiscal policy views that our analysis uncovers has important political implications. In the short and medium terms, governments may be able to sell austerity to their electorates by highlighting the potential positive effects of deficit reduction (Barnes and Hicks 2018). The political discourse plays an important role: voters are more likely to support austerity if they are consistently exposed to arguments highlighting the benefits of these policies (Ferrara et al. 2021). In the long term, however, these policies need to have the alleged, desired effect and generate economic growth in order to secure political support from voters. If this is not the case, like in Italy, for example, it is likely that political back-lash follows. Germany, the country whose economic success heavily relies on export, also experiences significant changes of its political landscape. The combined vote shares the two: mainstream center-left and center-right have lost between 1990 and 2016 amounts to roughly 23% (SPD: -13% / CDU: -10%). A significant share of people previously voting for either of these parties now support challenger parties, such as *Die Linke*, the *Green Party* or the *AfD*, all of which call for changes (though different in nature) of macroeconomic policies.

There is an increasing amount of evidence that this is in fact the case in a broad range of countries. In Britain, for instance, the rising popularity of UKIP has been linked to the austerity policies of the past decade (Fetzer 2019). More broadly, austerity has detrimental effects on party systems and increases political polarization when mainstream parties converge on a policy of fiscal restraint (Hübscher et al. 2019). The transformation of party systems and the rise of populism in many countries, therefore, can be directly traced to the spread of neoliberal economic policies and the adverse economic effects of these policies on many voters (Hopkin 2020; Hopkin and Blyth 2019). With the spread of austerity to consumption-led and mixed economies during and after the Great Recession, public discontent with economic policymaking is likely to rise further. These ongoing developments are likely to complicate the formation of stable government coalitions needed to produce sustainable policy outputs.

Notes

1. Of course, exceptions in peculiar circumstances are possible. For instance, many Eastern European citizens accepted austerity in order to avoid currency devaluations, which would have increased their foreign currency denominated debt (Walter 2015).
2. There is a tendency toward more austerity by right governments, but this result depends on model specification and is not robust. There is also evidence that austerity packages by left governments are somewhat smaller, but these differences are small compared to differences in attitudes between left and right voters.
3. In the language of the previous view, this means that the "fiscal multiplier" is small or even reverse.

4. Accordingly, macroeconomic outcomes that are central to growth models, notably current accounts, are highly persistent and vary mostly across countries. This cross-country variation in current accounts and trade balances is much more significant than the within-country variation over time (Manger and Sattler 2020).

5. The fielding phase of the survey has been administered by *respondi*. For each country we have a total of roughly 1.200 respondents (stratified by age cohorts and gender). The survey has been in the field between August 2 and August 9, 2019.

6. The exact wording of the questions is the following: "To what extent do you approve the Prime Minister's announcement?," answer categories varied between 1 (strongly disapprove) to 5 (strongly approve); "How do you think this decision will affect the growth of the British [German] economy?," with answer categories varying between "negatively," "neither/nor," and "positively."

7. Assessing the impact of our policy treatments on a third outcome variable (whether respondents would vote for the prime minister after a given treatment) reveals the same results, the proportion of respondents who would vote for the incumbent is as low as 10% for Germany and roughly 25% for the United Kingdom.

8. This coincides with the period that Baccaro and Pontusson (2016) defines as a turning point, from 1993 up to the Great Recession.

9. The variables measuring fiscal deficits and growth are taken from the Comparative Institutional Dataset by Armingeon et al. Government ideology is operationalized as the government parties' position on the ideological left-right axis from the Comparative Manifestos Dataset (Volkens et al. 2013) weighted by its vote share. Lower values on the ideology variable signify a more leftist government. In order to control for institutional constraints we use Henisz's (2004) index of political constraints, which measures to what extent a government is constrained to implement its agenda. A higher level of political constraints implies that the government is meeting a veto point, that is, in the form of a different majority in the upper chamber.

10. This interpretation requires that we center the control variables at their means.

11. Finland deviates from this pattern due to extensive austerity measures in 1993/1994 in the wake of the EMS crisis and the resulting economic crisis. Apart from this peculiar episode, Finland did not implement any austerity

12. The government ideology variable varies from -5 to +5, with a higher number indicating more right governments.

13. We define a typical center-left (right) government as one that is one standard deviation, that is, 1.67 points, below (above) the mean.

14. In additional analyses, we disentangled the moderating effects of export-led from the effect of demand-led models. In line with our expectation, we find that in demand-led models, the partisanship effect works mostly through the behavior of right governments: right governments increasingly pursue austerity, while left governments continue to avoid austerity, when a heavily demand-led model becomes more balanced. In contrast, the partisanship effect mostly works through the behavior of left governments in export-led models: left governments become less austere, while right governments continue to pursue austerity, when a heavily export-led model becomes more balanced.

15. Average turnout at general elections in Western democracies declined from roughly 82.5% in 1980 to just about slightly more than 70% in 2016 (see Hübscher et al. 2019). This figure includes countries in which turnout hardly changed, such as Belgium, to countries, in which turnout declined dramatically. That is, Austria experienced a decline in turnout from 92% in 1979 to 75.6% in 2019. In Germany, turnout dropped from roughly 90% in 1980 to 70.8% in 2009 and increased to slightly over 76% in 2016. The recovery in turnout was largely due to citizens who were politically inactive and voted AfD in 2016.

16. Among the more prominent parties/movements founded after the financial crisis are *Podemos, Syriza, M5S*, and la *France Insoumise*.

17. Examples of parties in this category are *Die Linke* or *Lega*.

16

Welfare States and Growth Models: Accumulation and Legitimation

JULIA LYNCH AND SARA WATSON

Introduction

The standard models used in comparative political economy—be they varieties of capitalism or worlds of welfare—have their intellectual roots in the *Trente Glorieuses* of booming postwar growth. But the exhaustion of Fordist growth models (GMs), accelerating de-industrialization, the concomitant rise of service economies across the advanced industrial countries have challenged existing understandings of relatively stable capitalist relations.

The GMs approach elaborated in this volume offers a fresh perspective on the dynamics of change in the post-Fordist era. Its understanding of contemporary capitalism differs both from interpretations of post-Fordism as embodying a monolithic model of neoliberal capitalism (Fraser 2015), and also from dominant understandings of the relative stability of capitalist social relations (Hall and Soskice 2001). The GM perspective represents an important theoretical advance in that it sheds the equilibrium bias inherent in much political economy theorizing over the past 30 years. It decenters questions of coordination and path dependence, and instead returns us to an older critical tradition in political economy concerned with the demand side of political economies, and the conflicts inherent in capitalist development.

The GM perspective retains a focus on *varieties* of capitalism by identifying multiple solutions to the common problem of how countries manage the transition from wage-led growth—without, however, endorsing a strict typology of national approaches. Nevertheless, it does identify clusters of countries that roughly adhere to various strategies ("models") of post-Fordist capitalist development—for example, export-led, consumption-led, balanced, and failed GMs—each of which carries distinctive implications for patterns of inequality.

This chapter contributes to the broader intellectual GM project by asking how the welfare state (WS) shapes the politics of several of the main GMs. We take as our starting point classic arguments about the accumulation and legitimation problems that beset capitalist democracies and that WSs may—though need not—help resolve (Habermas 1973; O'Connor 1973; Offe 1984; Streeck 2014a). Growth is an imperative for elites because in democracies economic stagnation makes it difficult secure a winning political coalition. We ask how political and economic elites may use the WS in the pursuit of growth and political acquiescence; and which strategies are more or less successful.

Much of the emerging literature on how the WS supports GMs presumes a functional fit between welfare policies and the growth of specific sectors. For example, Thelen (2019) notes reforms to higher education in Scandinavia supported the shift to an export sector dominated by high-end ICT services; while Hassel and Palier (2021a) link the residualization of the US WS to the financialization of the economy. While economically functional linkages in particular areas are undoubtedly relevant, questions relating to the political and ideational uses of social policy are equally important. WSs may support GMs by being economically functional—but they can also serve to cement social groups with disparate interests into political coalitions, and even structure what citizens imagine to be a just social order. Attention to both economic and explicitly political dynamics should thus be a central part of any effort to understand whether and how WSs support emergent GMs.

In this chapter we examine what role WSs may play in supporting post-Fordist GMs, both economically and politically. The analysis proceeds in three steps. We begin with the economics of accumulation. After a brief discussion of some of the main GMs—those identified in Baccaro and Pontusson (2016)— and their dominant growth coalitions, we derive a series of baseline expectations about the economic functions of WSs in each of these types of GM. Part two explores the predictive power of this framework with respect to specific instances of welfare reform in four countries since the 1990s. We examine reform episodes in four major domains of social policy (unemployment protection, old-age pensions, disability insurance, housing, and family policy) in four countries (Sweden, Germany, the United Kingdom, and Italy). These cases mirror the four different growth models discussed in Baccaro and Pontusson (2016), and also represent the four major worlds of welfare (social democratic, Conservative-corporatist, liberal, and southern European) (Esping-Andersen 1990a; Ferrera 1996). We evaluate the degree to which reforms in the policy areas in question represented solutions to specific accumulation barriers associated with the GM that each of the countries most resembles (export-led, consumption-led, balanced, and failed). These empirical vignettes suggest that while WSs have an important function in enabling an economic consensus around distinctive GMs, reforms in particular policy areas are often concerned with strategies of political legiti-mation, rather than merely with questions of economic accumulation. The final section of the chapter elaborates conceptually five possible pathways through which social policy might encourage the political legitimation of GMs. We con-clude with reflections on the politics of legitimation in an era of mass politics.

The Accumulation Dimension: Linking Post-Fordist Welfare States and Accumulation

The claim that WSs can serve as instruments to regulate and maintain capi-talist growth has a long history in comparative political economy. For example, O'Connor argued in *The Fiscal Crisis of the State* (1973) that capitalist states used social policy to promote two aims—capital accumulation and the legitimation of capitalist social relations—that were often contradictory. O'Connor's early insight was echoed, albeit in a less direct manner, by authors in the French reg-ulation school, who called attention to how different regimes of capitalist ac-cumulation were buttressed by distinct modes of social regulation and political settlements (Boyer 1990; Lipietz 1997).

But how might WSs operate to solve the particular obstacles to accumula-tion in the post-Fordist GMs identified in this volume? At the core of arguments about the role of the WS and capitalist accumulation is the idea that employers may support social policies that enhance investment stability, firm profitability, and/or labor productivity. In order to embed this general insight temporally and spatially, we first identify the actors and sectors that make up the dominant po-litical coalition in the main GMs discussed in this book, and then derive a set of social policy preferences that are likely to conform to the economic interests of that GM's particular dominant coalition.

The GM approach is an effort to theorize the dynamics of capitalist devel-opment when the relationship between productivity growth and rising wage shares—characteristics of the "Golden Age" of Fordism, widespread collective bargaining and the Keynesian WS—has come uncoupled, risking insufficient aggregate demand to ensure economic growth or political stability. The GM par-adigm argues that advanced capitalist political economies have not responded to the insufficiency of aggregate demand in a uniform fashion. Instead, it identifies a diversity of contemporary GMs, which are not mutually exclusive.

Consumption-led GMs are similar in some ways to Fordist wage-led GMs, but access to consumer credit replaces real wage growth as the main driver of ag-gregate consumption. Export-led GMs, on in contrast, are characterized by the promotion of exports and the repression of household consumption. They may also be characterized by dualization, as core workers in manufacturing see their wages rise in line with national productivity increases while low-end service-sector workers see flat to declining wages. There is also the potential for balanced GMs that mix wage growth with elements of consumer credit and export orientation, as well as for economic models that simply fail to stimulate growth by any means. Who are the key members of the political coalition that support each GM, and what are their primary goals? Who are the "losers"—that is, those groups excluded from the dominant coalition? And what would a WS that promotes the interests of the dominant social coalition for each GM look like?

The GM perspective is inspired by, but not beholden to, the Gramscian concept of hegemonic social blocs. The group of actors that pushes for a particular GM is termed the dominant growth coalition. Growth coalitions are often cross-class coalitions, but not coalitions among equals. Instead, the owners and managers of large companies in key economic sectors occupy a privileged position within the coalition. Other members of the growth coalition—for example, the types of workers whose labor generates the highest returns—may benefit from the GM in some ways but are also likely to be affected negatively by other dimensions.

In order to think about how social policy might reinforce (or not) a given GM, we need to clearly identify who is within and who is outside of a dominant coalition, and why. Here, we briefly distinguish between the "core" members of the coalition—those whose interests are directly benefited by the GM—and those who are less clearly advantaged, or even disadvantaged, by the GM. We then generate a set of propositions, summarized in Table 16.1, about how WSs may help support a given GM, based on how welfare policies affect these different groups.

The dominant partner in the credit-fueled *consumption-led GM's* growth coalition is the financial sector, which profits from the expansion of household and consumer debt. The central economic goal of actors in this sector is to maintain consumer demand for easy access to credit. It is harder to identify who is left out of the dominant growth coalition in this GM since, economically, nearly everyone benefits (at least in the short term) from rising consumption enabled by becoming financial-sector "adjacent" (van der Zwan 2014). Nevertheless, this GM generates inequality due to high incomes in the finance sector and housing-generated wealth, and lower income earners and those in areas with stagnant home prices may come to see themselves as excluded.

In a consumption-led GM, then, an economically functional WS would likely involve interventions to promote (debt-fueled) domestic consumption and investment and protect the finance sector. Low tax rates on high incomes, especially in the finance sector, militate for a residual WS—which also benefits the GM by reducing the ability of workers in other sectors to maintain consumption without recourse to credit. A return to the principle of "less eligibility" and

Table 16.1 **Welfare Policies and Economic Accumulation in Different GMs**

Consumption-Led Growth	*Export-Led GM*
Dominant Growth Coalition: Finance sector; middle-class homeowners	**Dominant Growth Coalition:** Export Sector
Economically functional social policy: Reduction in social protection to support credit-based consumption	**Economically functional social policy:** Dualization of social protection to support export competitiveness
Balanced GM	*Failed GM*
Dominant Growth Coalition(s): Export sector employers and unions; domestic service-sector unions; middle-class homeowners	**Dominant Growth Coalition:** None (unstable coalition)
Economically functional social policy: Support export-led and wage-led growth (plus debt-financed consumption)	**Economically functional social policy:** NA

a shift from passive benefits to "activation" policies serve the dual function of restricting wages to promote debt-financed consumption, and of assuring profits for the employers in other sectors who are "junior partners" in the coalition.

The *export-led* GM's dominant coalition is simpler to identify. Export-oriented manufacturers are the senior partner, while employees in this sector are the junior partner. The economic goals of this coalition are to moderate growth in real wages and suppress domestic consumption, in order to ensure export competitiveness in global markets. The core groups whose interests are opposed are low-wage service-sector workers and labor market "outsiders," who are both markedly disadvantaged in this GM.

The key economic concern in the export-led GM is to suppress wages, but without demoralizing skilled workers in the export sector. A functional WS would thus be a dualized one. Favored workers in the export sector might receive various forms of deferred compensation in return for wage restraint and the smooth functioning of collective bargaining; investments in human capital such as vocational training and subsidized education would benefit employers in the export sector. Meanwhile, in order to sustain the purchasing power of export workers domestically in the face of wage moderation, social policies in this model might encourage lower wages in the domestic service sector through activation policies aimed at making work pay, and a low minimum wage. In an export-led GM, we might also expect pressure to minimize reliance on payroll taxes to finance benefits, in order to reduce the fiscal wedge on employers.

The dominant coalitions in the remaining two categories of balanced growth and failed growth are somewhat different. In the *balanced* GM, which mixes growth through exports with some degree of wage- and debt-led consumption growth, the dominant coalition is catch-all, composed of employers and unions in the export sector, sheltered-sector unions, the banking industry and middle-class homeowners.[1] Theorizing the ideal social policy cluster for the balanced GMs is somewhat complicated, as the dominant growth coalition is large and varied. On the one hand, the export sector—which in Scandinavia at least involved the shift to a knowledge-intensive service sector—might be expected to support a strategy of flexicurity, to support human capital investment, labor market flexibility, and (perhaps) financialization in order to support innovation. Nevertheless, although unions representing low-skilled service workers may be supportive of the shift toward flexicurity, they may also continue to support traditional social programs that shore up consumption.

Finally, a distinguishing characteristic of the *failed* GM is the absence of a dominant growth coalition. Since there is no stable coalition, there is also no obviously preferred social policy model. One outcome could be a WS that preserves growth-inhibiting rigidities that benefit labor market "insiders" but do not bolster consumption by labor market outsiders; another could be austerity policies that lower both consumption and investment in human capital. In both scenarios, social policy may in fact block growth by discouraging export competitiveness without promoting consumption.

Welfare Reform and GMs: From Accumulation to Legitimation

Having deductively theorized a set of WS policies that are economically functional in different types of GMs, we now turn to a series of brief empirical studies of welfare reforms since the 1990s. Each case vignette asks whether the process of reform in that policy area is consistent with attempts to ensure economic accumulation and/or political legitimation in post-Fordist GMs. To preview, we find that when welfare reforms are undertaken mainly to ensure the success of a GM (which is not always the case), they are just as often informed by attempts to politically legitimate the GM as by a drive to enable accumulation beneficial to the dominant growth coalition.

We consider four countries associated with different types of GMs—export-led (Germany), debt-led (United Kingdom), balanced (Sweden), and failed (Italy)—and examine recent reforms to some of the main social insurance programs of mature WSs. In Germany we consider efforts to activate the unemployed; in the UK activation of the disabled; in Sweden, pension reform; and in Italy, family policy. Our focus on single social policy areas, rather than examining the entire panoply of policies associated with a given county's model of welfare capitalism (including labor market regulation and fiscal policy), is entirely pragmatic. Future research should examine all of these policy areas (and more) across a full range of WSs and GMs, to harness the leverage allowed by robust cross-national comparison—and some recent studies have already examined the relationship between GMs and WSs comparatively in areas such as housing and youth activation (see, e.g., Chevalier 2021; Reisenbichler and Wiedemann 2022). The present analysis has a more limited aim: to probe how episodes of WS reform may illuminate the possible tensions between accumulation, legitimation and democracy in several GMs.[2] Nevertheless, our choice of policy areas and countries is not random. The range of policy areas we selected allow us to probe a range of WS functions that affect men and women across the entire life course. And in each case, the reforms we examine were highly salient in the country in question, making them "most likely" cases in which to observe accumulation dynamics at play.

The Activation of the Unemployed in Germany's Export-Led Model

Germany is the archetypical export-led GM, in which wage repression enables a price-sensitive export sector to thrive. Industrial relations liberalization has done much to support accumulation in this GM (Baccaro and Benassi 2017), but welfare reform aimed at activating the unemployed also played an important role in mediating the shift from the Fordist to the export-led GM. Although Germany is now viewed as an economic powerhouse, this was not the case in the early 2000s. German reunification, which involved the merging of two very different economies, was costly. Between 1991 and 2003 German GDP grew by only 18%, half the growth rate of the United Kingdom or the Netherlands during that same period. Low growth rates went hand in hand with low employment creation and rising unemployment rates: nearly 10% in the West and 18% in the East (Jacobi and Kluve 2006).

At the turn of the 21st century, unemployment benefits in Germany still reflected Bismarckian commitments, with transfers linked to previous earnings designed to maintain workers' social status and firms' investments in training during spells of unemployment. Unemployment benefit payments were unlimited in duration, and replacement rates for the long-term unemployed were higher than in any other OECD country (OECD 2004). This system, once viewed as appropriate, came under fire starting in the late 1990s for undermining work incentives. Many voters in the former West German Länder, who increasingly viewed the social insurance system as a transfer from West to East, became especially hostile to generous benefits (Rehm 2016, 148).

After a series of failed efforts by the social partners to negotiate a solution to persistently high unemployment, the government of social democratic Gerhart Schröder imposed a reform package, known as the Hartz Reforms, aimed at fostering labor demand by activating the unemployed. The duration of unemployment benefits was shortened from 32 to 12 months (up to 24 months for older workers), and work conditionality tightened. Another dimension of the Hartz reform deregulated temporary employment by raising the wage ceiling on part-time jobs eligible for tax and social security exemptions (Weinkopf 2009). After 2003, Germany saw an explosion of low-paying part-time employment (mini-jobs) made possible by Hartz II and the absence of a national minimum wage before 2015 (Jacobi and Kluve 2006).

Taken together, these activating reforms to Germany's system of unemployment protection had important consequences for its shift to, and then maintenance of, an export-led GM. The reforms worked both economically and politically. Wage moderation, driven by bargaining decentralization and concessionary bargaining, improved the competitiveness of Germany's tradables sector. But the Hartz II reforms were also essential in facilitating the political stability of the GM. Mini-jobs, in particular, provided a workaround for stagnant wages for low-income households. Carillo-Tudeolo et al. (2018), for example, show that individuals directly affected by wage moderation (both skilled tradables workers and their low-skilled wives) were more likely to take on a second mini-job. The growth of mini-jobs, then, politically stabilized the German GM by providing low-wage workers with a mechanism for complementing their otherwise stagnant-to-declining household income without threatening the competitiveness of Germany's price-sensitive export sector. This aspect of the Hartz eforms, rather than directly contributing to stable accumulation, arguably played an important legitimation role by managing the economic dysfunction emerging from Germany's emergent GM.

Disability Activation in the UK's Debt-Led Model

If Germany is the archetype of the export-led GM, the UK exemplifies credit-fueled consumption-led growth. In this case study we analyze another effort at activation via social policy, one aimed at the disabled rather than the unemployed. An analysis of activation in disability policy is relevant to the study of accumulation dynamics in GMs because, prior to the wave of welfare reforms beginning in the 1990s, in many countries disability benefits effectively served a dual purpose, providing support not only for the disabled but also for the long-term unemployed (Burkhauser, Daly, and Ziebarth 2016).

In early postwar Britain, state support for the disabled was relatively limited and often took the form of institutional care. This began to change in the 1970s, when cash support programs were introduced. By the 1990s, the two main policies providing support to the disabled were Incapacity Benefit (IB) and the Disability Living Allowance (DLA) (Royston 2017; Spicker 2011). IB was a contributory benefit mainly for persons with occupational injuries, while DLA provided cash assistance for those requiring regular adult supervision and care with bodily function.

In 1997, Tony Blair's New Labour government initiated a broad set of "New Deal" reforms representing an important philosophical shift in policy. Rather than the prior rights-based approach to welfare policy, Blair's reforms were premised on the assumption that paid employment was the best way out of poverty, and used a series of supply-side programs to activate people outside the labor market. This work-based, conditional approach to welfare was applied broadly: to the unemployed, single mothers and the disabled (Watson 2015a).

The proximate cause for the disability reforms undertaken by the Blair government was the persistent rise in disability rolls, even as overall health levels were improving. In 1997, nearly 2.3 million working-age individuals were receiving sickness and/or disability benefits, and benefit duration on IB in particular was creeping upward (Considine et al. 2015, 72–73; McVicar 2008). Discursively, the Labour government painted IB as contributing to a "dependency culture," pushing the disabled into idleness through the very structure of the benefit (Grover and Piggott 2007). It was this alleged culture of dependency that the reform aimed to change.

In theory, reforms to disability benefits in the Blair era involved *personalized* conditionality, but overall the approach to activation was one of "labor market attachment" (with a focus on rapid re-entry into work) rather than a "human resources approach" (focusing on claimants' resources) (Dwyer, McNeill, and Scullion 2014; Nybom 2011). After a Work Capability Assessment (WCA), the disabled were divided into three groups, depending on their distance from work. Those whom caseworkers determined not to have an employment-limiting disability were placed onto unemployment benefit, which had very stringent work-search expectations. Those with a disability that limited their work activity were placed into either a "Support Group" or a "Work Related Activity Group." These latter beneficiaries were expected to attend regular meetings with a personal adviser to discuss work readiness. Benefit levels were periodically reduced if a claimant did not meet their required responsibilities without good reason.

Work-search requirements operated in conjunction with the Employment and Support Allowance (ESA), which in 2007 replaced the existing IB, and substantially reduced benefits for younger recipients and for couples (Piggott and Grover 2009).[3]

While the Blair government worked to activate the disabled through the imposition of work-related conditionality, the Tory-Liberal Democratic coalition government elected in 2010 went one step further, combining conditionality with austerity. The government continued Blair-era efforts to reduce the disability employment gap by expanding the number of people with disabilities subject to its work assessments and instituting gradual benefit cuts, equalizing the monthly benefit paid to unemployed and disabled people; and replacing the DLA (aimed at those with caring needs) with the Personal Independence Payment, in which eligibility was determined according to the impact of the condition on a claimant's ability to engage in paid work, rather than on the nature of their condition.[4]

At the same time, the government imposed cuts on local government, which were responsible for providing social care for disabled children and adults (Saffer, Nolte, and Duffy 2018); and ended supports for high-needs disabled people in England and Wales (Machin 2017). Taken together, the combination of more stringent work assessments and cuts to disability benefits, in the context of broader austerity cuts to other benefits (e.g., to housing benefits, or the creation of a benefit cap), meant that welfare reform since 2010 disproportionally affected people with disabilities (Butler 2016).

What does the experience of welfare reforms affecting people with disabilities in the United Kingdom tell us about the role of welfare politics in the consumption-led GM? To the degree that reforms to disability policy in the United Kingdom have focused on re-commodifying workers with long-term health problems, we have a story that is broadly consistent with the GMs' logic. In disability policy, just as in unemployment policy, the consequences of reforms have been to remove and demean alternatives to low-wage work, encouraging the financing of consumption via debt.

At the same time, the components of the reform imposing work requirements and austerity on the truly disabled suggest that activation was also, at least in part, a top-down ideological project aimed more at legitimation than at solving any clear obstacle to accumulation in the British economy. There is little evidence, for example, that activation of people with disabilities was a key priority of employers or of other private-sector members of the growth coalition. Indeed, Damien Green, head of Department of Works and Pension, in 2016 spoke of the importance of *changing* the mindset of businesses: "We want them to realise that there's a huge pool of talented people who are disabled and want to work and can contribute fully in the workplace" (BBC 2016). Similarly, the language of "supports" used in the British version of activation arguably served as a useful discursive strategy to justify the bitter pill of austerity, deflecting attention from the fact that any supports offered to claimants were largely secondary to organizational pressure to push recipients off benefits (Gingrich and Watson 2016).

Given that both Germany and the UK embraced major reforms organized around the concept of activation, it is worth reflecting on their experiences in tandem. At a general level, of course, activating reforms in both countries worked to recommodify labor through a combination of 'Fordern und Fördern'— demanding and enabling elements (Eichhorst, Grienberger-Zingerle, and Konle-Seidl 2008). Nevertheless, the approaches of the two countries toward activation were rather different, with Germany investing substantially in 'enabling' elements such as work-based retraining while Britain privileged rapid job entry. This may be partially explained by the different constraints imposed by the twin demands of accumulation and legitimation in these specific political economies. In Germany's export-led growth model, both the need for labor productivity and the need to buy the consent of workers in the tradeables sector pushed in the direction of 'enabling' activation strategies; while in the UK's debt-fueled consumption model, where neither workers' productivity nor their acquiescence to sub-standard market wages were necessary to sustain the dominant growth coalition's hold on power, principles of 'less eligibility' drove activation policies.

Pension Reform in Sweden's Balanced Model

Within the GM paradigm, Sweden is often held up as a model of balanced growth, combining domestic and export-driven components of growth and consumption. Sweden has maintained a competitive export sector in the post-Fordist era, in part by moving into high-end ICT services, but export competitiveness did not come at the expense of suppressing domestic demand. Much of the existing GM analysis of the Swedish case focuses on the preconditions for the shift to a "balanced" GM.[5] In terms of maintaining consumption, for example, Baccaro and Pontusson (2016) point to the existence of a large WS and strong service-sector unions disinclined to permit a steep drop in the wages of low-skilled workers.

Here, we explore the politics of balanced growth in the Swedish political economy through the lens of pension policy. Financialization has been linked to the rise of consumption-led growth in high-inequality Anglo-American countries, where financial markets encourage low-income citizens to take on mortgage and personal debt to maintain consumption (Ahlquist and Ansell 2017). In Sweden, financialization in the form of the rise of pre-funded defined-contribution plans managed by private financial services providers has coincided with relatively low inequality. But high levels of mortgage debt are also present, especially among higher earners (Anderson and Kurzer 2020). To what extent did Sweden's reform of its pension system support the rise of a consumption-based model?

Historically, relatively generous public pensions dominated pension provision in Sweden (Esping-Andersen 1990). Collectively bargained occupational pensions, covering approximately 90% of the workforce, topped up public provision. However, when a deep economic recession hit Sweden in the early 1990s, resulting in a massive rise in unemployment, the government began a reform effort aimed at restraining social spending, and pension reform moved high on the political agenda. Reforms aimed to improve the financial stability of the system (through the introduction of a lifetime expectancy index and other balancing mechanisms), while also reducing the redistributive nature of the system by tying benefits more tightly to contributions (Anderson 2019, 631). The old earnings-related state pension was to be slowly reduced, and in the long run replaced by new premium reserve funds—individual pension investment accounts that are part of the public system (Anderson 2004).

The relationship between pension reform and the consumption-led component of the Swedish GM is ambiguous. On the one hand, the 1998 pension reform likely propped up consumption by stabilizing pensioner incomes, and its notional defined-contribution design means Swedish workers have not faced rising pension contribution rates, as is happening in Germany. It is also true that the "financialized" component of the reform promoted the creation of individual investment accounts within the public system. On the other hand, these funds are too new to have substantially contributed directly to household incomes, nor do individuals own the capital in these individual investment accounts; they are only entitled to the income generated by the capital in that account.[6]

Some have additionally argued that there exists a link between Sweden's 1998 pension reform and the growth of household debt in Sweden (Belfrage and Kallifatides 2018), but an exploration of the timing and mechanisms suggests no strong functional relationship between the two. Instead, the rise in mortgage debt—one of the two pillars of consumption-led growth—seems largely attributable to a shift in housing policy in the early 1980s. The liberalization of mortgage credit in 1982 opened the door for more household indebtedness (Anderson and Kurzer 2020), but it is unclear that this alone would have driven mortgage debt absent "push" factors: the decline in social (public) housing investment starting in the early 1990s, as well as fiscal measures aimed at encouraging higher rates of home ownership among the middle class (Christophers 2013; Grundström and Molina 2016). These policies were initiated by a bourgeois government but subsequently embraced by the Social Democrats.

Around the margins, pension reform arguably supported consumption by assuring that workers' incomes would not be eroded by rising contributions. Similarly, some reform elements promoted by bourgeois parties—especially the creation of individualized pensions—perhaps played a constructivist role in acclimating Swedish citizens to financialized social relations in which high mortgage debt was socially acceptable (Belfrage 2008; Belfrage and Ryner 2009). However, reforms to this classic social insurance program of the WS (pensions) seem in fact to have been economically and politically orthogonal to Sweden's specific GM. If anything, Sweden's consumption-led growth seems to be one in which the strong blue-collar union LO fought to prop up wages on the low end of the income distribution, while electorally motivated governments of all political stripes pushed housing policies incentivizing middle-class homeowners to take on high levels of mortgage debt. Both unions and governments advocated policies that directly supported consumption, but the two types of consumption-enabling policies had substantially different distributional consequences. Whether this outcome reflected the interests of a stable dominant growth coalition, or the more unstable politics of a political stalemate between two sets of powerful actors with quite different preferences (Baccaro and Pontusson 2016; Erixon and Pontusson 2022), remains an open but important question.

Family Policy in Italy's Failed GM

We turn now to Italy, an exemplar of a "failed" GM mired in economic stagnation. For more than 20 years, Italian wages have remained flat, as have GDP and productivity growth. Italian export industries have failed to follow the German trajectory of increasing their share in global markets. This section explores child allowances, a policy used in many European countries to support the incomes of families with children, and which arguably could support a broader strategy of domestic demand-led growth (Avlijaš, Hassel, and Palier 2021a).

Historically, child allowances in Italy were quite generous. Fascist governments introduced child allowances in the mid-1930s for pronatalist and anti-poverty reasons. Child allowances were also popular with early postwar governments, so that by the early 1950s their value exceeded those in the heyday of fascist pro-natalism. The 1960s marked a turning point, however. After 1964, child allowances saw a steadily decline, in large part because unions traded off increases in the value of contributory child allowances for improvements in pensions and other policy gains (Lynch 2006, 96–97). Over time, party competition between the Christian Democrats and the left promoted the extension of family allowances to new groups (such as farmers and the self-employed), without addressing the problem of the benefit's declining ability to actually counter child poverty.

By the 1990s, after decades of Christian Democratic dominance, the center-left regained power. Child poverty was high—nearly 15%, compared to a 5% average elsewhere in Europe (Van Mechelen and Bradshaw 2013)—and Italian women had one of the lowest labor force participation rates in Europe. Although the center-left moved to address these two problems by expanding child benefits and childcare, they met substantial resistance from unions. Unions opposed a wholesale expansion of child benefits because they were financed through the social insurance (contributory) portion of the WS but were granted to populations who did not contribute to the system. As a compromise, Romano Prodi's government moved child benefits off the social insurance books and into the general-revenue-financed, social assistance realm of the WS (Matsaganis et al. 2003, 2006). Due to the constraints of EMU-driven balanced budgets, however, they were unable to fully fund even this means-tested system.

Austerity, and the inability to expand the WS in much-needed areas, opened up the space for a far more pro-natalist and nativist approach under Silvio Berlusconi. Low fertility, which by the 1990s was below 1.3 per woman, became increasingly politicized. Declining fertility was framed by right-wing parties and the Lega Nord as a threat to the survival of Italian culture, especially in light of rising rates of immigration. The solution offered by the right emphasized the need to provide benefits for *non-immigrants* to have babies (Naldini and Jurado 2013). In 2007, Berlusconi's government created a Ministry for Policies on the Family to address the "crisis" of falling birthrates and increased migration. The government offered "baby bonuses" to mothers of multiple children, but restricted eligibility to EU citizens (Brostoff 2019). In the intervening decade, as birthrates continued to plummet—in 2016, Italy had lowest birthrate since the country's unification in 1861—the left has increasingly come to accept the right's diagnosis of the problem. Rather than attacking the root of low fertility (a nearly nonexistent job market for young people), Renzi's center-left government in 2016 doubled the standard "baby bonus" and increased the allowance for second and third children born to long-term residents.

The links between the politics of family policy and the politics of GMs are non-obvious. At one level, the history of Italian family policy is not mainly a story about the WS supporting a particular model of capitalist accumulation. In its fascist origins, and in its evolution since 2005, it has largely been driven by nationalism and populism. But of course, there is an accumulation story in terms of constraints. Both in the late 1990s and today, Italy's adherence to European monetary rules has meant that debt-financed expansion of a consumption-oriented family policy (and of the WS more generally) has been off the table. Still, we find

no evidence that family policy in Italy worked to solve either a general accumulation problem, nor a more specific one of promoting export competitiveness or
consumption. Instead, family policy appears to have been largely driven by the
electoral concerns of political parties, who have not been particularly attentive
to growth imperatives. Indeed, the Italian case suggests that in the absence of a
stable growth coalition, politicians may seek legitimation for policy goals quite
apart from growth, and from sources outside of the dominant growth coalition.[7]

The Politics of Legitimation: How Welfare States Help Create and Sustain a Dominant Coalition

The vignettes analyzed in the previous section provided some support for the
idea that shifts in welfare provision over the past 30 years contributed to the economic functioning of GMs. But we saw little systematic evidence that reforms
reflected consistent efforts to move or keep countries on a particular growth
path. Instead, the case studies suggest that in many instances welfare reforms
serve explicitly political ends, which may or may not be related to the GM at all.

One of the strengths of the GM approach is its attention to political legitimation as a central analytic task. Comparative political economists agree that
growth requires some form of institutional regulation, but capitalism as a social formation relies just as much on the political management of dissent and
opposition as on the maintenance and enforcement of property rights. A focus
on political legitimation is useful in that it offers scholars the opportunity to incorporate ideational and discursive elements—the construction of what Nancy
Fraser (2015, 173) terms "political commonsense"—into explorations of how
dominant coalitions are formed and how they endure.

In this section we turn our attention to questions of legitimation, offering
reflections on how welfare policies may work politically to either sustain or undermine political conditions that support a GM's dominant coalition. Drawing
on the case studies discussed earlier, as well as other illustrative examples, we
identify five pathways through which social policy might encourage the political legitimation of a given GM. Welfare policies, we argue, may (1) signal the
managerial competence of the elites in the dominant growth coalition; (2) be
exchanged for support from subordinate groups in the coalition; (3) structure
the interests and identities of groups available for coalition; (4) create wedge issues, that is, divisions in society that can be mobilized to distract from problems
created by the GM; and (5) maintain inequality within socially acceptable
bounds. Greater attention to these mechanisms, we believe, can lead to deeper
understanding of how growth coalitions may encourage the requirements of
capitalist legitimation, while also leaving room for the autonomy of the political.

Welfare Policies Signal Managerial Competence to Capital Holders

An important structural precondition for maintaining any GM is securing and/ or maintaining investment from domestic or foreign sources that can be used to generate growth and productivity. While economic policies help elites in this task, so too do welfare policies. And in the latter case, the pathways through which the policies work are often overtly political and ideational, rather than acting directly to affect economic outcomes. In contemporary GMs, signaling managerial competence via welfare policies allows political elites to demonstrate to capital holders that their capital is safe from both expropriation and a collapse in demand. Promises to restrain social spending via benefits reductions, cuts to social budgets, or commitments to restrain future growth in social spending signal that a government is committed to maintaining a fiscal environment favorable to capital accumulation.

This type of signaling has been evident both in Italy and the United Kingdom since the 1990s. For example, reallocating spending within a fixed social budget, as in Italy, signaled a commitment to minimize future expenditure, as well as broadcast the government's efforts to discipline labor in ways that may facilitate downward pressure on wages, benefits, and worker control. Governments' willingness to comply with the expectations of external actors about appropriate social spending patterns and modes of welfare governance—conveyed, for example, via the open method of coordination, European semester, or communications from the Troika—sends important signals about the managerial "competence" of the government and a country's suitability for investment. Similarly, the British Labour Party's 1997 manifesto promise to keep spending within existing Conservative departmental ceilings for spending for the first two years upon assuming power was designed to convince the British press that Labour were competent to govern (Hopkin and Shaw, 2016). Nevertheless, the contrasting narratives of Italy and the United Kingdom suggest that successful signaling of managerial competence is no guarantee of growth.

Welfare Policies Buy Support for Voters

Another way in which welfare policies work to sustain particular GMs politically is by exchanging welfare goods for the loyalty of voters. This may take the form of rewarding voters in the core of the dominant growth coalition for their support, compensating voters in the periphery of the coalition, or preventing voters excluded from the coalition from rebelling against the GM and overturning the socioeconomic order.

Voters in the core of the dominant growth coalition are those who are advantaged by the GM and would be inclined to support it even in the absence of other inducements. If we think of welfare policies as exogenous to GMs, we might consider welfare benefits as "side payments" that reward core voters for showing up at the polls. In many instances, though, welfare benefits are simultaneously rewards for electoral support and constitutive of the GM, and make it clear that welfare policies need to be endogenized in GM theory. In the United States, for example, one could view policies such as the home mortgage tax deductions as examples of government social welfare provision that target benefits at middle- and upper-middle-class voters who are, by definition, already advantaged by the GM. At the same time, government subsidies for financialization of the housing sector contribute to debt-led consumption, which is integral to the GM in the United States.

Voters who are not naturally members of the core of a GM's coalition but whose support is needed to maintain a ruling coalition can be induced to support it through welfare policies. This was clearly the dynamic at work in Italy with family policy under Berlusconi and the *Lega Nord*, and arguably describes the political role played by mini-jobs in Germany. There, side payments in the form of family allowances and/or mini-jobs helped to secure the electoral support of female voters with weak ties to the formal labor market. Female voters are not the only out-groups who may be bought off via policy, however. Weak hypothecation of social insurance funds across industries and de facto non-enforcement of social insurance payments can provide significant benefits to, for example, the self-employed in agriculture and may induce them to support GMs that are really mainly oriented around the needs of the industrial sector (Lynch 2006).

Finally, voters who are actively disadvantaged by the GM may receive welfare payments to prevent disorder. This is the critical insight of Piven and Cloward's (2012) work showing that social assistance benefits tend to expand when slack demand for labor elevates the probability of social conflict, and to contract when the need for labor increases. More recent scholarship by Soss, Fording, and Schram (2011) and Watson (2015b) shows that the way in which social benefits are provided—for example, the level of stigmatization and surveillance with which both recipients and front-line providers of benefits are confronted—can itself serve to politically demobilize those economically disenfranchised groups that might otherwise be prone to protest the GM.

Welfare Policies Structure the Groups and Identities Available for Coalition

Welfare policies, in addition to signaling managerial competence to capital holders and providing incentives for political support to coalition members and potential disruptors, can also structure political identities in ways that render groups available for coalition formation in support of a GM. Social policies can facilitate the formation of new political groups with collective interests and identities aligned with the regime, and/or reinforce existing collective interests and identities.

The case studies highlighted a salient example of this dynamic in Sweden, where policy helped to construct a new salient political identity: homeowners. Prior to the 1990s, Swedish housing policy was tenure neutral, favoring neither renters nor homeowners. This began to change in the 1990s, when both the center-left and center-right began to actively advocate home ownership. Home ownership became a desired end of social policy, and successive governments supported generous fiscal subsidies to encourage middle-class households to enter the owner-occupied market. Eager to retain middle-class homeowners in their electoral coalition, Social Democrats showed themselves unwilling to rein in mortgage subsidies, despite their regressive character (Anderson and Kurzer 2016).

Of course, welfare policies can also reinforce already existing collective interests and identities. The paradigmatic example of this from the political economy literature is the Ghent system of unemployment benefits, in which unions administer statutory unemployment insurance schemes and are responsible for disbursing benefits. The Ghent system is associated with higher union density and greater resilience of unionization rates in the face of countervailing tendencies (see, e.g., Ebbinghaus and Visser 1999; Scruggs 2002) and case study research (e.g., Bockerman and Uusitalo 2006) finds a causal link between union management of unemployment insurance schemes and workers' propensity to join unions. Ghent systems—and other types of welfare benefits administered by economic associations, as in the Italian system of *patronati*—offer selective benefits that make membership more appealing. Ebbinghaus et al. (2011) show, however, that Ghent systems foster union membership and identification not only by offering the selective benefit of unemployment insurance. Instead, Ghent systems create a macro-level context in which "embeddedness in union-friendly social networks (family, circle of friends, neighbourhood and colleagues at workplace)" reinforce "positive beliefs about trade unions" (p. 109), leading to a greater propensity to identify as a union member. For this very reason, the Swedish bourgeois government in the early 2000s deliberately reformed the

Swedish unemployment benefit system with an eye to weakening the unions (Gordon 2019)

Discursive framings and the institutional structure of the WS, then, as much as one's structural location in the economy, are likely to shape how actors perceive their interests—and the ease with which they might be incorporated into coalition. This suggests the importance of a non-essentialist reading of economic interests.

Welfare Policies Can Serve as Political "Wedge" Issues

Welfare policies may also affect identities and mobilization in a more exclusionary way, however. The design of social policies can give pivotal electoral actors a sense that they have a stake in society—or they can stigmatize and marginalize these actors. In this way, social policy can be used as a wedge to prevent alternative political coalitions to the dominant coalition from forming. Groups may be marked as inappropriate for inclusion in a broad political coalition through welfare policies that stigmatize recipients as undeserving.

We saw such efforts at dividing and conquering in the Italian right's emphasis on excluding non-Italians from eligibility for baby bonuses. Similar dynamics can also be a facet of activation policies, such as those utilized in the United Kingdom in disability policy. Whereas historically the disabled had been incorporated via a contributory, insurance-based program that portrayed recipients as virtuous and deserving, the New Labour and Austerity governments channeled many of the disabled to a means-tested, highly conditional regime that implied a lack of deservingness. It is likely no coincidence that public support for policies aimed at the disabled unable to work—by far the most popular group of welfare recipients in the public imagination–fell by one-third between 1999 and 2013 (Harding 2017, 25).

Beyond these particular cases, other research suggests that racialized imagery, stringent means-testing, requirements for frequent or excessive documentation of eligibility, or demeaning interpersonal interactions with welfare bureaucracies all mark social welfare beneficiaries as inherently undeserving until proven otherwise. Some of these policy features serve the function of reinforcing the idea of "less eligibility"—a principle dating to 19th-century British Poor Law that induces labor market participation by making receipt of relief less appealing than even the worst paying job. However, they also make it difficult for those who may be disadvantaged by the GM to mount a unified resistance. A contemporary example is the 2010 US Affordable Care Act, in which means-testing of access to subsidized health insurance triggered resentment toward recipients among people just above the income cutoffs, who could ill-afford health insurance on their own (Chattopadhyay 2018). In sum, welfare policies can be used to divide and distract in order to prop up the politics of a precarious GM's dominant coalition. The mirror image may also be the case, however. When welfare regimes work successfully to contain inequality within socially acceptable bounds, they can be powerful tools for maintaining the legitimacy of a GM.

Esping-Andersen's *The Three Worlds of Welfare Capitalism* (1990) is best known among political economy scholars for its grouping of countries according to the level of decommodification provided by social policies. However, Esping-Andersen is equally explicit that postwar welfare regimes were designed to produce and reproduce social *stratification*; and that their political fates depend on their doing so in ways and to degrees that were acceptable to the various groups that make up a welfare regime's cross-class support coalition. The level of inequality that is acceptable to society varies across welfare regimes, which in turn maintain inequality at societally permissible levels through different combinations of taxation and redistribution; public spending; and regulation of markets for labor, goods, services, and finance. All of these policy strategies have come under pressure in an era dominated by a neoliberal policy paradigm, but politicians are nevertheless still held to account for delivering not just economic growth but also some level of equality (Lynch 2020).

Welfare regimes thus both reflect and generate certain expectations on the part of societal actors for what level of inequality is permissible. When a dominant growth coalition responds to societal demand for equality, the GM is also more likely to be politically acceptable. Thus, welfare policies that reproduce societally acceptable levels of inequality may be a critical mechanism through which coalition leaders can create and maintain a GM as *politically* hegemonic. It stands to reason that different GMs, like different welfare regimes, might require different combinations of redistributive taxation, spending, and market regulation to generate hegemony.

Connecting Legitimation Pathways and Growth Models

The GM literature identifies at least four distinctive GMs. Above, we highlighted five potential pathways through which the welfare state can be used to legitimate a given GM. How are GMs and legitimation pathways connected? One possibility is that all five pathways matter more or less equally across GMs. Another is that different GMs have different accumulation needs, and hence are more likely to rely on some legitimation pathways than others. Although we cannot settle this matter empirically, here we offer some initial reflections on these questions.

Our view is that the relevance of different legitimation pathways is likely to vary across the type of GM. Some legitimation pathways are more likely in some GMs than others. Consider the *signaling of managerial competence*. While governments everywhere likely wish to signal fiscal prudence to financial markets, financialized consumption-led GMs face more pressure to use retrenchment to signal that they can pay back debt. For similar reasons, the use of *welfare as a political wedge* issue should be more often at play in consumption-led regimes, as such strategies legitimize the reduction of social protection for 'undeserving' groups.

In contrast, other legitimation mechanisms are likely to be at work across all GMs, but will push in different directions depending on the GM. For example, although *the use of welfare to structure political identities* is likely to be a popular strategy everywhere, the *types* of identities mobilized should vary across types of GM. In export-led GMs, where the underlying accumulation model does not require limiting the organizational power of labor movements, welfare policies that support the continued salience of extant producer- and/or class-based identities are more likely. In contrast, GMs that create new opportunities for consumption outside of the welfare state are more likely to facilitate citizens' identities as consumers. Margaret Thatcher's privatization of council housing in the early 1980s, for example, was part of an explicit effort to create a new Gramscian common-sense among the British working classes: investment in homeownership as an aspirational ideal. In the balanced and failed GM models, elites may well make efforts to facilitate the formation of new group identities and to reinforce existing identities at the same time. In balanced GMs, while there may be concerted efforts by elites to weaken class-based political projects through the mobilization of new identities, the relative strength of labor organizations means this transformation remains incomplete. In contrast, failed GMs likely result from a failure of incorporation, as multiple identities are mobilized but not articulated into an economically coherent model. Of course, the pathologies of failed GMs may also be driven by other political and institutional factors such as a highly fragmented political system or very low trust in government.

A similar argument could be made about other pathways. Efforts to use the WS to *maintain inequality within acceptable bounds* should happen everywhere, but the level of acceptable inequality takes on different forms in export-led versus consumption-led GMs. Likewise, political leaders in all GMs may have an interest in using welfare to buy voters and strengthen their electoral coalition, but which voters they target will depend both on the GM and on autonomous political dynamics.

Reflections on Welfare, Legitimation and Mass Politics

The GM perspective on politics presented in the introduction to this volume argues for the centrality of both elite and mass politics in shaping GMs because stable economic governance requires coalition building among both producer groups and mass electorates. Although "quiet" producer group politics are likely important when it comes to many accumulation policies, especially in the realm of financialization or macroeconomic policy, our view is that any serious analysis of legitimation via the WS requires sustained engagement with the dynamics of party politics. Parties are crucial actors insofar as they help frame shared understandings of the legitimate use of state power in the service of private interests.

As the editors of this volume rightfully note, the politics of dominant growth coalitions and of electoral coalitions will not necessarily be congruent. In some contexts, parties may naturalize the worldview of core actors in the dominant coalition; in others, they may embrace counter-hegemonic views. It is through the push and pull of electoral politics that "political commonsense" (Fraser 2015) about the role of public versus private power, about just social orders, and about feasible alternatives are defined and redefined. The fit between the politics of growth coalitions and the politics of electoral coalitions will therefore frequently be messy and beset by tensions—a useful reminder that even stable GMs contain elements of indeterminacy.

This chapter's elaboration of the channels through which welfare policies can politically legitimate GMs offers some entry points for thinking more systematically about how parties' efforts to shift the balance between commodification and self-protection intersect with the dynamics of growth. In particular, our emphasis on the many uses to which parties may put welfare policies permits us to better integrate ideational concerns into the political economy of GMs. To the extent that welfare programs often involve embedded (if contested) messages about the deservingness of different constituencies, they play an important role in discursive battles over the definition of interests and direction of GMs, especially during "interregnums"—transitions from one era of ideological hegemony to another (Stahl 2019).

Our focus on potential mechanisms through which welfare might support the political legitimation of GMs represents only a starting point, however. Attention to variation in the nature of parties, party competition *and* to the legacies of how WSs and industrial relations were implemented in the Fordist era will also be crucial elements in any Gramscian-inflected story of how consent is mobilized. Fortunately, in contrast to other areas of political economy (VOC, Regulation School), the WS literature has a long tradition of considering how various dimensions of electoral politics—including changing electorates and cleavages, patterns of party competition, and party-society linkages and electoral institutions—create incentives for parties' design and provision of social programs (Lynch 2006, 2009; Gingrich 2011; Hausermann, Picot, and Geering 2013; Gingrich and Häusermann 2015; Watson 2015).

Notes

1. An alternative view is that there is no "dominant" coalition, but rather a balance of power between two equally strong coalitions: export-sector employers and unions, on the one hand; and sheltered-sector unions on the other.
2. Some of the "accumulation work" done in post-Fordist GMs might be also be achieved via reforms to industrial relations institutions. For example, a combination of sectoral bargaining and firm-level decentralization seems to have been important in generating wage repression to fuel Germany's export-led growth. Similarly, in financialized consumption-based regimes, capital may be less tolerant of labor-friendly institutions.
3. IB had been a contributory benefit. With the shift to ESA, there was a one-year limit on the contributory portion of the benefit; after that, recipients were put into a lower-paying means-tested version. See https://publications.parliament.uk/pa/cm201012/cmselect/cmworpen/1015/101509.htm#a18
4. https://www.bbc.com/news/uk-politics-37810701
5. There is debate about periodization for the Swedish case—whether it was always a balanced model, or whether it shifted from a predominantly export-led model in the pre-GFC period to a more consumption-led model post-GFC. We do not weigh in on that debate here, but see the Erixon and Pontusson chapter in this volume for a compelling explication of the latter view..
6. We thank Karen Anderson for clarifying this point.
7. Of course, the nativist slant documented in Italian policy is emerging across all the different GMs (even if articulated somewhat differently across countries), and perhaps speaks to the limitations of *all* post-Fordist growth models.

17

Green Growth Models

JONAS NAHM

Introduction

Over the past three decades, a broad scientific consensus has emerged around the need to drastically reduce global emissions of greenhouse gases to avoid the worst consequences of climate change. According to the Intergovernmental Panel on Climate Change (IPCC), limiting global warming to 1.5°C will require a 45% reduction of greenhouse gas emissions over 2010 levels by 2030 and net-zero emissions by 2050.[1] Achieving emissions reductions that even remotely approximate these goals will require states worldwide to enact unprecedented interventions in virtually every sector of the economy. To date, governments around the world have announced ambitious emissions reductions targets as part of the Paris Climate Accords. In practice, however, they have differed significantly in their ability to meet self-imposed climate goals against the opposition from incumbent interests invested in the status quo.[2]

A popular strategy among those trying to build political coalitions in support of climate policy has been the promise of "green growth." This strategy has recently gained popularity. Advocates pushing for a "Green New Deal" in the United States and those arguing for a "Green Deal" in the European Union have sought to combine climate policy with economic and social policies that create new jobs, industries, and sources of prosperity in the transition to a zero-carbon economy. In the past, this combination of economic goals and climate objectives has been particularly pronounced in renewable energy. Policymakers hoped that renewable energy policies would lead firms to invest in technological innovation and ultimately co-locate manufacturing to commercialize and produce wind and solar technologies domestically.

The link between renewable energy policy and the promise of material benefits in industrial development followed a broader political logic. Public investments in R&D and subsidies for the deployment of clean energy technologies were easier to justify politically when these investments promised local economic returns, particularly in the form of manufacturing jobs. Governments subsequently combined policies to support R&D with demand subsidies, often explicitly tied to local content regulations and other means to attract local industrial activity. Policies that offered the possibility of supporting growth and employment were attractive to policymakers also because they provided an opportunity to create new interest groups supporting climate policy from industrial sectors that benefited from emissions reduction goals. In countries where green industrial policies led to the growth of new industries, the development of political coalitions supporting climate policies enabled more consistent and widespread regulatory strategies to reduce greenhouse gas emissions.[3]

This chapter examines the feasibility of creating such economic coalitions in support of decarbonization in the context of debates about divergent national growth models. Building on the growth models (hereafter GM) framework at the core of this volume, I show that differences in the composition of domestic economic demand shapes the types of climate strategies that states can pursue.[4] I argue that whether economic growth primarily stemmed from exports or was dominated by domestic consumption affected the kinds of economic actors that could benefit from green industrial policies and the relative size of the political coalitions that could mobilize in support of—or opposition to—decarbonization. In particular, I propose that countries with export-driven GMs, notably China and Germany, which early and aggressively moved to dominate the production of clean energy technologies, can more easily realize economic co-benefits from climate policy. By contrast, consumption-driven GMs have so far proven to be less compatible with the green industrial development strategies promised as part of broader climate agendas. Consequently, they have been unable to build the outsized economic coalitions that export nations can mobilize behind decarbonization agendas.

The chapter proceeds as follows. I begin by reviewing existing research on the drivers of cross-national variation in climate policymaking. Such literatures have focused on factors ranging from developmental status to state capacity but have overlooked the constraints imposed by states' broader macroeconomic integration into the global economy. I propose that the domestic industrial composition as expressed in a country's GM shapes the decarbonization strategies that nations can pursue. The following sections illustrate this argument empirically, showing that economies with export-led GMs (Germany, China) have been able to build broader political coalitions supporting decarbonization than consumption-led economies (the United Kingdom, United States).

I conclude with a discussion of what this means for climate policy going forward. My most counterintuitive finding is that export-led manufacturing economies such as Germany and China—those with the types of legacy manufacturing industries that we would expect to oppose a green transition— actually have the potential to build broader domestic coalitions of economic supporters through export-led growth strategies. Non-export-driven growth models may face less domestic opposition from vested interests, but they crucially lack the kinds of material benefits that would unite broad political coalitions behind climate policy in the long run. Since not everyone can be an exporter, and economies such as Germany and China already dominate export production for many green technologies, prospects for aggressive global climate action based upon such "green growth" strategies in non-export-driven GM's remain dim.

The Political Economy of Climate Policy

A growing body of research in comparative politics and comparative political economy has examined both constraints and opportunities for climate policy, adding to a field of scholarship that until recently was dominated by scholars of international relations interested in the efficacy of global climate governance.[5] The comparative turn in climate policy research has yielded three broad research trajectories that have prioritized distinct sets of explanatory mechanisms to account for cross-national variation in decarbonization strategies.

The first group of research agendas has privileged public opinion and the determinants of public preferences, seeking to explain both when the public becomes concerned with climate change and when such concerns translate into political action. Although primarily focused on Western democracies, survey research in this tradition has debunked assumptions rooted in modernization theory by showing that concern about climate change is greatest among populations in Latin America and Africa.[6] While commitment to democratic values appears to be a strong predictor of concern about anthropogenic climate change, democratic factors appear to vary widely.[7] In the United States, at least, public attitudes toward climate change align with party identification and political ideology. Perhaps not surprisingly, demographic factors such as gender, age, and income suggest that younger and richer women are most likely to show concern about climate change. At the same time, more religious voters are less concerned about global warming.[8]

However, as many scholars have argued, public opinion does not easily translate into public policy, especially not if legislators systematically underestimate public demand for climate action and when vested interests capture the policymaking process.[9] More recent research has revived classic political science debates on state capacity to show when such opposition can be overcome.[10] Given the necessity to rapidly transform every sector of the economy to meet decarbonization goals, climate policy presents a test for state capacity precisely because of the comprehensive need for state intervention. Research in this vein has shown that corporatist systems of state-business relations can be also vulnerable to regulatory capture. In contrast, pluralist states have outmaneuver vested interests.[11] Public engagement, consultation, and democratic decision-making can open the doors to influence from vested interests. At the same time, the delegation of policymaking to autonomous bureaucracies can yield more consistent climate policy across economic sectors, including in pluralist systems known for their permeability to interest group influence.[12] Authoritarian governments supportive of efforts to reduce carbon emissions have also not always been immune to opposition from vested interests and have at times failed to enforce climate policy, including in the state-owned energy sector.[13]

To better understand when and where opposition to climate policy is particularly powerful, a third strand of the comparative climate policy literature has examined domestic interests. The economic reliance on industrial sectors most threatened by a transition away from fossil fuels—including energy, automotive, and energy-intensive manufacturing industries—has led some governments to encourage industrial upgrading to preserve national competitiveness in a zero-carbon future. More generally, however, the presence of energy-intensive industries has harmed the prospects of ambitious climate policy.[14] In this context, climate policies pursued in the correct order have also created opportunities to grow enterprises supporting decarbonization. In countries where green industrial policies led to the growth of green industries, the development of political coalitions in support of climate policies enabled more consistent and widespread regulatory strategies to reduce greenhouse gas emissions.[15]

This body of research has offered essential lessons for those trying to build broader political coalitions supporting decarbonization. Yet, such research has thus far paid less attention to the macroeconomic factors that shape domestic coalitions in support of climate policy. This chapter shifts the focus to the role of domestic growth models and their links to the international economy. It proposes that differences in the underlying growth drivers of the local GMs—themselves linked by different ties to the global economy—shape the makeup of domestic political coalitions and the types of climate politics that governments can pursue.[16]

Greening Growth Models

Climate policymaking presents a stern test for state capacity as states attempt to develop effective emission reductions against the opposition from incumbent interests. Opposition can stem from those with investments in assets likely to lose value due to decarbonization policies, labor unions predicting job losses in declining legacy industries, and energy-intensive sectors concerned about rising energy prices and increasing cost of regulatory compliance. However, state efforts to reduce greenhouse gas emissions can also draw support from those likely to benefit from climate policy. In addition to citizens, the majority of whom already show overwhelming concern about climate change in most parts of the world, support can come from business interests likely to benefit from decarbonization. Emissions reductions yield growing markets for clean energy firms, including producers of wind and solar panels, manufacturers of batteries and electric vehicles, and service sector businesses ranging from software to maintenance of low carbon energy technologies, among others. Not only do such companies form a political counterweight to incumbent interests, but the double promise of economic growth and decarbonization has made public investments in emissions reductions more palatable politically.

Public investments in low carbon energy technologies began as state initiatives to support scientific discovery. The scientific rationale behind such early support for renewable energy technologies did not immediately connect to profit expectations. That changed during the 1990s when improvements in wind and solar technologies opened up new prospects for economic growth and industrial development.[17] As policymakers discovered the economic potential of clean energy sectors, public investments in R&D and subsidies for the deployment of clean energy technologies became easier to justify politically. These investments promised local economic returns, particularly in the form of manufacturing jobs. Governments subsequently combined policies to support R&D with demand subsidies, often explicitly tied to local content regulations and other means to attract local industrial activity.

Not least because of the growth trajectory of renewable energy markets and the size of such public investments, few governments were content to just be consumers of clean energy technologies. Neither were they satisfied to attract individual segments of global renewable energy supply chains. Policymakers hoped that climate policy would lead firms to invest in technological innovation and ultimately commercialize and produce clean energy technologies domestically.[18] Among state initiatives to promote the reduction of greenhouse gas emissions, policies that offered the possibility of supporting growth and employment were attractive to policymakers precisely because they allowed for creating political coalitions behind renewable energy that extended beyond the core group of environmental advocates.

Such political support was significant for policies that entailed large public expenditures and additional financial burdens for electricity consumers to offset the cost differential between traditional energy sources and the higher-priced wind and solar technologies. Among policy options to address climate change, green industrial policies that pursued the dual objective of achieving emissions reductions while creating new sources of growth were easier to implement politically while also providing an opportunity to create new interest groups in support of energy sector transformation.[19] Public investments in the creation of industries that could invent, produce, and possibly export wind and solar products followed the goal of strategically modifying the local GM with future growth potential. The political logic of clean energy transitions in the context of broader climate policies frequently led to a focus on manufacturing clean energy technologies and the goal of exporting these technologies to stimulate industrial development beyond what domestic consumption alone could sustain.

The Politics of Green Coalitions: The Manufacturing Paradox

Although governments worldwide have connected climate policymaking to the broader premise of "green growth," few have successfully built large economic coalitions in support of decarbonization. The ability to forge such alliances hinged on two sets of macroeconomic forces largely independent of climate policy itself. First were the structural composition of the domestic economy, which shaped the distribution of supporters and opponents of climate policy, and, second, the demand drivers of that economy, which determined the types of industrial capabilities on which green industries could be established.

Within the discussion of GMs in general, it is useful to distinguish between manufacturing-intensive economies and those where service industries are the dominant industrial actors. The presence of sizable and politically powerful manufacturing sectors was frequently a central impediment to climate policy. Manufacturing industries were generally more energy and emissions intensive than service services, and more vulnerable to having stranded assets as a result of climate policy. Many manufacturing sectors, including the global automotive industry, were vested in technologies that competed with the low carbon alternatives promoted by climate policies and regulation. Manufacturing industries were therefore, on balance, more likely to be vested in the status quo and often had substantial political clout due to the large number of jobs they provided and their dominant role in R&D.

At the same time, however, manufacturing-intensive economies had the industrial capabilities needed to produce many of the new technologies required to reduce emissions rapidly. Service sector industries, by contrast, were more easily able to reduce emissions—including by switching to cleaner sources of energy—but less likely to create the manufacturing jobs often promised as part of green growth strategies. Service sector industries are generally not large energy consumers. They are also more likely to comprise new industrial sectors that had already internalized the need to reduce emissions and were, therefore, less likely to suffer from the risk of stranded assets. While the structural composition of the economy shaped the balance of interests and the types of industrial capabilities available domestically, aggregate sources of economic demand determined the size of such coalitions. Building on the growth model theory outlined in the introduction to this volume, I show that the composition of demand drivers in the local GM shapes opportunities for building economic coalitions in support of climate policy.

As the introduction and subsequent chapters note, over the postwar period a set of Fordist employment institutions generated productivity gains and distributed them through collective bargaining, cementing wages as the primary source of growth in Western economies. As wage-led growth models decayed at the end of the 20th century a shift from wage to capital income prompted stagnation in economies that had previously relied on wages as the primary source of demand.[20] Depressed wages and the associated decline in consumption led firms in some economies to replace domestic demand with exports, establishing foreign demand as the primary source of growth. Others replaced wages with an increasing reliance on household debt to shore up domestic spending, maintaining consumption-led growth strategies focused on domestic demand.[21]

The relevance for the politics of greening GMs lies in the fact that such differences in the sources of aggregate demand ultimately determine the size of the potential industrial coalitions that can be marshaled in support of climate policy, even if they emerged independently from climate considerations.[22] Export-led economies focused on supplying global markets were—given their outsized export sectors (see Schwartz and Blyth in this volume)—able to build green industries that could not be sustained solely from domestic demand. They benefited instead from consumption in other parts of the world. Export-led economies were more likely to fulfill the dual promise of economic growth and decarbonization touted by advocates of green growth strategies than consumption-led economies that were more likely to fuel the creation of jobs in other parts of the world. Pro-climate industrial coalitions were more prominent in export-led economies than in economies primarily reliant on consumption.

In short, cross-national differences in the composition of demand and the makeup of the domestic economy yielded distinct politics of decarbonization. In export-led manufacturing economies, industrial policies were more likely to produce green manufacturing sectors that could coalesce behind climate goals. Existing manufacturing industries provided the industrial capabilities on which green industries could be established since they already had export networks that could be utilized by emerging industrial enterprises and sectors. Export-led

manufacturing economies were also more likely to possess the institutional resources necessary to help new firms enter export markets.[23] In such a context,
the politics of emissions reductions were structured by a competition between
green growth coalitions versus vested interests in legacy industries, which were
more prevalent in export-led manufacturing economies. In consumption-led
manufacturing economies constrained by the size of the domestic economy,
and more likely to rely on imported technologies for decarbonization, vested
interests were better able to contest decarbonization goals, as their lack of export
markets prevented competition from sizable industrial coalitions in support of
climate policy.

Service industries were generally less resistant to emissions reductions and
more likely to advocate strongly in favor of emissions reductions.[24] Global internet giants, financial institutions invested in green lending, green tech firms,
and information technology providers lobbied to support active decarbonization and encouraged governments to reduce emissions rapidly. Consumption-
led service economies could also rely on deindustrialization for much of their
emissions reductions, as is the case with the United Kingdom in particular.
Political conflict in such contexts was more likely centered on the politics of deindustrialization and the shift from manufacturing to service sector jobs than on
climate policy itself. As a result, climate policy under consumption-led demand
drivers can find it hard to muster the supporting coalitions of labor and industry
that underpinned broad climate coalitions in export-led economies.

The remainder of this chapter illustrates the climate politics of export and
consumption-led green growth models empirically. The goal is not to make
probabilistic claims about the likelihood of emissions reductions under different growth models, but to illustrate instead how decarbonization faces different challenges depending on the structural composition of the domestic
economy and the sources of aggregate demand in other words—on the underlying GM. Climate policy has been successfully passed in different macroeconomic contexts, but it was backed by quite different political coalitions in
consumption-led service economies than in export-led manufacturing nations.

Export-Led Decarbonization in Germany and China

Export-led manufacturing economies are in part comprised of vested interests
strongly opposed to climate policy. But they also possess industrial capabilities
that allow for the development of manufacturing industries centered on the
production of new clean energy technologies. These competitive dynamics, in
which legacy sectors compete for political influence with growing clean energy

sectors, are structuring the clean energy transitions in Germany and China, where growing renewable energy sectors defended climate policy against opposition from the fossil fuel industry and legacy auto manufacturers. In both instances, the size of domestic green growth coalitions was linked to the scale of export production, allowing green technology industries to grow without always directly competing with vested interests domestically. Crucially, and tellingly, in both economies, the first far-reaching national climate legislation was passed after an export-driven renewable energy industry had been established domestically—in 2000 in Germany and 2007 in China.

Since the early 2000s, the regulatory requirements for power utilities and subsidies for renewable energy markets created a rapidly growing demand for wind turbines and solar panels. Global installations for solar panels soared from 319 MW in 2001 to 713,970 MW in 2018; over the same period, global wind turbine installations increased from 6,500 MW to 733,226 MW.[25] Exponential growth in international markets provided incentives for firms to enter renewable energy sectors, yet domestic industries that emerged in response differed sharply in their industrial footprint.

Germany

In Germany, large numbers of small- and medium-sized suppliers from existing, export-oriented industrial sectors diversified into renewable energy sectors by focusing on developing complex componentry and production equipment. The absence of specialized suppliers in renewable energy industries had previously required wind and solar firms to resort to improvisation, repurposing of equipment, and modifying components from other industrial sectors for application in wind turbines and solar PV modules.[26] Germany's existing manufacturing firms possessed a rich fabric of capabilities applicable to the development of wind turbine components and production lines for the solar industry that could address these needs. German firms subsequently responded to this opportunity by applying their niche capabilities to global renewable energy sectors. Firms entered from various existing industries, including machine building, automation and laser processing equipment, metal fabrication, and shipbuilding.

By 2011, VDMA, the German Engineering Federation, listed more than 170 member firms active in the wind industry. The majority of firms developed towers, blades, mechanical components, hydraulics systems, and production equipment for the wind industry.[27] Similarly, in the PV sector, more than 70 firms offered production lines, automation equipment, coatings, and laser processing machines. In 2010, the roughly 41,000 employees in solar PV equipment and component manufacturing far surpassed the 12,000 jobs in Germany's solar module producers.[28] Of the four vertically integrated solar manufacturers operating in Germany in 2011, only two remained in 2014. Their combined annual production capacity amounted to less than a single Chinese PV manufacturing plant.[29] This small number of domestic wind turbine and solar PV manufacturers made Germany's renewable energy suppliers highly dependent on global markets. Export quotas of more than 50% in the solar sector, and up to 80% in the wind industry, underline the tight integration of Germany's wind and solar firms into global renewable energy supply chains.[30]

The entry of export-oriented Mittelstand firms into renewable energy sectors had two broad consequences for climate politics in Germany. First, firms engaged a set of legacy institutions, including vocational training systems, R&D institutions for collaborative research, and relationships with local credit unions to secure financing. Such institutions retained relevance in these emerging industries not because of institutional complementarities and subsequent lock-in, but because of their continued utility to firms in new sectors.[31] As such, new industrial sectors became part of the economic coalitions that sustained legacy institutions long at the core of the German economy.[32] Second, Mittelstand firms brought with them political clout, both through their organization in Germany's most powerful industry associations and their relationships with organized labor. When conservative policymakers threatened to reduce renewable energy subsidies and to lower emissions reductions targets in the late 1990s and in the mid-2000s, it was a broad political coalition of renewable energy installers, environmentalists, and industrial interests from Mittelstand firms that prevented changes to Germany's long-standing renewable energy legislation. As Germany's feed-in-tariff emerged as a political third rail attempts to withdraw or adjust the legislation failed until 2014, nearly 25 years after it first passed in parliament.[33] By that point German renewable energy industries had created some 400,000 jobs and were on track to rival the automotive sector in terms of employment and importance for the German economy.[34]

The economic weight and the political connections of Mittelstand firms in clean energy industries allowed climate policy in the power sector to weather opposition from legacy utility firms, whose coal and gas assets were increasingly unable to compete with wind and solar. After posting record profits in the aftermath of the deregulation of the European power market in the early 2000s, rapidly falling prices for wind and solar technologies, and decreasing power prices on German spot markets, made coal increasingly uncompetitive. Eon and BWE—Germany's largest electric utilities and collectively responsible for some 40% of domestic power generation—booked net losses of EUR 2.4 billion and EUR 6.4 billion in 2013 and 2015. Eon lost 70% and RWE 80% of market capitalization in spectacular destruction of value due to losses stemming from coal and nuclear assets between 2011 and 2015. Both utilities responded by spinning out their renewable energy businesses into separate entities, essentially creating bad banks for fossil fuel and nuclear assets that have since traded at record lows.[35]

Pushing for continued decarbonization in the renewable energy sector despite such losses among the largest utility companies in the nation was not just a domestic service industry centered on the installation and mainte-nance of wind and solar, but also a broad network of manufacturing firms that had used domestic markets as a springboard for export production. As the production of solar panels and wind turbines became dependent on global markets, domestic manufacturers used their political clout not just to advo-cate for climate legislation but defended the open trading system itself. In 2012, European solar industry associations began to call for trade barriers to prevent import competition from Chinese competitors, filing anti-dumping cases with the European Union.[36] Fearing retaliation, Germany's export-oriented wind and solar firms vehemently and ultimately successfully op-posed plans to enact anti-dumping measures in Brussels.[37] Not only did wind and solar suppliers from Germany's Mittelstand use their political clout to maintain policy support for domestic renewable energy markets, but they were also instrumental in ensuring that these markets remained tightly linked to the global economy.

China

In China, wind and particular solar firms focused on commercialization and scaling up to mass production before creating large domestic markets. The ma-jority of wind turbine producers were spun off from state-owned or formerly state-owned manufacturing firms. In the solar industry, firms were frequently founded by Chinese scientists educated in solar PV research laboratories abroad.[38] In the late 1990s and early 2000s, when these firms entered wind and solar PV sectors, few manufacturers of wind turbines and solar panels were producing new energy technologies at scale. Chinese firms subsequently fo-cused their efforts on building innovative capabilities and engineering know-ledge around the commercialization and rapid scale-up of complex wind and solar technologies. Key in doing so was utilizing China's extensive domestic in-frastructure for mass production in its high-tech developing zones and export processing clusters.

Aggressive domestic industrial development of the wind industry spurred both export production for components and increasing consumption domesti-cally. By 2007, China had become the world's largest installer of wind turbines, with local content rates of over 80%. Chinese component suppliers were producing generators and gearboxes for wind turbine installations around the world.[39] By 2012, China's renewable energy firms accounted for over 60% of the global production of solar PV modules and nearly half of the world's wind turbines.[40] Seven of the 10 largest solar manufacturers and 4 of the 10 largest wind turbine producers in the world were Chinese firms.[41]

In the solar industry, China's export focus initially obviated the need for the domestic consumption of the solar panels manufactured in high-tech development zones. Chinese solar PV manufacturers exported up to 98.5% of their production, most of it to Europe, where more than 70% of global solar PV installations occurred between 2009 and 2011. Domestic installations of solar PV accounted for less than 2% of domestic production. After the decline of European export markets in the wake of the global financial crisis and ongoing tariff disputes with the United States starting in 2012, China's solar manufacturers actively lobbied to expand domestic markets. By 2013, China was the largest market for solar PV installations, and by 2018 it accounted for more than half of global sales. Today, China continues to produce nearly two-thirds of the world's solar panels.[42] China makes more than one-third of global wind turbines (and a far larger share of wind turbine components), is the world's largest producer of (and market for) electric cars, and commands more than two-thirds of global production capacity for lithium-ion batteries.[43]

The ability to achieve economic co-benefits from domestic climate policy encouraged China to take on a more constructive role in international climate negotiations, at least in part motivated by the prospect of growing export markets due to global decarbonization goals. China's role in global climate negotiations changed dramatically as its domestic clean energy sectors grew to dominate global markets. While China was a steadfast advocate for exempting developing economies from strict emissions reduction requirements during the Kyoto and Copenhagen negotiations, it became central to the passing of the Paris Accords in 2015. More recently, China announced a goal to reach net-zero-carbon emissions by 2060 and reemphasized the need to peak its greenhouse gas emissions before 2030 in its most recent Five-Year Plan. China committed to these goals despite the enormous size of its domestic coal industry, a large part of which is directly owned by the Chinese state itself.[44]

The success of China's renewable energy sectors led to the adoption of similar green growth strategies in other industries, most notably in electric vehicles, where China combined stringent regulatory incentives to create domestic demand with financial support for a growing number of electric vehicle manufacturers.[45] The attempt to bolster domestic electric vehicle manufacturers at the expense of established auto joint ventures with foreign firms also changed domestic climate policy in Germany, where export-dependent car manufacturers had long opposed climate policies for the transportation sector. The need to supply clean vehicle technologies for the Chinese market changed the political calculus for German car manufacturers, which began to support behind climate goals for Germany's domestic transportation sector.[46]

In sum, the competitive nature of decarbonization in manufacturing-intensive export GMs suggests that climate policy battles take on an increasingly sectoral nature, as green growth advocates prevail in some sectors, including the German power sector and China's auto industry, but are nonetheless not guaranteed political victories. The failure to forge decarbonization in the German transportation sector before China's policy reversal, and the ongoing investments in coal power generation in China indicate that vested interests can also defend their interests against economic coalitions in favor of emission reductions. Nonetheless, in Germany and China, ambitious climate agendas were backed by politically powerful clean energy industries that relied on exports for a sizable share of their revenue.

Consumption-Led Decarbonization in the United Kingdom and the United States

The possibilities for economic coalitions behind climate policy were decidedly less favorable in consumption-led economies, where producers of clean energy technologies were constrained by domestic demand. In the United States, to this day one of the world's largest manufacturing economies despite a long-standing trade deficit, renewable energy industries were predominately populated by startup firms with capabilities in inventing new technologies, but with minimal in-house production facilities and expertise. Renewable energy sectors mirrored the broader trajectory of US manufacturing, as the US share of global manufacturing value-added declined from 28% in 2002 to 16.6% in 2016. The US trade deficit soared to more than USD 800 million and growth in merchandise imports continued to outpace export gains.[47]

Although several multinational energy and defense firms had conducted wind and solar R&D in the 1970s and 1980s, a lack of demand eventually prompted most to shut their renewable energy divisions.[48] The majority of firms entering the US wind and solar sectors in the late 1990s and early 2000s were startups seeking to lower the cost of renewable energy through technological breakthroughs. Patent counts reflect this focus on invention. US firms and research institutes account for approximately 25% of cumulative wind and solar energy patents until 2009, roughly twice the number of China or the European Union.[49] In the solar sector, many of the new firms focused on developing thin-film technologies, which promised to lower prices by replacing silicon, an expensive raw material, with cheaper alternatives.[50] By 2009, out of 100 solar companies operating in the United States, at least 73 were startups.[51] Although fewer in number, US wind startups also attempted to decrease the cost of wind energy with radically different designs.[52] Yet, the relative lack of production capabilities and focus on upstream research activities in US renewable energy sectors prevented the emergence of the broad political coalitions comprising producers and labor organizations that supported climate policy in Germany and China. Nearly all solar panels installed in the United States were imported. In the wind sector, only components that were too heavy and too large to be shipped economically were produced domestically, keeping local content rates far below those in Germany and China. Particularly high-value components inside the turbine nacelle, including generators and gearboxes, were predominately sourced from abroad.[53]

The reliance on imported renewable energy technologies made US renewable energy sectors vulnerable to partisan battles over climate policy. It allowed policymakers to question the economic value of public investments in clean energy, particularly in the context of high federal deficits. The primary federal incentive program to clean energy technologies consisting of a series of production and investment tax credit was regularly on the brink of elimination. Between 1992 and 2006 alone, the Production Tax Credit for wind energy was renewed in five separate instances, often only for one or two years. On three different occasions, the PTC expired before it was restored, leading to periods of up to nine months during which no federal support was available at all.[54] Thus, the persistent threat of tax credit expiration made for a highly uncertain investment climate for renewable energy technologies.

This problem remained acute until the late Obama administration, when the tax credits were renewed one final time before a bipartisan agreement to phase them out progressively.[55] Import dependence and persistent trade deficits with China in energy sectors have also sparked several trade disputes that have resulted in punitive tariffs on wind turbine towers, and more recently, on solar panels.[56] While these tariffs did little to relocate manufacturing to the United States, they harmed domestic wind and solar jobs in the installation, maintenance, and operation of renewable energy installations, undermining potential support still further.

Federal tax credits for renewable energy—as intermittent as they were—nonetheless opened the door to political arguments that public funds were spent primarily on imported technologies. Although the Obama administration had ambitions to compete with China and Germany on the development of a domestic clean energy industry, an export-oriented coalition of clean energy manufacturers comparable to either Germany or China failed to emerge in the United States—perhaps except for Tesla, America's premier electric vehicle manufacturer.[57] Emissions reductions—nearly 10% between 2005 and 2018—were attributable primarily to falling natural gas prices, which forced utility companies to switch uncompetitive coal plants to natural gas plants with lower emissions.[58] Yet the abundance of domestic natural gas, and the resulting pressure on prices, was itself reflective of the contested nature of decarbonization. The US gas boom resulted from government R&D subsidies and regulatory changes that aided the commercialization of unconventional exploration, most notably new fracking technologies such as horizontal drilling, that allowed existing oil and gas firms to tap previously unexplored resources. US emissions reductions, centered primarily on the power sector, resulted from subsidies for fossil resources rather than an economic coalition supporting decarbonization.

Service Economies and Greening GMs: English Lessons

In manufacturing economies, political conflict over climate policy primarily pitted vested interests against coalitions of supporters that included industrial sectors benefiting from climate policy. Service-intensive economies, by contrast, were less likely to suffer from stranded assets that would become obsolete because of aggressive climate policy while having fewer energy-intensive sectors that were concerned about rising energy costs in the transition to renewables. In sharp contrast to the political battles about decarbonization in the United States, emissions reductions also came about simply due to deindustrialization and an increasing reliance on imports of industrial goods in consumption-led economies dominated by services.

For instance, in the United Kingdom, carbon emissions peaked in 1973 and have declined by nearly 40% since 1990, more than in any other developed economy.[59] In 2017, British emissions fell to levels last seen in 1890, at the height of the Industrial Revolution.[60] Yet Britain's impressive emissions reductions were initially less the result of ambitious domestic climate policy than the byproduct of a broader shift in the composition of the domestic economy going back to the early Thatcher years.

Throughout the 1980s, the Thatcher government's emphasis on regressive redistribution of the tax burden and a focus on a declining role for the state in the economy set in motion shifts in the demand drivers of the domestic GM. Thatcher's policies continued under subsequent prime ministers, encouraging a withdrawal of the state from the economy and widespread privatization of domestic industries. Such shifts in economic policymaking were amplified by changes in industrial relations as the collapse of industry-level wage bargaining and the abolition of wage councils diminished the influence of organized labor and led to a decline in union membership by 40% over the 1980s and 1990s.[61] Without government backing and now fully exposed to market sources, privatization led to widespread deindustrialization, particularly in energy and labor-intensive industries that were no longer competitive in the global economy.[62] As wage repression resulting from changes in industrial relations and shifts in economic policymaking led to a decline in domestic consumption, consumers increasingly relied on household debt to shore up domestic spending on a growing share of imported manufacturing goods.[63]

Although these changes in Britain's domestic economic policy preceded concerns about carbon emissions, they prompted widespread and early decarbonization. One of the earliest and most consequential victims of these changes was Britain's coal industry, which had fueled Britain's industrialization throughout the 1800s. In the context of market liberalization, the British mining industry lost competitiveness. Domestic power generation shifted from coal to cheaper and more practical natural gas with far lower carbon emissions. Between 1990 and 2017, the share of coal in power generation fell from 65% to 7%, largely independent of climate policymaking itself.[64] The political conflict surrounding these shifts in Britain's domestic energy mix and the opposition from labor and the coal industry to market liberalization took place in the context of broader debates about domestic economic policymaking. It was not tied to carbon emissions.

The transition toward a low carbon economy further accelerated as Britain increasingly substituted a domestic manufacturing sector with imported goods. While the decline of coal power generation contributed some 37% of Britain's emissions reductions between 1990 and 2017, another 31% of emissions reductions were caused by lower non-electric energy use in residential and industrial sectors. Until 2007, such energy savings were primarily offset by increased emission embedded in imported goods as Britain's domestic manufacturing sector declined and imports substituted domestic production.[65]

By the time Britain passed the 2008 Climate Change Act with cross-party consensus, structural changes in the British economy had not only drastically reduced domestic emissions but had also eliminated significant sources of industrial opposition to climate policy that remained influential in other economies. The legislation, which mandated emissions reductions of 34% over 1990s levels by 2020 and 80% reductions by 2050, spurred further investments in decarbonization, not least the build-out of wind and solar installations that now make up a quarter of domestic power generation. But such shifts occurred with little opposition from vested industrial interests and in the context of natural gas demand that far exceeded what could be supplied domestically.[66] Although aggressive climate targets also came under attack from the British right after the 2010 election, such opposition was primarily ideological. It did not stem from those losing out economically because of progressive decarbonization.[67]

Conclusions

A common political strategy to overcome vested interest opposition to climate policy has been to promise "green growth" to build coalitions of decarbonization supporters that expect material benefits from green industrial change. As I have argued in this chapter, states have varied dramatically in the types of green growth strategies that they have been able to choose, with important implications for the kinds of political coalitions that have emerged in support of decarbonization. The ability to forge economic coalitions in support of climate change has so far hinged on forces largely independent of climate policy itself. That is, on the structural composition of the domestic economy and broader shifts in the demand drivers of the local GM.

As I have illustrated in the cases of China, Germany, the United Kingdom, and the United States, export-led manufacturing economies were more likely to yield green manufacturing sectors that could coalesce behind climate goals. In both China and Germany, existing manufacturing industries provided the industrial capabilities on which green industries could be built, and they already had in place export networks that these new industries could utilize. Precisely the nations with large legacy manufacturing sectors that we would most likely expect to oppose a green transition could in fact build domestic coalitions of economic supporters through export-driven clean energy industries.

Germany and China continue to have much work to do to reduce carbon emissions. They have nonetheless been able to spearhead enormous investments in wind and solar power with the help of clean energy manufacturing industries. In the United States, in the context of a declining manufacturing sector and against the competition of formidable exporters, renewable energy policy has yielded economic results primarily in service sector jobs with less political influence. The US reliance on imported technologies for decarbonization has allowed vested interests to contest decarbonization goals. The "laissez-faire" approach to deindustrialization practiced in the United Kingdom indeed led to historic emission reductions by outsourcing carbon missions to export nations without an active policy framework. But this is probably not a replicable model. Calculating emissions by the location of consumption, not production, may still yield a far larger carbon footprint, and may ultimately prevent the types of industrial coalitions that could effectively advance climate policy in the long run.

Although consumption-led economies face less domestic opposition from vested interests, they often lack the material benefits from climate policy that export-led economies have enjoyed. Therefore, the establishment of export-led manufacturing industries was frequently a goal of policymakers seeking to marry economic and environmental goals, but such goals were hard to establish in practice. Since exports, by definition, must be consumed somewhere, pushing into global markets was significantly harder once existing exporters like China and Germany had already divided up global market markets.

More recently, consumption-led economies have begun to push back against their reliance on green technologies imports—not least through increasingly restrictive trade policies. The COVID-19 pandemic further accelerated such tendencies, highlighting not only the vulnerability of the world's economic supply chains to external shocks, but also strengthening mercantilist calls for national self-sufficiency in China, the United States, and elsewhere. The Biden administration, while retreating from the isolationist stands of the Trump administration, has thus far refrained from rolling back existing tariffs. Domestic policy initiatives, most notably the "American Jobs Plan," are explicitly framed as responses to competition with China, suggesting that the relationship will remain complex for the foreseeable future.[68]

Few industries have more at stake in these battles than those producing low carbon energy technologies, including wind turbines, solar panels, electric vehicles, and lithium-ion batteries that are increasingly needed for electric cars and on-grid storage. Because of China's unprecedented investment in manufacturing capacity in these sectors, the cost of these technologies has fallen sharply. Since 2009, prices for wind turbines and solar panels have decreased by 69% and 88%, respectively, making these technologies competitive with conventional energy sources in many parts of the world. Cost reductions are particularly steep when renewable energy technologies are deployed in conjunction with battery storage, where China's massive investments in new manufacturing capacity have also led to rapid cost declines.[69]

The unique geography of clean energy supply chains—some of the first industries to emerge after globalization led to a wholesale reorganization of the global economy in the 1990s—makes international collaboration and economic interdependence fundamental in any effort to avoid the worst consequences of climate change. Meeting the goals of the Paris Agreement will require net-zero emissions by 2050 and substantial reductions before then. By 2030, emissions must have peaked and begun declining among major industrialized economies given the limited remaining carbon budget.[70] In this time frame, it is unrealistic to expect that any other economy will be able to replicate or surpass China's capacity to produce clean energy technologies required to meet these goals. The structure of global supply chains is, of course, neither fixed nor inevitable. Yet, only long-term investments in domestic clean energy sectors will allow consumption-led economies to change their position in green technology sectors without jeopardizing global climate goals.

Two future avenues for research remain. The politics of labor that have accompanied domestic debates about climate policy in Germany and China and have been largely absent from debates in the United States until the emergence of the Green New Deal. Climate policy generates jobs and income even in non-producing contexts. Still, it is also clear that different jobs have different kinds of political influence and lead to both different incomes and social outcomes. Future research should investigate links between these different green growth models and their relationships to growth coalitions. More work also needs to be done to examine links between domestic green growth approaches and integration into the international economy. While national governments have almost universally aspired to create autonomous domestic industries, even export-led growth models have been highly specialized and relied on trade and collaboration with one another. This raises further questions about both the origins of different growth models and where and how they actually generate value added. China and Germany established their respective specializations because of existing clusters of firms and institutional resources that supported their green growth strategies. The United States failed to match these green growth strategies because of institutional differences and because China and Germany already dominated production.

Ultimately, green growth is unlikely to offer a universal shortcut to more ambitious climate policies, especially not in the time frame required to avoid the worst consequences of climate change. But greening the GM is now, nonetheless, front and center in political debate in the EU and increasingly in the United States. Just as the IT revolution led to productivity increases, growth, and wealth, not because of rapidly proliferating employment in computer manufacturing plants, but because it fundamentally changed the workings of the global economy, so greening GMs may do the same. Yet it is also possible that dashed hopes of establishing green industries have in many parts of the world given rise to a set of mercantilist politics and trade policies that are likely to be counterproductive in terms of both our ability to reach climate goals and to green different types of GM.

Notes

1. IPCC 2018, 95.
2. Meckling and Nahm 2018a, b.
3. Breetz et al. 2018, 500; Hughes and Urpelainen 2015; Meckling et al. 2015, 1170; Nahm 2017a, 711–713.
4. Baccaro and Pontusson 2016, 186.
5. Green 2013; Hale and Roger 2014; Keohane 2015,
6. https://www.pewresearch.org/global/2015/11/05/global-concern-about-climate-change-broad-support-for-limiting-emissions/
7. Lewis et al. 2019.
8. Konisky 2018; McCright et al. 2016.
9. Hertel-Fernandez et al. 2019; Meckling and Nahm 2018b.
10. Meckling and Nahm 2022.
11. Meckling and Nahm 2018b.
12. Gopinathan et al. 2019; Meckling and Nahm 2018a.
13. Eaton and Kostka 2014.

14. Aklin and Urpelainen 2018, ch. 5; Hughes and Urpelainen 2015; Meckling and Nahm 2019.
15. Breetz et al. 2018, 500; Hughes and Urpelainen 2015; Meckling et al. 2015, 1170; Nahm 2017a, 711–713.
16. Baccaro and Pontusson 2016, 186.
17. Meckling and Allan 2020, Nahm 2021, ch. 2.
18. Nahm 2021, ch. 2.
19. Breetz et al. 2018, 500; Meckling et al. 2015, 1170; Nahm 2017a, 711–713.
20. Blyth and Matthijs 2017.
21. Baccaro and Pontusson 2016.
22. This is of course complicated by party politics in each GM. See Hopkin and Voss in this volume for more details.
23. Nahm 2021, ch. 3.
24. Meckling and Nahm 2018a.
25. Earth Policy Institute 2015; IRENA 2021.
26. Nahm 2017b.
27. Germany Trade & Invest 2010 Arbeitsgemeinschaft Windenergie-Zulieferindustrie 2012.
28. Germany Trade & Invest 2011b, c.
29. Germany Trade & Invest 2011a, 2014.
30. Fischedick and Bechberger 2009, 26.
31. See Nahm 2021.
32. Nahm 2017b.
33. Meckling and Nahm 2018a.
34. van Mark and Nick-Leptin 2011, 4–6.
35. See Hörnlein 2019.
36. Bullis 2012.
37. Wessendorf 2013.
38. See Alexander 2013.
39. Nahm and Steinfeld 2014.
40. Earth Policy Institute 2015.
41. Bebon 2013, IHS Solar 2013.
42. Earth Policy Institute 2015.
43. Helveston and Nahm 2019.
44. Nahm 2019.
45. Meckling and Nahm 2019, 476.
46. Meckling and Nahm 2018b, 10–12; 2019, 476.
47. Congressional Research Service 2019; Levinson 2018.
48. Colatat et al. 2009; Heymann 1995, 349–354.
49. Bettencourt et al. 2013, 3.
50. Morton 2006.
51. Knight 2011, 176.
52. Goudarzi and Zhu 2013, 199.
53. Department of Energy, Appendix E, 18 It is important to note that most regulatory requirements for renewable energy were passed at the state level, even though federal tax credits were central to making such state-mandated renewable energy targets economical for utilities.
54. Wiser et al. 2007, 79.
55. Righter 2011, 80–81.
56. Lewis 2014.
57. The White House 2009.
58. EPA 2020.
59. Hausfather 2019.
60. Hausfather 2018.
61. Howell 2005, ch. 5.
62. Carstensen and Matthijs 2018; Matthijs 2011, ch. 5.
63. Baccaro and Pontusson 2016.
64. Isoaho and Markard 2020, 7.

65. Hausfather 2019.
66. Carter 2014.
67. Gillard 2016.
68. Farrell and Newman 2020.
69. Lazard 2018.
70. IPCC 2018.

BIBLIOGRAPHY

A

Aalbers, Manuel B. 2008. "The Financialization of Home and the Mortgage Market Crisis." *Competition & Change* 12(2): 148–166.

Aalbers, Manuel B. 2017. "The Variegated Financialization of Housing." *International Journal of Urban and Regional Research* 41(4): 542–554.

Aalbers, Manuel B., Rodrigo Fernandez, and Gertjan Wijburg. 2020. "The Financialization of Real Estate." In *The Routledge International Handbook of Financialization*, edited by Philip Mader, Daniel Mertens, and Natascha van der Zwan, 200–212. London: Routledge.

Aalbers, Manuel B. 2019. "Financial Geography II: Financial Geographies of Housing and Real Estate." *Progress in Human Geography* 43(2): 376–387.

Adascalitei, Dragos, and Stefan Guga. 2016. "Tensions in the Periphery: Dependence and the Trajectory of a Low-Cost Productive Model in the Central and Eastern European Automotive Industry." *Budapest: Center for Policy Studies, Central European University* 27(1): 18–34.

Adler, David, and Ben Ansell. 2020. "Housing and Populism." *West European Politics* 43(1): 344–365.

Afonso, Alexandre, and Fabio Bulfone. 2019. "Electoral Coalitions and Policy Reversals in Portugal and Italy in the Aftermath of the Eurozone Crisis." *South European Society and Politics* 24(2): 233–257.

Agénor, Pierre-Richard, and Otaviano Canuto. 2012. "Middle-Income Growth Traps." World Bank Policy Research Working Paper 6210.

Aglietta, Michel, and Régis Breton. 2001. "Financial Systems, Corporate Control and Capital Accumulation." *Economy and Society* 30(4): 433–466.

Ahlquist, John S., and Ben W. Ansell. 2017. "Taking Credit: Redistribution and Borrowing in an Age of Economic Polarization." *World Politics* 69(4): 640–675.

Aiginger, Karl, and Dani Rodrik. 2020. "Rebirth of Industrial Policy and an Agenda for the Twenty-First Century." *Journal of Industry, Competition and Trade* 20(2): 189–207.

Aikman, David, Andrew G. Haldane, and Benjamin D. Nelson. 2015. "Curbing the Credit Cycle." *The Economic Journal* 125: 1072–1109.

Aklin, Michaël, and Johannes Urpelainen. 2018. *Renewables: The Politics of a Global Energy Transition*. Cambridge, MA: MIT Press.

Albu, Nora, Alexander Herzog-Stein, Ulrike Stein, and Rudolf Zwiener. 2018. "Arbeits- und Lohnstückkostenentwicklung 2017 im Europäischen Vergleich." IMK Report 142. Düsseldorf: IMK in der Hans Böckler Stiftung.

465

Alesina, Alberto, Dorian Carloni, and Giampaolo Lecce. 2011. "The Electoral Consequences of Large Fiscal Adjustments." NBER Working Paper No. 17655.

Alesina, Alberto, Carlo Favero, and Francesco Giavazzi. 2015. "The Output Effect of Fiscal Consolidation Plans," *Journal of International Economics* 96: 19–42.

Alesina, Alberto, Carlo Favero, and Francesco Giavazzi. 2019. *Austerity: When It Works and When It Doesn't.* Princeton, NJ: Princeton University Press.

Alesina, Alberto, Roberto Perotti, and José Tavares 1998. "The Political Economy of Fiscal Adjustments." *Brookings Papers of Economic Activity* 1: 197–248.

Alexander, Cathy. 2013. "Carbon Cutters. http://www.crikey.com.au/thepowerindex/carbon-cutters/(accessed May 28, 2014).

Alexius, Annika, and Erik Post. 2008. "Exchange Rates and Asymmetric Shocks in Small Open Economies." *Empirical Economics* 35(3): 527–541.

Allen, Franklin, Krzysztof Jackowicz, Oskar Kowalewski, and Łukasz Kozłowski. 2017. "Bank Lending, Crises, and Changing Ownership Structure in Central and Eastern European Countries." *Journal of Corporate Finance* 42 (February 1, 2017): 494–515.

Álvarez, Ignacio, Jorge Uxó, and Eladio Febrero. 2018. "Internal Devaluation in a Wage-Led Economy: The Case of Spain." *Cambridge Journal of Economics* 43(2): 335–360.

Amable, Bruno. 2017. *Structural Crisis and Institutional Change in Modern Capitalism.* Oxford: Oxford University Press.

Amable, Bruno, Elvire Guillaud, and Stefano Palombarini. 2011. "The Political Economy of Neo-Liberalism in Italy and France." Documents de travail du Centre d'Economie de la Sorbonne 2011.51. Université Panthéon-Sorbonne.

Amable, Bruno, and Bob Hancké. 2001. "Innovation and Industrial Renewal in France in Comparative Perspective." *Industry and Innovation* 8(2): 113–133.

Amable, Bruno, and Stefano Palombarini. 2009. "A Neorealist Approach to Institutional Change and the Diversity of Modern Capitalism." *Socioeconomic Review* 7(1): 123–43.

Ambroziak, Łukasz. 2018. "The CEECs in Global Value Chains: The Role of Germany." *Acta Oeconomica*, April 19, 2018. https://doi.org/10.1556/032.2018.68.1.1.

Amsden, Alice H. 2001. *The Rise of the Rest: Challenges to the West from Late-Industrializing Economies.* Oxford: Oxford University Press.

Anderson, Karen M. 2004. "Pension Politics in Three Small States: Denmark, Sweden and the Netherlands." *The Canadian Journal of Sociology / Cahiers canadiens de sociologie* 29(2): 289–312.

Anderson, Karen M. 2019. "Financialisation Meets Collectivisation: Occupational Pensions in Denmark, the Netherlands and Sweden." *Journal of European Public Policy* 26(4): 617–636.

Anderson, Karen M., and Anke Hassel. 2015. *Winner-Take-All Politics in Europe? The Political Economy of Rising Inequality in Germany and Sweden.* Rochester, NY: Social Science Research Network. SSRN Scholarly Paper. (accessed April 29, 2021).

Anderson, Karen, and Paulette Kurzer. 2016. "The Politics of Mortgage Financing and Regulation in Denmark, the Netherlands and Sweden." Unpublished manuscript.

Anderson, Karen, and Paulette Kurzer. 2020. "The Politics of Mortgage Credit Expansion in Small Coordinated Market Economies." *West European Politics* 43(2): 366–389.

Andersson, Björn, Magnus Jonsson, and Henrik Lundvall. 2020. "Den nya makroekonomiska miljön efter finanskrisen," *Penning- och valutapolitik* 2020(1): 71–100.

Andersson, Fredrik, and Lars Jonung. 2015. "Krasch, boom, krasch? Den svenska kreditcykeln." *Ekonomisk Debatt* 43(8): 17–31.

Andrew, Dan, Chiara Criscuolo, and Peter Gal. 2016. *The Best Versus the Rest: The Global Productivity Slowdown, Divergence Across Firms and the Role of Public Policy.* Paris: OECD.

Ang, Yuen Yuen. 2016. *How China Escaped the Poverty Trap.* Ithaca, NY: Cornell University Press.

Ansell, Ben. 2014. "The Political Economy of Ownership: Housing Markets and the Welfare State." *American Political Science Review* 108(2): 383–402.

Ansell, Ben W., J. Lawrence Broz, and Thomas Flaherty. 2018. "Global Capital Markets, Housing Prices, and Partisan Fiscal Policies." *Economics & Politics* 30(3): 307–339.

Ansell, Ben, and David Samuels. 2014. *Inequality and Democratization: An Elite-Competition Approach*. Cambridge: Cambridge University Press.

Anselmi, Guido, and Serena Vicari. 2020. "Milan Makes It to the Big Leagues: A Financialized Growth Machine at Work." *European Urban and Regional Studies* 27(2): 106–124.

Arbeitsgemeinschaft Windenergie-Zulieferindustrie. 2012. "Komponenten, Systeme und Fertigungstechnik für die Windindustrie." Frankfurt: VDMA.

Acharya, Viral, Matthew Richardson, Stijn van Nieuwerburgh, and Lawrence White. 2011 *Guaranteed to Fail: Fannie Mae, Freddie Mac, and the Debacle of Mortgage Finance*. Princeton, NJ: Princeton University Press.

Arestis, Philip, and Ana Rosa González. 2014. "Bank Credit and the Housing Market in OECD Countries." *Journal of Post Keynesian Economics* 36(3): 467–490.

Arestis, Philip, Kevin. McCauley, and Malcolm Sawyer. 2001. "An Alternative Stability Pact for the European Union." *Cambridge Journal of Economics* 25: 113–130.

Armingeon, Klaus, and Lucio Baccaro. 2012. "Political Economy of the Sovereign Debt Crisis: The Limits of Internal Devaluation." *Industrial Law Journal* 41(3): 254–275.

Armingeon, Klaus, Kai Guthmann, and David Weisstanner. 2016. "Choosing the Path of Austerity: How Parties and Policy Coalitions Influence Welfare State Retrenchment in Periods of Fiscal Consolidation." *West European Politics* 39(4): 628–647.

Armstrong, Philip, Andrew Glyn, and John Harrison. 1991. *Capitalism since 1945*. Cambridge, MA: Basil Blackwell.

Aron, Janine, John V. Duca, John Muellbauer, Keiko Murata, and Anthony Murphy. 2012. "Credit, Housing Collateral, and Consumption: Evidence from Japan, the U.K., and the U.S." *Review of Income and Wealth* 58(3): 397–423.

Aslund, Anders. 2017. "Latvia's Banks: The Story from the Beginning." sites.krieger.jhu.edu/iae/files/2018/03/Final-2-Oct-2017-Latvian-Banks.pdf.

Aslund, Anders, and Valdis Dombrovskis. 2011. *How Latvia Came Through the Financial Crisis*. 1st ed. Institute of International Economics.

Assous, Michael, and Krishna Dutt. 2013. "Growth and Income Distribution with the Dynamicy of Power in Labour and Goods Markets." *Cambridge Journal of Economics* 37(6): 1407–1430.

Atkinson, Anthony B., Thomas Piketty, and Emmanuel Saez. 2011. "Top Incomes in the Long Run of History." *Journal of Economic Literature* 49(1): 3–71.

Atoyan, Ruben, Lone Engbo Christiansen, Allan Dizioli, Christian Ebeke, Nadeem Ilahi, Anna Ilyina, Gil Mehrez, Haonan Qu, and Faezeh Raei. 2016. *Emigration and Its Economic Impact on Eastern Europe*. International Monetary Fund.

Autor, David. 2019. Work of the Past, Work of the Future. NBER Working Paper No. 25588.

Autor, David, David Dorn, Gordon Hanson, and Kaveh Majlesi. 2020. "Importing Political Polarization? The Electoral Consequences of Rising Trade Exposure." *American Economic Review* 110(10): 3139–3183.

Avlijaš, Sonja, Anke Hassel, and Bruno Palier. 2021. "Growth Strategies and Welfare Reforms in Europe." In *Growth and Welfare in Advanced Capitalist Economies* edited by Anke Hassel and Bruno Palier, 372–436. Oxford: Oxford University Press.

B

Baccaro, Lucio. 2020. "Is There a Mediterranean Growth Model?" Unpublished Document, MPIfG.

Baccaro, Lucio, and Chiara Benassi. 2017. "Throwing Out the Ballast: Growth Models and the Liberalization of German Industrial Relations." *Socio-Economic Review* 15(1): 85–115.

Baccaro, Lucio, and Benjamin Braun. 2020. "Growth Models and IPE." Manuscript in progress, MPIfG.

Baccaro, Lucio, and Massimo D'Antoni. 2020. "Has the "External Constraint" Contributed to Italy's Stagnation? A Critical Event Analysis." MPIfG Working Paper 20/9.

Baccaro, Lucio, and Chris Howell. 2011. "A Common Neoliberal Trajectory: The Transformation of Industrial Relations in Advanced Capitalism." *Politics & Society* 39(4): 521–563.

Baccaro, Lucio, and Chris Howell. 2017. *Trajectories of Neoliberal Transformation: European Industrial Relations After the 1970s*. Cambridge: Cambridge University Press.

Baccaro, Lucio, and Erik Neimanns. 2021. "Determinants of Wage (Dis-)Satisfaction: Trade Exposure, Export-Led Growth, and the Irrelevance of Bargaining Structure." MPIfG Discussion Paper 21/3.

Baccaro, Lucio, and Jonas Pontusson. 2016. "Rethinking Comparative Political Economy: The Growth Model Perspective." *Politics & Society* 44(2): 175–207.

Baccaro, Lucio, and Jonas Pontusson. 2018. "Comparative Political Economy and Varieties of Macroeconomics." Max-Planck-Institut für Gesellschaftsforschung Discussion Paper 18/10. Köln: Max Planck Institute.

Baccaro, Lucio, and Jonas Pontusson. 2019. "Social Blocs and Growth Models: An Analytical Framework with Germany and Sweden as Illustrative Cases." Unequal Democracies Working paper n°7, April.

Baccaro, Lucio, and Jonas Pontusson. 2021. "European Growth Models Before and After the Great Recession. In *Growth and Welfare in Advanced Capitalist Economies*, edited by Anke Hassel and Bruno Palier, 98–134. Oxford: Oxford University Press.

Bai, Chong-en, Chang-Tai Hsieh, and Zheng Song. 2016. "The Long Shadow of China's Fiscal Expansion." *Brookings Papers on Economic Activity* 47(2): 129–181.

Baker, Dean. 2012. "First Time Underwater: The Impact of the First-Time Homebuyer Tax Credit." Working Paper, Center for Economic and Policy Research.

Baldenius, Till, Sebastian Kohl, and Moritz Schularick. 2019. "Die neue Wohnungsfrage: Gewinner und Verlierer des deutschen Immobilienbooms." MacroFinance Lab Working Paper.

Baldini, Massimo, and Teresio Poggio. 2014. "The Italian Housing System and the Global Financial Crisis." *Journal of Housing and the Built Environment* 29(2): 317–334.

Ban, Cornel. 2012. "Brazil's Liberal Neo-developmentalism: New Paradigm or Edited Orthodoxy?" *Review of International Political Economy* 20(2): 1–34.

Ban, Cornel. 2016. *Ruling Ideas: How Global Neoliberalism Goes Local*. Oxford: Oxford University Press.

Ban, Cornel. 2019. "Dependent Development at a Crossroads? Romanian Capitalism and Its Contradictions." *West European Politics* 42(5): 1041–1068.

Ban, Cornel, and Dragos Adascalitei. 2020. "The FDI-Led Growth Models of the East-Central and South-Eastern European Periphery." Unpublished Manuscript.

Ban, Cornel, and Dorothee Bohle. 2021. "Definancialization, Financial Repression and Policy Continuity in East-Central Europe." *Review of International Political Economy* 28(4): 874–897.

Ban, Cornel, and Oddný Helgadóttir. 2019. "Financialization and Growth Regimes." Unpublished Paper, Copenhagen Business School.

Ban, Cornel, Gabor Scheiring, and Mihai Vasile. 2021. "The Political Economy of National-Neoliberalism." *European Politics and Society* (published online August 10). https://doi.org/10.1080/23745118.2021.1956241.

Barbosa-Filho, Nelson, and Lance Taylor. 2006. *Distributive and Demand Cycles in the US Economy—a Structuralist Goodwin Model. Metroeconomica* 57(3): 389–411.

Barnes, Lucy. 2016. "Private Debt and the Anglo-Liberal Growth Model." *Government and Opposition* 51(4): 529–552.

Barnes, Lucy, and Timothy Hicks. 2018. "Making Austerity Popular: The Media and Mass Attitudes Towards Fiscal Policy." *American Journal of Political Science* 62(2): 340–354.

Barrios, Salvador, Viginta Ivaškaitė-Tamošiūnė, Anamaria Maftei, Edlira Narazani, and Janos Varga. 2019. "Progressive Tax Reforms in Flat Tax Countries." *Eastern European Economics* (October 21, 2019). https://doi.org/10.1080/00128775.2019.1671201.

Barry, Frank. 2019. "Aggressive Tax Planning Practices and Inward-FDI Implications for Ireland of the New US Corporate Tax Regime." *The Economic and Social Review* 50(2): 325–340.

Barta, Zsófia. 2011. "Flirting with Disaster: Explaining Excessive Public Debt Accumulation in Italy and Belgium." PhD diss, The London School of Economics and Political Science (LSE).

Barta, Zsófia. 2018. *In the Red: The Politics of Public Debt Accumulation in Developed Countries.* Ann Arbor: University of Michigan Press.

Bartels, Larry. 2016. *Unequal Democracy.* 2nd ed. Princeton, NJ: Princeton University Press.

Barth, Erling, Alex Bryson, James Davis, and Richard Freeman. 2014. "It's Where You Work: Increases in Earnings Dispersion across Establishments and Individuals in the US." NBER Working Paper No. 20447.

Barwell, Richard, and Oliver Burrows. 2014. "Growing Fragilities? Balance Sheets in the Great Moderation." In *A Flow-of-Funds Perspective on the Financial Crisis,* edited by Bernhard Winkler, Ad van Riet, and Peter Bull, 40–109. London: Palgrave Macmillan.

Baumol, William J. 1967. "The Macroeconomics of Unbalanced Growth." *American Economic Review* 52(3): 415–426.

Bawn, Kathleen, Martin Cohen, David Karol, Seth Masket, Hans Noel, and John Zaller. 2012. "A Theory of Political Parties: Groups, Policy Demands and Nominations in American Politics." *Perspectives on Politics* 10(3): 571–597.

BBC. 2016. "Work Capability Assessment Overhaul for Disabled." BBC News. https://www.bbc.com/news/uk-politics-37810701 (April 28, 2021).

Bebon, Joseph. 2013. "Top Wind Turbine Supplier in 2012: Vestas or GE." *North American Wind Power,* March 26. https://nawindpower.com/top-wind-turbine-supplier-of-2012-vestas-or-ge.

Beck, Mareike. 2021. "Extroverted Financialization: How US Finance Shapes European Banking." *Review of International Political Economy.* (online first). https://doi: 10.1080/09692290.2021.1949375.

Becker, Joachim, and Johannes Jäger. 2010. "Development Trajectories in the Crisis in Europe." *Debatte: Journal of Contemporary Central and Eastern Europe* 18(1): 5–27.

Becker, Joachim, and Johannes Jäger. 2012. "Integration in Crisis: A Regulationist Perspective on the Interaction of European Varieties of Capitalism." *Competition & Change* 16 (3): 169–187.

Becker, Joachim, Johannes Jäger, and Rudy Weissenbacher. 2015. "Uneven and Dependent Development in Europe: The Crisis and Its Implications." In *Asymmetric Crisis in Europe and Possible Futures,* edited by Johannes Jäger and Elisabeth Springler, 101–117. London: Routledge.

Behrens, Martin, and Markus Helfen. 2016. "Sachzwang oder Programm? Tarifpolitische Orientierungen und OT-Mitgliedschaft bei Deutschen Arbeitgeberverbänden." *WSI-Mitteilungen* 69(6): 452–459.

Belfrage, Claes. 2008. "Towards 'Universal Financialisation' in Sweden?" *Contemporary Politics* 14(3): 277–296.

Belfrage, Claes, and Markus Kallifatides. 2018. "Financialization and the New Swedish Model." *Cambridge Journal of Economics* 42: 875–899.

Belfrage, Claes, and Magnus Ryner. 2009. "Renegotiating the Swedish Social Democratic Settlement: From Pension Fund Socialism to Neoliberalization." *Politics & Society* 37(2): 257–287.

Bell, Daniel. 1973. *The Coming of Post-Industrial Society.* New York: Basic Books.

Bengtsson, Erik. 2014. "Labour's Share in Twentieth-Century Sweden: A Reinterpretation." *Scandinavian Economic History Review* 6(3): 90–314.

Bengtsson, Erik. 2015a. "Wage Restraint in Scandinavia: During the Postwar Period or the Neoliberal Age?" *European Review of Economic History.* https://doi: 10.1093/ereh/hev008.

Bengtsson, Erik. 2015b. "Wage Restraint and Wage Militancy: Belgium, Germany and the Netherlands, 1950–2010." Unpublished Manuscript, Economic History Unit, University of Gothenburg.

Beramendi, Pablo, Silja Häusermann, Herbert Kitschelt, and Hanspeter Kriesi. 2015. *The Politics of Advanced Capitalism.* Cambridge: Cambridge University Press.

Bergen, Mark, and Josh Eidelson. 2018. "Inside Google's Shadow Workforce," *Bloomberg*, July 25, 2018. https://www.bloomberg.com/news/articles/2018-07-25/inside-google-s-shadow-workforce.

Berger, David W., Kyle Herkenhoff, and Simon Mongey. 2019. "Labor Market Power." NBER Working Paper No. 25719.

Bergh, Anders, and Gissur Erlingsson. 2009. "Liberalisation without Retrenchment." *Scandinavian Political Studies* 32(1): 71–93.

Berghoff, Hartmut. 2016. "Varieties of Financialization? Evidence from German Industry in the 1990s." *Business History Review* 90(1): 81–108.

Bergholt, Drago, Francesco Furlanetto, and Nicolò Maffei-Faccioli. 2022. "The Decline of the Labor Share: New Empirical Evidence." *American Economic Journal: Macroeconomics*. https://doi.org/10.1257/mac.20190365 (online first).

Bernstein, Jeremy. 2008. *Physicists on Wall Street and Other Essays on Science and Society*. New York: Springer Science & Business Media.

Bershidsky, Leonid. 2018. "Latvia's Post-Soviet Money Pipeline Is Closing," *Bloomberg*, March 9, 2018. https://www.bloomberg.com/opinion/articles/2018-03-09/latvia-s-post-soviet-money-pipeline-is-closing.

Bértola, Luis, and José Antonio Ocampo. 2012. *The Economic Development of Latin America Since Independence*. Oxford: Oxford University Press.

Bessembinder, Hendrik. 2018. Do Stocks Outperform Treasury Bills? *Journal of Financial Economics* 129: 440–457.

Bessembinder, Hendrik, Te-Feng Chen, Goeun Choi, and Kuo-Chiang. Wei. 2019. Do Global Stocks Outperform US Treasury Bills? Available at https://ssrn.com/abstract=3415739.

Bettencourt, Luis M. A., Jessika E. Trancik, and Jasleen Kaur. 2013. "Determinants of the Pace of Global Innovation in Energy Technologies." *Plos ONE* https://doi.org/10.1371/journal.pone.0067864.

Bezemer, Dirk. 2014. "Schumpeter Might Be Right Again: The Functional Differentiation of Credit." *Journal of Evolutionary Economics* 24(5): 935–950.

Bhaduri, Amit, and Marglin, Stephen 1990. "Unemployment and the Real Wage: The Economic Basis for Contesting Political Ideologies." *Cambridge Journal of Economics* 14: 375–393.

Bhattacharyya, Sambit, and Jeffrey G. Williamson. 2016. "Distributional Consequences of Commodity Price Shocks: Australia Over a Century." *Review of Income and Wealth* 62: 223–244.

Bick, Christopher. 2021. "The Party Politics of Crisis: The Technologies of Partisan Communication and Institutional Instability." Paper presented at 27th Conference of Europeanists, June 2021.

Bierut, Beata K., and Kamila Kuziemska-Pawlak. 2017. "Competitiveness and Export Performance of CEE Countries." *Eastern European Economics* 55(6): 522–542.

Bishop, Matthew Louis. 2012. "The Political Economy of Small States: Enduring Vulnerability?" *Review of International Political Economy* 19(5): 942–960.

Bitard, Pierre, Charles Edquist, Leif Hommen, and Annika Rickne. 2008. "Reconsidering the Paradox of High R&D Input and Low Innovation: Sweden." In *Small Country Innovation Systems*, edited by Edquist and Hommen, 237–280. Cheltenham: Edward Elgar.

Blair, John. 1976. *Control of Oil*. New York: Pantheon Books.

Blair, Tony, and Gerhard Schroeder. 1998. "Europe: The Third Way/Neue Mitte." *Friedrich Ebert Stiftung*. https://library.fes.de/pdf-files/bueros/suedafrika/02828.pdf.

Blanchard, Olivier. 2019. "Public Debt and Low Interest Rates." Presidential Lecture to the American Economic Association, January.

Blanchard, Olivier, Eugenio Cerutti, and Lawrence Summers. 2015. "Inflation and Activity–Two Explorations and Their Monetary Policy Implications." NBER Working Paper No. 21726.

Blanchard, Olivier, Giovanni Dell'Ariccia, and Paolo Mauro. 2010. "Rethinking Macroeconomic Policy." IMF Staff Position Note 10/03.

Blanchard, Olivier, and Daniel Leigh, 2013. "Growth Forecast Errors and Fiscal Multipliers." International Monetary Fund Working Paper WP13/1.

Blanchard, Olivier, and Larry Summers. 2017. "Rethinking Stablization Policy: Back to the Future." PIIE Working Paper, October.

Blecker, Robert. 2016. Wage-Led versus Profit-Led demand Regimes: The Long and the Short of It. *Review of Keynesian Economics* 4(4): 373–390.

Blecker, Robert, Michael Cauvel, and Yun Kim. 2020. "Systems Estimation of a Structural Model of Distribution and Demand in the US Economy." PKES Working Paper 2012.

Blecker, Richael, and Mark Setterfield. 2019. *Heterodox Macroeconomics. Models of Demand, Distribution and Growth*. Aldershot: Edward Elgar.

Block, Fred L., and Matthew R. Keller, eds. 2015. *State of Innovation: The US Government's Role in Technology Development*. London: Routledge.

Blyth, Mark. 2002. *Great Transformations; Economic Ideas and Institutional Change in the Twentieth Century*. Cambridge: Cambridge University Press.

Blyth, Mark. 2003. "Structures Do Not Come with an Instruction Sheet: Interests, Ideas, and Progress in Political Science." *Perspectives on Politics* 1(4): 695–706.

Blyth, Mark. 2006. "Great Punctuations: Prediction, Randomness, and the Evolution of Comparative Political Science." *American Political Science Review* 100(4): 493–498.

Blyth, Mark. 2013. *Austerity: The History of a Dangerous Idea*. New York: Oxford University Press.

Blyth, Mark. 2016. "Policies to Overcome Stagnation: The Crisis, and the Possible Futures, of All Things Euro." *European Journal of Economics and Economic Policies: Intervention* 13(2): 215–228.

Blyth, Mark, and Richard Katz. 2005. "From Catch-All Politics to Cartelisation: The Political Economy of the Cartel Party." *West European Politics* 28(1): 33–60.

Blyth, Mark, and Matthias Matthijs. 2017. "Black Swans, Lame Ducks, and the Mystery of Ipe's Missing Macroeconomy." *Review of International Political Economy* 24(2): 203–231.

Bockerman, Petri, and Roope Uusitalo. 2006. "Erosion of the Ghent System and Union Membership Decline: Lessons from Finland." *British Journal of Industrial Relations* 44(2): 283–303.

Bofinger, Peter,, Sebastian Debes, Johannes Gareis, and Eric Mayer. 2013. "Monetary Policy Transmission in a Model with Animal Spirits and House Price Booms and Busts." *Journal of Economic Dynamics and Control* 37: 2862–2881.

Bohle, Dorothee. 2014. "Post-Socialist Housing Meets Transnational Finance: Foreign Banks, Mortgage Lending, and the Privatization of Welfare in Hungary and Estonia." *Review of International Political Economy* 21(4): 913–948.

Bohle, Dorothee. 2018. "European Integration, Capitalist Diversity and Crises Trajectories on Europe's Eastern Periphery." *New Political Economy* 23(2): 239–253.

Bohle, Dorothee, and Béla Greskovits. 2006. "Capitalism without Compromise: Strong Business and Weak Labor in Eastern Europe's New Transnational Industries." *Studies in Comparative International Development* 41(1): 3–25.

Bohle, Dorothee, and Béla Greskovits. 2007. "Capitalist Diversity in Eastern Europe." *Economic Sociology_the European Electronic Newsletter* 8(2): 3–9.

Bohle, Dorothee, and Béla Greskovits. 2012. *Capitalist Diversity on Europe's Periphery*. Ithaca, NY: Cornell University Press, 2012.

Bohle, Dorothee, and Wade Jacoby. 2017. "Lean, Special, or Consensual? Vulnerability and External Buffering in the Small States of East-Central Europe." *Comparative Politics* 49(2): 191–212.

Bohle, Dorothee, and Aidan Regan. 2021. "The Comparative Political Economy of Growth Models: Explaining the Continuity of FDI-Led Growth in Ireland and Hungary." *Politics & Society* 49(1): 75–106.

Bohle, Dorothee, and Leonard Seabrooke. 2020. "From Asset to Patrimony: The Re-emergence of the Housing Question." *West European Politics* 43(2): 412–434.

Boix, Carles. 2019. *Democratic Capitalism at the Crossroads: Technological Change and the Future of Politics*. Princeton, NJ: Princeton University Press.

Bojar, Abel, Björn Bremer, Hanspeter Kriesi, and Chendi Wang (2022). "The Effect of Austerity Packages on Government Popularity During the Great Recession." *British Journal of Political Science* 52(1): 181–199.

Boldrick, Isabel. 2021. "Die Konjunkturreagibilität öffentlicher Investitionen am Beispiel der Deutschen Schuldenbremse." CIW Discussion Paper 1/2021.

Borio, Claudio. 2014. "The Financial Cycle and Macroeconomics: What Have We Learnt?" *Journal of Banking & Finance* 45: 182–198.

Bowles, Samuel, and Robert Boyer, 1990. "A Wage-Led Employment Regime: Income Distribution, Labour Discipline, and Aggregate Demand in Welfare Capitalism." In *The Golden Age of Capitalism: Reinterpreting the Postwar Experience*, edited by S. Marglin and J. Schor, 187–217. Oxford: Clarendon.

Bown, Chad, and Melina Kolb. 2021. "Trump's Trade War Timeline: An Up-to-Date Guide." *Peterson Institute for International Economics*. https://www.piie.com/sites/default/files/documents/trump-trade-war-timeline.pdf.

Boyer, Robert. 1987. "Formalizing Growth Regimes within a Regulation Approach: A Method for Assessing the Economic Consequences of Technological Change." CEPREMAP Working Papers 8715.

Boyer, Robert. 1990. *The Regulation School: A Critical Introduction*. New York: Columbia University Press.

Boyer, Robert. 2000. "Is a Finance-Led Growth Regime a Viable Alternative to Fordism? A Preliminary Analysis." *Economy and Society* 29(1): 111–145.

Boyer, Robert. 2004. *Théorie De La Régulation, 1. Les Fondamentaux*. Paris: La découverte.

Boyer, Robert, and Pascal Petit. 1991. "Kaldor's Growth Theories: Past, Present and Prospects for the Future." In *Nicholas Kaldor and Mainstream Economics: Confrontation or Convergence?*, edited by Edward J. Nell and Willi Semmler, 485–517. London: Palgrave Macmillan UK.

Boyer, Robert, and Yves Saillard, eds. 2005. *Regulation Theory: The State of the Art*. London: Routledge.

Braun, Benjamin, and Richard Deeg. 2020. "Strong Firms, Weak Banks: The Financial Consequences of Germany's Export-Led Growth Model." *German Politics* 29(3): 358–381.

Braunstein, Elissa, Irene van Staveren, and Daniele Tavani. 2011. "Embedding Care and Unpaid Work in Macroeconomic Modelling: A Structuralist Approach." *Feminist Economics* 17(4): 5–31.

Brazys, Samuel, and Aidan Regan. 2017. "The Politics of Capitalist Diversity in Europe Explaining Ireland's Divergent Recovery from the Euro Crisis." *Perspectives on Politics* 15(2): 411–427.

Brazys, Samuel, and Aidan Regan. 2021. "Small States in Global Markets. The Political Economy of FDI-Led Growth in Ireland." In *Handbook of Irish Politics*, edited by David Farrell and Niamh Hardiman, 405–422. Oxford: Oxford University Press.

Breetz, Hanna, Matto Mildenberger, and Leah Stokes. 2018. "The Political Logics of Clean Energy Transitions." *Business and Politics* 20(4): 492–522.

Bremer, Björn, and Reto Bürgisser. 2018. "Are Voters Austerians? Evidence from Survey Experiments on Budgetary Trade-Offs and Priorities." Paper presented at the Annual Meeting of the Conference for Europeanists (CES), Chicago, April 5–8.

Bremer, Björn, Donato Di Carlo, and Leon Wansleben. 2021. "The Constrained Politics of Local Public Investments under Cooperative Federalism." MPIfG Discussion Paper 21/4.

Bremer, Björn, and Sean McDaniel. 2020. "The Ideational Foundations of Social Democratic Austerity in the Context of the Great Recession," *Socio-Economic Review* 18(2): 439–446.

Brender, Adi, and Allan Drazen. 2008. "How Do Budget Deficits and Economic Growth Affect Reelection Prospects? Evidence from a Large Panel of Countries." *American Economic Review* 98(5): 2203–2220.

Brenner, Aaron, Robert Brenner, and Cal Winslow, eds. 2010. *Rebel Rank and File: Labor Militancy and Revolt from Below during the Long 1970s*. London: Verso.

Brenner, Neil, Jamie Peck, and Nik Theodore. 2010. "Variegated Neoliberalization: Geographies, Modalities, Pathways." *Global Networks* 10(2): 182–222.

Brenner, Robert. 1977. The Origins of Capitalist Development: A Critique of Neo-Smithian Marxism. *New Left Review* 104: 25–92.

Bresser-Pereira, Luiz Carlos. 2015. "The Macroeconomic Tripod and the Workers' Party Administrations." In *The Brazilian Economy Today: Towards a New Socio-Economic Model?*, edited by Anthony W. Pereira and Lauro Mattei, 121–134. London: Palgrave/Macmillan.

Bresser-Pereira, and Luiz Carlos. 2018. "Neutralizing the Dutch Disease." Textos Para Discussão 476. Fundação Getulio Vargas.

Breuer, Sebastian, and Jens Klose. 2015. "Who Gains from Nominal Devaluation? An Empirical Assessment of Euro-Area Exports and Imports." *The World Economy* 38(12): 1966–1989.

Brooks, Sarah. M., Raphael Cunha, and Layna Mosley, L. 2015. "Categories, Creditworthiness, and Contagion: How Investors' Shortcuts Affect Sovereign Debt Markets." *International Studies Quarterly* 59(3): 587–601.

Brostoff, Ari M. 2019. "How White Nationalists Aligned Themselves with the Antiabortion Movement." *Washington Post* (August 27, 2019). https://www.washingtonpost.com/outl ook/2019/08/27/how-white-nationalists-aligned-themselves-with-antiabortion-movem ent/ (accessed April 27, 2021).

Broz, J. Lawrence, Jeffry Frieden, and Stephen Weymouth. 2008. "Exchange Rate Policy Attitudes: Direct Attitudes from Survey Data." *IMF Staff Papers* 55(3): 417–444.

Bruno, Michael, and Jeffrey Sachs. 1985. *Economics of Worldwide Stagflation*. Cambridge, MA: Harvard University Press.

Bruszt, Laszlo, and Visnja Vukov. 2017. "European Integration and the Evolution of Economic State Capacities in Southern and Eastern Europe." In *Reconfiguring European States in Crisis*, edited by Desmond King and Patrick Le Galès, 158–178. Oxford: Oxford University Press.

Brzezinski, Michal. 2018. "Income Inequality and the Great Recession in Central and Eastern Europe." *Economic Systems* 42(2): 219–247.

Buendía, Luis. 2020. "A Perfect Storm in a Sunny Economy: A Political Economy Approach to the Crisis in Spain." *Socio-Economic Review* 18(2): 419–438.

Buendia, Luis, and Pedro Rey-Araújo. 2021. "This Time Was Different: The Crisis That Went Past Sweden." In *Institutional Change After the Great Recession: European Growth Models at the Crossroads*, edited by Luis Cárdenas and Javier Arribas, 246–272. London: Routledge.

Bulfone, Fabio. 2019. "The State Strikes Back: Industrial Policy, Regulatory Power and the Divergent Performance of Telefonica and Telecom Italia." *Journal of European Public Policy* 26(5): 752–771.

Bulfone, Fabio. 2020. "New Forms of Industrial Policy in the Age of Regulation: A Comparison of Electricity and Telecommunications in Italy and Spain." *Governance* 33(1): 93–108.

Bulfone, Fabio, and Arianna Tassinari. 2021. "Under Pressure. Economic Constraints, Electoral Politics and Labour Market Reforms in Southern Europe in the Decade of the Great Recession." *European Journal of Political Research* 60(3): 509–538.

Bullis, Kevin. 2012. "The Chinese Solar Machine." *MIT Technology Review* 115(1): 46–49.

Bullough, Oliver. 2018. "The Rise of Kleptocracy: The Dark Side Of Globalization." *Journal of Democracy* 29(1): 25–38.

Bulow, Jeremy, John Geanakoplos, and Paul Klemperer 1985. Holding Idle Capacity to Deter Entry. *The Economic Journal* 95(377): 178–182.

Bundesministerium für Wirtschaft und Energie. 2020. *Fakten Zum Deutschen Außenhandel.* Berlin: BMWi.

Burkhauser, Richard V., Mary C. Daly, and Nicolas R. Ziebarth. 2016. "Protecting Working-Age People with Disabilities: Experiences of Four Industrialized Nations." *Journal for Labour Market Research* 49(4): 367–386.

Burrows, Oliver, Katie Low, and Fergus Cumming. 2015. "Mapping the UK Financial System." *Bank of England Quarterly Bulletin* (June 18, 2015). https://www.bankofengland.co.uk/ quarterly-bulletin/2015/Q2/mapping-the-uk-financial-system.

Busch, Andreas, and Philip Manow. 2001. "The SPD and the Neue Mitte in Germany," In *New Labour*, edited by Stuart White, 175–189. London: Palgrave Macmillan.

Busemeyer, Marius, Julian Garritzmann, and Erik Neimanns. 2020. *A Loud but Noisy Signal? Public Opinion and Education Reform in Western Europe*. Cambridge: Cambridge University Press.

Busemeyer, Marius, and Kathleen Thelen. 2020. "Institutional Sources of Business Power." *World Politics* 72(3): 448–480.

Butler, Patrick. 2016. "UK Austerity Policies 'Amount to Violations of Disabled People's Rights.'" *The Guardian* (November 7, 2016). http://www.theguardian.com/business/2016/nov/07/uk-austerity-policies-amount-to-violations-of-disabled-peoples-rights (accessed April 28, 2021).

Byrne, Stephen, and Martin O'Brien. 2015. "The Changing Nature of Irish Exports: Context, Causes and Consequences. *Bank of Ireland Quarterly Bulletin Articles* 2015 (April): 58–72.

C

Caballero, Ricardo J., Emmanuel Farhi, and Pierre-Olivier Gourinchas. 2017. "The Safe Assets Shortage Conundrum." *Journal of Economic Perspectives* 31(3): 29–46.

Cabrera, Mercedes, and Fernando del Rey. 2007. *The Power of Entrepreneurs: Politics and Economy in Contemporary Spain*. New York: Berghahn Books.

Cai, Peter. 2017. "Understanding China's Belt and Road Initiative." *Lowy Institute for International Policy*, published online March 22. https://www.lowyinstitute.org/publications/unders tanding-belt-and-road-initiative#:~:text=Understanding%20China's%20Belt%20and%20R oad%20Initiative%20China's%20Belt,not%20all%20of%20which%20can%20be%20eas ily%20reconciled.

Callaci, Brian. 2018. "Control Without Responsibility: The Legal Creation of Franchising 1960–1980." *Washington Center for Equitable Growth*. Available at https://equitablegrowth.org/working-papers/control-without-responsibility-the-legal-creation-of-franchising-1960-1980/ (accessed December 13, 2018).

Calomiris, Charles, Stanley Longhofer, and William Miles. 2012. "The Housing Wealth Effect: The Crucial Roles of Demographics, Wealth Distribution and Wealth Shares." NBER Working Paper 17740.

Cameron, David. 1984. "Social Democracy, Corporatism, Labour Quiescence, and the Representation of Economic Interests in Advanced Capitalism." In *Order and Conflict in Contemporary Capitalism: Studies in the Political Economy of Western European Nations*, edited by J. H. Goldthorpe, xii, 143–178. Oxford: Clarendon Press.

Campbell, John, and Joao Cocco. 2007. "How Do House Prices Affect Consumption? Evidence from Micro Data." *Journal of Monetary Economics* 54(3): 591–621.

Campello, Daniella. 2014. "The Politics of Financial Booms and Crises Evidence from Latin America." *Comparative Political Studies* 47(5): 589–602.

Cardenas, Amalia. 2013. "The Spanish Savings Bank Crisis: History, Causes and Responses." IN3 Working Paper Series.

Cárdenas, Luis, Paloma Villanueva, Ignacio Álvarez, and Jorge Uxó. 2021. "In the Eye of the Storm: The "Success" of the Spanish Growth Model." In *Institutional Change after the Great Recession*, edited by L. Cárdenas and J. Arribas, 202–244. London: Routledge.

Cardoso, Eliana, and Ann Helwege. 1991. "Populism, Profligacy, and Redistribution." In *The Macroeconomics of Populism in Latin America*, edited by Rudiger Dornbusch and Sebastian Edwards, 45–74. Chicago: University of Chicago Press.

Cardoso, Fernando Henrique, and Enzo Faletto. 1979. *Dependency and Development in Latin America*. Berkeley: University of California Press.

Carlin, Wendy, and David Soskice. 2006. *Macroeconomics: Imperfections, Institutions, and Policies* New York: Oxford University Press.

Carlin, Wendy, and David Soskice. 2009. "German Economic Performance." *Socio-Economic Review* 7: 67–99.

Carlin, Wendy, and David Soskice. 2015. *Macroeconomics*. Oxford: Oxford University Press.

Carlin, Wendy, and David Soskice. 2018. "Stagnant Productivity and Low Unemployment: Stuck in a Keynesian Equilibrium." *Oxford Review of Economic Policy* 34(1–2): 169–194.

Carrillo-Tudela, Carlos, Andrey Launov, and Jean-Marc Robin. 2018. "The Fall in German Unemployment: A Flow Analysis." IZA Working Paper.

Carrión, Miguel. 2021. "The Fiscal Rules Killed Public Investment Dead." *Across the Euro Area.* https://europeriphery.wordpress.com/2021/03/08/the-fiscal-rules-killed-public-investment-dead/

Carstensen, Martin B., and Matthias Matthijs. 2018. "Of Paradigms and Power: British Economic Policy Making since Thatcher." *Governance* 31(3): 431–447.

Carter, Neil. 2014. "The Politics of Climate Change in the UK." *WIREs Climate Change* 5(3): 423–433.

Case, Karl E., John M. Quigley, and Robert J. Shiller. 2013. "Wealth Effects Revisited 1975–2012." *Critical Finance Review* 2(1): 101–128.

Castles, Francis. 1978. *The Social Democratic Imagine of Society.* Boston: Routledge & Kegan Paul.

Cauvel, Michael 2019. "The neo-Goodwinian Model Reconsidered." PKES Working Paper 1915.

Celi, Giuseppe, Andrea Ginzburg, Dario Guarascio, and Annamaria Simonazzi. 2018. *Crisis in the European Monetary Union. A Core-Periphery Perspective.* London: Routlege.

Chandler Alfred D. 1977. *The Visible Hand: The Managerial Revolution in American Business.* Cambridge, MA: Harvard University Press.

Chang, Michele and Patrick Leblond. 2015. "All In: Market Expectations of Eurozone Integrity in the Sovereign Debt Crisis." *Review of International Political Economy* 22(3): 626–655.

Chappe, Raphael, and Mark Blyth. 2020. "Hocus Pocus: Debating the Magic Money." *Foreign Affairs* (November/December). https://www.foreignaffairs.com/articles/2020-10-13/hocus-pocus.

Chari, Raj S. 1998. "Spanish Socialists, Privatising the Right Way?" *West European Politics* 21(4): 163–179.

Charles, Sebastien. 2008. "Teaching Minsky's Financial Instability Hypothesis: A Manageable Suggestion." *Journal of Post Keynesian Economics* 31(1): 125–138.

Charnock, G., Thomas Purcell, and Ramon Ribera-Fumaz. 2014. *The Limits to Capital in Spain.* Basingstoke: Palgrave Macmillan.

Chattopadhyay, Jacqueline. 2018. "Is the Affordable Care Act Cultivating a Cross-Class Constituency? Income, Partisanship, and a Proposal for Tracing the Contingent Nature of Positive Policy Feedback Effects." *Journal of Health Politics, Policy and Law* 43(1): 19–67.

Chevalier, Tom. 2021. *Growth and Welfare in Advanced Capitalist Economies Fighting Youth Unemployment: Growth Strategies and Youth Welfare Citizenship.* Oxford: Oxford University Press.

Chinn, Menzie D., and Eswar S. Prasad. 2003. "Medium-Term Determinants of Current Accounts in Industrial and Developing Countries: An Empirical Exploration," *Journal of International Economics* 59(1): 47–76.

Chowdhury, Anis, and Iyanatul Islam. 2012. "The Debate on Expansionary Fiscal Consolidation: How Robust Is the Evidence?" *The Economic and Labour Relations Review* 23(3): 13–38.

Christophers, Brett. 2013. "A Monstrous Hybrid: The Political Economy of Housing in Early Twenty-First Century Sweden." *New Political Economy* 18(6): 885–911.

Christophers, Brett. 2016. *The Great Leveler: Capitalism and Competition in the Court of Law.* Cambridge, MA: Harvard University Press.

Christophers, Brett. 2020. *Rentier Capitalism: Who Owns the Economy and Who Pays for It?* London: Verso Press.

Ciarini, Andrea. 2019. "Trajectories of Welfare Financialisation in Europe. A Comparison between France, Italy and the United Kingdom." *International Review of Sociology* 29(3): 464–483.

Cimoli, Mario, and Gabriel Porcile. 2014. Technology, Structural Change and BOP-Constrained Growth: A Structuralist Toolbox. *Cambridge Journal of Economics* 38(1): 215–223.

Cioffi, John, and Martin Höpner. 2006. "The Political Paradox of Finance Capitalism: Interests, Preferences, and Center-Left Party Politics in Corporate Governance Reform." *Politics & Society* 34(4): 463–502.

Clarke, Harold D., David Sanders, Marianne C. Stewart, and Paul Whiteley 2004. *Political Choice in Britain*. Oxford: Oxford University Press.

Cloyne, James, Kilian Huber, Ethan Ilzetzki, and Henrik Kleven. 2019. "The Effect of House Prices on Household Borrowing: A New Approach." *American Economic Review* 109(6): 2104–2136.

Coates, David, ed. 2005. *Varieties of Capitalism, Varieties of Approaches*. London: Palgrave.

Coe, Neil M., Peter Dicken, and Martin Hess. 2008. "Introduction: Global Production Networks—Debates and Challenges." *Journal of Economic Geography* 8(3): 267–269.

Cohen, Benjamin J. 2015. *Currency Power: Understanding Monetary Rivalry*: Princeton, NJ: Princeton University Press.

Colatat, Phech, Georgeta Vidican, and Richard K Lester. 2009. "Title." IPC Working Paper Series. Cambridge, MA.

Colli, Andrea. 2010. "Dwarf Giants, Giant Dwarfs. Reflections about the Italian 'Industrial Demography' at the Beginning of the New Millennium." *Journal of Modern Italian Studies* 15(1): 43–60.

Colli, Andrea, Alberto Rinaldi, and Michelangelo Vasta. 2016. "The Only Way to Grow? Italian Business Groups in Historical Perspective." *Business History* 58(1): 30–48.

Collier, David. 1979. "Overview of the Bureaucratic-Authoritarian Model." In *The New Authoritarianism in Latin America*, edited by David Collier, 19–32. Princeton, NJ: Princeton University Press.

Collier, David, and Ruth Berins Collier. 1991. *Shaping the Political Arena: Critical Junctures, the Labor Movement, and Regime Dynamics in Latin America*. Notre Dame, IN: University of Notre Dame Press.

Collignon, Stefan. 2016. "Wage Imbalances in the European Labour Market." In *Europe in Crisis*, edited by Leila Simona Talani, 65–88. London: Palgrave Macmillan.

Committee for the Study of Economic and Monetary Union. 1989. "Report on Economic and Monetary Union in the Community." Brussels: Committee for the Study of Economic and Monetary Union.

Congressional Research Service. 2019. "U.S. Trade: Recent Trends and Developments." *Congressional Research Service*. https://crsreports.congress.gov/product/pdf/IF/IF11189.

Considine, Mark, Jenny M. Lewis, Siobhan O'Sullivan, and Els Sol. 2015. *Getting Welfare to Work: Street-Level Governance in Australia, the UK, and the Netherlands*. Oxford: Oxford University Press.

Constantinescu, Cristina, Aaditya Mattoo, Alen Mulabdic, and Michele Ruta. 2018. *Global Trade Watch 2017: Trade Defies Policy Uncertainty–Will It Last?* Washington, D.C.: World Bank Group.

Cooper, Andrew F., and Timothy M. Shaw. 2009. "The Diplomacies of Small States at the Start of the Twenty-First Century: How Vulnerable? How Resilient?" In *The Diplomacies of Small States: Vulnerability and Resilience*, edited by Andrew F. Cooper and Timothy M. Shaw, 1–18. Basingstoke, UK: Palgrave Macmillan.

Cordonnier, Laurent. 2006. "Le profit sans l'accumulation: La recette du capitalisme dominé par la finance." *Innovations, Cahiers d'économie de l'innovation* 23(1): 51–72.

Cornia Giovanni Andrea, Juan Carlos Gómez-Sabaíni, and Bruno Martorano. 2011. "A New Fiscal Pact, Tax Policy Changes and Income Inequality." WIDER Working Paper 2011/70.

Costa, Francisco, Jason Garred, and João Paulo Pessoa. 2016. "Winners and Losers from a Commodities-for-Manufactures Trade Boom. *Journal of International Economics* 102: 50–69.

Costigliola, Frank. 1984. *Awkward Dominion: American Political, Economic, and Cultural Relations with Europe, 1919–1933*. Ithaca, NY: Cornell University Press.

Crouch, Colin. 2004. *Post-Democracy*. Cambridge: Polity.

Crouch, Colin. 2009. "Privatised Keynesianism: An Unacknowledged Policy Regime." *The British Journal of Politics & International Relations* 11(3): 382–399.

Cséfalvay, Zoltán. 2019. "Robotization in Central and Eastern Europe: Catching Up or Dependence?" *European Planning Studies* (November 28, 2019). https://doi.org/10.1080/09654313.2019.1694647.

Cukierman, Alex. 1992. *Central Bank Strategy, Credibility, and Independence: Theory and Evidence.* Cambridge, MA: MIT Press.

Culpepper, Pepper. 2011. *Quiet Politics and Business Power.* Cambridge: Cambridge University Press.

Cunningham, Colleen, Florian Ederer, and Song Ma. 2019. "Killer Acquisitions." Washington Center for Equitable Growth Working Paper. https://equitablegrowth.org/working-papers/killer-acquisitions/.

Curtice, John, Miranda Phillips, and Liz Clery. 2015. *33 British Social Attitudes: Work and Welfare.* London: NatCen Social Research.

Curtis, Simon. 2016. *Global Cities and Global Order.* Oxford: Oxford University Press.

D

Dafermos, Yannis, Maria Nikolaidi, and Giorgos Galanis. 2017. "A Stock-Flow-Fund Ecological Macroeconomic Model." *Ecological Economics* 131: 191–207.

Damgaard, Jannick, Thomas Elkjaer, and Niels Johannesen. 2019. "Phantom Investments. Empty Corporate Shells in Tax Havens Undermine Tax Collection in Advanced, Emerging Market, and Developing Countries." *Finance & Development* 5(3): 11–13.

Danninger, Stephan, and Fred Joutz. 2008. "What Explains Germany's Rebounding Export Market Share?" *CESifo Economic Studies* 54(4): 681–714.

Dauth, Wolfgang, Sebastian Findeisen, and Jens Suedekum. 2017. "Trade and Manufacturing Jobs in Germany." *American Economic Review* 107(5): 337–342.

Davis, Leila, and Özgür Orhangazi. 2021. Competition and Monopoly in the US Economy: What Do the Industrial Concentration Data Show? *Competition & Change* 25(1): 3–30.

Dawisha, Karen. 2015. *Putin's Kleptocracy: Who Owns Russia?* New York: Simon and Schuster.

de Boef, Suzanna, and Jim Granato. 1999. "Testing for Cointegrating Relationships with Near-Integrated Data." *Political Analysis* 8(1): 99–117.

De Cecco, Marcello. 2007. "Italy's Dysfunctional Political Economy." *West European Politics* 30(4): 763–783.

Deeg, Richard. 1999. *Finance Capitalism Unveiled: Banks and the German Political Economy.* Ann Arbor: The University of Michigan Press.

Deeg, Richard. 2005. "Remaking Italian Capitalism? The Politics of Corporate Governance Reform." *West European Politics* 28(3): 521–548.

Deeg, Richard, and Iain Hardie. 2016. "What Is Patient Capital and Who Supplies It?" *Socio-Economic Review* 14(4): 627–645.

De Grauwe, Paul, and Corrado Macchiarelli. 2015. "Animal Spirits and Credit Cycles." *Journal of Economic Dynamics & Control* 59, 95–117.

Dellepiane-Avellaneda, Sebastian 2014. "The Political Power of Economic Ideas: The Case of 'Expansionary Fiscal Contractions,'" *British Journal of Political Science* 17(3): 391–418.

Dellepiane-Avellaneda, Sebastian, Niamh Hardiman, and Jon Las Heras. 2021. "Financial Resource Curse in the Eurozone Periphery." *Review of International Political Economy* (published online March 23). https://doi.org/10.1080/09692290.2021.1899960.

De Loecker, Jan, and Jan Eeckhout. 2018. "Global Market Power." NBER Working Paper No. 24768.

DeLong, Bradford, and Lawrence H. Summers. 2012. "Fiscal Policy in a Depressed Economy." *Brookings Papers on Economic Activity* 44(1): 33–297.

Dendrinou, Viktoria, Niko Chrysoloras, and Milda Seputyte. 2020. "EU Finance Chiefs Dodge Coronabonds in $590 Billion Rescue." *Bloomberg Economics,* April 10, 2020. https://www.

bloomberg.com/news/articles/2020-04-10/eu-finance-chiefs-dodge-coronabonds-in-590-billion-rescue-deal.

Department of Energy. 2018. *Wind Vision: A New Era for Wind Power in the United States.* Washington, D.C.: U.S. Department of Energy.

De Paula, Luiz Fernando, Barbara Fritz, and Daniela Prates. 2017. "Keynes at the Periphery: Currency Hierarchy and Challenges for Economic Policy in Emerging Economies." *Journal of Post Keynesian Economics* 40(2): 183–202.

Detzer, Daniel. 2018. "Inequality, Emulation and Debt: The Occurrence of Different Growth Regimes in the Age of Financialization in a Stock-Flow Consistent Model." *Journal of Post Keynesian Economics* 41(2): 284–315.

Detzer, Daniel, and Eckard Hein. 2014. "Financialisation and the Financial and Economic Crisis: The Case of Germany." FESSUD Studies in Financial Systems No. 18.

Detzer, Daniel, and Eckhard Hein. 2017. "Financialisation and Income Distribution." In *The German Financial System and the Financial and Economic Crisis,* edited by D. Detzer and E. Hein, 257–273. Cham, Switzerland: Springer International Publishing.

Detzer, Daniel, Nina Dodig, Trevor Evans, Eckhard Hein, Hansjörg Herr, and Franz Prante 2017. *The German Financial System and the Financial and Economic Crisis.* Berlin: Springer International Publishing.

Deutsche Bundesbank. 2009. "Zur Entwicklung der staatlichen Investitionsausgaben." *Monatsberichte der Deutschen Bundesbank* 61(10): 15–34.

Deutsche Bundesbank. 2018. "Die Maastricht-Schulden: Methodische Grundlagen sowie die Ermittlung und Entwicklung in Deutschland." *Monatsberichte der Deutschen Bundesbank* 70(4): 59–81.

Deutscher Bundestag. 2019. "Antwort der Bundesregierung auf die Kleine Anfrage der Abgeordneten Pascal Meiser, Fabio De Masi, Susanne Ferschl, weiterer Abgeordneter und der Fraktion Die Linke. Entwicklung der Allgemeinverbindlicherklärung von Tarifverträgen in Deutschland." Drucksache 19/8626. Berlin: Deutscher Bundestag.

Deutsches Aktieninstitut, Aktionärszahlen des Deutschen Aktieninstituts. 2014. *Tabellen* (Frankfurt, 2015), 4. https://www.dai.de/files/dai_usercontent/dokumente/Statistiken/2015-02-12%20Aktionaerszahlen%202014%20Datentabellen%20Web%20FINAL.pdf.

Deutsches Aktieninstitut. 2022. "Deutschland und die Aktie: weiter auf hohem Niveau." https://www.dai.de/fileadmin/user_upload/220119_Aktionaerszahlen_2021_Deutsches_Akt ieninstitut.pdf.

Devries, Pete, Jaime Guajardo, Daniel Leigh, and Andrea Pescatori, A. 2011. "A New Action-Based Dataset of Fiscal Consolidation." IMF Working Paper 11/128 (June).

Dewey, Matías. 2018. "Domestic Obstacles to Labor Standards: Law Enforcement and Informal Institutions in Argentina's Garment Industry." *Socio-Economic Review* 16(3): 567–586.

Dewey, Matías, and Donato Di Carlo. 2021. "Governing through Non-Enforcement: Regulatory Forbearance as Industrial Policy in Advanced Economies." *Regulation & Governance* (ahead of print). https://doi.org/10.1111/rego.12382.

Di Carlo, Donato. 2018. "Does Pattern Bargaining Explain Wage Restraint in the German Public Sector?" MPIfG Discussion Paper 18/3.

Di Carlo, Donato. 2021. "Regulation & Deregulation: Public Sector Wage-Setting Systems and the Two Models of State-Led Wage Restraint in Western Europe." Max Weber Programme Working Paper 21/02.

Di Carlo, Donato, and Martin Höpner. 2020. "Germany's Silent Rebalancing Has Been Undone by Covid-19." *LSE European Policy and Society Blog.* https://blogs.lse.ac.uk/europpblog/2020/11/26/germanys-silent-rebalancing-has-been-undone-by-covid-19/ (accessed April 8, 2021).

Dicken, Peter. 2015. *Global Shift: Mapping the Changing Contours of the World Economy.* 7th ed. Thousand Oaks, CA: Sage Publications.

Dieci, Roberto, and Frank Westerhoff. 2012. A Simple Model of a Speculative Housing Market. *Journal of Evolutionary Economics* 22: 303–329.

Diessner, Sebastian, Niccolo Durazzi, and David Hope. 2021. "Skill-Biased Liberalization: Germany's Transition to the Knowledge Economy." *Politics & Society*. https://doi.org/10-1177/00323292211006563.

Disney, Richard, John Gathergood, and Andrew Henley. 2010. "House Price Shocks, Negative Equity, and Household Consumption in the United Kingdom." *Journal of the European Economic Association* 8(6): 1179–1207.

Doctorow, Cory. 2014. *Information Doesn't Want to Be Free: Laws for the Internet Age*. San Francisco: McSweeney's.

Doellgast, Virginia, and Ian Greer, I. 2007. Vertical Disintegration and the Disorganization of German Industrial Relations. *British Journal of Industrial Relations* 45(1): 55–76.

Dornbusch, Rudiger, and Sebastian Edwards. 1991. *The Macroeconomics of Populism in Latin America*. Chicago: University of Chicago Press.

Doucette, Jamie, and Bongman Seo. 2011. "Limits to Financialization?" *Economy and Society* 29(1): 146–159.

Downs, Anthony. 1957. *An Economic Theory of Democracy*. New York: HarperCollings.

Draghi, Mario. 2012. "Speech by Mario Draghi, President of the European Central Bank at the Global Investment Conference," July 26. *European Central Bank*. https://www.ecb.europa.eu/press/key/date/2012/html/sp120726.en.html.

Draghi, Mario 2019. "Press Conference: Introductory Statement. European Central Bank." https://www.ecb.europa.eu/press/pressconf/2019/html/ecb.is190912~658eb51d68.en.html.

Drahos, Peter, and John Braithwaite. 2003. *Information Feudalism: Who Owns the Knowledge Economy?* London: Routledge.

Drakos, Anastassios A., Georgios P. Kouretas, and Chris Tsoumas. 2016. "Ownership, Interest Rates and Bank Risk-Taking in Central and Eastern European Countries." *International Review of Financial Analysis* 45: 308–319.

Draut, Tamara. 2005. *The Plastic Safety Net: The Reality Behind Debt in America*. New York: Demos and the Center for Responsible Lending.

Drehmann, Mathias, Claudio E. Borio, and Kostas Tsatsaronis. 2012. "Characterising the Financial Cycle: Don't Lose Sight of the Medium Term!" BIS Working Papers 380.

Dünhaupt, Petra. 2017. "Determinants of Labour's Income Share in the Era of Financialisation." *Cambridge Journal of Economics* 41(1): 283–306.

Dullien, Sebastian, Ekaterina Jürgens, and Sebastian Watzka. 2020. "Public Investment in Germany: The Need for a Big Push." In *A European Public Investment Outlook*, edited by F. Cerniglia and Francesco Saraceno, 49–96. Cambridge: Open Book Publishers.

Dunleavy, Patrick, and Christopher T. Husbands. 1985. *British Democracy at the Crossroads: Voting and Party Competition in the 1980s*. London: Taylor & Francis.

Dunleavy, Patrick, and Hugh Ward. 1981. "Exogenous Voter Preferences and Parties with State Power: Some Internal Problems of Economic Theories of Party Competition." *British Journal of Political Science* 11(3): 351–380.

Dunning, Thad. 2008. *Crude Democracy: Natural Resource Wealth and Political Regimes*. New York: Cambridge University Press.

Durand, Cédric, and William Milberg. 2020. "Intellectual Monopoly in Global Value Chains." *Review of International Political Economy* 27(2): 404–429.

Dustmann, Christian, Bernd Fitzenberger, Uta Schönberg, and Alexandra Spitz-Oener. 2014. "From Sick Man of Europe to Economic Superstar: Germany's Resurgent Economy." *The Journal of Economic Perspectives* 28(1): 167–188.

Dutt, Amitava, 1990. *Growth, Distribution, and Uneven Development*. Cambridge: Cambridge University Press.

Dutt, Amitava. 2006. "Aggregate Demand, Aggregate Supply and Economic Growth." *International Review of Applied Economics* 20(3): 319–336.

Dutt, Amitava. 2010. "Reconciling the Growth of Aggregate Demand and Aggregate Supply." In *Handbook of Alternative Theories of Economic Growth*, edited by M. Setterfield, 220–240. London: Edward Elgar.

Duverger, Maurice. 1954. *Political Parties: Their Organization and Activity in the Modern State.* London: Metheun & Co. Ltd.

Dwyer, Peter, Jenny McNeill, and Lisa Scullion. 2014. *Conditionality Briefing: Disabled People.* ESRC September. http://www.welfareconditionality.ac.uk/wp-content/uploads/2014/09/Briefing_Disability_14.09.10_FINAL.pdf.

Dynan, Karen, Douglas Elmendorf, and Daniel Sichel. 2012. "The Evolution of Household Income Volatility." *The B.E. Journal of Economic Analysis & Policy* 12(2): 1–42.

E

Earth Policy Institute. 2015. "Climate, Energy, and Transportation Data." http://www.earth-policy.org/data_center/C23 (accessed August 1, 2017).

Eaton, Sarah, and Genia Kostka. 2014. "Authoritarian Environmentalism Undermined? Local Leaders' Time Horizons and Environmental Policy Implementation in China." *The China Quarterly* 218: 359–380.

Ebbinghaus, Bernhard, Claudia Göbel, and Sebastian Koos. 2011. "Social Capital, 'Ghent' and Workplace Contexts Matter: Comparing Union Membership in Europe." *European Journal of Industrial Relations* 17(2): 107–124.

Ebbinghaus, Bernhard, and Jelle Visser. 1999. "When Institutions Matter: Union Growth and Decline in Western Europe." *European Sociological Review* 15(2): 135–158.

Economic Policy Institute. 2017. "Inequality Is Slowing U.S. Economic Growth." Report. Washington, D.C.: Economic Policy Institute, December 12, 2017.

Economic Policy Institute. 2018. "America's Slow-Motion Wage Crisis." Report. Washington, D.C.: Economic Policy Institute, September 13, 2018.

Economic Policy Institute. 2021. "Working Economics Blog: Wage inequality continued to increase in 2020." https://www.epi.org/blog/wage-inequality-continued-to-increase-in-2020-top-1-0-of-earners-see-wages-up-179-since-1979-while-share-of-wages-for-bottom-90-hits-new-low/ (accessed January 17, 2022).

The Economist. 2019. "A Money-Laundering Scandal Costs Swedbank's Boss Her Job." *The Economist*, March 28, 2019. https://www.economist.com/finance-and-economics/2019/03/28/a-money-laundering-scandal-costs-swedbanks-boss-her-job.

Edquist, Charles, and Bengt-Åke Lundvall. 1993. "Comparing the Danish and Swedish National Systems of Innovation." In *National Systems of Innovation,* edited by Richard Nelson, 265–298. Oxford: Oxford University Press.

Edquist, Harald. 2009. "Hur länge förblir IKT avgörande för svensk produktitivitetsutveckling?" *Ekonomisk Debatt* 37(1): 31–40.

Edvinsson, Rodney. 2005. *Growth, Accumulation, Crisis: With New Macroeconomic Data for Sweden, 1800–2000.* PhD diss, Stockholm Studies in Economic History 41 (Stockholm University).

Efken, Josef, and Jörg Rieger. 2015. "Der Markt für Fleisch und Fleischprodukte." *German Journal of Agricultural Economics* 64 (Supplement): 31–48.

Égert, Balázs, and Amalia Morales-Zumaquero. 2008. "Exchange Rate Regimes, Foreign Exchange Volatility, and Export Performance in Central and Eastern Europe: Just Another Blur Project?" *Review of Development Economics* 12(3): 577–593.

Eggertsson, Gauti B., and Paul Krugman. 2012. "Debt, Deleveraging, and the Liquidity Trap: A Fisher-Minsky-Koo Approach." *The Quarterly Journal of Economics* 127(3): 1469–5113. Doi: 10.1093/qje/qjs023.

Eglitis, Gatis, Balazs Forgo, Radoslav Krastev, Ingrid Toming, and Christian Weise. 2014. "Assessing Business Practices in Latvia's Financial Sector." *ECFIN Country Focus: Economic Analyses from European Commission´s Directorate General for Economic and Financial Affairs* 11(6): 1–9.

Eichengreen, Barry. 2010. *Exorbitant Privilege: The Rise and Fall of the Dollar and the Future of the International Monetary System.* Oxford: Oxford University Press.

Eichengreen, Barry, and Nachiket Shah. 2020. "The Correlates of International Financial-Center Status." *Review of International Economics* 28(1): 62–81.

Eichhorst, Werner, Maria Grienberger-Zingerle, and Regina Konle-Seidl. 2008. "Activation Policies in Germany: From Status Protection to Basic Income Support." In *Bringing the Jobless into Work?*, edited by Werner Eichhorst, Otto Kaufmann, and Regina Konle-Seidl. 17–67. Berlin, Heidelberg: Springer.

Eichhorst, Werner, Paul Marx, and Verena Tobsch. 2015. "Nonstandard Employment Across Occupations in Germany: The Role of Replaceability and Labour Market Flexibility," In *Non-Standard Employment in Post-Industrial Labour Markets: An Occupational Perspective*, edited by Werner Eichhorst and Paul Marx, 29–51. Cheltenham: Edgar Elgar.

Eihmanis, Edgars. 2018. "Cherry-Picking External Constraints: Latvia and EU Economic Governance, 2008–2014." *Journal of European Public Policy* 25(2): 231–249.

Eliasson, Kent, and Pär Hansson. 2016. "Are Workers More Vulnerable in Tradeable Industries?" *Review of World Economics* 152(2): 283–320.

Elkjaer, Mads, and Torben Iversen. 2020. "The Political Representation of Economic Interests: Subversion of Democracy or Middle-Class Supremacy?" *World Politics* 72(2): 254–290.

Elsässer, Lea, Senja Hense, and Armin Schäfer. 2020. "Not Just Money: Unequal Responsiveness in Egalitarian Democracies." *Journal of European Public Policy* (online first). https://doi.org/10.1080/13501763.2020.1801804.

EPA. 2020. *Inventory of U.S. Greenhouse Gas Emissions and Sinks.* Washington, D.C.: United States Environmental Protection Agency.

Erixon, Lennart. 1985. "What's Wrong With The Swedish Model? An Analysis of its Effects and Changed Conditions 1974–1985." Swedish Institute for Social Research Working Paper No. 12/1985.

Erixon, Lennart. 1987. *Profitability in Swedish Manufacturing: Trends and Explanations.* Stockholm: Almvist & Wiksell International.

Erixon, Lennart. 1989. "Den tredje vägen: Inlåsning eller förnyelse?" *Ekonomisk Debatt* 17(3): 181–195.

Erixon, Lennart. 1997. "The Golden Age of the Swedish Model. The Coherence Between Capital Accumulation and Economic Policy in Sweden in the Earl Postwar Period." *Report 97:9*, Oslo: Institutt for Samfunnsforskning (Institute for Social Research).

Erixon, Lennart.2008. "The Swedish Third Way: An Assessment of the Performance and Validity of the Rehn-Meidner Model." *Cambridge Journal of Economics* 32(3): 367–393.

Erixon, Lennart. 2011. "Under the Influence of Traumatic Events, New Ideas, Economic Experts and the ICT Revolution: The Economic Policy and Macroeconomic Performance of Sweden in the 1990s and 2000s." In *Comparative Social Research 28: The Nordic Varieties of Capitalism*, edited by Lars Mjøset, 265–330. Oslo: Emerald.

Erixon, Lennart. 2015a. "Can Fiscal Austerity Be Expansionary in Present-Day Europe? The Lessons from Sweden." *Review of Keynesian Economics* 3(4): 567–601.

Erixon, Lennart. 2015b. "Den solidariska lönepolitikens betydelse för strukturomvandlingen och tillväxten I dagens Sverige – teorier och belysningar." In *Lönebildning bortom NAIRU*, edited by Tony Johansson, 26–85. Stockholm: Landsorganisationen I Sverige.

Erixon, Lennart. 2022. "Industriavtalet: Luftslott eller riksintresse?" (An Illusion or a National Interest?). Department of Economics, Stockholm University (mimeo).

Erixon, Lennart, and Jonas Pontusson. 2022. "Rebalancing Balanced Growth: The Evolution of the Swedish Growth Model since the Mid-1990s." In *Diminishing Returns: The New Politics of Growth and Stagnation*, edited by Lucio Baccaro, Mark Blyth, and Jonas Pontusson, 268–292. New York: Oxford University Press.

Ertürk, Ismail, and Stefano Solari. 2007. "Banks as Continuous Reinvention" *New Political Economy* 12(3): 369–388.

Esping-Andersen, Gøsta. 1990. *The Three Worlds of Welfare Capitalism.* Princeton, NJ: Princeton University Press.

Estevez-Abe, Margarita, Torben Iversen, and David Soskice. 2001. "Social Protection and the Formation of Skills: A Reinterpretation of the Welfare State." In *Varieties of Capitalism: The*

Institutional Foundations of Comparative Advantage, edited by Hall and Soskice, 145–183. Oxford: Oxford University Press.

Etchemendy, Sebastián. 2004. "Revamping the Weak, Protecting the Strong, and Managing Privatization: Governing Globalization in the Spanish Takeoff." *Comparative Political Studies* 37(6): 623–651.

European Commission. 2011. "EU Economic Governance Six-Pack Enters into Force." Press Release, Brussels, December 12. https://ec.europa.eu/commission/presscorner/detail/en/MEMO_11_898.

European Commission. 2014. "Quarterly Report on the Euro Area." *Economic and Financial Affairs* 13(3): 27–33.

European Commission. 2014. "The EU's Economic Governance Explained." *European Commission, Brussels,* November 28. https://ec.europa.eu/commission/presscorner/detail/en/MEMO_14_2180.

European Commission. 2019. "Macroeconomic Imbalances Procedure Scorecard." *European Commission,* Brussels. https://ec.europa.eu/info/business-economy-euro/economic-and-fiscal-policy-coordination/eu-economic-governance-monitoring-prevention-correction/macroeconomic-imbalance-procedure/scoreboard_en.

European Commission's Directorate General for Economic and Financial Affairs. 2019. *Annual Macro-economic Database (AMECO).* Available at https://ec.europa.eu/economy_finance/ameco/user/serie/SelectSerie.cfm.

Eurostat. 2019a. "International Investment Position Statistics." *Eurostat.* https://ec.europa.eu/eurostat/statistics-explained/index.php/International_investment_position_statistics.

Eurostat. 2019b. "Current Account Balance – Annual Data." *Eurostat.* https://ec.europa.eu/eurostat/web/products-datasets/-/tipsbp20.

Evans, Peter. 1987. "Class, State and Dependence in East Asia: Some Lessons for Latin Americanists." In *The Political Economy of the New Asian Industrialism,* edited by F. Deyo, 203–226. Ithaca, NY: Cornell University Press.

Evans, Peter, and Gary Gereffi. 1981. "Transnational Corporations, Dependent Development, and State Policy in the Semiperiphery: A Comparison of Brazil and Mexico." *Latin American Research Review* 16(3): 31–64.

F

Fairfield, Tasha. 2011. "Business Power and Protest: Argentina's Agricultural Producers Protest in Comparative Context." *Studies in Comparative International Development* 46 (4): 424–453.

Fairfield, Tasha, and Candelaria Garay. 2017. "Redistribution under the Right in Latin America: Electoral Competition and Organized Actors in Policymaking." *Comparative Political Studies* 50(14): 1871–1906.

FAO. 2015. "The State of Agricultural Commodity Markets (SOCO)." Rome, Italy.

Farrell, Henry, and Abraham L. Newman. 2014. "Domestic Institutions beyond the Nation-State: Charting the New Interdependence Approach." *World Politics* 66(2): 331–363.

Farrell, Henry, and Abraham L. Newman. 2015. "The New Politics of Interdependence: Cross-National Layering in Trans-Atlantic Regulatory Disputes." *Comparative Political Studies* 48(4): 497–526.

Farrell, Henry, and Abraham L. Newman. 2016. "The New Interdependence Approach: Theoretical Development and Empirical Demonstration." *Review of International Political Economy* 23(5): 713–736.

Farrell, Henry, and Abraham L. Newman. 2018. "Linkage Politics and Complex Governance in Transatlantic Surveillance." *World Politics* 70(4): 515–554.

Farrell, Henry, and Abraham L. Newman. 2019. "Weaponized Interdependence: How Global Economic Networks Shape State Coercion." *International Security* 44 (1): 42–79.

Farrell, Henry, and Abraham L. Newman. 2020. "Will the Coronavirus End Globalization as We Know It?" *Foreign Affairs* (published online March 26). https://www.foreignaffairs.com/articles/2020-03-16/will-coronavirus-end-globalization-we-know-it.

Fazzari, Steven, Piero Ferri, and Edward Greenberg. 2008. "Cash Flow, Investment, and Keynes–Minsky Cycles." *Journal of Economic Behavior & Organization* 65: 555–572.

Fazzari, Steven, Piero Ferri, and Aanna Maria Variato. 2020. "Demand-Led Growth and Accommodating Supply. *Cambridge Journal of Economics* 44(3): 583–605.

Felipe, Jesus, and Matteo Lanzafame. 2018. "The PRC's Long-Run Growth through the Lens of the Export-Led Growth Model." ADB Economics Working Paper Series No. 555.

Ferguson, Thomas. 1995. *Golden Rule: The Investment Theory of Party Competition and the Logic of Money-Driven Political Systems.* Chicago: University of Chicago Press.

Fernandez, Rodrigo. 2016. "Financialization and Housing: Between Globalization and Varieties of Capitalism." In *The Financialization of Housing,* edited by Manuel B. Aalbers, 81–100. New York: Routledge.

Fernandez, Rodrigo, and Manuel B. Aalbers. 2017. "Capital Market Union and Residential Capitalism in Europe: Rescaling the Housing-Centred Model of Financialization." *Finance and Society* 3(1): 32–50.

Fernández Milmanda, B. 2019a. *On the Ballots, in the Streets or Under the Table. Agrarian Elites Political Strategies in Latin America.* PhD diss., Harvard University.

Fernández Milmanda, Belén. 2019b. "Agrarian Elites and Democracy in Latin America after the Third Wave." In *Oxford Research Encyclopedia of Latin American Politics.* Oxford: Oxford University Press. https://doi.org/10.1093/acrefore/9780190228637.013.1652.

Ferrara, Federico M., Jörg Haas, Andrew Peterson, and Thomas Sattler. 2021. "Exports vs. Investment: How Political Discourse Shapes Support for External Imbalances." *Socio-Economic Review* (online first). https://doi.org/10.1093/ser/mwab004.

Ferrera, Maurizio. 1996. "The Southern Model of Welfare in Social Europe." *Journal of European Social Policy* 6(1): 17–37.

Ferrera, Maurizio, and Elisabetta Gualmini. 2004. *Rescued by Europe?: Social and Labour Market Reforms in Italy from Maastricht to Berlusconi.* Amsterdam: Amsterdam University Press.

Fetzer, Thiemo. 2019. "Did Austerity Cause Brexit?" *American Economic Review* 109 (11): 3849–3886.

Fichtner, Jan. 2016. "Perpetual Decline or Persistent Dominance? Uncovering Anglo-America's True Structural Power in Global Finance." *Review of International Studies* (43)1: 3–28.

Fischedick, Manfred, and Mischa Bechberger. 2009. "Die ökologische Industriepolitik Deutschlands am Beispiel der Solar- und Windindustrie. Musterschüler oder Problemkind?" Moderne Industriepolitik 2/2009. Berlin: Friedrich-Ebert-Stiftung.

Fischer, Andrew M., 2015. The End of Peripheries? On the Enduring Relevance of Structuralism for Understanding Contemporary Global Development. *Development and Change* 46(4): 700–732.

Fishlow, Albert. 1973. "Some Reflections on Post-1964 Brazilian Economic Policy." In *Authoritarian Brazil: Origins, Policies, and Future,* edited by Alfred Stepan, 69–118. New Haven, CT: Yale University Press.

Fisk, Catherine L. 2009. *Working Knowledge: Employee Innovation and the Rise of Corporate Intellectual Property, 1800–1930.* Chapel Hill: University of North Carolina Press.

Fiss, Peer C., and Edward J. Zajac. 2004. "The Diffusion of Ideas over Contested Terrain: The (Non) Adoption of a Shareholder Value Orientation among German Firms." *Administrative Science Quarterly* 49(4): 501–534.

Flamm, Kenneth. 1988. *Creating the Computer: Government, Industry, and High Technology.* Washington, D.C.: Brookings Institution Press.

Flanagan, Robert J., David W. Soskice, and Lloyd Ulman. 1983. *Unionism, Economic Stabilization, and Incomes Policies: European Experiences.* Washington, DC.: Brookings.

Fleming, Alex, and Samuel Talley. 1996. "The Latvian Banking Crisis: Lessons Learned." WPS1590. *The World Bank.* http://documents.worldbank.org/curated/en/67531146877 2206366/The-Latvian-banking-crisis-lessons-learned.

Fligstein, Neil, and Adam Goldstein. 2012. A Long Strange Trip: The State and Mortgage Securitization, 1968–2010. In *The Oxford Handbook of the Sociology of Finance,* edited by Alex Preda and Karin Knorr-Cetina, 339–356. Oxford: Oxford University Press.

Fligstein, Neil, and Adam Goldstein. 2015. "The Emergence of a Finance Culture in American Households, 1989–2007." *Socio-Economic Review* 13(3): 575–601.

Florini, Ann, Hairong Lai, and Yeling Tan. 2012. *China Experiments from Local Innovations to National Reform*. Washington, D.C.: Brookings Institution Press.

Foley, Duncan, and Thomas Michl. 1999. *Growth and Distribution*. Cambridge, MA: Harvard University Press.

Forbes, Kristin J. 2010. "Why Do Foreigners Invest in the United States?" *Journal of International Economics* 80(1): 3–21.

Frank, Robert H., Adam Seth Levine, and Oege Dijk. 2014. "Expenditure Cascades." *Review of Behavioral Economics* 1(1–2): 55–73.

Franke, Reiner, Peter Flaschel, and Christian Proaño. 2006. "Wage-Price Dynamics and Income Distribution in a Semi-structural Keynes-Goodwin Model." *Structural Change and Economic Dynamics* 17(4): 452–465.

Franke, Reiner, and Frank Westerhoff. 2017. Taking Stock: Rigorous Modeling of Animal Spirits in Macroeconomics. *Journal of Economic Surveys* 31(5): 1152–1182.

Franzese, Robert J. 2001. "Institutional and Sectoral Interactions in Monetary Policy and Wage/Price-Bargaining." In *Varieties of Capitalism: The Institutional Foundations of Comparative Advantage*, edited by P. A. Hall and D. Soskice, 100–144. New York: Oxford University Press.

Fraser, Nancy. 2015. "Legitimation Crisis? On the Political Contradictions of Financialized Capitalism." *Critical Historical Studies* 2(2): 157–189.

Freeman, Christopher, and Francisco Louçã. 2001. *As Time Goes By: From the Industrial Revolutions to the Information Revolution*. New York: Oxford University Press.

Frenkel, Roberto, and Martin Rapetti. 2012. "Exchange Rate Regimes in the Major Latin American Countries since the 1950s: Lessons from History." *Journal of Iberian and Latin American Economic History* 30(1): 157–188.

Freyssenet, Michel, and Yannick Lung. 2000. "Between Globalisation and Regionalisation: What Is the Future of the Motor Industry?" In *Global Strategies and Local Realities*, edited by John Humphrey, Yvveline Lecler and Mario Sergio Salerno, 72–94. London: Palgrave Macmillan.

Freytes, Carlos. 2015. *The Cerrado Is Not the Pampas: Explaining Tax and Regulatory Policies on Agricultural Exports in Argentina and Brazil (2003–2013)*. PhD diss., Northwestern University.

Frieden, Jeffry. 2015. *Currency Politics: The Political Economy of Exchange Rate Policy*. Princeton, NJ: Princeton University Press.

Frieden, Jeffry, Lawrence Broz, and Stephen Weymouth. 2008. "Exchange-Rate Policy Attitudes: Direct Evidence from Survey Data." *IMF Staff Papers* 55(3): 417–444.

Frieden, Jeffry A., and Ronald Rogowski. 1996. "The Impact of the International Economy on National Policies." In *Internationalization and Domestic Politics*, edited by R. O. Keohane and H. V. Milner, 25–47. Cambridge: Cambridge University Press.

Frieden, Jeffry, and Sefanie Walter. 2017. "Understanding the Political Economy of the Eurozone Crisis." *Annual Review of Political Science* 20(1): 371–390.

Froud, Julie, Colin Haslam, Sukhdev Johal, and Karel Williams. 2000. "Shareholder-Value and Financialization: Consultancy Promises, Management Moves." *Economy and Society* 29(1): 80–110.

Fuller, Gregory W. 2018. "Exporting Assets: EMU and the Financial Drivers of European Macroeconomic Imbalances." *New Political Economy* 23(2): 174–191.

Fuller, G. W. 2019. *The Political Economy of Housing Financialization*. Newcastle: Agenda Publishing.

Fuller, Gregory W., Alison Johnston, and Aidan Regan. 2019. "Housing Prices and Wealth Inequality in Western Europe." *West European Politics* 43(1):297–320.

G

Gabbi, Giampaolo, Elisa Ticci, and Pietro Vozzella. 2014. "Financialisation and Economic and Financial Crises: The Case of Italy. No. 23." Financialisation, Economy, Society & Sustainable Development (FESSUD) Project.

Gabor, Daniela. 2010a. *Central Banking and Financialization: A Romanian Account of How Eastern Europe Became Subprime*. London: Palgrave Macmillan.

Gabor, Daniela . 2010b. Wind Energy Industry in Germany. Berlin.

Gabor, Daniela. 2011a. Leading PV Manufacturers Produce in Germany. Berlin.

Gabor, Daniela. 2011b. Photovoltaic Equipment. Berlin.

Gabor, Daniela. 2011c. Photovoltaics—Made in Germany. Berlin.

Gabor, Daniela. 2012. "The Road to Financialization in Central and Eastern Europe: The Early Policies and Politics of Stabilizing Transition." *Review of Political Economy* 24(2): 227–249.

Gabor, Daniela. 2014. Leading PV Manufacturers in Germany. Berlin.

Gabor, Daniela. 2021. "The Wall Street Consensus." *Development and Change* 6(1): 45–55.

Gabor, Daniela, and Cornel Ban. 2016. "Banking on Bonds: The New Links between States and Markets." *JCMS: Journal of Common Market Studies* 54(3): 617–635.

Galbraith, John Kenneth. 1967. *The New Industrial State*. New York: Houghton Mifflin.

Galgoczi, Béla. 2017. "Why Central and Eastern Europe Needs a Pay Rise." SSRN Scholarly Paper. Rochester, NY: Social Science Research Network, May 9, 2017. https://papers.ssrn.com/abstract=2965393.

Gallagher, Kevin P. 2014. *Ruling Capital: Emerging Markets and the Reregulation of Cross-Border Finance*. Ithaca, NY: Cornell University Press.

Gallagher, Kevin P., and Daniela Magalhães Prates. 2014. "Financialization and the Resource Curse: The Challenge of Exchange Rate Management in Brazil." GEGI Working Paper Series, September.

Gamble, Andrew. 1994. *The Free Economy and the Strong State: The Politics of Thatcherism*. London: Palgrave Macmillan.

Garay, Candelaria, and Sebastian Etchemendy. 2011. "Argentina: Left Populism in Comparative Perspective, 2003–2009." In *The Resurgence of the Latin American Left*, edited by Steven Levitsky and Kenneth M. Roberts, 283–305. Baltimore, MD: Johns Hopkins University Press.

Garcia-Bernardo, Javier, Jan Fichtner, Frank Takes, and Eelke M. Heemskerk. 2017. "Uncovering Offshore Financial Centers: Conduits and Sinks in the Global Corporate Ownership Network." *Scientific Reports* 7(1): 1–10.

Garcia-Herrero, Alicia, and Santiago Fernandez de Lis. 2008. "The Housing Boom and Bust in Spain: Impact of the Securitisation Model and Dynamic Provisioning." BBVA Working Paper No. 0808.

Garrett, Geoffrey. 1998. *Partisan Politics in the Global Economy*. Cambridge: Cambridge University Press.

Gelman, Andrew, and Jennifer Hill. 2007. *Data Analysis Using Regression and Multileve/Hierarchical Models*. Cambridge: Cambridge University Press.

Gereffi, Gary, John Humphrey, and Timothy Sturgeon. 2005. "The Governance of Global Value Chains." *Review of International Political Economy* 12(1): 78–104.

German Federal Government. 2020. "Pressemitteilung: A French-German Initiative for the European Recovery from the Coronavirus Crisis," Number 173/20. May 18. Online available at: https://www.bundesregierung.de/breg-en/news/dt-franz-initiative-1753890.

Germann, Julian. 2021. *Unwitting Architect: German Primacy and the Origins of Neoliberalism*. Stanford, CA: Stanford University Press.

Gerschenkron, Alexander. 1962. *Economic Backwardness in Historical Perspective*. Cambridge, MA: Harvard University Press.

Giavazzi, Francesco, and Marco Pagano, M. 1990. "Can Severe Fiscal Contractions Be Expansionary? Tales of Two Small European Countries." NBER Working Papers 3372.

Gibbon, Peter, Jennifer Bair, and Stefano Ponte. 2008. "Governing Global Value Chains: An Introduction." *Economy and Society* 37(3): 315–338.

Gibbon, Peter, and Stefano Ponte. 2008. "Global Value Chains: From Governance to Governmentality?" *Economy and Society* 37(3): 365–392.

Gilens, Martin. 2012. *Affluence and Influence.* Princeton, NJ: Princeton University Press.

Gill, Stephen. 1998. "New Constitutionalism, Democratisation and Global Political Economy." *Global Change, Peace & Security* 10(1): 23–38.

Gillard, Ross. 2016. "Unravelling the United Kingdom's Climate Policy Consensus: The Power of Ideas, Discourse and Institutions." *Global Environmental Change* 40: 26–36.

Gilpin, Robert, and Jean M. Gilpin. 1987. *The Political Economy of International Relations.* Princeton, NJ: Princeton University Press.

Gingrich, Jane. 2011. *Making Markets in the Welfare State: The Politics of Varying Market Reforms.* New York: Cambridge University Press.

Gingrich, Jane, and Silja Häusermann. 2015. "The Decline of the Working-Class Vote, the Reconfiguration of the Welfare Support Coalition and Consequences for the Welfare State." *Journal of European Social Policy* 25(1): 50–75.

Gingrich, Jane, and Sara Watson. 2016. "Privatizing Participation? The Impact of Private Welfare Provision on Democratic Accountability." *Politics & Society* 44(4): 573–613.

Glassner, Vera. 2010. "The Public Sector in the Crisis." European Trade Union Institute Working Paper 2010.07.

Glyn, Andrew. 2006. *Capitalism Unleashed: Finance, Globalization, and Welfare.* Oxford: Oxford University Press.

Goldthorpe, John H., ed. 1984. *Order and Conflict in Contemporary Capitalism: Studies in the Political Economy of Western European Nations.* Oxford: Clarendon Press.

González Casanova, Pablo. 1982. "System and Class in Latin American Studies." *Latin American Perspectives* 9(3): 104–110.

Goodfriend, Marvin. 2007. "How the World Achieved Consensus on Monetary Policy." *Journal of Economic Perspectives* 21(4): 47–68.

Goodhart, Charles, and Dirk Schoenmaker. 2016. "The Global Investment Banks Are Now All Becoming American: Does That Matter for Europeans?" *Journal of Financial Regulation* 2(2): 163–181.

Goodhart, David. 2017. *The Road to Somewhere: The Populist Revolt and the Future of Politics.* Oxford: Oxford University Press.

Gopinathan, Narayan, Narayan S. Subramanian, and Johannes Urpelainen. 2019. "Mid-Century Strategies: Pathways to a Low-Carbon future?" *Climate Policy* 19(9): 1088–1101.

Gordon, Joshua C. 2019. "The Perils of Vanguardism: Explaining Radical Cuts to Unemployment Insurance in Sweden." *Socio-Economic Review* 17(4): 947–968.

Gordon, Robert J. 2014. "The Demise of US Economic Growth: Restatement, Rebuttal, and Reflections." NBER Working Paper No. 19895.

Górnicka, Lucyna, Christophe Kamps, Gerrit Köster, and Nadine Leiner-Killinger. 2018. "Learning About Fiscal Multipliers During the European Sovereign Debt Crisis: Evidence from a Quasi-Natural Experiment." ECB Working Paper 2154.

Gospel, Howard F., and Andrew Pendleton. 2005. *Corporate Governance and Labour Management: An International Comparison.* Oxford: Oxford University Press.

Goudarzi, Navid, and Weidong. Zhu. 2013. "A Review on the Development of Wind Turbine Generators Across the World." *International Journal of Dynamics and Control* 1(2):192–202.

Gourevitch, Peter. 1986. *Politics in Hard Times.* Ithaca, NY: Cornell University Press.

Gourinchas, Pierre-Olivier, and Hélène Rey. 2007. "From World Banker to World Venture Capitalist: U.S. External Adjustment and the Exorbitant Privilege." In *G7 Current Account Imbalances: Sustainability and Adjustment*, edited by R. H. Clarida, 11–66. Chicago: University of Chicago Press.

Gourinchas, Pierre-Olivier, Hélène Rey, and Maxime Sauzet. 2019. "The International Monetary and Financial System." *Annual Review of Economics* 11(1): 859–893.

Gracia, Manuel, and María J. Paz. 2017. "Network Position, Export Patterns and Competitiveness: Evidence from the European Automotive Industry." *Competition & Change* 21(2): 132–158.

Grahl, John, and Paul Teague. 2000. "The Regulation School, the Employment Relation and Financialization." *Economy and Society* 29(1): 160–178.

Gramsci, Antonio. 1992. *The Prison Notebooks*. New York: Columbia University Press.

Grant, Wyn. 2001. "Pressure Politics: From 'Insider' Politics to Direct Action?" *Parliamentary Affairs* 54(2): 337–348.

Grasl, Maximilian, and Markus König. 2010. "Von außen Getrieben. Die Finanzpolitik der Großen Koalition 2005–2009." In *Die Zweite Große Koalition. Bilanz der Regierung Merkel 2005–2009*, edited by C. Egle and Reimut Zohlnhöfer, 205–233. Wiesbaden: VS Verlag.

Greco, Antonio. 2018. "Connections. Money Laundering in Latvia and the Role of Trust and Company Service Providers." *Transparency International Latvia*. https://www.google.com/url?sa=t&rct=j&https://delna.lv/en/about-delna/publications/.

Green, Jessica F. 2013. *Rethinking Private Authority: Agents and Entrepreneurs in Global Environmental Governance*. Princeton, NJ: Princeton University Press.

Green, Richard K., and Susan M. Wachter. 2005. "The American Mortgage in Historical and International Context." *Journal of Economic Perspectives* 19(4): 93–114.

Greenspan, Alan, and James Kennedy. 2008. "Sources and Uses of Equity Extracted from Homes." *Oxford Review of Economic Policy* 24(1): 120–144.

Grittersová, Jana. 2017. *Borrowing Credibility: Global Banks and Monetary Regimes*. Ann Arbor: University of Michigan Press.

Gros, Daniel. 2012. "Macroeconomic Imbalances in the Euro Area: Symptom or Cause of the Crisis?" *CEPS Policy Brief*, April 25, 2012. https://www.ceps.eu/ceps-publications/macroeconomic-imbalances-euro-area-symptom-or-cause-crisis/.

Grover, Chris, and Linda Piggott. 2007. "Social Security, Employment and Incapacity Benefit: Critical Reflections on A New Deal for Welfare." *Disability & Society* 22(7): 15.

Grundström, Karin, and Irene Molina. 2016. "From Folkhem to Lifestyle Housing in Sweden: Segregation and Urban Form, 1930s–2010s." *International Journal of Housing Policy* 16(3): 316–336.

Guajardo, Jaime, Daniel Leigh, and Andrea Pescatori. 2014. "Expansionary Austerity: New International Evidence." *Journal of the European Economic Association* 12(4): 949–968.

Günther, Wolfgang. 2021. *Staatliche Stützung der Tarifpolitik. Die Allgemeinverbindlicherklärung in Deutschland, den Niederlanden und Finnland*. Wiesbaden: Springer VS.

Guschanski Alexander, and Özlem Onaran. 2018. "Determinants of the Wage Share: A Cross-Country Comparison Using Sectoral Data." *CESifo Forum* 19(2). Ifo Institute for Economic Research eV.

Guschanski Alexander, and Özlem Onaran. 2021. "The Decline in the Wage Share: Falling Bargaining Power of Labour or Technological Progress? Industry Level Evidence from the OECD." *Socio-Economic Review*, forthcoming.

H

Haberly, Daniel, & Dariusz Wójcik, eds. 2021. *Global Financial Networks: What They Are and Where They Come From*. Oxford: Oxford University Press.

Habermas, Jürgen. 1973. "What Does A Crisis Mean Today? Legitimation Problems in Late Capitalism." *Social Research* 40(4): 643–667.

Hacker, Jacob S. 2019. *The Great Risk Shift: The New Economic Insecurity and the Decline of the American Dream*. 2nd ed. New York: Oxford University Press.

Hacker, Jacob S., and Paul Pierson. "Winner-Take-All Politics: Public Policy, Political Organization, and the Precipitous Rise of Top Incomes in the United States." *Politics & Society* 38(2): 152–204.

Hacker, Jacob S., and Paul Pierson. 2011. *Winner-Take-All Politics*. New York: Simon and Schuster.

Haffert, Lukas. 2019. "Permanent Budget Surpluses as a Fiscal Regime." *Socio-Economic Review* 17(4): 1043–1063.

Haffert, Lukas, and Daniel Mertens, D. 2021. "Between Distribution and Allocation: Growth Models, Sectoral Coalitions and the Politics of Taxation Revisited." *Socio-Economic Review* 19(2): 487–510.

Haggard, Stephan. 1990. *Pathways from the Periphery: The Politics of Growth in the Newly Industrializing Countries*. Ithaca, NY: Cornell University Press.

Hale, Thomas, and Charles Roger. 2014. "Orchestration and Transnational Climate Governance." *The Review of International Organizations* 9(1):59–82.

Hall, Peter. 1986. *Governing the Economy. The Politics of State Intervention in Britain and France*. New York: Oxford University Press.

Hall, Peter. 1993. "Policy Paradigms, Social Learning and the State." *Comparative Politics* 25: 275–296.

Hall, Peter. 2014. "Varieties of Capitalism and the Euro Crisis." *West European Politics* 37(6): 1223–1243.

Hall, Peter. 2020. "The Electoral Politics of Growth Regimes." *Perspectives on Politics* 18(1): 185–199.

Hall, Peter A., and Robert J. Franzese. 1998. "Mixed Signals: Central Bank Independence, Coordinated Wage Bargaining, and European Monetary Union." *International Organization* 52(3): 505–535.

Hall, Peter A., & Gingerich, Daniel W. 2004. *Varieties of Capitalism and Institutional Complementarities in the Macroeconomy: An Empirical Analysis*. Köln: Max-Planck-Institut für Gesellschaftsforschung.

Hall, Peter A., & Gingerich, Daniel W. 2009. "Varieties of Capitalism and Institutional Complementarities in the Political Economy: An Empirical Analysis." *British Journal of Political Science* 39(3):449–482.

Hall, Peter A., and David Soskice, eds. 2001. *Varieties of Capitalism: The Institutional Foundations of Comparative Advantage*. Oxford: Oxford University Press.

Hall, Peter, and David Soskice, D. 2001. "An Introduction to the Varieties of Capitalism," In *Varieties of Capitalism: The Institutional Foundations of Comparative Advantage*, edited by Hall and Soskice, 1–68. Oxford: Oxford University Press.

Hall, Peter A., and Kathleen Thelen. 2009. "Institutional Change in Varieties of Capitalism." *Socio-Economic Review* 7(1): 7–34.

Hallerberg, Mark, and Scott Basinger 1998. "Internationalization and Changes in Tax Policy in OECD Countries—the Importance of Domestic Veto Players," *Comparative Political Studies* 31(3): 321–352.

Halperin, Sandra. 2015. "Imperial City States, Nation States and Post-National Spatialities." In *Legacies of Empire: Imperial Roots of the Contemporary Global Order*, edited by Sandra Halperin and Ronen Palan, 69–96. Cambridge: Cambridge University Press.

Halperín Donghi, Tulio. 1969. *Historia Contemporánea de América Latina*. Madrid: Alianza Editorial.

Hamel, Eugene A. 1980. The Comparative Method in Anthropological Perspective. *Comparative Studies in Society and History* 22(2): April, 145–155.

Hamilton, Gary G., and Gary Gereffi. 2009. "Global Commodity Chains, Market Makers, and the Rise of Demand-Responsive Economies." In *Frontiers of Commodity Chain Research*, edited by Jennifer Bair. 136–161. Palo Alto, CA: Stanford University Press.

Hamilton, Nora. 1982. *The Limits of State Autonomy*. Princeton, NJ: Princeton University Press.

Hancké, Bob. 2013. *Unions, Central Banks, and EMU. Labor Market Institutions and Monetary Integration in Europe*. Oxford: Oxford University Press.

Hancké, Bob, Martin Rhodes, and Mark Thatcher, eds. 2007. *Beyond Varieties of Capitalism*. Oxford: Oxford University Press.

Hancké, Bob, Martin Rhodes, and Mark Thatcher, eds 2009. "Beyond Varieties of Capitalism." In *Debating Varieties of Capitalism. A Reader*, edited by Bob Hancké, 273–300. Oxford: Oxford University Press.

Hardie, Iain, and David Howarth. 2009. "Die Krise but not La Crise? The Financial Crisis and the Transformation of German and French Banking Systems." *JCMS: Journal of Common Market Studies* 47(5): 1017–1039.

Hardie, Iain, and David Howarth. 2013. "A Peculiar Kind of Devastation: German Market-Based Banking." In *Market-Based Banking and the International Financial Crisis*, edited by I. Hardie and D. Howarth, 103–127. Oxford: Oxford University Press.

Hardie, Iain, David Howarth, Sylvia Maxfield, and Amy Verdun. 2013. "Banks and the False Dichotomy in the Comparative Political Economy of Finance." *World Politics* 65(4): 691–728.

Harding, Roger. 2017. *British Social Attitudes Survey: The 35th Report*. London: The National Centre for Social Research.

Hartwig, Jochen. 2014. "Testing the Bhaduri–Marglin Model with OECD Panel Data." *International Review of Applied Economics* 28(4): 419–435.

Harvey, David. 1982. *The Limits to Capital*. London: Verso.

Haskel, Jonathan, and Stian Westlake, S. 2017. *Capitalism Without Capital*. Princeton, NJ: Princeton University Press.

Hassel, Anke. 2014. "The Paradox of Liberalization. Understanding Dualism and the Recovery of the German Political Economy." *British Journal of Industrial Relations* 52(1): 57–81.

Hassel, Anke, and Bruno Palier, eds. 2021a. *Growth and Welfare in Advanced Capitalist Economies: How Have Growth Regimes Evolved?* Oxford: Oxford University Press.

Hassel, Anke, and Bruno Palier. 2021b. "Tracking the Transformation of Growth Regimes in Advanced Capitalist Economies." In *Growth and Welfare in Advanced Capitalist Economies*, 3–56. Oxford: Oxford University Press.

Hassel, Anke, and Christof Schiller. 2010. *Der Fall Hartz IV: Wie es zur Agenda 2010 kam und wie es weitergeht*. Frankfurt a.M.: Campus.

Häusermann, Silja, and Hanspeter Kriesi. 2015. "What Do Voters Want? Dimensions and Configurations in Individual-Level Preferences and Party Choice." In *The Politics of Advanced Capitalism*, edited by P. Beramendi, S. Häusermann, H. Kitschelt, and H. Kriesi, 202–230. Cambridge: Cambridge University Press.

Häusermann, Silja, Georg Picot, and Dominik Geering. 2013. "Rethinking Party Politics and the Welfare State—Recent Advances in the Literature." *British Journal of Political Science* 43(1): 221–40.

Häusermann, Silja, and Schwander, Hanna 2012. Varieties of Dualization? Labor Market Segmentation and Insider-Outsider Divides Across Regimes. In *The Age of* Dualization, edited by P. Emmenegger, S. Häusermann, B. Palier, and M. Seeleib-Kaiser, 27–52. New York: Oxford University Press.

Hausfather, Zeke. 2018. "Analysis: UK Carbon Emissions in 2017 Fell to Levels Last Seen in 1890." CarbonBrief.

Hausfather, Zeke. 2019. "Analysis: Why the UK's CO2 Emissions Have Fallen 38% since 1990." CarbonBrief.

Hausmann, Ricardo, and Dani Rodrik. 2003. "Economic Development as Self-Discovery." *Journal of Development Economics* 72(2): 603–633.

Hay, Colin. 2007. *Why We Hate Politics*. Cambridge: Polity.

Hay, Colin. 2009. "Good Inflation, Bad Inflation: The Housing Boom, Economic Growth and the Disaggregation of Inflationary Preferences in the UK and Ireland." *The British Journal of Politics & International Relations* 11(3): 461–478.

Hay, Colin. 2011. "Pathology without Crisis? The Strange Demise of the Anglo-Liberal Growth Model." *Government and Opposition* 46(1): 1–31.

He, Hui, Feng Huang, Zheng Liu, and Dongming Zhu, 2018. "Breaking the 'Iron Rice Bowl': Evidence of Precautionary Savings from the Chinese State-Owned Enterprises Reform." *Journal of Monetary Economics* 94: 94–113.

Heath, Anthony F., Roger M. Jowell, and John K. Curtice 1985. *How Britain Votes*. Oxford: Pergamon.

Heath, Anthony F., Roger M. Jowell, and John K. Curtice. 2001. *The Rise of New Labour: Party Policies and Voter Choices*. Oxford: Oxford University Press.

Heath, Anthony et al. 1991. *Understanding Political Change: The British Voter 1964–1987*. Oxford: Pergamon.

Hedin, Karin, Eric Clark, Emma. Lundholm, and Gunnar. Malmberg. 2012. "Neoliberalization of Housing in Sweden: Gentrification, Filtering, and Social Polarization." *Annals of the Association of American Geographers* 102(2): 443–463.

Heilmann, Sebastian. 2008. "Policy Experimentation in China's Economic Rise." *Studies in Comparative International Development* 43(1): 1–26.

Hein, Eckhard 2012. "Financialization," Distribution, Capital Accumulation, and Productivity Growth in a Post-Kaleckian Model." *Journal of Post Keynesian Economics* 34(3): 475–496.

Hein, Eckhard. 2012. *The Macroeconomics of Finance-Dominated Capitalism and Its Crisis*. Cheltenham: Edward Elgar.

Hein, Eckhard 2013. "The Crisis of Finance-Dominated Capitalism in the Euro Area, Deficiencies in the Economic Policy Architecture, and Deflationary Stagnation Policies." *Journal of Post Keynesian Economics* 36(2): 325–354.

Hein, Eckhard, Petra Dünhaupt, Marta Kulesza, and Ayoze Alfageme. 2017. "Financialization and Distribution from a Kaleckian Perspective: The United States, the United Kingdom, and Sweden Compared—Before and After the Crisis." *International Journal of Political Economy* 46(4): 233–266.

Hein, Eckhard, Walter P. Meloni, and Pasquale Tridico. 2020. "Welfare Models and Demand-Led Growth Regimes Before and After the Financial and Economic Crisis." *Review of International Political Economy* 28(5): 1196-1223.

Hein, Eckhard, and Matthias Mundt. 2013. "Financialisation, the Financial and Economic Crisis, and the Requirements and Potentials for Wage-Led Recovery." In *Wage-Led Growth. An Equitable Strategy for Economic Recovery*, edited by M. Lavoie and E. Stockhammer, 153–186. London: Palgrave Macmillan.

Hein, Eckhard, and Christian Schoder, 2011. "Interest Rates, Distribution and Capital Accumulation—A Post-Kaleckian Perspective on the US and Germany," *International Review of Applied Economics* 25(6): 693–723.

Hein, Eckhard, and Arthur Tarassow. 2010. Distribution, Aggregate Demand and Productivity Growth—Theory and Empirical Results for Six OECD Countries Based on a Post-Kaleckian Model. *Cambridge Journal of Economics* 34: 727–754.

Hein, Eckhard, and Lena Vogel. 2008. "Distribution and Growth Reconsidered—Empirical Results for six OECD Countries," *Cambridge Journal of Economics* 32: 479–511.

Heipertz, Martin, and Amy Verdun. 2010. *Ruling Europe: The Politics of the Stability and Growth Pact*. Cambridge: Cambridge University Press.

Helgadóttir, Oddný. 2016. "Banking Upside Down: The Implicit Politics of Shadow Banking Expertise." *Review of International Political Economy* 23(6): 915–940.

Helgadóttir, Oddný . 2021. "The New Luxury Freeports: Offshore Storage, Tax Avoidance, and 'Invisible' Art." *Environment and Planning A: Economy and Space*. https://doi.org/10.1177%2F0308518X20972712 (online first).

Helleiner, Eric. 1994. *States and the Reemergence of Global Finance: From Bretton Woods to the 1990s*. Ithaca, NY: Cornell University Press.

Helleiner, Eric. 2011. "Understanding the 2007–2008 Global Financial Crisis: Lessons for Scholars of International Political Economy." *Annual Review of Political Science* 14: 67–87.

Helveston, John, and Jonas Nahm. 2019. "China's Key Role in Scaling Low-Carbon Energy Technologies." *Science* 36 (6467): 794.

Hemerijck, Anton. 2013. *Changing Welfare States*. Oxford: Oxford University Press.

Henisz, Witold J. 2004. "Political Institutions and Policy Volatility." *Economics & Politics* 16(1): 1–27.

Henry, James S. 2016. "Taxing Tax Havens." *Foreign Affairs*. https://www.foreignaffairs.com/artic les/panama/2016-04-12/taxing-tax-havens.

Hermann, Christoph. 2014. "Structural Adjustment and Neoliberal Convergence in Labour Markets and Welfare: The Impact of the Crisis and Austerity Measures on European Economic and Social Models." *Competition & Change* 18(2): 111–130.

Herrigel, Gary. 1996. *Industrial Constructions: The Sources of German Industrial Power*. Cambridge: Cambridge University Press.

Hertel-Fernandez, Alexander, Matto Mildenberger, and Leah C Stokes. 2019. "Legislative Staff and Representation in Congress." *American Political Science Review* 113(1): 1–18.

Heymann, Matthias. 1995. *Die Geschichte der Windenergienutzung 1890–1990*. Frankfurt: Campus.

Hibbs, Douglas A. 1977. "Political Parties and Macroeconomic Policy." *American Political Science Review* 71(4): 1467–1487.

Hicks, John. 1937. Mr. Keynes and the Classics: A Suggested Interpretation. *Econometrica* 5: 147–59.

Hilber, Christian A. L., and Olivier Schöni. 2016. "Housing Policies in the United Kingdom, Switzerland, and the United States: Lessons Learned." *Cityscape* 18(3): 291–332.

Hilmarsson, Hilmar Þór. 2018. "Iceland Alone and Latvia Captured: The Role of Sweden in the Icelandic and Latvian Financial Crises." *EUROPP* (blog). February 21, 2018. https://blogs. lse.ac.uk/europpblog/2018/02/21/iceland-alone-and-latvia-captured-the-role-of-sweden-in-the-icelandic-and-latvian-financial-crises/.

Hirschman, Albert O. 1945. *National Power and the Structure of Foreign Trade*. Berkeley: University of California Press.

Hirschman, Albert O. 1968. "The Political Economy of Import-Substituting Industrialization in Latin America." *Quarterly Journal of Economics* 82(1): 1–32.

Hodgson, Geoffrey. 2021. "Financial Institutions and the British Industrial Revolution: Did Financial Underdevelopment Hold Back Growth?" *Journal of Institutional Economics*, 17(3): 429–448.

Höpner, Martin. 2018. "The German Undervaluation Regime under Bretton Woods, 1950–1973: How Germany Became the Nightmare of the World Economy." MPIfG Discussion Paper 19/1.

Höpner, Martin. 2021. "Proportionality and Karlsruhe's Ultra Vires Verdict: Ways out of Constitutional Pluralism?" MPIfG Discussion Paper 21/1.

Höpner, Martin, and Mark Lutter. 2018. "The Diversity of Wage Regimes: Why the Eurozone is Too Heterogeneous for the Euro." *European Political Science Review* 10(1): 71–96.

Holland, Alisha, and Ben Ross Schneider. 2017. "Easy and Hard Redistribution: The Political Economy of Welfare States in Latin America." *Perspectives on Politics* 15(4): 988–1006.

Hope, David, and David Soskice. 2016. Growth Models, Varieties of Capitalism, and Macroeconomics. *Politics and Society* 44(2): 209–226.

Hopkin, Jonathan. 2004. "The Problem with Party Finance: Theoretical Perspectives on the Funding of Party Politics." *Party Politics* 10(6): 627–651.

Hopkin, Jonathan. 2020. *Anti-System Politics: The Crisis of Market Liberalism in Rich Democracies*. Oxford: Oxford University Press.

Hopkin, Jonathan, and Kate Alexander Shaw. 2016. "Organized Combat or Structural Advantage? The Politics of Inequality and the Winner-Take-All Economy in the United Kingdom." *Politics Society* 44(3): 345–371.

Hopkin, Jonathan, and Mark Blyth. 2019. "The Global Economics of European Populism: Growth Regimes and Party Change in Europe." *Government and Opposition* 54(2): 193–225.

Hopkin, Jonathan, and Caterina Paolucci. 1999. "The Business Firm Model of Party Organisation: Cases from Spain and Italy." *European Journal of Political Research* 35(3): 307–339.

Horan, Hubert. 2019. Uber's Path of Destruction. *American Affairs* 3(2): 108–133.

Horn, Gustav A., Fabian Lindner, Sabine Stephan, and Rudolf Zwiener. 2017. "The Role of Nominal Wages in Trade and Current Account Surpluses: An Econometric Analysis for Germany." *IMK Report* 125e: 1–18.

Hörnlein, Lena. 2019. "Utility Divestitures in Germany: A Case Study of Corporate Financial Strategies and Energy Transition Risk." Available at https://papers.ssrn.com/sol3/papers.cfm?abstract_id=3379545.

Hou, Yue. 2019. *The Private Sector in Public Office: Selective Property Rights in China.* Cambridge: Cambridge University Press.

Hozic, Aida. 2001. *Hollyworld: Space, Power, and Fantasy in the American Economy.* Ithaca, NY: Cornell University Press.

Howard, Christopher. 1997. *The Hidden Welfare State: Tax Expenditures and Social Policy in the United States.* Princeton, NJ: Princeton University Press.

Howell, Chris. 2005. *Trade Unions and the State: The Construction of Industrial Relations Institutions in Britain, 1890–2000.* Princeton, NJ: Princeton University Press.

Huang, Yasheng. 2008. *Capitalism with Chinese Characteristics: Entrepreneurship and the State.* Cambridge: Cambridge University Press.

Huber, Evelyne, and John D. Stephens. 2012. *Democracy and the Left: Social Policy and Inequality.* Chicago: University of Chicago Press.

Hübscher, Evelyne. 2016. "The Politics of Fiscal Consolidation Revisited." *Journal of Public Policy* 36(4): 573–601.

Hübscher, Evelyne. 2018. *The Clientelistic Turn in Welfare State Policy-Making: Party Politics in Times of Austerity.* London: ECPR Press.

Hübscher, Evelyne, Achim Kemmerling, and Thomas Sattler. 2015. "Austerity for the Win? The Effect of Fiscal Consolidation on Political Support for the Government." Paper presented at the Annual Meeting of the European Political Science Association, Vienna, June 25–27.

Hübscher, Evelyne, and Thomas Sattler. 2017. "Fiscal Consolidation under Electoral Risk." *European Journal of Political Research* 56(1): 151–168.

Hübscher, Evelyne, Thomas Sattler, and Markus Wagner.2019. "Does Austerity Cause Polarization?" Paper presented at the Annual Meeting of the American Political Science Association, Washington D.C., August 29–September 1.

Hübscher, Evelyne, Thomas Sattler, and Markus Wagner. 2020. "Voter Responses to Fiscal Austerity." *British Journal of Political Science* 51(4): 1751–1760.

Hughes, Llewelyn, and Johannes Urpelainen. 2015. "Interests, Institutions, and Climate Policy: Explaining the Choice of Policy Instruments for the Energy Sector." *Environmental Science & Policy* 54: 52–63.

Hünnekes, Franziska, Moritz Schularick, and Christoph Trebesch. 2019. "Exportweltmeister: The Low Returns on Germany's Capital Exports." CEPR Discussion Paper No. DP13863.

Hunter, Wendy. 2010. *The Transformation of the Workers' Party in Brazil, 1989–2009.* Cambridge, MA: Cambridge University Press.

Huntington, Samuel P. 1993. *The Third Wave: Democratization in the Late Twentieth Century.* Norman: University of Oklahoma Press.

Hurst, William. 2009. *The Chinese Worker after Socialism.* Cambridge: Cambridge University Press.

I

Ibsen, Christian L., Trine P. Larsen, Jørgen S. Madsen, and Jesper Due. 2011. "Challenging Scandinavian Employment Relations: The Effects of New Public Management Reforms." *The International Journal of Human Resource Management* 22 (11): 2295–2310.

IHS Solar. 2013. *Integrated PV Market Tracker – Q1 2013.* Englewood, CO: IHS.

ILO. 2008. *World of Work Report.* Geneva: ILO.

Imbs, Jean, and Romain Wacziarg. 2003. "Stages of Diversification." *American Economic Review* 93(1): 63–86.

IMF (International Monetary Fund). 2018. *Global Financial Stability Report.* Washington, D.C.: IMF.

Immergut, Ellen M. 1992. *Health Politics: Interests and Institutions in Western Europe*: Cambridge: Cambridge University Press.

Ingham, Geoffrey. 2004. *The Nature of Money.* Cambridge: Polity Press.

IPCC. 2018. "Global Warming of 1.5°C." Geneva: Intergovernmental Panel on Climate Change.

IRENA. 2021. "Renewable Capacity Statistics 2021." Abu Dhabi: International Renewable Energy Agency.

Isoaho, Karoliina, and Jochen Markard. 2020. "The Politics of Technology Decline: Discursive Struggles over Coal Phase-Out in the UK." *Review of Policy Research.* 37(3): 342–368.

Iversen, Torben. 1999. *Contested Economic Institutions: The Politics of Macroeconomics and Wage Bargaining in Advanced Democracies.* Cambridge: Cambridge University Press.

Iversen, Torben, and David Soskice. 2001. "An Asset Theory of Social Preferences." *American Political Science Review* 95(4): 875–893.

Iversen, Torben, and David Soskice. 2006. "Electoral Institutions and the Politics of Coalitions: Why Some Democracies Redistribute More Than Others." *American Political Science Review* 100(2): 165–181.

Iversen, Torben, and David Soskice. 2009. "Distribution and Redistribution: The Shadow of the Nineteenth Century." *World Politics* 61(3): 438–486.

Iversen, Torben, and David Soskice. 2019. *Democracy and Prosperity: Reinventing Capitalism through a Turbulent Century.* Princeton, NJ: Princeton University Press.

Iversen, Torben, David Soskice, and David Hope. 2016. "The Eurozone and Political Economic Institutions." *Annual Review of Political Science* 19: 163–185.

Iversen, Torben, and Anne Wren. 1998. Equality, Employment, and Budgetary Restraint: The Trilemma of the Service Economy. *World Politics* 50(4): 507–546.

J

Jackson, Gregory, Martin Höpner, and Antje Kurdelbusch. 2006. "Corporate Governance and Employees in Germany: Changing Linkages, Complementarities, and Tensions." In *Corporate Governance and Labour Management: An International Comparison,* edited by H. Gospel and A. Pendleton, 84–121. Oxford: Oxford University Press.

Jacobi, Lena, and Jochen Kluve. 2006. *Before and After the Hartz Reform: The Performance of Active Labour Market Policy in Germany.* RWI Discussion Paper. No. 41.

Jacoby, Wade. 2020. "Surplus Germany." *German Politics* 29(3): 498–521.

Jain-Chandra, Sonali, Niny Khor, Rui Mano, Johanna Schauer, Philippe Wingender, and Juzhong Zhuang. 2018. *Inequality in China—Trends, Drivers and Policy Remedies.* IMF Working Paper No. 18/127.

Jakab, Zoltan, and Michael Kumhof. 2015. "Banks Are Not Intermediaries of Loanable Funds— and Why It Matters." Bank of England Working Paper 529.

Jaros, Kyle A., and Yeling Tan. 2020. "Provincial Power in a Centralizing China: The Politics of Domestic and International 'Development Space.'" *The China Journal* 83(1): 79–104.

Jenkins Rhys. 2015. "Is Chinese Competition Causing Deindustrialization in Brazil?" *Latin American Perspectives* 42(6): 42–63.

Jennings, Will, and Gerry Stoker. 2019. "The Divergent Dynamics of Cities and Towns: Geographical Polarisation and Brexit." *The Political Quarterly* 90: 155–166.

Jessop, Bob. 1990. *State Theory: Putting the Capitalist State in Its Place.* College Park, PA: Penn State Press.

Johnson, Chalmers A. 1982. *MITI (Ministry of International Trade and Industry) and the Japanese Miracle: The Growth of Industrial Policy, 1925–1975.* Stanford, CA: Stanford University Press.

Johnston, Alison. 2012. "European Economic and Monetary Union's Perverse Effects on Sectoral Wage Inflation: Negative Feedback Effects from Institutional Change?" *European Union Politics* 13(3): 345–366.

Johnston, Alison. 2016. *From Convergence to Crisis: Labor Markets and the Instability of the Euro.* Ithaca, NY: Cornell University Press.

Johnston, Alison. 2021. "Always a Winning Strategy? Wage Moderation's Conditional Impact on Growth Outcomes." In *Growth and Welfare in the Knowledge Economy*, edited by A. Hassel and B. Palier, 291–319. Oxford: Oxford University Press.

Johnston, Alison, Gregory Fuller, and Aidan Regan. 2020. "It Takes Two to Tango: Mortgage Markets, Labor Markets and Rising Household Debt in Europe." *Review of International Political Economy* 28(4): 843–873.

Johnston, Alison, Bob Hancké, and Suman Pant. 2014. "Comparative Institutional Advantage in the European Sovereign Debt Crisis." *Comparative Political Studies* 47(13): 1771–1800.

Johnston, Alison, and Paulette Kurzer. 2020. "Bricks in the Wall: The Politics of Housing in Europe." *West European Politics* 43(2): 275–296.

Johnston, Alison, and Aidan Regan 2016. "European Monetary Integration and the Incompatibility of National Varieties of Capitalism." *JCMS: Journal of Common Market Studies* 54(2): 318–336.

Jones, Erik. 2015a. "The Forgotten Financial Union: How You Can Have a Euro Crisis Without a Euro." In *The Future of the Euro*, edited by M. Matthijs and M. Blyth, 44–69. Oxford: Oxford University Press.

Jones, Erik. 2015b. "Getting the Story Right: How You Should Choose Between Different Interpretations of the European Crisis (and Why You Should Care)." *Journal of European Integration* 37(7): 817–832.

Jones, Erik. 2016. "Macroeconomic Imbalances and Sovereign Debt Markets." In *Europe, Canada and the Comprehensive Economic and Trade Agreement*, edited by Kurt Hübner, 305–321. London: Taylor & Francis.

Jones, Erik. 2021. "The Financial Consequences of Export-Led Growth in Germany and Italy." *German Politics* (online first). https://doi.org/10.1080/09644008.2021.1881955.

Jones, Erik, R. Daniel Kelemen, and Sophie Meunier. 2016. "Failing Forward? The Euro Crisis and the Incomplete Nature of European Integration." *Comparative Political Studies* 49(7): 1010–1034.

Jones Luong, Pauline, and Jazmin Sierra. 2015. "The Domestic Political Conditions for International Economic Expansion: Lessons from Latin American National Oil Companies." *Comparative Political Studies* 48(14): 2010–2043.

Jordá, Oscar, Moritz Schularick, and Alan M. Taylor. 2016. The Great Mortgaging: Housing Finance, Crises and Business Cycles. *Economic Policy* 31(85): 107–152.

Jordà, Oscar, and Alan M. Taylor. 2016. "The Time for Austerity: Estimating the Average Treatment Effect of Fiscal Policy." *The Economic Journal* 126(590): 219–255.

Jordana, Jacint. 2014. "Multiple Crises and Policy Dismantling in Spain: Political Strategies and Distributive Implications." *Political Studies Review* 12(2): 224–238.

K

Kaldor, Nicholas. 1982. The Scourge of Monetarism. Oxford: Oxford University Press.

Kalecki, Michal. 1943. Political Aspects of Full Employment. *Political Quarterly* XIV 4: 322–31.

Kalinowski, Thomas. 2013. "Regulating International Finance and the Diversity of Capitalism." *Socio-Economic Review* 11(3): 471–496.

Kalyvas, Stathis. 2015. *Modern Greece: What Everyone Needs to Know®*. Oxford: Oxford University Press.

Kaplan, Greg, Giovanni L. Violante, and Justin Weidner. 2014. "The Wealthy Hand-to-Mouth." *Brookings Papers on Economic Activity* 2014(1): 77–138.

Kaplan, Stephen, and Kaj Thomsson. 2016. "The Political Economy of Sovereign Debt: Global Finance and Electoral Cycles." *Journal of Politics* 79(2): 605–623.

Karabarbounis, Loukas, and Brent Neiman. 2014. "The Global Decline of the Labor Share." *The Quarterly Journal of Economics* 129(1): 61–103.

Karwowski, Ewa, Mimoza Shabani, and Engelbert Stockhammer. 2020. "Dimensions and Determinants of Financialisation: Comparing OECD Countries since 1997." *New Political Economy* 25(6): 957–977.

Katz, Richard S., and Peter Mair. 1995. "Changing Models of Party Organization and Party Democracy: The Emergence of the Cartel Party," *Party Politics* 1(1): 5–28.

Katz, Richard S., and Peter Mair. 2009. "The Cartel Party Thesis: A Restatement," *Perspectives on Politics* 7(4): 753–766.

Katzenstein, Peter J., ed. 1978. *Between Power and Plenty: Foreign Economic Policies of Advanced Industrial States.* Madison: University of Wisconsin Press.

Katzenstein, Peter J., ed. 1985. *Small States in World Markets. Industrial Policy in Europe.* Ithaca, NY: Cornell University Press.

Kaufman, Robert. 1979. "Industrial Change and Authoritarian Rule in South. America: A Concrete Review of the Bureaucratic-Authoritarian Model." In *The New Authoritarianism in Latin America,* edited by David Collier, 165–254. Princeton, NJ: Princeton University Press.

Kaufman, Robert R., and Alex Segura-Ubiergo. 2001. "Globalization, Domestic Politics, and Social Spending in Latin America: A Time-Series Cross-Section Analysis, 1973–97." *World Politics* 53(4): 553–587.

Kaufman, Robert R., and Barbara Stallings. 1991. "The Political Economy of Latin American Populism." In *The Macroeconomics of Populism in Latin America,* edited by Rudiger Dornbusch and Sebastian Edwards, 15–44. Chicago: University of Chicago Press.

Kay, Cristóbal. 2002. "Why East Asia Overtook Latin America: Agrarian Reform, Industrialization and Development." *Third World Quarterly* 23(6): 1073–1102.

Kazen Orrefur, Samuel. 2019. "Förstatliga pengarna – så stoppar vi bankerna från att skapa finanskriser." Katalys report no. 68. Stockholm: Katalys.

Keohane, Robert O. 1984. *After Hegemony: Cooperation and Discord in the World Political Economy.* Princeton, NJ: Princeton University Press.

Keohane, Robert O. 2015. "The Global Politics of Climate Change: Challenge for Political Science." *PS: Political Science & Politics* 48(1):19–26.

Keynes, John. 1973 [1936]. *The General Theory of Employment, Interest and Money. The Collected Writings of John Maynard Keynes, Volume VII.* Cambridge: Macmillan.

Kiefer, David, and Codrina Rada. 2015. Profit Maximizing Goes Global: The Race to the Bottom. *Cambridge Journal of Economics* 39(5): 1333–1350.

Kindleberger, Charles P. 1973. *The World in Depression, 1929–1939.* London: Allen Lane.

Kindleberger, Charles P. 1978. *Manias, Panics, and Crashes: A History of Financial Crises.* New York: Basic Books.

King, John 2002. *A History of Post Keynesian Economics since 1936.* Cheltenham: Edward Elgar.

Kinsella, Stephen. 2012. Is Ireland Really the Role Model for Austerity? *Cambridge Journal of Economics* 36(1): 223–235.

Kirchheimer, Otto. 1966. "The Transformation of the Western European Party Systems." In *Political Parties and Political Development,* edited by Joseph La Palombara and Myron Weiner, 177–200. Princeton, NJ: Princeton University Press.

Kitschelt, Herbert 1991. Industrial Governance Structures, Innovation Strategies, and the Case of Japan. *International Organization* 45(4): 453–493.

Kitschelt, Herbert. 1994. *The Transformation of European Social Democracy.* Cambridge, MA: Cambridge University Press.

Kitschelt, Herbert. 2000. "Citizens, Politicians, and Party Cartellization: Political Representation and State Failure in Post-Industrial Democracies." *European Journal of Political Research* 37(2): 149–179.

Kitschelt, Herbert, and Philipp Rehm, 2014. "Occupations as a Site of Political Preference Formation," *Comparative Political Studies* 47(12): 1670–1706.

Kitschelt, Herbert, and Philipp Rehm. 2015. "Party Alignments: Change and Continuity." In *The Politics of Advanced Capitalism*, edited by Kriesi, Kitschelt, Beramendi, and Häusermann, 179–201. Cambridge: Cambridge University Press).

Klein, Herbert, and Francisco Vidal Luna. 2018. *Feeding the World: Brazil's Transformation into a Modern Agricultural Economy*. Cambridge: Cambridge University Press.

Klein, Matthew C., and Michael Pettis. 2020. *Trade Wars Are Class Wars: How Rising Inequality Distorts the Global Economy and Threatens International Peace*. New Haven CT: Yale University Press.

Klier, Thomas, and James Rubenstein. 2008. *Who Really Made Your Car? Restructuring and Geographic Change in the Auto Industry*. Kalamazoo, MI: WE Upjohn Institute.

Kline, Patrick, Neviana Petkova, Heidi Williams, and Owen Zidar. 2019. "Who Profits from Patents? Rent-Sharing at Innovative Firms." *The Quarterly Journal of Economics*, 134(3): 1343–1404.

Knight, Chris P. 2011. "Failure to Deploy: Solar Photovoltaic Policy in the United States." In *The State of Innovation: The U.S. Government's Role in Technology Development*, edited by Fred Block and Matthew Keller, 181–203. London: Paradigm Publishers.

Kohl, Sebastian. 2017. *Homeownership, Renting and Society: Historical and Comparative Perspectives*. London: Routledge.

Kohler Karsten, Alexander Guschanski, and Engelbert Stockhammer. 2019. How Does Financialisation Affect Functional Income Distribution? A Theoretical Clarification and Empirical Assessment. *Cambridge Journal of Economics* 43(4): 937–974.

Kohler, Karsten, and Engelbert Stockhammer. 2021. "Growing Differently? Financial Cycles, Austerity and Competitiveness since the Global Financial Crisis." *Review of International Political Economy* (online first). https://doi.org/10.1080/09692290.2021.1899035.

Kollmeyer, Christopher, and John Peters. 2019. "Financialization and the Decline of Organized Labor: A Study of 18 Advanced Capitalist Countries, 1970–2012." *Social Forces* 98(1): 1–30.

Konisky, David M. 2018. "The Greening of Christianity? A Study of Environmental Attitudes over Time." *Environmental Politics* 27(2): 267–291. doi: 10.1080/09644016.2017.1416903.

Koo, Richard C. 2011. "The World in Balance Sheet Recession: Causes, Cure, and Politics." *Real-World Economics Review* (58):19–37.

Kordalska, Aleksandra, and Magdalena Olczyk. 2019. "Is Germany a Hub of Factory Europe for CEE Countries? The Sink Approach in GVC Decomposition." GUT FME Working Paper Series A No. 4/2019 (56).

Korpi, Walter. 1974. "Conflict and the Balance of Power." *Acta Sociologica* 17(2): 99–114.

Korpi, Walter. 1983. *The Democratic Class Struggle*. London: Routledge & Kegan Paul.

Korpi, Walter. 2006. "Power Resources and Employer-Centered Approaches in Explanations of Welfare States and Varieties of Capitalism: Protagonists, Consenters, and Antagonists." *World Politics* 58(2): 167–206.

Krahnen, Jan P., and Reinhard H. Schmidt, eds. 2004. *The German Financial System*. Oxford: Oxford University Press.

Krajewska, Anna, and Magdalena Kapela. 2018. "Minimum Wage Impact on the Polish Economy." *Olsztyn Economic Journal* 13(3): 227–244.

Kranendonk, Henk, and Johan Verbruggen. 2008. "Decomposition of Gdp Growth in Some European Countries and the United States." *De Economist* 156(3): 295–306.

Kremers, Jeroen J. M., Neil R. Ericsson, and Juan J. Dolado. 1992. "The Power of Cointegration Tests." *Oxford Bulletin of Economics and Statistics* 54(3): 325–348.

Krippner, Greta R. 2011. *Capitalizing on Crisis: The Political Origins of the Rise of Finance*. Cambridge, MA: Harvard University Press.

Kristal, Tali. 2010. "Good Times, Bad Times: Postwar Labor's Share of National Income in Capitalist Democracies." *American Sociological Review* 75(5): 729–763.

Kristal, Tali, and Yinon Cohen. 2017. "The Causes of Rising Wage Inequality: The Race Between Institutions and Technology." *Socio-Economic Review* 15(1): 187–212.

Krugman, Paul. 2017. "Leprechaun Economics and Neo-Lafferism." *The New York Times*. https://krugman.blogs.nytimes.com/2017/11/08/leprechaun-economics-and-neo-lafferism/.

Krugman Paul, and Venables Anthony 1995. Globalization and the Inequality of Nations. *Quarterly Journal of Economics* 110(4): 857–880.

Kumhof, Michael, Romain Rancière, and Pablo Winant. 2015. "Inequality, Leverage, and Crises." *American Economic Review* 105(3): 1217–1245.

L

Lagna, Andrea. 2015. "Italian Municipalities and the Politics of Financial Derivatives: Rethinking the Foucauldian Perspective." *Competition & Change* 19(4): 283–300.

Lake, David. 2009. "Open Economy Politics: A Critical Review," *Review of international Organizations* 4(3): 219–244.

Lane, Philip. 2011. "The Irish Case." In *The Euro Area and the Financial Crisis*, edited by Beblavy, Cobman, and Odor, 59–80. Cambridge: Cambridge University Press.

Lane, Philip. 2020. Keynote speech by Philip R. Lane, Member of the Executive Board of the ECB, at the Joint European Central Bank, Irving Fisher Committee and Banco de Portugal conference on "Bridging measurement challenges and analytical needs of external statistics: Evolution or revolution?"

Lardy, Nicholas R. 2019. *The State Strikes Back: The End of Economic Reform in China?* Washington, D.C.: Peterson Institute for International Economics.

Lavoie, Marc. 2009. *Introduction to Post-Keynesian Economics*. London: Palgrave.

Lavoie, Marc. 2014. *Post-Keynesian Economics: New Foundations*. Cheltenham: Edward Elgar.

Lavoie, Marc. 2017. "The Origins and Evolution of the Debate on Wage-Led and Profit-Led Regimes." *European Journal of Economics and Economic Policies* 14(2): 200–221.

Lavoie, Marc. 2018. "Rethinking Macroeconomic Theory before the Next Crisis." *Review of Keynesian Economics* 6(1): 1–21.

Lavoie, Marc, and Engelbert Stockhammer. 2012. "Wage-Led Growth: Concept, Theories and Policies." ILO Conditions of Work and Employment Series *No. 41*.

Lavoie, Marc, and Engelbert Stockhammer. 2013. *Wage-Led Growth*. London: Palgrave.

Layard, Richard, Stephen Nickell, and Richard Jackman. 2005. *Unemployment: Macroeconomic Performance and the Labour Market*. Oxford: Oxford University Press.

Lazard. 2018. "Lazard's Levelized Cost of Energy Analysis." *Lazard*. https://www.lazard.com/media/450784/lazards-levelized-cost-of-energy-version-120-vfinal.pdf.

Lazonick, William. 1990. *Competitive Advantage on the Shop Floor*. Cambridge, MA: Harvard University Press.

Lazonick, William. 2010. "Innovative Business Models and Varieties of Capitalism: Financialization of the US Corporation." *Business History Review* 84(4): 675–702.

Lazonick, William, and Mary O'Sullivan. 2000. "Maximizing Shareholder Value: A New Ideology for Corporate Governance." *Economy and Society* 29(1): 13–35.

Leamer, Edward. 2015. "Housing Really Is the Business Cycle: What Survives the Lessons of 2008–09?" *Journal of Money, Credit and Banking* 47(S1): 43–50.

Lee, Ching Kwan. 2018. *The Specter of Global China: Politics, Labor, and Foreign Investment in Africa*. Chicago: University of Chicago Press.

Leeper, Eric M. 2018. "Sweden's Fiscal Framework and Monetary Policy." Report to the Swedish Fiscal Policy Council 2018/3.

Levinson, Marc. 2018. *U.S. Manufacturing in International Perspective*. Washington, D.C.: Congressional Research Service.

Levitsky, Steven, and Kenneth Roberts. 2011. *The Resurgence of the Latin American Left*. Baltimore, MD: Johns Hopkins University Press.

Lewis, Gregory B., Risa Palm, and Bo Feng. 2019. "Cross-National Variation in Determinants of Climate Change Concern." *Environmental Politics* 28(5): 793–821.

Lewis, Joanna I. 2014. "The Rise of Renewable Energy Protectionism: Emerging Trade Conflicts and Implications for Low Carbon Development." *Global Environmental Politics* 14(4): 10–35.

Lin, Ken-Hou, and Donald Tomaskovic-Devey. 2013. "Financialization and US Income Inequality, 1970–2008." *American Journal of Sociology* 118(5): 1284–1329.

Lindblom, Charles. 1977. *Politics and Markets*. New York: Basic.

Lipietz, Alain. 1997. "The Post-Fordist World: Labour Relations, International Hierarchy and Global Ecology." *Review of International Political Economy* 4(1): 1–41.

Lipset, Seymour Martin, and Stein Rokkan, eds. 1967. *Party Systems and Voter Alignments: Cross-National Perspectives*. Vol. 7. New York: Free Press.

Lipton, Michael. 1977. *Why Poor People Stay Poor: A Study of Urban Bias in World Development*. Cambridge, MA: Harvard University Press.

Liu, Chang, and Wei Xiong. 2020. "China's Real Estate Market." In *The Handbook of China's Financial System.*, edited by Marlene Amstad, Guofeng Sun, and Wei Xiong, 181–207. Princeton, NJ: Princeton University Press.

Locke, Richard M. 1995. *Remaking the Italian Economy*. Ithaca, NY: Cornell University Press.

Lonergan, Eric, and Mark Blyth. 2020. *Angrynomics*. Newcastle: Agenda Publishing.

Looney, Kristen. 2020. *Mobilizing for Development: The Modernization of Rural East Asia*. Ithaca, NY: Cornell University Press.

López, Isidro, and Emmanuel Rodríguez. 2011. "The Spanish Model." *New Left Review* 69(3): 5–29.

Lukes, Steven. 2004. *Power: A Radical View*. London: Macmillan International Higher Education.

Lunz, Patrick. 2013. "What's Left of the Left? Partisanship and the Political Economy of Labour Market Reform: Why Has the Social Democratic Party in Germany Liberalised Labour Markets?" LSE 'Europe in Question' Discussion Paper Series, Paper No. 65/2013.

Lynch, Julia. 2006. *Age in the Welfare State*. New York: Cambridge University Press.

Lynch, Julia. 2009. "Italy: A Christian Democratic or Clientelist Welfare State?" In *Religion, Class Coalitions and Welfare States*, edited by Kees Van Kersbergen and Philip Manow, 91–118. New York: Cambridge University Press.

Lynch, Julia. 2019. "Populism, Partisan Convergence, and Mobilization in Western Europe." *Polity* 51(4): 668–677.

Lynch, Julia. 2020. *Regimes of Inequality: The Political Economy of Health and Wealth*. New York: Cambridge University Press.

M

Machin, Richard. 2017. "Made to Measure? An Analysis of the Transition from Disability Living Allowance to Personal Independence Payment." *Journal of Social Welfare and Family Law* 39(4): 435–453.

Mader, Philip, Daniel Mertens, and Natascha Van der Zwan, eds. 2020. *The Routledge International Handbook of Financialization*. London: Routledge.

Madonna. 1984. "Material Girl," *Like a Virgin*. London: Sire Records. https://www.youtube.com/watch?v=6p-lDYPR2P8.

Maggiori, Matteo, Brent Neiman, and Jesse Schreger. 2020. "International Currencies and Capital Allocation." *Journal of Political Economy* 128(6): 2019–66.

Maier, C. S. 2015. *Recasting Bourgeois Europe: Stabilization in France, Germany, and Italy in the Decade after World War I*. Princeton, NJ: Princeton University Press.

Mair, Peter. 2011. "Bini Smaghi vs. the Parties: Representative Government and Institutional Constraints." EUI Working Paper RSCAS 2011/22.

Mair, Peter. 2013. *Ruling the Void: The Hollowing of Western Democracy*. London: Verso.

Manger, Mark S., and Sattler, Thomas 2020. "The Origins of Persistent Current Account Imbalances in the Post-Bretton Woods Era." *Comparative Political Studies* 53(3-4): 631–64.

Mangonnet, Jorge, Maria Victoria Murillo, and Julia Rubio. 2018. "Local Economic Voting and the Agricultural Boom in Argentina, 2007–2015." *Latin American Politics and Society* 60(8): 27–53.

Mankiw, Gregory, and David Romer.1991. *New Keynesian Economics*. 2 vols. Cambridge, MA: MIT Press.

Manzi, James, David Tesher, Geoffrey Wilson, Leonard Grimaldo, Arthur Wong, and Faheem Khan. 2017. "U.S. Corporate Cash Reaches $1.9 Trillion but Rising Debt and Tax Reform Pose Risk," *S&P Global*, May 25, 2017. https://www.spglobal.com/en/research-insights/articles/us-corporate-cash-reaches-19-trillion-but-rising-debt-and-tax-reform-pose-risk.

Mares, Isabela. 2001. "Firms and the Welfare State: When, Why and How Does Social Policy Matter to Employers?" In *Varieties of Capitalism: The Institutional Foundations of Comparative Advantage*, edited by Peter A. Hall and David Soskice, 184–212. Oxford: Oxford University Press, Oxford.

Marglin, Stephen A., and Juliet B. Schor, eds. 1990. *The Golden Age of Capitalism: Reinterpreting the Postwar Experience*. Oxford: Oxford University Press.

Martin, Cathie Jo and Duane Swank. 2012. *The Political Construction of Business Interests: Coordination, Growth, and Equality*. Cambridge: Cambridge University Press.

Marx, Paul. 2011. "The Unequal Incidence of Non-Standard Employment Across Occupational Groups: An Empirical Analysis of Post-Industrial Labour Markets in Germany and Europe." IZA Discussion Paper No. 5521.

Matsaganis, Manos et al. 2006. Reforming Family Transfers in Southern Europe: Is There a Role for Universal Child Benefits? *Social Policy and Society* 5: 189–197.

Matsaganis, Manos, Maurizio Ferrera, Luis Capucha, and Luis Moreno. 2003. "Mending Nets in the South: Anti-Poverty Policies in Greece, Italy, Portugal and Spain." *Social Policy & Administration* 37(6): 639–655.

Matthijs, Matthias. 2011. *Ideas and Economic Crises in Britain from Attlee to Blair (1945–2005)*. London: Routledge.

Matthijs, Matthias. 2016a. "Powerful Rules Governing the Euro: The Perverse Logic of German Ideas." *Journal of European Public Policy* 23(3): 375–391.

Matthijs, Matthias. 2016b. "The Euro's "Winner-Take-All" Political Economy: Institutional Choices, Policy Drift, and Diverging Patterns of Inequality." *Politics & Society* 44(3): 393–422.

Matthijs, Matthias. 2017. "Integration at What Price? The Erosion of National Democracy in the Euro Periphery." *Government and Opposition* 52(2): 266–295.

Matthijs, Matthias. 2020. "The Right Way to Fix the EU: Put Politics Before Economics," *Foreign Affairs* 99(3): 160–170.

Matthijs, Matthias, and Mark Blyth. 2015. *The Future of the Euro*. New York: Oxford University Press.

Matthijs, Matthias, and Mark Blyth. 2018. "When Is It Rational to Learn the Wrong Lessons? Technocratic Authority, Social Learning, and Euro Fragility." *Perspectives on Politics* 16(1): 110–126.

Matthijs, Matthias, and Kathleen McNamara. 2015. "The Euro Crisis' Theory Effect: Northern Saints, Southern Sinners, and the Demise of the Eurobond." *Journal of European Integration* 37(2): 229–245.

Mazzucato, Mariana. 2015. *The Entrepreneurial State: Debunking Public vs. Private Sector Myths*. London: Anthem Press.

McCarty, Nolan M., Keith T. Poole, and Howard Rosenthal. 2013. *Political Bubbles: Financial Crises and the Failure of American Democracy*. Princeton, NJ: Princeton University Press.

McCauley, Robert, Patrick McGuire, and Vladyslav Sushko. 2015. Global Dollar Credit: Links to US Monetary Policy and Leverage. *Economic Policy* 30(82): 187–229.

McCright, Aaron M., Sandra T. Marquart-Pyatt, Rachael L. Shwom, Steven R. Brechin, and Summer Allen. 2016. "Ideology, Capitalism, and Climate: Explaining Public Views about Climate Change in the United States." *Energy Research & Social Science* 21: 180–189.

McDowell, Daniel. 2012. "The US as 'Sovereign International Last-Resort Lender': The Fed's Currency Swap Programme During the Great Panic of 2007–09." *New Political Economy* 17(2): 157–78.

McGuire, Shawn K., and Charles B. Delahunt. 2020. "Predicting United States Policy Outcomes with Random Forests." Institute for New Economic Thinking working Paper Series, N. 138, October.

McLeay, Michael, Amar Radia, and Ryland Thomas. 2014. Money Creation in the Modern Economy. BoE Quarterly Bulletin 54(1): 14–27.

McNamara, Kathleen R. 1998. The Currency of Ideas: Monetary Politics in the European Union. Ithaca, NY: Cornell University Press.

McVicar, Duncan. 2008. "Why Have UK Disability Rolls Grown So Much?" Journal of Economic Surveys 22(1): 27.

Meckling, Jonas, and Bentley B. Allan. 2020. "The Evolution of Ideas in Global Climate Policy." Nature Climate Change 10(5):434–438.

Meckling, Jonas, Nina Kelsey, Eric Biber, and John Zysman. 2015. "Winning Coalitions for Climate Policy." Science 349(6253):1170–1171.

Meckling, Jonas, and Jonas Nahm. 2018a. "The Power of Process: State Capacity and Climate Policy." Governance 31(4): 741–757.

Meckling, Jonas, and Jonas Nahm. 2018b. "When Do States Disrupt Industries? Electric Cars and the Politics of Innovation." Review of International Political Economy 25(4): 505–529.

Meckling, Jonas, and Jonas Nahm. 2019. "The Politics of Technology Bans: Industrial Policy Competition and Green Goals for the Auto Industry." Energy Policy 126: 470–479.

Meckling, Jonas, and Jonas Nahm. 2022. "Strategic State Capacity: How States Counter Opposition to Climate Policy." Comparative Political Studies 55(3): 493–523.

Medve-Bálint, Gerggo, and Vera Šćepanović. 2020. "EU Funds, State Capacity and the Development of Transnational Industrial Policies in Europe's Eastern Periphery." Review of International Political Economy 27(5), 1063-1082.

Meltzer, Allan H., and Scott F. Richard. 1978. "Why Government Grows (and Grows) in a Democracy." Public Interest 52(1): 111–118.

Mendoza, Enrique, Vincenzo Quadrini, and Jose-Victor Rios-Rull. 2009. "Financial Integration, Financial Development, and Global Imbalances." Journal of Political Economy 117(3): 371–416.

Merkel, Angela. 2010. "Speech in the Bundestag," May 19. Online available at https://www.bund esregierung.de/Content/DE/Bulletin/2010-2015/2010/05/55-1-bkin-bt.html (accessed on August 16, 2019).

Merler, Silvia. 2018. "Latvia's Money Laundering Scandal | Bruegel." (April 9, 2018). http://brue gel.org/2018/04/latvias-money-laundering-scandal/.

Mertens, Daniel. 2015. Erst sparen, dann kaufen? Privatverschuldung in Deutschland. Frankfurt a.M.: Campus.

Meyer, Henry, Aron Eglitis, and Irina Reznik. 2018. "The Face of Latvia's Financial System Is Caught in a Corruption Case." (September 25, 2018). https://www.bloomberg.com/news/ features/2018-09-25/the-face-of-latvia-s-scandal-ridden-financial-system-is-caught-in-a-corruption-case.

Mian, Atif, and Amir Sufi. 2011. "House Prices, Home Equity-Based Borrowing, and the US Household Leverage Crisis." American Economic Review 101(5): 2132–2156.

Mian, Atif, and Amir Sufi. 2014. House of Debt: How They (and You) Caused the Great Recession, and How We Can Prevent It from Happening Again. Chicago: University of Chicago Press.

Mian, Atif, Amir Sufi, and Francesco Trebbi. 2010. "The Political Economy of the US Mortgage Default Crisis." American Economic Review 100(5): 1967–1998.

Minsky, Hyman. 1986. Stabilizing an Unstable Economy. New Haven, CT: Yale University Press.

Minsky, Hyman. 2008. John Maynard Keynes, New York: McGraw-Hill.

Minsky, Hyman. 2016, "The Financial Instability Hypothesis: A Restatement." In Can 'It' Happen Again? Essays on Instability and Finance, edited by Hyman Minsky, 59–71. London and New York: Routledge.

Mishel, Lawrence, Josh Bivens, Elise Gould, and Heidi Shierholz. 2012. *The State of Working America*. 12th ed.New York: ILR Press.

Mishel, Lawrence. 2018. "Uber and the Labor Market." Economic Policy Institute. https://www.epi.org/publication/uber-and-the-labor-market-uber-drivers-compensation-wages-and-the-scale-of-uber-and-the-gig-economy/.

Molina, Oscar. 2014. "Beyond De-Centralization: The Erosion of Collective Bargaining in Spain During the Great Recession." *Stato e Mercato* 102(3): 397–422.

Molina, Óscar, and Martin Rhodes. 2007. "The Political Economy of Adjustment in Mixed Market Economies: A Study of Spain and Italy." In *Beyond Varieties of Capitalism: Conflict, Contradictions, and Complementarities in the European Economy*, edited by B. Hancké, Martin Rhodes, and M. Thatcher, 223–252. Oxford: Oxford University Press.

Montgomerie, Johnna, and Mirjam Büdenbender. 2015. "Round the Houses: Homeownership and Failures of Asset-Based Welfare in the United Kingdom." *New Political Economy* 20(3): 386–405.

Moore, Basil J. 1988. *Horizontalists and Verticalists: The Macroeconomics of Credit Money*. Cambridge: Cambridge University Press.

Morgan, Kimberly J., and Andrea Louise Campbell. 2011. *The Delegated Welfare State: Medicare, Markets, and the Governance of Social Policy*. New York: Oxford University Press.

Morgan, Kimberly, and Alexander Reisenbichler. 2021. "Riding the Tiger: Managing Risk in U.S. Housing Finance and Health Insurance Welfare Markets." *Socio-Economic Review* (advanced online access): 1-24.

Morton, Oliver. 2006. "Solar Energy: A New Day Dawning?: Silicon Valley Sunrise." *Nature* 443(7107): 19–22.

Moschella, Manuela. 2016. "Negotiating Greece. Layering, Insulation, and the Design of Adjustment Programs in the Eurozone." *Review of International Political Economy* 23(5): 799–824.

Muellbauer, John, and Anthony Murphy. 2008. "Housing Markets and the Economy: The Assessment." *Oxford Review of Economic Policy* 24(1): 1–33.

Mügge, Daniel, and Lukas Linsi. 2020. "The National Accounting Paradox: How Statistical Norms Corrode International Economic Data." *European Journal of International Relations* 27(2): 403–427.

Müller, Wolfgang C., and Kaare Strøm, eds. 1999. *Policy, Office, or Votes? How Political Parties in Western Europe Make Hard Decisions*. Cambridge: Cambridge University Press.

Murie, Alan. 2016. *The Right to Buy?: Selling Off Public and Social Housing*. Bristol: Policy Press.

Murillo, Maria Victoria, Virginia Oliveros, and Milan Vaishnav. 2011. "Economic Constrains and Presidential Agency." In *The Resurgence of the Latin American Left*, edited by Steven Levitsky and Kenneth M. Roberts, 52–70. Baltimore, MD: Johns Hopkins University Press.

Murphy, Brendan. 1999. "European Integration and Liberalization: Political Change and Economic Policy Continuity in Spain." *Mediterranean Politics* 4(1): 53–78.

Murray, Joshua, and Michael Schwartz. 2019. *Wrecked: How the American Automobile Industry Destroyed Its Capacity to Compete*. New York: Russell Sage Foundation.

Mutz, Diana. 2011. *Population-Based Survey Experiments*: Princeton, NJ: Princeton University Press.

Myant, Martin. 2016. "Unit Labour Costs: No Argument for Low Wages in Eastern and Central Europe." ETUI Research Paper-Working Paper, 2016.

Myant, Martin. 2018a. "The Limits to Dependent Growth in East-Central Europe." *Revue de La Régulation. Capitalisme, Institutions, Pouvoirs* 24. http://journals.openedition.org/regulation/13351.

Myant, Martin 2018b. "Why Are Wages Still Lower in Eastern and Central Europe?" ETUI Research Paper—Working Paper No. 2018.01.

N

Naastepad, C.W.M., and Servaas Storm. 2006/07. "OECD Demand Regimes (1960–2000)." *Journal of Post-Keynesian Economics* 29(2): 213–248.

Nachtwey, Oliver. 2018. *Germany's Hidden Crisis: Social Decline in the Heart of Europe*. London: Verso Books.

Naczyk, Marek. 2021. "Taking Back Control: Comprador Bankers and Managerial Developmentalism in Poland." *Review of International Political Economy* published online June 28. https://doi.org/10.1080/09692290.2021.1924831.

Nahm, Jonas. 2017a. "Exploiting the Implementation Gap: Policy Divergence and Industrial Upgrading in China's Wind and Solar Sectors." *The China Quarterly* 231: 705–727.

Nahm, Jonas. 2017b. "Renewable Futures and Industrial Legacies: Wind and Solar Sectors in China, Germany, and the United States." *Business and Politics* 19(1): 68–106.

Nahm, Jonas. 2019. "The Energy Politics of China." In *The Oxford Handbook of Energy Politics*, edited by Kathleen J. Hancock and Juliann Emmons Allison, 507–532. New York: Oxford University Press.

Nahm, Jonas. 2021. *Collaborative Advantage: Forging Green Industries in the New Global Economy*. New York: Oxford University Press.

Nahm, Jonas, and Edward S. Steinfeld. 2014. "Scale-up Nation: China's Specialization in Innovative Manufacturing." *World Development* 54: 288–300.

Naldini, Manuela, and Teresa Jurado. 2013. "Family and Welfare State Reorientation in Spain and Inertia in Italy from a European Perspective." *Population Review* 52(1): 43–61.

Natali, David. 2018. "Occupational Pensions in Europe: Trojan Horse of Financialization?" *Social Policy & Administration* 52(2): 449–462.

Naughton, Barry. 2007. *The Chinese Economy: Transitions and Growth*. Cambridge, MA: MIT Press.

Naughton, Barry. 2016. "Supply-Side Structural Reform: Policy-Makers Look for a Way Out." *China Leadership Monitor Winter* 49.

Naughton, Barry, and Hai Weng. 1999. "China's Dual Trading Regimes: Implications for Growth and Reform." In *International Trade Policy and the Pacific Rim*, edited by John Piggott and Alan Woodland, 30–58. London: Macmillan.

Neumann, Henriette. 2020. "The Determinants of German Exports—An Analysis of Intra- and Extra-EMU Trade." *International Review of Applied Economics* 34(1): 126–45.

Nienaber, Michael. 2022. "'We Won't Waste the Crisis': Germany's New Finance Minister Open to EU Reforms." *Reuters News Agency*. (January 10, 2022). https://www.reuters.com/markets/europe/we-wont-waste-crisis-germanys-new-finance-minister-open-eu-reforms-2022-01-10/.

Nikolaidi, Mmaria, and Engelbert Stockhammer. 2017. "Minsky Models. A Structured Review." *Journal of Economic Surveys* 31(5): 1304–1331.

Noble, David 1984. *Forces of Production: A Social History of Automation*. New York: Knopf.

Nölke, Andreas. 2016. "Economic Causes of the Eurozone Crisis: The Analytical Contribution of Comparative Capitalism." *Socio-Economic Review* 14(1): 141–161.

Nölke, Andreas. 2021. *Exportismus: Die deutsche Droge. Eine Entzugsstrategie für gesundes Wachstum*. Frankfurt a.M.: Westend.

Nölke, Andreas, and Arjan Vliegenthart 2009. "Enlarging the Varieties of Capitalism: The Emergence of Dependent Market Economies in East Central Europe." *World Politics* 61(4): 670–702.

Norris, Pippa, and Ronald Inglehart. 2019. *Cultural Backlash: Trump, Brexit, and Authoritarian Populism*. Cambridge: Cambridge University Press.

Nybom, Jenny. 2011. "Activation in Social Work with Social Assistance Claimants in Four Swedish Municipalities." *European Journal of Social Work* 14(3): 339–61.

O

Oatley, Thomas. 2019. "Toward a Political Economy of Complex Interdependence." *European Journal of International Relations* 25(4): 957–978.

Oatley, Thomas et al. 2013. "The Political Economy of Global Finance: A network Model." *Perspectives on Politics* 11(1): 133–153.

Oatley, Thomas, Sarah Bauerle-Danzman, and William K. Winecoff. 2017. "All Crises are Global: Capital Cycles in an Imbalanced International Political Economy." *International Studies Quarterly* 61(4): 907–923.

Obst, Thomas, Özlem Onaran, and Maria Nikolaidi. 2020. The Effects of Income Distribution and Fiscal Policy on Aggregate Demand, Investment and the Budget Balance: The Case of Europe. *Cambridge Journal of Economics* 44(6): 1221–1243.

Ocampo, José Antonio. 2017. "Commodity-Led Development in Latin America." In *Alternative Pathways to Sustainable Development: Lessons from Latin America*, edited by Gilles Carbonnier, Humberto Campodónico, and Sergio Tezanos Vázquez, 51–76. Leiden: Brill.

Ocampo, José Antonio, and Jaime Ros. 2011. *The Oxford Handbook of Latin American Economics*. Oxford: University of Oxford Press.

O'Connor, James. 1973. *The Fiscal Crisis of the State*. New York: Transaction Publishers.

O'Donnell, Guillermo. 1973. *Modernization and Bureaucratic-Authoritarianism: Studies in South American Politics*. Berkeley: University of California Press.

O'Donnell, Guillermo. 1978. "State and Alliances in Argentina, 1956–1976." *Journal of Development Studies* 15(1): 3–33.

O'Donnell, Guillermo.1988. *Bureaucratic Authoritarianism: Argentina 1966–1973 in Comparative Perspective*. Berkeley: University of California Press.

OECD. 2004. *Benefits and Wages*. Paris: OECD.

OECD. 2008. Growing Unequal? Income Distribution and Poverty in OECD Countries. Paris: OECD.

OECD. 2017. *Labour Market Resilience: The Role of Structural and Macroeconomic Policies*. Chapter 2 of *OECD Employment Outlook 2017*. Paris: OECD Publishing.

OECD. 2018. *Economic Outlook No 104 - November 2018*. Paris: OECD.

OECD. 2019. *Under Pressure: The Squeezed Middle Class*. Paris: Organisation for Economic Co-operation and Development.

OECD. 2020. *Economic Outlook No. 2 - December 2020*. Paris: OECD.

OECD. 2021a. *Strictness of Employment Protection*. URL: https://stats.oecd.org/Index.aspx?Data SetCode=EPL_OV (Accessed April 8).

OECD. 2021b. *Involuntary Part Time Workers*. URL: https://stats.oecd.org/Index.aspx?DataSetC ode=INVPT_I# (Accessed April 8).

Oellerich, Nils. 2021. "Promoting Domestic Bank Ownership in Central and Eastern Europe: A Case Study of Economic Nationalism and Rent-Seeking in Hungary." *East European Politics* published online June 16. https://doi.org/10.1080/21599165.2021.1937137.

Offe, Claus. 1984. *Contradictions of the Welfare State*. London: Routledge.

Office for National Statistics. 2018. "Making Ends Meet: Are Households Living Beyond Their Means?" Report London: Office for National Statistics, July 26.

Onaran, Özlem, and Valerie Boesch. 2014. "The Effect of Globalization on the Distribution of Taxes and Social Expenditures in Europe: Do Welfare State Regimes Matter?" *Environment and Planning A* 46(2): 373–397.

Onaran, Özlem, and Giorgos Galanis. 2014. "Income Distribution and Growth: A Global Model." *Environment and Planning A* 46(10): 2489–2513.

Onaran, Özlem, and Thomas Obst. 2016. "Wage-Led Growth in the EU15 Member States: The Effects of Income Distribution on Growth, Investment, Trade Balance, and Inflation." *Cambridge Journal of Economics* 40(6):1517–1551.

Onaran, Özlem, Cem Oyvat, and Euridyke Fotopoulou. 2019. "The Effects of Gender Inequality, Wages, Wealth Concentration and Fiscal Policy on Macroeconomic Performance." Greenwich Papers in Political Economy 71.

Onaran, Özlem, Cem Oyvat, and Eurydike Fotopoulou. 2022. A Macroeconomic Analysis of the Effects of Gender Inequality, Wages, and Public Social Infrastructure: the Case of the UK. Feminist Economics 28:Forthcoming.

Onaran, Özlem, Engelbert Stockhammer, and Lucas Grafl. 2011. The Finance-Dominated Growth Regime, Distribution, and Aggregate Demand in the US. Cambridge Journal of Economics 35(4): 637–661.

Oren, Tami, and Mark Blyth. 2019. "From Big Bang to Big Crash: The Early Origins of the UK's Finance-Led Growth Model and the Persistence of Bad Policy Ideas." New Political Economy 24(5): 605–622.

Orhangazi, Özgur. 2008. Financialisation and Capital Accumulation in the Non-financial Corporate Sector: A Theoretical and Empirical Investigation on the US Economy: 1973–2003. Cambridge Journal of Economics 32(6): 863–86.

Ornston, Darius. 2013. "Creative Corporatism: The Politics of High-Technology Competition in Nordic Europe." Comparative Political Studies 46(6): 702–729.

Ostrom, Elinor. 2019. Governing the Commons: The Evolution of Institutions for Collective Action. Cambridge: Cambridge University Press.

P

Pagano, Ugo. 2014. The Crisis of Intellectual Monopoly Capitalism. Cambridge Journal of Economics 38(6): 1409–1429.

Palan, Ronen. 2006. The Offshore World: Sovereign Markets, Virtual Places, and Nomad Millionaires. Ithaca, NY: Cornell University Press.

Palan, Ronen, Richard Murphy, and Christian Chavagneux. 2013. Tax Havens: How Globalization Really Works. Ithaca, NY: Cornell University Press.

Palley. Thomas. 1996. Aggregate Demand in a Reconstruction of Growth Theory. Review of Political Economy 8: 23–35.

Palley. Thomas. 2015. "Escaping Stagnation and Restoring Shared Prosperity: A Macroeconomic Policy Framework for Job-Rich Growth." ILO Working Papers 994874713402676.

Palley. Thomas. 2016. Financialization: The Economics of Finance Capital Domination. Basingstoke: Palgrave Macmillan.

Palley. Thomas. 2017. "Wage- vs. Profit-Led Growth: The Role of the Distribution of Wages in Determining Regime Character." Cambridge Journal of Economics 41(1): 49–61.

Palley. Thomas. 2019. "The Fallacy of the Natural Rate of Interest and Zero Lower Bound Economics: Why Negative Interest Rates May Not Remedy Keynesian Unemployment." Review of Keynesian Economics 7(2): 151–70.

Panebianco, Angelo. 1988. Political Parties: Organization and Power. Cambridge: Cambridge University Press.

Paniagua, Victoria. 2018. Protecting Capital: Economic Elites, Asset Portfolio Diversification, and the Politics of Distribution. PhD diss., Duke University.

Pariboni, Riccardo, Walter Paternesi Meloni, and Pasquale Tridico. 2020. "When Melius Abundare Is No Longer True: Excessive Financialization and Inequality as Drivers of Stagnation." Review of Political Economy 32(2): 216–242.

Pasquino, Gianfranco. 2007. "The Five Faces of Silvio Berlusconi: The Knight of Anti-Politics." Modern Italy 12(1): 39–54.

Pautz, Hartwig. 2010. "Think Tanks in the United Kingdom and Germany: Actors in the Modernisation of Social Democracy," British Journal of Politics and International Relations 12(2): 274–294.

Pavlínek, Petr. 2020. "Restructuring and Internationalization of the European Automotive Industry." Journal of Economic Geography 20(2): 509–541.

Pearson, Margaret. 2015. "State-Owned Business and Party-State Regulation in China's Modern Political Economy." In *State Capitalism, Institutional Adaptation, and the Chinese Miracle*, edited by Barry Naughton and Kellee S. Tsai, 27–45. New York: Cambridge University Press.

Pearson, Margaret, Meg Rithmire, and Kellee Tsai. 2020. "Party-State Capitalism in China." HBS Working Paper No. 21–065.

Peinert, Erik. 2021. "Cartels, Competition, and Coalitions: The Domestic Drivers of International Orders." *Review of International Political Economy* 28(6): 1652–1676.

Perez, Carlota. 2009. "The Double Bubble at the Turn of the Century: Technological Roots and Structural Implications." *Cambridge Journal of Economics* 32: 779–805.

Pérez, Sofia.1997. *Banking on Privilege: The Politics of Spanish Financial Reform*. Ithaca, NY: Cornell University Press.

Perez, Sofia, and Manos Matsaganis, M. 2018. "The Political Economy of Austerity in Southern Europe." *New Political Economy* 23(2): 192–207.

Persson, Mikael. 2020. "What Explains Unequal Responsiveness?" Unequal Democracies Working Paper No. 18. University of Geneva.

Perzanowski, Aaron, and Jason Schultz. 2016. *The End of Ownership: Personal Property in the Digital Economy*. Cambridge, MA: MIT Press.

Pew Research Center. 2016. *Household Expenditures and Income*. Report Washington, D.C.: Pew Research Center.

Pharr, Susan J., and Robert D. Putnam. 2000. *Disaffected Democracies: What's Troubling the Trilateral Countries?* Princeton, NJ: Princeton University Press.

Philippon, Thomas. 2019. *The Great Reversal: How America Gave Up on Free Markets*. Cambridge, MA: Harvard University Press.

Piatanesi, Benedetta, and Josep-Maria Arauzo-Carod. 2019. "Backshoring and Nearshoring: An Overview." *Growth and Change* 50(3): 806–23.

Picot, Georg, and Arianna Tassinari. 2017. "All of One Kind? Labour Market Reforms under Austerity in Italy and Spain." *Socio-Economic Review* 15(2): 461–482.

Piggott, Linda, and Chris Grover. 2009. "Retrenching Incapacity Benefit: Employment Support Allowance and Paid Work." *Social Policy and Society* 8(2): 159–170.

Piketty, Thomas. 2014. *Capital in the Twenty-First Century*. Cambridge, MA: Belknap Press.

Piketty, Thomas. 2020. *Capital and Ideology*. Cambridge, MA: Harvard University Press.

Piore, Michael, and Charles Sabel. 1984. *The Second Industrial Divide: Possibilities for Prosperity*. New York: Basic Books.

Piroska, Dóra. 2017. "Funding Hungary: Competing Crisis Management Priorities of Troika Institutions." *Third World Thematics: A TWQ Journal* 2(6): 805–824.

Pistor, Katharina. 2013. A Legal Theory of Finance. *Journal of Comparative Economics* 41(2): 315–330.

Pistor, Katharina. 2019. *The Code of Capital: How the Law Creates Wealth and Inequality*. Princeton, NJ: Princeton University Press.

Piven, Frances Fox, and Richard Cloward. 2012. *Regulating the Poor: The Functions of Public Welfare*. New York: Knopf Doubleday.

Pizzorno, Alessandro. 1978. "Political Exchange and Collective Identity in Industrial Conflict." In *The Resurgence of Class Conflict in Western Europe since 1968*, edited by C. Crouch and A. Pizzorno, 277–298. London: Macmillan.

Pollin, Robert. 2019. Advancing a Viable Global Climate Stabilization Project: Degrowth versus the Green New Deal. *Review of Radical Political Economy* 51(2): 311–319.

Pollin, Robert. 1992a. *The Limits of Social Democracy: Investment Politics in Sweden*. Ithaca, NY: Cornell University Press.

Pollin, Robert. 1992b. "At the End of the Third Road: Swedish Social Democracy in Crisis." *Politics and Society* 20(3): 305–332.

Pollin, Robert. 2011. "Once Again A Model: Nordic Social Democracy in a Globalized Age." In *Futures of the Left*, edited by James Cronin, George Ross, and James Shoch, 89–115. Durham, NC: Duke University Press.

Pontusson, Jonas. 1992a. *The Limits of Social Democracy: Investment Politics in Sweden*. Ithaca, NY: Cornell University Press.

Pontusson, Jonas. 1992b. "At the End of the Third Road: Swedish Social Democracy in Crisis." *Politics and Society* 20(3): 305–332.

Pontusson, Jonas. 2011. "Once Again a Model: Nordic Social Democracy in a Globalized Age." In *Futures of the Left*, edited by James Cronin, George Ross, and James Shoch, 89–115. Durham, NC: Duke University Press.

Pontusson, Jonas, and Peter Swenson. 1996. "Labor Markets, Production Strategies, and Wage-Bargaining Institutions: The Swedish Employers' Offensive in Comparative Perspective." *Comparative Political Studies* 29(2): 223–250.

Prados de la Escosura, Leandro. 2007. "Inequality and Poverty in Latin America: A Long-Run Exploration." In *The New Comparative Economic History*, edited by Timothy J. Hatton, Kevin H. O'Rourke, and Alan M. Taylor, 291–315. Cambridge, MA: MIT Press.

Prasad, Monica. 2012. *The Land of Too Much: American Abundance and the Paradox of Poverty*. Cambridge, MA: Harvard University Press.

Prebisch, Raúl. 1962. "The Economic Development of Latin America and Its Principal Problems." *Economic Bulletin for Latin America* 7(1): 1–22.

Priewe, Jan. 2020. "Europäische Wirtschafts- und Währungsunion: Grenzwerte für Defizite und Schulden in der Kritik." *Wirtschaftsdienst* 100(7): 538–544.

Przeworski, Adam. 2019. *Crises of Democracy*: Cambridge: Cambridge University Press.

Purdue, David, and Hansi Huang. 2016. *Irish Exports: The Facts, the Fiction and the Risks*. Dublin: National Treasury Management Agency.

Q

Quaglia, Lucia, and Sebastián Royo. 2015. "Banks and the Political Economy of the Sovereign Debt Crisis in Italy and Spain." *Review of International Political Economy* 22(3): 485–507.

R

Radice, Giles. 1992. *Southern Discomfort*. Vol. 9. London: Fabian Society.

Raggett, Chris. 2019. "The Flawed Bank Redemption: Europe and the Politics of Money Laundering." *European Council on Foreign Relations*. https://www.ecfr.eu/article/commentary_europe_and_the_politics_of_money_laundering.

Rajan, Raghuram G. 2011. *Fault Lines: How Hidden Fractures Still Threaten the World Economy*. Princeton, NJ: Princeton University Press.

Rangone, Marco, and Stefano Solari. 2012. "From the Southern-European Model to Nowhere: The Evolution of Italian Capitalism, 1976–2011." *Journal of European Public Policy* 19(8): 1188–1206.

Reca, Lucio G. 2008. "El conflicto por el régimen de retenciones y el futuro de la agricultura argentina." Annual Meeting of the Asociación Argentina de Economía Política.

Redeker, Nils, and Stefanie Walter. 2020. "We'd Rather Pay Than Change the Politics of German Non-Adjustment in the Eurozone Crisis." *The Review of International Organizations* 15(3): 573–599.

Regalia, Ida, and Marino Regini. 1998. "Italy: The Dual Character of Industrial Relations." In *Changing Industrial Relations in Europe*, edited by A. Ferner and R. Hyman, 459–503. Malden, MA: Blackwell Publishers.

Regan, Aidan, and Samuel Brazys. 2018. Celtic Phoenix or Leprechaun Economics? The Politics of an FDI-Led Growth Model in Europe. *New Political Economy* 23(2): v223–238.

Regini, Marino. 1984. "The Conditions for Political Exchange: How Concertation Emerged and Collapsed in Italy and Great Britain." In *Order and Conflict in Contemporary Capitalism*, edited by J. H. Goldthorpe, 124–142. Oxford: Clarendon.

Rehm, Philipp. 2016. *Risk Inequality and Welfare States: Social Policy Preferences, Development, and Dynamics*. New York: Cambridge University Press.

Reinhart, Carmen, and Kenneth Rogoff. 2009. *This Time Is Different: Eight Centuries of Financial Folly*. Princeton, NJ: Princeton University Press.

Reisenbichler, Alexander. 2020. "The Politics of Quantitative Easing and Housing Stimulus by the Federal Reserve and European Central Bank, 2008–2018." *West European Politics* 43(2): 464–484.

Reisenbichler, Alexander. 2021a. "Entrenchment or Retrenchment: The Political Economy of Mortgage Debt Subsidies in the United States and Germany." *Comparative Politics* (online first). https://doi.org/10.5129/001041522X16314500561319.

Reisenbichler, Alexander. 2021b. Housing Finance Markets Between Social Welfare and Growth Strategies. In *Growth and Welfare in Advanced Capitalist Economies*, edited by Anke Hassel and Bruno Palier, 320–347. Oxford: Oxford University Press.

Reisenbichler, Alexander, and Andreas Wiedemann. 2022. "Credit and Consumption Led Growth Models." In *Diminishing Returns: The New Politics of Growth and Stagnation*, edited by Lucio Baccaro, Mark Blyth, and Jonas Pontusson, 213–237. New York: Oxford University Press.

Rezai, Armon, Lance Taylor, and Duncan Foley. 2018. "Economic Growth, Income Distribution, and Climate Change." *Ecological Economics* 146: 164–172.

Rhodes, Martin. 2000. Restructuring the British Welfare State: Between Domestic Constraints and Global Imperatives. In *Welfare and Work in the Open Economy*, edited by Fritz Scharpf and Vivien A. Schmidt, 19–68. Oxford: Oxford University Press.

Richardson, Neal P. 2012. *The Politics of Abundance: Export Agriculture and Redistributive Conflict in South America*, Ph.D diss., University of California, Berkeley.

Righter, Robert W. 2011. *Windfall: Wind Energy in America Today*. Norman: University of Oklahoma Press.

Rithmire, Meg. 2015. *Land Bargains and Chinese Capitalism: The Politics of Property Rights under Reform*. New York: Cambridge University Press.

Rithmire, Meg. 2017. "Land Institutions and Chinese Political Economy: Institutional Complementarities and Macroeconomic Management." *Politics & Society* 45(1): 123–153.

Rivera-Quiñones, Miguel. 2014. "Macroeconomic Governance in Post-Neoliberal Argentina and the Relentless Power of TNCs: The Case of the Soy Complex." In *Argentina since the 2001 Crisis: Recovering the Past, Reclaiming the Future*, edited by Cara Levey, Daniel Ozarow, and Christopher Wylde, 67–86. London: PalgraveMacmillan.

Rixen, Thomas. 2015. "Hehre Ziele, wenig Zählbares. Die Steuer- und Fiskalpolitik der schwarz-gelben Regierung, 2009–13." In *Die Politik im Schatten der Krise. Eine Bilanz der Regierung Merkel 2009–2013*, edited by R. Zohlnhöfer and Thomas Saalfeld, 327–351. Wiesbaden: Springer VS.

Rixen, Thomas. 2019. "Die Verwaltung des Überschusses. Die Fiskalpolitik der Großen Koalition, 2013–17." In *Zwischen Stillstand, Politikwandel und Krisenmanagement. Eine Bilanz der Regierung Merkel 2013–2017*, edited by R. Zohlnhöfer and Thomas Saalfeld, 345–372. Wiesbaden: Springer VS.

Rodrigues, João, Ana C. Santos, and Nuno Teles. 2016. "Semi-Peripheral Financialisation: The Case of Portugal." *Review of International Political Economy* 23(3) 480–510.

Rodrik, Dani. 2004. "Industrial Policy for the Twenty-First Century." CEPR Discussion Papers No 4767.

Rodrik, Dani. 2016. "Premature Deindustrialization." *Journal of Economic Growth* 21(1): 1–33.

Rose, Richard, and Ian McAllister. 1986. *Voters Begin to Choose: From Closed Class to Open Elections in Britain*. Beverly Hills: Sage Publications.

Royston, Sam. 2017. *Broken Benefits: What's Gone Wrong with Welfare Reform?* Bristol: Policy Press.

Rueschemeyer, Dietrich, Evelyne Huber, and John Huber. 1992. *Capitalist Development and Democracy*. Chicago: University of Chicago Press.

Ruggie, John Gerard. 1982. "International Regimes, Transactions, and Change: Embedded Liberalism in the Postwar Economic Order." *International Organization* 36(2): 379–415.

Ruiz, Juan Rafael, Patricia Stupariu, and Ángel Vilariño. 2015. "The Crisis of Spanish Savings Banks." *Cambridge Journal of Economics* 40(6): 1455–77.

Ryoo, Soon 2016. "Household Debt and Housing Bubbles: A Minskian Approach to Boom-Bust Cycles." *Journal of Evolutionary Economics* 26: 971–1006.

S

Sacchi, Stefano. 2015. "Conditionality by Other Means: EU Involvement in Italy/Structural Reforms in the Sovereign Debt Crisis." *Comparative European Politics* 13(1): 77–92.

Saez, Emmanuel, and Gabriel Zucman. 2019. *The Triumph of Injustice: How the Rich Dodge Taxes and How to Make Them Pay*. New York: WW Norton.

Saffer, Jessica, Lizette Nolte, and Simon Duffy. 2018. "Living on a Knife Edge: The Responses of People with Physical Health Conditions to Changes in Disability Benefits." *Disability & Society* 33(10): 1555–1578.

Salento, Angelo. 2016. "The Financialisation of Companies in Italy." *Oñati Socio-Legal Series* 6(3): 795–815(3).

Salento, Angelo, Giovanni Masino, and Domenico Berdicchia. 2013. "Financialization and Organizational Changes in Multinational Enterprises." *Revue d'économie industrielle* 144: 145–176.

Sánchez-Ancochea, Diego. 2021. "The Surprising Reduction of Inequality during a Commodity Boom: What Do We Learn from Latin America?" *Journal of Economic Policy Reform* 24(2): 95–118.

Sandbu, Martin. 2019. "Almost Two-Thirds of Irish FDI Is 'Phantom'—IMF Study." *The Irish Times*, September 9, 2019. https://www.irishtimes.com/business/economy/almost-two-thirds-of-irish-fdi-is-phantom-imf-study-1.4012191.

Sanderson, Henry, and Michael Forsythe. 2013. *China's Superbank: Debt, Oil and Influence—How China Development Bank Is Rewriting the Rules of Finance*. Singapore: John Wiley & Sons.

Santana, Andrés, and José Rama. 2018. "Electoral Support for Left Wing Populist Parties in Europe: Addressing the Globalization Cleavage." *European Politics and Society* 19(5): 558–576.

Sartori, Giovanni. 1976. *Parties and Party Systems: A Framework for Analysis*. New York: Cambridge University Press.

Sassen, Saskia. 2016. "The Global City: Strategic Site, New Frontier." In *Managing Urban Futures*, edited by Marco Keiner, Martina Koll-Schretzenmayr, and Willy A. Schmid, 73–88. London: Routledge.

Šćepanović, Vera, and Dorothee Bohle. 2018. "The Institutional Embeddedness of Transnational Corporations: Dependent Capitalism in Central and Eastern Europe." In *Handbook of the International Political Economy of the Corporation*, edited by Andreas Nölke and Christian May, 152–166. Cheltham: Edward Elgar Publishing.

Schakel, Wouter. 2021. "Unequal Political Responsiveness in the Netherlands." *Socio-Economic Review* 19(1), 37–57.

Schanzenbach, Diane Whitmore, Ryan Nunn, Lauren Bauer, and Megan Mumford. 2016. *Where Does All the Money Go: Shifts in Household Spending Over the Past 30 Years*. Technical Report Brookings: The Hamilton Project.

Scharpf, Fritz W. 1991. *Crisis and Choice in European Social Democracy*. Ithaca, NY: Cornell University Press.

Scharpf, Fritz W. 2003. "Problem-Solving Effectiveness and Democratic Accountability in the EU." MPIfG working paper 03/1.

Scharpf, Fritz W. 2011. "Monetary Union, Fiscal Crisis and the Preemption of Democracy." MPIfG Discussion Paper 11/11.

Scharpf, Fritz W. 2018. "International Monetary Regimes and the German Model." MPIfG Discussion Paper 18/1.

Schattschneider, Elmer Eric. 1960. *The Semisovereign People: A Realist's View of Democracy in America*. Belmont, CA: Wadsworth Publishing Company.

Scheiring, Gábor. 2021. "Varieties of Dependency, Varieties of Populism: Neoliberalism and the Populist Countermovements in the Visegrád Four." *Europe-Asia Studies* 73(9): 1569–1595.

Schelkle, W. 2017. *The Political Economy of Monetary Solidarity: Understanding the Euro Experiment*. Oxford: Oxford University Press.

Schelkle, Waltraud, and Dorothee Bohle. 2020. "European Political Economy of Finance and Financialization." *Review of International Political Economy* 28(4): 1–14.

Schiller, Christof, and Anke Hassel. 2010. *Der Fall Hartz IV: Wie es zur Agenda 2010 kam und wie es weitergeht*. Frankfurt: Campus Verlag.

Schipani, Andres. 2019. *Strategies of Redistribution: The Left and the Popular Sectors in Latin America*, PhD diss., University of California, Berkeley.

Schiumerini, Luis and David Steinberg. 2020. "Black Market Blues: The Political Costs of Illicit Currency Markets." *Journal of Politics* 82(4): 1217–1230.

Schmidt, Manfred G. 1987. "West Germany: The Policy of the Middle Way." *Journal of Public Policy* 7 (2): 135–177.

Schmidt, Vivien A. 2008. "Discursive Institutionalism: The Explanatory Power of Ideas and Discourse." *Annual Review of Political Science* 11(1): 3033–26. doi: doi:10.1146/annurev.polisci.11.060606.135342.

Schoeller, Magnus G. 2018. "The Rise and Fall of Merkozy: Franco-German Bilateralism as a Negotiation Strategy in Eurozone Crisis Management." *JCMS: Journal of Common Market Studies* 56(5): 1019–1035.

Schulten, Torsten, and WSI-Tarifarchiv. 2020. *Collective Bargaining in Germany 2020: Annual Report of the WSI Collective Agreement Archive*. Düsseldorf: Wirtschafts- und Sozialwissenschaftliches Institut der Hans-Böckler-Stiftung.

Schumpeter, Joseph A. 1942. *Capitalism, Socialism and Democracy*. New York: Harper & Brothers.

Schwan, Michael. 2017. "Which Roads Lead to Wall Street? The Financialization of Regions in the European Union." *Comparative European Politics* 15(4): 661–683.

Schwartz, Herman. 2009. *Subprime Nation: American Power, Global Capital, and the Housing Bubble*. Ithaca, NY: Cornell University Press.

Schwartz, Herman M. 2007. Dependency or Institutions? Economic Geography, Causal Mechanisms and Logic in Understanding Development. *Studies in Comparative International Development* 42(1): 115–135.

Schwartz, Herman M. 2011. *Subprime Nation: American Power, Global Vapital, and the Housing Bubble*. Ithaca, NY: Cornell University Press.

Schwartz, Herman M. 2014. "Global Imbalances and the International Monetary System." In *Handbook of the International Political Economy of Monetary Relations*, edited by T. Oatley and W. K. Winecoff, ch. 5. Cheltham: Edward Elgar.

Schwartz, Herman M. 2016. "Wealth and Secular Stagnation: The Role of Industrial Organization and Intellectual Property Rights." *RSF: The Russell Sage Foundation Journal of the Social Sciences* 2(6): 226–249.

Schwartz, Herman M. 2017a. "Elites and American Structural Power in the Global Economy." *International Politics* 54(3): 276–291.

Schwartz, Herman. 2017b. "Club Goods, Intellectual Property Rights, and Profitability in the Information Economy." *Business and Politics* 19(2): 191–214.

Schwartz, Herman M. 2019a. "American Hegemony: Intellectual Property Rights, Money, and Infrastructural Power," *Review of International Political Economy* 26(3): 490–519.

Schwartz, Herman M. 2019b. *States Versus Markets: Understanding the Global Economy*. London: Macmillan International Higher Education.

Schwartz, Herman M. 2020. "Covering the Private Parts: The (Re-)nationalisation of Housing Finance." *West European Politics* 43(2): 485–508.

Schwartz, Herman M., and Leonard Seabrooke. 2009. "Varieties of Residential Capitalism in the International Political Economy: Old Welfare states and the New Politics of Housing." In *The Politics of Housing Booms and Busts*, edited by H. M. Schwartz and L. Seabrooke, 1–27. London: Palgrave Macmillan, London.

Schwartz Herman, and Bent Sofus Tranøy. 2019. "Thinking about Thinking about Comparative Political Economy." *Politics & Society* 47(1): 23–54.

Scruggs, Lyle. 2002. "The Ghent System and Union Membership in Europe, 1970–1996." *Political Research Quarterly* 55(2): 275–292.

Seabrooke, Leonard 2006. *The Social Sources of Financial Power: Domestic Legitimacy and International Financial Orders*. Ithaca, NY: Cornell University Press.

Seabrooke, Leonard, and Duncan Wigan. 2014. "Global Wealth Chains in the International Political Economy." *Review of International Political Economy* 21(1): 257–263.

Seabrooke, Leonard, and Duncan Wigan. 2017. "The Governance of Global Wealth Chains." *Review of International Political Economy* 24(1): 1–29.

Seeheimer Kreis. 2003. "Mut zur Veränderung—Agenda 2010: Reformen für Deutschland," *Seeheim Eckpunktepapier*, Berlin.

Segal, Adam, and Eric Thun. 2001. "Thinking Globally, Acting Locally: Local Governments, Industrial Sectors, and Development in China." *Politics & Society* 29(4): 557–588.

Seguino, Stephanie 2010. "Gender, Distribution, and Balance of Payments Constrained Growth in Developing Countries." *Review of Political Economy* 22(3): 373–404.

Sell, Susan. 2003. *Private Power, Public Law: The Globalization of Intellectual Property Rights*. Cambridge: Cambridge University Press.

Serrano, Francisco, and Ricardo Summa. 2012. "Macroeconomic Policy, Growth and Income Distribution in the Brazilian Economy in the 2000s." *Investigación Económica* 71: 55–92.

Sgambati, Stefano. 2019. "The Art of Leverage: A Study of Bank Power, Money-Making and Debt Finance." *Review of International Political Economy* 26(2): 287–312.

Sharman, Jason C. 2017a. "Illicit Global Wealth Chains after the Financial Crisis: Micro-States and an Unusual Suspect." *Review of International Political Economy* 24(1): 30–55.

Sharman, Jason C. 2017b. "Sovereignty at the Extremes: Micro-States in World Politics." *Political Studies* 65(3): 559–575.

Shaxson, Nicholas. 2019a. *The Finance Curse: How Global Finance Is Making Us All Poorer*. London: Grove Press.

Shaxson, Nicholas. 2019b. "Tackling Tax Havens. The Billions Attracted by Tax Havens Do Harm to Sending and Recieving Nations Alike." *Finance & Development* 5(3): 7–10.

Shelley, Louise I. 1997. "Stealing the Russian State." *Demokratizatsiya* 5(4): 482–482.

Shih, Victor. 2007. *Factions and Finance in China: Elite Conflict and Inflation*. New York: Cambridge University Press.

Shleifer, Andrei, and Lawrence H. Summers. 1990. "The Noise Trader Approach to Finance." *Journal of Economic Perspectives* 4(2): 19–34.

Shonfield, Andrew. 1965. *Modern Capitalism: The Changing Balance of Private and Public Power*. Oxford: Oxford University Press.

Sierra, Jazmin. 2015. *Partners at Home and Abroad. How Brazil Globalized State-Led Development*, PhD diss., Brown University.

Sierra, Jazmin, and Kathryn Hochstetler. 2017. "Transnational Activist Networks and Rising Powers: Transparency and Environmental Concerns in the Brazilian National Development Bank." *International Studies Quarterly* 61(4): 760–773.

Simoni, Marco. 2020. "Institutional Roots of Economic Decline: Lessons from Italy." *Italian Political Science Review/Rivista Italiana di Scienza Politica* 50(3): 382–397.

Sinn, Hans-Werner. 2014. *The Euro Trap: On Bursting Bubbles, Budgets, and Belief*. Oxford: Oxford University Press.

Skocpol, Theda, and Alexander Hertel-Fernandez. 2016. "The Koch Network and Republican Party Extremism." *Perspectives on Politics* 14(3): 681–699.

Skott, Peter. 2005. "Fairness as a Source of Hysteresis in Employment and Relative Wages." *Journal of Economic Behavior and Organization* 57: 305–331.

Skott, Peter. 2015. "Growth Cycles with or without Price Flexibility." *Review of Keynesian Economics* 3(3): 374–386.

Slobodian, Quinn. 2020. "The Law of the Sea of Ignorance: FA Hayek, Fritz Machlup, and other Neoliberals Confront the Intellectual Property Problem." In *Nine Lives of Neoliberalism*, edited by Philip Mirowski, Dieter Plehwe, and Quinn Slobodian, 70–90. London: Verso Books.

Smart, Alan, and James Lee. 2003. "Financialization and the Role of Real Estate in Hong Kong's Regime of Accumulation." *Economic Geography* 79(2): 153–171.

Sobolewska, Maria, and Robert Ford. 2020. *Brexitland: Identity, Diversity and the Reshaping of British Politics*. Cambridge: Cambridge University Press.

Sommers, Jeffrey. 2014. "Austerity, Internal Devaluation, and Social (in)Security in Latvia." In *The Contradictions of Austerity: The Socio-Economic Costs of the Neoliberal Baltic Model*, edited by Jeffrey Sommers and Charles Woolfson, 17–43. London: Routledge.

Song, Jae, David Price, Fatih Guvenen, Nicholas Bloom, and Till von Wachter. 2019. Firming Up Inequality. *Quarterly Journal of Economics* 134(1): 1–50.

Sørensen, Vibeke 2001. *Denmark's Social Democratic Government and the Marshall Plan, 1947–1950*. Copenhagen: Museum Tusculanum Press.

Sorge, Arndt, and Wolfgang Streeck. 2018. "Diversified Quality Production Revisited: Its Contribution to German Socio-Economic Performance over Time." *Socio-Economic Review* 16(3): 587–612.

Soskice, David. 1990. "Wage Determination: The Changing Role of Institutions in Advanced Industrialized Countries." *Oxford Review of Economic Policy* 6(4): 36–61.

Soskice, David. 1999. "Divergent Production Regimes: Coordinated and Uncoordinated Market Economies in the 1980s and 1990s." In *Continuity and Change in Contemporary Capitalism*, edited by H. Kitschelt, P. Lange, G. Marks and J. D. Stephens, 101–134. Cambridge: Cambridge University Press.

Soskice, David. 2007. "Macroeconomics and Varieties of Capitalism." In *Beyond Varieties of Capitalism*, edited by Bob Hancké, Martin Rhodes, and Mark Thatcher, 89–121. Oxford: Oxford University Press.

Soss, Joe, Richard C. Fording, and Sanford F. Schram. 2011. *Disciplining the Poor: Neoliberal Paternalism and the Persistent Power of Race*. Chicago: University of Chicago Press.

Spicker, Paul. 2011. *How Social Security Works: An Introduction to Benefits in Britain*. Bristol: Policy Press.

Stack, Graham. 2015. "Baltic Shells: On the Mechanics of Trade-Based Money-Laundering in the Former Soviet Space." *Journal of Money Laundering Control* 18(1): 81–98.

Stahl, Rune Møller. 2019. "Ruling the Interregnum: Politics and Ideology in Nonhegemonic Times." *Politics & Society* 47(3): 333–360.

Stahn, Kerstin. 2006. "Has the Impact of Key Determinants of German Exports Changed? Results from Estimations of Germany's Intra Euro-Area and Extra Euro-Area Exports." Deutsche Bundesbank Discussion Paper Series 1: Economic Studies (No 07/2006).

Stallings, Barbara. 1990. "The Role of Foreign Capital in Economic Development: A Comparison of Latin America and East Asia." In *Manufacturing Miracles: Patterns of Development in Latin America and East Asia*, edited by Gary Gereffi and Donal L. Wyman, 55–89. Princeton, NJ: Princeton University Press.

Standard & Poor's Rating Service. 2015. "Banking Disintermediation in Europe." Frankfurt: Standard and Poor's.

Stansbury, Anna M., and Lawrence H. Summers. 2020. "The Declining Worker Power Hypothesis: An Explanation for the Recent Evolution of the American Economy." NBER Working Paper No. 27193.

Steindl, Josef. 1952. *Maturity and Stagnation in American Capitalism*. New York: Monthly Review.

Stenfors, Alexis, Eric Clark, Ilia Farahani, Anders Lund Hansen, and Marco Passarella. 2014. "The Swedish Financial System." https://pure.port.ac.uk/ws/portalfiles/portal/4085624/The_S wedish_financial_system.pdf.

Stetser, Brad. 2018. "A Few Words on China's Holdings of U.S. Bonds." *Council on Foreign Relations*. https://www.cfr.org/blog/few-words-chinas-holdings-us-bonds.

Stiglitz, Joseph. 2009. *Freefall: Free Markets and the Sinking of the Global Economy*. London: Penguin.

Stockhammer Engelbert. 2004. "Financialization and the Slowdown of Accumulation." *Cambridge Journal of Economics* 28(5), 719–741.

Stockhammer, Engelbert. 2005/06. "Shareholder Value-Orientation and the Investment-Profit Puzzle." *Journal of Post Keynesian Economics* 28(2): 193–216.

Stockhammer, Engelbert, 2008a. "Is the NAIRU a Monetarist, New Keynesian, Post Keynesian or Marxist Theory?" *Metroeconomica* 59(4): 479–510.

Stockhammer, Engelbert. 2008b. "Some Stylized Facts on the Finance-Dominated Accumulation Regime." *Competition & Change* 12(2): 184–202.

Stockhammer, Engelbert. 2011. "Wage Norms, Capital Accumulation and Unemployment. A Post Keynesian View." *Oxford Review of Economic Policy* 27(2): 295–311.

Stockhammer, Engelbert. 2013. "Why Have Wage Shares Fallen? An Analysis of the Determinants of Functional Income Distribution." In *Wage-Led Growth*, edited by M. Lavoie and E. Stockhammer, 40–70. London: Palgrave.

Stockhammer, Engelbert. 2015. "Rising Inequality as a Cause of the Present Crisis." *Cambridge Journal of Economics* 39(3): 935–958.

Stockhammer, Engelbert. 2016. "Neoliberal Growth Models, Monetary Union and the Euro Crisis. A Post-Keynesian Perspective." *New Political Economy* 21(4): 365–379.

Stockhammer, Engelbert. 2017a. "Determinants of the Wage Share. A Panel Analysis of Advanced and Developing Economies." *British Journal of Industrial Relations* 55(1): 3–33.

Stockhammer, Engelbert. 2017b. "Wage-Led versus Profit-Led Demand: What Have We Learned? A Kalecki-Minsky View." *Review of Keynesian Economics* 5(1): 25–42.

Stockhammer, Engelbert. 2021. "Post-Keynesian Macroeconomic Foundations for Comparative Political Economy." *Politics and Society*, https://journals.sagepub.com/doi/full/10.1177/00323292211006562.

Stockhammer, Engelbert, Cedric Durand, and Ludwig List. 2016. "European Growth Models and Working Class Restructuring before the Crisis. An International Post-Keynesian Political Economy Approach." *Environment and Planning A* 48(9): 1804–1828.

Stockhammer, Engelbert, Eckhard Hein, and Ludwig Grafl. 2011. "Globalization and the Effects of Changes in Functional Income Distribution on Aggregate Demand in Germany." *International Review of Applied Economics* 25(1): 1–23.

Stockhammer, Engelbert, and Karsten Kohler. 2020. "Financialization and Demand Regimes in Advanced Economies." In *The Routledge International Handbook of Financialization*, edited by Philip Mader, Daniel Mertens, and Natascha van der Zwan, 149–161. London: Routledge.

Stockhammer, Engelbert, and Özlem Onaran. 2004. "Accumulation, Distribution and Employment: A Structural VAR Approach to a Kaleckian Macro Model," *Structural Change and Economic Dynamics* 15: 421–447.

Stockhammer, Engelbert, Özlem Onaran, and Stefan Ederer. 2009. Functional Income Distribution and Aggregate Demand in the Euro Area. *Cambridge Journal of Economics* 33(1): 139–159.

Stockhammer, Engelbert, Joel Rabinovich, and Niall Reddy. 2021. "Distribution, Wealth and Demand Regimes in Historical Perspective: The USA, the UK, France and Germany, 1855–2010." *Review of Keynesian Economics* 9(3): 337–367.

Stockhammer, Engelbert, and Rafael Wildauer. 2016. "Debt-Driven Growth? Wealth, Distribution and Demand in OECD Countries." *Cambridge Journal of Economics* 40(6): 1609–1634.

Stockhammer, Engelbert, and Rafael Wildauer. 2018. "Expenditure Cascades, Low Interest Rates or Property Booms? Determinants of Household Debt in OECD Countries." *Review of Behavioral Economics* 5(2): 85–121.

Stockhammer, Engelbert, and Christina Wolf. 2019. "Building Blocks for the Macroeconomics and Political Economy of Housing." *Japanese Political Economy* 45(1–2): 43–67.

Stokes, Susan. 2001. *Mandates and Democracy: Neoliberalism by Surprise in Latin America.* Cambridge: Cambridge University Press.

Stopford, John M., and Susan Strange with John S. Henley. 1991. *Rival States, Rival Firms: Competition for World Market Shares.* Vol. 18. Cambridge: Cambridge University Press.

Storm, Servaas. 2017. "The New Normal: Demand, Secular Stagnation, and the Vanishing Middle Class." *International Journal of Political Economy* 46(4): 169–210.

Storm, Servaas. 2019. "Lost in Deflation: Why Italy's Woes Are a Warning to the Whole Eurozone." *International Journal of Political Economy* 48(3): 195–237.

Storm, Servaas. 2020. "Secular Stagnation, Loanable Funds and Demography: Why the Zero Lower Bound Is Not the Problem." In *Economic Growth and Macroeconomic Stabilization Policies in Post-Keynesian Economics,* edited by H. Bougrine and L.-P. Rochon, 90–106. Cheltenham: Edward Elgar.

Storm, Servaas, and C. W. M. Naastepad. 2012. *Macroeconomics Beyond the NAIRU.* Cambridge, MA: Harvard University Press.

Storm, Servaas, and C. W. M. Naastepad. 2013. Wage-Led or Profit-Led Supply: Wages, Productivity and Investment. In *Wage-Led Growth. An Equitable Strategy for Economic Recovery,* edited by Mark Lavoie and Engelbert Stockhammer 100–124. London: Palgrave Macmillan.

Streeck, Wolfgang. 1991. "On the Institutional Preconditions of Diversified Quality Production." In *Beyond Keynesianism: The Socio-Economics of Production and Full Employment,* edited by E. Matzner and W. Streeck. 21–61. Aldershot: Elgar.

Streeck, Wolfgang. 1997. "Beneficial Constraints: On the Economic Limits of Rational Voluntarism." In *Contemporary Capitalism: The Embeddedness of Institutions,* edited by R. Boyer and R. J. Hollingsworth, 197–219. Cambridge: Cambridge University Press.

Streeck, Wolfgang. 2009. *Re-Forming Capitalism: Institutional Change in the German Political Economy.* Oxford: Oxford University Press.

Streeck, Wolfgang. 2011. "Taking Capitalism Seriously: Towards an Institutionalist Approach to Contemporary Political Economy." *Socio-Economic Review* 9(1): 137–167.

Streeck, Wolfgang. 2012. "How to Study Contemporary Capitalism?" *European Journal of Sociology/Archives Européennes de Sociologie* 53(1): 1–28.

Streeck, Wolfgang. 2014a. *Buying Time: The Delayed Crisis of Democratic Capitalism.* London: Verso Books.

Streeck, Wolfgang. 2014b. "How Will Capitalism End?" *New Left Review* 87(May/June): 35–64.

Streeck, Wolfgang, and Kathleen Thelen. 2009. "Institutional Change in Advanced Political Economies." In *Debating Varieties of Capitalism,* edited by Hancke, 95–134. Oxford: Oxford University Press.

Streeck, Wolfgang, and Kozo Yamamura, eds. 2001. *The Origins of Nonliberal Capitalism: Germany and Japan in Comparison.* Ithaca, NY: Cornell University Press.

Summers, Lawrence. 2014a. "U.S. Economic Prospects: Secular Stagnation, Hysteresis, and the Zero Lower Bound." *Business Economics* 49(2): 65–73.

Summers, Lawrence. 2014b. "Reflections on the 'New Secular Stagnation Hypothesis.'" In *Secular Stagnation: Facts, Causes and Cures,* edited by C. Teulings and R. Baldwin, 27–38. London: CEPR Book.

Summers, Lawrence 2014c. "U.S. Economic Prospects: Secular Stagnation, Hysteresis, and the Zero Lower Bound." *Business Economics* 4(2): 65–73.

Svallfors, Stefan, and Anna Tyllström. 2019. "Resilient Privatization: The Puzzling Case of For-Profit Welfare Providers in Sweden." *Socio-Economic Review* 17(3): 745–765.

Swenson, Peter. 1991. "Bringing Capital Back in, or Social Democracy Reconsidered" *World Politics* 43(4): 513–544.

Swenson, Peter. 2002. *Capitalists against Markets*. Oxford: Oxford University Press.

T

Tan, Yeling. 2021. *Disaggregating China, Inc.: State Strategies in the Liberal Economic Order*. Cornell Studies in Political Economy. Ithaca, NY: Cornell University Press.

Tang, Frank. 2020. "What Is China's Dual Circulation Economic Strategy and Why Is It Important?" *South China Morning Post*, November 19, 2020. https://www.scmp.com/economy/china-economy/article/3110184/what-chinas-dual-circulation-economic-strat egy-and-why-it.

Tarantelli, Ezio. 1986. "The Regulation of Inflation and Unemployment." *Industrial Relations* 25(1): 1–15.

Tavani, Daniele, and Luca Zamparelli. 2017. "Endogenous Technical Change in Alternative Theories of Growth and Distribution." *Journal of Economic Surveys* 31(5): 1272–1303.

Temesvary, Judit, and Adam Banai. 2017. "The Drivers of Foreign Bank Lending in Central and Eastern Europe: The Roles of Parent, Subsidiary and Host Market Traits." *Journal of International Money and Finance* 79: 157–173.

Teulings, Coen, and Richard Baldwin, eds. 2014. *Secular Stagnation: Facts, Causes and Cures*. London: CEPR Book.

Thelen, Kathleen. 2014. *Varieties of Liberalization and the New Politics of Social Solidarity*. New York: Cambridge University Press.

Thelen, Kathleen. 2019. "Transitions to the Knowledge Economy in Germany, Sweden and the Netherlands." *Comparative Politics* 51(2): 295–315.

Theodoropoulou, Sotiria, and Andrew Watt. 2015. "An Evaluation of the Austerity Strategy in the Eurozone: Was the First Greek Bailout Program Bound to Fail?" In *The Politics of Extreme Austerity: Greece in the Eurozone Crisis* edited by Karyotis et al., 71–90. London: Palgrave Macmillan.

Thirlwall, Anthony. 1979. "The Balance of Payments Constraint as an Explanation of International Growth Rate Differences." *BNL Quarterly Review* 32 (128): 45–53.

Thirlwall, Anthony. 2011. "Balance of Payments Constrained Growth Models: History and Overview." *PSL Quarterly Review* 64(259): 307–351.

Thompson, Helen. 2012. "The Limits of Blaming Neo-liberalism: Fannie Mae and Freddie Mac, the American State and the Financial Crisis." *New Political Economy* 17(4): 399–419.

Thomson, Henry. 2019. *Food and Power: Regime Type, Agricultural Policy, and Political Stability*. Cambridge: Cambridge University Press.

Thorbecke, Willem, and Atsuyuki Kato. 2012. "The Effect of Exchange Rate Changes on Germany's Exports." RIETI Discussion Paper Series 12(E-081).

Thurston, Chloe N. 2018. *At the Boundaries of Homeownership: Credit, Discrimination, and the American State*. New York: Cambridge University Press.

Tolliday, Steven. 1995. "From 'Beetle Monoculture' to the 'German Model': The Transformation of Volkswagen, 1967–1991." *Business and Economic History* 24(2): 111–132.

Tooze, Adam. 2018. *Crashed: How a Decade of Financial Crises Changed the World*. London: Penguin.

Toplišek, Alen. 2019. "The Political Economy of Populist Rule in Post-Crisis Europe: Hungary and Poland." *New Political Economy* 25(3): 388–403. CBDS Working Paper 2020/2 45.

Tori, Daniele, and Özlem Onaran. 2018. "The Effects of Financialization on Investment: Evidence from Firm-Level Data for the UK." *Cambridge Journal of Economics* 42(5): 1393–1416.

Tori, Daniele, and Özlem Onaran. 2020. "Financialisation, Financial Development, and Investment: Evidence from European Non-financial Corporations, *Socio-Economic Review* 18(3): 681–718.

Torres, Raymond. 2019 . "Export-Led Growth in the Euro Area: Benefits and Costs." *Funcas SEFO* 8(4). https://www.funcas.es/wp-content/uploads/Migracion/Articulos/FUNC AS_SEFO/044art02.pdf.

Tortella, Gabriel, and José Luis García Ruiz. 2013. *Spanish Money and Banking: A History.* London: Palgrave.

Tridico, Pasquale, and Riccardo Pariboni. 2018. "Inequality, Financialization, and Economic Decline." *Journal of Post Keynesian Economics* 41(2): 236–259.

Tsai, Kellee S. 2007. *Capitalism Without Democracy: The Private Sector in Contemporary China.* Ithaca, NY: Cornell University Press.

Tschoegl, Adrian E. 2000. "International Banking Centers, Geography, and Foreign Banks." *Financial Markets, Institutions & Instruments* 9(1): 1–32.

V

Van der Zwan, Natascha. 2014. "Making Sense of Financialization." *Socio-economic Review* 12(1): 99–129.

Van Doorslaer, Hielke, and Mattias Vermeiren. 2021. "Pushing on a String: Monetary Policy, Growth Models and the Persistence of Low Inflation in Advanced Capitalism." *New Political Economy* 26(5): 797–816.

Van Gunten, Tod, and Edo Navot. 2018. "Varieties of Indebtedness: Financialization and Mortgage Market Institutions in Europe." *Social Science Research* 70: 90–106.

van Mark, Michael, and Joachim Nick-Leptin. 2011. *Renewably Employed—Short and Long-Term Impacts of the Expansion of Renewable Energy on the German Labour Market.* Berlin: Bundesministerium für Umwelt, Naturschutz und Reaktorsicherheit.

Van Mechelen, Natascha, and Jonathan Bradshaw. 2013. "Child Poverty as a Government Priority: Child Benefit Packages for Working Families, 1992–2009." In *Minimum Income Protection in Flux*, edited by Ive Marx and Kenneth Nelson, 81–107. London: Palgrave Macmillan.

Van Treeck, Till. 2009. "The Political Economy Debate on 'Financialization'—A Macroeconomic Perspective." *Review of International Political Economy* 16(5): 907–944.

Veblen, Thorstein. 1904. *The Theory of Business Enterprise* Clifton, NJ: A. M. Kelley.

Veblen, Thorstein. 1908. "On the Nature of Capital." *The Quarterly Journal of Economics* 22(4): 517–542.

Veblen, Thorstein. 1908b. "On the Nature of Capital: Investment, Intangible Assets, and the Pecuniary Magnate." *The Quarterly Journal of Economics* 23(1): 104–136.

Vergeer, Robert, and Alfred Kleinknecht. 2011. "The Impact of Labor Market Deregulation on Productivity: A Panel Data Analysis of 19 OECD Countries (1960–2004)." *Journal of Post-Keynesian Economics* 33(2): 369–404.

Vesper, Dieter. 2016. "Was Kann Die Fiskalpolitik? Erfahrungen, Perspektiven Und Handlungsspielräume." WISO Diskurs 13.

Visser, Jelle. 2019. ICTWSS Database, version 6.1, University of Amsterdam. https://www.oecd.org/employment/ictwss-database.htm.

Vitols, Sigurt. 2002. "Shareholder Value, Management Culture and Production Regimes in the Transformation of the German Chemical-Pharmaceutical Industry." *Competition and Change* 6(3): 309–325.

Volkens, Andrea, Pola Lehmann, Nicolas Merz, Sven Regel, and Annika Werner. 2013. "The Manifesto Data Collection." *Manifesto Project (Mrg/Cmp/Marpor)*, \urlhttps://manifesto-project.wzb.eu/ (July).

von Weizsaecker, Carl Christian. 2013. "Public Debt and Price Stability." *German Economic Review* 15(1): 42–61.

Vukov, Visnja. 2020. "European Integration and Weak States: Romania's Road to Exclusionary Development." *Review of International Political Economy* 27(5): 1041–1062.

W

Wade, Robert. 2003. "What Strategies Are Viable for Developing Countries Today? The World Trade Organization and the Shrinking of 'Development Space." *Review of International Political Economy* 10(4): 621–644.

Wagschal, Uwe. 2007. "Auf dem Weg zum Sanierungsfall? Die rot-grüne Finanzpolitik seit 2002." In *Ende des rot-grünen Projektes. Eine Bilanz der Regierung Schröder 2002–2005*, edited by Christoph Egle and Reimut Zohlnhöfer, 241–270. Wiesbaden: Springer VS.

Walker, Christopher, and Melissa Aten. 2018. "The Rise of Kleptocracy: A Challenge for Democracy." *Journal of Democracy* 29(1): 20–24.

Wallace, Jeremy. 2014. *Cities and Stability: Urbanization, Redistribution, and Regime Survival in China*. New York: Oxford University Press.

Wallerstein, Immanuel. 1974. *The Modern World-System I: Capitalist Agriculture and the Origins of the European World-Economy in the Sixteenth Century*. New York: Academic Press.

Walter, Stefanie. 2015. "Crisis Politics in Europe: Why Austerity Is Easier to Implement in Some Countries Than in Others." Comparative Political Studies 49(7): 841–873.

Walter, Stefanie. 2021. "The Backlash Against Globalization." *Annual Review of Political Science* 24(20): 1–20.22. https://doi.org/10.1146/annurev-polisci-041719-102405.

Walter, Timo, and Leon Wansleben. 2020. "How Central Bankers Learned to Love Financialization: The Fed, the Bank, and the Enlisting of Unfettered Markets in the Conduct of Monetary Policy." *Socio-Economic Review* 18(3): 625–653.

Walters, Alan. 1990. *Sterling in Danger*. London: Fontana/Collins.

Wang, Orange, and Zhou Xin. 2018. "Xi Jinping Says Trade War Pushes China to Rely on Itself and 'That's Not a Bad Thing." *South China Morning Post*, September 26, 2018. https://www.scmp.com/economy/china-economy/article/2165860/xi-jinping-says-trade-war-pushes-china-rely-itself-and-thats.

Watson, Matthew. 2010. House Price Keynesianism and the Contradictions of the Modern Investor Subject. *Housing Studies* 25(3): 413–426.

Watson, Sara. 2015a. "Does Welfare Conditionality Reduce Democratic Participation?" *Comparative Political Studies* 48(5): 645–686.

Watson, Sara. 2015b. *The Left Divided: The Development and Transformation of Advanced Welfare States*. Oxford: Oxford University Press.

Weber, Isabella. 2021. *How China Escaped Shock Therapy: The Market Reform Debate*. Routledge Studies on the Chinese Economy. New York: Routledge.

Weber, Max. 1978. *Economy and Society*. Trans. Gunther Roth and Claus Wittich. Berkeley: University of California Press.

Weil, David. 2014. *The Fissured Workplace: Why Work Became so Bad for so Many and What Can Be Done to Improve It*. Cambridge, MA: Harvard University Press.

Weinkopf, Claudia. 2009. "Germany: Precarious Employment and the Rise of Mini-Jobs." In *Gender and the Contours of Precarious Employment*, edited by Leah F. Vosko, Martha MacDonald, and Iain Campbell,, 177–193. New York: Routledge.

Wessendorf, Florian. 2013. "VMDA Photovoltaik Produktionsmittel: VDMA begrüßt Einigung im Solarhandelsstreit."http://www.vdma.org/article/-/articleview/1989046(accessedApril11,2014).

Westermark, Andreas. 2019. "Lönebildningen i Sverige: med Tyskland som kompass?" *Penning-och Valutapolitik* 2019(2): 90–113.

White, Jonathan, and Lea Ypi. 2016. *The Meaning of Partisanship*. Oxford: Oxford University Press.

The White House. 2009. "Remarks by the President Challenging Americans to Lead the Global Economy in Clean Energy." edited by Office of the Press Secretar. Washington, D.C.

Wiedemann, Andreas. 2021a. *Indebted Societies: Credit and Welfare in Rich Democracies*. New York: Cambridge University Press.

Wiedemann, Andreas. 2021b. "A Social Policy Theory of Everyday Borrowing. On the Role of Welfare States and Credit Regimes." *American Journal of Political Science*. https://doi.org/10.1111/ajps.12632 (online first).

Wiedemann, Andreas. 2022. "How Credit Markets Substitute for Welfare States and Influence Social Policy Preferences: Evidence from US States." *British Journal of Political Science* 52(2): 829–849.

Williams, Brendan, and Nedovic-Budic, Zorica 2016. "The Real Estate Bubble in Ireland. Policy Context and Responses." *Urban Research & Practice* 9(2): 204–218.

Williamson, Jeffrey G. 2011. *Trade and Poverty: When the Third World Fell Behind.* Cambridge, MA: MIT Press.

Williamson, Jeffrey G. 2015. "Latin American Inequality: Colonial Origins, Commodity Booms or a Missed Twentieth-Century Leveling?" *Journal of Human Development and Capabilities* 16(3): 324–341.

Wiser, Ryan, Mark Bolinger, and Galen Barbose. 2007. "Using the Federal Production Tax Credit to Build a Durable Market for Wind Power in the United States." *The Electricity Journal* 20(9):77–88.

Wiß, Tobias. 2019. "Reinforcement of Pension Financialisation as a Response to Financial Crises in Germany, the Netherlands and the United Kingdom." *Journal of European Public Policy* 26(4): 501–520.

Wong, Julia. 2019. "'A White Collar Sweatshop': Google Assistant Contractors Allege Wage Theft," *The Guardian*, May 28, 2019. https://www.theguardian.com/technology/2019/may/28/a-white-collar-sweatshop-google-assistant-contractors-allege-wage-theft.

Wood, James. 2018. "The Integrating Role of Private Homeownership and Mortgage Credit in British Neoliberalism." *Housing Studies* 33(7): 993–1013.

Wood, James. 2019. "Mortgage Credit: Denmark's Financial Capacity Building Regime." *New Political Economy* 24(6): 833–850.

Wood, Stewart. 2001. "Business, Government, and Patterns of Labor Market Policy in Britain and the Federal Republic of Germany." In *Varieties of Capitalism: The Institutional Foundations of Comparative Advantage*, edited by Peter Hall and David Soskice, 247–274. Oxford: Oxford University Press.

Woodford, Michael D. 2003. *Interest & Prices.* Princeton, NJ: Princeton University Press.

Woodruff, David M. 2016. "Governing by Panic: The Politics of the Eurozone Crisis," *Politics & Society* 44(1): 81–116.

World Inequality Database. 2022. https://wid.world/ (accessed January 17, 2022).

Wray, Randall. 2016. *Why Minsky Matters. An Introduction to the Work of a Maverick Economist.* Princeton, NJ: Princeton University Press.

Wren, Anne, ed. 2013a. *The Political Economy of the Service Transition.* New York: Oxford University Press.

Wren, Anne. 2013b. "The Political Economy of the Service Transition." *Renewal: A Journal of Labour Politics* 21(1): 67–76.

Wren, Anne. 2021. "Strategies for Growth and Employment Creation in a Services-Based Economy: Skill Formation, Equality, and the Welfare State." In *Growth and Welfare in Advanced Capitalist Economies. How Have Growth Regimes Evolved?* edited by Anke Hassel and Bruno Palier, 255-288. Oxford: Oxford University Press.

X

Xinhua. 2020a. "Premier Li Keqiang's Government Work Report at the 13th National People's Congress." http://www.xinhuanet.com/politics/2020lh/2020-05/22/c_112 6018545.htm.

Xinhua. 2020b. "Summary Communique of the Fifth Plenum of the 19th Party Congress." October. http://www.xinhuanet.com/2020-10/29/c_1126674147.htm.

Y

Yan, Xiaojun, and Jie Huang. 2017. "Navigating Unknown Waters: The Chinese Communist Party's New Presence in the Private Sector." *China Review* 17(2): 37–63.

Yang, Hongxing, and Dingxin Zhao. 2014. "Performance Legitimacy, State Autonomy and China's Economic Miracle." *Journal of Contemporary China* 24(91): 1–19.

Z

Zalewski, David. A., and Charles J. Whalen. 2010. "Financialization and Income Inequality: A Post Keynesian Institutionalist Analysis." *Journal of Economic Issues* 44(3): 757–777.

Zezza, Gennaro. 2018. "Introduction to the Special Issue on Financialization, Growth and Distribution." *Journal of Post Keynesian Economics* 41(2): 161–164.

Zhu, Yuchao. 2011. "'Performance Legitimacy' and China's Political Adaptation Strategy." *Journal of Chinese Political Science* 16(2): 123.

Zohlnhöfer, Reimut. 1999. "Institutions, the CDU and Policy Change: Explaining German Economic Policy in the 1980s." *German Politics* 8(3): 141–160.

Zohlnhöfer, Reimut. 2003. "Rot-grüne Finanzpolitik zwischen traditioneller Sozialdemokratie und neuer Mitte." In *Das rot-grüne Projekt. Eine Bilanz der Regierung Schröder 1998–2002*, edited by Christoph Egle, Tobias Ostheim, and Reimut Zohlnhöfer, 193–214. Wiesbaden: Springer VS.

Zoomers, Annelies. 2002. "Rural Development Policy in Latin America: The Future of the Countryside." *Social Scientist* 30(11/12): 61–84.

Zuboff, Shoshana. 1988. *In the Age of the Smart Machine: The Future of Work and Power.* New York: Basic Books.

Zucman, Gabriel. 2015. *The Hidden Wealth of Nations.* Chicago: University of Chicago Press.

Zucman, Gabriel. 2017. "How Corporations and the Wealthy Avoid Taxes (and How to Stop Them) | Gabriel Zucman." *New York Times*, November 10, 2017. https://gabriel-zucman. eu/how-corporations-avoid-taxes/.

Zysman, John. 1983. *Governments, Markets, and Growth: Financial Systems and the Politics of Industrial Change.* Ithaca, NY: Cornell University Press.

INDEX

Note: Tables and figures are indicated by *t* and *f* following the page number and "n" refers to endnote numbers.

Printed in the USA/Agawam, MA
October 11, 2022

799611.026